Pedagogy and Place

Robert A. M.
Stern

Jimmy
Stamp

Pedagogy and Place

100 Years of Architecture Education at Yale

Yale University Press
New Haven and London

yalebooks.com/art

Designed by Pentagram
Set in Stanley by Ludovic Balland
and Neue Haas Unica Pro by
Toshi Omagari
Printed in China by Regent
Publishing Services Limited

Library of Congress Control
Number: 2015930492
ISBN 978-0-300-21192-4

A catalogue record for this book is
available from the British Library.

This paper meets the requirements
of ANSI/NISO Z39.48-1992
(Permanence of Paper).

10 9 8 7 6 5 4 3 2 1

Frontispiece: Paul Rudolph,
Art and Architecture Building,
1963 (fig. 4.40, detail)

Contents

Acknowledgments

The initial impulse for this book came about as a result of Robert Stern's appointment by Yale University President Richard C. Levin as the William Clyde DeVane Professor in 2001, when Stern delivered the series of public lectures and graduate seminars "Ideals without Ideologies." Stern's lectures, supplemented by lectures from notable alumni of the school, addressed key issues of architectural pedagogy by examining the impact and influence of the Yale School of Architecture through its history and the professional work of leading faculty and graduates. Afterward, President Levin encouraged Stern to undertake a history of the school and provided research funds to assist with the work. The authors would like to thank President Levin for initiating this project, President Peter Salovey and Provost Ben Polak for their continued advocacy, and Edward P. Bass, as well as other trustees of the Fourth Century Trust, whose subsequent generosity made this publication possible.

In writing the history of the Yale School of Architecture, we had a great start thanks to the work of Bimal Mendis (b. 1976; B.A. 1998, M.Arch 2002), who as a graduate student provided core research for the DeVane lectures and assisted in the accompanying seminars, which together served as the foundation for our subsequent work. The partners at Robert A. M. Stern Architects were also very generous in helping to see this project through by making available assistance from Sarah Acheson and the members of the firm's research department.

We also owe an enormous debt of gratitude to the entire staff of Yale University Manuscripts and Archives, particularly Public Services Manager Stephen Ross, Chief Research Archivist Judith Schiff, Architectural Records Archivist Suzanne Noruschat, and Library Service Assistant Michael Frost, as well as the staff of Yale's Robert B. Haas Family Arts Library. Additionally, we would also like to thank Monica Robinson, Senior Director of Development at the Yale School of Architecture, Paul Rudolph Foundation Co-Directors

Dan Webre and Sean Khorsandi (b. 1981; M.Arch 2006); founding Director of the Charles Moore Foundation Kevin Keim; Curator and Collections Manager William Whitaker of the University of Pennsylvania Archives and Records Center; Director of Research at the Van Alen Institute Anne Guiney; Michael Shulman at Magnum Photos; the Library of Congress; and the many individuals who shared their collections and assisted in our research. Thanks also to Timothy Rohan, Associate Professor of Art History and Graduate Program Director at the University of Massachusetts–Amherst, whose insight into the mind and work of Paul Rudolph was essential to understanding the importance of this key figure in Yale's history.

The authors wish to acknowledge Michael Bierut and the talented designers at Pentagram for their book design, and we wish to acknowledge the support and vision of Michelle Komie, Patricia Fidler, Amy Canonico, and Mary Mayer at Yale University Press for their skilled editorial guidance and production assistance. We would also like to recognize the editorial contributions of Heidi Downey and Tamara Schechter.

Finally, though they are too numerous to mention by name, we would like to thank the many alumni, former and present faculty members, and other associates of the Yale School of Architecture who so generously shared their time, their work, and their memories during the writing of this book, and whose talent, creativity, and strength of character shaped the Yale School of Architecture into the venerable institution it is today.

Robert A. M. Stern
Jimmy Stamp

Introduction

"A distinguished school of architecture is important to Yale and to the nation. Yale is concerned, more than most universities, with the conservation and the constant restatement of human values in a society containing so many dehumanizing forces. Architecture is concerned with the kind of visual life we all will lead. It is thus an indispensable component of humane education, and indeed of civilized human existence as well.

"The Yale School of Architecture continues to influence this country to a degree quite out of proportion to its small size. It is not an easy task which such a school has to perform. The undertaking to recruit the most talented young men and women of each generation and give them personal exposure to the best faculty of their times will always be expensive. Throughout man's history, however, there has been no other way to teach the best and teach them well.

"Such schools are generations in the making, yet . . . can be lost overnight."

J. Irwin Miller

The Yale School of Architecture was founded on the conviction that architecture is the art of building. Over its one-hundred-year history, the definition of the art of architecture has broadened and deepened, but as the school's program has grown to encompass the interrelated technological and cultural issues surrounding the discipline, it has never lost sight of its principal mission: to empower students with the skills necessary to shape the built environment. As architecture has evolved, so too has the way architecture is taught. Examining the development of architecture education at Yale, from a Beaux-Arts–inspired academic Classicism to the current era of digital postmodernity, reveals an institution that has successfully navigated the shifting currents of architectural discourse by adopting an inclusive pedagogical approach that fosters interdisciplinary collaboration, while maintaining a steadfast commitment to training individual students to become leaders in the profession. With this in mind, this book presents a chronological history of architecture education at Yale that has its tentative beginnings in 1879, when the School of the Fine Arts initiated a course in architecture to meet the demands of aspiring architects from Yale College—well before the formal inauguration of a Department of Architecture in 1916—and spans to the present day, when the school not only offers full graduate-level architecture courses and two research programs, but is also responsible for a pre-architecture program that still offers courses to aspiring architects from Yale College.

In the United States, architecture began to be recognized as a profession in the 1840s, and the first American architecture programs, founded shortly after the Civil War, were all situated within schools of applied science or engineering. But when the Yale School of the Fine Arts opened in 1869 as the first art school in the United States affiliated with an institution of higher learning, its founding director, John Ferguson Weir (1841–1926), deliberately modeled it on the École des Beaux-Arts, intending courses in sculpture, painting, and architecture, leading to an interdisciplinary, arts-focused approach that gave Yale the distinct character that is still a defining aspect of its identity. As the School of the Fine Arts grew, expanding into separate departments and new buildings, the ideal of teaching the various arts was pursued in the belief that studying painting, sculpture, and architecture side-by-side had distinct advantages, especially in offering design studios that encouraged collaboration among the disciplines.

Yale's architecture program was slow to develop, and it was not until 1916 that it became fully formalized as a department offering professional training within the School of the Fine Arts, with Everett Victor Meeks (1879–1954; B.A. 1901, B.F.A. 1917), a graduate of the École des Beaux-Arts, as its first chair and, after 1922, also the dean of the school. Meeks, who served as architecture chairman for almost thirty years, worked with his faculty and visiting critics to develop a program that balanced modernist methods and styles with a knowledge of history and an understanding of Beaux-Arts design and composition. As other schools, inspired by the German Bauhaus, went "modern" they typically eschewed the study of the past and adopted rigid pedagogies based exclusively on function and technology. In so doing they advocated a single approach to style. At Yale, however, no single style was allowed to dominate and a multitude of methods and styles were accepted. This pluralist approach led many modernists to dismiss it as a school that had lost its way. But with the breakup of hegemonic modernism in the post–World War II era, things began to change dramatically, and Yale embarked on a startling if quixotic search for a synthesis of the Beaux-Arts and Bauhaus traditions with the appointments of the prominent Beaux-Arts–trained American modernist architect George Howe (1886-1955) as chairman of the Department of Architecture, and Josef Albers (1888-1976), formerly a master at the Bauhaus, as chairman of the Department of Art. Although some may argue that their attempts to synthesize the craft-based curriculum of the German school with the arts-based approach of the French did not work, it is generally agreed that the Howe-Albers years elevated Yale to the forefront of art education.

Since the appointment of Meeks in 1916, responsibility for Yale's program and control of its curriculum have typically been placed in the hands of a chairman or dean with strong roots in professional practice. For this reason, *Pedagogy and Place* is largely structured around the individuals whose leadership has been critical to the school's success. Moreover, the school's reliance on a succession of senior critics, chairmen, and deans who were recognized as prominent practitioners—rather than professional academics— has ensured that the choir of dissenting voices and influences pervading an architecture school at any given moment doesn't descend into disharmonic chaos. Under Yale's strong dean model, the school's culture and curriculum have evolved according to the interests and ideas of its leaders, who have consistently steered clear of the profession's propensity for amnesia and, instead, endeavored to keep the program focused on the larger discourse of architecture in a manner consistent with the historic trajectory of the discipline.

Almost as important as the succession of strong design leaders has been the succession of architecturally significant buildings that have housed the program. At Yale, pedagogy and place have been inextricably linked. While the studios of many American architecture programs have been situated in spaces initially designed for other purposes, Yale's program has been fortunate enough to be housed in facilities that were deliberately intended for arts education, in buildings deliberately conceived to be important reflections of prevailing architectural tastes at the time they were built—beginning with the program's inauguration in the cramped basement room of the Ruskinian Gothic Street Hall, bridging across High Street to the Beaux-Arts–inspired Romanesque Yale Art Gallery, to the Collegiate Gothic cloister of Weir Hall, then to the modern forms of Louis I. Kahn's (1901–1974) Art Gallery extension, and culminating in the spatially complex, canonical work of Brutalism that is the Art and Architecture Building designed by Paul Rudolph when he was chairman of the Department of Architecture. For this reason, the story of Yale's arts buildings, like that of the various administrative leaders, is central to this text.

Institutional memory—the continuous preservation and transmission of policies, practices, and pedagogies—is critical to the success of any academy, but a school must also open itself to new ideas and methods as a prerequisite to innovation. As deans and faculty retire and are replaced, curricula evolve, and new facilities are built to house the programs, it becomes easy for a school to lose itself, to change completely instead of growing while retaining its unique identity. Balancing consideration of an evolving pedagogy and the testimony of the school's physical settings, this book is intended as a reaffirmation of the distinct identity of the Yale School of Architecture, and an inspiration for its future.

1

Beginnings: Toward an American Beaux-Arts 1869–1916

"The Yale School of the Fine Arts embraces in its object the cultivation and promotion of the Arts of Design, viz: Painting, Sculpture, and Architecture, both in their artistic and aesthetic aims, through practice and criticism."

Statement on the Objects of the Yale School of the Fine Arts, 1875

1.1 Peter B. Wight, Yale School of the Fine Arts (1866), New Haven. The building was renamed Street Hall in 1928 in honor of its benefactor, Augustus Russell Street.

1.2 John Ferguson Weir, artist and inaugural director of the Yale School of the Fine Arts (ca. 1910).

Of all American institutions of higher education, Yale enjoys the longest commitment to the arts, beginning with the opening of the Trumbull Art Gallery in 1832. The Yale School of the Fine Arts, the first school of art on an American college campus, opened in a new, dedicated building (Peter B. Wight, 1866) in 1869 (1.1). The new building replaced the Trumbull Art Gallery as the university's art museum and at the same time housed new programs in studio art. Initially intended to teach all "the Arts of Design," the school focused exclusively on painting until 1879, when a course in architecture was added to its curriculum. A more extensive architecture curriculum was introduced in 1908, but it would not be until 1916 that a full-fledged professional program in architecture was established, and not until 1959 that the department, then part of the Yale School of Art and Architecture, was made a fully professional graduate school; finally in 1972, architecture was formally constituted as an independent faculty within the university. Thus, compared to its peers, Yale's program in architecture is comparatively young: MIT began to teach architecture in 1865, followed by Cornell (1870), the University of Illinois (1873), Columbia (1881), Syracuse (1889), the University of Pennsylvania (1890), and Harvard (1895).[1] In these other schools architecture was taught within a school of science or engineering. What is significant about education in architecture at Yale is that from its inception as a single course of instruction, it was undertaken under the aegis of an art school. This simple but crucial difference would profoundly influence the school's pedagogy. Yale's relative lateness in establishing architecture as an independent curriculum comes as something of a surprise given the desires of Augustus R. Street (1794–1866; B.A. 1812) and his wife, Caroline Leffingwell Street (1790–1877), whose 1864 gifts financed the construction of a building to house a School of the Fine Arts and the endowment of programs in art education. Augustus Street can also be credited with selecting the name "The School of the Fine Arts"—a literal translation of *L'École des Beaux-Arts*—but it was John Ferguson Weir, a landscape painter and the school's founding director (serving 1869–1913), who shaped the unique program, combining painting, and eventually architecture and sculpture, as an American version of the French institution (1.2).

Weir's enthusiasm for the French school was influenced in part by the experiences of his younger brother, the painter Julian Alden Weir (1852–1919), who began his study of art "in the barn at home with the man of all work for a model" but went on to Paris, "where he remained four years, a pupil of Gérome in the *École des Beaux-Arts* [Weir's emphasis]." In John F. Weir's view, the advantage of his brother's experience was "not simply the merit of technical instruction under a French master, but the stimulus of working beside serious

1.3 Studio painting class with both male and female students in Street Hall (ca. 1900).

students attracted to that centre with a common aim and earnest purpose." He was particularly impressed by the shared learning environment that was at the core of the Beaux-Arts system: "The affinity of sincerity and individual earnestness is a strong one, more exacting than the standard of a class and more potent than can be the influence of any instructor passing from easel to easel twice a week with verbal criticism."[2] To Weir, the rewards and competitions were secondary to the long-lasting, close friendships formed in studio during the shared pursuit of truth and beauty. For him, the new school at Yale would be a community imbued with the esprit de corps of the École, emphasizing an openness and inclusiveness among independent-minded students.

When the School of the Fine Arts was established, Yale was just embarking on its transformation from a relatively provincial college into a national university. By the time he retired as director, Weir was able to see the Yale School of the Fine Arts recognized "as a distinct department of the University with its own dean and faculty," one able to take its place "beside the departments of Law, Medicine, and Theology."[3] Moreover, Weir would point out that while other departments occupied generic facilities, the school's new home, named Street Hall in 1928 to honor its benefactor, was the first building to be constructed on an American campus for the specific purpose of arts education. Street Hall enjoyed another distinction: built at a time when Yale College was replacing its nineteenth-century Brick Row, it did not follow Yale's emerging pattern of enclosed quadrangles, but rather stood in isolation as the first Yale building to face both inward to the campus quadrangle and outward to the city, with a prominent entrance on Chapel Street.

Despite the curricular embrace of disciplines that would transform the exclusively male college into a major university, late nineteenth-century Yale remained provincial in many ways. Undergraduate students and, to a considerable extent, faculty regarded the professional schools with thinly veiled disdain, in part because students who completed the program were only offered either a course certificate or honor certificate for satisfactorily completing the required work. Nonetheless, the prestige of the School of the Fine Arts grew throughout the 1880s, so that a bachelor of fine arts degree was formally established in the school, elevating its status as a professional program.

The School of the Fine Arts was also viewed with suspicion as the first division at Yale to admit women (1.3). Female art students not only outnumbered male students, but often outshone them. The first bachelor of fine arts degree was awarded in 1891 to painting student Josephine Lewis.[4] And when the Winchester Prize was established in 1897—the "largest of its kind offered in America," funding two years of study, at least one of which was to be spent in Europe—the first recipient was painting student Mary Foote.[5] The presence of women in the school may well have been one of the reasons the puritanical faculty of the all-male college discouraged undergraduates from taking courses there, despite the fact that a significant number of them were interested in the arts, including architecture. Weir was all too aware that there was a "prejudice of some kind to be overcome" and worked tirelessly to integrate the school's offerings into the college curriculum, and by century's end he succeeded in establishing "technical art electives" for juniors and seniors.

Weir was not only a tireless advocate for the serious treatment of the School of the Fine Arts by the central administration, he was also vocal in his belief that its significance transcended its place in the university; for Weir, the Yale School of the Fine Arts was to rival the École des Beaux-Arts as the only American institution of higher education "where the Arts of Design are all assembled in one school because of their mutually related interests; but in separate ateliers . . . with their different courses of instruction under their respective professional masters." In so conceiving the school, Weir set himself a difficult task. While the French school was supported by the state, Weir's intention to establish an American equivalent was dependent on "practical conditions and developments"—that is to say, funds for endowment, although "contributions to the funds were seldom solicited."[6]

Weir's ambitions for the school as an American Beaux-Arts notwithstanding, a lack of sufficient funding largely limited its curriculum to instruction in painting during its first forty years. However, the 1879 bulletin for Yale College noted that in order for Yale "to carry out the idea of a 'School of the Fine Arts,' Sculpture and Poetry or Belles-Lettres should evidently be included, that it may have the completeness which the title implies, and may fulfill the ends of an aesthetical department in the University."[7] And while the Streets and Weir had from the first hoped that architecture would be a core discipline in the school, Weir believed that technical courses in architecture should be provided in the Sheffield Scientific School, Yale's parallel undergraduate college for engineering and applied science that for a short time endeavored to serve as a home to architecture education. According to the 1871 bulletin, the Sheffield Scientific School offered a "thorough preparatory course for the study of [architecture] . . . consisting of mathematics, mechanical engineering, and studies relating to the nature and strength of materials." Thus, it can be seen that Weir's intentions for an architectural program were holistic—rooted in both the sciences and the humanities.

On January 1, 1879, instruction in architecture commenced in the School of Fine Arts under the guidance of architect Harrison Wheeler Lindsley (1853–1893; Ph.B. 1872).[8] Fresh from three years at the École des Beaux-Arts, the young Lindsley had established a practice in New Haven. As Lindsley was to write, his experience at the École had led him to embrace "the idea that in order to compose in a branch of art a student must first have considerable knowledge of such good compositions as have already been made." As a result, his courses were a direct reflection of those at the École des Beaux-Arts, consisting "chiefly in making the students copy the most characteristic examples of the more important styles of Architecture and read the History of these styles."[9] Lindsley's curriculum began its "First Division" with "Drawing—from the flat and from casts of Architectural ornaments: India-ink and water-color drawing," and "Mathematics—plane descriptive geometry: isometric projection: linear perspective; Architecture—the five orders; studies of classical details; projects—doors, windows, porticoes, etc." It was followed in its "Second Division" with "Drawing—Casts of architectural ornament: water colors" and "Mathematics—descriptive geometry, including warped surfaces and stone-cutting: resistance of materials." In the Second Division, students were introduced to the "history of architecture; the various styles; studies of details in various styles; projects—dwelling-houses, stores, public-buildings, etc." and began to undertake projects "given out once a month (or once in two months)," with the finished drawings "placed on exhibition for comparison at the end of the year," when examinations were held. At the end of the course, a program was given for a final project and thesis.[10] In 1879, only two students, Howard Sibley and William Jewett, took up Lindsley's curriculum.[11]

When Lindsley relocated his practice to New York in 1887, John H. Niemeyer (1839–1932; M.A. 1874), instructor of drawing, took over some of his classes, but the program clearly suffered without an architect's leadership. The program appears to have been in danger of being dropped, despite growing student interest in architecture, leading the *Yale Daily News,* in April 1889, to urge that it continue, writing that "the course was not established as an experiment, but rather in answer to an expressed want on the part of a number of members of the present Junior class. With success assured, the course will we hope be permanent, for if the course be thorough and suited to the needs of the profession, it cannot fail to obtain due recognition through the country."[12] The *News* also reported that President (1886–99) Timothy Dwight V (1828–1916; B.A. 1849) supported the idea of the architecture course.

In 1891, Weir, faced with Lindsley's resignation but determined to keep architecture as a discipline, was willing to have it taught in the Sheffield

1.4 A drawing room for engineering students in North Sheffield Hall (ca. 1872).

Scientific School, where a drafting room was already in place to meet the needs of engineering students (1.4), and courses in descriptive geometry, shades and shadows, perspective, mechanics, construction, architectural drawing, and the principles of architecture could be fielded.[13] However, no action was taken by the Scientific School—largely due to the dearth of funding. This may have been for the best, ensuring that architectural education once properly undertaken would be conducted within a setting devoted to art, and that the French fine arts approach would prevail over the German technical one, like that advocated by Nathan Ricker (1843–1924) at the University of Illinois, where the program began with years of mathematics and science before design work was undertaken by students.[14] To be fair, although architecture, as previously noted, was typically taught in American schools of engineering or applied science, many, beginning with MIT, embraced the French studio system to give students "the flavor of the atelier experience," by hiring a French graduate of the École—in the case of MIT, it was Eugène Létang (1842–1892), who became its chief design critic in 1872. Nonetheless, the absence of the other arts at MIT and other early programs and the great emphasis on technical issues of construction led many students to seek a French architectural education firsthand by studying in Paris.[15]

As the century drew to a close, Yale—now led by President (1899–1921) Arthur Twining Hadley (1856–1930; B.A. 1876), the university's first president who was not an ordained minister—used the occasion of its bicentennial in 1901 to celebrate its evolution from a narrow community of like-minded faculty deeply imbued with the puritanical values of New England's "theocracy" into a cosmopolitan research university with a multitude of departments and diverse offerings. An early symptomatic expression of Yale's emerging cosmopolitanism was the 1879 decision of James Mason Hoppin (1820–1906; B.A. 1840) to resign his professorship in the Divinity School in favor of one in the Art School, where he taught courses in art and architectural history until his retirement in 1899. Hoppin, who took no salary, "brought Ruskinian passion and belief in the moral purpose of art to his courses in architectural history and to his books about the early Renaissance and Greek architecture."[16]

Another reflection of Yale's evolution into a modern university was the increasing number of undergraduates who would regard college not as the end of their education but as the first step in their professional development. This led Weir to redouble his efforts to establish architecture as a distinct discipline in the school, beginning in 1899, when he, for the first of many times, lobbied President Hadley for the establishment of a full program that would "strengthen and complete the effective development of this Art School, giving it a place in advance of any similar institution of its kind in this country and making it closely resemble in its scheme the '*École des Beaux-Arts*' [Weir's emphasis]—which includes Painting, Sculpture, and Architecture." In writing to Hadley, Weir emphasized that Yale's "scheme of instruction [was] based on that School [the École des Beaux-Arts] and our plan of development has been shaped to a degree with reference to that well considered plan."[17]

Weir continued to insist that architecture's correct place was "among the fine arts," and that the failure to include it "would seriously cripple the development and stultify" the school's future: "These arts gain naturally when they are brought in close affiliation and the courses of instruction already supplied in the Art school would have a direct bearing on a course in architecture." To Weir "the element of *design*" distinguished architecture from "statistical and mechanical engineering." In his view, since the École was "the leading school of its kind in the world," it provided the proper model by which "the study of design is pursued throughout the entire course without interruption."[18] Weir not only admired the French atelier system for its sense of community, he also held in high regard the École's requirement that students enter at least two design competitions per year, alternating between a simple, twelve-hour sketch problem (*esquisse*), which taught students how to get to the essence of a problem quickly, and a more ambitious "rendered" project (*projet rendu*), requiring students to first make a sketch and then refine the idea it embodied over a two-month period before submitting the design.[19] Also central to the French approach was the discipline of the *parti,* requiring that a student, in undertaking a projet rendu, sketch out his design intention—plan, section, and principal elevation—at the outset and hold to that over the two-month period as he developed the design. To not do so would render the project *hors concours*—out of the running. As students frequently stopped working on a project when they or their instructors lost faith in the possibilities of the esquisse and its parti, the time taken to complete the course of study in Paris was not fixed. However, students were required to graduate by the time they reached thirty years of age.

While Weir's program in painting was considered to be fully professional, with its own degree, his intention for architecture was different: as a first step, he was willing to settle for a program suited to the needs of undergraduates in a liberal arts college who would like to pursue professional architectural studies after graduation, a strategy calculated to win President Hadley's support for a class in architectural drawing distinctly intended "as preparatory to a course in Architecture."[20] To overcome the distrust of visual studies among Yale College faculty, Weir made it clear that the architecture program he envisioned would incorporate both "design" and "engineering and construction," as well as various history and archeology classes, and would require that each design project be accompanied by a written thesis, "with references to domestic, commercial, civic and ecclesiastical architecture."[21] Hadley supported Weir in this, but he insisted that a full program in architecture could not be established until a chaired professorship was endowed.

Eager to get an architecture program going, Weir suggested to Hadley that, as "the original terms of agreement in founding a department of the fine arts in the University specifies the arts of Painting, Sculpture, and Architecture as properly associated in a School of Fine Arts," the university had in some significant way failed to honor Caroline Street's intentions. But Hadley held his ground on the matter of an endowment. Weir was able to move closer to establishing an architecture program in 1904, when a conditional offer of $5,000 (equivalent to approximately $130,000 in 2015) was made anonymously by a friend of the school toward endowing a chair in architecture. Though the offer was generous, it was not enough to establish a chair, which Hadley insisted on as necessary to establish both an architecture program and one in sculpture, the other foundational discipline that was also not yet established at the school. Weir kept up the pressure, aided by influential recent college alumni such as Grosvenor Atterbury (1869–1956; b.a. 1891) and William Adams Delano (1874–1960; b.a. 1895, b.f.a. 1908, m.a.h. 1930), who had been unable to pursue their interests in architecture while undergraduates and resented the fact that they had to go to Columbia for postgraduate preparation in order to qualify for entrance to the École des Beaux-Arts.[22] Atterbury and Delano were but two of Yale's "architects before architecture," undergraduates from the 1890s who went on to significant careers in the field but resented their inability to complete their professional training in New Haven. (A list of these architects appears at the end of this chapter.) Encouraged by Atterbury and Delano, Weir pushed on as best he could, reporting to the president in 1906 that "while elementary courses are provided in modeling and architectural design, the School is urgently in need of thoroughly equipped departments of Sculpture and Architecture under professionally qualified directory heads."[23]

Weir continued to badger President Hadley about Yale's potential as the only American institution of higher learning capable of providing the kind of education in the arts that could be found in Paris at the École—while acknowledging that much more money was needed, saying "two hundred thousand dollars [approximately $5 million in 2015] would place a department of Architecture here well in advance of any other school of the kind in this country"[24]—and remained adamant in his belief that the potential value to the university of "the association under one roof of the class-room instruction and the collections of an art museum" would give "to this Art School a distinct advantage in connection with a university, not found elsewhere."[25] As if to goad President Hadley, Weir pointed out that Columbia was contemplating a comprehensive program in the arts, which would include architecture, but that Columbia had to put its program together from various separate entities, while Yale had a school intended for all the arts already in place.[26] To get the program started, Weir once again suggested compromising his vision by splitting the coursework between the School of the Fine Arts and the Sheffield Scientific School, telling President Hadley that he could see "no reason why correlative departments of architecture should not be provided" in each "to their initial advantage," but "under one competent directing head, as may be agreed upon between the Art School and the Scientific School—a professional architect of acknowledged merit and reputation."[27] According to Weir's plan, after successfully completing the two-course track, with classes in the Scientific School and in the Art School, architecture students would earn a bachelor of fine arts degree.[28] The sense that Yale was losing ground to Columbia, combined with Weir's willingness to accept a program with "correlative departments" in both the Scientific and Art schools, led President Hadley in 1905–6 to authorize a "Department of Architecture," but one that would only provide "provisional instruction" and was not professional, but "intended chiefly as an elective for undergraduates, and for those who wish some preparation for entering an architect's office."[29] From the time the program was established in 1906 until 1929, when the Department of Architecture began to field its own technical courses, the dual arrangement prevailed.

The death of retired Professor James Mason Hoppin in 1906 changed everything. In his will, Hoppin, who had anonymously promised the $5,000 gift, left the school his library and art collection, as well as $60,000 (approximately $1.5 million in 2014) dedicated toward the endowment of a chair in architecture, subsequently named in his honor.[30] Two years later, Professor John H. Niemeyer, who had been offering courses in architectural drawing, retired after thirty-seven years as Street Professor of Drawing.[31] Hoppin's bequest and Niemeyer's retirement got things moving in earnest, and, in March 1908, the Yale Corporation authorized the appointment of Richard H. Dana, Jr. (1879–1933; b.f.a. Hon. 1912), as instructor in architecture, in charge of a course "arranged for those having a professional aim, or for those desiring a general knowledge of the subject."[32]

Dana, a 1901 graduate of Harvard College and a 1904 graduate of Columbia (B.S. in architecture) who had also studied at the École des Beaux-Arts (1904–6), would commute from New York, where he was establishing a partnership with one of the Yale College "architects before architecture," Henry Killam Murphy (1877–1959; B.A. 1899, B.F.A. 1913). Dana's appointment marked the first time a newly established, well-educated architect from outside New Haven was invited to serve as an instructor—a policy that continues to this day and helps ensure that Yale School of Architecture students are exposed to current architectural ideas from some of the discipline's most highly esteemed practitioners. From his appointment in 1908 until 1916, Dana conducted a "Technical course in Architectural Design and the fundamental principles and historic development of architecture," as well as an undergraduate elective course. In 1908–9, the course had two regular students, one special student, and seven undergraduates who, "taking the course as an elective," could be given "little outside work beyond our four hours a week together."[33] According to Dana, "The course was thus, in a way, two courses in one—suitable to the two kinds of men taking [it]": those who "were seriously preparing to be architects and took this as an introductory elementary course in their technical training," and those "who wished to have a first-hand knowledge of architecture as part of their general culture, but were planning to go into other professions." By the next year (1909–10), the course had matured considerably, with Dana joined by assistants. The studio met weekly for four hours and included the "study of styles and orders, of the details of architectural construction, and of the rendering of original projects, supplemented by readings in the History of Art."[34] Dana would also offer "*projets*" and "*sketch projets,*" described as "a thorough study of the principles of plan and facade composition."[35] Accommodations for the new program were barely adequate. Dana particularly regretted the absence of a suitable library, noting the lack of "useful books accessible in our room, not enough illustrations of the right sort. This gave a rather 'amateurish' atmosphere to part of our work."[36]

Despite Dana's sense that the course was amateurish, some of the work appears to have been sufficiently promising, as three architecture students received honorable mentions in the competition for the Alice Kimball English Prize, a traveling fellowship established in the Art School in 1893: Harold H. Griswold (1886–1950; B.A. 1909), Henry Dennis Hammond (B.A. 1909), and Herman Loth (B.A. 1912). Additionally, a "special prize for merit in several classes" went to John Frederick Kelly (1888–1947; B.F.A. 1915), who would go on to a prominent career specializing in the restoration of Colonial-era houses in Connecticut and would write several important histories of Connecticut

1.5 John Frederick Kelly (B.F.A. 1915), India Ink Rendering (ca. 1915).

1.6 John Frederick Kelly, Order Problem (ca. 1915).

1.7 John Ferguson Weir, Addition to the School of the Fine Arts (ca. 1911), New Haven.

1.8 Drafting room in the School of the Fine Arts (ca. 1911).

architecture.[37] In 1911–12, Kelly would be the first architecture student to win the coveted William Wirt Winchester Fellowship (1.5, 1.6).[38]

Hoppin's bequest appears to have encouraged others to open their pocketbooks in support of the nascent architecture department. In 1908–9, Henry F. English made a gift of $5,000 (approximately $130,000 in 2015); he was joined by an unnamed source who contributed $16,000 (approximately $420,000 in 2015), along with $35,000 (approximately $920,000 in 2015) for an addition to the Art Building (Street Hall) to be undertaken as a memorial to Richard S. Fellowes, class of 1832.[39] Later, the donor's identity was revealed to be J. Davenport Wheeler (Ph.B. 1858).[40] The 1911 Fellowes Memorial addition to Street Hall, designed by Weir, provided "a comfortable drafting room, a library which can be used for informal lectures and recitation, and an office room for the Faculty" (1.7, 1.8).[41] It also allowed for the expansion of the Art Gallery. But even before the addition was complete, Weir was looking further into the future, writing in his 1909–10 annual report that ground had been reserved for the school's expansion to accommodate a fully equipped Department of Architecture at the northwest corner of Chapel and High streets, where a new building could "possibly connect with the present building by a covered archway over the street"—a scheme that would be realized in 1928.[42]

In 1912, Weir retired after forty-four years as the founding director of the School of the Fine Arts. Though he can be credited with championing the instruction of architecture at Yale, he retired without realizing his hope to establish a full professional course of study in the field. He had, however, prevailed upon the Yale Corporation to provide a new measure of academic recognition for all graduates of the School of the Fine Arts: replacing the certificate with the degree of bachelor of fine arts, one "based primarily on technical acquisitions in the practice of the Arts of Design—painting, sculpture, or architecture." Though not a "literary degree," it required a thesis and therefore promised to enjoy the same consideration as degrees in the humanities.[43] For Weir, the initiation of the bachelor of fine arts degree fulfilled his longtime objective to elevate arts education to the same status as that enjoyed by the other professional schools within the university. He rejoiced in the fact that the school, distinct among other "similar institutions both here and abroad," was "primarily a technical and professional School of Art" modeled after the École des Beaux-Arts, and that "it is now widely recognized that these arts have certain mutual relations and affiliations that make it desirable to bring them in closer touch in schools of practice, as they are now being brought into close relation in the professional experience with the enlargement in this country of the field of art in all branches of design, especially in architecture."[44]

In anticipation of his retirement, Weir helped in the search for his successor. Weir had maintained his studio while serving as director and was able to persuade President Hadley that a new director would "not have to give up outside professional work or be closely tied down as to days and hours. It is for the interest of both the school and the university as a whole that he should continue and if possible, enlarge his outside work."[45] This would come to be a defining characteristic of virtually all leaders of all Yale's arts programs. The search ultimately led to William Sergeant Kendall (1869–1938), a respected painter, who was appointed director of the School of the Fine Arts in June 1913.

Appendix:
Architects before Architecture

Students who attended and typically graduated from Yale College or, in some cases, the Sheffield Scientific School, before going on to the École des Beaux-Arts.

Walter Cook (1846–1916) briefly attended Yale, class of 1869,
    before transferring to Harvard and then going on to
    Poly Munich and then the École
Walter Boughton Chambers (1866–1945; B.A. 1887)
Emil Baumgarten (1865–1922; B.A. 1886)
Charles A. Valentine (1868–1947; B.A. 1889)
Evarts Tracy (1865–1922; B.A. 1890)
Howard Van Doren Shaw (1869–1926; B.A. 1890)
Grosvenor Atterbury (1869–1956; B.A. 1891)
Egerton Swartwout (1870–1943; B.A. 1891)
Clarence C. Zantzinger (1872–1954; Ph.B. 1892)
Donn Barber (1871–1925; Sheffield Scientific School, Ph.B. 1893)
John MacIntosh Lyle (1872–1945; B.A. 1894)
William Adams Delano (1874–1960; B.A. 1895, B.F.A. 1908, M.A.H. 1930)
Robert Austin Hamlin (1874–1901; Sheffield Scientific School 1895)
Louis Rochat Metcalfe (1874–1946; B.Phil. 1895)
William Edward Parsons (1872–1939; B.A. 1895)
Charles H. Collens (1873–1958; B.A. 1896)
Francke Huntington Bosworth, Jr. (1875–1949; B.A. 1897)
George Shepard Chappell (1877–1946; B.A. 1899)
John Cameron Greenleaf (1878–1958; Sheffield Scientific School 1899)
Henry Killam Murphy (1877–1959; B.A. 1899, B.F.A. 1913)
John Cross (1878–1951; B.A. 1900)
Edward Clarence Dean (1879–1966; B.A. 1900)
Stowe Phelps (1869–1952; B.A. 1900)
Everett Victor Meeks (1879–1954; B.A. 1901)
James Layng Mills (1878–1955; B.A. 1901)
Paul F. Mann (1881–1943; B.A. 1903)
Henry Corwith Dangler (1881–1917; B.A. 1904)
Franklin W. Glazier (B.A. 1904)
Frederick Burnham Chapman (1883–1935; B.A. 1905)
Charles Lanier Lawrence (1882–1950; B.A. 1905)
Frederick Augustus Godley (1886–1961; B.A. 1906)
Philip Lippincott Goodwin (1885–1958; B.A. 1907)
Heathcote Morrison Woolsey (1884–1957; B.A. 1907)

2
An American Beaux-Arts 1916–1947

"It is worthy of note that the mental atmosphere of the School of
the Fine Arts, in which the three great branches, Architecture,
Painting, and Sculpture, are studied side by side, should properly
have a more advantageous effect upon the student of any one
of these professions than a school limited to the consideration of
one branch alone. Each student is cognizant of the work done in
the other courses and can follow and be inspired by the work of the
whole school."

Bulletin of the School of the Fine Arts, Department of Architecture, 1916–17

The appointment in June 1913 of William Sergeant Kendall as director of the School of the Fine Arts coincided with the establishment of a new professional program in architecture that would see its first graduates in 1916. The program was a significant expansion of Richard Dana's one-year preparatory course, now restructured as a three-year course with an optional fourth year of advanced work. Entry requirements were established that were in line with those of the Sheffield Scientific School—which, indirectly, was responsible for the technical courses—and students who successfully completed their senior year would receive a special "fourth-year certificate." Similarly, the courses in painting and sculpture were also extended by the addition of an optional fourth year. As a result, "students in any of the departments of the School who previous to the year 1913–1914 have completed the course with honors, and have thereafter spent at least two years in professional practice as specified in the regulations," were eligible for the bachelor of fine arts degree.[1] In all disciplines within the school, a preparatory year was required for those students who failed to meet the entrance requirements for the first year's work.[2] In the university *Bulletin* for 1914–15, the goals of the course in architecture were stated in detail, making clear that the thrust was an art-oriented professionalism: "A thorough technical training in Architecture [that] proposes to develop a student not merely into a clever draughtsman, but into a fully equipped architect. It places its emphasis on Design and Art, while giving enough training to enable the student to understand the structural needs for design, and to cooperate intelligently with the Architect-Engineer."[3]

In 1915, the corporation voted to adopt stricter conditions for degrees to be conferred upon students of architecture. Certificates were dropped in favor of exclusively awarding students the bachelor of fine arts degree. However, certificates of accomplishment were still awarded to so-called "special students," who were admitted to the school without passing any entry examinations, based strictly on evidence of ability. These students likely came into the program with office experience as draftsmen and completed an abbreviated curriculum consisting of design but not technical subjects. The program for special students continued until 1930. One special student, Donald McNutt Douglass (1899–1971), a member of the class of 1925, did not successfully earn his certificate, but went on to pursue a career as an architectural illustrator, initially working in the office of Raymond Hood, who "admired his work and used it whenever he could."[4]

With stricter requirements for the bachelor of fine arts degree, the course of study was changed to a basic four-year course that could be finished in three years, according to the student's ability.[5] A 2,500-word thesis was required, and the degree would be granted "only to such students as give evidence of high attainments in their special field."[6] Additionally, it was strongly recommended, though not yet required, that students interested in attending the School of the Fine Arts first receive a general college education. With these changes in place, the new Department of Architecture—formally named as such in the 1916 university *Bulletin*—was, in Kendall's view, equipped to offer "full professional training of the highest sort,"[7] comparable to that offered at Columbia, where entering students were required to have had two years of college before undertaking the four-year architecture program, but not so rigorous as at Harvard, which was unique among American programs in offering only a three-year, graduate-level education while also fielding an undergraduate preparatory program in architectural science.[8]

Kendall expected "slow but steady growth" in the new department's development, given that it initially consisted of only two faculty members, Richard Dana and Franklin Jasper Walls (1880–1964), a graduate of Columbia's School of Architecture appointed in 1914.[9] Its diminutive size notwithstanding, the new department vigorously promoted itself: architecture's section in the School's *Bulletin* now contained a generous selection of illustrations of student work, including a Museum of the Fine Arts by third-year student John Louis Barletta (B.F.A. 1916), a measured drawing of a Colonial doorway, "A Large City Apartment House"—both also by Barletta—and "A Memorial Monument" by John Frederick Kelly (2.1, 2.2).

The 1915–16 *Bulletin* also illustrated a "Correlated Design Problem"—the term "collaborative" would subsequently be adopted for this kind of problem—that was a "composition of Sculpture, Painting, and Architecture," with contributions by students in each of the disciplines. The Correlated Design Problem was a unique innovation in American architecture education, made possible by the situation of the Architecture Department within the School of the Fine Arts. It was likely based on the annual four-week long, "vital but unstructured" interdisciplinary team competitions held at the American Academy in Rome that were "critical in demonstrating [its] original goals and ideals."[10] Yale's first correlated problem was an "Entrance to Museum of Ceramic Art," with Barletta as the architect member of the team (2.3).[11]

Like Weir, Kendall embraced architecture as the essential ingredient needed to fulfill the promise of the School of the Fine Arts as an American counterpart to the École des Beaux Arts. Reporting to President Hadley, he spoke of the school's hope for the future: "The great opportunity of the School, as a technical school, lies in the way of advanced instruction—the giving to competent students an opportunity to learn the creative side of art by carefully

2.1 John Louis Barletta (B.F.A. 1916), A Museum of the Fine Arts, elevation (ca. 1914).

COMPOSITION OF SCULPTURE PAINTING ARCHITECTURE
ENTRANCE TO MUSEUM OF CERAMIC ART
SCALE 1 IN 4 FT

2.3 John Louis Barletta and others, Entrance to Museum of Ceramic Art, elevation. Correlated Design Problem (ca. 1914).

2.2 John Frederick Kelly (B.F.A. 1915), A Memorial Monument, elevation (ca. 1914).

2.4 Everett Victor Meeks (n.d.).

guided experiments in production . . . the direct solving of practical problems for the architects. This is non-existent in other schools [of the fine arts] in this country, so far as I know, and only by the institution of this much needed study can we hope to make the School an essential and important element in art education."[12]

To help propel the new department into the front rank, Kendall set out to beef up the faculty with additional hires. In 1916, while still retaining Dana's services, he appointed Everett Victor Meeks as assistant professor of architecture and head of the now-formalized Department of Architecture. In 1920, Meeks was joined by Shepherd Stevens (1880–1962), a Columbia graduate who had also studied at the École and had met Meeks while they were both working in the office of Carrère & Hastings. The two men would share responsibility for the introductory course intended for majors in Yale College and also help students with thesis research. Meeks would also teach "Building Materials," "Working Drawings and Specifications," and a survey in architectural history, and also handle the design theses. Delighted to be invited to join the faculty of his alma mater, but concerned that his time as teacher would prevent him from pursuing professional practice in New York, Meeks made it clear to President Hadley that he would not tolerate what he perceived to be "the long-standing prejudice within our University against our Art School," which might "continue to militate against the proper carrying out of a program of architecture teaching."[13]

Everett Victor Meeks was a New Yorker who came from an affluent family of cabinetmakers and bankers, although his father was a successful lawyer (2.4). After his graduation from Yale College, he went to Columbia for pre-architectural training in 1902–3 and then on to the École des Beaux-Arts, enrolling in the studio of Henri-Adolphe-Auguste Deglane in 1905. According to Elisabeth Hodermarsky, in her brief account of his career, Meeks's thesis at the École "amazed the conservative French critics with its especially daring utilization of reinforced concrete—a material only in use since 1875, which had recently proved its great strength in a two-story building that withstood the 1906 San Francisco earthquake"[14] (2.5, 2.6). A likely influence was Anatole de Baudot's pioneering work in reinforced concrete, as seen in his Church of Saint Jean de Montmartre, Paris, completed in 1904.

Meeks returned to the United States in 1908 and entered the firm of Carrère & Hastings, the architects of Yale's 1901 Bicentennial Buildings (Commons, Civil War Memorial Rotunda, and Woolsey Hall); Meeks would complement the complex with a cenotaph honoring Yale's World War I dead in 1927 (2.7).[15] Meeks stayed with the firm until 1914, when he established

2.5 Everett Victor Meeks, Guardhouse for a Large Property, plan, section, elevation, and perspective (1908).

2.6 Everett Victor Meeks, A Plan for the Manufacture of Mosaics and Stained Glass. Thesis project at the École des Beaux-Arts, awarded First Medal (1908).

2.7 Everett Victor Meeks, Yale Alumni War Memorial Cenotaph (1927), New Haven.

an independent practice while simultaneously teaching at Cornell, before coming back to Yale as faculty in 1916. When the United States entered World War I, Meeks embarked on a tour of duty as assistant director of the Fine Arts Department of the Army University in France, returning in 1918 to Yale, where he remained on the faculty as a professor, as director of the department until 1945, and as dean of the School of the Fine Arts from 1922 until his age-mandated retirement in 1947.

Though Everett Meeks's appointment as chairman of architecture and subsequently as dean would have a transformative effect on the school, his decision to stay at Yale after war service was not a foregone conclusion. Cornell was aggressively recruiting him to return to its faculty, offering a full professorship and the "maximum salary paid by that University." At the same time, Meeks also had "a definite offer of partnership for the active practice of architecture in New York."[16] However, his interest in maintaining a private practice in New York and his sentimental attachment to his alma mater made Yale's offer more attractive than Cornell's. Moreover, he believed that Yale's department could develop into "an effective School of Architecture." To this end, in December 1918 he wrote directly to President Hadley to request an appointment that would allow him to be in New York for two days each week, clearly something a position at remotely located Cornell would not permit.[17] Given the university's postwar revenue problems, Hadley was relieved to know that salary was not the primary issue—Meeks had an independent income.[18] The real sticking point in Meeks's negotiations proved not to be the issue of money or time, but of title—Meeks wanted Yale to match Cornell's offer of full professorial rank. Kendall supported this demand, suggesting that Meeks's current title, assistant professor of architecture, was "a handicap, not only in the eyes of the students, but also of the Alumni."[19] In a letter to Anson Phelps Stokes (1874–1958; B.A. 1896, M.A. 1900), secretary of the university, Kendall, blending expectations for academic excellence with sound fiscal realities, reported that "Cornell, which has under way great preparations for the developing of its department," was "making determined attempts to secure" Meeks, offering a full professorship and enhancing their previous offer of a generous salary. Kendall expressed his fear that, should Yale lose Meeks, "we shall find it impossible to get another man of equal power and distinction, also supplied with the private fortune which makes it possible to do the work here for the meager remuneration which we are able to give."[20]

At the time of the negotiations with Meeks, Yale was grappling with insufficient endowments and a lingering Victorian fustiness. But the soon-to-retire Hadley, with his legacy in mind, was pushing the university toward a massive administrative reorganization, which saw the appointment of its first provost, the formation of a University Council, and a new focus on the graduate and professional schools. Against this backdrop of postwar planning, on January 7, 1919, Kendall again brought the matter of Meeks's appointment to Hadley's attention, expressing his belief "that it is Yale University and its Administration, rather than the Art School and its Director, which will be judged eventually by the result."[21] Kendall deemed Meeks's promotion to full professor essential to the school's reputation and future: "If Yale is to hold its place among the great universities, the Department of Architecture must be strengthened. It is this feature of the Art School work which makes the largest appeal to the constructive American mind and brain and binds us both to the College and the Sheffield Scientific School. Such important work should be directed by a man with the rank of full professor." Additionally, Kendall asked that the university "continually draw attention to the work being done in the Art School, and particularly that of the Department of Architecture." He also asked that when the university publicized its plans for its postwar restructuring "a disproportionate amount of recognition and attention should be given to the affairs of the Art School, which, from the standpoint of publicity, have been consistently neglected." Kendall wanted Art School news to be "disseminated within the University," a request he deemed by far the most difficult "because of the lack of coordination in the University."[22]

Soon enough, Kendall had worked things out and Meeks was appointed professor, effective January 1919.[23] A year later, perhaps on his own volition but quite likely with Meeks's encouragement, Franklin Jasper Walls resigned, and Meeks pushed for the appointment of Shepherd Stevens as assistant professor.[24] Meeks believed that the widely traveled Stevens, with whom he had taught at Cornell, would bring to Yale "a background of Culture and refinement" not to mention "a certain amount of independent means." Such would be the case. Once ensconced on the faculty, Stevens and his first wife, Mary Wilder Breckenridge, entertained often at their New Haven residence on Saint Ronan Terrace, with Stevens reporting on parties to his aunt Charlotte S. Davenport, from whom he would inherit the considerable wealth that, in 1958, he passed on to the school to form the William B. and Charlotte Shepherd Davenport Fund, which since 1966 has been used to support a visiting professorship in architectural design and other teaching appointments.[25]

Although the Architecture Department graduated its first students in 1916, it was the United States' entry into World War I in 1917 that proved to be the most powerful stimulus to Yale's full commitment to architectural education. Even before the United States joined the Allies in their fight against Germany and Austria, A. Kingsley Porter (1883–1933), professor of art history, had somewhat presumptuously reported that the Architecture Department, though the youngest in the university, was vitally important not only to the university, but also to American architectural education as a whole, because the war, having forced the closing of the École des Beaux-Arts in Paris, made "more felt than ever, the need of [an] architectural school of the very first rank in America."[26] In so saying, Porter—reflecting the views of Weir, Kendall, and in all likelihood Meeks, who was then in France—expressed his disdain for established architecture programs at other American universities on the grounds that they were either part of engineering schools or because they lacked connections to the arts. Porter argued that no American art school except Yale's merited comparison with the École des Beaux-Arts, and that Yale, with its unique constellation of studio programs as well as an art gallery with substantial holdings, had the opportunity to establish an American equivalent of the French program and, by implication, to usurp its authority for Americans.

Writing in 1918, Kendall reiterated this point in his annual report to President Hadley:

> Until four years ago there was no real professional instruction in architecture. We had a one year's course, excellent in itself, but serving merely as an introduction to the study; and our men, in default of what we might have given them, were compelled to go to Harvard, Cornell, Pennsylvania, or Columbia, for their professional education.
>
> We are now offering not only a full four year course in architecture, complete in every detail, but also following the example of the great École des Beaux-Arts in Paris, by giving to the students of the three arts, with manifest advantages from the true architect's point of view, the opportunity of working together in the same school. It is hard to overestimate the effect for good upon each one of these departments of the active presence of the others. Painters and sculptors should properly relate their work to architecture, and architects should find in painting and sculpture inspiration and suggestion for the beauty of their design.[27]

As chairman of the department, Meeks was even more outspoken. In a 1918 interview with a reporter from the *Yale Daily News,* he went to some length to situate architecture within the broad context of education: "The mistake . . . has been made until recently in this Country, of establishing schools of architecture as outgrowths of schools of engineering," which has placed "them amidst an atmosphere of didactic methods of design founded on mathematical principles, with the consequent tendency to bring about a state of affairs in which the designer adds the architectural covering as a veneer to an already determined scheme, itself the result of mathematical inspiration." However, Yale's Department of Architecture was "fortunate in having . . . procured the hearty cooperation of other departments in the University; more especially fortunate in having won the confidence of that very important department indeed, the College. It has consequently become possible for students in the College to 'major and minor' in architecture and thus anticipate, while working for the Bachelor of Arts degree, a year of work in the professional School."[28] Thus from its inception, the program in architecture, though dedicated to professional training in the field, was also situated in the wider, humanistic culture of the university.

Just as Meeks was getting the department going in earnest, Princeton announced plans for a new "School of Fine Arts" to be organized along similar lines to Yale's. Kendall welcomed this news as "proof of a general awakening, not only to the real need of the architect to work in close conjunction with decorative artists, but also to the right of schools of the Fine Arts to be important branches of our great Universities."[29] Meeks—although happy to note "that to-day Yale has, and tomorrow Princeton will have, the advantage of the numerous other American universities that teach architecture"—saw distinct differences between the two new programs: at Yale, as opposed to Princeton, there is the additional advantage "afforded by existing excellent equipment, an established artistic tradition, and a splendid collection of pictures and drawings to frame her work in architecture."[30]

In one way, Meeks's somewhat dismissive assessment of Princeton was unwarranted: Princeton had, in fact, a longer tradition of offering subjects in architecture than Yale. Beginning in 1832, the same year that Yale's Art Gallery opened, Joseph Henry, a professor and amateur architect, offered Princeton students a course in architectural history covering architectural styles and classifications; Henry's course, continuing for five years, was in fact the first humanities course taught at Princeton, which like Yale, Harvard, and most other colleges of the period, still focused on recitation of the classics and on courses in theological discourse. After Henry, architecture was taught intermittently at Princeton, and in 1882 a Department of Art and Archaeology was founded, offering a course on the history of Christian architecture and, beginning in 1892, a course in the elements of architecture and historical drawing. Systematic design courses, however, weren't taught at Princeton until 1915, seven years after Yale began to do so in earnest.

The establishment of Princeton's architecture program within the Department of Art and Archaeology made it different from Yale's in a significant way: Yale's was closely connected to studio instruction in painting and sculpture, as well as art history, and was intended as a professional program, while Princeton's program, with no tradition of studio art programs, was integrated with instruction in art history and archaeology. Also, Yale's program was led by practitioners—first Dana and then Meeks—and after 1916, it enjoyed full departmental status. Princeton's architecture program, on the other hand, was led by an historian, Sherley Warner Morgan, and did not constitute its own department. Nonetheless the two programs shared common values: like Yale's, Princeton's was predicated "on the belief that architects should have a well-rounded education in liberal studies; approach their profession primarily as an art; understand and appreciate the other arts in relation to architecture; and be taught the science of building construction as a part of their training in design rather than as an end in itself."[31]

Meeks, backed by Kendall, set the bar very high for the fledgling department. In fact, he aimed to make sure that Weir's adoption of the name, "the School of the Fine Arts," was not only an English-language translation of the French, but also the clear expression of his intention to make Yale its American counterpart—perhaps even, given France's postwar near economic collapse, its successor. An unsigned 1917 paper devoted to a "Program for Expansion" of the School of the Fine Arts, written by either Meeks or Kendall, but probably by Meeks, argued that the "faculty of the Architecture Department believes that in the Yale Art School, design should be taught better than anywhere else in America and at least as well as in the École des Beaux-Arts at Paris. It believes that Yale has the opportunity of establishing a school of architecture truly national in the broadest meaning of the word."[32]

In 1919, Kendall's title was changed from director to dean of the School of the Fine Arts, and with the title change came a further elevation of the school's status to one more in line with the university's other professional divisions. In his report for the year, Kendall noted that "it now seems evident that the University at large is beginning to understand and appreciate the rightful functions of such a school in its relation to other schools of the University. We hold that the justification of a professional school's existence as part of a university consists mainly in its offerings to the undergraduates; we hold, also, that in order to have vitality in its offerings it must, in every sense of the word, be a professional school, that is, one actively engaged in fitting students to become trained workers in their chosen profession, and because of this, having in its theoretic teaching, the life and authority possessed by the man who is engaged in creative or original research work in the subjects upon which he is instructing his students."[33]

Under Kendall, the school exhibited increased academic rigor: for the first time, lecture courses counted for credit, and records of attendance were kept. Previously, under Weir, "the atmosphere had been free and easy, no discipline, no credits, etc."[34] While Kendall was determined to situate the school as a rival, or even successor, to the École des Beaux-Arts, he was also wise enough to recognize that its future depended on the cooperation of various other divisions in the university, especially Yale College. To this end, the new four-year program offered thirty-eight different subjects leading to a bachelor of fine arts, with engineering and mathematics handled by faculty in the Sheffield Scientific School. Meeks was in charge of design, while also teaching a series of history courses—first with Porter, who left in 1919, and then with his replacement, Henry Davenport (1882–1965), an architect and painter who was a graduate of Harvard and former student of Victor Laloux's at the École des Beaux-Arts. Davenport's appointment was "part of the general plan of University reconstruction" that in February 1923 would combine all undergraduate departments into a single undergraduate Faculty of Arts and Sciences, supplanting the three undergraduate divisions—Yale College, the Sheffield Scientific School, and the Freshman Year—that had been administered separately. Davenport would remain on the faculty until 1926.

Virtually from its inception, the new department taught design along strict Beaux-Arts lines, using design problems proposed by the Beaux-Arts Institute of Design (BAID), an organization founded in 1916 as an outgrowth of the Society of Beaux-Arts Architects, which was first formed in 1894 in New York by young graduates of the École who, finding "a dearth of good designers and draftsmen," established an *atelier* system.[35] Because many of those who took the society's classes had the intention of improving their job situations in large offices, very few completed the course until the Paris Prize was instituted in 1904, at the suggestion of Samuel B. T. Trowbridge, promising entrance to and financial support at the École des Beaux-Arts.[36]

From the first, the Yale Department of Architecture and the Beaux-Arts Institute of Design enjoyed a close relationship, so that as early as 1917, Kingsley Porter was able to report that Yale students "have so far obtained, in these general competitions . . . exceedingly gratifying ratings."[37] The purpose of the BAID was in effect to elevate American arts education by standardizing curricula in schools across the country using the pedagogical methods of the École des Beaux-Arts—especially its competition system and its format for judgment. Because the BAID issued standard programs to participating schools and judged the top submissions from each school in New York, its program of interscholastic competitions quickly took root and, after 1924, with the publication of a monthly journal illustrating top designs, its ambitions to raise national standards began to be realized. Prize-winning submissions were also published along with their programs in *The American Architect and Building News*. In addition to those studying at recognized architecture schools, BAID competitions could also be entered by anyone—typically ambitious draftsmen seeking to elevate their professional status—who belonged to a participating club or atelier such as the T-Square Club in Philadelphia or the Atelier Masqueray New York, and the BAID's Paris Prize competition was open to all citizens under the age of twenty-seven.[38] With students across the country entering the same competitions, which were evaluated by the same judges, American architecture education for the first time assumed a national character. In 1956, the BAID was renamed the National Institute for Architectural Education (NIAE) in response to nationwide shifts in architecture education, and in 1995 it was again renamed, this time in honor of a significant benefactor, William Van Alen, the architect of the Chrysler Building. Today, the activities of the Van Alen Institute are largely confined to expanding the awareness of architecture in the public realm through lectures and exhibitions.[39]

The programs of the BAID encompassed mural painting, decorative arts and sculpture, as well as architecture—all disciplines within the School of the Fine Arts. After screening projects at their home bases, architectural schools, including MIT, Columbia, Harvard, Pennsylvania, Illinois, Syracuse, and Yale, would send the best work on for judgment by the BAID in New York. According to Rosemarie Haag Bletter, "The peak of this activity was in 1929–30 when forty-four schools sent in almost 10,000 drawings."[40] The BAID remained active, but with diminishing influence, until its role in establishing standards for all schools was usurped by the National Architectural Accrediting Board (NAAB), founded jointly by the American Institute of Architects, the Association of Collegiate Schools of Architecture, and the National Council of Architectural Registration Boards in 1940. Whereas the BAID was concerned with aesthetic standards, the NAAB was principally concerned with issues related to preparing students for professional licensure.

Although Yale's new program was small, it quickly attracted a number of outstanding students who would go on to successful careers in the profession. One of the first to receive a degree in the new program was Douglas Orr (1892–1966; B.F.A. 1919, M.F.A. 1927), who began his architectural practice in

2.8   Douglas Orr (B.F.A. 1919, M.F.A. 1927), Model Village Block, elevation and plans (ca. 1916).

2.9   Hyman I. Feldman, (B.F.A. 1919), Proposed School of Fine Arts, Chapel Street elevation (1919).

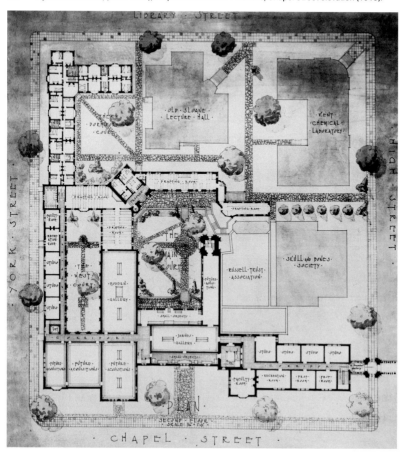

2.10   Hyman I. Feldman, Proposed School of Fine Arts, second-floor plan (1919).

New Haven in 1926 and would become the city's leading architect as well as a figure of national importance as president of the American Institute of Architects (1947), during which time he initiated the annual Honor Awards program that continues to this day. The quality of Orr's traditional work was excellent, beginning with early student projects such as the Model Village Block, reflecting the most advanced thinking about the Garden Suburb movement (2.8), to his realized buildings such as the inventively designed, Georgian-style New Haven Lawn Club (1931) and the Art Deco–inspired Southern New England Telephone Company Administration Building (1938). However, his output suffered after World War II, when he unsuccessfully attempted to transition his approach to that of stylistic modernism, as evidenced by his firm's postwar work for Yale, including Helen Hadley Hall (1958) and the Dunham Laboratory Annex (1958). However, Orr, a consummate professional, brilliantly served as associate architect on Louis I. Kahn's extension to the Yale University Art Gallery (1953).[41]

Another early student in the department, Gilbert Stanley Underwood (1890–1960; B.A. 1920), became the highly accomplished designer of national park structures. Born in Oneida, New York, but raised in San Bernardino, California, Underwood did not finish high school, instead electing to work as a draftsman for a local architect before enrolling at the University of Illinois, from which he eventually dropped out. Six years later, he enrolled at Yale to finish his undergraduate studies, winning a competition sponsored by the Société des Architectes Diplômés par le Gouvernement of France offering a year's study at the École des Beaux-Arts. Already married and with a young child, Underwood could not afford to go to Paris and instead enrolled at Harvard as a graduate student in architecture. After graduating from Harvard in 1923, he moved to Los Angeles to open his own office, designing stations for the Union Pacific Railroad and Wilshire Tower, a prominent Los Angles office building in the Art Deco style, as well as lodges for the National Park Service, of which the best known is the Ahwahnee Hotel (1927) at Yosemite National Park. In 1934, Underwood became a consulting architect for the federal government, designing post offices, courthouses, and the San Francisco Mint.[42]

Hyman I. Feldman (1897–1981; B.F.A. 1919), another early graduate, also pursued an unconventional route to Yale. Born in Szczerzec, now Ukraine, Feldman immigrated to New York at an early age, attending City College and then studying landscape architecture at Cornell before enrolling at Yale, only to have his education interrupted by the onset of World War I. Returning to Yale after the war to finish his degree, he then went on to establish his own practice in New York, eventually designing more than twenty-five hundred developer-built apartment buildings in the metropolitan area. In 1955, Feldman endowed what is now the top design prize in the School of Architecture, the Feldman Prize, "awarded annually to the student who demonstrates the best solution to an architectural problem in an advanced studio, taking into consideration the practical, functional, and aesthetic requirements of the problem."[43]

In 1919, Feldman's thesis, a proposal for the expansion of the university's arts facilities developed in close collaboration with Meeks, would prove critical to the school's physical expansion during the 1920s (2.9, 2.10). While the 1911 expansion of Street Hall was useful to the fledgling department, it had not solved certain basic problems of space. Of particular concern was the housing of the Art Gallery and the various studios under one roof, which was proving a bad idea "because of the danger of giving access to the valuable works of art contained in the galleries," and because the late-night studio hours demanded by architecture students—some things never change—presented security problems for the gallery.[44] In 1917, an iron grille erected to separate the Architecture Department from the rest of Street Hall made it possible to open "the architectural rooms for the students in the evening after the building is closed." It was a dramatic improvement, though it didn't address the fundamental problem: lack of space. Arguing that the strategy of converting galleries in Street Hall to classrooms would deprive the public of "one of the most extraordinary picture collections in America," Meeks lobbied the university to expand its art facilities.[45]

Feldman's thesis design addressed all these issues, proposing the construction of an entirely new quadrangle, bounded on the west by a new residential college facing York Street intended for art students (realized in 1924 as Dickinson and Wheelock halls, made part of Jonathan Edwards College in 1932), on the north by an incomplete building known as the Miller Property that was being used for storage, and a massive new art gallery on Chapel Street stretching all the way from High Street to York Street. Feldman proposed to connect this new gallery to the Fine Arts Building with a bridge over High Street—an idea generally believed to have come from Weir, but first formally articulated in President Timothy Dwight's 1898 annual report, which noted that "if the two buildings were to be connected by a bridge or covered passageway, constructed after some fine architectural design, the whole combined edifice belonging to the school would be an ornament to the city as well as a useful and beautiful home of the Fine Arts in the University."[46] The need to join the Fine Arts Building with a new art gallery derived in part from the Trumbull will, which required that the colonel and his wife be buried with their art—hence the bridge would fuse the two buildings into one, permitting flexibility in the disposition of the collections.[47]

Meeks used Feldman's plans to help goad the university into action. In a 1920 letter to Kendall accompanying photographs of the thesis drawings, Meeks stated that "much more study has been put on the plans than on the elevations, but the latter, while somewhat hastily prepared, show how readily the scheme could be developed along the lines of 'University Gothic'"—the style then being adopted by Yale College as the result of the enormous success of the Harkness Memorial Quadrangle, designed by increasingly influential alumnus James Gamble Rogers (1867–1947; B.A. 1889).[48] Meeks told Kendall that "one by one the other Universities are leaving us behind. You are doubtless well acquainted with Nelson Robinson, Jr. Hall at Harvard [McKim, Mead & White, 1902], which houses her school of Architecture, and have probably seen the splendid plan adopted by Princeton for her own fine arts group, and now I hear that Cornell is planning a School of Fine Arts in connection with her College of Architecture."[49] Meeks's letter to Kendall and the photographs of Feldman's thesis were forwarded to John V. Farwell, chairman of the corporation's Committee on Architectural Plan, who stated that they "should form the basis of one of the schemes which we shall have to consider in the near future."[50] The university was convinced, authorizing $50,000 (approximately $600,000 in 2015) to renovate the Miller Property as the first phase of the arts expansion plan.[51]

The Miller Property had an unusual history dating back to 1911, when George Douglas Miller (1847–1932; B.A. 1870), a Skull and Bones man, commissioned Evarts Tracy and Egerton Swartwout to reconstruct a version of Alexander Jackson Davis's Alumni Hall (1851–53), then being demolished, to be used as a dormitory for seniors in the secret society (2.11). Construction on the new building, located behind the society's High Street tomb, was begun, but the plan proved too ambitious. According to Catherine Lynn, Miller "had the stones of the old building disassembled, numbered, and taken there, but ran out of money and sold it all unfinished to Yale."[52] With the $50,000 from the corporation, the renovation of the Miller Property proceeded quickly under Meeks's supervision and included the reconstruction of the original towers, which formed a backdrop to the society's tomb but are "nearly invisible to the rest of the community."[53] When it opened in 1925, the building, later named Weir Hall, in honor of the school's founding director, was the first building on campus dedicated exclusively to a single art school program, providing space for one hundred architecture students in three drafting rooms, as well as a common room, faculty offices, and a departmental library (2.12, 2.13).[54] Weir Hall would serve as home to the Department of Architecture until 1963.

2.11 Alexander Jackson Davis, Alumni Hall (1853; demolished 1911), New Haven.

2.12 Everett Victor Meeks, after a design by Evarts Tracy and Egerton Swartwout, Weir Hall (1925), New Haven.

2.13 First-year design students working in Weir Hall studio (ca. 1926).

The centerpiece of the expanded arts plan as conceived by Meeks and Feldman was a new art gallery for which James Gamble Rogers was asked to make sketches. Rogers, who had been appointed campus architect in 1920 with the stipulation that he undertake no university building commissions, recommended Egerton Swartwout, who, developing Feldman's master plan, proposed a block-long gallery twice the size of what would ultimately be constructed. However, in contrast to Feldman's modestly scaled Collegiate Gothic design, Swartwout's gallery was to be a monumental, Romanesque-inspired structure with a symmetrical facade of seventeen arches, bracketed by towers, and a grand entrance located at its center (2.14, 2.15). Two anonymous donors contributed $1 million (approximately $12 million in 2015) for the construction of the first half of the gallery building (1928), which would be the only portion of Swartwout's scheme to be realized (2.16, 2.17). Though a powerful design, the new Art Gallery was, as Patricia E. Kane has pointed out, quickly "viewed as out of date, even by Dean Meeks," who admitted to the corporation's Committee on Museums in 1939 that "our lighting and ventilation, to mention only two aspects, are not in any sense contemporary."[55]

When Meeks succeeded Kendall as dean in 1922, he continued with his modest professional practice in New York, telling the president that it brought a "definite benefit to academic teaching."[56] As dean, Meeks redoubled his efforts to establish Yale as an American École des Beaux-Arts, moving so quickly and successfully toward this goal that in March 1924 the Groupe Américain of the Société des Architectes Diplômés par le Gouvernement, an organization of American graduates of the French school, awarded its gold medal to the Department of Architecture for 1922–23, symbolizing excellence in the teaching of architecture along the lines followed by the École.[57]

Meeks's attempts to maintain a practice while running the school as dean and serving as architecture chair quickly proved to be too much. With little time to teach in the architecture studios, at the suggestion of James Gamble Rogers, he appointed Otto Faelten (1884–1945) as assistant professor, commencing in the spring 1922 term. The German-born, New York–raised Faelten was a 1902 graduate of MIT, winner of the Rotch Traveling Scholarship (1907), and a distinguished student in the atelier of Victor Laloux at the École des Beaux-Arts. As Rogers's senior partner and principal designer, Faelten was largely responsible for the design of Yale's widely acclaimed Harkness Memorial Tower and Quadrangle (1921).[58]

Faelten, who rose to the rank of associate professor of architectural design in 1927, would teach in the department for twelve years and was,

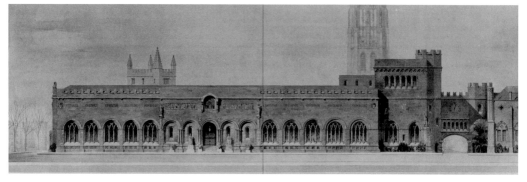

2.14 Egerton Swartwout, Proposed Art Gallery, Chapel Street elevation (1925).

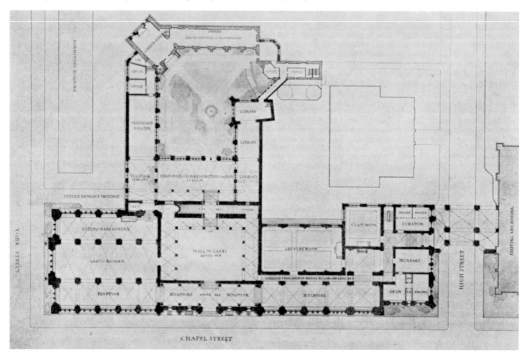

2.15 Egerton Swartwout, Proposed Art Gallery, first-floor plan (1925).

2.16 Egerton Swartwout, Yale Art Gallery (1928), New Haven. Today, the building, which is part of the larger Yale Art Gallery, is known simply as Swartwout.

2.17 Yale Art Gallery Sculpture Hall (1928). At the end of the hall stands the statue of Minerva, which was moved into Paul Rudolph's Art and Architecture Building in 1963.

as much as Meeks, responsible for propelling Yale into the first rank of architecture programs, serving in all but name as "chief critic," a term that would not be adopted until 1947. Faelten was an inspiring teacher. For Paul Schweikher (1903–1997; B.F.A. 1929), who would one day serve as chairman of the Architecture Department (1954–56) (see Chapter 3), there "was never any question of his suzerainty and we thrived under it."[59] Near the end of his life, Schweikher recalled two stories about Faelten. As one of his projects during his first year, Schweikher produced an ink sketch of a horse-riding academy:

> When I showed it to Faelten he shook his head, sat there for a while. He and I hadn't met before and he said, "Schweikher, you'd better go HC." That was hors concours, out of the running. That was permissible and you could get a grade on it but it meant that you only got a standard mention, you only got part of a value. . . . It meant you weren't going to work for six weeks on something if you weren't going to get any value. We had an assistant by the name of Andy Euston [Andrew F. Euston, 1902–1982; B.F.A. 1929], assistant to the critic . . . [who] only came once a week. During the weekdays Andy would go around in our class and help, usually because he was following the esquisse, the sketch . . . which had been made. Andy would simply help you to fulfill the requirements of your esquisses and the program. And he had stood by as he was supposed to when the critic was there, to help you interpret the criticisms. Andy looked at it after Faelten left and he sat down.

Euston offered what Schweikher "thought . . . was great instruction" about how to develop the sketch, and suggested that, with some revisions, Schweikher could submit the design. When Faelten returned, he saw the studies and, according to Schweikher, "said: 'You're going to keep to the great half-smile are you? Just a great big half-smile, non-architecture.' I said, 'Yes sir! I think I will!' Faelten said, 'All right' . . . turned around and left, never came near me." Schweikher submitted the project and earned a first mention, getting his design published in the BAID bulletin (2.18). "Faelten was furious. He said, 'I was on the jury, but I didn't give any award.' That was all. He said, 'You don't follow my advice,' and he just left."[60]

Faelten's attitude changed by the time of Schweikher's thesis, a design for "Chicago as an International City upon development of the St. Lawrence Waterways." This was the basis for his receipt of the Matcham Prize, one of the department's two traveling fellowships for graduating students. As Schweikher was rushing to complete his thesis drawings, Faelten came by

2.18 Paul Schweikher (B.F.A. 1929), A Riding School, elevation, plan, and section (1928). Awarded First Mention by the BAID.

and said: "How are you getting along?" He didn't say more, he just took off his coat, picked up a brush and got to work. He spent all that night working on my project, which is the most flattering thing. I could have wept at the time, I was so delighted. It set me up so much I knew damn well I was going to win the prize. When morning came I was ready to go over and be awarded the prize, and I was. Faelten wasn't present. He didn't come up [from New York] for the awards. Ted Lamb [Theodore Lamb, 1902–1943; B.F.A. 1930] came in after the awards were over and said, "I have a message from Faelten. He wants you to come down and see [James Gamble] Rogers, for employment."[61]

There was a darker side to Faelten as well. He could be emotionally volatile. Julian H. Whittlesey (1906–1995; Sheffield Scientific School 1927, B.F.A. 1930) remembered him as "best in his cups."[62] To George Nelson (1908–1986; B.A. 1928, B.F.A. 1931), he was "a very mixed-up and incomplete man, but with tremendous vitality and quite clearly a man of fantastic talent, and we all worshipped him. He would come in drunk, and he did all those things that we as kids associated with a free-thinking, free-living person. He was a tremendous influence."[63] So memorable was Faelten's behavior that, twenty-five years later, the engineer-inventor R. Buckminster Fuller (1895–1983) recalled a Yale cocktail party at which Faelten "entered through the window of one of the students' rooms, having been jetted from below with a liquid fuel blast off."[64]

Faelten's "cups" may have eventually led to his downfall at Yale. After his resignation was demanded in 1933, he joined the faculty at the University of Pennsylvania in 1936, first as professor and then as chairman of its Architecture Department. Until his death in 1945, Faelten continued to inspire students at Pennsylvania, which held on to the Beaux-Arts system a bit longer than Yale.[65] Writing in the 1970s, Joseph Esherick—San Francisco architect, UC Berkeley faculty member, and one of Faelten's students at Penn—remembered him as "an extraordinarily clever man and ideal for training people to win prizes in Beaux-Arts competitions." He went on to say that Faelten "was flexible" and "an observant and quick critic" who was "given to as much good living as one could conceive and enjoyed enormously parties with the students." Esherick remembered "once being in the Dean's office . . . when Faelton [sic] walked in with an enormously heavy overstuffed briefcase, which he swung up to the Dean's desk with the announcement 'Documents for the boys, Dean.' After a few words he struggled off with his load, and Dean Koyl turned to me and said, 'Wonderful man, Mr. Faelton [sic], wonderful man.'" At the end of his meeting with the dean, Esherick went to the drafting room, where Faelten "was opening up his great briefcase of documents. It was filled with Scotch."[66]

With the design studios under Faelten's control, Meeks was free to attend to his administrative duties and, as a teacher, his undergraduate lecture course that by 1929 was among Yale's most popular, attended by three hundred students, causing a then-cheeky, Yale-centric *Time* magazine to describe him as "Merry Meeks," a "roly-poly little man with a swarthy moon-face, merry squinting eyes, black mustache and knobby goatee—a small Sultan in mufti." According to *Time,* Meeks's course demanded "plenty of attention and reading . . . in architecture history" as well as "fat notebooks with multitudes of clipped illustrations. It is not an easy course. Yet it is crowded, relished."[67]

With Meeks in full control of the school, the new department grew rapidly in size and stature, with about twenty-five students in each class.[68] Meeks also tried to expand the program into new areas. In 1922, he instituted a program in interior decoration that ultimately did not prove successful and was dropped from the curriculum in 1927, perhaps related to the impending resignation in 1928 of Edwin Avery Park (1891–1978), a specialist in interior architecture, decorative arts, and ornament who had been appointed assistant professor of architecture in 1925–26.[69] Also important for the department's meteoric rise in stature, as Arthur Clason Weatherhead wrote in his 1941 history of architectural education in America, was the close relationship at Yale between architecture, painting, and sculpture: "During the years of greatest emphasis on collaboration of the arts [Yale] was the recognized leader. It was one of the first schools to demonstrate that it was possible to maintain successfully a thoroughly professional school of the Fine Arts in connection with architecture in a university program."[70]

As the program hit its stride in the 1920s, Meeks tightened standards and developed a curriculum that was "as comprehensive and quite as thorough as that which [the university] offers in engineering, in medicine, in law, or in the church."[71] Studios began focusing more on common building types that students could expect to encounter in professional practice, such as offices, residences, and churches, and enrollment was now limited to two categories: "those who pass fifteen units of College Entrance Board Examinations and those who are college graduates or who have had one or more years of satisfactory work at a college of recognized standing." According to Meeks, "In the case of the former, it has become increasingly apparent that the four years' professional course does not provide for certain instruction which the degree of Bachelor of Fine Arts should signify and require."[72] With this in view, Meeks implemented a more extensive five-year course for those incoming students who lacked collegiate experience.

From the program's outset, both Kendall and Meeks had reservations about the partnership with the Sheffield Scientific School: "while comprehensive," the school's courses "may be open to the criticism" that they occupy "too great a proportion of the student's time, inasmuch as the courses are not specially arranged for architects."[73] In 1930, the department took on responsibility for the necessary technical courses under the direction of architectural engineer Theodore Crane (1886–1961), who transferred from the Sheffield School. From the first, Crane taught in a classroom adjacent to the studios, a strategy intended to represent "a coordination with the design side of the curriculum . . . [that] is particularly fortunate in these days of apparently developing style forms modifying and growing to meet modern materials and methods of construction."[74]

By the end of the 1920s, Yale was enjoying a national reputation for excellence. Although many students came from various liberal arts colleges, the program was principally made up of a steady stream of Yale undergraduates like George Nelson, one of the department's most important graduates from the early 1930s, who would enjoy great success as a modernist architect, product designer, and polemicist. Coming from modest circumstances, Nelson entered Yale when he was just sixteen years old. A year into his collegiate career, he experienced what he later remembered as a revelation. Seeking to stay dry amidst a sudden rain shower, Nelson, then a sophomore, had cut through Weir Hall, where he was attracted to "a series of ten-day design projects by some student architects. The title of the project was 'A Cemetery Gateway,' and the presentations were watercolor and tempera renderings. They were the most exquisitely beautiful and exciting things I had ever seen in my life. I fell in love instantly with the whole business of creating designs for cemetery gateways. That was when, without any further question on my part, I decided I had to be an Architect."[75]

Seeking entry into the program, Nelson soon met with Dean Meeks, "a pretty wise old bud [who] knew a number of things that I didn't know. One was that the student projects were really awful. . . . He wasn't worried about talent because he was accustomed to students who seemed to have no talents at all. Furthermore, this was in the mid-twenties, and he was very hard up for students because everybody wanted to be a customer's man on Wall Street and get rich overnight. So I had no trouble getting accepted."[76] The curriculum placed a high priority on drawing and rendering, skills that Nelson soon mastered.[77] In the American Beaux-Arts system, short "sketch" design problems lasting a

2.20 Homer Fay Pfeiffer (B.F.A. 1926), A Small Art Museum, section and plan (1926).

2.19 George Nelson (B.A. 1928, B.F.A. 1931), Sketch (1930).

2.21 George Nelson, Elevation (1932). Winning entry for the Rome Prize.

few hours were typical as limbering-up exercises, forcing students to be able to quickly seize on and represent an idea. Nelson remembered a particular sketch problem asking students to design "A Residence for a Western Diplomat on the Outskirts of Peking," replete with enough social space to "be like a huge embassy." Nelson, like many of his generation, saw the exercise in functionalist terms: "Well, what a bunch of nineteen-year-old kids from small towns in America and mostly middle-class parents knew about an ambassador's establishment on the outskirts of Peking—that was a little difficult to figure out."[78] On reflection, he would later see the wisdom of the exotic and seemingly preposterous design problems: "At that point if someone had come to me and said, 'Would you like to redesign Venezuela?' I would have said, 'I need a lot of information, but I'll do it!' And that marvelous inability to realize that here is a project you weren't equipped to cope with was one of the things that made it possible to switch from architecture to publishing to industrial designing without even realizing I was making a transition."[79]

Between 1928 and 1931, Nelson pursued his bachelor in fine arts degree. Presumably on the strength of his draftsmanship (2.19), he was made a teaching assistant but was dropped after only one year, when the school's budget began to reflect the collapse of the national economy. Out of a job and looking to earn some extra money, Nelson began doing renderings for the New York firm Adams & Prentice, architects of Yale's Gothic-style Briton Hadden Memorial (1932), home of the *Yale Daily News*. After graduation in 1931, Nelson set out to win the Paris Prize. Fearing disappointment, he did not go after the more prestigious Rome Prize, which many Yale painting students, but only three architecture students, had captured: architecture student William Douglas (B.A. 1918, B.F.A. 1928) garnered the prize in 1924 before completing his professional training at Yale; Homer Fay Pfeiffer (1898–1981; B.F.A.1926) won in 1927, when he was a postgraduate student with a bachelor in science in architecture from the University of Illinois (2.20); and in 1930, the prize went to Burton Kenneth Johnson (1907–1979; B.Arch 1929), who after four years studying at the University of Illinois had won honorable mention, but then he came to Yale to complete the final year of his studies and, as *Time* magazine put it, "the honor of turning him to prize-winning pitch was Yale's."[80]

Nelson felt that he would have a better shot at the Paris Prize if he enrolled at Catholic University, "a bedraggled school on the outskirts of Washington, D.C.," that he erroneously believed produced prize winners.[81] This view is surprising given that the Paris Prize, through Faelten, had a particularly strong Yale connection beginning in 1922, when it was won by Cornell graduate Roger Bailey (1897–1985), who prepared his entry with the advice of

Meeks and Faelten; in 1926, it was awarded to Carnegie Institute of Technology graduate Carl E. Landefeld, who also had Faelten as a "patron"; and finally, in 1928, four out of the five Paris Prize finalists—Arthur J. Kelsey, A. F. Euston, D. A. White, and F. W. Dunn—were from Yale, although none of them were winners and the prize was awarded to a Catholic University graduate, Thomas H. Locraft.[82] Nelson followed through with his plan and in 1931–32 pursued graduate work at Catholic while he also went after the Prix de Rome. Ironically, he was turned down for the Paris Prize but was selected as winner of the Rome Prize (2.21).[83]

Nelson's two-year stay in Rome did not have the effect intended by the academy's founders, Charles F. McKim, J. P. Morgan, John D. Rockefeller, and William K. Vanderbilt. Instead of deepening his commitment to traditional Classicism, it allowed him the time to explore the emerging modernism of a dozen European architects ranging from Marcello Piacentini to Ludwig Mies van der Rohe, many of whom he had the opportunity to meet and interview. Upon his return to the United States, Nelson published his conversations with these architects as a series in *Pencil Points*.[84] He then went on to a prominent career that combined architecture, city planning, industrial design, design journalism, teaching—including first at Yale in 1941—and exhibition design. In 1988, Nelson's widow, along with his principal industrial design patron, Herman Miller, Inc., established a scholarship in Nelson's name, awarded each year to second-year students to support independent, travel-related research and an exhibition.[85]

In contrast to Nelson's fond recollections, Julian H. Whittlesey was decidedly negative about his time in the school. In 1986, at the end of a long career as a well-regarded New York architect specializing in large-scale housing and planning projects, Whittlesey wrote Dean Thomas Beeby about the "heady days" of the late 1920s, when projects focused on summer houses and embassies and there were "Beaux-Arts medals and the Rome and Paris prizes to be won" but "so little to be learned" in Weir Hall. "From Everett V. Meeks, our dean, we learned about styles, and from Shepherd Stevens about the history of ornament . . . and from each other we learned how to draw, but from none what to draw. Our favorite critic who taught us how to win medals was the great Otto Faelten." With over fifty years' hindsight, Whittlesey remembered the school as "a pretty good stopping off place, but little more than that, for the majority of us whose cultural and academic backgrounds were likely to help carry us on in the changing times we were about to face in the '30s."[86] Whittlesey's studio neighbor, Standish (Stanley) Meacham (1889–1949; Ph.B. 1913, B.F.A. 1928), "kept drawing 'housing' of all things. We had not been told about that. We also learned that he and his wife worked in 'community services.' We had not been told about that either. What was Stanley up to?" As it turned out, after graduating, Meacham was up to something very different from the social housing he was exploring at Yale; returning to his native Cincinnati, he started a firm with his father-in-law, Walter L. Rapp, specializing in traditional homes designed in the Colonial Revival style.[87]

Though it is widely but somewhat uncritically believed that the call for a modern approach to architectural design was not heard by the American academic establishment until after the 1925 Exposition des Arts Décoratifs in Paris, such was not quite the case, at least at Yale. For example, during the 1923–24 academic year, under Meeks's direction, the School of the Fine Arts held a lecture series investigating "The Trend of Architecture in America," with talks by traditional architects such as Benjamin Wistar Morris, Charles Z. Klauder, Dwight James Baum, and William Adams Delano, as well as the provocatively modern-minded architect-urbanist Harvey Wiley Corbett, and by Dean Meeks, who revealed himself not to be the archconservative later generations chose to label him. The series was, in all likelihood, a follow-up to the April 1923 exhibition in the Art Gallery of the entries to the well-publicized *Chicago Tribune* competition (1922).[88] Meeks's chosen topic, "The Modern Trend in Architecture," addressed the stylistic eclecticism of American architecture, which he believed was encouraged by the introduction of industrialized building techniques. Meeks identified three separate directions in contemporary practice, each of which he considered to be a "school": the "School of Specialization," intent on developing one particular style; the "School of Eclecticism," requiring familiarity with all the styles; and the "No Style School," an attempt to discover a new school as embodied in the work of Eliel Saarinen (1873–1950), the Finnish-born architect who had leapt to prominence in the United States in 1922 with his second-prize–winning design for the Chicago Tribune Tower before settling near Detroit, where he soon became the founding head and architect of the Cranbrook Academy, which included a new school of art and design.[89]

Meeks, though quick to recognize that the Stock Market Crash of 1929 and the ensuing Depression brought with them changing social and economic circumstances requiring new approaches to design, remained uncomfortable with the European modernism being promoted as a more socially responsible approach than that typical in American practice.[90] Many students from the late 1920s and early 1930s were impatient with his conservatism, although some, like Paul Schweikher, would come to appreciate it: "We were taught under a system, the Beaux-Arts system," remembered Schweikher. "It was faulty in that it was too rigidly programmatic, too tied to its past, too regimenting toward the uniformity of all schools participating in it, but it had the virtue of orderly sequential acquisition: a system."[91] Carroll L. V. Meeks (1907–1966; Ph.B 1928, B.F.A. 1931, M.A. 1934), another student in the school at the time—one who would join the faculty in 1930—remembers being frustrated during this transitional period: "We knew about Hitchcock's book [*Modern Architecture,* 1929], and we knew about Le Corbusier, but this did not appear in the work in the drafting room."[92] In 1930, as a growing number of students began to pressure the school to give up Classical and traditional forms in favor of a modernist approach, Meeks shrewdly and diplomatically hedged his bets, stating that the modern movement was "a distinct advantage to architects, because it gives them a choice of paths, whereas previously they had but one pattern to follow."[93] In 1931, as the featured speaker at a dinner marking the fiftieth anniversary of the Architectural League of New York, he emphasized his ostensibly nonideological, pluralist approach, valuing aesthetics over the literal functionalism and technological determinism typically insisted on by modernists: "I permit myself one basic principle for future architecture. In all the intolerance that the ultra-conservative may feel today for the confirmed radical, and particularly, in a contrary sense, in all the impatience that the imaginative experiments may have with the 'style man,' let us remember that there is a broad common ground upon which they may meet, respect one another, inspire one another. And it is the only stable ground—I venture to say—upon which either may build his philosophy of design. It is beauty."[94]

The *Art Digest* reported that at the school's 1932 graduation exercises, Meeks told students, "It is erroneous to expect a school to teach stylism in creative work. This should come afterward as an individual development; and by 'stylism' I mean not only historic style but modern style as well."[95] Later that same year, Meeks participated in a symposium on the arts held at Brown University. Other speakers included Frank Lloyd Wright. In his talk, "The Fine Arts in Education," Meeks, acknowledging the revolution in art represented by modernism, argued for a comprehensive approach combining technical study of fundamentals with a study of works of art of the past and the present: "We are now beginning to take our heads out of the sand and face and recognize contemporary art—a difficult matter, it is true, for present-day art has not been classified with finality and pigeonholed with certainty. What hope would there be for the art of the future, however, should the great centres of art instruction fail to recognize the art forces about them?"[96]

A further example of Meeks's open approach was his early recognition of Raymond Hood (1881–1934), a graduate of MIT who had spent four years at the École des Beaux-Arts, and, with John Mead Howells, had been awarded first prize for his Gothic-inspired tower designed for the Chicago Tribune competition. When Meeks invited him to lecture at the school in February 1925, Hood's design sensibility was evolving away from historicism and toward a style that was modern, if not explicitly "modernist." Soon, Hood would become an outspoken enthusiast for the work of Le Corbusier, whose ideas about urbanism he adapted to New York in a series of hypothetical projects that were significantly more radical than the Rockefeller Center group of buildings (1930–39) for which he was the chief designer.[97] Hood's Daily News (1930) and McGraw-Hill (1931) buildings, along with an unrealized but more innovative project for a suburban apartment tower, were included by Philip Johnson and Henry-Russell Hitchcock in *Modern Architecture—International Exhibition* at the Museum of Modern Art in 1932.[98]

Meeks embraced Hood's modernity because it was rooted in French academicism. When Hood lectured at Yale in 1925, Meeks told editors of the *Yale Daily News* that Hood was "a leader among the younger architects in the movement of developing architectural style to more logically fit modern conditions of building construction. In this he has been highly influenced by his training at the École des Beaux-Arts in Paris, where he had a brilliant record as a student." Meeks was particularly impressed by Hood's second skyscraper, the black-granite- and brick-clad American Radiator Building (1924) in New York, which marked a notable break from tradition to embrace a more streamlined, modern design: "In this building he has been able not only to use forms which suggest our steel skeleton construction, but has tried the experiment of introducing strong color into architecture. It is through the efforts of such men as Mr. Hood that our American style will develop."[99]

Hood returned to Yale in spring 1933 as a replacement for Otto Faelten. The appointment proved popular with students, who welcomed Hood's "inspiring criticism."[100] Unfortunately, shortly after his appointment he was stricken with a serious illness that sent him to the hospital. Hood seemed to recover sufficiently to attempt to teach in fall 1933, but he was, as Meeks reported to President (1921–37) James Rowland Angell (1869–1949), "again stricken after the year began," this time with so serious an illness "as to completely incapacitate him leading to his resignation."[101] Hood died on August 14, 1934.

After Hood's death, the department drifted as Meeks tried to appoint design faculty who he hoped could adapt Beaux-Arts principles to modern conditions, notably Frederick Godley (1886–1961), a former partner of Hood's who had studied at MIT and the École des Beaux-Arts. Godley remained on the faculty until 1948. Meeks also appointed Roger Bailey, the Cornell graduate whom Faelten and Meeks had coached in his successful bid for the Paris Prize and who, after a brief time at Yale, joined the faculty of the University of Michigan, where he was to teach and influence a young Charles Moore.

The onslaught of the Depression brought with it not only challenges to the program's emphasis but also to the school's economic stability as "altered circumstances" led to reduced enrollments, although Meeks was able to report in 1931 that "few have had to withdraw, however, meeting their new problems with courage and success."[102] Despite the drain on students' time caused by the financial crisis, Meeks held to university standards, even contemplating program initiatives, including a program in landscape and town planning. However, as Meeks reported to President Angell in 1931, the school would be unable to develop instruction in those fields until the university could provide "additional space, although a promise has been made for the founding of a professorship to handle the major portion of such work." Meeks believed that Yale was "peculiarly fitted to carry on instruction in Town Planning and landscape, due to the existence within the University not only of the School of Fine Arts, but the School of Forestry, the Botanical Gardens, and the Department of Economics."[103] However, given the deepening economic crisis, he realized that plans for new programs would have to be postponed. Meeks also saw to the initiation in 1931 of a two-year postgraduate master of fine arts degree to be conferred by the School of the Fine Arts (rather than the Graduate School). To be admitted to the program, applicants were required to hold a bachelor's degree "from a school of architecture in good standing" and must present examples of their drawings and architectural designs. The degree was to be conferred upon the recommendation of the faculty after the completion of a thesis representing a "complete study and presentation of an extensive architectural problem, such as a monumental building or group of buildings or a comprehensive study in town planning."[104] The new program failed to attract students.

Despite the Depression, students from well-heeled families could afford to enroll in the department, including Eero Saarinen (1910–1961; B.F.A. 1934), who would become one of its most distinguished graduates. Saarinen's qualifications for admission were unusual, to say the least. Son of the distinguished Finnish architect Eliel Saarinen, he had studied sculpture (1929–30) in the Académie de la Grande Chaumière in Paris before deciding to pursue a career in architecture.[105] As a high school graduate with no college-level credits, Saarinen's son needed a little help to get into the right school. On January 15, 1930, Eliel wrote to Meeks to ask that his "boy" be admitted to the program for two or three years as a special student. Though Meeks had tightened admissions requirements, he made room for this exceptional candidate, welcoming the younger Saarinen, who took advantage of the department's offerings, enrolling during his first semester in a variety of courses, including "Introduction to Architecture" taught by Carroll L. V. Meeks, and one on Greek and Roman architecture, while also preparing designs for a variety of projects in his first year, including that of a water tower, a police station, a memorial tunnel entrance, a residence for a college dean, a place for an exiled monarch, a garden club, and a synagogue—all of which earned recognition from the BAID.[106] Clearly, Eliel's "boy" had talent (2.22–2.25). Saarinen studied elementary design with Shepherd Stevens, as well as freehand drawing, engineering mechanics, medieval architecture, and economics. In recognition of his studies in Paris, Saarinen was advanced to his final year in fall 1933, pursuing "Archeology Research" with Raymond Hood. In his last semester (spring 1934), he studied scenic design with Donald Oenslager (1902–1975), who had been appointed to the school's Drama Department as instructor in scenic design in 1926 and then assistant professor of lighting in 1927. Oenslager often included architecture as part of his lectures.[107] It's likely that while at Yale, Saarinen also got to know Stanley McCandless (1897–1967) who, after earning a bachelor of art degree from the University of Wisconsin and a master of architecture degree from Harvard in 1923, directed his career to theatrical and architectural lighting design. McCandless was associate professor of stage lighting and was known to have "lectured regularly in the architecture department."[108] Saarinen would work closely with McCandless later on, beginning with Kleinhans Music Hall (1938), designed in collaboration with his father, in Buffalo, New York.[109]

Despite his packed schedule of classes and studio projects, Saarinen found enough time for college life, which he embraced heartily. As a member of the Decorating Committee of the biennial Beaux-Arts Ball, Saarinen, Donal McLaughlin (1907–2009; B.F.A. 1933) recalls, transformed the Sculpture Hall of the Art Gallery "into a circus," designing "a screen that surrounded a cast of the Venus de Milo, shielding her from the navel on down. Then, using his sculptor's knowledge, he sketched a full-sized trompe l'oeil of a dancer delicately poised on a thimble."[110] Though Saarinen excelled in BAID competitions, he almost always came just short of winning the First Medal, earning him the nickname Second-Medal Saarinen. His thesis project, completed in spring 1934, for a new facility for the "Stevens Institute of Technology," received the silver medal of the Société des Architectes Diplômés par le Gouvernement.

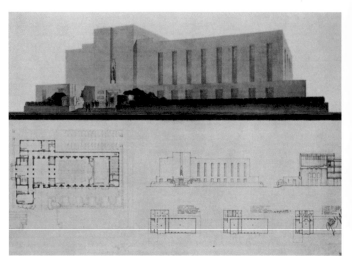

2.22 Eero Saarinen (B.F.A. 1934), A Monument to Johann Sebastian Bach, plan and elevation (1933). Awarded Second Medal by the BAID.

2.23 Eero Saarinen, A Small County Court House, perspective, plans, elevation, and section (1933). Awarded Second Medal by the BAID.

2.24 Eero Saarinen, A New Thousand-Dollar Bill (1934). Awarded First Medal by the BAID.

2.25 Eero Saarinen, An Industrial City, plan (1934). Awarded First Medal by the BAID.

Despite growing agitation for a more modern approach, Saarinen, along with many other Yale students, did so well in the BAID competitions that in 1933 the department was awarded, for the third time, the medal of the Société des Architectes Diplômés par le Gouvernement—the alumni association of the American graduates of the Beaux-Arts.[111] Saarinen capped his Yale career with the Charles Arthur and Margaret Ormrod Matcham Fellowship, providing him with $1,000 (approximately $18,000 in 2015) for European travel. Terms of the award required him to document his trip with measured drawings submitted to Dean Meeks, yet Saarinen, "intrigued by the atmospheric qualities of the sites," opted to submit watercolors instead.[112] Some of these paintings have survived in the collection of the Yale Art Gallery despite a shocking misappropriation of the school's archives during the Moore years (2.26).

During World War II, Saarinen's classmate Donal McLaughlin (2.27) was recruited into the Office of Strategic Services (OSS), a United States intelligence agency that was a precursor to the CIA. As chief of its graphics division, McLaughlin's duties included designing cigarette packages that surreptitiously illustrated diagrammatic instructions for acts of espionage. McLaughlin also played a key role in designing the United Nations' logo.[113] McLaughlin brought Saarinen into the OSS as a civilian consultant to work on graphics for defusing bombs, designs for "the situation room," as well as other projects.[114]

In addition to Schweikher, Nelson, Whittlesey, and Saarinen, many graduates from the late 1920s and early 1930s would go on to notable careers, though not always in architecture. Harold Rome (1908–1993; B.A. 1929, M.F.A. 1934) (2.28) and Leslie Cheek, Jr. (1908–1992; B.F.A. 1935), shared a passion for the theater. Although he headed to New York after graduating to begin a career in architecture, Rome's hobby—writing and performing music—soon became more lucrative than his profession, and he dedicated himself to it full time as author of popular socially and politically minded musicals and musical revues, including *Pins and Needles* (1937) and *Wish You Were Here* (1952). "I was an architect with no buildings to build, a painter with no patrons," Rome recalled near the end of his life, "but hidden in my subconscious mind there was always a tune and a catch-line of social significance."[115]

Leslie Cheek, Jr., was a 1931 graduate of Harvard College who chose to study architecture at Yale over his alma mater, presumably because the School of the Fine Arts included a department of drama. Cheek came from great wealth—he grew up in Nashville, Tennessee, where his family had created the Maxwell House Coffee Company and subsequently sold it to General Foods. Between his graduation from Harvard and his arrival at Yale, Cheek had taken an active role in the construction of his parents' substantial house

2.26 Eero Saarinen (B.F.A. 1934), *Acropolis* (ca. 1935). Watercolor and charcoal on paper. Yale University Art Gallery, New Haven.

2.27 Donal McLaughlin (B.F.A. 1933), A Synagogue, elevation, plan, and section (ca. 1930).

2.28 Harold Rome (B.A. 1929, M.F.A. 1934), A Greek Doric Hexastyle-Peripteral Temple (1933). Awarded Second Medal by the BAID.

in Nashville, Cheekwood (Bryant Fleming, 1932). At Yale, Cheek took several courses in the Department of Drama, including one in set design taught by Oenslager, who, along with the rest of the drama faculty, selected him to design sets that would actually be built—a rare opportunity (2.29). Cheek may not have been as strong a designer as Saarinen, but he could work effectively with artists and sculptors in the collaborative projects. In 1934, his third year at Yale, Cheek joined painting student Leonard Haber (1912–1992; B.F.A. 1936) and sculpture student Raymond G. Barger (1906–2001; B.F.A. 1935) in preparing drawings and a model for submission to a collaborative problem competition sponsored by the Association of the Alumni of the American Academy in Rome, which challenged entrants to redesign a public space in New York's Times Square.[116] The collaboration was typical of the time: Cheek determined the massing and distribution of the structures, as well as the over-all style of the project; Haber designed the lighting, including electric signs and marquees, and created the dramatic renderings; and Barger focused on ornamentation for the buildings and the public square (2.30). Cheek and his teammates tied for first place with two other teams, one of which also came from Yale and included J. T. Howard as architect, painter G. Banever, and sculptor G. M. Proctor.[117] In spring 1935, Cheek's final term, he and some other students created the setting for the biennial Beaux-Arts Ball, transforming the Art Gallery's Sculpture Hall into a medieval abbey with black-cloth-covered Gothic arches trimmed in gold (2.31). Dean Meeks, costumed as an abbot, was persuaded to preside over the festivities from an imitation stained-glass window. Like Harold Rome, Cheek did not pursue a career in architecture. Instead, he embarked on a long career as director of the Virginia Museum of Fine Arts (1948–68), where he was known for highly theatrical exhibitions, reflecting McCandless's belief that light "should be thought of as a new mate-rial to serve definite functions. . . . It is a plastic medium which fills space very much like clay, brick, or stone."[118]

In the early 1930s, the abstracted, modern Classicism that Paul Cret (1876–1945), professor at the University of Pennsylvania, had established in his Folger Shakespeare Library (1932) in Washington, D.C., began to influence the work of many Yale students. This could be seen in the work of Yen Liang (1908–2000; B.F.A. 1931) (2.32), the department's first Chinese-born student, who went on to become Frank Lloyd Wright's first apprentice at Taliesin, where from 1932–34 he not only worked alongside the master, but also plowed his fields and entertained guests and fellow students with violin sonatas by Vivaldi.[119] When he returned to China in 1934, Liang designed the International Club in Nanjing, the Yunnan Trust Building, and the Bank of Yunnan Mining

2.29 Leslie Cheek, Jr. (B.F.A. 1935), Set Design for Act II of Edward Reveaux's *Names in Bronze* (1934).

2.30 Leslie Cheek, Jr. architect; Leonard Haber (B.F.A. 1936), painter; and Raymond G. Barger (B.F.A. 1935), sculptor, Proposal for Times Square, perspective. Collaborative Project (1934).

2.31 Leslie Cheek, Jr., Design for the Yale School of the Fine Arts Beaux-Arts Ball, interior perspective (1935).

2.32 Yen Liang (B.F.A. 1931), A Private Banking House, elevation plan and section (1931). Awarded Second Medal by the BAID.

Industries. After World War II, Liang settled in New York, where he first worked for the United Nations Planning Office before joining Harrison & Abramovitz. After retiring from practice in 1973, he embarked on a career as a children's book writer and illustrator.[120] In 2002, the Yen and Dolly Liang Scholarship Fund was established as the bequest of Dolly Liang.

Other notable graduates from the early 1930s include John Graham (1908–1991; B.F.A. 1931),[121] who revealed early on a mastery of large-scale commercial design in his project for an office building (2.33), anticipating his successful corporate practice in Seattle that specialized in shopping centers but might be best known for the design of the Space Needle created for the 1962 World's Fair. German-born Max O. Urbahn (1912–1995; M.F.A. 1937) began his studies at the University of Illinois before transferring to Yale, where he embraced stylistic modernity, as seen in two of his projects published by the BAID (2.34). Urbahn founded an office specializing in massive infrastructural projects, including the NASA Vehicle Assembly Building and Launch Control Center at Cape Canaveral, Florida.[122]

As the decade of the 1930s evolved, Meeks, like other Beaux-Arts deans, faced mounting student pressure for curricular reform. Students wanted to "go modern." As a stop-gap measure, in 1935, Meeks mounted a series of lectures by modernists of various stripes, beginning with Frank Lloyd Wright and Le Corbusier, during his inaugural visit to the United States.[123] Meeks also tried to include Walter Gropius in the series, hoping to share travel costs from England with other schools. When they pleaded lack of funds, Meeks offered a $100 honorarium (approximately $1,800 in 2014) plus a $25 travel supplement (approximately $435 in 2014). Gropius declined the invitation, asking for a year's postponement, but even without him, the series provided a broad overview of the current scene, including Ralph Walker, Eliel Saarinen, John A. Holabird, Eric Gugler, Philip N. Youtz, and George Howe.[124] Writing to MIT Dean William Emerson that although "students are quite excited," Meeks expressed reservations about the series: "I wonder whether from these they are going to discover the 'new philosophy' of design."[125]

Frank Lloyd Wright's talk, delivered on October 16, resonated with students, who relished his iconoclastic attack on American philistinism, and on the architecture of his contemporary and bête noir from Chicago, James Gamble Rogers, whose work at Yale was then derided by many students as "Girder Gothic."[126] But Le Corbusier's talk on modern residential architecture, to be delivered two weeks later, on October 30, 1935, was the anticipated high

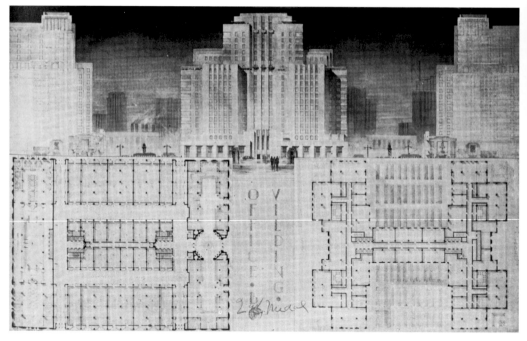

2.33   John Graham (B.F.A. 1931), Project for an Office Building, elevation and plans (1930).

2.34   Max O. Urbahn (M.F.A. 1937), A Banquet and Ballroom, interior perspective, plan, and sections (1937).

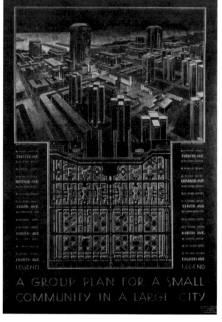

2.35   Richard G. Hartshorne, Jr. (B.F.A. 1937), A Group Plan for a Small Community in a Large City, perspective and plan (1936).

point of the series, attracting, as the *Yale Daily News* noted, "the attention which is usually reserved for Hollywood stars and visiting statesmen."[127] However, despite the Swiss-French architect's bravura technique of drawing while speaking, his ideas, delivered in rapid-fire French and translated by architect Robert Allan Jacobs (1905–1993), were not understood by many in the audience. Even those who did understand him seemed skeptical. In her book documenting Le Corbusier's encounters with America, Mardges Bacon has suggested that the talk "failed to resonate with the students because Dean Everett Meeks continued to keep a firm rein on the Beaux-Arts curriculum."[128] This is an exaggeration; clearly many students were turned off by Le Corbusier's take-no-prisoners approach and put off by his arrogant manner. As George Nelson was to put it in his interview with the Swiss-French architect, published a few months before the Yale lecture in the July 1935 issue of *Pencil Points*, Le Corbusier could be "impossibly exasperating."[129]

Realizing that lectures by modernists were not enough to meet student demands for reform, Meeks, perhaps fearing, or at least seeking to ward off, the kind of seismic shift about to take place at Harvard, attempted an evolutionary approach to change that maintained the curriculum's Beaux-Arts methodology in the introductory studios where *analytiques* and other typical problems continued to be offered, but allowed for a shift in emphasis in the advanced studios, where design assignments were closely tied to contemporary conditions and new forms were tolerated—as could be seen in some of Saarinen's student work or in Richard G. Hartshorne, Jr.'s (1912–1949; b.f.a. 1937) Le Corbusier–inspired "Group Plan for a Small Community in a Large City"[130] (2.35). Surely Meeks was against the full replacement of Beaux-Arts Classicism with International modernism, but in particular he objected to the narrow-focused and intolerant aestheticism of the modernists, arguing that "The [Yale] school does not pretend nor does it intend, to enter into instruction in the various 'isms' or fields of specialization."[131]

At its core, Yale remained wedded to the values of the Beaux-Arts system, so much so that in 1937, for the fourth time, it received the medal of the Société des Architectes Diplômés par le Gouvernement Français Groupe Américain.[132] This proved to be something of a last hurrah, as students were beginning to take note of the dramatic changes Joseph Hudnut (1884–1968) had initiated during his brief time as dean at Columbia (1934–36) and afterward at Harvard, where he became dean in fall 1936.[133] Hudnut's Harvard appointment, and the appointment a year later of Walter Gropius as chairman of the Department of Architecture (in what Hudnut had already reorganized as the Graduate School of Design, or GSD, incorporating landscape architecture and city planning), inaugurated a sea change in American architectural education that could not be ignored by Meeks.

With Hudnut's tacit support, Gropius conveyed the impression that Harvard's GSD was an American Bauhaus, mirroring Meeks's claim of twenty years before that Yale was an American École des Beaux-Arts. But in reality, Yale had been far closer to its prototype in France than Harvard was to its in Germany. Gropius soft-pedaled the fact that under his leadership the Bauhaus had been an interdisciplinary arts and crafts school, which did not include an architecture department until after his resignation in 1928. As a result, the idea that the GSD, with no related programs in painting, sculpture, crafts, or industrial design, was an American Bauhaus was a myth Gropius devised to serve his own ambitions for his work at the school, a point initially made by architect and historian Turpin C. Bannister (1904–1982) in the introduction to his 1954 book *The Architect at Mid-Century.* Pointing to Gropius's role in sweeping aside Harvard's Beaux-Arts curriculum, Bannister suggested that the change was more one of style than of methodology, that one form of "esthetic movement" had simply given way to another: "Despite Gropius' assertion that the Bauhaus intended to establish only an attitude and method of working," Bannister wrote, "much of its impact on students and practitioners has been to promulgate a new style with its own clichés."[134]

Only a few students at Harvard caught on to Gropius's sleight-of-hand, one of whom was Bruno Zevi (1918–2000), who would go on to become an outspoken historian and critic in his native Italy. In a document entitled "An Opinion on Architecture" (1941), dedicated to Dean Hudnut, Zevi stated that "life in the school [was] not fundamentally different from that of any Beaux-Arts School," and that "instead of having a conception of architecture based on common ideas, able to answer the new collective needs of society—to find something new (not something good) has largely become our aim."[135] As Zevi saw it, the GSD was infused with a "drive towards originality" to the extent that it was in danger of "becoming a workshop of mannerism, or a playhouse of individualistic preference. . . . Have we substituted for the 'art for art's sake' of the [Beaux-Arts] 'rendered project' the 'art for art's sake' of the abstract model?"[136] A similar point was also made in 1941 by historian Donald Drew Egbert (1902–1973), assistant professor in Princeton's Department of Architecture, who wrote that the Harvard program under Gropius was essentially Cubist, initiating "a new kind of formal composition . . . very different from the Renaissance version predominant at the École des Beaux-Arts," which "tended to produce a new kind of traditional academicism of its own."[137] Though Gropius sought to deny this, the catalogue that he helped edit for the

Bauhaus exhibition in 1938 at the Museum of Modern Art in New York proclaimed "the genuine unity of form which all Bauhaus products achieved in later years."[138]

Despite the dramatic changes taking place at Harvard, Yale still remained attractive to students seeking fresh challenges. In 1936, Harry Weese (1915–1998), "apparently in a spur-of-the-moment decision," transferred from MIT to Yale, in part because Eero Saarinen was a recent graduate.[139] Weese knew Saarinen's student work from BAID publications and, according to his biographer, Robert Bruegmann, "decided that any school that had produced a student like Saarinen could teach him something important." In later years, Weese, who went on to become an important architect in Chicago and a close friend of Saarinen's, "remembered learning [at Yale] about acoustics, illumination, and concrete from professionals who came up from New York City, and . . . a history professor named [Shepherd] Stevens who delivered stimulating lectures on the importance of saving historic buildings."[140] After a year at Yale, Weese returned to MIT to complete his education.

Gropius's arrival at Harvard had a profound impact on American architecture education that Meeks could not ignore. In 1938, at the suggestion of Frederick Godley, he took the dramatic step of appointing Wallace K. Harrison (1895–1981) as associate professor of architectural design and, for all intents and purposes, "chief critic." In Harrison, who was to remain at Yale until 1942, when wartime assignments required him to withdraw from teaching, Meeks found a meaningful way to meet the growing demands for a modern approach without betraying the educational and professional principles he valued. In Meeks's view, Harrison's modernism was marinated in the Beaux-Arts. According to George Dudley (1914–2005; B.A. 1936, B.F.A. 1938, M.F.A. 1940), a student who would go on to have a close working relationship with Harrison, when Meeks first met Harrison in the spring of 1938, "The Dean couldn't resist sharing his memories of his salad days in Paris and New York. He told them of the complaints in the School, of its falling behind the times and, though he couldn't go along with what Gropius was doing at Harvard, he thought the School needed a new approach."[141] Meeks found an almost ideal antidote to Gropius in Harrison, whom he admired as "an American architect who has his roots in the soil of this country," but also someone who valued France and its role in the arts. Harrison was the key to what Meeks proclaimed to be "an American System of Architectural Education."[142] Harrison was no modernist ideologue. As he was to put it fifteen years later: "Americans are always trying to do something new, but with a sense of balance. We're sort of a halfway post between radicalism and reaction. . . . You can over-refine and over-systematize the life out of anything, and Beaux-Arts thinking had a tendency to do just that. Still, it seems to me the modernists went too far in their wholesale censuring of the approach the Beaux-Arts stood for. . . . There's something to the Beaux-Arts approach. . . . You really can't dismiss all traditional building with glib avant-garde phrases."[143]

Born in Worcester, Massachusetts, Wallace Kirkman Harrison followed a somewhat unusual career path, given his professional prominence. He did not have any formal academic training beyond high school but learned to draft while working in the offices of a contractor. He then apprenticed at a number of architecture firms, including McKim, Mead & White, Cram, Goodhue & Ferguson, and the partnership of Frank J. Helmle and Harvey Wiley Corbett, before going on to Paris in 1920 to join the atelier of Gustave Umbdenstock as the first step toward entry into the École des Beaux-Arts, to which he was admitted in March 1921. Impatient with the École's conservative approach, Harrison embarked on a tour of historic architectural sites with two other Americans, Robert Perry Rodgers (1895–1934) and Paul Nelson (1895–1979), before returning to New York when his funds ran out, eventually joining the Associated Architects group charged with the design of Rockefeller Center and, after the death of Raymond Hood in 1934, becoming the project's principal designer. Harrison's sympathies with European modernism began to emerge in the early 1930s, but his own work, as represented by the Rockefeller Apartments (1935) in New York, eschewed the extreme mechano-morphological approach then characteristic of Le Corbusier or Gropius, in favor of a gentler manner that can be compared with Erich Mendelsohn's work in Palestine or Willem Dudok's in Holland.[144] Harrison considered himself "a modern architect," who, given his experience as someone "who has gone through the mill," would never go "in for complete revolt. When you leave your drawing board and start getting your hands dirty, you stop thinking of your buildings as a challenge to your ability to create absolute art. You're happy to settle for good buildings that get built, in the hope they'll lead to progressively better buildings."[145] Meeks admired Harrison as someone "particularly qualified to train American architects in the best aspects of the International Style and all that it has meant in architectural development in the world of today, supplemented by his wide knowledge and experience of American customs, practices, and standards."[146]

In his professional work, Harrison was an insecure designer who relied on close associates, especially Max Abramovitz (1908–2004), his University of Illinois- and Columbia-trained partner, who joined him at Yale.

Harrison and Abramovitz's arrival at the school brought "a slight breath of fresh air," remembers Carroll L. V. Meeks. "And they did start things up, I must say, in quite a novel way. In fact, it was so novel it was unpopular with the administration. They did, however, follow an ancient American tradition in architecture schools, because they constantly brought Europeans into the drafting room."[147]

One of these Europeans was Oscar Nitzchke (1900–1991), whom Harrison met in spring 1938 on one of his frequent trips to Paris and invited to join the faculty, where he remained until 1948, making a profound impact on a generation of Yale students. While Harrison can be credited with moving Meeks away from Beaux-Arts historicism toward modernism, it was Nitzchke who was the real source of inspiration for students—just as Marcel Breuer (1902–1981) was for students at Harvard, where Gropius, like Harrison not a confident designer, maintained his distance in the design studios. Harrison had learned of Nitzchke after speaking to a number of his friends in the Paris art world about the important opportunity for establishing a fresh direction at Yale. Among those whom Harrison consulted was Christian Zervos, founder of the magazine *Cahiers d'Art,* who was enthusiastic about Nitzchke, the German-born but Swiss-raised architect, and his "amazing" unrealized project for the Champs-Elyseés, the Maison de Publicité (1934–36), incorporating illuminated signage on its facade (2.36). Nitzchke—who had worked for Le Corbusier and had spent some time in New York working for Paul Nelson, Harrison's friend from his Beaux-Arts days, on a project for the Columbia Broadcasting System—welcomed the opportunity to return to the States to work with Harrison in his office, where he became director of research, and to teach at Yale, rather than at Harvard under Gropius or as a "regional envoy of Le Corbusier's."[148]

Harrison was not a great studio critic. Hugh Moore (b. 1920; B.Arch 1943) recalls one evening when he "was finishing up a sketch problem of an aquarium, turquoise on black paper [and] Harrison walked by, took a quick look, threw his arms wide, saying, 'An entrance should be welcoming.' With that he took a yellow crayon and slashed an irreparable concave circle across my drawing. I could have killed him. But I got the message."[149] Nitzchke, on the other hand, was inspiring. He arrived in New Haven in early 1939 to take up his appointment as assistant professor of architectural design (although he had no academic degree), quickly proving himself to not only excel as a studio critic, but also as a link to some of the most interesting trends in contemporary art. Because of his wide-ranging group of friends and professional connections— Le Corbusier, the sculptress Mary (Meric) Callery, Paul Nelson, and Fernand

2.36   Oscar Nitzchke, Maison de Publicité (1936).

2.38   The 1938 "Conference on Housing" held in the
Yale Art Gallery.

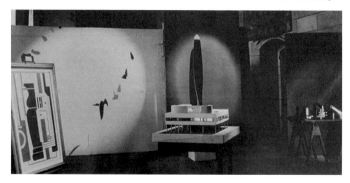

2.37   *Modern Exhibition—Painting and Architecture,* installation,
Yale Art Gallery (1943).

Léger, to name but a few—he brought a cosmopolitanism hitherto unknown to Yale, connecting the school with an international art scene that, as the result of the political situation in Europe, was shifting from Paris to New York. Together with Harrison, he persuaded the French painter Léger to lecture twice, and Le Corbusier's sometime collaborator, the painter Amédée Ozenfant, to lecture on "Form from Prehistoric to Modern Times." Thirty-five years after his student days, Porter McCray (1908–2000; M.Arch 1941) recalled that it was not "the Bauhaus" which was brought to Yale, but a different kind of Continental modernism. Dress designer Elsa Schiaparelli "gave a marvelous course on color and interiors, she was absolutely terrific. . . . Bucky Fuller was coming on very strong on the scene at that point. So it was really a very stimulating, exciting moment, actually. . . . And everyone . . . in the school . . . was awakening to a whole new world and it was inevitable that Beaux-Arts would collapse."[150] Nitzchke's enthusiasm helped make these visits meaningful for students. As Dudley recalled: "Oscar exuded the qualities that he, an architect, got from the work of such men, and we absorbed his love of the creative integration of all the arts. His own enthusiasm and admiration generated open-mindedness in students seeing work far ahead of the academic teaching at the school."[151] Nitzchke split his time between New York and New Haven. George Dudley recalls, "An important and unique arrangement for him was to have a small room and bath in Weir Hall. . . . Cloistered away along steps leading up into the courtyard, hard by the windowless Egyptian mass of the secret society Skull and Bones, this retreat afforded him both privacy and accessibility to students, in an arrangement reflecting perfectly the role he would play at the School."[152]

According to Dudley, Nitzchke personified "the productive interdisciplinary fun-loving avant-garde," becoming, like Faelten in the late 1920s, the focal point of the Advanced Design studios. Nitzchke never spent weekends in New Haven, preferring his Eighth Street apartment in New York's Greenwich Village, from which he would return to New Haven with recharged exuberance because of what he had experienced in the city's museums, art galleries, and bookstores, bringing students "a sense of sharing in the turbulence at the cutting edge. He always had the best records, avant-garde journals, and catalogues of exhibits we might never have heard of otherwise."[153] Nitzchke was inclusive in his appreciation of both people and architecture and, rather than dictating his personal beliefs, he led by example. "Some students hungry for hard information or turned off by his 'bohemianism' gained little from this," notes Dudley, "but others were inspired to become passionately involved in his forward-looking modernism and more understanding of its clear expression in his approach to design. Again memory's image seems to reflect the larger reality—a bohemian, yes, but a proper Swiss bohemian, in white shirt, blue serge suit and black shoes."[154]

The lack of a clear and singular direction, such as that demanded by Gropius at Harvard or Mies at IIT, encouraged Yale students to make their own discoveries in the broad area of modern art and architecture. The physical intimacy between the architecture studios in Weir Hall and the Art Gallery where many classes were taught—forcing students to walk past great works of art "every day for some reason or other"[155]—combined with the fluid culture of connections that Nitzchke enabled, encouraged students to curate their own exhibits of contemporary art and architecture. With space at a premium, halls and stairways were enlisted as places of display: "In those days, you could put out a room of Picasso etchings and let the students walk through it and leave it open all night and nothing ever happened to it."[156] New York architects, as well as John McAndrew, architecture curator at the Museum of Modern Art, were "very helpful in the early stages in lending us stuff every fall, just photographs, to put in shows on modern architecture. It was very informal and very inexpensive. We would borrow a station wagon usually and come down to pick the stuff up, never insured it or anything else."[157]

Hugh Moore chose the work of the Czech-born architect Antonin Raymond (1888–1976) for his exhibit. Raymond had settled in Japan after working with Frank Lloyd Wright on the Imperial Hotel (1923), but had recently returned to New York as war clouds gathered. To reflect Raymond's Japanese-inflected modernism, Moore "painted the walls barn red overlaid with bold plaids in white adhesive tape. Shadows of Bamboo played on shoji screens and Mrs. Raymond's hand-blocked fabrics draped over the stair rails." But when Raymond came to New Haven to give a talk, "he said nothing of his Japanese work, spending the whole time on his experimental low-cost housing. Although I was pretty mad at him at the time [I] ended up myself in public housing which of course is not 'low cost' but 'low income.'" Moore recalls that "fellow classmate Mel Schnall [b. 1919; B.Arch 1943], brother of noted architectural photographer Ben Schnall, did not fare so well with his exhibit. Schnall had gotten hold of a collection of watercolor renderings of Rambusch Lighting Fixtures. Pure Renaissance! Nitzchke . . . was furious. He said (recalling his rebellious student days in Paris) we should take them down, smash them up and burn them. The Administration had them taken down, ostensibly for 'security reasons.'"[158] For those who could afford it, Depression economics made travel cheap and, with work in architects' offices not readily available, students toured Europe during the summer recess in search of modern buildings. Advised by Hugo Van Kuyck (1902–1975), a young Belgian architect who taught at Yale from 1936 to 1940, Dudley and Maynard (Mike) Meyer (1913–1993; B.F.A. 1935, M.F.A. 1939) visited Dudok's work in Hilversum, Holland, where they "stumbled on the beautiful Grand Hotel Gooiland by [Bernard] Bijvoet and [Jan] Duiker, completed in 1936. Such new work was never mentioned at Yale before Oscar's arrival."[159] Dudley and Meyer also traveled to Switzerland to discover "what [Karl] Moser, the Roths, Max Bill and others were doing there." Returning to Yale, Dudley and Meyer, advised by Nitzchke, who put them in touch with Sigfried Giedion and Alfred Roth, curated a Constructivist-inspired exhibition in March 1940 of what they had seen: *Modern Architecture in Switzerland Presented by the Graduate Group in Architecture to Show the Voices-Methods-Aims of the Movement in Switzerland.*[160]

The exhibit of Swiss architecture inspired Henry Kibel (b. 1919; M.Arch 1947) to organize an exhibition in 1943, *Modern Exhibition—Painting and Architecture,* also displayed in the Sculpture Hall of the Art Gallery (2.37).[161] As Dudley recalled, the motivation behind the show "was the exciting new notion of an inclusive, unprejudiced and inspirational juxtaposition of the best of many disciplines." The exhibit, which was lit by Richard Kelly (1910–1977; B.Arch 1944), a pioneer of modern architectural lighting design, consisted of paintings and sculpture from the gallery's collection, including work by Alexander Calder, Alberto Giacometti, Fernand Léger, Joan Miró, Juan Gris, Piet Mondrian, Paul Klee, Amédée Ozenfant, Jacques Lipchitz, and Pablo Picasso, as well as photographs by Herbert Matter, Harold Edgerton, Barbara Morgan, and Man Ray, and architectural models borrowed from the Museum of Modern Art, such as Le Corbusier's Villa Savoye, Mies van der Rohe's Tugendhat House, and Paul Nelson's Suspended House.[162] The show also included industrial parts and models of molecules and mathematical formulae along with urbanism projects by Nitzchke, Mike Meyer, and Maurice Rotival. All of this was accompanied by sound recordings by Duke Ellington, Edgard Varèse, Paul Hindemith, James Joyce, Darius Milhaud, and Igor Stravinsky. As Dudley recollected forty years later: "The list of exhibited material speaks for itself and speaks also of Oscar's enthusiastic participation."[163] But, as Henry Kibel was to point out to Dudley, "It was not only Oscar's closeness to important people in the arts but his creativity, incisive criticism and sensitivity to the *esprit du temps* that made him an inspiration and prime-mover in . . . [its] conception."[164]

Hugh Moore was stimulated by the mix of pedagogical systems: "We got the best of both old and new. The first year we were given programs like mausoleums and temples. I took Shepherd Steven's course on Italian Renaissance. . . . We were the last class to do renderings in multiple layers of Chinese ink."[165] But Porter McCray felt that the transition from Beaux-Arts to modern made for "a very painful year." Nonetheless Dean Meeks, "who was a perfectly extraordinary man," proved himself to be "remarkably open minded, considering all the blasphemes that were leveled against the Beaux-Arts at that time." McCray, as president of the student body in 1940, "had to do an awful lot of persuading with the students to even tolerate the continuation of some of the faculty who were on tenure," including Stevens, "who was brilliant in all of that vocabulary," but whom the students demanded be removed. "It was a very trying moment."[166] Stevens would retire as professor along with Meeks in 1947.[167]

For some students, Meeks's hesitant embrace of modernism was too little too late, leading them to follow their undergraduate education in New Haven with graduate work at Harvard. One of those was Benjamin Thompson (1918–2002; B.F.A. 1941), who after Harvard would become a partner in Gropius's practice, the Architects' Collaborative, a member of the Harvard faculty, and, eventually, chairman of its Department of Architecture (1964–68), during which time he surprised many by reflecting positively on his time at Yale, remembering it as "a good school," albeit one that "never did have a serious formulation of its purpose, but it exposed you to many influences, which was fine."[168] Another student, Norman Fletcher (1917–2007; B.F.A. 1940), also moved on to Cambridge—not to study under Gropius, but to join him as a founding partner in the Architects' Collaborative.

With Harrison and Nitzchke encouraging innovative thinking in design, Meeks took a second stab at introducing town-planning courses into the curriculum. Like the move to "the modern" in the design studios, the decision to initiate a planning program was a reactive one. Now, with the architect-planner Hudnut leading Harvard and the statistic-minded German émigré planner Martin Wagner (1885–1957) also on its faculty, Meeks felt obliged to restart the program at Yale; in 1938, he appointed Yale College and École des Beaux-Arts graduate William E. Parsons (1872–1939; B.A. 1895, B.F.A. 1905), of the Chicago firm of Bennett, Parsons & Frost, to teach courses in housing and planning.[169] Parsons had been the master planner of Manila and the Pasadena, California, Civic Center, among other notable projects. At the announcement of his appointment, Meeks stated, "The day of design of single individual buildings without regard to their neighbors is over."[170] Unfortunately, Parsons died before he could take up his Yale post, but the planning program nonetheless got going when Dudley and Meyer decided to remain at Yale as postgraduate students and work under Harrison, organizing a master's program in the field. Along with William S. Evans (1913–1999; B.A.

1937, B.F.A. 1939, M.Arch 1940), Wallace R. Lee, Jr. (1914–2000; B.F.A. 1939), and James L. Murphy, Jr. (1916–2009; M.F.A. 1940), Dudley and Meyer formed "the Yale Graduate Group in Architecture" to undertake a study of Bridgeport, Connecticut, with, as Dudley recalled, "only our homegrown instruction in city planning!" He arranged a discussion with Bridgeport's Socialist mayor, Jasper McLevy, while Nitzchke "brought us the documentation developed by the CIAM [Congrès Internationaux d'Architecture Moderne] in its systematization of the analysis of cities . . . so that comparative studies could be made. Oscar blindly took our team of a half dozen graduate students and put it amongst experienced planning groups around the world."[171] Harrison arranged with the *Bridgeport Herald* to help the postgraduate students financially and to publish the study.[172]

In 1938, at Harrison's instigation, housing experts were invited to Yale to explore the latest technical developments in the field at a conference convened by the department in collaboration with *Life*, the highly successful picture magazine reinvented two years before by Henry R. Luce (1898–1967; B.A. 1920). Attended by two hundred people, the conference was accompanied by an exhibition "of new housing and building techniques, including two trailer-mounted bathrooms designed by Bucky Fuller"[173] (2.38). It was the first of many exhibitions designed by George Nelson. Luce addressed the group, as did Meeks and Harrison; Richmond H. Shreve, codesigner of the Empire State Building and architect of Parkchester, the Metropolitan Life Insurance Company's new super-scale Bronx, New York, housing project; Deputy Administrator of Federal Housing Miles Colean; and Beardsley Ruml, treasurer of R. H. Macy & Co.[174]

Increasingly involved in Harrison's practice, Nitzchke frequently brought "work from the office back to his study/bedroom at Yale," and to the pleasure of many students, afforded them an "opportunity to see how he worked." Dudley remembers in particular the project for Hotel Avila for Caracas, Venezuela, which was to have direct consequences for the postwar redevelopment of the city of New Haven and for the city planning program at Yale. While working on the Hotel Avila, Max Abramovitz encountered Maurice Rotival (1892–1980), whom he invited to the States to meet Harrison and to teach at Yale, beginning in 1941, first as lecturer in city planning and later as associate professor—a position he held until 1945 (2.39). With Rotival's appointment, along with the appointments of Dudley and Meyer as instructors in city planning, a systematic graduate program in planning was at last initiated, offering "several new courses in fundamental theory of design, of unit building, and of group and

2.39 Maurice Rotival (1951).

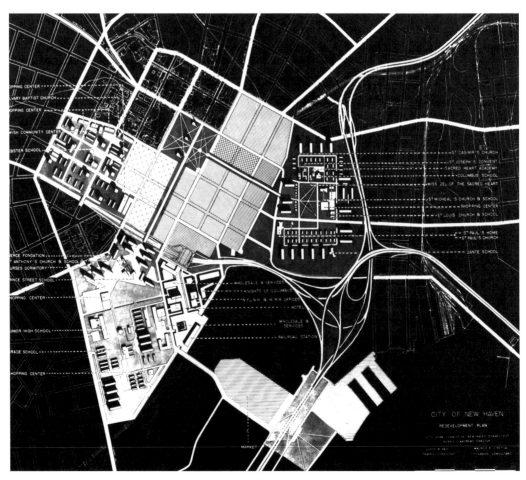

2.40 Maurice Rotival, City of New Haven Redevelopment Plan (ca. 1942).

regional planning . . . added in order that each student may have a thorough understanding of the nature and scope of the problems which he may be called upon to face in a world in which an architect's responsibilities as a planner are being constantly enlarged."[175]

"Rotival made an immediate impression," Dudley has written, "with his Gallic flair, his international experience, and a planning approach that was more intuitive than exclusively analytical." Known for his monumental, Beaux-Arts–style plans, Rotival adapted these to the needs of high-speed roadways that he proposed to circle the city. When New Haven Mayor (1932–35, 1940–41) John Murphy invited proposals for a new master plan for the city, Rotival, Meyer, and Dudley were selected, asking Nitzchke to join their team since "we realized that proposals would have to be convincingly presented and the diagrammatic representation of our research and conclusions would have to be communicated with the greatest possible clarity and visual interest."[176] Rico Cedro has pointed out in the catalogue to his 1988 exhibition, *Modern Visions: Twentieth Century Urban Design in New Haven,* that it was Rotival and Meyer, collaborating in 1941, who supplied "all of the elements and techniques of [New Haven's redevelopment in] the 1950s and 60s . . . regional expressways driven to the threshold of the [original] nine squares, reorganized street patterns, downtown reconstruction and new waterfront land" (2.40). Although the plan took into consideration the Frederick Law Olmsted, Jr., and Cass Gilbert plan of 1910, it introduced a "new ascendancy, some would claim the supremacy, of roads as the framework of the city."[177]

Dean Meeks was impressed by the work being produced by Yale planners, and by Rotival, whose bold approach contrasted with the statistically based planning that Martin Wagner was advocating at Harvard. Moreover, as Hugh Moore has put it, Rotival "was good company."[178] Meeks saw Rotival as someone who shared his values. Announcing the planner's appointment to the faculty, Meeks quoted Rotival: "Yale did not and does not believe that there is a distinct demarcation enclosing planning within absolute limits, neither does the university consider that there is necessarily a special science of city planning . . . [which] is one of the phases of [a] broad human problem—planning for common living." Rotival emphasized the need for broad studies rather than specialization with the observation that Yale's willingness to "attach foremost importance to design is to be expected, since it considers that design is to the planner the most practical way of expressing himself." In the fall 1943 term, the planning program was formalized within the Department of Architecture, offering a twelve-lecture course, the first of its kind to be given in New England, focusing on the postwar era.[179]

With the department seeming to regain its momentum, in May 1941 Meeks wrote to Provost Edgar Furniss to request that the faculty in architecture "be permitted to award the degree of Bachelor of Architecture . . . in order that the degree may more clearly describe the professional education of our respective students."[180] The new degree was conferred for the first time in 1942, replacing the bachelor of fine arts in architecture. To meet the needs for post-professional study, a one-year program leading to a master of architecture was once again instituted in 1943.[181]

The entrance of the United States into World War II late in 1941 encouraged Meeks's mildly xenophobic antimodernism. Within a matter of months after the Japanese attack on Pearl Harbor he announced "a unique new curriculum" that would, according to a somewhat jingoist university press release, break "off the shackles of European tradition in American architecture while adapting itself to the needs of the war."[182] Whether he meant a break with Beaux-Arts academicism, Bauhaus functionalism, or both was not made clear, but the new curriculum was intended to fit in with the university's "accelerated" war program, condensing five calendar years of study into three and a half years. The change was a realization of significant aspects of the curricular reform that Meeks seemed to have advocated in 1937, when he shared the platform with Gropius at the annual meeting of the American Institute of Architects: "It is time that the two 'fetishes' of architecture education—the credit system and the planning of courses on a yearlong basis—be discarded and buried forever. There should be no such thing as specific credit toward a total of say 132 units and then the degree. As for the other artificial measure, the academic year, I believe it an absurdity."[183]

Meeks's "accelerated" curriculum anticipated the integrated program George Howe would attempt to implement in the early 1950s. For Meeks, "the pattern of the new architecture is going to be not only democratic but humanistic," and Yale's accelerated "program will stress the interrelation of every course in the department, providing automatic synchronization of the work in theory, design and construction."[184] Architectural problems would be accompanied by related course work, meaning that students designing houses would at the same time study the historical development of housing, the theory of planning houses and town planning, as well as the practical issues of construction. Meeks justified the accelerated curriculum as a response to the country's role as an arsenal of democracy: "It is up to the armed forces to decide whether they need an individual more than the arsenal." But he emphasized that, at the very least, it was "every professional man's duty to perfect his professional training."[185]

When addressing graduating students less than a year after the accelerated program had been implemented, Meeks put great emphasis on the postwar future, when a pent-up demand for projects would require the services of architects. As significant, if not more so, was the "new order of life" Meeks believed would soon be developing: "He would be a bold man who would dare to prophesy its nature in full; but at least we do know that we are going to have to provide not only materially but intellectually and artistically for a far broader clientele and far wider public." Meeks was in many ways clear-seeing about what the postwar years would be like, stating that as far as the architect was concerned, there would be a responsibility to carry forward large-scale housing and urban redevelopment programs. And he did anticipate the extent to which old cities would be redeveloped: "I do not mean that we are going to tear down completely to build anew. But we are going to modify existing buildings in a scope far wider than ever experienced before. The shaking of society on its very foundations means not only rebuilding socially but physically as well." Meeks was confident that the "architect by training and viewpoint is particularly fitted to share in—yes, perhaps to lead—such comprehensive physical and social rehabilitation."[196]

Among the curricular reforms was a dramatic change of policy initiated, in part at least, to make up for the loss of male students to the war effort: women would be admitted into the Architecture Department for the first time.[187] Although the School of the Fine Arts had, from its inception, admitted women into its programs in painting and sculpture, the Architecture Department had been an exclusively male domain. Meeks's decision to admit women students into architecture had little immediate effect, but after the war, an increasing number of women enrolled, including Nancy Pan Sun (M.Arch 1949) and Sonia Albert Schimberg (1925–1981; M.Arch 1950); Schimberg went on to a rewarding career in the office of architect Charles Luckman, where she designed hotel interiors (2.41). In 1981, an award was initiated in Schimberg's name to recognize the achievements of top female students.[188] Other pioneering women students include Vica Schneiwind Emery (b. 1925; M.Arch 1955), Estelle Thompson Margolis (b. 1926; M.Arch 1955) (2.42, 2.43), and Leona Annenberg Nalle (M.Arch 1956).

Wallace Harrison went to Washington, D.C., in 1942 to aid in the war effort, taking George Dudley along as his assistant. Together, they set out to help improve the standard of living in twenty Central and South American countries. After Harrison's departure, his place as chief design critic was taken by Richard Marsh Bennett (1907–1995), who had joined the faculty as assistant professor of architectural design in 1940. A graduate of Harvard (B.F.A.

2.41 Sonia Albert Schimberg (fourth from right, M.Arch 1950) in front of a hotel designed with Luckman Architects (1955).

1928, M.Arch 1931), Bennett had worked with Edward Durell Stone (1902–1978) during the 1930s while also teaching at Rensselaer Polytechnic Institute, Columbia, and Vassar, as well as at Yale. His work at the time was heavily influenced by Le Corbusier and unabashedly modernist, as evidenced by his "ideal scheme" for New York, developed in 1940 with Granville Hicks, that proposed razing the entire city and building regularly spaced towers. Bennett left Yale in 1943 to join the retail giant Montgomery Ward, as head of its Bureau of Style and Design. Shortly after Bennett's resignation, Meeks told President (1937–50) Charles Seymour (1885–1963; B.A. 1908, Ph.D. 1911), "We were reluctant and profoundly disturbed to lose him. He not only showed outstanding ability in teaching Design, but also interested himself in fundamental problems of education."[189] Bennett's departure was a blow for the program, calling attention to the fact that busy architects were only willing to commit to teaching for shorter and shorter periods. Harvard was also experiencing faculty instability, but to a lesser extent because many of its staff were able to live and practice in the Boston area while remaining on the faculty. Yale, situated in a small city with limited opportunities for architectural practice, was forced to import talent from New York, as it had been doing since the time of Harrison Wheeler Lindsley.

Bennett's role as chief critic was taken up by Morris Ketchum, Jr. (1904–1984), in 1943–44, and then William W. Wurster (1895–1973), who decided to return to active practice in California after only one term. Writing to President Seymour, Meeks attributed design faculty instability to "the calls of growing and successful practices in the case of such high quality men on the one hand, and the very slim recompense available through continually reduced budgets. Such constant changing is bad not only for continuity in design but for student morale."[190] Following Wurster's abrupt departure and an extensive search yielding more than twenty-five names, Meeks asked Bennett to return as professor of design, effective February 1945. Meeks believed Bennett to be the right man "to develop the School along contemporary lines . . . a man who is thoroughly in sympathy with the modern development but who has a complete general background and training and who is in no sense a faddist . . . a man of necessary power and qualifications, young enough to be with us during our period of postwar development."[191] In advocating Bennett's reappointment, Meeks made it clear that now-modernist Yale, just as it had done in the largely Beaux-Arts past, would not follow the practice of its peer schools by turning to foreign teachers to lead the design program: "The Yale School has been essentially American in composition and ideals to provide the best possible training for young architects to practice in America. With this in mind, as

2.42   Estelle Thompson Margolis, A Post Office in New Haven, model. Thesis project (1955).

2.43   John Lee (M.Arch 1954), Estelle Thompson Margolis (M.Arch 1955), and Paul Pozzi (M.Arch 1954) building a house in Weston, Connecticut, for client George Brunjes (ca. 1954).

far as possible, we are not planning to call upon foreigners." For Meeks, it was important for Yale that an American take charge of the Department of Architecture, as "even the most brilliant foreigner is almost always out of sympathy with American traditions, backgrounds and the demands of the American public."[192] In this, Meeks was echoing his long-standing position with regard to employing "resident Frenchmen" as senior design faculty. Nonetheless, Meeks's statement, given the wartime context, could also be deemed jingoistic. In a thinly disguised reference to Gropius, Breuer, and Mies, he continued: "It is true that there are a number of refugee foreigners, mostly from Germany, who are now teaching in America. And heretofore there has been what now seems an unfortunate tendency to overestimate the value of a foreigner with a consequent under-estimation of the outstanding ability of American teachers of design."[193] Bennett returned to Yale as full professor, effective February 1945, not only serving as professor of design, but also assuming Meeks's position as department chairman in June.[194] However, after a promising start, he was lured back into full-time practice in 1947, joining a Chicago firm that would become Loebl, Schlossman & Bennett, with responsibilities for a massive suburban development called Park Forest.

As Meeks approached Yale's mandatory retirement age, with his exit scheduled for July 1, 1947, he offered some thoughts on the school's future, including an evaluation of the effort to unify the introductory programs within the school, which had already begun with a "first realistic step"—the establishment of a new comprehensive course, "Theory I," that, as a requirement for all students in the school and an elective open to Yale College undergraduates, would examine "the principles of vision, design and art by means of lectures given by men from various parts of the University supplemented by a regular schedule of laboratory and studio experiments."

Meeks hoped the new course would be the first of a three-term series devoted to ancient, Gothic, and Renaissance art, as well as contemporary movements and problems of modern art. Meeks also proposed to reduce the specialization that came with the school's independent departments by admitting students into the larger Art School, rather than the various disciplines within it, allowing students a degree of flexibility with regard to their specific interests as they developed.[195]

As the university prepared for Meeks's retirement after twenty-five years as dean, it began a search for his replacement, considering L. Bancel LaFarge (1900–1989; B.F.A. 1925), a practicing architect in New York; Charles Nagel (1899–1992; B.A. 1923, B.F.A. 1926), an architect turned museum director;

and Charles Sawyer (1906–2005; B.A. 1929), whose background was also in arts administration. Sawyer had served as curator of the Addison Gallery of American Art at Phillips Academy, Andover, before succeeding Francis Henry Taylor as head of the Worcester Art Museum in 1942, when Taylor became director of the Metropolitan Museum of Art in New York. During World War II, Sawyer served in the Office of Strategic Services (OSS), where, as one of the "Monuments Men," he documented works of art stolen by the Nazis and helped return them to their rightful owners.[196] By late 1946, Sawyer, having risen above the other contenders, was asked to offer observations about the school. He responded with a memorandum almost exclusively devoted to the departments of Painting and Sculpture and to the Art Gallery, but opened with the observation that he had the "general impression . . . that the School of Architecture is the focal point of the School of Fine Arts and the Department on which its reputation very largely rests." However, Sawyer continued,

> it is also my impression that the School of Architecture has not developed or materially enhanced its reputation during the past ten years. In a time of drastic changes in the building profession and in the whole role of the architect in connection with it, it would seem as if the Yale School has adjusted itself less successfully than some of the others to the problems of new materials and structural principles. One feels a survival of Beaux-Arts principles and practice that have, in some measure at least, outlived their usefulness. I realize that changes have been made in recent years to answer in part such criticism, but it seems to be the opinions [*sic*] of a considerable section of the architectural profession that these changes have not penetrated far enough into the fabric of the Architecture School as a whole.[197]

In March 1947, Charles Sawyer was appointed Meeks's successor as dean of the Yale School of the Fine Arts; he was also given the title of director of the newly organized Division of the Arts, with responsibility for the overall direction of the Art Gallery, the Art History Department, and the departments of Drama, Painting and Sculpture, and Architecture, each to be administered by strong leaders who were to become "responsible for general supervision of their student bodies and for their own curriculum."[198] Over the next decade, this independence would be crucial to the advancement of all the arts programs, but it would also result in conflict and controversy with Yale College, particularly in the case of architecture. Upon his selection as the new dean, Sawyer was invited to meet with Meeks. The meeting went quite well, and afterward Meeks wrote to President Seymour that though he "had expected to leave the School in a veil of mourning," he would "now go out greatly cheered on by the prospect."[199]

Everett Meeks spent his last years in New York, where he died on October 27, 1954, at the age of seventy-five.[200]

3

An American Bauhaus? 1947–1958

"Each discipline [in the School of Architecture and Design] is united by basic courses common to all and by occasional collaborative projects, cross-department electives, and lectures which encourage in each student an awareness of the essential unity of the visual and spatial arts. Training for the practice of architecture at Yale is based on the concept that architecture is the art of building, and that the art of building is the fertilizing principle that makes the trade, the science, and the business of building bear fruit in significant form."

Bulletin of Yale University, Division of the Arts, 1953

3.1 Harold Hauf (ca. 1945).

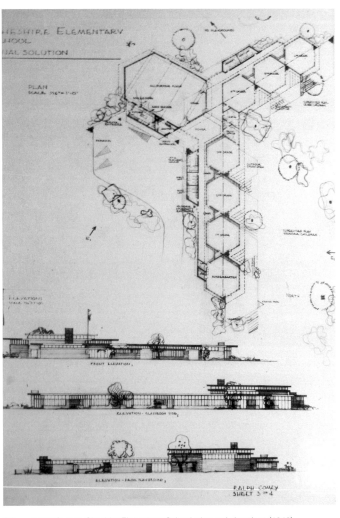

3.2 Ralph Comey, Cheshire Elementary School, plan and elevations (1948).

In October 1947, Sawyer made the odd decision to ask Harold D. Hauf (1905–2003; M.S. 1932), professor of architectural engineering, to serve as chairman of the Department of Architecture, thereby placing the program, for the first time, in the hands of someone whose inclinations were more technical than artistic.[1] G. Holmes Perkins (1904–2004), then the Charles Dyer Norton Professor of Regional Planning at Harvard's Graduate School of Design, had been seriously courted for the position, but after demonstrating a keen interest in coming to Yale, Perkins declined the offer, leading Sawyer to speculate that he had "probably received definite assurance that he will succeed Dean Hudnut at the GSD, and this, with his keen interest in the development of the planning department at Harvard, probably turned the scales against us."[2] Perkins did not become the Harvard dean. When Hudnut stepped down in 1952, Perkins had recently left Cambridge, decamping to the University of Pennsylvania to become its dean of the School of Fine Arts (1951–74).[3] Gropius also stepped down in 1952 as chairman of Harvard's Department of Architecture, and José Luis Sert (1902–1983) was appointed both dean and chairman.

Harold Hauf (3.1) had a long history at Yale that began with his years as a graduate student in the School of Engineering in the early 1930s, when he also served as an instructor, rising in 1939 to the rank of associate professor of architectural engineering. After wartime service as a lieutenant in the U.S. Naval Reserve, Hauf briefly returned to the university in 1945, only to leave again—this time to serve as director of the Technical Branch of the National Housing Agency in connection with the Veterans' Emergency Housing Program in Washington, D.C.[4] After only six months in that position, he returned to Yale in September 1946 as acting chairman before being appointed professor and chairman.[5]

As chairman, Hauf was not exactly beloved. Peter Millard (1924–2009; B.Arch 1951), a veteran naval aviator who would later become an influential teacher at the school, remembered him as "a man with a former lieutenant commander's engineering mentality still very much in charge. He was impatient with his mostly veterans student body's casual attitude toward rules." Millard elaborated on Hauf's temperament in relation to the general mood of the day: "One morning he entered his office that overlooked Weir Courtyard, which was full of students eating their brown bag lunches. He saw an open casement window with two-inch green footprints proceeding across the sill, down the inside wall behind the radiator, across the floor, up the leg of his desk, over the desktop and the papers on it, down the other side, and then back out the window. His swivel chair had been replaced with a seatless toilet bowl in which floated a folded paper boat with 'USNR' printed on it. With a howl of rage, he picked up the toilet and flung it across the room. It had been sealed at the floor with modeling clay, and the bowl of water opened all over. It took Louise Britton—the school's 'mother' [school secretary]—all afternoon to calm him down."[6]

Sawyer and Hauf, recognizing that the department needed strong design leadership, undertook a search for a professor of design. Sawyer's choice for this appointment was Eero Saarinen, "who is probably the school's most distinguished graduate in the past twenty years. . . . Such an appointment would be widely proclaimed in the profession."[7] Saarinen declined the appointment. He did, however, agree to join the newly instituted University Council, serving on its Committee on the Division of the Arts—a position he held until 1954. The main function of the University Council was "to study the major activities of the University at close range and make plans and recommendations for their improvement." Council members appointed by the corporation were to constitute visiting committees, "each devoted to a special interest."[8] Committee members were asked to become "intimately acquainted with the aims and needs of the particular parts of the University to which they are assigned, to make the acquaintance of their officers and faculties, to inspect their work and equipment, to appraise their national standing, and to assemble evidence upon which to base plans for their welfare and betterment."[9] Saarinen also served on the Committee on the Yale Center for Fine Arts (1958–61) and, importantly, on President (1950–63) Alfred Whitney Griswold's (1906–1963; B.A. 1929, Ph.D. 1933) Architectural Advisory Committee (1960–61), while also working on campus planning projects and proposing ideas for new buildings.

As they awaited Saarinen's decision whether or not to accept the invitation to become professor of design, the faculty decided that should he decline and no other suitable person could be found, it was important to fill a "subordinate position before the opening of the fall season. Mr. Hauf and all the members of the School faculty are in agreement that the current situation in Design is not satisfactory and that we should not carry through another year without an additional appointment."[10] Unable to attract Saarinen as professor, Sawyer and Hauf set out to regularize the informal policy of visiting critics by asking them to work under the leadership of a senior critic. The visiting critics would serve as architects in residence for a limited time, usually about five or six weeks in a term.[11] In his effort to recapture the department's luster, Hauf asked Edward Durell Stone to become the department's first senior critic in Advanced Design, charged with "giving coordination and coherence to the whole design program."[12]

Before coming to Yale, Stone had taught at New York University's short-lived (1928–42) School of Architecture and Allied Arts, which was run in conjunction with the Beaux-Arts Institute of Design. At NYU he established a close professional friendship with Henry A. Pfisterer (1908–1972), who was responsible for the structural engineering of the Radio City Music Hall (1932) for which Stone had been the lead designer.[13] Pfisterer, who joined the Yale faculty as assistant professor in 1941, may well have promoted Stone for the job. Stone may also have had the support of Philip Goodwin (1885–1958; B.A. 1907), an influential Yale alumnus and his co-architect in the design of the Museum of Modern Art's first permanent home in New York (1939). Stone served in the military from 1942 to 1945, earning the rank of major before returning to private practice. Short on funds, he gladly accepted Yale's invitation, remaining on the faculty until 1951, proving himself to be an effective and well-liked studio critic who, according to his former student R. Paige Donhauser (1923–2012; B.A. 1945, M.Arch 1950), was "amusing, interested, and serious about taking his students' work at face value."[14] For Donhauser and other Yale students, Stone's role as mentor would continue beyond academia. Donhauser went on to become a partner in Stone's office, as did another graduate, John C. Hill (B.A. 1949), while William Guy Garwood (M.Arch 1949) and Edward Lloyd Flood (M.Arch 1947) would join the office as senior designers, causing it to be referred to as a "rough and tumble Yale finishing School."[15] Shortly after graduation, Flood would join Stone's office as senior draftsman and also serve under him at Yale, teaching first-year Basic Design with another newly minted architect, Eugene Nalle (1916–2008; B.Arch 1948), who would make a dramatic and controversial impact on the school in the 1950s (see Chapter 3). Flood's student work reflected the stylistic uncertainty of the immediate postwar years, as did Stone's own work, which moved from International Style modernism to a "hair shirt" manner heavily influenced by Frank Lloyd Wright and, to an extent, by Harwell Hamilton Harris (1903–1990).[16] These new influences are also reflected in student work such as Ralph Comey's (b. 1924; B.Arch 1951) hexagonal design for an elementary school (3.2) and William Guy Garwood's senior thesis for a "Small Hawaiian House." That a modest-size, single-family suburban house should be deemed appropriate as a thesis project testifies to the virtually complete rejection of the Beaux-Arts approach, with its emphasis on monumental public architecture, leading Vincent Scully (b. 1920; B.A. 1940, M.A. 1947, Ph.D. 1949) to call his essay on the period "Doldrums in the Suburbs."[17]

Under Hauf and Stone, the program took on a literal pragmatism that George Howe would severely criticize a few years later.[18] For example,

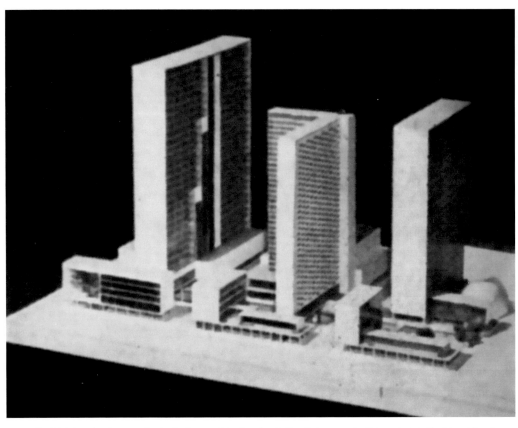

3.3 Model of the redevelopment plan for the Avenue of the Americas in New York, created by Yale students led by Edward Durell Stone (spring 1947). From left to right: Mexican Building designed by Edward Lloyd Flood (M.Arch 1947); Argentine Building by Paul Webb, Jr. (M.Arch 1947); and Brazilian Building by John Caproni (M.Arch 1947).

in 1947, thesis students worked under Stone's direction and that of Colonel V. Clement Jenkins, president of New York's Avenue of the Americas Association, to propose a plan that in many ways anticipated the westward expansion of Rockefeller Center under Harrison & Abramovitz in the 1960s.[19] The students were asked to line Manhattan's Sixth Avenue, newly rechristened the Avenue of the Americas, with low-rise buildings designed to house consulates, behind which a high-rise hotel and office towers were to be accessed via a below-grade pedestrian promenade linking all the buildings (3.3). In 1948, Stone invited hospital specialist Alfred L. Aydelott (1916–2008), from Memphis, Tennessee, to join him in teaching a hospital studio, certainly a pragmatic topic, which became a staple during the 1950s. Stone and Aydelott, who had met while serving on a hospital competition jury, became fast friends, earning a reputation as "big drinkers whose encouragement of each other's inclination for good times and boozing for a number of years would become a source of pain and regret to their families. For the moment, though [while at Yale], Stone remained sober."[20]

With Stone serving as chief critic, the first cohort of visiting critics in residence was appointed (1947–48): Louis I. Kahn, Paul Schweikher, Carl Koch (1912–1998), Gardner Dailey (1895–1967), and Antonin Raymond. Kahn's appointment was something of a fluke, coming at the last minute when the scheduled visiting critic, Brazilian modernist Oscar Niemeyer (1907–2012), under terms of the 1918 Immigration Law, was denied entry into the United States because of his Communist sympathies, a controversial decision that was widely reported in the press.[21] The school had extended its invitation to Niemeyer during the summer of 1947, when he was in the United States in conjunction with his work, from 1947 to 1949, as part of the ten-member Board of Design responsible for the United Nations Headquarters (1952) in New York. But at the time he was to assume his position at Yale, the board's work was over and the State Department refused him further entrance, despite Sawyer's appeals. The controversy came at the height of the Red Scare, when artists, writers, and Hollywood personalities were asked to testify before Congress about their political affiliations.[22]

Ten alumni wrote to President Seymour to express their concern about Yale's stand in the case, saying: "We are often asked what the general position of Yale is in the matter of associating political beliefs with intellectual qualifications, and whether the university will plead for a re-examination of Sr. Niemeyer's case with the State Department."[23] Sawyer, acknowledging the letter on behalf of Seymour, outlined the situation:

Sr. Niemeyer was originally invited to serve as one of the visiting critics in Advanced Architectural Design when he was in the country last summer [summer 1947] as a member of the Architectural Advisory Board for the United Nations. It was our understanding that he would return to this country in September in connection with his services as a member of the Board. When he was not able to reach the country in September, we renewed the invitation for January, as we were informed that he would be coming in to the country at that time under a United Nations passport. In this connection, we would like to make it clear that Sr. Niemeyer was invited to Yale because of his distinction as an architect and regardless of his political affiliations.

We regret that what was intended as a professional appointment should now enter the realm of international politics. . . . It is, I am told, a clearly established University policy that the political affiliations of a candidate for such an appointment are not of concern.[24]

William Huff (b. 1927; B.A. 1949, M.Arch 1952) remembers "the outrage expressed by students over Niemeyer's exclusion. What a disappointment for that class!"[25] Meanwhile, Kahn's appointment went virtually unacknowledged. He was largely unknown to students, although Hauf knew his housing work, in partnership with George Howe and Oscar Stonorov, from publications and was also familiar with Kahn's service to the American Society of Planners and Architects.[26]

In 1948, Hauf, recognizing that the presence of so many disparate design personalities came at the expense of a coherent curriculum, established a Design Council—a somewhat informal committee made up of four instructors who, under his oversight, would each take responsibility for a different year. Eugene Nalle was put in charge of Basic Design and Robert Coolidge (1915–1955), appointed assistant professor in 1946, was given charge of Intermediate Design. Kahn led the Advanced Design students, and Stone, who guided the thesis students, was also charged with overall coordination. In his first report as chairman, Hauf expressed pleasure with the new arrangement: "The first year's experience with this system indicates that bringing advanced students into contact with such practicing architects stimulates their interest and imagination and at the same time tempers their thinking by apprising them of some of the realities encountered in professional practice."[27]

The 1948–49 academic year saw Louis I. Kahn given a full faculty appointment as critic in architectural design and the appointment of Eliot Noyes

(1910–1977) as critic, with additional responsibilities as a curator of special exhibits in the Art Gallery.[28] Visiting critics in 1948–49 included Eero Saarinen, Sven Markelius (1889–1972), Pietro Belluschi (1899–1994), John Sloan (1871–1951), and Hugh Stubbins (1912–2006). Saarinen, whose design, "The Gateway to the West," won the competition for the Jefferson National Expansion Memorial the previous spring, asked the students to study "a dormitory for professional students" at Yale to be located on a site near the Medical School; many of the designs, such as the proposal by Nancy Pan Sun and E. N. Chamberlain, reflect the predominant but increasingly diagrammatic International Style favored for large-scale student projects. Markelius was an architect and town planning director of Stockholm, in his native Sweden, and, like Niemeyer, had been a part of the U.N. design team. He offered as a problem the design of a civic and shopping center for the town of Hamden, Connecticut, which Hauf regarded as an excellent opportunity "to demonstrate the inter-relationship of architecture and city planning." Briefly reviewing the ongoing objective to strengthen the city planning program, the faculty petitioned Dean Sawyer to explore with the administration "the question of authorizing the award of a master's degree in this field," which was approved by the Yale Corporation in 1950.[29]

Fall 1948 also saw the reinstatement of the collaborative problem between advanced architects, painters, and sculptors, with Sawyer welcoming what had been "for many years an important part of the Yale tradition."[30] That year, Kahn expressed interest in leading the "problem," which had also been a hallmark of the American Academy in Rome.[31] Ironically, just as the collaborative problem was being revived in New Haven, it was abandoned in Rome by the fellows of the American Academy, some of whom objected to it as being too linked to Renaissance sensibilities.[32] According to Hauf, "When collaborative problems [at Yale] were given before the war, there was a tendency for the architectural students to design the building independently, leaving some area for mural decoration for the painters and a site for a suitable work of sculpture."[33] Things were to be different under Louis Kahn, assisted by Jean Charlot (1898–1979), a painter on leave for six weeks from the Fine Arts Center at Colorado Springs, and sculptor Gilbert Switzer (1912–1976). The studio was composed of sixteen teams, each consisting of two architects, two painters, and a sculptor. Kahn's project brief was for a "National Center of UNESCO."[34] The proposed facility was intended for the site in Fairmount Park, in Philadelphia, that the United Nations had considered for its headquarters.

Selected projects from the studio, published in the pages of *Progressive Architecture*, in a distinct contrast with the flaccid pictorial work then characteristic of the department, are notably inventive, with a rigorous use of

3.4 Bliss Woodruff (M.Arch 1949) of Team 16 discussing the design for "A National Center of UNESCO" with Louis Kahn. Collaborative Project (1949).

3.5 Unidentified student work, An Idea Center for Plastics (1949).

structure to determine form (3.4). Team 7, with Edward Dupaquier Dart (1922–1975; M.Arch 1949) and George Allen Hinds (b. 1922; B.Arch 1949, M.C.P. 1953) as architect members, produced what was, in terms of form, surely the boldest design, consisting of "three cantilevered trusses: the forces involved acting one against the other to produce a light, balanced composition with a minimum of constructive effort."[35] Dart would go on to become a partner in Richard Bennett's Chicago firm. Team 14's project, also illustrated, had as its sculptor member Evans Woollen (b. 1927; M.Arch 1952), who would go on to a successful career as an architect and artist in Indianapolis.

The 1949 collaborative problem, taught by Kahn, Josef Albers (1888-1976), now a visiting critic in the Department of Art and a member of the University Council for Art and Architecture, and Elliot Noyes, who had recently curated an exhibition on plastics in art, called for "An Idea Center for Plastics." As Sarah Goldhagen has written:

> Kahn was principally responsible for conceptualizing the studio prob-
> lems in which students would seek better designs for a material that
> was omnipresent but often visually unappealing. They were instructed
> to design "a showroom demonstrating to consumers potential uses of
> this new material"—namely, plastic—"in varying environmental circum-
> stances." Kahn, synthesizing Albers' ideas, wrote in his prospectus that
> an abstract aesthetic should prevail, in which students would explore the
> inherent qualities of different kinds and colors of plastic in changeable
> light. In a distinctly Albersian directive, Kahn instructed his students that
> the "principles of optics are of primary importance."[36]

To help ensure that architects didn't dominate the project, the brief was written to "provide equal design scope and responsibility for each member of the team" and did not specifically require a building, per se. Instead, students were tasked with designing a structure adjacent to a plastics manufacturing plant that would "[dramatize] the visual and structural potentialities of plastics by devising a *setting for the demonstration* of the effect that light, color and force can have on plastics of various shapes and textures" (3.5).[37] The broader aim of the project was to examine "the growing opportunities now developing in all the arts in Design for Industry."[38] Rohm and Haas, the Philadelphia-based chemical company that introduced the world to Plexiglas in 1936, readily supplied the materials for the students.[39] Architecture student Edward Nelson (b. 1918; M.Arch 1950) remembered that "the plastic materials were given to us in sheets of different thicknesses, blocks, rods, and cylinders, to encourage us to create

3.6 William Huff (B.F.A. 1949, M.Arch 1952) and Warren Peterson (M.Arch 1953), Zoo Collaborative, model (1951).

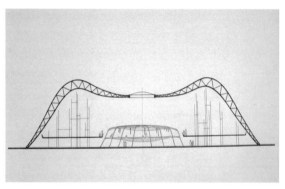

3.7 William Huff and Warren Peterson, Zoo Collaborative, section (1951).

3.8 Student building a geodesic dome on the roof of Weir Hall, designed with Visiting Critic R. Buckminster Fuller (1952).

3.9 Geodesic dome on the roof of Weir Hall (1952), New Haven.

new forms. Our creations could be sculpture or useful objects which might lead the company to find new uses for their products."[40] The studio proved to be quite challenging, with students producing wildly inconsistent work. While Kahn seemed to appreciate what Brenda Danilowitz refers to as "the conceptual notion of plastic as a modern material that the architect could use to forge a new and dramatic monumentality," Albers was not pleased with the results, which "were in sharp contrast to [the critics'] insistence of simplicity, rigor, and order."[41] Moreover, as Eeva-Liisa Pelkonen notes, "Albers was surely uninterested in the basic premise in the studio of working with new materials and new industries, since it distracted from what he saw was the basic function of all art education: learning to see."[42]

Albers's response to the studio theme should not have been surprising. In 1944, he had articulated his position on new materials in an essay concluding the influential book *New Architecture and City Planning,* which also contained an essay by Kahn. In contrast to his former Bauhaus colleague László Moholy-Nagy, Albers "emphasized the importance of manual labor and craft [over new materials], giving architecture and weaving as examples of the persistence of traditional technologies."[43] As he put it in the 1944 essay: "One thing seems sure, the more new architecture gains the quality of old handicraft, the more it will fulfill its task, the more it will contribute and lead to better living."[44] The message of the essay was clear, as Pelkonen notes: "Albers did not believe that modern architecture could be aligned with newness and progress."[45] It is this message that would carry over to the Core curriculum Howe would devise in collaboration with Eugene Nalle.

In 1951, a collaborative project led by Frederick Kiesler (1890–1965) challenged students to design a zoo (3.6, 3.7). Then, in October and November 1952, R. Buckminster Fuller led a collaborative of thirty-two architecture and thirty-two painting students. When Fuller arrived in New Haven, he was told that "in the past years the 'collaboration' usually consisted of the architects designing a building and, when they were all through, asking the painters to illustrate their solutions."[46] After much debate and discussion, Fuller puzzled out a way to avoid this, encouraging each participant to make his or her own contribution toward the design of an "environment control device." The studio engaged in prototyping studies, and little in the way of conventional design emerged. But in the spring term, a group of seven architecture thesis students organized themselves as the Fuller Study Group, with the intention of continuing the work by constructing a thirty-foot cardboard geodesic dome on the roof of Weir Hall (3.8, 3.9). "It fit together perfectly, it was strong and stout," remembers Roy Harrover (b. 1928; M.Arch 1953). "We went inside—a

3.10 James Wilder Green (M.Arch 1952) and John David Erickson (M.Arch 1952), Design for a Zoo (1952).

3.11 James Jarrett (M.Arch 1935), Beach House (1950).

great space. We climbed on top and took pictures. Then it rained. The dome melted."[47] Though Fuller was not often seen in New Haven, his influence was pervasive, as can be seen in a 1952 project for a zoo by James Wilder Green (1927–2005; M.Arch 1952) and John David Erickson (B.A. 1945; M.Arch 1952) (3.10) and, most importantly, in the triangulated structure of Kahn's Art Gallery extension.

The diverse visiting faculty ensured that student work at Yale in the late 1940s was more varied than that coming out of Harvard.[48] But to some observers, this was hardly an advantage, indicating that Yale students were failing to grasp the basics of the discipline. Even the work of some of the best students, such as James Jarrett's (1926–2010; M.Arch 1955) first-year project for a beach house, seemed confused in its combination of Marcel Breuer's so-called Butterfly House, then recently displayed in the garden of the Museum of Modern Art in New York, with a circular pavilion of vaguely Wrightian origins (3.11).[49] In April 1948, the newly formed University Council for Art and Architecture, concerned with the seemingly unfocused nature of student work, outlined a "Possible Basic Curriculum," so similar to the so-called Vorkurs workshop at the Bauhaus introduced by Johannes Itten and later led by Albers that it is likely to have been written by Albers, a committee member. Like Meeks's planned Basic Curriculum, the council's proposal called for a three-stage Core to be taken by all students, but it differed in that it was to be rooted in crafted abstractions rather than history. The first stage of Yale's Vorkurs was to be "devoted to the establishment of a visual vocabulary by direct study of the basic elements of visual expression. . . . The visual vocabulary having been obtained, the second stage of the curriculum would lead the student to begin using his vocabulary by free organization of the various basic elements into three-dimensional compositions . . . the purpose of these being the investigation of the relations of surface and volume to space. Any tendency to imitate accepted stereotypes would be avoided, lest the student's personal development be retarded." The third stage "would take place in well-equipped workshops," where the student would leave abstraction and "begin the solution of a problem with roots in everyday life. . . . The 'making' process, the complete creative cycle—problem, sketching, planning, criticism, execution—would be the important thing at this point."[50]

Confined to only one semester, the new Core was adopted for fall 1948. It was required for all students in the school, including Yale College majors in art, architecture, and art history.[51] In point of fact, a version of it had already been initiated a year before when, in fall 1947, with Meeks retired, Herbert Gute (1907–1977), a painter, and Gilbert Switzer, a sculptor, were given responsibility for "a reorganization of our basic introductory course in the practice of arts for undergraduates." They were not successful, perhaps because what they proposed was too experimental.[52] William Huff, an undergraduate architecture student in the new introductory course, wrote to his parents in 1947: "My art class is a little puzzling. . . . In that class we aren't painting, aren't drawing, aren't etching, no—we're 'filling space': Filling space with planes, lines and solids. Our media are cardboard, wire and clay. But it isn't quite as crazy as it may seem, for it fits in perfectly with architecture (which in itself is filling space). It gives us some theories of composition."[53] Nonetheless it marked an important new direction and began to suggest that Yale was recasting itself as an American Bauhaus, at the very time that the "Harvard Bauhaus" was beginning to lose focus with the withdrawal of Marcel Breuer from the faculty in 1946, and Gropius and Hudnut disagreeing about just about everything. When Paul Rudolph, future chairman of Yale's Department of Architecture and perhaps the most talented of Gropius's American students, honored his teacher in 1950 with the publication, in the important French journal *L'Architecture d'aujourd'hui,* of a broad selection of work by recent Harvard graduates, his tribute would mark the apogee of Gropius's influence as an educator, but also reveal the limited scope of design typical of the master's students.[54] Two years later, a group of ninety-five Harvard students "deeply concerned with the existing quality of work in the School" signed a petition urging Breuer to return to his teaching there. Though he did not return, "the petition hung framed in Breuer's New York office for many years."[55]

With news of trouble in Cambridge becoming more widespread and dramatic new initiatives beginning to take effect in New Haven, the playing field between the two rival architecture programs was leveling and perhaps beginning to tip in New Haven's favor, especially after April 1949, when the University Council acknowledged that some of its curricular suggestions had resulted in the expansion of "Visual Fundamentals." However, the council lacked confidence in the faculty to effect necessary changes in the overall program: "new staff leadership" was needed in both the Art and Architecture departments. With regard to the Department of Architecture, the committee, though "impressed by the fresh reality provided by the presence of the various visiting professional architects," expressed the need for a "full-time, resident head in the person of an architect and designer of proven distinction and wisdom to provide the unity of a continuing philosophy of design," and also "recommended the discontinuation of life tenure [in the school] in all future contractual agreements by the University. Though security through tenure may produce rare scholarship," they stated it "was more often than not a stultifying element for teachers concerned with artistic production."[56] In 1949, it was becoming increasingly clear that Harold Hauf was not the right person to lead the Department of Architecture, and he resigned to accept an appointment as editor in chief of *Architectural Record*. Within two weeks of his departure, the university announced that George Howe had agreed to succeed him, effective January 1950.[57] At approximately the same time, Josef Albers accepted Sawyer's invitation to become chairman of the Department of Art.

Credit for Yale's postwar reemergence as a powerful force in art education is generally attributed to Alfred Whitney Griswold (3.12). Though respected as an administrator and admired for his wide-ranging scholarship, Griswold was in many ways an enigmatic figure with a complex and sometimes contradictory attitude toward modernity that combined nostalgia for the halcyon days of Dink Stover's Yale with a determination to keep the university at the forefront of American higher education.[58] With a firm belief in architecture as an expression of cultural values, Griswold set out to rebuild the campus, not from the ground up as had twice before been the case—first in the mid-nineteenth century, when the Brick Row was demolished, and again in the early twentieth century, when many of the university's nineteenth-century buildings were replaced—but rather by peppering its inherited physical fabric with high-wire examples of stylistic modernism. Griswold understood the symbolic importance of architecture and viewed Yale's new buildings as manifestations of a reinvigorated university. During his tenure, Yale's campus was transformed with the addition of twenty-six new buildings, many of them mediocre, but some of international significance, including structures designed by Louis I. Kahn, Eero Saarinen, Paul Rudolph, Gordon Bunshaft, and Philip Johnson. As a result of the dramatic changes made to Yale's physical structure during his presidency, Griswold is also typically credited with reinvigorating arts education at Yale. However, it was actually his predecessor, Charles Seymour, who made the three most critical appointments associated with the dramatic transformation of the School of the Fine Arts: Charles H. Sawyer, appointed dean in 1947; George Howe, appointed chairman of the Department of Architecture in August 1949; and Josef Albers, already a visiting critic and member of the University Council Committee for Art and Architecture, appointed chairman of the Department of Art, effective July 1950.

When George Howe was appointed, he was the most prominent American-born architect associated with the modern movement to be offered a position of administrative and philosophical importance in American architectural education (3.13, 3.14). Since 1947, Howe had been serving as the

3.12 Yale University President Alfred Whitney Griswold (ca. 1959).

3.13 George Howe, chairman of the Department of Architecture (ca. 1950).

3.14 From left to right: Unknown, Louis Kahn, and George Howe examine a student model (n.d.).

first resident architect at the American Academy in Rome, while simultaneously working on the design of a new building for the U.S. consulate in Naples. Howe's presence at the academy, which had been forced to close during the war, was deemed crucial to its postwar renewal as it shifted its emphasis from academic Classicism to stylistic modernism.[59] In a recent study of Howe's time in Rome, Denise R. Costanzo has observed that Howe's academy appointment "constituted a public declaration of its new artistic identity and was instrumental in convincing recent architecture graduates to apply for Academy fellowships."[60]

There's no doubt that Howe was important to the American Academy, but being in Rome was just as important to Howe. He wittily described his Roman routine in a letter to his daughter Helen Howe West: "I lie in a toga, while Maria (the cook) makes proper pasta, eating and drinking like a true Roman. When I overeat or drink, like a true Roman, I throw up and start all over again!"[61] While at the academy, he only made occasional, brief return visits to the United States. Indeed, when first approached by Dean Sawyer, he stated that he had "no intention of entering the academic field but had rather made up [his] mind to live in Europe and take up a long deferred project to write a book."[62] Sawyer persisted in his efforts to lure Howe to New Haven, recruiting Howe's old friends Louis I. Kahn and Edward Durell Stone to the cause, with Stone telling Howe that "the only thing that the Department has lacked has been overall leadership by an architect such as yourself."[63] Howe eventually relented, accepting the appointment in part because it provided him with an escape from the looming threat of a possible second marriage, in part because he needed the money, and in part because Yale just seemed right to him. "Isn't that a break?" he wrote to his daughter. "If you had asked me which school I would like to head I'd have picked Yale."[64] George Howe assumed his new role on January 1, 1950, and by fall 1950, he was firmly in command.[65]

At the time of his appointment, Howe was an accomplished architect with almost no experience as an educator. Massachusetts-born and -educated (Harvard; B.A. 1908), Howe attended the École des Beaux-Arts (1908–12), before settling in his wife's hometown of Philadelphia, where he worked for the once-dynamic but by then stodgy firm of Furness, Evans & Co. His first independent work of consequence was his own house, High Hollow (1914).[66] In 1916, Howe became partner in the Philadelphia firm of Mellor, Meigs & Howe, where, after service in World War I, he would design widely admired traditional country houses and branch banks until the late 1920s, when, becoming disenchanted with his work—later describing it as his romantic "Wall-Street Pastorale" period (3.15)—he switched artistic direction, leaving

3.15 Mellor, Meigs & Howe, Newbold Estate (1922), Laverock, Pennsylvania. This image, captioned "Wall-Street Pastorale," accompanied Howe's article in *Perspecta* 2.

3.16 George Howe, on the balcony of Fortune Rock (1939), Mount Desert Island, Maine.

3.17 Josef Albers in his studio in New Haven (1954).

his partnership to open his own office with the intention of designing in the modern style.[67] That decision was reinforced in a year's time when he joined William Lescaze (1896–1969), who had come to the United States from Switzerland in 1920. Although Lescaze's early work was also in traditional styles, he and Howe established a remarkably successful practice in the newly accepted vocabulary of what William Jordy has isolated as the "European phase" of the International Style, which might more easily be called the "machine style."[68] The firm attracted wide attention, especially for its design of the now-canonical skyscraper home of the Philadelphia Saving Fund Society (1932).

Howe returned to individual practice in 1934. His design for Fortune Rock (1939), a house on Mount Desert Island, Maine, became an icon of modern American domestic architecture, an abstract design combining vernacular references with technological bravura in the form of a pair of dramatically cantilevered, reinforced concrete beams carrying the living room over the tidal Somes Sound (3.16). Reportedly, Dean Meeks found the house quite provocative and would show it to students at the culmination of his historical survey course, amiably exclaiming, "This, gentlemen, is an example of the cantilever gone mad!" Presumably for its similar show of structural bravura, Frank Lloyd Wright's Fallingwater (1938) also couldn't escape Meeks's good-natured scorn. While discussing that house, Meeks famously told his class: "Gentlemen. If you ask me, I think this looks like an airplane wreck in the woods!"[69]

In 1939, Howe formed a partnership with Oscar Stonorov (1905–1970), who had worked in Le Corbusier's atelier and edited *Oeuvre Complète, 1910–1929*, the first volume of the master's standard-setting monograph series. A year later, Louis I. Kahn joined them as partner to work on projects for the U.S. Defense Housing program. Between 1942 and 1945, Howe was supervising architect of the U.S. Public Buildings Administration—the first modernist to hold an important government appointment. Despite his Saul to Paul conversion, Howe enjoyed wide professional respect among both traditionalists and modernists alike, and by the late 1940s, he was considered a senior statesman among American architects. Joseph Esherick, the Bay Area architect and dean of the School of Architecture at the University of California, Berkeley (1977–81), recalled that when he was a student at the University of Pennsylvania in the early 1930s, Howe had frequently been a guest lecturer, tolerated by the Beaux-Arts faculty as "the principal representative of what could then be confidently called modern architecture." Esherick, who after graduation worked for Howe and remained close to him thereafter, found him to be "diffident and urbane on the surface . . . a heroic, gentlemanly anti-hero" who "was witty and incisive and much more deeply concerned than he seemed to want to let on."[70]

Charles Sawyer recalls that it was Kahn who initially suggested Howe's name as a possible chairman.[71] Kahn, who had served as visiting critic in 1947 and joined the faculty of the Architecture Department in 1948, felt that Yale would be propelled forward by the luster of Howe's reputation as a first-rate American architect who embraced the modern movement without being an ideologue.[72] Howe's appointment was welcomed by many who hoped that Yale would assert a pedagogical position for itself different from its traditional rival in Cambridge. As architecture critic Paul Goldberger was to put it fifty years later, Howe was suited to Yale's "indifference to ideology as compared to other architecture programs in those years. Howe's ability to welcome modernism without using it as a club of moral superiority with which to bludgeon those of more cautious bent, his reluctance to sneer at everything else as beneath contempt, was important, and very characteristic of Yale's general tendency to avoid an excessive degree of dogma."[73]

Howe's appointment was part of a larger strategy intended to reassert the school's preeminent position in art and architecture education, and combat the perception that it had become unfocused since the late 1930s. The almost simultaneous appointment of Josef Albers was another critical aspect of that strategy (3.17).[74] And it almost didn't happen. Albers, with his wife, Anni (1899–1994), a weaver, emigrated from Germany to the United States in 1933. Albers was teaching at Black Mountain College, a small, experimental school in North Carolina, when, in 1936, Joseph Hudnut—newly appointed dean of Harvard's architecture school, which he renamed the Graduate School of Design—invited the artist to give a series of workshops in Cambridge. Hudnut was also courting Walter Gropius to join the faculty as chairman of the GSD's Department of Architecture. Gropius, in turn, pressed for Albers's appointment to the faculty during the negotiations leading to his own appointment, believing him to be the right man to indoctrinate the students into the basic tenets of form and color via a required Basic Design course similar to the famous Vorkurs at the Bauhaus.[75]

Hudnut, however, believed that the study of history, which Gropius abhorred, and not Basic Design, was fundamental to professional training in architecture. While Hudnut extended a limited invitation to Albers, he told Gropius that as a painter and designer, Albers's potential appointment to the faculty was dependent on Harvard's Division of Fine Arts and not on the GSD. Hudnut, who had "definite misgivings about the approach to design that Albers, as a non-architect, might bring to Harvard's architects, planners, and landscape architects," did not want the GSD to become an American Bauhaus, a point of contention between him and Gropius that, by the mid-1940s, led to a fairly public battle, ultimately terminating their relationship.[76] In the end, Gropius's attempt to promote an American Bauhaus at Harvard failed—not only because of the battle over the issue of Basic Design, but also because Harvard, unlike Yale, lacked requisite programs in painting, sculpture, drama, and crafts.

With the active encouragement of Sawyer, Albers and Howe set out "to dust off Yale's Beaux-Arts cobwebs and shepherd the oldest university art school in America into the modern era."[77] At Yale, Albers found a situation that held the potential for a renewed Bauhaus—not only did the School of the Fine Arts encompass programs in art and architecture, it also encouraged collaboration between them and other disciplines. But there was a rub: the work of the art students and the department's entrenched faculty were still in the traditional Beaux-Arts manner, and disinclined to support the Vorkurs-like course that Albers, as a key member of the University Council Committee, proposed. For Albers, who was at this point a respected educator though not yet recognized as a major artist, Basic Design was about students "learning to see," by using paper, wood, metal, plastics, and glass, to create three-dimensional compositions before advancing to a "making" stage where they would "begin the solution of a problem with roots in . . . everyday life," such as simple furniture. A student in the Basic Design course "would acquire the self-confidence that comes only through elementary knowledge, and realize gradually the design powers resting within himself."[78] After this stage, students would begin to pursue their various disciplinary interests in design "perhaps with common grounding in appropriate Social Studies and Sciences." Complementing the gradual introduction of disciplinary specialization, the University Council's Basic Design proposal also called for "yearly collaborative exercises" addressing "some visual problem of our industrial age."[79] Additionally, the University Council, no doubt reflecting Albers's view, saw to the redesignation of the Department of Art as the Department of Design.

Key to Albers's Basic Design approach were his drawing and color classes. Jaquelin T. Robertson (b. 1933; B.A. 1955, M.Arch 1961), who has enjoyed prominence as an architect, planner, and educator, considers Albers to have been his greatest teacher. Though an undergraduate majoring in Chinese studies, Robertson "was able to talk myself into his drawing class. . . . It was the single best course I had ever taken. It taught you how to see. Albers, all he was trying to do was break your bad visual habits—to teach you how to draw what you saw. . . . One week, you had to draw an umbrella sitting on its side. The next week, he brought in a bicycle or ten other things and you had to draw it. The kids in there who all wanted to be artists and were in the art school were so terrified of him, they'd just break down."[80] Robertson remembers discovering "the mystery of seeing for the first time your own hand at work exploring (with eraserless pencil) the differences between paper and stone, under that hawk-like unrelenting gaze . . . always half afraid of your own clumsiness yet excited at the magic of self-revelation and the power of the teacher."[81] Albers had a particularly profound impact on Robertson: "One day, near the end of the year, he came up to me and said, 'Hey boy, what you do?' I told him I was studying then as an undergraduate to go into foreign service. I was a Chinese major. He said, 'No, no, no. You be architect. I been watching you. You see. You see. You see.'"[82] From that moment, Robertson's path was set.

In 1950, the Department of Architecture may have been primed for change, and Howe, despite his lack of experience as an educator, was intent on stripping away the banal pragmatism that Hauf had encouraged. As Howe saw it, Yale's architecture program was unfocused, with a curriculum that included "all that is stupidest and most vicious in accepted practice."[83] Gradually, under his direction, the departments of Architecture and Design (as the programs were for a time denoted) followed "parallel and related objectives," so that each was able to "serve the other in many ways not previously possible."[84] But it was one thing to criticize the previous program, another to create something new and better.

From the first, Howe, conflicted about the extent of the role technical training should play in the curriculum, seemed to move in multiple directions, stressing the importance of architecture as a design profession with its own protocols, as well as one with key relationships to various disciplines outside it, especially to the practice of visual art. He derived this view of interdisciplinarity in large part from Alfred N. Whitehead's *The Aims of Education,* a text he read during his first year as chairman that would become his pedagogical bible.[85] But he also drew upon his four years at the École des Beaux-Arts, insisting that the architect is morally bound to master basic, time-honored principles: "He may, indeed must, study the principles of design and the aesthetic aspects displayed in any work that he admires, to enlarge his own store of knowledge through the experience of others and to fill his mental gallery with images, but these principles and these images he must absorb into his personal experience, not apply them to it."[86]

After just six weeks on the job, using his preferred method of communication, the formal lecture, Howe addressed alumni on February 22,

1950, stating: "We must not lose sight of the fact that the primary purpose of architectural schools is to create architects not to prepare draftsmen for office work." Design was paramount: "Over-emphasis on technological preparation must not be allowed to interfere," yet the technical training of artists must not be neglected because an "artist who is not technically competent in his art is no artist."[87] Howe was concerned that the program lacked discipline, and although he expressed his support for "independent thought in design," he was not convinced by "the philosophy firmly established at Yale that men shall learn by trial and error, by bouncing off their own mistakes so to speak, rather than by imposed discipline." As a result, he set out to address the "generally acknowledged" lack of discipline among students without unduly curtailing their individuality, and to instill a respect for rigor among the faculty, who Howe believed were failing to "make students conscious of the direct relation" between their instruction and "their ultimate professional development."[88] In support of this observation, he noted that a member of the National Architectural Accrediting Board, which inspected the department in spring 1950, had said to him personally that "he found the training process of Yale exciting but confusing."[89]

A few years later, as Howe reflected back on his first days as chairman, he would be far more blunt in describing the department as he had found it. The first-year students were, he reported, "neglected by the administration," while their instructor, Eugene Nalle, was restrained by an "unimaginative" program. The second-year students were "confused and discontented" and encouraging their younger peers to leave en masse for another school. In the third and fourth years, things were even worse, with students "in general, incapable of three-dimensional thinking and prone to 'slap an elevation' on a plan at the last minute."[90]

At the end of his first term as chairman, Howe proposed significant revisions to the curriculum, intended to take place over four years so that their full impact could not be measured until 1953–54, when the first class to have experienced it in its entirety would graduate, and Howe would be sixty-eight years old and thereby forced into retirement. Once the new curriculum began to be implemented, Howe, in September 1951, felt confident enough to offer some general ideas about education in a talk called "Training for the Practice of Architecture," a title originally used in a lecture given thirty years before by Charles Herbert Moore (1840–1930), Howe's teacher at Harvard.[91] In his talk, Howe threw down the gauntlet against Gropius's Harvard and probably against Mies van der Rohe's approach at IIT as well. Echoing Dean Meeks's efforts in the early 1940s to craft a distinct approach that was both modern and American, Howe stated his intention to work with students and faculty to "evolve together a way of training for the practice of architecture peculiarly our own, peculiarly Yale's, based on no doctrine or theory but worked out from day to day by experience, in a thoroughly American way. When our training becomes so stabilized in form as to amount to a system it will be time to begin again from the starting point."[92]

Howe's approach to design education was full of contradictions. As a "principle" undergirding training at Yale, Howe, somewhat contradicting his emphasis on skills in his February 1950 talk, stated his intention to "consider the trade, the business and the science of building always as the servants of the art of building, which is the particular province of the architect, and that we shall consider them always as significant form," a term coined by the art critic Clive Bell.[93] And as the art of building must triumph over the science of building, imagination must never be limited by technique or restrained by accepted practices: "The artist must adapt his technique to the tools he has to use. But let us never admit that our tools can dominate our thought and our imagination. Let us never . . . be product-minded, process-minded, standard-minded. The standards of today are the bad habits of tomorrow."[94]

Though Howe was never entirely consistent or clear about what the measure of "significant form" was, he was quite precise about his view on modernity, which was never a simple matter of the fashionable formal solution. From the onset of his personal break with tradition-based design in the late 1920s, he had undertaken to define modern architecture in broad terms—not based on a concern for new shapes, but rather on a way of building in the twentieth century that would be a "return to sound tradition . . . that is to say, to the interpretation of function, spiritual as well as material, logically and imaginatively, in terms of modern materials, internally structural as well as visible."[95] For Howe, the "higher purpose" of architectural practice was simple: "produce good architecture." But what did that mean? He also struggled with the concept of style. After considering definitions from Ruskin, Nietzsche, and Whitehead, he seized on Oswald Spengler's attempt to define style: "Only the art of great Cultures, the art that has ceased to be only art and begun to be an effective unit of expression and significance, possesses style."[96] Howe questioned whether modern art and architecture had yet become "an 'effective unit of expression and significance' for our time," going on to state that "architecture particularly is assailed by doubts." Yet he held out hope that true innovators would persevere despite the missteps that have been taken in the pursuit of significant modern form:

The trail beaten into the wilderness by the great architectural innovators from the turn of the last century has become rutted by their followers. A rut is a comfortable line to follow. Anyone can throw the reins on the mule's back and go to sleep. This is the way of commercial hacks.

A great style is not made by uttering great words. . . . A great style is not made at all. It is discovered by a host of explorers with their minds and hearts full of the thoughts and feelings of their day. When it is discovered it becomes the property of a whole culture, to draw on as it will, until it has been sucked dry of meaning in its turn.

The time for the discovery of a great style may be ripe. The opportunity, not only to share, but to lead in the exploration is ours.[97]

Drawing from his readings of John Dewey and Whitehead, Howe made explicit his own commitment to a humanistic approach to design education: "[The purpose of the university is] not so much to educate as to set the student on the way to self-education." Quoting Whitehead's observation that "fools act on imagination without knowledge, [while] pedants act on knowledge without imagination," Howe stated that the "task of the University is to weld together imagination and experience." Professing not to much like "the mechanical implications of the word weld," he offered "the organic notion that the task of the University is to fertilize imagination with experience and experience with imagination."[98] Howe's September 1951 lecture was part an expression of doubt and part a call to arms. He was clearly proud of it and arranged for printed copies of it to be distributed to students and a version to be published in the pages of the first issue of the student-edited journal *Perspecta*, the foundation of which he actively encouraged.

With his mission laid out and the troops thusly rallied, it now fell to Howe to lead the charge toward curricular reform. His proposed changes lay in two basic areas: philosophy of teaching and methods. With regard to the former, he recognized that students need to pursue their own ideas freely, but guided by instructors, particularly in regards to history and the proper use of precedent and of contemporary "architectural attitudes"—or what today would be called "theory," a term not then much used in architectural discourse. Howe believed it was essential to carry the lessons learned in lectures and seminars into the studio as "Drafting Room Philosophy." To do this, he not only brought art historians and philosophers into the design studio, but also into drawing and structural design classes.[99]

With regard to methods, Howe acknowledged that each instructor and critic needed to teach "according to his own knowledge and vision."[100]

3.18   King-lui Wu (ca. 1978).

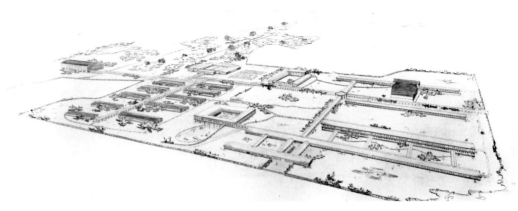

3.19   King-lui Wu, Yali Middle School (1947).

3.20   King-lui Wu, Irving Rouse House (1955), North Haven, Connecticut. Fireplace design by Josef Albers.

But he also insisted on shared objectives and students in each studio. To take advantage of faculty individuality, he initially divided design classes into groups, with one critic in charge of each group of students for a prescribed period, after which the critic would rotate to the next group; this would continue throughout the year so that, while undertaking identical design problems, students would benefit from a number of different points of view, a system that forced students to make their own decisions and form their own opinions.

Initially, he assigned Robert Coolidge, Eliot Noyes, and Joseph N. Boaz (b. 1917), an architectural engineer who trained at the University of Oklahoma and Columbia, to lead the Intermediate Design studios, and Edward Durell Stone to continue as senior critic, teaching with Karl Holzinger, while Lloyd Flood and King-lui Wu (1918–2002) were charged with advising and, when necessary, directing the visiting critics who would also lead Advanced Design studios.

The Chinese-born Wu would enjoy a forty-three-year-long career at Yale, although he was never admitted to the ranks of the tenured faculty (3.18). Having earned both his bachelor's and master's degrees from Harvard, Wu, probably in the hope of designing buildings in China through Yale-in-China, moved to New Haven in 1945 to begin teaching in the department as instructor in architectural design.[101] Wu maintained a modest practice in New Haven. Working with Yale-in-China in the wake of World War II, he designed the Changsha Medical Center and thirty-seven buildings for the Yali Middle School (1947) (3.19), projects that went unrealized as the result of the 1949 revolution. In New Haven, his work included houses for Yale anthropology professor Irving Rouse (1955) (3.20) and Benjamin DuPont (1959). The Rouse House was undertaken to prove that an architect could design a high-quality house at moderate cost—less than $20,000 (approximately $175,000 in 2015). "It is always easy to build a cheap house," Wu said, "but it is a great challenge to an architect to build a good inexpensive house: one of solid construction and of good materials."[102] The centerpiece of the Rouse House was a brick fireplace designed by Albers. This would be Wu's first collaboration with the artist, who also designed a brick fireplace for the elegant and technically ingenious DuPont House and the decorative intaglio mural for the Manuscript Society (1965), which has the distinction of being the only modernist-style senior society "tomb" at Yale.[103]

Wu, who came from a privileged background, was, in the words of his former student Alexander Purves (b. 1935; B.A. 1958, M.Arch 1965), "very conscious of personal deportment and politeness."[104] His meticulous nature was reflected in work that emphasized carefully designed details and the artistic manipulation of daylight, which would become one of his teaching specialties after Richard Kelly was no longer able to find time to teach. Wu's "Daylight and Architecture" course was especially important in a time when many were becoming alarmed by architecture's energy dependency. However, he did not approach the topic from the point of view of energy conservation, but instead emphasized that buildings needed to breathe and that natural light brought them to life.

In contrast to the increasing emphasis on gestural design in the 1950s and 1960s, Wu's studio teaching emphasized meticulous detailing and fastidious proportions. As a student in the early 1960s, Purves worked for Wu "drawing an entire building at three-inch scale. Every single intersection. . . . Most of it was like a Chinese puzzle—how do I fit all these on a sheet of 18-x-24 paper? You do it by drawing the intersection and quickly making a cutline. But you learned that if you start a reveal somewhere you know where it's going. All the way around the room until it comes back."[105] As the discipline of the 1950s and early 1960s gave way to the more ad-hoc approach of the late 1960s and 1970s, students found Wu's insistence on careful planning and craft off-putting. His critiques were seen as less "cutting edge" than those of the visiting critics coming into the school, but the wise students recognized that though "he was very traditional in many ways . . . his traditionalism bought into modernism."[106] Wu's longtime presence in the postwar Department of Architecture, comparable only to Peter Millard's, would prove critical. "I don't think the school of architecture would have maintained its stability if it wasn't for him," former Wu student Charles Gwathmey stated. "Really, he was the rock through all the transitions, all the ups and downs."[107]

Although Howe's charm took him a long way, more was needed to propel the school forward. His search for teachers who could shake things up did not always work out. While Kiesler seemed to work well as part of the collaborative studio, the Austrian-born, New York–based, Surrealist-inspired artist-architect who had conducted a much-admired experimental design lab at Columbia (1937–43), proved unsuccessful with beginning students, who resisted his approach.[108] John Field (b. 1930; B.A. 1952, B.Arch 1955), who would go on to lead a prominent San Francisco practice, recalled that Kiesler's two-week design course was "more memorable than useful. . . . Kiesler was a small man who kept telling us how lucky we were to have him there to teach us. . . . Our assignment was to design a chair based on the relative pressure different areas of our buttocks exerted on the surface we sat on. . . . After two weeks of such scientific experiment, I was delegated to go to George Howe to complain that we were wasting our time. He listened with a slight smile on his face and Kiesler's class was cut short."[109]

Soon enough, Howe settled on three very different architects whom he would rely on to help shape the department's future: Philip Johnson (1906–2005), Louis I. Kahn, and Eugene Nalle, each representing a different leg of Howe's philosophy of teaching, with Johnson as the historian in the drafting room, Kahn as the engaged artistic architect struggling through teaching to find his way, and Nalle as the primitive rule maker. Howe had known Johnson since the early 1930s, when Johnson and Henry-Russell Hitchcock's *Modern Architecture—International Exhibition* (1932) show at the Museum of Modern Art included Howe and Lescaze's Philadelphia Saving Fund Society Building. Howe and Johnson's friendship blossomed in the early 1940s, when both were stationed in Washington, D.C.[110]

Johnson had studied philosophy as a Harvard undergraduate before beginning his career as a curator, but his early professional accomplishments were darkened by a disturbing turn as a Nazi sympathizer in the 1930s. Taking stock of his priorities at the end of that decade, Johnson redirected his energies to a career in architecture, returning to Harvard, where he received his master of architecture degree in 1942. When Howe came to Yale, Johnson had just finished his Glass House in New Canaan (1949) and was principally occupied as director of the Department of Architecture at New York's Museum of Modern Art, while seeking to establish himself as an independent practitioner. Johnson's sister Theodate (1907–2002) was at the time romantically involved with Howe, so the young architect saw a great deal of his old friend, for whom he had the utmost respect and considered to be "the greatest gentleman we've ever had in architecture . . . the first of my real architectural friends whom I could talk shorthand with, whom I always depended on. We could always get right to the essence. . . . Howe was not a common man with a common touch. He was an elitist from way back."[111]

As a studio instructor, Johnson pushed students out of their functionalist comfort zones by asking them to design a house three times over—once in the style of each modern master: Frank Lloyd Wright, Le Corbusier, and Mies van der Rohe (3.21). For this exercise, he presented students with an established floor plan. "The challenge was to develop the architectural expression," Johnson told Ralph H. Comey, Jr., who found his teacher to be "always interesting and provocative."[112] But studio instruction wasn't Johnson's strong suit. Instead he proved to be brilliant on juries and in the lecture hall, where,

3.21 Duncan Wray Buell (M.Arch 1953), House in the Manner of Frank Lloyd Wright, perspective (1951).

3.22 Philip Johnson lecturing to Yale students (ca. 1954).

as Vincent Scully has recalled, his lectures were "regarded as pronouncements of the Devil. He stood up on the platform . . . and he said to a shocked hush across the room, 'I would rather sleep in the nave of Chartres Cathedral with the nearest john two blocks down the street than I would in a Harvard house with back-to-back bathrooms!'"[113] (3.22).

At Howe's instigation, Johnson and Kahn co-taught the Collaborative Studio in fall 1953 consisting of two design problems: "a new sign for the Museum of Modern Art involving the architectural changes necessary for the idea" and "a poster board for the new Gallery at Yale"—both projects representing the growing importance of graphic design in the Department of Art under Albers. Johnson and Kahn were not very fond of one another, despite each man's individual friendship with Howe, and the studio seems not to have been a success. Kahn found the project "a bit stupid because col-laboration amongst the graphic art's section the painters and the architects is somewhat cloudy. However that is Yale—no system—all freedom."[114] Johnson was anathema to some faculty, especially Eugene Nalle, but he had a profound impact on students, in particular James Jarrett, whose house project of fall 1951 is remarkably similar to Johnson's Wiley House (3.23), then under design. Jarrett's counterproposals for Helen Hadley Hall (1958), Yale's first women's residence, were developed with the encouragement of Vincent Scully, who abhorred Douglas Orr's bland design (3.24, 3.25). "Doug Orr's office had been a brilliant office back in the '20s and the early '30s" says Scully, "but when Orr came into Modernism, he lost the thread. He really did." President Griswold wasn't pleased with Orr's design either and called Scully and his fellow art his-tory professor, Charles Seymour, Jr. (1912–1977; B.A. 1935, Ph.D. 1938). "We said, 'It's disgusting,'" remembers Scully. "You've got to remember that we were intolerant in ways that I can't apologize for enough. But we were. So he said, 'Well, can you do any better?'"[115] For the first, but not last, time Scully, then junior faculty, had a chance to directly influence Yale's building program.[116] Scully brought in Jarrett to come up with alternatives. While one of Jarrett's proposals is quite conventionally "modern," the other was much more inter-esting, bearing a strong resemblance to Edwin Lutyens's Page Street Houses (1930) in London, then a little-known work. Both the president and Scully were excited about the new designs. Unfortunately, Jarrett made the unforgivable mistake of sharing the commission with his students, and word quickly got back to Orr, who was understandably displeased that the university was going behind his back. President Griswold was also upset—not at Scully or Jarrett exactly, but at the fact that Jarrett's indiscretion forced him to go forward with Orr's design. Scully said, "He wanted to do better. He was always ashamed.

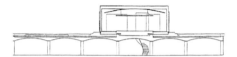

3.23 Top: James Jarrett (M.Arch 1955), A Residence, section (1951). Bottom: Philip Johnson, Wiley House, New Canaan, Connecticut, section (1953).

3.24 Douglas Orr, Helen Hadley Hall (1958), New Haven.

3.25 James Jarrett, counterproposal for Helen Hadley Hall (ca. 1955).

Our plan was for a much better building."[117] Jarrett would go on to work for Johnson, who considered him a "dynamo," playing a decisive role in some of his most important projects of the late 1950s, especially the Roofless Church in New Harmony, Indiana (1960).[118] In the 1980s, Jarrett returned to Yale to teach history and theory.

Johnson's influence on Yale students was most clearly represented by the "Yale Box," a seemingly universal design strategy that swept the school, consisting of refined, often symmetrical structures that were well detailed, well proportioned, and could accommodate almost any function. In a 1958 article for *Progressive Architecture,* graduating student Herbert McLaughlin (1934–2015; B.A. 1956, M.Arch 1958), who would go on to found a major practice in San Francisco, saw the Yale Box, clearly influenced by the Glass House and other early Johnson houses, as "pseudo-Miesian" with "an element of romanticism and concern with spatial play and more dramatic structure." McLaughlin goes on to say: "But what the arrival of Johnson himself and this style signified, more than anything else, was the beginning of an attempt on the part of the student to establish himself as an artist. This architecture, while symbolizing the classic and serene, also symbolized a rejection of the function of the architect as solely a social and sun-angle coordinator. Here was an architecture of aloof perfection"[119] (3.26).

Looking back after forty years, Johnson took a certain pride in his "box" being the subject of so much student attention, recalling that when he took the design portion of his Connecticut state licensing exam in Weir Hall, the drafting room was adorned with student graffiti depicting versions of his Glass House: "The students made very good fun of it; and for very good reasons, so anti-symbolic was it and Miesian. . . . . And they did it by these humorous graffiti sketches all over the wall. So there I was, feeling so humiliated and drag-ass, since I didn't have a license yet, and I look up on the walls and my house is all over the place."[120]

Johnson's impact on Yale extended beyond the boundaries of the campus, as students were often invited to visit him in New Canaan at the Glass House. "Surrounded by sunlit open space with a wall of trees as a lecture hall, I looked up from my seat to view a . . . Poussin [*The Burial of Phocion*]. What pleasure!" says R. Edward Harter (b. 1929; B.Arch 1953), who remembers Johnson as a "a giant of cultural fertilization."[121] Johnson, in turn, had a great respect for the level of student sophistication—so much so that, with characteristic overkill, he enthusiastically claimed that were he to go to architecture school over again, Yale would be the place "because it is a greater madhouse than the rest and has fine 'gentlemen' working there."[122]

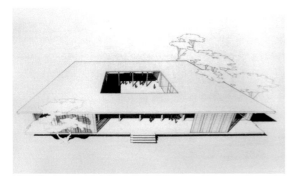

3.26 Edwin William de Cossy (M.Arch 1957), An Elementary School, perspective (1955).

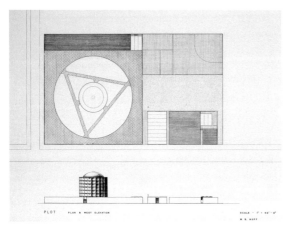

3.27 William Huff (B.A. 1949, M.Arch 1952), An Urban Church, plan and elevation. Thesis project (1952).

3.28 William Huff, An Urban Church, perspective. Thesis project (1952).

3.29 Philip Johnson, Soreq Nuclear Research Center (1960), Yavne, Israel.

One of the earliest memories that Marshall D. Meyers (1931–2001; M.Arch 1957) had of his time at Yale was an informal "session" in a fellow student's apartment, where Johnson was engaged in conversation with Louis Kahn: "Johnson was remarkably articulate in contrast to Kahn who fought to make his words come out right. Kahn was saying that, to him, building—making a building—which was not just constructing—was a struggle and that this struggle should be evident in the work."[123] Vincent Scully believed that the dialogue between the two very different men during their time at Yale was "very important for the formulation of their ideas." Like Johnson, Kahn was also interested in architecture as an art: "The main point is the focus on architecture, the unique capacity of the visual arts to teach us through visual experience. That's what Lou was always after—what Johnson has always been after. To me, this is the link between them."[124]

Although Louis I. Kahn's ten-year stint at Yale began before George Howe's arrival, and extended beyond Howe's retirement, it is probably safe to assume that Kahn's success at Yale was largely the result of Howe's support. Kahn was a highly regarded graduate (1924) of the University of Pennsylvania, where he had studied under the Beaux-Arts–trained master teacher and architect Paul Cret, in whose office he was briefly employed (1929–30), until he was let go with the onset of the Depression. During the 1930s, Kahn, stirred by social issues, abandoned his Classical training in favor of modernism, though he never really seemed comfortable with its stylistic tropes, especially its lack of spatial precision and tectonic rigor.

Howe became aware of Kahn in the early 1930s as a result of their shared interest in social housing. As the United States prepared for its inevitable entry into World War II, Kahn joined Howe and Oscar Stonorov to work on federal housing for war workers, including Carver Court (1943) for black steelworkers, on the site of a former racetrack in Coatesville, Pennsylvania.[125] There were a number of other government-sponsored housing projects for Howe, Stonorov, and Kahn to design, but after the United States entered the war, this kind of work dried up, as did most nonessential construction. Kahn's poor eyesight excused him from military service, and so he embarked on a search for a way to reconnect architecture with its own history, as evidenced by the Gothic-inspired drawings he produced to accompany his essay, "Monumentality," published in Paul Zucker's widely circulated book *New Architecture and City Planning*.[126]

According to Eugene Nalle, Kahn, in his early years at Yale, was just as much adrift as anyone else in the department. Indeed, when Kahn first joined the Yale faculty, as Scully remembers, he seemed to be searching for some greater truth:

> It was clear that here was a man who'd lost an order and was looking for it everywhere. What that order was nobody knew. He didn't know himself, but he constantly talked about it—not about flow diagrams and flow patterns, the kind of thing they were then talking about at Harvard, but about order, especially the order of crystals. It was as if he, like a lot of people in architecture and art history in the late forties, wanted to get outside art, to something that would sanction art. . . . Kahn felt there had to be some kind of scientific basis for his work. It was a curious time in our lives, when we lost confidence in the things that we live by.[127]

Surprisingly, despite his comparative inarticulateness, Kahn proved to be effective with students, and in 1950 was promoted to full faculty. After a residency at the American Academy in Rome from December 1950 to February 1951, he was asked to take over from Edward Durell Stone as chief critic in architectural design. It was during his tenure at the academy that Kahn was said to have been first introduced to the powerful forms of ancient Roman architecture by Yale Professor of Archaeology Frank E. Brown (1908–1988; Ph.D. 1938), who was serving as professor in charge of the Classical School and director of excavations during Kahn's residency.[128] Contrary to many historians of the time who celebrated the utilitarian and tectonic nature of Roman architecture, Brown taught his students to see it as "a poetry of space, of light and water."[129] Kahn took Brown's lessons to heart in his projects in the late 1950s and 1960s— some of his greatest work—particularly the unrealized community building at the Salk Institute for Biological Studies (1959–65), the Kimbell Art Museum (1966–72), and the National Assembly Building in Dhaka (1961–82).

When Kahn returned from Rome, Howe, together with Professor of Philosophy Paul Weiss (1901–2001), nursed, indulged, and stimulated him, not only as architect but as philosopher, which had the effect of increasing his abstract and oracular way of speaking, both in his lectures and desk-side criticism. "Most of the students loved him," remembers Scully, "though many didn't understand what he was talking about, which I think was natural since many times he used to talk to try to feel for the idea. At times he didn't even know what he was talking about, which is lovely. It is like designing or drawing."[130] Estelle Thompson Margolis describes Kahn as contradictorily "shy and bombastic all at the same time. He was an impatient genius and a very patient teacher."[131] For certain students, such as William Huff, Kahn had a transformative effect. "He was a dedicated teacher who, when not working, was with us at the drafting tables in the Weir Hall architectural department or at the coffee table in the Chapel Street greasy spoon."[132]

Significantly, Kahn's influence is not as large as one might expect. For example, Huff's 1952 thesis project for an urban church, while it reflects Kahn's influence in the well-articulated plan, strong geometric forms, and choice of materials (3.27, 3.28), reveals other influences at play as well, with references to Piranesi and to the Classicizing modernism of Philip Johnson, whose Soreq Nuclear Research Center in Yavne, Israel (1960) would take on a similar shape (3.29).[133] Scully suspects that Kahn's inability to permanently influence the department's direction could be explained by the fact that he was "the farthest from being an academic man."[134] Though Kahn spent a lot of time talking with fellow critics and students, as much as anything, it was his buildings that inspired students like Huff and Irving Colburn (1923–1992; M.Arch 1951) with a sense of what architecture, at its best, could be. As Jaquelin T. Robertson suggests, Kahn would talk "lovingly, with his hands about the 'idea of architecture'; and *show* you by the building you were in that he had built [the Yale Art Gallery extension], that somehow that idea *could* survive, at least in part, its translation 'from becoming into being.'"[135]

James Polshek (b. 1930; M.Arch 1955), who would supervise construction of Kahn's posthumous Roosevelt Memorial in New York in 2012, remembers being frustrated by his teacher's quasi-mystic opacity. Kahn's "verbal poetics were often obscure and his scribbled notations usually illegible. But these mysteries stimulated the studio and the work that was generated was as iconoclastic as the man himself. . . . Except for a small group of students to whom he paid special attention, the rest of us were in an almost constant state of anxiety. The early years of a rigorous and systematic pedagogy [under Eugene Nalle] had given way to an arcane laissez-faire randomness, which was uncomfortable."[136]

Howe was determined to break the department's "trade school" pattern by introducing dramatic pedagogical reform as the coordinator of first-year design.[137] Assisted by Eugene Nalle, Joseph Boaz, and Robert Russell (B.Arch 1948), a classmate of Nalle's and a former recipient of the Winchester Prize, he was determined to institute "one course of instruction implementing education . . . in which, as Alfred N. Whitehead puts it, 'Interrelated truths are utilized en bloc, and the various propositions are employed in any order.'"[138] But such high-flying philosophizing does not necessarily translate into a methodology suited to beginning architects, and Howe turned to Nalle to

3.30 From left to right: Thomas R. (Tim) Vreeland, Jr. (B.A. 1950, M.Arch 1954), George R. Brunjes, Jr. (M.Arch 1954), and Eugene Nalle (B.Arch 1948), working in Weir Hall (ca. 1950).

3.31 Eugene Nalle, Department Store, perspective (1946).

help develop "a system of ordered exercises which would prepare the minds of the students *in general* for independent thought and work." Then, "with this end in view," Howe saw to it that the new first-year program experimented "with such general ideas as space, movement in space, composition, color, drawing, and so forth, without regard to specific function or dry contemporary technics."[139] In this, he relied heavily on Eugene Nalle, who was in many ways the most significant of the three leading teachers in the department (3.30). Though most closely associated with Howe, Nalle actually served under five different chairmen: Meeks; Richard Bennett, whom Nalle considered the department's "first policy maker" and the "first true chairman"; Harold Hauf; Howe; and Paul Schweikher.

Nalle was a primitivist. While Kahn and Johnson shared a commitment to architecture as a formal system rooted in history, Nalle seemed unwilling to be bound by rules or precedents, except those that could be deduced from elemental tectonics. Raised in Dallas, Texas, Eugene Nalle attended Highland Park High School, where the principal often remarked that "all of life is enigma and contradiction," something that became Nalle's mantra."[140] Nalle's initial training as a cabinetmaker was interrupted by military service, during which he sustained injuries as the result of a plane crash. After recuperating, he enrolled in Yale's architecture program in 1944. Dean Meeks admitted the less-than-credentialed young Texan on the strength of his skills as a draftsman. Later, Meeks asked him to join the faculty to "help out" with drawing, beginning Nalle's teaching career, which he claims to have "drifted" into.[141] Scully described Nalle's early draftsmanship work as "late Bauhaus," in which "space is constructed purely by graphic tricks: a little bit of shadow up above, and the *snap* of the black plane below (3.31). Passage, transparency, flux, flow, no weight, no symmetry, and in front, demonstrating . . . a good deal of the distrust with which Western civilization as a whole was held by practitioners of this period, what is apparently the head of a Fiji Islander heaves into sight—so introducing in the project the necessary purity of primitive art."[142]

When Howe first came to Yale, "it was a little bit of a rough go" for Nalle.[143] Initially, Howe did not recognize Nalle's talents, but he soon came to see him as "a dedicated teacher, an artist-philosopher begotten by Yale out of carpentry and building."[144] Like other faculty members, Nalle had reservations about Howe, whom he came to regard as something of a split personality. "When he got on his Homburg and his Chesterfield, he was George Howe, the eminent architect of the Philadelphia Saving Bank. [If] you knew George Howe personally, he had on his Tyrolean hat and sports coat, he was an entirely different person. Really. He really was two people." The Howe that arrived at Yale

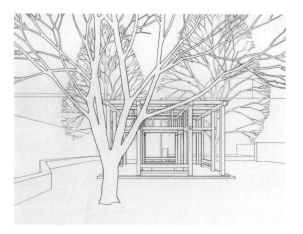

3.32 Harold Fredenburgh (M.Arch 1958), Weir Court Pavilion, perspective (1954).

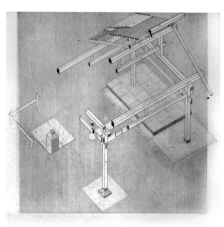

3.33 Phillip Brodrick (M.Arch 1956), assembly isometric (ca. 1955)

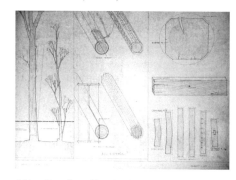

3.34 Unattributed Drawing Illustrating How to Source and Prepare Material for a Wood Pavilion (1953), likely drawn by Nalle or one of his assistants as an example for students.

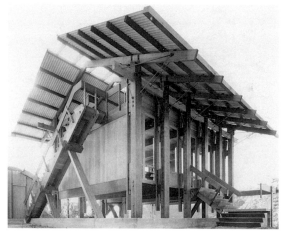

3.35 Frederic P. Lyman III (B.A. 1950, B.Arch 1953), Malibu Residence (1960), California.

3.36 James Polshek (M.Arch 1955), Project for a Pavilion (left, 1951), and Long Island Park Shelter (right, 1966), Baldwin, Long Island, New York.

was wearing a Homburg and made it clear that "he felt our little projects were awfully provincial."[145]

By spring 1951, Howe, working with Nalle, had extended his curriculum reform to the first two years, conceived as a lower school "to integrate instruction and education in a succession of related and interlarded experiences with exercises in design as their nucleus," so that, "the student . . . will educate himself by illustrating in his own designs and in his own way the principles inculcated step by step by instruction in history, technics, the arts and methods of systematic thought."[146] An integrated "lower school" curriculum would "prepare the student for his first essays in independent and personal architectural composition, during his last two or upper school years, under the guidance of visiting critics, more adequately than he has been prepared in the past. Needless to add," Howe continued, "lessons drawn from the past, both near and remote, will be directed throughout to the clarification of contemporary architectural design."[147]

Working with Nalle, Howe developed exercises designed "to inculcate notions of the place of Perception, Conception and Modulation in the Design Process" on what Howe called "the Path of the Feet and the Eyes." They asked beginning students to locate three elements—a portal, a platform, a bench—in relation to the trees and boundaries of Weir Court, before going on to more abstract concepts such as "pageantry," which emphasized the importance of "ceremony" in even the simplest building.[148] "The Path of the Feet and the Eyes," an explicit criticism of Sigfried Giedion's abstract conceptual emphasis on spatial flow, was rooted in Howe's faith in a perceptual approach to architecture and a conviction that, "in thinking of human scale," one should think of man "as a mobile eye, supported on a pair of feet, and remember that the roving eye can experience only that to which the feet conduct it."[149] Howe had begun to develop this idea in the 1930s and used it as the basis of his plans for a large country house, Square Shadows (1934), in Whitemarsh, Pennsylvania.[150] So convinced was Howe of his spatial idea that he reported to the University Council that he expected it would "run through the following three years of the Architecture Course."[151]

"The Path of the Feet and the Eyes" notwithstanding, the principal thrust of the two-year Basic Design course, reflecting Albers's original vision and Nalle's background as a skilled cabinetmaker, was a "hands-on" approach rooted in elemental tectonics with students working directly with wood and masonry, often using the actual materials in the drafting room in a manner many felt more appropriate to the engineering laboratory or to the contractor's shed. Very different from the abstract functionalism advocated by

Gropius at Harvard, Nalle's method led to what Harold Fredenburgh (b. 1933; M.Arch 1958), a first-year student in 1954–55, has described as "stick and stone architecture." Fredenburgh found Nalle's "a remarkable discipline," with a building seen as "an articulate assemblage of elements. . . . Almost from the start we drafted (ever so precisely) details of materials being put together. This is quite different in approach, say, than designing a house with 2×4s and wood siding wherein, however simple the program, the structure is obscure."[152] In some cases, Nalle had students not only draft material assemblies but also account for material sourcing—students had to draw the type of tree used, the tools necessary, and the milling process (3.32–3.34).

The two-year sequence Howe encouraged Nalle to develop had its greatest appeal to students like Frederic P. Lyman III (1927–2005; B.A. 1950, B.Arch 1953) and James Polshek. Lyman, more than many other students, absorbed Nalle's methods into his subsequent work—particularly the Malibu, California, house he built for himself in 1960 (3.35).[153] Polshek's work also reflected Nalle's teaching (3.36). Polshek came to Yale as a graduate student with no prior experience of architecture; he received his undergraduate education at Case Western Reserve University, where he prepared for a career in medicine before deciding to change professional direction. Polshek flourished under Nalle's rigorous and restrictive approach, which, he recalls, was not about ideas so much as principles: "Over and over again the catechism was drummed into our heads—earth slab, support, span, envelope, connections. Over and over the basic elements that made up the hut or the high rise. And it was, for me, extraordinarily stimulating and they are lessons I have not forgotten to this day."[154] Under Nalle's guidance, there was also a deliberate effort to see specific building programs as generic types: a "library would be called an archive. A bank was a repository. Magazines in the studio were discouraged. It was actually somewhat cultish but in that if you were willing to suspend belief for a year or two, the advantages were absolutely enormous." Reflecting on his student work, after fifty years of experience as a leading architect and educator, Polshek, dean of Columbia's Graduate School of Architecture, Planning, and Preservation from 1972 to 1987, was struck by "the absence of glass, the awareness of sun and wind, long before it became fashionable and necessary."[155]

If Kahn was a guru for advanced students, Nalle was a cult leader for initiates. His inarticulateness and uncommunicative nature were regarded by some as indications of remarkable depth; but to some, his seemingly mystical devotion to architecture, to quote Thurlow Merrill (Tim) Prentice, Jr. (b. 1930;

B.A. 1953, M.Arch 1960), "did not so much involve the students in a craft or art or service to society, as in a religion."[156] Nalle's primitivist problems left little room for design creativity. As John Field recalls: "We focused on the assignments to draw first a path and then a gateway, followed by a series of designs for very simple structures, each an exercise in wood joinery and weather protection. No focus was ever placed on how the plan worked but how you kept the water out and how you put the pieces of the building together was paramount. Our efforts were sometimes rewarded with Gene Nalle bringing in photographs of fifteen examples of other situations with architecture without architects where our problem was solved well. Any flights of romantic fantasy were brutally rejected."[157]

Nalle deplored precedents from the grand tradition, but he did have distinct artistic passions, as reflected in his collection of postcards that were constantly passed around to introduce the students to their master's preferred color, graphic, and compositional strategies, while any outside materials were strictly verboten. His studios became worlds unto themselves. Polshek recalled, "'Determined originality' was the enemy and the design *process* was emphasized over the design *product*."[158]

Soon enough, concerns about Nalle's methods and his control over two years of studio began to arise. Ironically, the initial negative reaction to the Basic Design curriculum was not philosophical but administrative. Those students with four years at another college needed four graduate years to receive the bachelor of architecture degree, but Yale College juniors and seniors were able to enroll in the first and second years of the graduate program, so that in six years' time they could earn both a bachelor of arts and a bachelor of architecture degree. As a result, undergraduates spent a large part of their time in the Architecture Department, giving Nalle considerable power over them.[159] Not everyone thought this wise, especially members of the art history faculty, who felt that Nalle's pedagogical approach was overly deterministic. As Polshek has written, Nalle's approach "posed a significant threat to the art historians (in particular Vincent Scully)."[160] Initially, Scully admired Nalle, even briefly engaging him to design a house. (Scully also considered hiring Frank Lloyd Wright, who prepared a design. Realizing that he couldn't afford to build the master's design, Scully decided to design the house himself.[161] Wright's design was posthumously realized by Taliesin Architects as the West House in 1987.) Scully soon clashed with Nalle, later calling him "a real monster," a "primitive law-giver to oversophisticated people like George Howe." Scully and other art historians particularly objected to Nalle's ostensible anti-intellectualism: he "didn't actually burn books but he wouldn't let people go to the library."[162] In reality, he encouraged students to read, but selectively, from authors he approved of, including Giedion, Spengler, and José Ortega y Gasset.[163]

Ralph Comey recalls one particular moment of conflict between the two instructors during one of Scully's lectures in 1948: "From the start, he [Scully] was an exciting, dynamic lecturer, restlessly pacing the [stage], using the pointer like a rapier. . . . His stylist [sic] descriptions were vivid, and his observations and comparisons were perceptive and brilliant. . . . During one lecture on the Renaissance Mannerist period when he was analyzing a Giulio Romano facade, there was a shout from the darkness, 'But that architecture is dishonest. It's a stage set!' I recognized Gene Nalle's voice. Vince patiently explained that this was a style, honest in its own terms, but as far as I know the argument was never resolved."[164]

Nalle's obsessive thoroughness was reflected in the careful way he prepared each new design exercise. According to Polshek, all problems were "done in advance by the critics—literally, done by the critics. He and his small but ardent staff."[165] Nalle, his co-teachers, and their teaching assistants formed a kind of monastic order that would spend the summer working out the design exercises he would assign in the following year.[166] The problems and requirements were dictated in great detail: "Everything was 18×24. There was a module that broke down into the next scale and the next scale. Notebooks were kept, things were handed out, a certain amount of tracing was required, which is actually a kind of Beaux-Arts system, but at that time, there was little to draw upon. There was Wright and Taliesin, there was Mies and there was Le Corbu." But Nalle "leaned eastward rather than westward, so that became a very important influence. [He] was so diligent. . . . He and his staff were there all the time. He could be found at the studio at midnight, 1:00, 2:00 in the morning, working over a student's drawing, rubbing Prismacolor. So there was this intensity to it."[167] Mark Hardenbergh (b. 1930; B.A. 1952, M.Arch 1957, M.C.P. 1958) remembers that Nalle would "come in while you were gone and erase and redo half of your drawing. This used to drive some people up the wall and out of the room for at least the rest of the day. But he had a knack of redoing your drawing in the same style you were attempting and hence showing you how to do better what you wanted to do." However, Hardenbergh admits that Nalle's approach wasn't always successful: "I don't know that he taught us very much about design."[168]

It is a sad irony of Howe's tenure that, as Yale's only post–World War II chairman or dean to attempt a systematic pedagogy for beginning students, his efforts ended up being regarded as contrary to Yale's tradition of open inquiry.

Howe was slow to see that Nalle's approach stood in sharp contradiction to prevailing university standards, especially as they pertained to undergraduate education. Indeed, the deterministic nature of Nalle's pedagogy, like that of Albers, brought into sharp focus as never before what many would see as the inherent contradiction of professional art training in a humanities-based university. As early as June 1952, Howe, forced to acknowledge that his two-year Basic Design curriculum had resulted in "some confusion," fell back on his wit, saying, "As in other art areas, the romantic counter-revolution following the realist revolution has set in," and recognizing that the dissidents "felt they were being cribbed, cabined and confined by the intellectual, functional and structural disciplines." Howe was sympathetic up to a point and promised that the reforms to be introduced in the second year of the new curriculum would meet the students' concerns "before discontent became vocal."[169]

Initially, Dean Sawyer respected Chairman Howe's new curriculum and Nalle's near-total control of its first two years, as did the Visiting Committee of the University Council. But with Howe's retirement approaching, Sawyer's enthusiasm began to give way to doubt, and in his annual report to President Griswold for 1953–54, he expressed his reservations: "I have been concerned, lest the specific demands of a professional curriculum absorb an undue proportion of an undergraduate's time."[170] But Howe, with a certain degree of either innocence or naiveté, given Griswold's fierce dedication to traditional scholastics, defended Nalle's primitivism to the president in his final report as chairman: "Glib verbal knowledge is a dangerous possession, I am convinced, to the budding visual artist, whose proper medium of expression is the image, not the word, whose natural endowment is intuition, not intellect. . . . Filled with sketchy theories of all kinds, the Yale major is convinced that talking architecture, science, economics, sociology, is the way to create three-dimensional form in the Modern World."[171] Proudly, and amazingly, Howe went on to tell Griswold that, working with Nalle, he had virtually banished verbal and written discourse from the typical Yale architecture major in order to force students to design basic structures using only form, space, and color. Therefore, "All the so-called 'contemporary' problems, around which the verbiage of modern architecture has gathered, together with all the familiar associative images presented by everyday life and current publications, could no longer be argued about and imitated."[172]

Howe died on April 16, 1955, less than a year after stepping down as chairman. Charles Sawyer, traveling through Italy when he learned of Howe's death, took the occasion to assess his accomplishments at Yale: "George was

3.37   The retiring George Howe being honored by colleagues at Yale. From left to right: Paul Weiss,
Louis McAllister, Howe, Vincent Scully handing Howe a medal, Charles Sawyer, and Louis Kahn
holding a painting by Josef Albers, presented as a gift to Howe.

3.38   The cover of the first issue of *Perspecta* (1952),
designed by Norman Ives.

a brave and gay spirit and one of our most cultivated men, in the full sense, I ever knew. He made a rich contribution to Yale in his comparatively brief term with us: the final party which his students gave in his honor was a warm and rather rare tribute to a very generous personality (3.37). George had his faults and limitations—who hasn't," but he was someone to whom Sawyer deferred "in matters involving the policy of his department, for his appointment and that of Albers represented a firm effort to appoint Chairmen of mature experience and professional stature and then give them our full support. . . . George Howe did extremely well with the limited teaching staff available and at hand, and his authority with the students was such that they accepted with grace the somewhat spartan and limited educational fare which was handed them."[173]

There is no doubt that Howe believed the Basic Design curriculum to be his most important contribution as chairman. But he failed to see that a Bauhaus-like, obsessively focused Vorkurs, such as he and Nalle had fashioned, could not be sustained in an environment of a liberal arts university. Nalle's approach was inflexible and inaccessible, as the sole written expression of his design philosophy made clear, or, rather, unclear: "Architecture, with its irrationally complex yet deep roots of personal discipline, demands an extremely broad and viable outlook. It must encompass intuitive sensibility to the immediate situation observable in short range fact; this must be combined with a 'moral behavior' (in the largest sense of the word) beyond egocentric sentimentality which demands a continual intellectual wrestling with theory—a philosophic study of relationships between the inner and outer worlds of reality."[174]

Within a year of Howe's death, the controversy over Basic Design and Nalle would bring the department to near collapse.

Howe's most enduring contribution to the program proves not to have been in the area of curricular innovation but in the area of what may best be described as architectural culture. For example, in response to student concerns about the Beaux-Arts–style jury system, in which faculty and visiting jurors met *in camera* to review projects and determine student grades, he introduced reforms that, while retaining the closed-door judgment and grading of the Beaux-Arts system, permitted students to present their work publicly in front of the jury. At the same time, the age-old Beaux-Arts method of publicly affixing grades to student drawings was abolished in favor of sending private written commentary to students.[175]

Outside the studios, Howe treated the students as young professionals and encouraged them to meet informally with practicing architects after lectures or juries. Oftentimes, he would invite a group of students to his rooms in Jonathan Edwards College for conversation and drinking. These meetings of what he called the Digressionist Club were highly appreciated by students and fondly recollected by them in later years. Howe's ambition to cultivate a sense of community would extend beyond the public juries of student work and conversations of the Digressionist Club. Early in his second term, he embarked on a project that would profoundly affect the culture and reputation of the school: the founding of *Perspecta: The Yale Architectural Journal,* which would become Howe's most enduring legacy, providing students with the means to engage with the profession in a meaningful way—not by broadcasting their own jejune ideas but by publishing in a professional-caliber journal the writings and design work of scholars and architects whom they admired. From the publication of its first issue in 1952, *Perspecta*'s student editors have gathered together historical as well contemporary material in an ongoing effort to shape the future of architecture, publishing at the time of this writing forty-seven issues of the journal. *Perspecta* did not push any single agenda. As Howe famously put it, "To all architects, teachers, students *Perspecta* offers a place on the *merry-go-round.*"[176]

The first issue of *Perspecta* was edited by Norman F. Carver, Jr. (b. 1928; B.A. 1951, B.Arch 1954), who would go on to a notable career as an architectural photographer known for documenting vernacular architecture around the world.[177] The issue set a high standard for content and for its layout (3.38). It was designed by Norman Ives (1923–1978), faculty in the newly established Department of Graphic Design, who would continue to shape the magazine until *Perspecta 4*, when students in the graphic design program took on that responsibility under the supervision of Graphic Design Chairman Alvin Eisenman (1921–2013). According to Eisenman, the name "Perspecta" was also the journal's raison d'être: "*Perspecta* is the past participle of *perspicio* and it doesn't mean to see, it means to see through."[178] Eisenman recalls that the idea for starting a student-edited magazine was probably first conceived at a university party given to celebrate the five-hundredth anniversary of the printing of the Gutenberg Bible, where Howe and the distinguished surgeon John Fulton had a conversation about the importance of student magazines in professional schools. Subsequently, Eisenman got some tips about organizing and running a student magazine from one of his clients, the editors of the *Yale Law Journal,* and passed them along to Howe. "*Perspecta* was as far as I could see really based primarily on the intense enthusiasm George Howe had for the ideas of students. . . . He was meeting regularly with students at the time. . . . And out of that came the notion that there could be a magazine, I believe."[179]

As Howe told it, the first issue of *Perspecta* grew out of his

custom to listen to the complaints of my students and discuss with them the problems of contemporary architecture beyond the limits of the drafting room. When I returned from a weekend in the summer of 1950 I reported to them that Mies van der Rohe had said to me, "We know what design is." When I returned from a New Year's excursion in 1951 I reported to them that Frank Lloyd Wright had said to me, "I am the background." While expressing their admiration of these two eminent architects the students refused to accept their judgments as final.

Yet, inexperienced as they are in life and even in their trade, they were unable to offer alternatives to these expressions of personal satisfaction. So we came to the conclusion that they should create a medium of expression for themselves through which the potentialities of contemporary expression in architecture might be explored without programmatic implications.[180]

In Howe's view, it was students, and not practitioners or academics, who were best able to seize upon new ideas or discern the work of the past circumstances that would help illuminate contemporary trends. The early numbers of *Perspecta* had an influence wildly disproportionate to the comparatively few copies printed for each issue. For example, three young English architects, Colin St. John Wilson (1922–2007), Peter Carter (1927–2012), and Alan Colquhoun (1921–2012), were introduced to the work of Louis I. Kahn in 1955 when a visitor from Yale showed them a copy of *Perspecta* 3, illustrating the Yale Art Gallery. Years later, Wilson recalled that "the shock of recognition of a new presence in the world of architecture was immediate."[181]

The department's culture during the Howe years became fodder for a mildly sensational novel in 1956, when Edwin Gilbert published *Native Stone*, the first of a series of place-and-profession-specific novels he would write.[182] *Native Stone* drew on Gilbert's direct observation of the department and on bits of information and gossip supplied to him by departmental secretary Louise Britton, whom William Huff has described as a "sex goddess to some, mother to all, unofficial vice-chairman to at least three official and one or two interim chairmen in Yale's Department of Architecture."[183] In Gilbert's novel, the character Matthew Pierce is modeled on Howe ("tall, frosty-eyed chairman with the inimitable aura of dark elegance"), as is the character of Vern Austin. The hero of the book was, as Huff has written, "a sort of F. L. W. [Frank Lloyd Wright] devotee—representative of the actual maverick, Gene Nalle . . . fighting in a last ditch stand against an archaic Establishment but [also] against Philip Johnson's new order and its pallid presentment proliferated by the emerging SOM [Skidmore, Owings & Merrill] giant. In the background was painted one of the more identifiable personalities," the "'almost gnome-like' professor-master Homer Jepson. 'Louie' Kahn, of course."[184] As Gilbert envisioned Jepson/Kahn, he had given up a major practice to remain at Yale as chief design critic "to imbue and jab and incite his students with his knowledge, his gifts of erudition and experience."[185]

Howe's last term was spring 1954, but he had begun to plan for his successor two years earlier, according to William Huff, offering the chairmanship to Kahn, who was supposedly intrigued, but wary of leaving his practice to enter academia full-time: "Finally, one day, as his patience waiting on Lou's decision wore thin, Howe pushed him once more. 'Lou,' he said, 'you are, after all, more a teacher than an architect.' 'It was in that moment,' Lou related, 'that I realized I was more an architect than a teacher' (or, at least, aspired to be); and he turned Howe's offer down—making, probably, the most crucial decision of his career."[186] Kahn's decision led Howe to propose that Paul Schweikher take over: "He has proved his worth here as Visiting Critic on several occasions. He is devoted to the Department. There is probably no better man for the job in the country, available or not."[187]

A Denver, Colorado, native, Paul Schweikher initially enrolled in the College of Engineering at the University of Colorado in 1921 before changing his field of study to architecture in the next year. In 1922, he left the university to take a job as a draftsman in the Chicago firm of Granger & Bollenbacher while attending night classes at the Art Institute, the Armour Institute, and the Chicago Atelier. After five years of professional experience and academic training in Chicago, he enrolled at Yale and received his bachelor of fine arts degree in 1929, before returning to Chicago to start his own practice. In 1934, he joined up with fellow Yale alumnus Theodore W. Lamb, and in 1937 the two brought in Winston Elting (1907–1968) as partner in a firm that specialized in suburban houses.[188] The firm suspended practice during World War II, but in 1945 reopened as Schweikher & Elting, with Schweikher leading the design effort, while Elting focused on administration and construction management.[189]

Many faculty and alumni of the school, including Eero Saarinen, agreed with Howe that Schweikher would be right for the job. Reflecting on Schweikher's selection twenty years later, Dean Sawyer remembered that "While his reputation was as something of a 'loner' he seems to have been generally respected by his contemporaries. We thought we were fortunate in his acceptance of the chairmanship."[190] Schweikher's appointment was announced on June 22, 1953, shortly after he had broken with Elting to open an independent practice in which he was responsible for both design and project management. Schweikher's newly independent, Chicago-based practice began to take off, keeping him away from New Haven a great deal of the time. With his business booming, he was only too happy to rely on Eugene Nalle to an even greater extent than his predecessor, not only embracing Nalle's controlled approach to learning in the first- and second-year Core curriculum, but also giving him increased responsibility by placing him in charge of the third year. The story of Schweikher's brief chairmanship is, therefore, inextricably linked to his relationship to Nalle, with unfortunate consequences for them both.

As soon as Schweikher took over, the faculty, rent by conflicts—some petty, some personal, many truly reflective of the uncertain state of American architecture and architectural education at the time—began to publicly express their displeasure with Howe's curriculum, as delivered by Nalle, which they believed not only thwarted the individual creativity of students but also demeaned their own. As the faculty began to rebel, Schweikher's personality did not help. He was brusque and impatient, with a disposition that did not make him particularly well suited for dealing with divergent views on architectural practice and pedagogy.

Richard Nininger (b. 1929; B.A. 1951, M.Arch 1957) experienced the school's transition from Howe to Schweikher firsthand. As a senior in Yale College, Nininger had taken first-year design under Howe and Nalle. After two years of military service and a year in Douglas Orr's office, he returned to Yale in fall 1954, entering into Nalle's second-year class, where, he later observed, "there was still much of the regimen of my first year in terms of the discipline of the craft, which was further enhanced by such hands-on exercises as the explanation of forces in the form of sticks and wire, which we would assemble into large 'snowflake' designs." However, according to Nininger, there was a notable change in the department, which had recently consolidated its studios from Weir Hall, the Sculpture Gallery, and the Chapel Street storefront, to the fourth floor of Kahn's extension of the Yale Art Gallery: "There was a decided lack of the wonder [and] explorative freedom that had prevailed in the old Chapel Street storefront. I cannot put my finger on it. Perhaps it was the missing midnight bull sessions, or of the father figure of George Howe. Maybe it was being on the inaccessible top floor of Kahn's Art Gallery. But somehow that *joie de vivre* was missing. It wasn't the students' lack of enthusiasm or spontaneity, but rather an underlying discontent of something lacking, perhaps an alternative voice of debatable opposition."[191]

This lack of "debatable opposition" may have been a direct result of Nalle's tendency to steamroll over those who disagreed with him. As Dean Sawyer succinctly put it, "Eugene Nalle was no diplomat."[192] His trenchant criticism and rigid principles gradually divided the students into two opposing camps: zealous disciples and vehement detractors. When William Huff paid a postgraduate visit to Yale during Schweikher's tenure, he found a very different department from the one he had left: "The glamor of what was left of Howe's Yale was fast waning. Gene Nalle, intense, neurotic, charismatic, making his very last stand under Schweikher's wing, reclaimed Weir Hall and built the school-within-school 'squirrel cage' lock-in for his band of 'Native Stone' followers."[193]

Students took sides. Lee Mogel (b. 1933; M.Arch 1957) failed to see any humor in the situation and looked back on the program after fifty years as "probably among the most uncreative periods of my life."[194] Walter Kaplan (b. 1927; B.Arch 1955), on the other hand, defended Nalle's methods in a passionate letter to the *Yale Daily News* attributing students' discontent to their impatience "with themselves and the slow process of growth, as well as with the errors of the school in this vital period of its development." Kaplan countered claims that the program was an un-Yale-like vocational monoculture, arguing that although one might wish "for as great a variety of architectural influences and personalities as the school can assemble . . . this, in actual practice, results in a series of rather episodic experiences adding up to an education unrelated to an orderly process of development." He continued: "To call the school a 'vocational school' is, I think, to say more about the student using the epithet than about the school. Architecture, as do the other arts, invites a craft and technique as its basis which are to be acquired only through arduous disciplining. A student of the piano who aspires to play Bach before having mastered the scales may do well perhaps to reconsider his vocation. It is he who is on shaky ground, not his teacher who insists on such mastery."[195]

Students may have been divided about Nalle and his methods, but the faculty was, for the most part, united against him. With Howe gone, and Schweikher's professional work distracting him from his duties as chairman, the resident faculty pushed for administrative changes, including the hiring of additional faculty to mitigate Nalle's influence. Schweikher was slow to realize that there was a problem. In his annual report for 1954–55, documenting his first full year as chairman, he confessed that he had "apparently missed the undercurrent of disagreement among the faculty and the effort on the part of some to expel another" and had failed to "anticipate the dissatisfaction of the Course of Studies Committee of Yale College with the existing program for the major in Architecture or the compulsions implicit in the inquiry of the President's Committee or the emphasis to be given to courses in the liberal arts."[196]

The situation became so dire that in November 1954—just five months after his retirement to Philadelphia—Howe was asked by Dean Sawyer to return to New Haven to meet with faculty members, prepare a report on the condition of the school, and make suggestions for ways to bring people together. Howe reluctantly obliged, noting in his report that although the faculty considered Nalle to be "dictatorial, unfair and vindictive, confused, narrow, psychopathic," there were many students who were enthusiastic about his teaching. Addressing claims from the faculty that the "whole method of instruction evolved by Mr. Nalle, at my suggestion, is too analytical, not free enough, distorted, unhumanistic [*sic*], contrary to the Yale ideal of the free exchange of ideas," Howe tried to defend his pedagogical legacy, but his response to what was becoming a vote of no confidence in his chosen successor was simplistic and bitter—that of a tired, disengaged man leaning on his charm:

> When I was in New Haven, I listened patiently, answering only here and there with a protest that not the new Chairman but the old was responsible for much of what they found to criticize. That, they said, was somehow different. Why? Only, I suspect, because they were used to his weird ways. However that may be, the longer I think about it the more indignant I become at the parochial behavior, the petty vanity, the lack of generosity and understanding, of patience and forbearance, the seemingly unconscious disloyalty to their beloved Yale of my former colleagues.
>
> None of this, smiling diplomat that I am, will I say to their faces. I shall tell them only that I have reported their sentiments to you as best I could and retire from the scene. They complained that you [Dean Sawyer] and Paul [Schweikher] would not listen to them. One of them said to me that he felt better already after talking to me. If that is the feeling of others my purpose in injecting myself into the argument will have been fulfilled.
>
> On reading over this hasty script I find I have failed to mention one interesting point. When the Department was really in confusion a few years ago the humanists found no fault with the system. Only the idea of a professional discipline seems to shock them. Shall I laugh or cry?[197]

Howe sent a copy of his memorandum to Schweikher, who appreciated Howe's support while seeming to confess to his own deficient leadership skills, writing to Sawyer: "I think that my job as Chairman is one of doing more than talking: every word of explanation seems to me one too many and carries with it an implication of apology and defense that I do not feel." In a memorandum, Schweikher affirmed his continuing support for the direction of Howe's curriculum by, characteristically, deferring to Nalle, who had produced a chart describing in great detail the step-by-step process by which students would acquire the fundamental skills needed by all architects. Schweikher explained to Sawyer that though the chart was often derided by faculty as "a kind of occultism . . . it is nothing more than the thoughtful production of an orderly mind."[198]

Schweikher's memorandum to Dean Sawyer was pitiful in some ways—obsessively detailed and defensive—but it also revealed a keen intelligence and a civilized demeanor, describing the Howe-Nalle curriculum in minute detail and responding to its critics on the faculty. But it came too late. The damage had been done, and in the months following Howe's return visit, Carroll Meeks, Louis Kahn, and King-lui Wu grew more vocal in their opposition to Nalle. Foremost among his opponents was Wu, who believed that Nalle, having put the students into the darkness, offered them one magnificently glowing light at a time, while never revealing to them the complexity and interdependence of the issues. Significantly, no doubt sensing Wu's antipathy to Nalle, both Howe and Schweikher had refused to advance him to tenure.[199] Kahn was also public in his opposition to Nalle, telling a reporter for the *Yale Daily News* that "students should be given a consciousness of the whole. They should be presented with a wider span of criticism. They should never be allowed to lose sight of the whole problem of architecture during each of their four years. They should not be taught one part one year, one part the next, etc." Kahn advocated for a more open and flexible curriculum, launching a thinly veiled tirade against Nalle's pedagogy: "The present conception is that a strict program will lead to more learning. I believe that no man is big enough to impose a single approach."[200]

If Nalle's methods had been confined to graduate students, his downfall might have been avoided or, at least, postponed, but his control was regarded as particularly inappropriate by undergraduate majors, who took the equivalent of five courses in the department, all graded by Nalle. Undergraduate criticism focused on four points: "1) inadequate criticism by the instructors, 2) the arbitrary grading of creative projects by one man, 3) the absence of diversity and depth within the course, and 4) the insufficient number of instructors."[201] In fall 1954, Schweikher agreed to participate more regularly in the grading process, but that concession was not enough to stem the tide of opposition.

Schweikher's decision to rely on Nalle was, in his own view, a carefully considered choice between supporting the controversial educator or giving the department over to the school's art historians.[202] Indeed, Carroll Meeks had been angling for advancement within the department, possibly even the chairmanship, and was doing quite a bit to stir the pot. Like Kahn, Meeks shared his grievances with the *Yale Daily News:* "The aim of a school is to develop independence of thought, self-reliance, adaptability in its graduates," he said. "The atmosphere of the school should be liberal, hospitable to new conceptions, adventurous in ideas, tolerant, and free of cant and dogma. . . . It should never become so abstract that it loses touch with such realities as the living function of the building, the human client, and the ultimate ends of architecture, aesthetic and spiritual."[203]

According to Sawyer, by the time Schweikher assumed responsibility for the collapse, it was too late: "'the fat was in the fire,' and in a remarkably short time the whole morale and effectiveness of the Department deteriorated."[204] Aside from the inappropriateness of a monocultural approach within a humanities-driven university, Nalle's primitivism was increasingly out of step with trends in the profession as a whole, which was beginning to throw off the narrow functionalism of Gropius in favor of an increasing diversity of approaches, including Miesian Classicism as well as structurally innovative form-making, "usually involving a thin shell, folded planes, paraboloids, and other shapes," as Scully's student Herbert McLaughlin put it, drawing attention to the prevalence of space frames and tensile structures in Yale student work that may "foreshadow development in another direction, in that their total forms approach abstract sculpture." This could be seen in the evolution of Duncan Wray Buell's (b. 1928; M.Arch 1953) early Frank Lloyd Wright–inspired work (see 3.21) to his 1953 thesis project for a railroad station in New Haven (3.39), which Carroll Meeks included in his book *The Railroad Station* as a dynamic example of new construction methods. Space frame enclosures ultimately derived from Buckminster Fuller could also be found in the 1954 fourth-year design problem of Avery Faulkner (1929–2007; B.A. 1951, M.Arch 1954) and Tim Vreeland (b. 1925; B.A. 1950, M.Arch 1954) for a "Theatre for Drama" in New Haven (3.40). Alternatively, the more sculptural approach of Thomas Green's (b. 1931; M.Arch 1959) 1957 sprayed-concrete church enclosed by folded planes (3.41) was inspired by the work of John M. Johansen (1916–2012), who joined the faculty as critic in architectural design in 1956. Johansen had recently been commissioned to explore the possibilities of sprayed, thin-shell concrete construction and would go on to use the technology in several projects, including his pavilion for the Zagreb International World's Fair

3.39   Duncan Wray Buell (M.Arch 1953), New Haven Railroad
Station, perspective. Thesis project (1953).

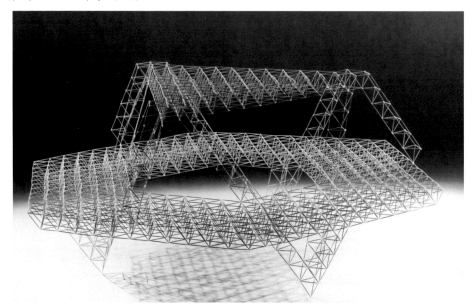

3.40   Avery Faulkner (B.A. 1951, M.Arch 1954) and Tim Vreeland (B.A. 1950, M.Arch 1954), A Theatre for Drama
in New Haven, structural model (1954).

3.41   Thomas Green (M.Arch 1959), Sprayed Concrete Construction, model (1957).

(1956) and a church in Norwich, Connecticut (1957).[205] While Nalle abhorred architectural history, students, influenced by Johnson and Scully, increasingly accepted historical precedent and began to embrace "past forms as valid in themselves," resulting in, as McLaughlin noted, "a great deal of effort [being] given to relating new buildings to old, not only in massing, but in texture and profile, something largely ignored before. Even ornament is returning."[206] With this sea change in student interests, the Howe-Nalle pedagogical program that was once seen as innovative and adventurous was now considered sterile and academic.

The negative 1955 report of a Visiting Committee of the National Architectural Accrediting Board (NAAB) forced President Griswold to take action. In its report, the committee recommended that architecture, still a department in the School of the Fine Arts, as it had been since 1916, be established "as a professional school . . . on a par with the other professional schools in the University." Concerned that the department was not taking advantage of the "full teaching resources" of the university and that students were insufficiently encouraged "to cross boundaries . . . and explore areas of study outside of the immediate field of Architecture," the committee went on to observe that "even the rich resources of general studies courses within the Department seem not to be utilized to their fullest extent." Though students "were not overly critical of the introductory portion of the program itself," the committee felt that "they resented the dominance of one faculty member over the direction of their work" and "felt extremely restricted to a particular pattern of performance, which limited to a serious degree the development of personal exploration and judgment."[207]

Taking note of the "lack of harmony" within the faculty, which was "unfortunately reflected in the morale of the students with whom we came into contact," the NAAB's Visiting Committee identified several of the same issues raised by the faculty, expressing its concern that the first-year curriculum was being extended "into the second and third years with the apparent intention of embracing the fourth year as well," thereby producing "an extreme reliance on predicted techniques" rather than imbuing students with an understanding of the broader principles of architecture. It went on to report that, with the exception of Nalle, the faculty had no sympathy with the school's pedagogy or curriculum, and little effort was made to integrate their talents into the department. Committee Chairman Thomas K. Kirkpatrick's letter to Griswold continued: "It is not the province of this committee to speculate on the dis-harmony which admittedly had developed within the staff recently but it is of extreme concern to the committee that this lack of common understanding reflects in the morale of the student body and seriously effects [*sic*] their devotion to and understanding of the underlying philosophy of the Department." In summary, the committee expressed its belief that the program "has a certain merit and future promise," but "that this promise is not and will not be fulfilled unless, first, the timing and balance of the curriculum is improved; second, its scope is broadened and its administration improved; and third, the various functions of the school's faculty are better organized and are better coordinated."[208]

Although the department was awarded continuing accreditation, it was only on a "provisional" basis lasting one academic year, 1956–57, at which time the NAAB would return.[209] This was a slap in the face, an aggressive gesture that threatened the very future of the program, given that students need to attend an accredited school in order to pursue professional licensure. Sawyer found the NAAB's action to be justified, expressing his own displeasure with certain members of the architecture faculty, whom he believed had forgotten "the best interests of the institution to carry a family quarrel outside its walls," thereby permitting "the interests of its students to be affected adversely." In his view, a "sharp rebuke" was necessary. While Sawyer was grateful to the committee for refusing "to pass judgment on the merits of the controversy until a proper climate was restored," he deemed it "unfortunate" that they "allowed themselves to be used by one group as a weapon against the other."[210]

Because the negative report was not only embarrassing, but also highly public, everyone was "unsettled, if not in an uproar."[211] In a letter to President Griswold, William Huff, after reporting that "some graduates" have described the situation in the department as "extremely degenerate," went on to say that "as the situation now stands, I could not conscientiously recommend the Yale School of Architecture to any new aspirant in the field; though only a couple of years ago it was one of the best schools in the world."[212] Obviously, drastic changes had to be made. However, if there was a silver lining to be found in this particular cloud, it was that the NAAB report left University Provost Edgar Furniss "with the impression that more funds should be directed to the department" to allow for additional instructors, thereby reducing Nalle's teaching load and his influence as well.[213]

Schweikher tried to restore his credibility by appointing a Faculty Executive Committee, consisting of Kahn, Meeks, Scully, and Wu, to plan for the school's future. The committee, which immediately set out to expel Nalle, initially met with resistance from Dean Sawyer, then on leave, Acting Dean Boyd Smith, and Provost Edgar Furniss—all of whom had supported Nalle and Schweikher. Sawyer seriously questioned "whether [Nalle] should be made the sacrificial calf of the current proceedings." In fact, he saw Carroll Meeks as the principal troublemaker, referring to the art historian as "my chief problem this year." In Sawyer's view, Meeks "made a full-time job of stirring up trouble, with students, faculty, alumni, accrediting committee, in fact any-body who would listen." Meeks's behind-the-scenes role in the Architecture Department led design faculty and students to underestimate his value as a scholar and his pioneering research into nineteenth-century eclecticism. But no one who knew him could deny his effectiveness at maintaining traditional academic standards. Nalle was relieved of authority over the first- and sec-ond-year program in the fall of 1955. In a letter to President Griswold, Sawyer acknowledged Nalle's accomplishments, calling him "our most dedicated and hardest working teacher," albeit one with "a prickly pear personality who has unhappily succeeded in antagonizing a considerable portion of the student body and faculty."

The NAAB report effectively ended Schweikher's tenure as chairman, although he continued to serve in a diminished capacity until February 1956, when he submitted his resignation in a curt two-sentence letter to President Griswold, who wrote back to regret "the fact that [Schweikher's] services at Yale should terminate in this fashion," while expressing his conviction that the decision was in Schweikher's "own best interests."[214] Schweikher's failure as chairman, combined with the poor reception of his Josiah Willard Gibbs Research Laboratories (1955) (3.42), constructed on Science Hill in confor-mance to a master plan by Eero Saarinen, severely tarnished his reputation at Yale, but not elsewhere. He went on to combine a successful practice in Pittsburgh with a teaching career at Carnegie Mellon Institute before retiring to Arizona in 1970. But he never seemed to come to terms with his failure to effectively lead the department. Looking back on the situation with thirty years of hindsight, he stood by his actions and seemed to have few regrets: "There were many times during the three [sic] years as chairman of the department at Yale that I could have found solutions that would have brought me into a very happy relationship with everybody, but I would have had to yield some of my own personal convictions and I found that difficult to do, so that it became a quite free choice. I don't think I walked into something that I should have known better about at all. . . . I had plenty of friends when I left and could have stormed it through as it were. I was advised by many faculty members, Lou Kahn among them, that I could stay and should stay, but I chose not to."[215]

Although many blame Howe for placing too much faith in Nalle, Sawyer ultimately put the blame for the department's near collapse on Schweikher, who "made a tactical mistake . . . in attempting to spread [Nalle's] type of

3.42   Paul Schweikher, Josiah Willard Gibbs Research Laboratories (1955), New Haven.

3.43   Temporary drafting studio in the Swartwout Sculpture Gallery (ca. 1946).

3.44   Temporary architecture studio in a Chapel Street storefront (ca. 1952).

curriculum into the third professional year." As Sawyer saw him, Schweikher was very different from the urbane Howe: he was "honest and sincere—if anything, too literal and determined in his objectives and approaches to them," someone who "does not bend easily" and whose approach "to decisions in the academic world were somewhat naive and ill-considered. He was not accorded by his colleagues that usual period of tolerance and grace that marks a honeymoon period and if he acted arbitrarily at moments it was under considerable provocation."[216] Schweikher was offered an opportunity to add a few words in a letter to Sawyer that was made part of the 1955–56 annual report, his last as chairman, but after reading his previous report and that of George Howe "in the hope of adding to them my thoughts and actions of the past year in a connected and continuing way," he found that his thoughts were "too negative, the actions too few to have meaning let alone connection and continuity."[217]

Regardless of who was to blame, the fracas over Nalle seriously damaged Louis Kahn's relationship with the department. In a letter to Anne Tyng, Kahn, who claimed to never have been sure of Schweikher's leadership, reported that when he first presented his ideas on "space-order design" to Schweikher, he "barely got the idea. He is far from stupid but somehow I find it difficult to warm up to him."[218] Moreover, Kahn did not feel that Schweikher supported him to the extent that Howe had and expressed concern that he was actively trying to diminish Kahn's influence in the department. Kahn told Tyng that "Schweikher's real intention showed itself . . . [when] I received my usual notice from the Yale Corporation announcing my re-employment for the year 1954–1955 but it did not indicate the usual raise in salary and dropped the 'Chief' in front of Critic in giving my title. I called G. H. [George Howe] (knowing he was in on the arrangements for next year) and [he] seemed 'not to remember' discussing that particular point with Schweikher." On Howe's advice, Kahn spoke with Schweikher, recounting the conversation in his letter to Tyng:

> [Schweikher said] that he thought I wouldn't mind his dropping "chief" from my title since he understood that I didn't give a damn one way or another and that if critic had been used in the catalogue as a title, mine would be the only one used in that way and the others would be known as assistant critics or associate critics or research assistants etc., etc.,—Then I said, "Why did you drop chief without my permission?" [H]e said he should [not] have done so but thought it made no difference to me. I agreed that it did not but to the outside world it would be taken as a demotion and that I was tired of explaining my worth to people. . . .

He [Schweikher] was very sorry, said he was rather misled by George [Howe]—he did not caution him about my possible reaction. He tried to get me to drop my objection—but I did not permit that. He said most likely the catalogues were being printed. I said they would have to correct the printing. He said he would try to do so. He was so sorry. Of course it is obviously an attempt on his part to minimize my importance. Everyone knows that a director is a desk man and I as "chief critic" would appear more important. He concocted all this business for purely selfish reasons and I will definitely quit if the catalogue cannot be altered.[219]

Kahn had his way. The 1954–55 *Bulletin* lists Kahn as "Chief Critic in Architectural Design."

In 1955, Kahn accepted an appointment at the University of Pennsylvania, but with Schweikher on the way out, efforts were immediately made to have him return to Yale—possibly as chairman. Griswold met with him on February 27, 1956, the day after Schweikher submitted his letter of resignation, and Sawyer talked with him "several times on the telephone," reporting to the president that Kahn "has expressed a definite desire to accept the invitation to return to Yale." On February 8, Sawyer reported to University Council member Robert Osborn that the school's Executive Committee had unanimously agreed to try to get Kahn back: "All are in equal agreement as to his inspiring qualifications as a teacher, but there is also a firm conviction on the part of [Henry] Pfisterer and others that he needs a strong balance wheel and a firm and unanimous conviction that there should be no administrative duties expressed or implied in his appointment." Sawyer believed "that with one more strong design staff appointment—and it might be Ed Barnes—we would have a faculty that could work with Lou effectively and at the same time hold him in bounds at the moment when he is inclined to indulge in complete tetrahedral fantasy. Lou's flights from the reservation are part of his charm as a human being, but they can be confusing to a class and disturbing to a faculty."[220] A week later, on February 14, Sawyer reported to Osborn that Kahn would consider returning to Yale in fall 1956, but would not give up his office in Philadelphia, where Kahn felt there were upcoming professional opportunities. "Since we want primarily the inspiration of his teaching rather than administrative services," Sawyer wrote, "I don't think this is a major factor," adding that even though he couldn't "give him any specific assurances here in reference to professional practice . . . it is my own guess the Yale appointment would open up more opportunities for him than he would be likely to secure in Philadelphia."[221]

Sawyer was prepared to allow Kahn to split his time between the University of Pennsylvania and Yale as "a transition," if it were "necessary or desirable from his standpoint." Kahn seemed willing to come back if, as Sawyer reported to Griswold, he would be asked to participate "in the future architectural planning and design of the University." While Sawyer "made it clear to Kahn" that he could "make no commitments" regarding this, he did discuss it with Provost Edgar Furniss and drafted a "letter outlining what we would propose by way of commitment to Kahn in this direction."[222] Sawyer's proposal, which Griswold did not endorse, was to have Kahn and Saarinen work together with Douglas Orr on the planning of two new residential colleges that eventually were given to Saarinen and Orr.[223]

Vincent Scully remembers that although Kahn was invited to take over as chairman, Griswold was not enthusiastic about the prospect:

> Whit [Griswold] didn't have a very strong relationship with Kahn, because he got a little bit disillusioned with Kahn during the [Art Gallery] building process. Lou was always a very slow designer; always agonizing, always changing everything all the time. And Yale has always been rather impatient with that kind of thing—most corporations are. . . . But at this time when we were looking for a new dean [chairman], Whit offered it—right at the beginning of the whole search—to Kahn, because by '57 or so, it was clear that Kahn was going to be a great man; that at least was clear enough. And though he wouldn't give him another building at that time, Whit did offer Kahn the job. Kahn refused unless he could be guaranteed another building, and Whit wouldn't do it. . . . I was trying hard to get Kahn to accept the thing, which was a mistake on my part. Kahn would have been a terrible dean [chairman]. He just couldn't focus on stuff like that; he was too preoccupied with his work.[224]

In his efforts to persuade Kahn to take the position, Scully echoed an argument made by Howe three years prior: "I said to him—which is the most terrible story I can possibly tell about myself—'Look, Lou, you are probably not going to build a lot of buildings. You are a great teacher, and you know the way it has gone up to now. This is probably the great chance for you—really take it.' He got mad, and replied, 'I am going to build a lot of buildings.' He was really mad at me, furious, because he was right. He was going to build a lot of buildings."[225] As things played out, on April 12, Kahn assured Sawyer that he would return in the fall to supervise the reinstated Master's Class, spending a minimum of one day a week at Yale while continuing to teach at Pennsylvania in the spring term and also maintaining his practice in Philadelphia. Kahn's appointment as professor of architecture was announced on June 1 and was to extend for one year only.[226] He had already begun to plan for his next year at Yale, including the selection of visiting critics.[227]

According to Sawyer, the invitation to Kahn to return carried with it "several desirable features," such as making it possible to postpone "the decision as to the selection of a Chairman." Not needing to hire a new chairman freed up funds "to appoint several visiting critics who may be prospects for continuing appointments," and it gave the program "the benefit of Kahn's teaching services without any implication of executive responsibilities," which Kahn did not wish to take on. However, Sawyer speculated to Griswold, if the transition year worked out favorably, Kahn might be persuaded to take on "responsibility for the entire design program and to work with the faculty as a whole in establishing a coherent educational policy. He sees this very clearly as a partnership and not a dictatorship."[228] It was hoped that Kahn would join the faculty on a long-term basis in 1957–58 and even move his practice to New Haven, were he given work in the area. With the new colleges off the table, Sawyer suggested to Griswold that Kahn "might be asked to participate in the Oak Street development,"[229] a massive redevelopment project that was intended as the showpiece of New Haven's urban renewal program. Subsequently, Kahn would unsuccessfully participate in the Oak Street Redevelopment (see Chapter 5).

With the conclusion of World War II, the department swelled with returning veterans taking advantage of the G. I. Bill to complete their education, so that enrollment for the 1946–47 academic year was more than double that of the previous year—an unprecedented 160 students. One such G. I. was George Hinds (b. 1922; B.Arch. 1949, M.U.P. 1953), who went on to a planning career in Philadelphia before relocating to Chicago to teach at the University of Illinois–Chicago.[230] To accommodate what John Field called a "flood of people," new drafting rooms were established in the tower of the art museum and the monumentally scaled Sculpture Gallery was hastily retrofitted into a studio with rickety wood drafting tables for forty students (3.43). The basement of Weir Hall was renovated into exhibition and jury space that Field remembers "could have depressed any but the most dedicated first year architecture students if they ever thought about the wood paneled libraries where their classmates in Yale College might be studying."[231] As more students enrolled, more space was needed, and a Chapel Street storefront was leased to accommodate the overflow (3.44), a dismal location that reminded Walfredo Toscanini (1928–2011;

B.A. 1952, M.Arch 1955) of "a ship's galley where everybody's going to be given an oar and start rowing, or a whip."[232] The space crunch, as Sawyer noted, "necessitated a complete restudy" of the 1941 proposal to extend the Art Gallery, with the idea that the addition should not only provide the exhibition storage and general museum space called for in the original plans, but also classroom, studio, and library space.[233] This study would lead to the decision to construct the Art Gallery extension (1951–53), designed by Kahn in association with Douglas Orr, as a flexible, loft-like facility serving the needs of both the Art Gallery and the various departments of the School of the Fine Arts (3.45). The Art Gallery extension enabled Street Hall to become exclusively devoted to the Department of Art, and for the Sculpture Hall in Swartwout's Art Gallery to be fitted out for the Arts Library (3.46). With the Art Gallery extension, the ideal of teaching all the arts under one roof—or, at least, interconnected roofs—once again became a reality. Architecture studios were located on the fourth floor of the gallery extension, then known as the Yale University Art Gallery and Design Center (3.47), but Weir Hall remained home to administrative offices as well as exhibition and jury space.

The completion of the Art Gallery extension marked the beginning of Louis Kahn's maturity as an architect. The design was also a milestone in the evolution of modern architecture away from the brittle forms characteristic of the 1940s. Ten years before Kahn's design broke ground in 1951, the university had determined that an Art Gallery extension would be built in a modern style and asked Philip Goodwin to prepare a design (3.48).[234] The university had no doubt selected the well-connected, Hartford-born, Yale College alumnus as a result of his successful collaboration with Edward Durell Stone on the new building for New York's Museum of Modern Art (1939). In the early 1940s, Goodwin had prepared preliminary designs for the extension, but by 1950 he was in semi-retirement and did not want the job, instead recommending Philip Johnson, who was as yet virtually untried as an architect. The university passed on Johnson but offered the commission to Eero Saarinen, who was too busy to take it on. George Howe then intervened and convinced Griswold that Kahn, though an as-yet-unfulfilled architect, ought to be given the job. Griswold agreed, and Kahn was hired, in association with Douglas Orr and structural engineer Henry Pfisterer. From this sequence, it is clear that Yale's willingness to commit to architectural modernism preceded Griswold's presidency, as Kahn would acknowledge by pointing out that Goodwin "fought the battle for modern architecture at Yale and he won!"[235] Initially, students weren't convinced about the decision. "When the news broke that George Howe had engineered Kahn's selection as architect for the Gallery addition, our hearts

3.45 Louis Kahn, Yale Art Gallery and Design Center (1953), New Haven.

3.46 Arts Library, temporarily housed in the Art Gallery Sculpture Hall (ca. 1955).

3.47 Drafting room on the fourth floor of the Yale University Art Gallery and Design Center (1953).

3.48 Philip L. Goodwin, one of several proposed designs for an extension to the Yale Art Gallery (1941).

sank," Huff has reported.[236] Students saw it as a missed opportunity to bring in an international designer of great repute like Mies van der Rohe or, at the very least, Yale's own Eero Saarinen. Kahn was thought of as a good teacher, but his skills as a designer were still untested.

Kahn worked in close collaboration with the Art Gallery's director, Lamont Moore, who, inspired by Mies's American work—particularly his theoretical project, Museum for a Small City (1941–43)—had already determined that the new wing should contain simple, rectangular, loft-like spaces, optimized for extreme flexibility. To provide for the walls absent in these new spaces, Howe, who kept a close eye on the progress of the design, contributed the "pogo panels"—five-foot-wide, "floating," floor-to-ceiling display panels carried on spring-mounted, synthetic rubber-tipped feet that could be easily rearranged by the curators. The Art Gallery extension formally opened on November 6, 1953. Though slow to gain favor with the public, it was from the first championed by Yale architecture students, faculty, and some critics—one of whom, George Sanderson, welcomed it as a "return to design fundamentals."[237]

Almost from the first, the juxtaposition of the various art departments and the Art Gallery in a single building proved ill-advised, raising the same problems of security and access that had plagued Street Hall during its first fifty years. But as the first modern-style building to be erected at Yale, its importance was undeniable, making the visible expression of the dramatic transformation of the campus that Griswold, aided by his trusted advisor Eero Saarinen (who first became involved with master planning at Yale in 1949), would become famous for. Saarinen's involvement with Yale continued until his death in 1961. To many who remembered the interwar years when James Gamble Rogers got the lion's share of campus commissions and also served as master plan advisor to President Angell, Griswold's approach to the selection of Saarinen for a large amount of work and his role as university planner may have held out the promise of a stylistically consistent approach. But Saarinen's was a restless talent searching for a unique solution to each specific building project, and he and Griswold invited other architects to do their own thing in building the new Yale, so that many found the result somewhat helter-skelter: "What are you trying to do," an undergraduate asked Griswold, "make an architectural arena out of Yale, picking a group of hot architects and letting them compete for effects?" To this, Griswold replied: "We don't want one teacher or one architect at Yale. A great university should look at architecture as a way of expressing itself. It can do this only by choosing to use the very best architects of its generation, men who see history as a continuous stream, not a stagnant pool."[238]

At the same time that the pivotal appointments of Howe and Albers were made, the school further strengthened its offerings in city planning under the leadership of Christopher Tunnard (1910–1979), who argued that although prior to 1950, Yale had trained only a few students in city planning, many of them were occupying prominent positions around the country, and that it was "extremely desirable that recognition for professional training be granted in the form of a professional degree; these men have graduated from Yale with Master of Arts and Master of Architecture degrees, which do not adequately recognize their specialized educational programs."[239] As previously mentioned in Chapter 2, city planning had first appeared at Yale in 1939, in the form of a course in "housing and town planning" that was to have been taught by William E. Parsons and was then informally advanced by George Dudley and others in the early 1940s, with Maurice Rotival providing faculty direction in the mid-1940s. At Tunnard's behest, the discipline was formalized in 1950 as a two-year graduate course of study within the Department of Architecture, leading to the degree of master of city planning.[240]

Christopher Tunnard had emigrated in 1929 from his native Canada to England, where he studied at the Royal Horticultural Society, worked with garden designer Percy Crane, and later, collaborating with Serge Chermayeff, worked as landscape designer for Bentley Wood, in Halland (1938), one of England's most important houses in the International Style.[241] While in England, Tunnard also wrote a series of articles on modernist landscape design, which were collected and published as *Gardens in the Modern Landscape,* one of the earliest books on the topic.[242] Tunnard migrated to the United States in order to take up a post at Harvard's Graduate School of Design, where, according to Philip Johnson, he was "the local head of the communist party" and "the only person I [Johnson] had trouble with."[243] At Harvard, despite his left-leaning politics, Tunnard came under the influence of Joseph Hudnut—both men were increasingly disillusioned with modernism and opposed to Gropius's view of urbanism, best captured by his chilling phrase "city desert."[244] Tunnard's Harvard career was interrupted by the outbreak of World War II and his conscription into the Royal Canadian Engineers, but his military career was cut short in 1943 by the development of an embolism in his eye. The declining student population at the GSD made his return to the faculty infeasible, and as compensation he was awarded an Arthur W. Wheelwright Fellowship for 1943–44, enabling him to pursue research in city planning.

Tunnard moved to New York, where, still quite the radical, he became associated with Henry Hope Reed, Jr. (1915–2013), recently appointed editor of the Harvard student journal *Task: A Magazine for the Younger Generation in Architecture.* Under Reed, *Task* attacked real-estate investors, speculators, and New York's "master builder," Robert Moses.[245] After a short stint as associate editor of *Architectural Forum,* Tunnard accepted an appointment to Yale as visiting lecturer in architecture, and in 1945 he was made assistant professor in city planning in the Department of Architecture.[246] In 1948, he was promoted to associate professor and began to campaign for an expansion of the city planning program.[247]

Tunnard's beliefs changed dramatically during his time at Yale (3.49). As Charles Brewer (b. 1926; B.Arch 1949) recalls, "He was a radical. . . . And he came [to Yale] and became one of the most conservative members of the faculty."[248] His radical streak would briefly reemerge in the late 1960s, in response to a crisis that would rock the university, but, as Jill Pearlman writes, "By the time he died in 1979, Tunnard had moved so far from his earlier beliefs that he had become a major figure in historic preservation in New Haven and a member of the International Committee on Monuments and Sites."[249] Regarding his conversion, Tunnard said that when he came to Yale he began "to learn how to fill the gaps" in his knowledge. He came to appreciate notions of "quality and value" thanks to the university's art historians, who taught him to "analyze and enjoy a work of art in its social context."[250]

Tunnard bolstered the reputation of the program with a continuous stream of well-regarded publications, including *City Planning at Yale: A Selection of Papers and Projects* (1954), which emphasized the interdisciplinary nature of his approach; but his most important early contribution was the 1952 Civic Art Conference, a two-day symposium that paralleled an exhibit, *Ars in Urbe,* co-curated with Assistant Professor in City Planning Henry Hope Reed, Jr., as radical as ever but now passionate about the inability of modernism to achieve the monumentality required of public architecture, along with Lamont Moore.[251] The iconoclastic exhibition confronted modernist architects, especially those engaged in urban renewal schemes, with the lost tradition of Classical city design. The *Hartford Courant* described the event as "centering mainly on the artistic possibilities in civic planning today," noting that it was "the first of its kind in the United States in more than 20 years."[252]

Following the Civic Art Conference, Tunnard and Reed collaborated on an influential history of architecture and urbanism, *American Skyline* (1953), the first in its field to be published in a popular paperback edition (1956). At a time when the academic Classicism of the decades leading up to World War I was routinely dismissed as a regressive dead end, the book offered a sympathetic treatment.[253] Reed's antimodernism struck a chord

3.49   Christopher Tunnard and students study a master plan for Westport, Connecticut (1947). From left to right: Joseph Tamsky (B.Arch 1948), Mario Torres, Assistant Professor Christopher Tunnard, James Ward (B.Arch 1948, M.C.P. 1951), Samuel Spielvogel (M.Arch 1948), and Howard Barnstone (B.Arch 1948).

3.50   Frank Lloyd Wright and Philip Johnson at Yale (1955).

with the editors of the first issue of *Perspecta,* who published his "Monumental Architecture—or the Art of Pleasing in Civic Design," a full-frontal attack on modernism's dismissal of ornament, and of its ethos of functional determinism. "We have sacrificed the past, learning, the crafts, all the arts on the altar of 'honest functionalism,'" he wrote. "In so doing we have given up . . . the very stuff which makes a city beautiful, the jewels in the civic designer's crown."[254] Reed followed his article with an even more dramatic essay, "For the 'Superfluous' in Buildings," published in the *New York Times Magazine* in 1956, which found considerable public support, while irritating many members of the architectural profession.[255] He further developed his ideas in *The Golden City* (1959), which, emulating A. W. N. Pugin's tract *Contrasts* (1836), juxtaposed photographs of functionally similar buildings in Classical and modernist styles.[256]

Though a fine scholar, Tunnard was not a great manager. Moreover, the program's reach did not seem to be broad enough. In the same 1955 letter to President Griswold in which he reported on the growing crisis in the Architecture Department, Dean Sawyer also expressed concern over the future of planning education at Yale:

> Chris Tunnard and the City Planning Section is the other perplexing problem and decision we face next year. You may recall, that like the Graphic Arts program in design, it was adopted in 1950 on a five-year experimental basis as a means of determining the University's program in this field. The coordination with architecture that was presumed, never really took effect and our Council Committee has been critical of the narrowness of the program which has stressed primarily the physical and visual aspects of planning. Now we have two questions before us: a) is the program in planning, as now constituted, one which the University wishes to continue to sponsor and support and b) has Tunnard established his professional stature sufficiently to warrant a permanent appointment (he is now on term appointment as Associate Professor) and consideration for a full Professorship? These two questions are obviously related but they are also distinguishable; my own opinion is possibly no in reference to the former, but a yes in relation to the latter, for Tunnard has been a productive scholar in the book sense and might make an effective contribution within his particular area to a more broadly conceived program in planning, operated, if that is possible, in cooperation with the Graduate and Law Schools.[257]

Sawyer's sense that an aesthetically driven planning program embedded in the architecture program was not sufficient to the task would become an issue in the late 1960s, leading, in part, toward its dissolution.

Amidst the crisis over the direction of the curriculum and Schweikher's failure as a leader, the department soldiered on, buoyed up in part by the memorable visit on September 20, 1955, of Frank Lloyd Wright, about which there are almost as many stories told as there were faculty and students who witnessed it.[258] The invitation to Wright apparently came about when Philip Johnson's nephew Andrew Dempsey (1934–1985; B.A. 1956), then taking Vincent Scully's "Modern Architecture" course, volunteered to Scully that his uncle would intervene in getting Wright to lecture at Yale. Scully supported the idea, and a date was set. But when the time came to escort the grand old man to his hotel, the students forgot to meet him at the train station. As Scully recalls, Wright "was traveling alone and, though full of vigor, was after all more than eighty-eight years old. He was plenty mad. Getting himself to the Hotel Taft— in front of which, not long before, Anne Baxter [Wright's granddaughter] had played a scene with George Sanders in [the 1950 film] *All About Eve*—he settled into a room on the top floor, from which he quite obstinately declined to descend despite all persuasion that the Yale students, who had finally discovered him there, could bring to bear upon him."[259]

In this extremity they got in touch with Scully, enlisting his assistance in trying to "talk him down," but, as Scully later put it, this task was rather "tricky." Though Scully was a passionate advocate of Wright's work, he was afraid that Wright might remember him as someone who had asked him to design a house for his family in 1948, which would of course work in his favor, but was unable to afford to build, which would not. He might also remember him as someone who in 1953 "published an article that tried to take Wright to task for a number of McCarthy-like comments of his about the International Style."[260] Asked by a student how he enjoyed the view from his Taft Hotel perch, Wright said he would have preferred a room in James Gamble Rogers's Harkness Tower so he wouldn't have to look at it. Wright was at once jealous and contemptuous of Rogers, who while an undergraduate at Yale mixed with the elite who would one day become his clients, while Wright was spending two desultory years as an engineering student at the University of Wisconsin. After graduating from Yale College, Rogers worked for Chicago architects until he had saved enough money to go on to the École des Beaux-Arts, while Wright dropped out of Wisconsin to take a job in a Chicago architect's office, married, and began a large family that prevented him from completing his education.

Once Wright was lured from his hotel room, Scully remembers that "everything went well enough." The lecture was preceded by a cocktail party held in Wright's honor in Hendrie Hall, where Kahn played Bach on the piano. Once Wright entered the pre-lecture party, he immediately spotted Philip Johnson in the crowd, walked up to him, and, as Scully recalls, "in a loud, clear voice exclaimed, 'Why, Philip, I thought you were dead!'" (3.50). The remark echoed one Johnson had made about Wright twenty-five years before, when his mentor, Henry-Russell Hitchcock, had proposed a visit to the master in connection with the 1932 exhibition *Modern Architecture—International Exhibition*, which they were arranging for the Museum of Modern Art. Wright's greeting, as Scully put it, "shook Johnson considerably, as well it might, there being so many resonances and reversals in it of old time critical relegations of Wright to a has-been role in modern architecture and even Johnson's own and per- haps not entirely well-meant description of Wright as 'the greatest architect of the nineteenth century.'"[261]

Wright, however, was not yet finished. Standing amid a group of students, "muttering to himself and not paying any attention to what they were saying, [he] suddenly turned toward Johnson, who was more or less skulking in another group, and uttered the immortal lines, 'Why Philip, little Phil, all grown up, building buildings and leaving them out in the rain,'" a remark that Scully considered to be "the funniest and most devastating thing [he] had ever heard one architect say about another."[262] Much later, after many retellings of this story to his Yale students, one of them appeared at the end of Scully's class with a copy of a book, *Tulsa Art Deco,* which included the uncharacteristic flat-roofed house Wright had designed in 1929 for his cousin Richard Lloyd Jones.[263] In the book, Jenkin Lloyd Jones, the client's son, tells about the house's perennially leaking roof: "During one cloudburst, while the family was dashing about the living room with buckets and pans trying to save the rugs, my mother stood in the middle of the disaster and said with an acid Irish wit, 'Well, this is what we get for leaving a work of art out in the rain!'"[264] So, as Scully concluded, "Wright had been carrying those words around with him for twenty-five years or more until he came upon Philip Johnson at the opportune moment and was able to unload them on him. Later that evening, Johnson paid Wright one of the most moving trib- utes I ever heard and Wright got up and said, 'Now you're on the right track, Johnson.' He turned and looked severely at me. 'And you too, Scully.' he said. At least, that's the way I remember it."[265]

Ralph H. Comey remembered that "the lecture hall was packed with students, and for one-and-half hours Wright strode the podium like the actor he was, speaking extemporaneously—proud, provocative, and insulting. He did not like educational institutions, Yale included, and he especially disliked the Yale buildings, which he thought were a cultural fraud. . . . The students, in turn, were not friendly, and there were many challenging questions and comments, but Wright held his ground."[266] In arguing for what he called organic architecture, Wright dismissed nearly everything else—academia, religion, and even his own followers. As noted in the *News,* "He was particularly distressed by the tendency of his followers to divide his work into 'phases,' to an extent where one can only end up 'phased.'"[267] Wright's fiery lecture was divisive but it ended with words of inspiration: "There is only one moral to all this: hell, let's be ourselves."[268]

After the lecture, students were invited to meet the great architect in the Timothy Dwight lounge, where his manner became completely different—quiet, unassuming, and refreshed. After "standing in line with students for his beer," as Comey recalls, Wright was seated in front of the fireplace with the students gathered around: "All at once, a strange young man started to speak. He was a draftsman in a New Haven architectural office whom I had never seen before. He went on and on, but Mr. Wright listened patiently until he was finished (I was embarrassed). Mr. Wright turned to counsel him: 'You should not feel boxed in. You can always make changes in your life. You might consider looking for another job.' I was surprised at Mr. Wright's compassion." Comey does not remember many of the specific questions and answers, but remembers Wright explaining "his principles and approach. . . . He was lucky to be there at the right time. These things were waiting to be discovered. He was not special—it could have been done by anyone. As he talked about organic architecture and some of the other things he loved, I saw a humility, an openness, even a vulnerability. I realized that Mr. Wright, near the end of his life, was visiting colleges and talking to students in order to explain it all to the next generation. At about 11:00 p.m., Mr. Wright said, 'We better stop, it's my bedtime.'"[269]

Shortly after Paul Schweikher stepped down in 1956, Dean Sawyer, also asked to leave Yale, moved on to the University of Michigan, where he renewed his career in arts museum administration. Boyd Smith of the Drama Department took over as acting dean, while the Department of Architecture's administrative void was filled by Henry Pfisterer, who presided over the Executive Committee that was busily preparing for an expected return visit of the NAAB slated for early 1957, at which time it was hoped that the provisional accreditation would be replaced by the typical five-year endorsement. Under

Pfisterer's brief leadership, the department not only recovered its status with the NAAB, but also assumed an air of professionalism that had been debunked by Nalle and, to a degree, by Howe. This aspect found expression through a renewed interest in the rigors of programmatic design; for example, the Magnus T. Hopper Fellowship in hospital design, instituted with funds donated by Charles F. Neergaard (1875–1961; B.A. 1897) in 1949, was successfully integrated into the third year as part of a revised curriculum introducing students to more complex architectural programs and the evolution of building typologies. To the amazement of Aaron N. Kiff (1903–1980), visiting critic in charge of the 1957 hospital problem, the normally dry building type was enthusiastically embraced by the students who, contrary to Kiff's expectations, demonstrated a level of studio work that one would normally expect "from experienced and specialized designers." When the NAAB Committee, consisting of Robert S. Hutchins, Walter H. Kilham, Jr., Hugh Stubbins, and the educator Elliot L. Whitaker, visited the department in February 1957, they found it to be much improved, although the committee was not impressed with aspects of the students' work: "Student maturity notwithstanding, the caliber of the technical work seen and exhibited, is what we found in other undergraduate programs in architecture." In May 1957, the NAAB agreed to remove the term "provisional" for Yale in its forthcoming published list of accredited schools, doing so "with the understanding that the accreditation is essentially an 'open end' accreditation rather than the normal five year accreditation, to allow the University reasonable time in which to make a selection of a permanent Dean and Head."[270]

The search for a new dean and a new chair really began in mid-summer 1956, when Robert Osborn, a member of the University Council, solicited Eero Saarinen's opinion about the school's future leadership. In a long letter of reply, Saarinen surely surprised the council with what was hardly a ringing endorsement: because of its "previous standing and through the high quality of some of its related departments, and partly through its relation to the University," the Architecture Department enjoyed a reputation "far above what it deserves."[271] Saarinen believed that in order to have "a first class professional School of architecture," it would be "necessary to make one of two choices— either the School of Architecture should be given authority over its own Dean . . . or it is necessary to make the Dean for the whole show a man who, first of all, has authority in and understanding of architecture, but in addition to this, is qualified and respected in other fields." Saarinen continued to say that "the reason Charlie Sawyer failed in his job was not his fault. He was simply ill equipped for the core of his problem."[272]

In his letter to Osborn, Saarinen listed the qualities he believed the dean should have:

1. He should be an architect of national (or international) reputation, who is respected by the student body. He should have a reputation for a *stand* [Saarinen's emphasis] in architecture.
2. He should be able to gather and hold a good faculty around himself.
3. He should be, in a sense, a frontman for the School, be a good speaker, and develop, if possible, a statesmanship [*sic*] for the profession.
4. He should be able to get along with the rest of Yale.
5. (If Dean of all departments) he should be a good administrator.
6. (If Dean of all departments) he should be of a mature wisdom so he can be respected by and have respect for the other faculties of the Fine Arts Department and the Gallery.
7. He should be able to give up psychologically and/or economically most of his private practice and make Yale his primary job.

Saarinen then went on to evaluate potential candidates, in the process revealing a knowing and comprehensive sense of the profession as a whole. Saarinen's assessment of various leading professionals is well worth repeating here as a document of the era. He endorsed the Milanese architect Ernesto Rogers (1909–1969), who was scheduled to come to New Haven as visiting critic in March 1957. Saarinen also endorsed G. Holmes Perkins who, though excellent, "is not of the same stature as Ernesto Rogers, nor has he, as Rogers, deep philosophical convictions about architecture." The third architect Saarinen endorsed was Henry Kamphoefner (1907–1990), who "in the sticks [North Carolina] . . . has built up an architectural school with lots of spirit."

Saarinen's fourth choice was I. M. Pei (b. 1917), "now chief architect for Zeckendorf [a New York developer]." Saarinen regarded Pei as a "brilliant designer" and "an absolutely marvelous diplomat—as somebody said, 'You would have to be a good diplomat to get along with Zeckendorf.'" Saarinen wryly observed that his "impression" was that Pei "would run the whole show" and that "his wife would be a marvelous Dean's wife." In the file copy of the letter, there is a penciled-in notation—"no"—presumably written by Griswold, whose invitation to Pei may have been rebuffed. Saarinen also listed former faculty member Eliot Noyes, "a man who manages admirably to work in both architecture and industrial design," as well as the Danish architect Kay Fisker (1893–1965). He also listed Minoru Yamasaki (1912–1986) ("a very good architect—one of the very best architects we have"), John Lyon Reid, Ernie Kump, and Harry Weese (who, "ten years from now . . . may be your best bet"), Hugh Stubbins, Elliot Brown (someone Griswold was interested in), and Philip Johnson (whom Saarinen considered "quick, brilliant, ambitious," someone who could create real enthusiasm in the school, but judging from his record at the Museum of Modern Art, there could be little room for any opinion diverging from his own").[273]

The search for a new dean, who was presumably to be an architect, dragged on for more than nine months after Sawyer's resignation, leading Boyd Smith, in his capacity as acting dean, to solicit Saarinen's opinion about John Knox Shear (1917–1958), editor of *Architectural Record,* and Ralph Rapson (1914–2008), of the faculty of the University of Minnesota.[274] Saarinen had only recently met Shear and was, therefore, "obviously not qualified to judge him," although he did know that "he has made a remarkable thing out of the *Record* in a comparatively short time." Because Rapson, recently appointed dean of the School of Architecture at the University of Minnesota, was, Saarinen's "very good, old friend," he asked that his assessment be kept "in strictest confidence." Saarinen sketched Rapson's career, including his "year as a student of my father's at Cranbrook" and "about three or four years" on the faculty at MIT at the invitation of William Wurster, where "he became an excellent teacher." Although he felt that "Rapson might be a very good choice," his endorsement was qualified with some serious reservations, such as the fact that "outside of his architecture, [Rapson was] a fairly simple farm boy."[275]

The position was offered to John Knox Shear, who declined it in a letter to President Griswold that was copied to the Search Committee consisting of Boyd Smith, Professor Sumner Crosby, and Vincent Scully.[276] On April 12, Saarinen wrote to Griswold that in "frankly and confidentially" attempting to assess "all the names that I have been thinking of as conceivable candidates," he had consulted "a good friend who knows the problems of being Dean of an architectural school intimately" but who wished to remain anonymous. Seemingly unaware that Shear had declined the appointment, Saarinen also assessed the viability of the journalist Douglas Haskell, the editor of the *Architectural Forum* who, Saarinen believed, "would be too old to reorient himself into architectural education," before going on to suggest G. Holmes Perkins, who "would make an extremely good Dean" except that it "might be that he is really too normal a person—he is not primarily a designer himself; he will not come to the school with a strong conviction that the architectural department will go in this or that direction; he would be a very good person to bring in a good faculty . . . and he would be a full time Dean." Perkins, who had previously been considered for the chairmanship in 1947, was interviewed but failed to impress the Search Committee.

Saarinen, after characterizing Hugh Stubbins as "a brilliant architect," went on to assess Ernesto Rogers, "one of the international statesmen" of architecture, whom in his letter to Robert Osborn he had ranked as his first choice, but now ranked number three. Saarinen rejected Sir William Holford, arguing that "for the job it probably would be best to stay within the USA," while dismissing Gardner Dailey (1895–1967), then approaching sixty years of age, as "too old for the job." Saarinen then briefly recapped, in somewhat softer language, his prior assessment of Ralph Rapson, before going on to Harry Weese, whom he viewed as "a brilliant architect and . . . probably the most charming person on the list." But after soliciting Weese's interest in the position, he came to the conclusion that he "would lack a certain strength which is necessary for this job. For this reason, we rule him out."

The last two Americans on Saarinen's list were Philip Johnson and a young architect with a rising reputation named Paul Rudolph. Saarinen believed that Johnson "of all the people on the list . . . might well be the most brilliant person, a very good speaker, a very good architect, and the best spokesman for a whole trend in architecture." Saarinen reported to Griswold that he had "questioned in my earlier letter to Bob Osborn whether [Johnson] was able to build a team or whether there might grow petty jealousies and things within that team." Now Saarinen didn't think such was the case: "I think his qualities and his brilliance would far out-shadow any of these hesitations one might have. He would always keep the school interesting."

Saarinen then went on to evaluate Paul Rudolph, who is "considered the fair-haired boy of the profession. I hesitate to use the word brilliant again, but perhaps he is the most brilliant designer of all. . . . His direction in architecture is very interesting, very provocative; he also writes very well; he gets along very well with students and has perhaps the best following. . . . He is a well-read educated person with an awareness of the other arts. Bringing him in as Dean would immediately in the eyes of the architectural students of the country make Yale rate with the very best if not the best school." Rudolph had been offered the opportunity to succeed Mies at IIT in 1955 and, according to Saarinen, "after a great deal of soul-searching turned down the job." According to Saarinen, Rudolph might "say yes to Yale, partly because of its prestige, partly because it would not be following a great man like Mies van der Rohe at Illinois Institute of Technology which is always a difficult job, and partly because he would be happier in the East. There are personal reasons [presumably Rudolph's homosexuality] of a similar nature as Philip Johnson why there might be some objection from Yale's point of view; however, it is my conviction that in Mr. Rudolph's case, even more than in Mr. Johnson's case, the qualities far outweigh the objections. I really believe I would put him in the first choice group with Stubbins and Rogers."[277]

Griswold worked closely with his Search Committee to find the best candidate. Scully recalls, "he interviewed everyone who was interested in the job, or whom we thought was important in the architecture professional. Everyone. He was absolutely available to us the whole time. He interviewed the candidates in his office . . . and he was very shrewd."[278] In the end, Rudolph was the obvious choice for chairman. "Rudolph turned out to be without question the candidate," says Scully, "the best one, the most intelligent, the most open and so on. He really embodied at that time the avant-garde of modernism. He seemed perfectly timed."[279] On June 11, 1957, Griswold wrote to the NAAB to report that Gibson A. Danes (1910–1992) had been appointed dean and Paul Rudolph chairman, both appointments effective January 1, 1958. Parallel with the new appointments, the School of the Fine Arts was reorganized as the School of Architecture and Design, but renamed a year later as the School of Art and Architecture. The job of dean was seen as largely administrative, while the chairmen were to provide curricular direction to the departments of Architecture and Art. The appointments of Danes and Rudolph met with almost instant approval from the NAAB.[280] With the leadership crisis resolved, and the dream of an integrated School of Art and Architecture housed under one roof seemingly accomplished, Yale seemed poised for a golden age and would be propelled into a position of international prominence in architecture education.

4

A Time of Heroics 1958–1965

"Training at Yale for the practice of architecture is based on the concept that architecture is the rational integration of the art and science of building. Architecture is a coordinating as well as a creative activity. . . . The humanities and the sciences form the background for creative work and technical disciplines. The student is encouraged to study the related arts and to collaborate with students in the other arts and sciences."

Bulletin of Yale University, School of Art and Architecture, 1961–62

Paul Rudolph assumed the position of chairman of the Department of Architecture in January 1958 (4.1).[1] In short order he not only rebuilt the program but elevated it to greater prominence than it had ever before enjoyed, drawing national and international acclaim and attracting a remarkable number of students who would go on to their own celebrated careers as independent practitioners. "When Rudolph came in he was the boy wonder," says Charles Brewer, a critic at the school since 1952. "He changed everything."[2]

Born in Elkton, Kentucky, to a Methodist minister father and an artistically inclined mother, Paul Marvin Rudolph (1918–1997) grew up in a series of small southern towns. Though an accomplished classical pianist, Rudolph decided to pursue a career in architecture instead of music and would go on to study at the Alabama Polytechnic Institute (now Auburn University), where he received his bachelor of architecture degree in 1940. However, in Rudolph's view, his architectural education didn't truly begin until he enrolled in the master's program at Harvard's Graduate School of Design. After only six months at Harvard, the outbreak of World War II interrupted Rudolph's education, prompting four years of service in the U.S. Naval Reserve. While stationed at the New York Naval Shipyard (widely known as the Brooklyn Navy Yard), Rudolph was introduced to new materials and construction techniques related to shipbuilding and repair that stayed with him throughout his career. He returned to Harvard in the fall of 1946, was awarded his degree in 1947, and immediately began professional practice in Sarasota, Florida, where he partnered with architect Ralph Twitchell (1890–1978), for whom Rudolph had previously worked after graduating from Auburn. After a year spent in Florida designing schools and private residences in the International Style favored by his alma mater, Rudolph left Florida in 1948 to travel through Europe for a year on a Wheelwright Traveling Fellowship—though he continued to work with Twitchell through correspondence.[3]

Writing for the inaugural issue of *Perspecta,* Rudolph described his time at Harvard, his time in the U.S. Navy, and his postwar travels through Europe as the "three major phases in my development as an architect."[4] Though he credited Gropius with giving him a sense of direction and a foundation on which he could begin to build his own set of design principles, he was not impressed with his teacher's work as an architect, especially after his European travels opened him to a profound appreciation for traditional architecture and urbanism, something that had been denied to virtually all GSD graduates of the time as a result of Gropius's belligerent attitude toward the study of history. In contrast to the functionalist Gropius, Rudolph expressed an interest in the "feeling and understanding" that is inherent in pre-modernist architecture. Europe had a transformative effect on the young architect, reinforcing the "conviction of the necessity of regaining the 'form sense' which helped to shape Western man's building until the nineteenth century. Other periods have always developed means of tying their architecture to previous works without compromising their own designs. This also is our task."[5] Much later, he said, "I don't learn from modern architecture by and large. . . . I don't like looking at most twentieth-century buildings. I love looking at Wright and Corbu, but I don't even like looking very much at Mies. I will make a special trip, if necessary, to see the Barcelona Pavilion, but I wouldn't go very far to look at another Mies office building."[6] After returning to the United States, Rudolph rejoined Twitchell in Florida before striking out on his own in 1951.

In Florida the demand for Rudolph's work was almost exclusively limited to small houses, yet he and his work became widely known within the profession, in part due to his extraordinary draftsmanship, perfectly suited as it was to the advancements in printing methods then being adapted by architectural magazines.[7] Rudolph further enhanced his reputation through teaching stints at important northern schools of architecture, where his quick rise to national prominence as a residential architect had an unexpected side effect: students "decided they wanted to become famous the way he did—by designing houses. That was the credential he came [to Yale] with. And that was what vaulted him to fame so quickly. That was a real shake-up."[8]

This wider exposure led to commissions for larger projects, including the Mary Cooper Jewett Arts Center at Wellesley College (1958) and the Blue Cross/Blue Shield office building in Boston (1960), commissions that coincided with his appointment at Yale, substantially burnishing his reputation. Yet even before the Yale appointment, Rudolph was so respected as an architect-teacher, despite his youth, that in 1955 he was asked to succeed Mies van der Rohe as head of the architecture program at the Illinois Institute of Technology. In a letter to his parents, Rudolph wrote: "This of course is for me a rather tremendous step, and I'm still very much on the fence about it. It is such a difficult problem in terms of human relations plus taking my own time. It is a real challenge for I know that it can be made the best in the Middle West and nothing else would be good enough."[9] Rudolph initially agreed to take over as Mies's successor, but after two weeks of thought, he reneged on his decision because, while he admired what Mies had accomplished, as head of the program, he would have felt obliged to take the school in a completely different direction.[10]

At the time of his appointment at Yale, Rudolph was thirty-nine years old—little more than a decade senior to some of the students who had seen

4.1   Paul Rudolph (ca. 1960).

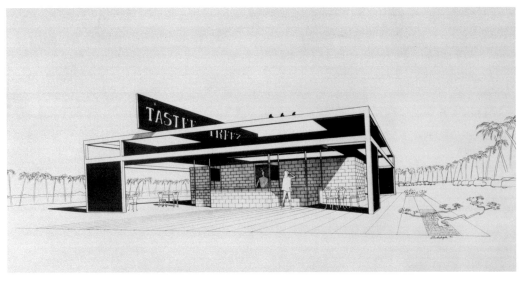

4.2   Paul Rudolph, Tastee-Freez Ice Cream Stand, Sarasota, Florida, perspective (1954).

military service in Korea. Though a well-known product of Gropius's Harvard, as is clearly evidenced by his Florida houses and, more significantly, the publication he edited in 1950 celebrating his teacher's accomplishments at Harvard, "Walter Gropius et Son École," Rudolph surprised many by proving to be much more, as it were, in the Yale mode—that is to say, romantic and individualistic.[11] "Let's face it, architects were never meant to design together," he said in a 1958 interview in *Architectural Forum*. "Architecture is a personal effort, and the fewer people coming between your work the better. . . . If an architect cares enough and practices architecture as an art, then he must initiate design—he must create rather than make judgments."[12]

Despite the heroic status that has been attributed to him, Paul Rudolph did not single-handedly save the department. Rather, he strengthened its best feature, the visiting critic system, by attracting a collection of talented architects from around the world. Taking advantage of the increasingly cheap, fast, and reliable long-distance air travel that began with the introduction of the Boeing 707's regular trans-Atlantic service in 1958—the same year Rudolph began as chairman—he saw to it that visiting faculty came from Europe as well as the West Coast and Latin America. As a result, the Department of Architecture became the most cosmopolitan design program in the United States, replacing Rudolph's alma mater, Harvard's GSD, as the "go-to" place to both study and teach architecture. Under Rudolph, in a well-earned reversal from Meeks's last years, Yale began to attract disaffected students who sought to transfer from Harvard, Columbia University, and elsewhere.[13] Additionally, the succession of high-wire modernist buildings commissioned by the university during Rudolph's tenure transformed Yale into a museum of architecture that included his masterpiece, the Art and Architecture Building, which opened in fall 1963, garnering media attention that would endure, for better and worse, for the next fifty years.

Before his appointment as chairman, Rudolph had taught at Yale as a visiting critic in fall 1955, famously assigning a week-long design problem for a Tastee-Freez ice cream stand. The project, based on a project he had recently completed in Florida (4.2), was somewhat aggrandized by Rudolph, who called it "the idea of the Pavilion in the Park." Yet that simplicity concealed what he believed was a conceptual richness, with "so many ironies about it. . . . [It was] a pavilion on a sea of asphalt." At the time of his initial visit, Rudolph was "absolutely shocked" with the elemental designs produced by the students, many of whom had been fully indoctrinated by the recently departed Eugene Nalle. Ultimately, if there was indeed any irony in the project, it was that twelve-inch-by-twenty-inch solid oak members were being used in the designs for something as ephemeral and inconsequential as an ice cream stand. "They had been doing it that way because he [Nalle] had been teaching that this is the way you start out learning architecture, because this is one of the first ways man built."[14]

Taking over, Rudolph found a department still reeling from the blow-up of Schweikher's tenure, with what Interim Chairman Henry Pfisterer described as a "bread and butter, meat and potatoes" curriculum.[15] Rudolph did not hold most of the resident design faculty in high regard, but he had the utmost respect for Pfisterer, whom he admired for his personal insight and no-nonsense approach. "After all these wild architects had ruined the School, [Pfisterer was] a good stable lovable person, [a] very good organizer, very good administrator [who] stabilized the thing . . . contrary to what outsiders were saying. . . . 'Yale was such a mess, you'll find yourself out in two years or want to leave, why do you do this?' I didn't find that at all and it was to a large degree due to Henry Pfisterer."[16] Students also had great respect for Pfisterer and enjoyed his humane approach to teaching structures. To John Jacobson (b. 1945; M.Arch 1970), who would work for a time in Pfisterer's office and also teach structures, he was "an amazing guy, an unbelievable storyteller," who always made the subject "interesting and humorous. He had worked on the Empire State Building, all the major buildings in New Haven. So he had all these stories. A lot of the class was just storytelling."[17]

Twenty years after taking over as chairman, reflecting on the state of the department as he first found it, Rudolph "thought that one of the reasons why the Department . . . was in rather sad condition [was] that it was overly dominated by the Department of [Art] History. I regarded it as a matter of bringing in a better balance."[18] With that observation, Rudolph was echoing Charles Sawyer's impression that some of the blame for the events leading up to the accreditation crisis of 1955 could be ascribed to what he regarded as meddling architecture-historians, especially Carroll L. V. Meeks, who held a joint appointment in the departments of Architecture and Art History. Although Rudolph valued historic architecture and urbanism, his attitude toward the discipline of architecture history itself was somewhat ambivalent, perhaps even hostile: "My feeling was that one had to be clear about the relationship or attitudes of the would-be architect as opposed to the would-be historian and to have a balance between the two and to make clear that one is not to be intimidated by history and that everybody lives in their own time and has their own attitudes and that these are absolutely valid and must be respected."[19]

George Howe had struggled to make history and theory part of the design process by inviting historians such as Meeks and Vincent Scully to lecture in the studios, but for Rudolph, trained at Harvard, such a strategy was outside his experience. In any case, by the time Rudolph took charge, there was no longer much integration between the two disciplines, with art history classes falling completely under the purview of an independent Department of Art History. Nonetheless, survey courses taught by Meeks and Scully continued to have a powerful influence over both undergraduate and graduate students. Meeks lectured on the history of nineteenth-century American architecture up to the Civil War, while post–Civil War American and twentieth-century "modern" architecture was taught by Scully. Spiro Kostof (1936–1991; Ph.D. 1961) was a junior faculty member in the late 1950s and early 1960s who was, like Scully, a spellbinding platform personality. He has written sympathetically about Meeks who, in his demeanor and dress, was very much an establishment type, but in his scholarship was an important counter-establishment voice who "had no patience with the inflated Modernist claims of architecture as an agency of social reform, and so, as a corollary, he refused to hold architects accountable for the failures of society."[20]

It was not Meeks but Scully who made Rudolph most uncomfortable, largely because Scully was becoming an important tastemaker with a national reputation, principally championing Wright, Le Corbusier, and Kahn. Rudolph sought Scully's favor, frequently inviting him to join design juries and often sitting in on his lectures—both those on modern and on Greek architecture.[21] But the two men never grew close. As Stanley Tigerman (b. 1930; B.Arch 1960, M.Arch 1961) put it, Rudolph's "determination to shine as a bright star in the architectural firmament precluded deep friendships within the field."[22]

Vincent Scully's rise to international prominence paralleled Rudolph's own (4.3). Acclaimed as "the Ruskin of the twentieth century," he was famed for the "impassioned, allusive, lyrical" language of his lectures. Few could deny that Scully's impassioned lecture style, his charismatic personality, and his powerful convictions helped set the moral compass of virtually all who studied with him; his articulation of formal relationships across the boundaries of time and culture exemplified the pluralism that has long since been Yale's strength. His passion for architecture was, as Spiro Kostof has written, "deeply moralistic, a heartfelt outpouring for the 'human act.' . . . His was a secular humanism that made buildings surrogates of our existential dilemma and the architects' agents of destiny."[23]

However, Scully was not without his detractors. Some architecture students were critical of his platform bravura. Etel Kramer (1938–2001; M.Arch

4.3   Vincent Scully (center) with students in the Law School auditorium.

1964), a graduate of Smith College, "arrived at Yale from beneath the waterfall of Henry-Russell Hitchcock's method of total immersion in all the buildings of most of the architects of Europe and America of the last 150 years." In Kramer's view, Scully seemed to believe that "we had no critical faculties but wanted to be told what was good architecture, especially his phrase 'act, love or die' exalting the elemental God-architect," which was a form of "anti-intellectualism." As a result, Kramer, influenced by "Peter Millard's attitude that nothing was to be learned from the past, [that] we must learn it all from our own actions" as well as by "Rudolph's incredible intensity and commitment to building bright ideas," began to assume that "it was right to make my own way in as original a manner as I could. I did not want to design anything resembling any building I had ever seen before."[24] Perhaps as a consequence, Kramer's early design promise was never fulfilled. Kostof shared Kramer's reservations, though he was nonetheless impressed by Scully's capacity to engage his students in architecture as a living art: "[Students were] swept up and almost palpably transfigured. This was puzzling in one sense, because there was nothing very tangible for them to carry away to the drafting table. The human act is not transferable. But they were moved by the affirmation of history that architecture cannot be practiced without consequences, that the act of design is a vehicle to wisdom. In the drudgery and self-doubt of those apprentice years that affirmation fed their hopes and gave them strength to persevere."[25]

Vincent Scully first rose to national attention as an "Architectural Spellbinder," a term coined by his former Yale College student David McCullough (b. 1933; B.A. 1955) in a 1959 article for *Architectural Forum,* written four years after the publication of Scully's first book, *The Shingle Style.* In this book, Scully had recast the prevailing view of American architecture as a colonial reflection of Europe by presenting it in terms of its own history as well as in terms of its interaction with Europe, spawning an attitude among an entire generation of students that affected virtually every aspect of their work, and which Scully himself discussed in a long essay published in 1974.[26]

Perhaps Scully's greatest influence was on his Yale undergraduate students who would go on to careers outside architecture, something Norman Foster (b. 1935; M.Arch 1962) pointed out: "Thinking back to those Yale days, I recall that Vincent Scully's lectures were dominated by a vast audience of undergraduates. Imagine the positive influence at this grassroots level on future civic and industrial leaders."[27] In addition to his importance as a herald of new American and modern architecture, Scully's lectures and book on ancient Greece brought to life for most students a subject that had been previously buried in the dreariest pedantry.[28] For many students, Scully's inspiring rhetoric opened the door to a modern architecture that could build upon tradition.

Scully and Meeks were the members of the art history faculty with the greatest influence on undergraduate and graduate architecture students. But it was the decidedly uncharismatic George Kubler (1912–1966; B.A. 1934, M.A. 1936, Ph.D. 1940)—a student of Yale's noted art history chair (1937–43) Henri Focillon (1881–1943)—who, despite the fact that his specialty in pre-Columbian and Latin American art and architecture was not of much general interest, enjoyed the greatest influence over architecture students. This influence was the result of his densely argued book, *The Shape of Time* (1962), which provided a broader view of art history than was typical of the time, uniting it with material culture, and thereby dramatically expanding the range of what can be understood as "art" while also opposing the notion of a linear trajectory in the historic development of art and architecture.[29]

In 1965, Kubler expounded on the relationship between historians and architects in an essay in *Perspecta* 9/10, stating that "the disastrous attempt [in the United States] for twenty years to banish all historical studies for architects clarified the question for nearly everyone more than a decade ago" so that there was "now no question that historical studies of his craft are useful to the practitioner of any art." Kubler went on to denounce the rejection of historical studies by many schools of architecture: "The self-evident truth, as we now see it, is that all good architects have been saturated with the history of their profession: only the Puritans and the second-rate designers and the peripheral people can afford the self-mutilation of ignoring the history of architecture." Kubler concluded his essay with three points that connected broad themes of *The Shape of Time* to the specific nature of professional practice and design pedagogy, and in so doing seemed the quintessential antidote to Rudolph's heroic individualism: "1) Works of art have little or no finality, being manifestations of process. 2). Every building has many authors. 3). The idea of style is only a convenient verbalism. Process and sequence are more relevant."[30]

Rudolph's popularity with students was immediate, as they quickly came to revere their new chairman for his rebellious stance against corporate practice, deterministic functionalism, and other "-isms" offered up as substitutes for genuine design insight. Both as an administrator and as a teacher, Rudolph's style, in fact his whole persona, was virtually opposite to that of his immediate predecessors. When he got to Yale, Rudolph immediately immersed himself in the design studio, where he was direct, brash, and refreshingly brusque.

His obvious passion for building was deep and pure, very different from the genteel aestheticism of previous chairmen. "He brought an *emotional* love for architecture," remembers Brewer. "He didn't come off as a practitioner. He came off as an artist. That shifted the emphasis. All the faculty suddenly looked very old-fashioned, and that became a problem."[31] Although unfailingly courteous, with a soft, southern voice, he was in no way a "gentleman of the old school" like Meeks or Howe, nor even an "Ivy League type" like Bennett or Schweikher. He was not scholarly in any way; but it can be said that what he lacked in cultivation, he made up for in curiosity and, perhaps above all else, hard work. Rudolph worked tirelessly, sometimes even obsessively, both at his architecture and his teaching, and expected everyone else around him to do the same. He was a phenomenon. His "architecture and life were inextricably intertwined. He lived, breathed, slept, taught and of course practiced architecture."[32] To this day, Allan Greenberg (b. 1938; M.Arch 1965) doesn't "believe Paul thought that there was a person called Paul Rudolph. There was only the architect Paul Rudolph. His capacity to work was unlimited. . . . He measured his personal integrity by the integrity of his buildings. I don't believe he thought of anything other than architecture."[33]

In February 1959, one year after Rudolph became chairman, the NAAB revisited the department, presumably to assess his impact on the program. Pleased with what they found, accreditation was extended for the standard five years, subject to annual interim reports.[34] The board's report, as Rudolph informed President Griswold, was "very favorable, even glowing," and "their negative comments" confirmed "some of our own opinions." Among these were the need to emphasize "environmental technologies, such as Mechanical and Electrical courses and Acoustics."[35] Rudolph also commented on the NAAB's concern about the teaching of drawing, noting that Austrian architect Wilhelm Holzbauer's (b. 1930) spring 1959 course "proved to be most effective," and that in 1959–60 the painter Neil Welliver (1929–2005; M.F.A. 1955), instructor in design in the Department of Art, would "organize a 'Sketch Book' procedure for the pre-architectural first year students."[36] What Rudolph neglected to say was that he had deliberately undermined drawing instructor Herbert Gute, who taught Frank Lloyd Wright–style rendering techniques. "At that time," notes Charles Brewer, "Wright was [seen as] a nineteenth-century architect. He was not in the game any longer. So there was this old curriculum that wasn't very interesting when Rudolph arrived. This idea of drawing, of making beautiful drawings, changed from the pastels of the kind that Frank Lloyd Wright used to do so beautifully to these black-and-white line drawings that Rudolph was so good at. It was a real shift."[37] Rudolph's marginalizing of

Gute reflected student dissatisfaction as well as his own stylistic preferences.[38]

The NAAB Visiting Committee also noted that "Mr. Rudolph needs additional assistance in the Master's Class to free him for his administrative and overall supervision requirements."[39] To help ease this burden, Rudolph reported to President Griswold that the eighteen-student enrollment in 1958–59 would be reduced by three in the following year and "additional use of Visiting Critics will be made," but that he felt "it most important to maintain as much contact with the students as possible," with "across the drafting board" criticism, reflecting "our strong conviction that the student has not really learned in the lecture courses until he can use it in his own designs."[40] The 1958–59 report also drew particular attention to what Rudolph saw as the department's "greatest problem," which was the need "to strengthen the City Planning Program, and redefine its relationship to Urban Design and Architecture." He observed, "At the present time, there is almost no real coordination between Planning and Architecture"—the two programs weren't even in the same building; architecture was taught in Kahn's Art Gallery extension, while city planning was located in the Center for Urban Region Planning at 295 Crown Street. Rudolph concluded his assessment of the department's progress, stating that the past year had been "one of intense activity and change" and that he "personally [was] much happier about [his] decision to come to Yale than at the time that [he] made it."[41]

Whereas Howe sought to narrow the field of design investigation for beginning students, Rudolph was intent on conveying, even to beginning students, a design approach that, though mindful of pragmatic issues, was also open to wide possibilities for formal expression. Despite his own strong personal style, Rudolph was never dogmatic, believing that the teaching of architecture should be approached "as a creative act, but [that] creativity cannot be taught." In *Perspecta* 5, he wrote, "The embryonic architect is seldom able to see that his own discoveries are usually restatements (often with complete validity). However, he has an uncanny ability to recognize that which is unique and significant in the work and thought of his peers."[42] To this end he endeavored to establish "an atmosphere and approach whereby the problems are defined and the students can commence the endless journey to find themselves."[43] He was largely successful, as Craig Whitaker (b. 1940; B.A. 1962, M.Arch 1965) has written: "The School rejected an *a priori* polemical position as a basis for design. In this sense [this] period at Yale is almost 'book-ended' between the functionalism of the Harvard School of Design of the late forties and early fifties and the sociological relevance which became the vogue in architecture schools in the late 1960s."[44]

As a critic, Rudolph was tough and he was brilliant. Thomas Beeby (b. 1941; M.Arch 1965) remembers that nothing escaped the chairman's well-trained eye: "[Rudolph] could just look at a drawing and read it—read it plus all of the details, the way it's structured. He would ask you questions like, 'What would you think about this building? Imagine walking down this hall and when you get to here, you look at the end and what do you see?' This is all about the perceptual grasp of what the spaces were like. He had an amazing grasp of three-dimensional space and it wasn't schematized the way Cornell [where Beeby received his bachelor of architecture degree in 1964] taught you to do it. He was a great teacher and he had an absolute standard; nothing was good enough."[45]

A renewed emphasis had been placed on the Master's Class for post-professional students beginning in fall 1956, led by Louis Kahn. English architect John Winter (1930–2012; M.Arch 1957) remembered it as "a very informal education," where sometimes "the whole class would drive out with Kahn for picnics. . . . [Kahn] was revered."[46] When he arrived, Rudolph took over the Master's Class and changed its character dramatically. Assisted by Arthur DeSalvo, Jr. (1926–1997; M.Arch 1950), during the first term and Peter Millard during the second, Rudolph immersed the post-professional students into a studio culture that demanded intense concentration and high production. Rudolph's impact was immediately recognized, and the Master's Class grew from ten students in 1957 to nineteen students in 1958. Picnics were a thing of the past. Rudolph would assign programs and projects with which he was professionally involved—a decision that proved to be somewhat divisive. Norman Foster "loved the way" Rudolph treated the Master's Class "as an extension of his office. . . . Literally, he'd gotten this commission for a house and he would say, 'I really want you to have a go. . . .' Or he came in one day and he said, 'You know, imagine there's this drug company and they've got this old building and you have to provide additional space. Do you think it's possible to skim that space across so that you can create a new facade?' He always got these ideas and you suddenly realized they [the students] were the tool, the extension of the office, to explore those ideas." But, as Foster recalled, "A lot of people thought that was really rather naughty."[47]

Beeby, who was a student in Rudolph's last Master's Class, has described his time at Yale as "the era of the great hero and everyone wanted to be a master architect." Kahn was leading the studios at Penn, Sert at Harvard, but under Rudolph, Yale was "the most energized place. . . . It was all about becoming a genius, you know, where you're going to hone your skills and become one of the great architects of your period."[48] Rudolph was determined to shake each Master's Class student out of a sense of security. On the first day of class, before students even settled into their desks, he assigned a week-long design problem for a high school—it was a seemingly impossible schedule, given the chairman's requirements for plans, sections, elevations, renderings, and details. "If you spent the entire semester you could not fulfill the requirements of that program," remembers Allan Greenberg:

> I stayed at the studio late. I'd come in at 7:00 or 8:00 and stay until 3:00 or 4:00 in the morning. I was having a lot of trouble just figuring it out. All I had for our review was a series of freehand drawings on tracing paper. . . . I had done one section and a site plan. I was so terrified. I was the last person to present and my hand was shaking so much I couldn't even get the pins in the tracing paper. Anyway, I stood in front of Rudolph and the jury and my tongue kept sticking to my palette. I was so nervous. Eventually, I got it together and I said, "I've organized this building on a split level—you can see it in the section." Rudolph stood up. And he said, "Guys, this is what I was after. I didn't need all the plans, sections, elevations, because I knew you couldn't do them. It was a year's worth of work. I just wanted a week's worth of exploration. And a potential solution."[49]

Greenberg had previously studied architecture at the University of Witwatersrand in his native South Africa, where he had been trained in both Classical architecture and European modernism. Parallel to his design courses at Wits "were five years of architectural history," with each term's class concluding in a five-hour-long examination, "during which we were required to answer written questions and draw—from memory, to scale, using a T-square and triangle—all the buildings we had studied." By graduation, Greenberg "had memorized about three hundred buildings" while learning to love "the intense immersion in scale, construction technology, symbolism and language of architectural form they provided."[50]

Fleeing the racial turmoil of South Africa, Greenberg went to work for the Danish architect Jørn Utzon, designer of the Sydney Opera House (1958–73), taking time to tour the work of the European masters of the interwar years including Le Corbusier and Mies van der Rohe. When Utzon moved to Australia, Greenberg spent a year in an office in Helsinki immersing himself in the work of Alvar Aalto, followed by a year in Stockholm working in an office. While in Stockholm he happened upon Henry Hope Reed's book *The Golden City,* which, in conjunction with his reading of Jane Jacobs's *The Death and Life of Great American Cities* and Vincent Scully's *The Earth, the Temple, and the Gods,* had a transformative effect on him, bringing into focus the intellectual conflict he was experiencing "about the role of architectural history in contemporary architecture and the relationship of new buildings to cities and to the landscape." Unclear about "how to move on" in his work as an architect, Greenberg applied to and was accepted into the master's program at Yale, which consisted of "twelve students, half of them American and half from abroad."[51]

Like his classmate Beeby, Greenberg was deeply impressed by Rudolph, finding him to be "the finest teacher [he] had ever encountered. Totally committed to architecture, he would often come into our studio at midnight to look at our designs and chat with the two or three students who were there." Although "he was considered a ruthless critic," Greenberg welcomed Rudolph's "honesty," which "stemmed from love of architecture and respect for his students." During one such midnight discussion, Rudolph examined Greenberg's designs for courtyard housing, such as those he had encountered in Copenhagen and Stockholm. Rudolph, who surmised that Greenberg had never walked through the courtyards of Yale's residential college, drew a map and said: "Walk through these courtyards on your way home tonight. Look at them again in the morning. They are superb."[52] It was something Rudolph suggested that other students do as well, reflecting his complex relationship with traditional architecture, which he admired not for its stylistic tropes, but for its ability to shape public space as well as its handling of scale and context.

Some students, such as Edwin William de Cossy (b. 1929; M.Arch 1957), who had worked closely with Rudolph in Florida before following him to Yale, Marvin Hatami (b. 1925; M.Arch 1961), Der Scutt (1934–2010; M.Arch 1961), David Fix (b. 1932; M.Arch 1962), and George Buchanan (b. 1937; B.A. 1959, B.Arch 1962), became experts at imitating Rudolph's aesthetic (4.4–4.6). Of these, Scutt was probably the most talented and definitely the most forceful. A graduate of Penn State, he was a powerful personality who is said to have changed his name from Donald Clark Scott to the more commanding Der Scutt, mastering Rudolph's design mannerisms, and perhaps even influencing them when Scutt worked closely with his master in his professional office during his student years and for some years afterward. Scutt's project for a housing village facing Davenport College across Park Street in New Haven (4.7) related to Rudolph's interest in European trends in housing design, as could be seen in his own Married Student Housing (4.8). Scutt's spring 1961 thesis—using the program for what would become Philip Johnson's Amon Carter Museum (1961) in Fort Worth—was also low-key, an early example of a non-building embedded in the landscape, though still in keeping with Rudolph's personal style (4.9). At the end of the spring 1961 term, when the

4.4   Marvin Hatami (M.Arch 1961), A Library of Science, elevation (1960).

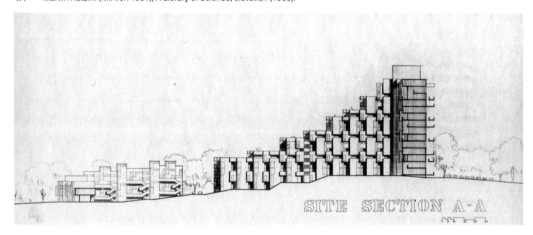

4.5   George Buchanan (B.A. 1959, M.Arch 1962), Housing in Baltimore, Maryland, elevation (1962).

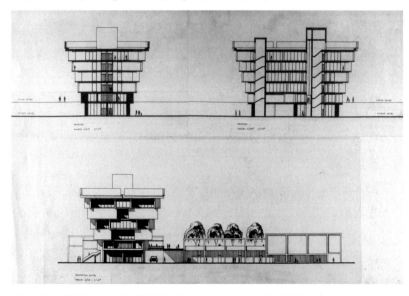

4.6   David Fix (M.Arch 1962), Office Building, sections and elevations (1961).

faculty could not decide whether the coveted Winchester Prize should be awarded to Scutt or to Jaquelin T. Robertson, for his radical redesign of Yale's Old Campus (4.10, 4.11), a "super-jury" was convened to review their two theses and other projects. Scutt ultimately won the Winchester, but most students who tried to emulate the master were treated derisively by him, as Stanley Tigerman points out: "Rudolph had little time for fawning students. . . . If you thought that pandering to Paul Rudolph's stylistic predilections by making them your own would confer upon you credibility in his eyes, you were in for a rude awakening. Whether or not your capabilities were effectively expressed in your architectural production, Rudolph would eschew your stylistic predilections as he criticized your work so as to help make it the best that it could be on your own terms, not his. He wasn't shy about informing you of your strengths and/or weaknesses in the context of design. . . . Brilliant yet brutal, his critiques unearthed fires that I never realized were burning."[53]

Tigerman was probably the most representative Master's Class student of the Rudolph era. Arriving at Yale as an experienced, licensed professional, he was not a college graduate, having studied at MIT for one year before dropping out and enlisting in the Navy. After military service, Tigerman worked for various architects, including Skidmore, Owings & Merrill in Chicago, and then embarked on a less than lucrative independent practice followed by the decision to return to school. Basically broke, Tigerman was in part able to pay his tuition thanks to the Chicago White Sox baseball team and a series of bets made with the "unsuspecting aesthetes" in SOM's design department that, Tigerman has written, "netted me more than one thousand dollars (half the Yale tuition at the time) when 'my beloved boys of summer' won the 1959 American League pennant. I gathered up my ill-gotten gains, packed our second hand, stick-shift Ford Falcon station wagon with what little we owned and headed east."[54]

There's more to the story of Tigerman's arrival at Yale than a well-made wager. Intent on completing his education, Tigerman had written to MIT, which would welcome his return providing he completed four years of undergraduate training before going on to architecture; to Harvard, which rejected him; to IIT, which never replied; and to Yale, from which he claims to have received a letter directly from the chairman stating, "I know I will live to regret this, but please find an enclosed application."[55] Tigerman filled out the application form and shortly afterward flew to New Haven to see Rudolph. Their meeting "did not start out on an especially promising note when he learned of my intention to acquire a Master's degree in just one year with no more than a single uncredited year of college behind me." Given the fact that

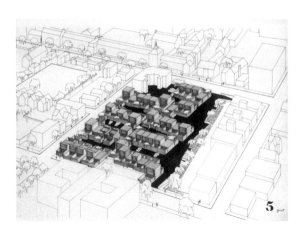

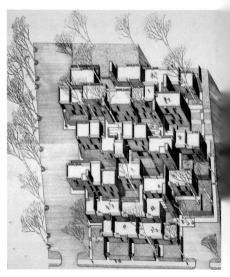

4.7 Der Scutt (M.Arch 1961), Housing in New Haven, axonometric (1960).

4.8 Paul Rudolph, Married Student Housing, New Haven, axonometric (1961).

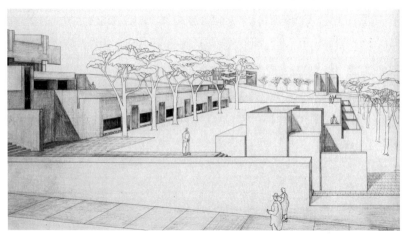

4.9 Der Scutt, Museum in Fort Worth, Texas, perspective (1961).

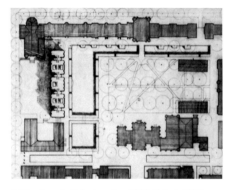

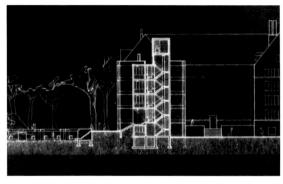

4.10 Jaquelin Robertson (B.A. 1959, M.Arch 1961), Dormitory for Old Campus, site plan (1961).

4.11 Jaquelin Robertson, Dormitory for Old Campus, section (1961).

he was already a registered architect, Tigerman argued that this requirement of a bachelor's degree should be waived. Rudolph, "rapidly losing patience," proposed a "non-negotiable compromise": Tigerman could matriculate into the bachelor's thesis year and, should he excel, he would be allowed to join the Master's Class in his second year.[56]

Rudolph, needless to say, remembered the story somewhat differently:

> Stanley came for an interview . . . and I didn't see him at that time because I had nothing to do with [admissions]. I did get on the train coming in to New York and there was Stanley. I didn't know who Stanley was but he knew me. We rode from New Haven to New York on the New Haven railroad. That was an hour and a half. I remember it quite well, he was very charming. Also, I always felt that a place like Yale should be, in a sense, the place of last resort. Yale would take all sorts of people: if it seemed so outrageous or so out of it then there was a place for it at Yale. Stanley never let me forget that hour and a half. I was asked about him and said, "Well, why don't we take a chance," or something like that.[57]

Once enrolled, Tigerman found the pressure almost unbearable. His status as a registered architect in no way assured him of passing studio grades. If anything, he had to work harder to meet Rudolph's exacting demands. Tigerman recalls being called into Rudolph's office in one particularly cruel act of intimidation when his work failed to meet expectations: "Referring to my last week's 'substandard grade,' Mr. Rudolph then said that I seemed to have lost interest in architecture. However, he told me that the architecture department would gladly undertake the responsibility of underwriting the cost of a battery of tests to ascertain what field I would be more suitably qualified for other than architecture."[58] Norman Foster was similarly admonished in a critique when Rudolph, rejecting work completed after a marathon studio session, simply said: "You don't care enough." The now-celebrated British architect was brought to the verge of tears. "Architecture," Foster recalls Rudolph saying, "is a process of finding out what you need to know." Rudolph demanded that his students produce: "If there wasn't something to look at, a model, or a set of drawings, there was no conversation."[59] That the pressure was intense is not surprising. The penalties for failing were much more severe than they are today. Only 50 percent of Tigerman's bachelor's thesis class graduated on time; some students had to complete a remedial summer studio, while others took an extra semester or year to complete their work. As well, there were always students who never received their degree.

4.12 Paul Rudolph (center) working with students at a drawing board (ca. 1964). From left to right: John Lucas (B.A. 1963, M.Arch 1968), David Childs (B.A. 1963, M.Arch 1967), Rudolph, and an unidentified student.

4.13 Stanley Tigerman's bachelor's thesis review (1960). From left to right: Vincent Scully, Henry Pfisterer, Stanley Tigerman (B.Arch 1960 , M.Arch 1961), and Paul Rudolph.

4.14 Stanley Tigerman, A New Campus for the University of Illinois, perspective. Master's thesis (1961).

4.15 Paul Rudolph working in his professional office at 31 High Street (1962). From left to right: Frank Chapman (M.Arch 1959), Jonathan Hall, Jim Weber (M.Arch 1959), Paul Rudolph, John Damico (M.Arch 1966), Bill Bedford, Andrew Nastri.

Students in Rudolph's studios could expect a "personal critique" at their drawing board each week (4.12). But this one-on-one interaction was a privilege, not a right. Should a student's work not be sufficiently developed over the course of a few weeks with site and building plans, sections and section perspectives, elevation studies at various scales, construction details, and study models, then that student "would never see him again until the final jury. By then it was too late and you could rest assured that danger would be up on the agenda when you publicly presented your project."[60] According to Tigerman, to survive Rudolph's "cathartic cauldron" of critique, a student was required to "to unearth resonant solutions to design problems with which individual preconceptions had little to do by digging deep into the reservoir of one's imagination." He has observed, "Curiously, not much has been written about that unique aspect of Rudolph's educational legacy, but his ability to critique others on their own terms while still requiring considerable amounts of work to flesh out their design was, for many of us, the most significant aspect of his tenure as a studio critic at Yale."[61]

Tigerman's bachelor's thesis, a luxury housing project for Chicago's lakefront, brought the Classicized rectangle of the mid-fifties, the so-called Yale Box, to a new sculptural, Rudolph-influenced level, by reconfiguring it as a pinwheeling tower that cut the structural "umbilical cord," which had hitherto tied Tigerman's work to Chicago modernism (4.13).[62] Presentation materials included fifteen twenty-inch-by-thirty-inch boards that he "had drawn immaculately in ink" together with a six-foot-high model; all represented at a scale of one-quarter inch equals one foot. Tigerman strategically situated the model under the vaulted ceiling of the lobby of Weir Hall, where it was unavoidable to those arriving to attend the jury. For one juror, John Hejduk (1929–2000), who would serve as instructor in architectural design from 1961 to 1964, the model was his introduction to Tigerman, with whom he was to become close friends: "There was this housing model—a big model, a strong presence. Paul Rudolph turned to me and smiled as he said, 'That's Tigger-man's. Do you know Stanley? Stanley is from Chicago.' It was obvious that Rudolph liked Stanley Tigerman."[63]

But things did not always go smoothly for Tigerman: he almost met his comeuppance at the end of his second year when, as his thesis in the Master's Class, he undertook a design for the University of Illinois's proposed Chicago campus, then slated to be built on Navy Pier (4.14). "I made a huge mistake," Tigerman recalls. "I finished . . . sixteen thirty-by-forty ink boards a day and a half early, and he [Rudolph] came around to my board before the jury and said, 'Why aren't you working?' And, like an asshole, I said, 'Well, I'm done.' He said,

'Really? Why don't I sit down and take a look at it. Do you mind?'"[64] Rudolph then "invited the rest of the Master's Class over to see the drawings since he felt there were some features he might like to discuss with [them] that could perhaps benefit the rest of the class generally and their own thesis presentations specifically." Tigerman had no choice but to agree to this, only to discover that Rudolph had invited the entire bachelor's thesis class as well. "It was then that I knew that I was about to be given considerable grief for both the thesis and my cavalier attitude about finishing early." With all the students gathered around Tigerman's desk, "Rudolph launched into an invective-laden tirade. He castigated me publicly, accusing me of treating both the architecture school and the project as if both came about as the result of a 'blueprint reading course' as part of a vocational trade school curriculum. He threatened to withhold my degree if I didn't make striking changes to improve the project and then stalked off leaving me, much diminished, as well as a stunned audience of both thesis classes in his wake."[65] So Tigerman, like many of his classmates whom Rudolph also criticized at the eleventh hour, went back to work "and drew like hell," changing everything. "Of course. I mean the guy was—he was great."[66]

In retrospect, Norman Foster believes the students ultimately benefitted from Rudolph's policy of terrifying eleventh-hour crits: "The one thing it really made you realize is that the more immersed you were in the issues of a design, the more you knew about it, you did have the ability, at the very last moment, to question everything you'd done and to reshape the project—either modify it or go back to square one. . . . I think that ability to really concentrate your energy, to make you question, and to challenge, I think is architectural but, in a way it's beyond architecture."[67] Under Rudolph, rhetoric and reasoning were no substitute for completed drawings and models. If it couldn't be pinned up, it didn't matter.

Foster credits the rigor of his Yale education under Rudolph with instilling in him a "a sense of confidence, freedom and self-discovery."[68] And indeed, the organization of his eventual worldwide practice was very much modeled on the Yale studio, as well as on Rudolph's private studio in New Haven (4.15). "Consciously or subconsciously," Foster has said, "there is a very strong connection between my time [at Yale] and the way we do what we do [in London]. . . . I think the two are inseparable in a way."[69] In his 1999 Pritzker Prize acceptance speech, Foster recalled Yale as a frenetic, inspiring environment: "Paul Rudolph had created a studio atmosphere of fevered activity, highly competitive, and fueled by a succession of visiting luminaries. The crits were open and accessible and often combative. And it was a can-do approach in which concepts would be shredded one day to be reborn overnight."[70]

Though Rudolph was typically regarded as a tough but sympathetic critic, from time to time he could be just plain mean, even destructive, "particularly if he was goaded on by the presence of somebody like Philip Johnson. . . . They would egg each other on, and be clever at the expense of students."[71] One particularly scathing critique came at the expense of Louis Skidmore, Jr. (b. 1934; M.Arch 1963), the son of one of the founding partners of the world's most admired and envied corporate architecture firm, Skidmore, Owings & Merrill, which was then fully committed to the formal vocabulary of Mies van der Rohe—although it never quite attained Mies's level of refinement, prompting the partners to be waggishly referred to as "three blind Mies." For his project, Skidmore, Jr., whose previous work had been Miesian, chose to explore Corbusian themes. By all accounts, his project was not particularly successful, prompting a confused Rudolph to reportedly say, "Mr. Skidmore, I don't understand this project. Up until now you were doing neo-Miesian kind of work and we all thought that was appropriate because we know where you came from and where you're going. Why are you doing this?" Skidmore replied, "Well, I wanted to study Mies for obvious reasons and I feel I've learned everything there is to know about Mies. And so, I want to study Corbusier." This did not sit well with the chairman. "You could see the blood rising into Rudolph's face," Tigerman remembers. Angered as he was, Rudolph calmly leveled a most severe threat against the younger Skidmore: "Mr. Skidmore, I can tell you know nothing about Mies, but I am going to give you a chance to find out, because as of right now, you're flunked out for one year."[72]

Rudolph made it a point to participate in design juries at all levels. As a result, he had a strong impact on all the students in the program, turning what had been a relatively low-key, gentlemanly pursuit into an intense, competitive blood sport. To M. J. Long (b. 1939; M.Arch 1964) (4.16), Rudolph "was tough as a critic, but he was very quick. Whereas most critics would sit around waffling, trying to find their way into something, he would very much more quickly than anybody say, . . . 'I see what you're trying to do, which is this, but in your own terms you're inconsistent, here, here and here.' . . . He would say, 'That stair doesn't correspond in plan and section.' Nobody else would be doing things like that."[73] Rudolph could be vehement in his opinions about a student's project, but he was even more so about criticism offered at the department's well-attended open reviews, where he might "sarcastically and explicitly" challenge guest jurors and faculty alike before graciously hosting them at his High Street townhouse apartment (4.17–4.20).

Despite the occasional parties, Rudolph was intensely private, actually quite shy. Norman Foster remembers when Rudolph "asked a group of us back

4.16 Rudolph and students (1962). From left to right: Paul Rudolph, Edward T. Groder (M.Arch 1964), M. J. Long (M.Arch 1964), and Robert A. M. Stern (M.Arch 1965).

4.17 Student review (1960). From left to right: Philip Johnson, George Buchanan (B.A. 1959, M.Arch 1962) (behind Johnson), Paul Rudolph, Charles Gwathmey (M.Arch 1962) (behind Rudolph), Vincent Scully, and Folke Nyberg (M.Arch 1960) (presenting in the foreground).

4.18 Student review (1960). From left to right: Jean Paul Carlhian, Philip Johnson, Leonard Perfido (B.A. 1959, M.Arch 1962), unidentified student, Paul Rudolph, and Henry Pfisterer review a project by Judith Chafee (M.Arch 1960).

4.19 View from Rudolph's courtyard into a cocktail party at his apartment at 31 High Street (1962).

4.20 View looking down into the double-height living space at Paul Rudolph's 31 High Street apartment (1962).

to his house one night. He got us there, sat us down, and then couldn't find anything to say to us. And as the silence dragged on it got harder and harder for anybody to break it. He was trying to be nice, but outside work, he felt lost, and it made him even more difficult."[74] In contrast to his shy manner, once the subject turned to architecture, especially the architecture of his own generation, himself included, Rudolph had a sharp wit and was capable of terrific one-liners. For example, Robert Stern remembers that when the wife of architecture student Robert Mittelstadt (b. 1935; M.Arch 1964), who would sometimes bring their two young children to visit their father in the studio, pointed out to Rudolph that the top-hinged, floor-level wood ventilating hoppers under each window of the recently dedicated Art and Architecture Building were dangerous for small children, who could fall through the openings, he looked her straight in the eye and said, "Well, that would only happen once!"

A hallmark of the Master's Class was the extensive amount of course credits that were available to students as elective subjects, which could be sampled from any of the university's offerings. As a result, many post-professional students broadened their education, "catching up," as it were, in the liberal arts subjects they were not free to study when they were immersed in their professionally focused undergraduate programs. As Tigerman has put it: "I knew what Yale University meant. In the architecture department, beyond Rudolph and the visiting critics, the faculty was . . . mostly ordinary. But it was Yale University. So there was this great wealth of coursework that you could do."[75] Despite the pressure of the design studio, and his need to work in Rudolph's office in the early morning hours to earn enough money to pay for living expenses for himself and his wife, Tigerman found time to broaden his education, studying with art historian George Heard Hamilton, philosopher Paul Weiss, literary critic Cleanth Brooks, and Josef Albers, whom Tigerman found to be "a great teacher. Another brutal, yet poetic teacher, a very tough guy," whose influence remained strong in Tigerman's paintings and sculpture of the 1960s and 1970s.[76]

Besides Tigerman, many other Yale students worked part-time for Rudolph in New Haven and later took full positions in his office after he moved to New York. For some, such as Scutt, who would manage the transfer of Rudolph's office to New York in 1964–65, Rudolph continued to act as a mentor long after graduation. In Rudolph's New York office, his former Yale students were "clearly the elite," says one former Rudolph employee, Anthony C. Antoniades (b. 1941), adding, "Most of them were in Charge of Design, they knew exactly how to make a 'Paul Rudolph' building out of a tiny sketch [from Rudolph]. . . . Two or three of them appeared to be actually on extremely personal good terms with Rudolph, sharing stories about parties, what was happening in New York, doing all the gossip about 'Philip' and some others."[77] Stanley Tigerman declined Rudolph's invitation to continue working in his office, choosing instead to return to Chicago, where he combined practice with teaching.

While it can be argued that Tigerman was in many ways Rudolph's most representative student, it was the Master's Class of 1961–62, the one following Tigerman's, that stands out as the most dazzling of the Rudolph years. That studio is now remembered as the "British Invasion," a term not coined until 1964, when the Beatles first toured the United States. In addition to the previously mentioned Norman Foster, the 1961–62 Master's Class included English students Eldred Evans (b. 1937), Richard Rogers (b. 1933; M.Arch 1962), and Robert Alan Cordingley (1926–2009; M.Arch 1962), who as an undergraduate student at Liverpool University had been an early collaborator with James Stirling.[78] Evans dropped out of the program after one term, having won a competition for the Civic Centre in Lincoln, England, which she had entered with Denis Gailey while still a student at the Architectural Association in London. It would unfortunately never be built, but Evans nonetheless made a profound impression on the department during her one Yale term.[79] To Richard Rogers, she was "the brightest student" in the class, "not Norman or I. She had very strong character, probably more formed than we had. Jim [Stirling] and she were intellectually well linked, wonderfully well. She was quite a lady—she could drink well, swear well, etc. they made a striking couple."[80]

Of the four Brits in the 1961–62 Master's Class, Foster and Rogers are the best known and are indeed among the most celebrated architects of the late twentieth century. Ironically, the two did not know each other in England, meeting for the first time in London at a gathering of Fulbright scholars headed for various American universities. Foster declined his Fulbright scholarship when he learned that its rules would prevent him from working in the United States. Instead, he was awarded a Henry Fellowship that would require him to "choose between Harvard and Yale, making his decision to attend Yale on the strength of its faculty, especially Rudolph." For Foster, Yale was a life-changing experience: "I came from a very kind of tough urban environment in the north of England, what would fashionably be called a mixed-use neighborhood in the sense that everything was close to everything else. It was the exact opposite of suburbia."[81] Arriving at Yale, the University of Manchester graduate found "the equivalent of a kind of Oxbridge environment which was almost a kind of European experience that was totally socially inaccessible" to a working-class English boy at that time. In Britain, Foster "was the odd one out who worked my way through the university, all the way supporting myself, paying the fees. Coming to the States for the first time I felt really at home."[82]

Richard Rogers, in many ways Foster's opposite, came from an upper-middle-class London family. His father was a doctor; his uncle, Ernesto Nathan Rogers, whom Saarinen nominated as a possible candidate for chairman of the Department of Architecture in 1956, was a partner in the internationally admired Milanese firm BBPR, then best known for the historicizing Torre Velasca (1958) in Milan. Richard Rogers was married to sociologist and urban planner Su Brumwell, and together they applied to five American universities, choosing Yale because it was the only one to admit both of them. The Rogerses sailed to New York on the *Queen Elizabeth*. So unusual was the arrival of foreign students to Yale in those days that, just before landing, a representative of the *New Haven Register* came on board from the pilot boat, sent by his paper to write about the couple and also to host them in New York. The ensuing article in the *Register Magazine* showed photographs of the Rogerses at various touristic spots in New York as well as reclining on the Branford College lawn with a view of the Harkness Tower rising above them.[83] Unfortunately, the couple arrived five days after classes had begun. As Rogers's biographer Bryan Appleyard observes, "Neither had been too concerned about this after the easygoing atmosphere of the LSE [London School of Economics] and the AA [Architectural Association] but at Yale it nearly resulted in their expulsion."[84] Rogers, who is dyslexic and also a poor draftsman, found Rudolph's Yale an almost unbearably frustrating pressure cooker of impossible deadlines. According to Appleyard, Yale "came as a shock after the ruminations of the AA. There, the agony was likely to be intellectual, at Yale it was practical."[85]

In late-night drafting room conversation, the quality of work produced by the Master's Class was typically questioned and contrasted with that of the four-year baccalaureate program, where students, though they may have lacked office experience, had four years of liberal arts college under their belts. During fall 1961, when Foster and Rogers arrived, their trial by fire began with the usual high school project, but then the class was thrown together with the fourth-year bachelor of architecture class and asked to prepare their own versions of Rudolph's Blue Cross/Blue Shield office building. Foster considers his solution the best of his Yale work, a cluster of towers with a structurally expressive profile using exposed service elements that owe more to the example of Louis Kahn than Rudolph (4.21, 4.22). For the next problem, Rudolph continued his experiment—assigning the design of a master plan for the Pierson-Sage science complex (Science Hill) at Yale that,

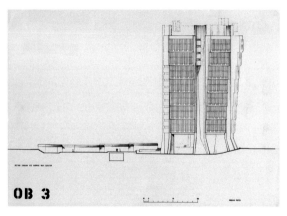

4.21 Norman Foster (M.Arch 1962), Design for an Office Building, elevation (1961).

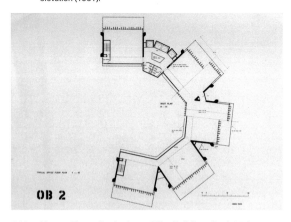

4.22 Norman Foster, Design for an Office Building, plan (1961).

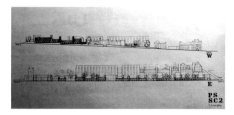

4.23 Robert Alan Cordingley (M.Arch 1962), Pierson-Sage Science Complex, elevation (1961).

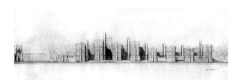

4.24 Carl Abbott (M.Arch 1962), Pierson-Sage Science Complex, elevation (1961).

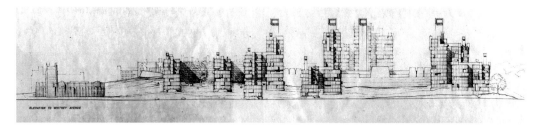

4.25 Norman Foster and Richard Rogers (M.Arch 1962), Pierson-Sage Science Complex, elevation (1961).

4.26 Norman Foster and Richard Rogers, Pierson-Sage Science Complex, site plan (1961).

unbeknownst to the students, was Philip Johnson's commission. Rudolph's program statement challenged students to consider not only pragmatic requirements, but also the deplorable state of contemporary architecture and urbanism: "This is an urban problem. It is also the problem of the architect, as planners and developers have failed to rebuild our cities. They are obsessed with numbers (people, money, acreage, units, cars, roads, etc.) and forget life itself and the spirit of man."[86]

Bold schemes were produced by Robert Alan Cordingley (4.23) and Carl Abbott (b. 1935; M.Arch 1962), a Florida native who would return to his home state after graduation to continue the legacy of Rudolph's achievements in Sarasota.[87] At Yale, Abbott became a close friend of both Foster and Rogers, and their schemes reflected their shared sensibilities: Abbott's called for a circulation spine running the length of the site (4.24); Foster and Rogers, who collaborated on the project, "to the horror of Paul Rudolph,"[88] also located car parking, classrooms, and food service in a low central spine off of which the various departments were housed in tentacular slabs that stepped down the hill to meet the surrounding streets (4.25, 4.26). But the Foster/Rogers scheme was much bolder in form than Abbott's. As Bryan Appleyard writes, although there was "a certain rationalist, AA [Architectural Association] quality about the plan," its "landscape and 'poetic' service towers were strictly American," with a strong debt to Kahn's recently completed Richards Medical Research Laboratories at the University of Pennsylvania. In its totalizing singularity, the Foster/Rogers design offered American students what was perhaps their first glimpse of the megastructural approach often associated with the Archigram group that would become a dominant trend in the late 1960s.[89] According to Foster's biographer, Deyan Sudjic, Rogers "still recalls Foster, in his commanding manner, presenting the projects that they had worked on together."[90]

Johnson was on the jury and "not entirely impressed" with the Foster/Rogers megastructural approach. He stared at their balsa wood model and then proceeded to crush its service towers in his fist, muttering: "Have to do something about these."[91] By contrast, the proposal of fourth-year student Charles Gwathmey (1938–2009; M.Arch 1962) had its basis in quadrangular prototypes like Yale's Old Campus (4.27). He would later develop a version of his design as a dormitory complex (1969) at the Purchase campus of the State University of New York (4.28).[92]

Charles Gwathmey was the outstanding member of the 1962 bachelor's class. As an undergraduate at the University of Pennsylvania, he had been encouraged by Louis Kahn to go to Yale in order to study under Rudolph (4.29, 4.30). In the summer vacation after his first year at Yale, he was able to renovate

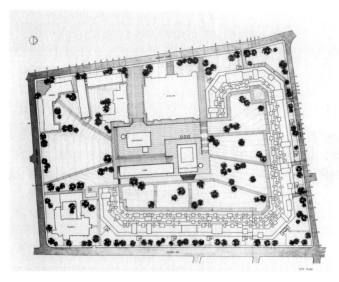

4.27   Charles Gwathmey (M.Arch 1962), Pierson-Sage Science Complex,
site plan (1961).

4.28   Gwathemy Siegel, Dormitory Complex at SUNY Purchase (1969), New York.

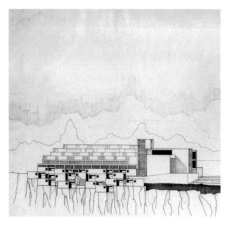

4.29   Charles Gwathmey, Hotel Project,
elevation (1961).

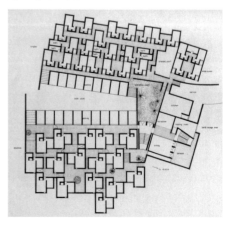

4.30   Charles Gwathmey, Hotel Project,
plans (1961).

a barn that George O'Brien published in the *New York Times Magazine*, a venue then normally reserved for traditional houses and interiors.[93] After graduation, Gwathmey worked in the office of Edward Larrabee Barnes—a preferred destination for many Yale graduates, including Giovanni Pasanella (1931–2010; M.Arch 1958), Jaquelin Robertson and Alexander Cooper (b. 1936; B.A. 1958, M.Arch. 1962). While still at Barnes's office, Gwathmey was also designing some small, independent projects on the side, including a shingled house on Fire Island (1965) designed with office-mate Richard Henderson that was featured in *Progressive Architecture;* and another, for his parents at Amagansett, New York (1966), that Gwathmey, now in independent practice, built with a few carpenters from Brooklyn. It became one of the most influential projects of the era.[94]

Despite their admiration for the uninhibited exuberance of the American scene, the English bridled at what they regarded as the mindless formalism of much of its architecture, or what M. J. Long, implicitly criticizing Rudolph's influence, has described as its "forced and rather blowsy monumentality." The open, loft-like studio at the top of the Art Gallery was the scene of memorable debates between the Brits and the Americans. As Deyan Sudjic has described the situation, there was something of a divide between the two groups: "The British were a little older, and preferred to debate and to argue rather than to draw. . . . After one episode of more than usually provocative Anglo-Saxon prevarication, a placard appeared over their drafting tables. 'Stop talking, start drawing,' it demanded. The British struck back with a slogan of their own on the other side of the studio that urged the Americans to 'Start Thinking.'"[95] Although it may have seemed that English students dominated the program, talented students came to Yale from all over the world. Bangladeshi architect and planner Muzharul Islam (1923–2012; M.Arch 1961), for example, went on to become one of the leading advocates of modernism in South Asia; and Shinichi Okada (b. 1928; M.Arch 1963) went on to become a prominent architect in his native country, best known as the designer of Japan's Supreme Court in Chiyoda, Tokyo (1974).[96]

Under Rudolph, the design faculty was also subject to a British invasion that began in spring 1959, when Rudolph invited James Stirling (1924–1992) to serve as visiting critic, and continued in fall 1960 with the arrival of Colin St. John Wilson (1922–2007). While Peter (1923–2003) and Alison Smithson (1928–1993) did not teach, together with the critic Reyner Banham (1922–1988), they participated in juries during spring 1961. Taken together, the Brits brought a much-needed cosmopolitanism to the program's lingering provincialism. For example, Alison Smithson, reviewing first-year projects for a natatorium to be built on New Haven's Long Wharf, embarrassed students by drawing attention to their ignorance of Middle-European interwar modernism, which, she argued, was exuberant in comparison to the dismal student projects.

Reyner Banham, an engineer turned architectural critic and historian, had a disproportionately strong, though negative, impression of Yale, given the brevity of his visits. He first came to New Haven in spring 1961 and returned late in the spring of 1962 to tour the nearly complete Morse and Stiles Colleges, a posthumous work of Eero Saarinen's, whose U.S. Embassy on Grosvenor Square, London, Banham had previously dismissed as the work of one of America's "most trivial performers."[97] Banham also dismissed Stiles and Morse residential colleges, which "disgusted" him and led him to say that there were "no extenuating circumstances" to justify the design for which "the client gave the architect plenty of rope."[98] Although Banham disliked Saarinen's use of concrete, he really saved his venom for the architect's romantic massing of the complex, dismissing its "Gordon Craig–type scenic effects (equally suitable for Macbeth or The Desert Song)," which he felt were achieved at the price of "medieval standards" of student accommodation. For many in New Haven, Banham's hatchet job on the residential colleges went too far in a too public way. Not content to take a swipe at the recently deceased Saarinen's design, he also went after the art critic Aline B. Louchheim Saarinen (1914–1972), dismissing her as the "formidable Saarinen widow." Returning to the colleges, he lamented "the creeping malady" of "gratuitous affluences irresponsibly exploited" that causes an increasing number of returning Europeans to say, "Yale is a very sick place."[99] The English critic Ian McCallum (1919–1987) was much more open to the Yale scene, taking up longtime residence, probably at the invitation of Carroll Meeks, as he developed a widely discussed series of articles about contemporary American architecture that he published in the *Architectural Review* and subsequently collected in the book *Architecture u.s.a.*[100]

Visiting critics not from Britain included the German Frei Otto (1925–2015), who visited in fall 1960; Bernard Rudofsky (1905–1988), originally from Moravia (now part of the Czech Republic), in 1960–61 and 1964; and Danish architect Henning Larsen (1925–2013), in fall 1964. Despite considerable effort on the part of King-lui Wu, Rudolph failed to make contact with Le Corbusier, but with the help of Phyllis B. Lambert (b. 1927), a reluctant Mies van der Rohe came to New Haven as visiting critic for a portion of the fall 1958 term (4.31).[101] Lambert had enrolled in the first year at Yale as a member of the class of 1961. Already a public figure, admired for her role in realizing the Seagram Building

(1958), she only stayed at Yale briefly, transferring to IIT to study with Mies.[102] Lambert does not have very fond memories of her time at Yale, and they do not correspond with the recollections of very many others:

> For example, a Japanese student there was interested in engineering and was not a very good designer in the sense that Yale accepted. He would get just slammed in juries. And then, when you were working on a project and got a good idea, they'd tell you, "Don't tell anybody, because they'll just copy your idea." I couldn't stand that. And Paul Rudolph . . . I had a drawing I was very proud of. It was a perspective section through a house, and I had every story in place, and all the sections through the house that you had to have. Lots of poché, lots of hours. And Rudolph just came over and said, "Where is your vapor barrier?" It seemed to me to be a school that had nothing to do with educating people, just with putting people down. Anyway, I wasn't learning what I wanted to learn. And there was all this posturing. For example: Should there be a campanile at the end of a campus or not? I thought issues like this could be interesting, but I would have preferred to know how to make a campus from scratch. So I went to IIT.[103]

Lambert's brief time at Yale has given rise to stories—some perhaps apocryphal, or at least exaggerated—about how the by-then world famous architectural patron fit into the program as a first-year student. One such story was Stanley Tigerman's recollection that a personal servant carried Lambert's pavilion model on a silver platter to the final project review (Lambert denies that the platter was silver) (4.32). "Equally entertaining," remembers Tigerman, "was watching the same Phyllis Lambert sauntering down Chapel Street on her way home to her refurbished town house on Crown Street with her chauffeur-driven Rolls Royce Silver Wraith following slowly at a discreet distance behind her."[104] Tigerman also remembers that, incensed by the lack of a women's toilet on the fourth floor of the Art Gallery extension, where the studios were located, Lambert "liberated" the men's room. Tigerman, and likely many other male architecture students of the time, was not amused by her habit of barging in "without so much as 'excuse me' and deliberately make her way to the water-closet stalls at the rear of the restroom. This bothersome behavior caused many [of] the male[s] to cringe causing stained chinos for those of us who had the misfortune to be utilizing the urinals as she so nonchalantly sauntered by."[105]

4.31 Ludwig Mies Van der Rohe reviews the work of architecture students at Yale (1958).

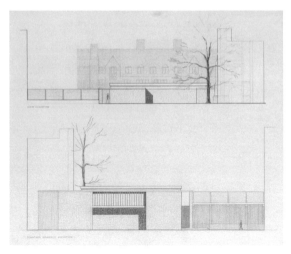

4.32 Phyllis Lambert, Weir Court Lecture Hall, elevations (1959).

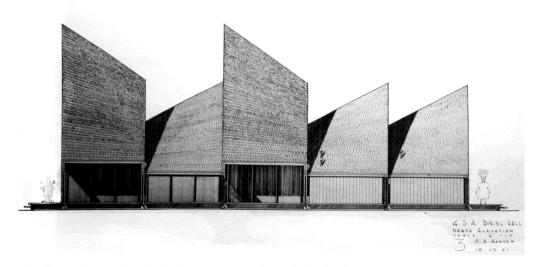

4.33 Margaret Hansen (M.Arch 1966), Dining Hall for Girl Scout Camp, elevation (1961).

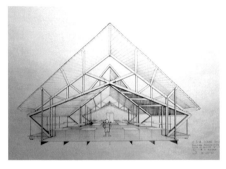

4.34 Margaret Hansen, Dining Hall for Girl Scout Camp, section perspective (1961).

If one looks for an explanation for the competitive self-consciousness of many students in the Rudolph years, one must look not only to Rudolph's intensity or Scully's emphasis on the individual act, but also to the composition of the student body, which under the guiding hand of Meeks, who oversaw admissions, was selected as much on the potential for leadership in the profession as on the basis of demonstrated design talent. When an alumnus complained that recent Yale graduates were not very useful as employees, Meeks replied that they were trained not to be employees but competitors. However, when it came to admissions, Meeks had one serious blind spot: women. M. J. Long, who would join the faculty in 1972, eventually came to admire Meeks but remembers that he "was definitely anti-women." When he was head of admissions, there would only be one or two women admitted a year, but in 1960, when Meeks was on a sabbatical leave, seven women were accepted into the four-year program for beginning professional students: Long, Etel Kramer, Judith Anderson (Lawler), Lucinda Cisler, Margaret Hansen (Smertenko) (4.33, 4.34), Joan Stouffer (Scharnberg), and Vivian Wei-Chu (Wu), who would transfer to graphic design. Like Long and Kramer, Stouffer had been an architecture major at Smith College.

After Meeks returned from sabbatical, Kramer and Long enrolled in his course on American colonial architecture, which "neither of us knew anything about." Long recalled: "It was one of those big courses, like the Scully courses—a large number of [male] undergraduates . . . plus a few graduate students. It was an interesting course. We had a midterm and he gave back the blue books—Etel and I, for no particular reason, had signed our names with our initials. I signed mine 'M. J. Long' and she signed hers 'E. T. Kramer,' although she didn't call herself E. T., she called herself Etel. So he handed back the books and said, 'Well, there were two really good papers. One was Mr. Kramer's and one was Mr. Long's.' The whole place erupted in laughter."[106] Looking back on it, Long doesn't think Meeks's antipathy toward women students was personal: "It's just that, for him, Yale was a male place and architecture was a male profession. . . . And once he found out that one or two of us were interested in what he was interested in, he was delightful."[107]

By far the most significant visiting critic was James Stirling, whom Rudolph first invited to Yale in 1959, and who would return at Rudolph's invitation several times before beginning an eighteen-year commitment as Davenport Visiting Professor in 1966. Stirling would have a decisive influence on generations of Yale students. When he was hired, he was a rising star on the British architecture scene who had just begun to design the Leicester Engineering Building with his professional partner, James Gowan

(1923–2015)—a project that would propel them to international fame. As was then customary for visiting critics, Stirling was asked to join teams of critics in various studios and, as Emmanuel Petit has observed, with so little of his own work to influence student designs, much of Stirling's impact came through his writings, published in *The Architectural Review* and *Perspecta,* as well as the sheer force of his personality. Over the years, Stirling's architecture evolved, but he never wavered in his core belief that the self-imposed inhibitions of modernist architecture were self-destructive. In his essay "The Functional Tradition and Expression," published in *Perspecta* 6 in 1960, Stirling made a plea for an expanded vocabulary of form, as could be seen in his early work in brick, especially his workers' housing at Preston in the north of England (1959), which was the inspiration behind many student projects.[108] Later, in an interview in *Perspecta* 11, amidst the increasingly restless late 1960s, he criticized the "slabs and plazas" of modernist urbanism.[109]

Stirling and Rudolph were competing architectural stars in the eyes of the students. But, as Vincent Scully points out, they were "very much alike. . . . They were both High Modern performers. Each one, each time, tried to do something that had never been seen on land or sea before, and to knock your eyes out. They were natural rivals."[110] And yet their personalities were completely different. George Buchanan put it this way: "If Paul was head, then Jim was heart." Whereas the intensely shy Rudolph was awkward when he chose to socialize with students, Stirling reveled in a shared camaraderie. As Buchanan has put it, Stirling "became 'Jim' to the students, where Rudolph, for the majority, remained 'Mr. Rudolph'"—although he was called "Big Daddy" behind his back.[111] Between Stirling and Rudolph, students, according to Buchanan, felt they "were at the epicenter of architectural thought and practice," and took their cues from the proclivities of both architects: "You know, we thought a great deal of ourselves. We were a pretty arrogant lot. We were heavy drinking, heavy working."[112]

At Yale, Stirling exhibited a behavioral freedom that connected with the "angry young man" sensibility of postwar England. Stories of his escapades abound and over time have taken on legendary proportions. On his first visit, Stirling took up with Barbara Chase (b. 1939; M.F.A. 1960), a black graduate student in the Sculpture Department. In her words, for a Yale professor to have an affair with a student, particularly a black student, was "a slap in the face of all Yale establishment conventions."[113] Stirling was reckless. According to his biographer, Mark Girouard: "One noisy and drunk party was raided by the police when Stirling and a girl were making love on the floor. The students pulled them apart and dumped Jim in a cupboard just in time. There was a

Vice Squad in New Haven in those days, which called itself, without irony, the SS Squad, and patrolled the town raiding motels to winkle out misbehaving businessmen."[114] When Chase and Stirling eventually broke up, Stirling took it quite badly—drinking and gaining a lot of weight, though "his architecture flourished."[115] Stirling later began a relationship with Master's Class student Eldred Evans, who was widely admired not only for her talent as a designer but also for her "very wild" behavior. George Buchanan, at the time in his third year of the first professional program, remembers Evans as "tough, assured, extraordinarily confident, unbelievably facile and . . . basically unapproachable."[116] In 1964, Stirling again pushed the limits when he used the dining table in the penthouse of the newly completely Art and Architecture Building to couple with a faculty member. From then on, students referred to it as the "Stirling Table."

The most notorious demonstration of Stirling's wild ways occurred during a party Rudolph gave in fall 1961 in his apartment. Richard Rogers remembers it vividly:

> [Rudolph] had this annoying . . . slightly Hollywood apartment, with steps coming in at the higher level, marble steps cantilevered off the wall. At the end there was a double-height wall of glass, and outside there was probably seven feet of open space before a big white wall. The wall had a great light on it as though it was the screen of a cinema, and the light reflected back into the room—absolutely white. And everybody else was there. There was a piano, and let's say a hundred people. An hour later, still no Jim. No Eldred. Doors open at high level, there's a commotion, yells and giggles and so on, and then suddenly come Eldred and Jim, down those cantilevered, slightly marbley steps, giggling because they're canned, literally just rolling down these goddamn steps, drunk. It was a great entry. Paralytic. And like a lot of those paralytic situations, they didn't hurt themselves. A few minutes later Jim says, "Where's the loo?" Somebody says, "Oh, it's upstairs." Jim says, "Fuck the loo" or something, goes into the space outside, in front of this unbelievably white screen, turns around and pisses against the glass, with about a hundred people who could look nowhere else. Like on a cinema screen.[117]

Mark Girouard, Stirling's biographer, has tried to make sense of the endlessly repeated story, "the best known" of the many about Jim: "All the versions are a little different . . . as everyone was well stocked up with drink when it occurred." Rudolph was loath to discuss it, but others had theories about why Jim did it: "Rudolph had flayed him at a crit . . . and this was Jim's way of getting back at him; it was a 'sod you' gesture against the Yale establishment; it was just because Jim was drunk and happy. Perhaps it was a bit of all three, perhaps mostly the last. Explanations vary, but the image remains: Jim, with a big grin on his face, peeing against the glass."[118]

Hijinks and bad behavior notwithstanding, both Stirling and Colin St. John Wilson brought to their studio crits a literateness about the history of architecture, and especially the history of early twentieth-century modernism, that was broader and deeper than that possessed by typical Yale design faculty—not to mention that of the American architecture profession as a whole. This went down very well with many students who carried forward Philip Johnson's admonition that "you cannot not know history," a declaration he had written on a chalkboard as part of a 1959 lecture delivered on the occasion of an exhibition of his work curated by Robert Finkle (b. 1936; M.Arch 1960), who designed the show specifically to show how the architect's style was diverging from that of Mies van der Rohe.[119] Finkle's own work, both as a student and a beginning professional, was strongly influenced by Johnson's post-Miesian Classicism.[120]

M. J. Long was particularly impressed with the British approach. After graduation, she moved to England, partnering on the design of the British Library (1998) in London with Colin St. John Wilson, whom she would eventually marry, before embarking on her own independent practice in the firm Long & Kentish. For Long, Yale's great failure was that its approach to history was overly formal: "There was a kind of distrust of theory." Yale "wasn't anti-intellectual, but it was anti-idea," so that form-making was emphasized but forms were not seen as combined with fixed or social meanings. "Yale just wasn't interested in ideas at all."[121] This was made clear early on by Rudolph who, commenting on the state of the profession in a speech delivered on Alumni Day in February 1958, stated that "Action has outstripped ideas and theory. The last decade [1950s] has thrown a glaring light on the omissions, thinness, paucity of ideas, naiveté with regard to symbols, lack of creativeness, and expressiveness of architectural philosophy as it developed during the twenties."[122] Believing that so-called "modern architecture" lacked the richness of the great historical styles, he advocated a theory that was fundamentally experiential: "We need desperately to relearn the art of disposing our buildings to create different kinds of space: the quiet, enclosed, isolated, shaded space; the hustling, bustling space, pungent with vitality; the paved, dignified, vast, sumptuous, even awe-inspiring space; the mysterious space; the transition space which defines, separates, and yet joins juxtaposed spaces of contrasting character. We need sequences of space which arouse one's curiosity, give a sense of anticipation, which beckon and impel us to rush forward to find that releasing space which dominates, which acts as a climax and magnet, and gives direction. Most important of all, we need those outer spaces which encourage social contact."

As Rudolph scholar Timothy Rohan (b. 1968; B.A. 1991) points out, theory to Rudolph pretty much meant having an artistic idea and not just helping to instrumentalize construction. In his speech Rudolph called for the need to adhere to four "forgotten fundamentals" that would be the focus of education at Yale: finding "ways of rendering our cities fit for humans"; searching "for more eloquent relationships between the conceptual aspects of buildings and techniques"; the "visual perception" of buildings; and "a renewed concern with visual delight."[123]

Rudolph frequently invited his Harvard contemporaries, including John M. Johansen, Ulrich Franzen (1921–2012), Edward Larrabee Barnes (1915–2004), and Henry (Harry) Cobb (b. 1926), to teach and to sit on juries. While Johansen would remember the department as "a vigorous center for modernism," in reality it was a place where modernism was being tested and frequently found wanting.[124] Rudolph's invitations also extended to outside the Ivy establishment, including self-educated designer Ward Bennett (1917–2003), as well as the then-little-known California architects Craig Ellwood (1922–1992) and Pierre Koenig (1925–2004). Howe and Kahn's former partner, Oscar Stonorov, was also a visiting critic. Historians and critics such as Walter McQuade (1922–1994) and the outspoken Sibyl Moholy-Nagy (1903–1971) were frequently asked to join project reviews.

Stanley Tigerman believes that Rudolph, as a young architect whose career had shot upward like a meteor, was inherently insecure and needed to surround himself with a wide array of rivals, whom he would seek to best at juries. Guests who didn't share Rudolph's beliefs "were often the recipient[s] of cutting commentary. He wasn't bashful about sharing his belief systems within ear shot of anyone and arguing vociferously on behalf of his position."[125] For students, the contact with so many wildly diverging points of view, always seen in relationship to Rudolph's own readily available opinions, was eye-opening, nurturing a depth of understanding and sophistication in the handling of architectural ideas that sometimes outstripped the students' ability to give them formal expression.

Rudolph generally got along with his faculty, with one very notable exception: Louis I. Kahn. During Rudolph's first term as a visitor, Kahn was leading the

Master's Class, but by the time Rudolph began his first term as chairman (spring 1958), Kahn had decided to confine his teaching to the University of Pennsylvania. As has been discussed in the previous chapter, Kahn chose to leave Yale for many reasons. Teaching at Penn, his alma mater, meant a good deal to him. Moreover, it enabled him to spend more time in his Philadelphia-based professional office. His exit was also motivated by his disappointment over the university's unwillingness to guarantee him a new commission. But it could also be directly attributed to a professional quarrel with Rudolph who, unbeknownst to Kahn, was asked to renovate portions of the Yale Art Gallery extension in 1958 to suit its new director (1957–71), Andrew C. Ritchie (1907–1978), who disliked its signature "pogo-panels" and its loft-like open spaces, and insisted on full-height partitions such as were typical at the Museum of Modern Art, where he was previously employed as a curator. Kahn "was furious," remembers Vincent Scully. "He never spoke to Paul again after that. And that's one reason why Louis designed the British Art Center on a small bay system, so that in fact they couldn't do that."[126]

William Huff had described the renovation as a "crushing blow" to Kahn, whom he encountered shortly after Rudolph "plaster-boarded . . . over the bricks, blocks and concrete of the Art Gallery (while Lou critted on the top floor)" and noted Rudolph's "later unconvincing flirtations to have Lou return as critic."[127] Clearly, it was unprofessional of Rudolph to undertake the renovation without consulting Kahn. Seeking to justify his intervention, he later expressed his belief that it was a "tribute to Mr. Kahn's gallery that it can absorb changes and still remain itself."[128] Charles Brewer, who worked with Rudolph on the gallery renovation, dismisses the stories of Kahn's negative reaction to the renovation as exaggerations. Brewer says he and Kahn "had a long talk on Chapel Street about architecture. I said I was part of desecrating the building. But he was absolutely wonderful about it." The building had been designed as a flexible loft space but, according to Brewer, "He didn't consider what would happen if you had to accommodate a large exhibition of Pre-Columbian Art that needed to be in glass cases. . . . It just didn't work for that exhibition." In the end, at least according to Brewer, Kahn was philosophical about the renovation: "What his feeling was that if he had done a museum that was good enough, then they wouldn't have had to revise it for that show."[129]

Nonetheless, there was no love lost between Kahn and Rudolph. In 1964, Stanley Tigerman and Rudolph traveled together to Dhaka, East Pakistan (now Bangladesh), at the invitation of Tigerman's classmate in the master's program, Muzharul Islam, who had worked with the World Bank to arrange meetings that led to significant commissions. Islam, as East Pakistan's chief architect, was also instrumental in securing Kahn's services as designer of the new capitol complex in Dhaka.[130] On March 16, 1974, during the course of one of his trips to East Pakistan, Tigerman encountered Kahn "in the international lounge at Heathrow Airport in London." After some debate over Islam's political passions—Kahn regarded them a pointless distraction from architectural practice—Kahn asked that when Tigerman next saw Rudolph, he tell him that he very much admired his work. The next day, Kahn, returning to Philadelphia, died in the men's room in New York's Penn Station. Several days later, Tigerman, on his way to Chicago, stopped in New York to see Rudolph and convey Kahn's sentiments, which now seemed especially poignant, but which Rudolph greeted with nothing but a "deadpan expression." Tigerman has written, "It seems that differences of opinion about architecture theory and practice die hard, if ever."[131]

With Kahn's departure, Rudolph assumed the role of chief critic, although the title was no longer used; instead Rudolph became the first J. M. Hoppin Professor, in recognition of the faculty member whose generous testamentary bequest had been critical to the founding of the Architecture Department. With Kahn no longer present and only a small, largely undistinguished resident faculty, Rudolph ran the department as ringmaster of an ever-changing circus of visitors. After stepping down from the chairmanship, Rudolph would take pride in his ability "to hold everything together. I am very proud that I never had a major argument although I had brought the most diverse representatives of architectural ideas together at one time or another. I tried to be two different people—one unopinionated, interested in other's ideas, helpful to their work, trying to relate everything to the general forces at play—but knowing all the time that this is the opposite of the life of a creative architect."[132]

Though increasingly well-known in professional and academic circles, Rudolph, who craved the kind of media attention that Philip Johnson was attracting, enjoyed his first notable appearance in the mass media when *Vogue* magazine, taking note of his impact on Yale and New Haven, dispatched Elliott Erwitt (b. 1928) to photograph him for a January 1963 profile (4.35), which Deyan Sudjic, the English critic, has analyzed in detail:

> *Vogue* opened the feature with an unforgettable double-page image of Rudolph taken with a lens long enough to bring down a helicopter gunship. Erwitt shows Rudolph standing entirely alone on the roof of one of the most extraordinary of his creations, New Haven's Temple Street car park, which was built to evoke the melancholy splendor of a ruined

4.35 Paul Rudolph on the roof of his Temple St. Parking Garage (1962), photographed by Elliot Erwitt for *Vogue*.

4.36 Serge Chermayeff working on housing concepts at Yale in front of a caricature of him created by students (1966).

Roman aqueduct in massive cast concrete. He is a tiny figure, almost lost in the background of the photograph, until you focus on him, caught standing proudly four-square, arms folded, next to his cherished Jaguar XK-150 coupe, with its white-wall tires and its wire wheel hubs [and, embarrassing to purists, automatic transmission], looking like a Roman general preparing for a triumph beside his chariot. Framed by his own monumental work, and with the city crowding in around him, it is the personification of the architect as a solitary hero in the Ayn Rand tradition: an individual with a vision, standing alone against the world, ready to follow the dictates of his own genius.[133]

Never again would Rudolph enjoy such flattering attention in the mass media.

After four years as the singular focus of Yale's resurgence, in 1962, Rudolph surprised everyone in the school by inviting Serge Chermayeff (1900–1996) to join the permanent faculty. Chermayeff was a brilliant if controversial teacher and one of the more amazing characters of twentieth-century modernism (4.36).[134] Born Sergius Issakovitch to a prosperous Jewish family in the Caucasus, he was sent to the Harrow School in England, where, after World War I, when his family fortunes dried up as the result of the Russian Revolution, he took the surname of his host/sponsor family. He then migrated to Argentina, where he established himself as a tango instructor in Buenos Aires before returning to England in the late 1920s to work as a decorator. He then moved on to a career as an architect in 1933, when he entered into a partnership with German émigré Erich Mendelsohn (1887–1953). Together they would design England's first modernist public building, the De La Warr Pavilion (1935), at Bexhill in East Sussex; later, Chermayeff worked alone on the design of the Bentley Wood house (1938), for which Christopher Tunnard provided the landscape design.[135]

In 1939, as war clouds gathered over England, Chermayeff decamped to the United States, where he taught in various design programs for short periods of time, frequently moving on because of his difficult personality: the San Francisco Art Institute (1940–41); Brooklyn College (1942–46); the Institute of Design at the Illinois Institute of Technology (1946–51); and the Massachusetts Institute of Technology (1951–53). In 1953, Chermayeff joined the faculty of Harvard's Graduate School of Design, where he was put in charge of the first year—an assignment given to him, according to his Yale student and collaborator Alexander Tzonis (b. 1937; M.Arch 1963), because the recently appointed dean, José Luis Sert (1902–1983), reacting against the narrow focus of Gropius's curriculum, believed "that an encyclopedically oriented person" like Chermayeff would be good for beginning students.[136] While at Harvard, Chermayeff maintained a small professional practice, designing houses. Before coming to Yale, William Grindereng (1925–2011; B.Arch 1956) worked in Rudolph's Boston office, which was "basically one big loft space" separated from Chermayeff's by a "a flimsy partition. . . . You could hear everything that went on [in] either office. Serge Chermayeff and his partner, [Hayward] Cutting, would get into horrendous arguments."[137]

As Chermayeff's interests began to shift from building design to urban research, teaching first year proved not to be a good fit, and by the early 1960s, Chermayeff had begun to wear out his welcome at Harvard. Although he and Sert were both dedicated urbanists, they disagreed on both methodology and focus, leading to a definitive split, with Sert seeing urbanism as a design problem, and Chermayeff convinced that large-scale solutions "could not and should not be posited in terms that were wholly physical."[138]

Seeking the opportunity to work with more advanced students, Chermayeff requested a sabbatical leave for 1961–62 in part, unbeknownst to Harvard, to accept Rudolph's invitation to lead Yale's Master's Class in the spring term, where he would encounter Norman Foster and Richard Rogers, who would become his committed disciples.[139] According to Tzonis, when Chermayeff returned to Harvard at the end of his sabbatical leave, he was "received at a faculty meeting in a very punitive way" because he had used the time to teach and not to pursue pure research. Chermayeff responded to this criticism by attacking Louis Bakanowsky (b. 1930), an architectural partner in the recently founded firm Cambridge Seven, where Chermayeff's sons Peter and Ivan were also partners. Chermayeff told Bakanowky: "When you take your sabbatical you run to your office."[140] Bakanowsky responded, and the confrontation escalated when "Serge raised up [to his considerable height] and said, 'Louis, not only is your English accent horrible, but you are also short.' That was a completely surrealistic, but a typically Chermayeff way of reacting to an absurd situation. . . . Well, the rest was history."[141] Rudolph offered Chermayeff a contract to lead the Master's Class as a research studio for three consecutive spring terms beginning in 1963. Peter Chermayeff urged his father to accept the invitation. Under Sert, Harvard's preeminence over Yale had been eroding significantly, and Chermayeff's departure followed up a 1962 report of the National Architectural Accrediting Board, which expressed concern that Sert, as dean, chairman of architecture, and design instructor, had too much responsibility. Moreover, Walter Gropius, retired but still influential, was no fan of his successor. In 1964, Sert resigned as chairman and, in 1969, as dean.[142]

Ideologically and pedagogically, Chermayeff was Rudolph's complete opposite. And that's exactly why Rudolph brought him in. "It was my notion to get people who didn't agree with me," Rudolph boasted, "and he was certainly a good candidate. It was never dull when you were near Serge."[143] For Rudolph, Chermayeff was "someone who perhaps makes more connections with society in general and a given subject. . . . He also had the ability to think beyond the problems of the moment. And he was there as a complement to the faculty, as a thoughtful provocateur."[144] Rudolph justified his invitation in a number of ways: to capture a leading Harvard faculty member with an international reputation was a coup; to bolster his own faculty in an area— urban theory—where it was notably weak was also a good thing. Rudolph also defended his invitation as an act of kindness by a younger man to a beleaguered senior colleague. Such was certainly the case, as Chermayeff's biographer, Alan Powers, makes clear. Not only had Chermayeff broken with standard practice by teaching at another institution during a paid sabbatical, but he had also antagonized his former colleagues, who received the news of his "defection in the form of a press release from Yale," leading Chermayeff to write "what must have been the most apologetic letters of his career to smooth over the affront."[145]

In the face of a pedagogy based on a content-free formalism that he seemingly opposed, why did Chermayeff come to Yale? For much the same reasons that Rudolph invited him. In a letter written to Rudolph in 1964, Chermayeff attributed his decision to the freedom the appointment would give him to complete "a line of enquiry which I hoped to finish before the rules of the game [forced retirement] closed the academic career I had deliberately chosen long ago, and while I could still be useful."[146] Seeing himself as "the loyal opposition," Chermayeff expressed his "unequivocal admiration" for Rudolph's gifts but also for his "integrity and forthright acceptance of other viewpoints as a deliberate policy for the school." Twenty years or so later, reflecting on his years at Yale, Chermayeff said, "I had a lovely time because [Rudolph] was a very nice man. I liked him very much and we got on very, very well."[147]

Harvard may have been relieved to be free of the divisive Chermayeff, but the prospect of his appointment did not go down particularly well with key Yale faculty. Faculty objections to Rudolph's invitation centered on Chermayeff's tendency toward pedagogical dogmatism and his dismissive attitude toward colleagues with whom he disagreed, including his former collaborator Christopher Tunnard, with whom, as Alan Powers has observed, "no friendship was rekindled."[148] Vincent Scully was concerned that Chermayeff's dogmatic tendencies would clash with the department's characteristic open-mindedness. While Rudolph probably did believe that Chermayeff would enrich the debate, the reality, as Scully and others had predicted, was to encourage divisiveness in the department's approach to architecture, transforming what had been a debate between "functionalists" and "formalists" into an argument. In response to faculty protests, Rudolph insisted that he could control Chermayeff. "But he didn't," remembers Scully. "Chermayeff destroyed every place he came. . . . Chermayeff just divided and conquered. He tried to tear everything apart. He'd invite you to dinner just to conspire. It was horrible. . . . He was compelled to do this; compelled to run things; compelled to be in charge."[149]

The faculty wasn't alone in objecting to Chermayeff's presence in the school. Students also took issue with his contrariness. At the end of the spring 1960 term, when Tigerman presented his bachelor's thesis to a stellar gathering of architects, including Gordon Bunshaft (1909–1990), Jean Paul Carlhian (b. 1919), Harry Cobb, Ulrich Franzen, and Philip Johnson, Chermayeff was the only juror to speak out against the project. As Tigerman recalls, Chermayeff concluded his critical assessment with a question: "Now, young man, just between you and I, if you had to do it over again, you wouldn't do it this way." Before Tigerman could say a word, Rudolph stood up and said, "Of course he would, you ass. Next project."[150] Students also witnessed Chermayeff's dogmatism during a jury in spring 1961, when he lashed out against the fenestration on Jaquelin Robertson's contextually responsive design for a new residence hall on the Old Campus, arguing that window mullions could "never have a cross pattern." Like many others, Robertson "ended up really disliking Chermayeff. He was the meanest son of a bitch. Really smart. And really mean." In 1964–65, Robertson returned to Yale as a critic, teaching alongside Rudolph and others in the third year in the fall term, and in the spring he was assisting in Chermayeff's studio, when Chermayeff "started beating up on a guy on a jury and the student burst into tears. I said, 'Ok, we'll take a break.' I walked outside and I looked at Chermayeff and I said, 'You really are a son of a bitch. And now I know why I didn't like you from the start. You're just all mean.' I said, 'Here's the deal: You will go back and apologize to this student in front of the class.'" Robertson then threatened to reveal some particularly embarrassing information about Chermayeff's past; Chermayeff relented. "He knew I wasn't kidding," says Robertson.[151]

When Thomas Beeby studied under Chermayeff during the spring 1965 term, he found that his teacher would "stop and snort and carry on endlessly about how stupid people were." More to the point, students "were not allowed to do design" but instead told to construct diagrams that would become the basis of a building, "a stadium complex. . . . It had to be a group project, it was part of the approach. 'Men don't work alone anymore because that is what geniuses do and architects are not geniuses'"[152] (4.37). A recently graduated Robert A. M. Stern (b. 1939; M.Arch 1965) described Chermayeff as "a police-man castigating those who have made light of functionalism, an evangelical minister saving young innocents from the temptations of 'prima donna' archi-tecture and returning them to their true responsibilities in a nuclear world which has little time for artistry, not to mention art. . . . But the strings of his bow are limited and the tune has an annoying familiarity to those who are acquainted with the pseudo-functionalism and the technological determinism of the Harvard-Bauhaus."[153]

In opposition to the American students, the British students who stud-ied under Chermayeff in spring 1962 largely saw the contrast with Rudolph as liberating, and also reassuring. Norman Foster contrasts the two: "Rudolph had his crew cut, the trousers stylishly high, the soles of the shoes slightly thick; Chermayeff was elegantly tall, with long hair and a tailored suit." But more importantly, beyond their physical differences were their ideological differences: "Chermayeff wouldn't want to look at a drawing. He would want to know why you were doing it: What was your motivation? Chermayeff insisted that students think through and analyse."[154] Chermayeff, Foster says, "was as European as Rudolph was American." Foster found him "philosophical to the point of 'a building—why design a building?'"[155] Richard Rogers, also Chermayeff's student in spring 1962, described him as someone who "could have persuaded us to do anything. He was a dominating figure, hugely intellectual in the best European mould and just as much of an influence as Rudolph."[156] Under Chermayeff, Rogers, with fellow students Norman Foster (M.Arch 1962), John Chisholm (M.Arch 1962) and Roy Mason (1938–1996; M.Arch 1963) (4.38), designed a new city, proposing a decidedly European solu-tion made up of rational, Siedlung-like row houses punctuated by towers; it strongly reflected ideas Chermayeff would set forth in the book he was writing with the Austrian-born California architect Christopher Alexander (b. 1936), *Community and Privacy* (1963).

Chermayeff's lessons would have an enduring effect on Rogers and Foster, especially in their early joint practice (with their wives, Su Brumwell Rogers and Wendy Cheeseman Foster) as Team 4. When attempting to secure work from the British developer-builder Wates, they modeled their design for a housing site in Croydon, Surrey, on Chermayeff's ideas. In a 1964 letter, Rogers and Foster told their mentor about "some grueling interviews where we

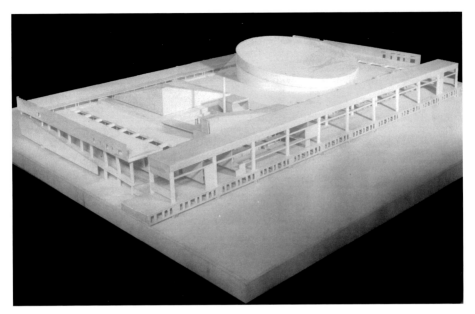

4.37 Thomas Beeby (M.Arch 1965), Glenn Garrison (M.Arch 1965), and Alan Greenberg (M.Arch 1965), Model. Master's class project completed under Chermayeff (1965).

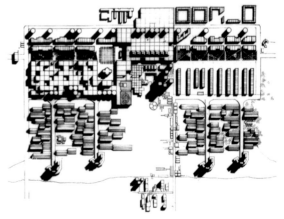

4.38 Norman Foster (M.Arch 1962), John Chisholm (M.Arch 1962), Richard Rogers (M.Arch 1962), and Roy Mason (M.Arch 1962), A New City, model and plan. Chermayeff studio (1962).

not only quoted your book ad infinitum but also gave them a copy. They were so impressed with our social mindedness as against our competitor's architectural art approach that with a little luck we shall get the job."[157] They did not. Nonetheless, the impact of Chermayeff's ideas on their work endured, leading Foster to write to Chermayeff in 1966 that "we're realising more and more the value of the Yale studies and now that the practice and our teaching here is a little more organized we'd like to follow some of the ideas further."[158]

Along with Foster and Rogers, Alexander Tzonis was a notable beneficiary of Chermayeff's research-oriented approach. A graduate of Athens College, before coming to Yale as a Ford Fellow, Tzonis studied architecture in his native Greece at the National Technical University and pursued a career in the theater and filmmaking that included the art direction of the 1960 film *Never on Sunday*. Originally admitted into the School of Drama, after a semester Tzonis transferred to the architecture Master's Class, where he studied under Chermayeff, and then in spring 1963 with Rudolph and his studio assistant, Robert Venturi (b. 1925), who took the class to Philadelphia to meet Louis Kahn. Tzonis recalls that "one of the things that Kahn spoke very vividly [about] and with a tremendous analytical power was the pre-war [residential] colleges and other teaching facilities of Yale," emphasizing "that you have to develop an architecture that recognizes through materials, through scale, through how one enters the building, and through maybe the way one proceeds through the building, the values, architectural and organizational, expressed by the pre-war architecture of Yale."[159] Eventually Tzonis, in partnership with Chermayeff, would develop ideas on campus planning and design research initiatives that would bear fruit in their book *Shape of Community: Realization of Human Potential* (1971);[160] according to Richard Plunz, the book summed up Chermayeff's work at Yale "quite precisely," reflecting "the particular confluence of political and environmental issues that directed much architectural thought toward the end of the sixties: misuse of technology, destruction of urban centers, and threats to natural and human ecology." The book did not succeed as *Community and Privacy* had. By the time it was published, it was out of synch with an architectural discourse that was turning away from environmental issues. As Plunz notes, "To be sure, the book suffered from other problems, most notably a lack of visual and textural clarity. In the United States, *Shape of Community* was greeted with the strongest possible critical reaction, which was silence."[161]

Disruptive though Chermayeff was, his contract was surprisingly renewed by Rudolph's successor, Charles Moore. Under Moore, Chermayeff, taking advantage of abundant federal grants then available, developed the "Yale Model," an innovative form of urban analysis and design involving collaborative work between architecture faculty, students, and visiting experts, including biologist Edward Deevey (1914–1988), the lawyer Charles Haar (1920–2012), the philosopher Paul Weiss (1901–2002), the naturalist Albert E. Parr (1900–1991), and others. These collaborative discussions were transcribed, edited in "mosaics" of commentary, and distributed. According to Chermayeff biographer Alan Powers, "It was a stimulating method, giving students an important role and narrowing the gaps between them and the staff, by giving them the feeling of doing work of real importance."[162]

Rudolph's influence at Yale could be felt not only in the architecture studios but in the university's extensive program of adventurous new buildings being undertaken with President Griswold's encouragement. Rudolph sat on the Building Committee of the Yale Corporation, advising on architect selection. The appointment was critical to his self-esteem, but also reflected Rudolph's belief that the leader of an architecture department should also be involved in setting the university's policies with regard to new buildings. "When it became clear [that] they wanted me to come to Yale," Rudolph told C. Ray Smith, "I made two demands. They were: 1) that I be allowed to continue practicing architecture, therefore I would spend half my time [at the school]; and 2) that I did not think that a department of architecture could be saying one thing, and the university [be building] in a completely different way. There had to be some relationship between the two things." Griswold "completely agreed and his way of carrying out that agreement was to put me on the Building Committee. This was a fascinating experience for me because I was, for the first time, sitting on the opposite side of the table. In practice this meant that they would ask me to suggest three architects for buildings coming up and they would select one of the three."[163]

Rudolph's participation in the university's architect selection process was a definite departure from previous practice, where only donors and certain members of the Yale Corporation were typically consulted by the president. The story of the selection of Gordon Bunshaft as architect of the Beinecke Rare Book and Manuscript Library (1963) illustrates how the new system did—and did not—work. According to Bunshaft, the selection process "started with Paul Rudolph calling me one afternoon and asking if I would be willing to be in a small group of four architects to do a competition to get the commission to do the Beinecke Rare Book Library. I remember two of the other architects. One was Eero Saarinen, who was doing work at Yale, and Ed Stone. I can't remember the fourth." This was probably Mies van der Rohe, who Rudolph claimed in conversation at the time to have been his preferred choice for the job. The Beinecke brothers also suggested that several far more conservative architects who had experience designing libraries—Robert O'Connor (1916–1993), Alfred Easton Poor (1899–1988), and the firm of Otto Eggers (1882–1964) and Daniel Higgins (1886–1953)—be considered. Bunshaft, however, believed that "it was Paul Rudolph's idea of having this competition. He had convinced the Yale University officials that this was a good way to select an architect. I told Paul immediately that I would have no part of it, that is not the way to do a good building."[164]

Rudolph was upset by the negative reaction to the competition idea, prompting Bunshaft to ask permission to discuss his reservations with Provost Norman Buck (1892–1964). Rudolph gave his blessing, and Bunshaft found Buck to be sympathetic: "Well, you're not the only one that's against this form of selecting an architect," Buck told him. "The chairman of the Building Committee of the Yale trustees was in this morning, and he heard about this competition, and he said, 'If Yale hasn't got brains enough to select an architect, they shouldn't build a building.'"[165] Bunshaft was asked to submit his credentials, and a few weeks later he received a call from Lou Crandall (1893–1978), head of the George A. Fuller Construction Company, who had the Beinecke brothers with him in his office at that very moment. "I think you have the job," Crandall told Bunshaft, "but don't say anything." A week later, Provost Buck confirmed the commission. Of course, it helped that the Beinecke brothers' father had owned the Fuller Company, and the family still had a financial interest in it.[166]

Bunshaft's design for the Beinecke Library was initially greeted with hostility, especially by Vincent Scully, who deemed it the type of "spectacular disaster" of American architects attempting to work in a monumental, urban style, creating "a world without human reference points, wherein no contact with things is possible. Indeed it is the true 'empty landscape of psychosis' about which Norman Mailer warned us in 1963."[167] Bunshaft could not accept Scully's objection to the building as a critical judgment, preferring to see it in personal terms. He attributed Scully's hostility to a thesis jury they had both attended, a claim that is hardly credible; Scully was not one to seek revenge (4.39). Nonetheless, Bunshaft, who was largely out of touch with architecture schools, found the way Yale ran its juries to be an unfamiliar and disturbing experience, in direct opposition to the closed-door silent juries of the Beaux-Arts that he knew from his student days at MIT. Bunshaft recalled the jury:

The man that had the thesis got up and explained it, and the jury sat and looked at it. Behind us was practically the whole class listening

4.39 Thesis review (1960). From left to right: Vincent Scully, Paul Rudolph, Jean Paul Carlhian, Philip Johnson, King-lui Wu, and Gordon Bunshaft (yawning). Presenting: James Baker (M.Arch 1960).

4.40 Paul Rudolph, Art and Architecture Building (1963), New Haven.

to us. These jurors really beat up the students, asking tough questions and made them feel they flunked. They were very rough on them. I didn't say much. The other architects on it were calm, but they asked tough questions.

We came to some fellow with a church. We were sitting there, just a small group and a lot of students behind. Some of the architects said something about it, and then Scully got up and started screaming at this kid. He was very excitable. He was shouting and asking, "Why this? Why this? Why this? This doesn't seem right. Why this?" If I were a student, I would have thought I was flunking, kicked out of school. I sat there, and I said to Scully, "What are you shouting about?" I could have shot him with a cannon. He was, of course, embarrassed in front of the student body. So that took care of our relationship.[168]

The year 1963 marks the apogee of Rudolph's positive influence on the Department of Architecture, coinciding with the completion of the Art and Architecture Building, which was to unite the various departments of the school under one roof for the first time since they were all squeezed together in Street Hall (4.40).[169] Though it was not part of his initial discussion with President Griswold, Rudolph was "delighted" when he was asked to design three buildings for the university shortly after his appointment as chairman: the Greeley Memorial Laboratory for the School of Forestry (1959), Married Student Housing (1961), and, most significantly, a new building for the School of Art and Architecture (1963). The "A&A" was an opportunity to finally realize an American Bauhaus. Though he worked with Josef Albers to program the building's spaces, Rudolph was, for all intents and purposes, both architect and client, placing him in "select company," as Timothy Rohan observes, with Karl Friedrich Schinkel and his Bauakademie in Berlin (1836), Walter Gropius and the Dessau Bauhaus (1926), and Mies van der Rohe with Crown Hall at IIT (1956). Like these architects before him, Rudolph intended the A&A to be not just a manifesto on the current state of architecture, but also a physical representation of a distinct philosophy of arts education. Rejecting the loft-like universal space of Crown Hall, Rudolph set out to arrange carefully defined spaces in an effort to unite students in all the disciplines of the arts in accord with a utopian, Bauhaus-like vision of interaction, if not collaboration. "Rudolph believed that students would learn from the architecture of the A&A Building itself, especially his carefully crafted and decorated interiors."[170] Unfortunately, this ambitious agenda proved ill-timed.

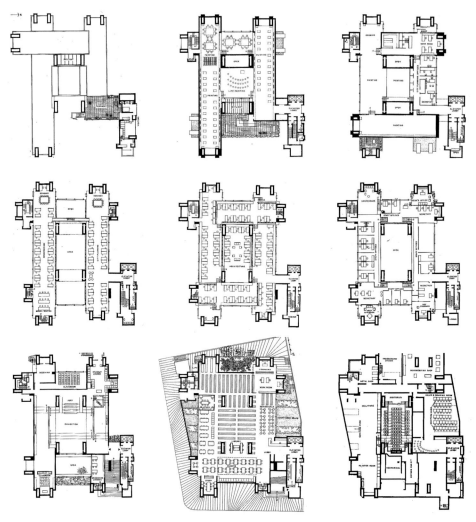

4.41 Paul Rudolph, Art and Architecture Building, basement through penthouse plans (1963).

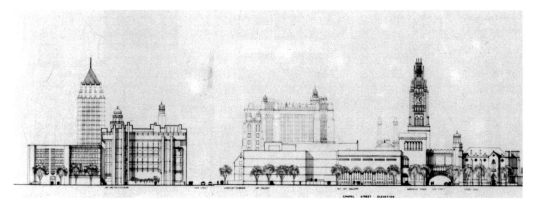

4.42 Paul Rudolph, Chapel Street elevation showing the Art and Architecture Building in relationship to other arts buildings (1963).

Planning for the building started almost immediately after Rudolph's arrival at Yale, spurred on by the 1959 NAAB report that criticized the department's ad-hoc space arrangements, including the loft-like fourth floor of Kahn's Art Gallery extension that then served as the architecture drafting studio and was beloved by students. The Accrediting Board, which was supposed to confine its findings to the architecture program, went beyond its mandate to state that the various spaces used by the whole school were "temporary in the sense that they are not designed for the purpose for which they are now used, and are scattered in four separate buildings"—Street Hall (painting and sculpture), Weir Hall (architecture), the Yale University Art Gallery and Design Center (architecture, graphic design, arts library), and 295–297 Crown Street (city planning). In response, Rudolph noted that "a building program is in progress."[171] At first, as Rudolph later recalled, the idea was to demolish Street Hall and construct a new building for the arts in its place, but this led to "much agitation and much concern on the part of . . . the Yale Corporation regarding putting a modern building on the Old Campus and after some soul searching the site at the corner of York and Chapel, which then had a filling station on it, was selected."[172]

Rudolph struggled with the design, producing no fewer than seven versions by the time the corporation demanded that work go forward. The spatially inventive and surprisingly contextual design completed in 1963 would become home to both the Architecture and Art departments; its "pinwheel" plan was the only consistent element throughout the design's many iterations, allowing Rudolph to conceptually "turn the corner" at York and Chapel streets while maintaining the building's integrity as an object (4.41). One of the key drawings in understanding the design of the Art and Architecture Building was an elevation illustrating all the Yale buildings along Chapel Street, which makes it abundantly clear that the architect was thinking urbanistically, something that Rudolph also emphasized in his teaching (4.42). "However much that building may be criticized," Vincent Scully wrote in 1992, "nobody can fault its siting: where Kahn's building is a cut-off box, Rudolph's opens in a great gesture to embrace it from across York Street, so concluding the impressive movement of Yale's art and architecture buildings down Chapel Street."[173] As Timothy Rohan has observed, several of Rudolph's contemporaries, including Ulrich Franzen, who was a frequent visitor to the school, believed that "the ongoing discussion of urbanism was [Rudolph's] main contribution to the Yale School of Architecture."[174]

Though it initially seemed an isolated sculptural object, the Art and Architecture Building was designed to accommodate future expansion, but

Rudolph chose not to spell out exactly what form an addition might take, preferring to intimate "what might be done. The environment constantly changes, as history shows." However, he did leave "the design open to expansion on its north side where an incipient courtyard might be completed."[175] Rudolph believed that "If the next architect is at all sensitive, he will complete the courtyard, thereby adding immeasurably to the whole. Implications in architecture are a twentieth century must."[176]

Rudolph devised the Art and Architecture Building's distinctive "corrugated" concrete surface to complement the traditional masonry of Yale's nearby residential colleges, but its rough materiality was seen by some as an overly aggressive expression of self-importance, earning the building its reputation as a canonical Brutalist structure. Scully, in his initial review of the building, dismissed the building's surfaces as "one of the most inhospitable, indeed physically dangerous, ever devised by man."[177] For Rudolph, the corrugated concrete—based, in part, on the work of Japanese architect Kenzo Tange (1913–2005), whose partially board-formed concrete Prefectural Government Office (1958) Rudolph had likely seen on a trip to Japan—was a way to break "down the scale of walls and [catch] the light in many different ways because of its heavy texture. . . . As the light changed the walls seemingly quivered, dematerialized, [and] took on additional solidity."[178] The corrugations also related to Rudolph's characteristic drawing style.[179]

The building's interior was notable for its complex organization of thirty-seven distinct levels over ten floors, as well as its decorative display of purposely created faculty art and an array of artifacts including bas reliefs and statuary from Yale's collection of Beaux-Arts–era plaster casts, which some interpreted as a call for a reintegration of history with new design, a frightening concept to many faculty who were, according to Scully, "mad with rage."[180] For Rudolph, the installation of these casts was not a way of advocating a return to tradition; they were motivated by his instincts as a decorator. "These works have been used to reduce the scale of the interiors," Rudolph explained, "which is, I believe, the basic relationship between all ornament and architectural space."[181] Similarly, the decision to place the Roman sculpture of Minerva, the Roman goddess of poetry, wisdom, and commerce, in the double-height architecture studio that occupied the building's fourth and fifth floors was defended by Rudolph in formal terms: "[I] didn't care what it was really—you must understand that [for] the architect, his principal interest is not—I should say my principal interest—is not only what it is, I would love that it be Athena directly from the Acropolis if she would fit, but if she wouldn't fit then I wouldn't want her, if she wasn't the right size and shape. I look at it not in terms of what it actually is in terms of her history. . . . I look at her and her shape and size and color and texture and where she is and whether . . . she is intrinsically right for that space. By right, I mean the right size, color, proportion."[182]

Charles Jencks (b. 1939), then a student at the Graduate School of Design, attacked the building's design in *Connection,* a student journal that he edited, focusing on Rudolph's "scattering sculpture around" as if to imply "that art (aside from its therapeutic effect) is meaningless." Jencks went on to state that there was "hope that [Rudolph] is a real antichrist about to deliver his heterodoxy in architectural terms: i.e. that modern architecture is a meaningless doctrine in a valueless world. But [Rudolph] doesn't have either the insight or the courage to support his action with that philosophy."[183] Many years later, Robert Stern would remind Jencks of his youthful publication when he introduced the historian and critic at a lecture: "Charlie [had] dismissed the plan of this building—our home—and its use of materials and all its stylistic inclusiveness, which he deemed 'a mélange with the integrity of pop art' that 'exhibited iconoclasm without verve' and was 'a mockery of modern architecture without the courage to be different or unique.' Charles dismissed both the A&A and the Gothic colleges of James Gamble Rogers as applications of 'form without content.' Needless to say, when copies of *Connection* were dumped in great quantity on the steps of the A&A Building in 1964, their arrival was not universally appreciated, especially not by Paul Rudolph, whose response to the criticism was casually caustic—possibly mumbling the old adage . . . 'You can always tell a Harvard man, but you can't tell him much.'"[184]

The A&A Building was certainly not without content. It was a challenge to "the orthodoxies of modernism" that, as Rohan notes, "provided an alternative to the gray, soulless world of the corporatized International Style."[185] But more than just a formal challenge to modernism, the A&A was a physical expression of a distinct pedagogical ideal: the integration of all arts under one roof, with the intention of fostering their interaction. But that ideal proved to be the building's undoing, as the various disciplines under its roof were in the process of dramatically moving further apart from each other—in particular the painters who were now working in a more gestural style on much larger canvases than the small-scale paintings preferred by Albers.

The building was not only a rigidly deterministic expression of a rejected pedagogy, it was also very undersized (4.43–4.45). The painting students felt betrayed. "It's very impressive," said Phyllis Rosenblatt (b. 1942; M.F.A. 1965), "but it's impossible to work in."[186] Disappointed with their new spaces, the

4.44 Subbasement sculpture studio, Art and Architecture Building (1963).

4.43 Seventh-floor painting studio, Art and Architecture Building (1963).

4.45 Fourth- and fifth-floor architecture studios, Art and Architecture Building (1963).

art students met with Rudolph days before the building's opening to air their grievances; little was done to appease them. As a result, a group of students, including Chuck Close (b. 1940; M.F.A. 1964), Nancy Graves (1939–1995; B.F.A. 1962, M.F.A. 1964), and Richard Serra (b. 1939; B.F.A. 1962, M.F.A. 1964), planned to picket in front of the school at the dedication to protest the cramped, garret-like lit quarters designed for them. Rudolph, who only learned of the proposed picket two days before the opening, when Robert Stern informed him, was "somewhat shocked."[187] The threat of a picket never became more than that, but to avoid embarrassment the university did what it could to screen the most outspoken critics from the press. After their protests, some painting students, including Close, Graves, and Serra, took more direct action by decamping to a more generously proportioned studio space in an old building on Crown Street. With the escape from the A&A came an escape from the sense of a comprehensive pedagogy. As Sasha M. Newman has noted, these painters "shared a sense that they could come and go as they pleased from the School's 'official' center at the A&A, but that they were not bound to its academic hierarchies."[188]

The design not only sought to achieve a Bauhaus-like unification of the arts under one roof, its spatial arrangement also reflected an attempt to recapture the Beaux-Arts ideal of architecture as the mother of the arts served by artistic handmaidens. When a reporter from the *Yale Daily News* suggested Rudolph was playing favorites, he defensively replied, "Look, I wasn't born yesterday; I knew this accusation would be raised. But the truth of the matter is that if you care to do the multiplication, you will find that there are more square feet per painter upstairs than there are for each architect down here. Actually, they got almost everything they asked for," Rudolph noted, before adding, perhaps somewhat spitefully, "You know, you couldn't very well get a painter to design the building."[189]

The new building garnered enormous press coverage, much of it favorable but not unreservedly so. *New York Times* architecture critic Ada Louise Huxtable described it as "an exceptionally handsome and provocative structure, which will set trends nationally and internationally. It will surely be one of the most influential buildings of this decade. . . . Its real significance," she continued, "is that it asks and answers some of the major questions facing the art of architecture today, at a time of crisis and transition in the development of the contemporary style. . . . The new building is a genuine creative achievement and a spectacular tour de force. It is willful, capricious, arbitrary, bold, brilliant and beautiful, and it may very possibly be great."[190]

For Peter Blake, managing editor of *Architectural Forum,* "The tremendous importance of Yale's new Art and Architecture Building is that it will challenge, disturb, possibly inspire the students within it as few other schools of architecture anywhere have done in recent times. It is not really important to decide whether this is a good building or a bad one."[191] Jan Rowan, editor of *Progressive Architecture,* devoted the cover of *P/A*'s February 1964 issue to Robert C. Damora's (1912–2009; M.Arch 1953) portrait photograph of Rudolph collaged over his photograph of the building—a rare example at that time of a professional journal featuring a picture of an architect on its cover. But in his text, Rowan took note of the art students' protests, pointing out that Damora, on his recent visit, had "noticed that the building had been splattered with eggs and one window pierced by a bullet from a zip gun."[192]

A thoughtful review by Vincent Scully in *Architectural Review* summarized the spatial politics of the building and the complex reaction to it: "The hysterical twittering of the ninety-four painters who are caged in what can only be regarded as its entablature, and the heavier, troglodytic resentments of the seventeen sculptors who have been driven down into its second basement, are more than matched by the euphoric beatitude of the one hundred and seventy-three architects and planners who, under the white-painted eyes of Minerva, are now expanding grandly through its airy middle floors." As Scully pointed out, there was a kind of opéra bouffe quality to the distribution of the various program spaces: painters were accommodated on the building's top floors in an almost comical reprise of nineteenth-century Paris and its *La Vie Bohème* attic ateliers; sculptors, working with heavy materials, were housed on the basement floors in rooms that were too small for their work; also in the basement spaces were the graphic designers and photography darkrooms; and architects were given pride of place with a light-filled, double-height drafting room sitting atop a double-height exhibition hall intended to also function as the setting for studio reviews. Near the end of his extensive review, Scully waxed philosophical on the humanist qualities of the building:

> The structure proliferates with its infinity of levels, as complicated as any human soul, as dark and tortuous in some places, as surprisingly generous in many others, lighted from unexpected sources, a never ending wonder to explore. . . .
>
> Whoever uses the building is caught up in that human complexity—in the curiously intimate scale of personal drama—in that insatiable will and unappeasable anxiety. This is, one imagines, the larger reason why the painters and sculptors hate it so, who wish to be caught up only in their own. . . .
>
> How raw and violent it [the A&A] is—that is, we are—how resourceful,

determined, and uneven in strength: all this so truly, openly, with so much talent, I think bravely, stated here.[193]

Scully's assessment was not published until six months after the building's formal dedication on November 9, 1963, when the German-born and trained English art and architecture historian Sir Nikolaus Pevsner (1902–1983) delivered the principal address (4.46, 4.47). The invitation to Pevsner, probably made at the behest of Carroll Meeks, although Rudolph attributed it to Dean Danes, was misguided. Many of the art history faculty feared that Pevsner, an unreconstructed modernist of the interwar era, "couldn't understand the building and wouldn't like it."[194] They were right. After describing the Art School's original home, Street Hall, as a less-than-inspired, Ruskinian reaction against Georgian architecture, and offering brief praise for Rudolph, whom he situated in the Pantheon of great American architects, along with Richardson, Sullivan, Burnham & Root, and Frank Lloyd Wright, Pevsner launched into a thinly veiled attack on the design, just as the art historians had predicted:

> So my message to the students is simple and short. You have the immense advantage of a controversial head. Students will be students. You will adore him or slash him. Both will be equally useful. But do promise me one thing. Don't imitate what you have now around you. Of course the young architect worth his salt does not imitate motifs anyway. But the International Modern of the thirties could at least be imitated with impunity. Something reasonable, serviceable, non-aggressive would come out. But woe to him who imitates Paul Rudolph, who imitates Saarinen, Yamasaki, or Philip Johnson. . . . The result is disaster. The great individual, the artist-architect concerned with self-expression primarily, is inimitable.[195]

Pevsner then went on to describe successful architecture as the result of a collaboration between the architect and the client—both are responsible. "Well, here we have the rare case that . . . the client was the architect and the architect was the client. . . . So, in walking round this building, as you have no doubt done, or are going to do, never forget that whatever you see and inspect is exactly as the brief demanded it. I find that a most stimulating and valuable lesson, and it is the lesson with which I want to end."[196]

M. J. Long, then in her fourth year, found the dedication ceremony "fascinating. I think very few people actually listened. You know the way openings

4.46 The crowd gathers in the second-floor gallery at the dedication of the Art and Architecture Building on November 9, 1963. Pictured in the foreground are Robert A. M. Stern (M.Arch 1965) and Aimée Brown (M.A. 1963, Ph.D. 1972).

4.47 Paul Rudolph, Nikolaus Pevsner, and Carroll L. V. Meeks at the dedication of the Art and Architecture Building.

are. Everybody was sitting there smiling, and Paul Rudolph was getting pinker and pinker. He absolutely was listening."[197] Not surprisingly, Rudolph did not react well to the address, interpreting Pevsner's comments as a personal attack. Although the dedication should have been Rudolph's crowning moment, according to Scully it was "at that moment he decided he had to leave Yale."[198]

Rudolph remained at Yale for almost two more years, until June 1965, during which time his influence over students seemed as strong as ever. Robert Mittelstadt's 1964 thesis for a monastery was "a full lockup with the formal principles of Paul Rudolph as I interpreted from then current work, notably the Boston Government Center" (4.48).[199] Like George Nelson before him, Mittelstadt's failure to win the Paris Prize was mitigated by a Prix de Rome. Shortly thereafter, he won a competition for a civic center in Fremont, California (1966–68, demolished 2004), with a design also based on Rudolph's Boston Government Center (4.49).[200] On the other hand, M. J. Long's thesis, also from 1964 and also a monastery but for an urban site, was a far less flamboyant, more introspective design featuring a monumental six-story-high space curled around a central courtyard (4.50).

Both Mittelstadt's and Long's, as well as a few other theses, were selected by the department to be entered in the Paris Prize competition. Long recalls that

Yale, in its usual way, only realized this thing was coming up the day before. So a couple of us said we'd drive the boards to New York. . . . We gave them [the sponsors, the National Institute for Architectural Education] the boards to put up around the walls and they told us to go away and come back to pick up our stuff around 4:00. So we went off and had a nice Italian lunch. . . . I think it was Caleb Hornbostel [1905–1991] who was running the jury, and I think he had been drinking all day and looking at these projects. He was feeling very cheery and he said to us, "One of your students has won the prize! He did a monastery." So both Bob and I assumed he won the prize. And then it turned out that the winner was Mr. Long. Again. That was a real lesson [about the place of women in the architectural profession]. The first thing this guy [Hornbostel] said to me, and I do think he was drinking because his guard was down, he said, "Oh well . . . the second prize goes to a man from Princeton. I'm sure he'll be happy to take the prize." I said, "What do you mean?" [He said,] "Well, you're a woman. You don't want to travel around Europe." And I said, "Are you kidding? Of course I want to

4.48 Robert Mittelstadt (M.Arch. 1964), A Monastery, perspective (1964).

4.49 Robert Mittelstadt, Fremont Civic Center (1968; demolished 2004), California.

4.50 M. J. Long (M.Arch. 1964), Monastery and School, model (1964).

travel around Europe!" And I decided I was M. J. Long from then on. There was no question in my mind that if I had put "Mary Jane" on the drawings, the result would have been different. And then when I said I want to go traveling, he said, "Oh. Oh I see. Oh, well . . . that's interesting." Then he started getting excited . . . [and] entered into the whole spirit of the thing. "Oh, this is a really groundbreaking thing we're doing here."

Reflecting on this turn of events, Long has stated: "I didn't want to be special, but I didn't want to be ruled out."[201]

Mittelstadt's and Long's topics and their meticulous presentations were typical of Yale's standards for theses at the time, but that of David Sellers (b. 1938; B.S. 1960, M.Arch 1965), for a new department store on a site facing New York's Lexington Avenue between Fifty-Eighth and Fifty-Ninth streets, was a startling departure from the values Rudolph espoused. The design consisted of a windowless box conceived with little regard to aesthetics, but more in tune with the city's infrastructure, including a new subway station. Anticipating the work of John Portman later in the decade, the proposal called for a cavernous interior public space crisscrossed by escalators and motorized conveyors connecting rapid transit lines, existing streets, and shopping floors above. Abandoning the de-rigueur, meticulous models and ink drawings character-istic of Rudolph-inspired student presentations, Sellers presented a slapdash model and pencil drawings on brown butcher paper. This provocation did not come as a surprise to Rudolph, or the faculty.

Sellers's incipient countercultural rebelliousness had already begun to make its mark on the department. Just before his thesis term, Sellers had taken a year off to pursue a hands-on approach to architecture, building a house for his brother near Poughkeepsie, New York. In this he was assisted on weekends by Peter L. Gluck (b. 1939; B.A. 1962, M.Arch 1965), Etel Kramer, and M. J. Long, who would "cut classes most Thursdays and [go] to Poughkeepsie to bang in nails and pour concrete. It was great and, in those days, probably the only way for a girl to get on-site building experience."[202] Another Rudolph student, Peter J. Hoppner (b. 1937; M.Arch 1965), also sought hands-on experience in order to "escape from an architecture of shape making, believing that kind of architecture to be overly willful and excessively obtrusive."[203] Surprisingly, his Mill House at Mad River Glen, Vermont (1966), was one of the first East Coast buildings to show a direct influence from Rudolph's successor, Charles Moore. Hoppner's house was published in the November 1965 *Progressive Architecture* in a colorful, comic-strip-like spread, its shed-like forms, simple wood construction, and bold supergraphics (4.51) anticipating much of the work that would emerge from Yale in the late 1960s.[204] These hands-on experiments were to be of immense importance to the future of the department itself, setting the stage for the Building Project initiated in 1967 by Moore.

Although Sellers's approach seemed diametrically opposed to Rudolph's professionalism, Charles Brewer believed him to be "probably the epitome of the Rudolph philosophy"—a charismatic individualist, good at generating personal publicity, who "organized people and organized students." Sellers's views brought him into direct conflict with his fellow student Robert A. M. Stern, who espoused a decidedly more intellectual and historically oriented approach to architecture. Indeed, Vincent Scully has identified the two students as polar opposites. When Sellers returned to school from his year off working on his brother's house, much to his chagrin, he found that Stern had emerged as a leader within the school. Their disagreements led to a now-legendary encounter that ended up with Sellers hanging Stern upside-down from the bridge that joined the fifth-floor studio trays. Speaking with students in 2001, Sellers said, "I want to dispel some rumors about my relationship with Bob Stern. Some of them are true . . . the one where I dangled him over a bridge, that was true. I don't know why I did that, but he had everyone listening to him in our class. He was sitting on a stool and he had everyone standing around him and listening to him. I was playing touch football with George Buchanan and [Charles] Gwathmey. I walked in and it was irritating. I don't know why I did this, but I just dangled him there. Oh, well. I saved your life when I pulled you back."[205]

Sellers's approach was perhaps the first significant manifestation of the countercultural trend that would increasingly characterize the department, and most other university architecture programs, in the late 1960s. But Sellers was not a nihilist, as many other students would be. For Sellers, the experience of hands-on construction was life changing and allowed him "to get involved in research, politics, education and community development." For him, "the real content of the Yale experience wasn't form or design or structure, but being. Chermayeff, [sculpture professor Robert] Engman, Millard, Chris Argyris [professor of industrial administration], Paul Weiss, Kahn, Scully, [art history Ph.D. candidate William H.] Woody [Jr.], all talked about this."[206] Countercultural Sellers may have been, but he could also be an active participant in mainstream architectural discourse. Hearing Philip Johnson lecture, he was inspired to seek out the Glass House during a return trip to New Haven from Christmas break in Chicago. After driving their rented truck around

New Canaan aimlessly, Sellers and a friend finally found the house around six in the morning:

> Philip Johnson comes to the door in his bathrobe. I knew I had time for one question. I said, "I'm an architecture student at Yale. What do you think?" His answer was classic. He said, "Don't do it." He invited us in for breakfast and we spent the whole morning there. His basic argument was that the only reason you would ever do it is because you can't help it. You won't make money. It is difficult. You're going to do things nobody wants. You're going to do something no one wants to pay for. You are going to do something that gets half built and then they change it. So it is going to be very difficult to survive. The only way you can is if you can't help it. I [Johnson] couldn't help it, so I continued.[207]

Sellers couldn't help it either. While he was finishing his last year at Yale, he was simultaneously operating a small construction company that was building two houses, remodeling another ranch house, and building a tree house for some kids. After presenting his thesis in January 1965, with four months to kill before graduation, he decided to go to Vermont to build a house out of ice sprayed over weather balloons. "I arrived, there was no snow or ice, so I looked into the possibilities of doing some building in Vermont. This evolved into lengthy discussions on the virtues of vacation-house building versus going into the cities where the action was. The conclusion was that if continuing education after architecture school involved one in actual construction (which was my opinion) that eliminated the inner city."[208] After much discussion and economic forecasting, Sellers and his classmate William Reinecke (b. 1938; M.Arch 1965) selected Vermont's Mad River Valley as their field of action, and the project that became known as Prickly Mountain was under way. Described in *Progressive Architecture* as an "architectural blast off," Prickly Mountain was a dramatic break from staid academia and overweening modernism, spearheaded by two recent graduates, "lumbering mountaineers" who were disenchanted by the typical path to professionalism. Twenty years later, Vincent Scully would write:

> Sellers has lived all his life in the myth of the pioneer and the myth of the north. He was one of the first generation of the sixties to take off for Vermont and Maine—a leader among the "kids" who lit out for the territories, leaving urban civilization behind in order to become craftsmen-architects, fellers of forests, joiners, cabinetmakers, rustic

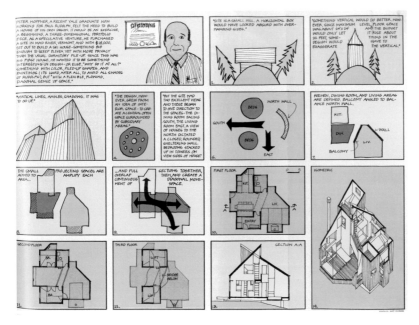

4.51 Peter J. Hoppner (M.Arch 1965), Mill House (1966), Mad River Glen, Vermont, as published in *Progressive Architecture* (November 1965).

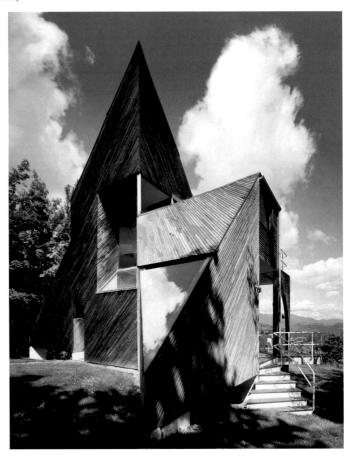

4.52 David Sellers (B.A. 1960, M.Arch 1965) and Bill Reinecke (M.Arch 1965), Sibley House (1967–72), Prickly Mountain, Vermont.

politicians and entrepreneurs. . . .

One of Sellers's motives in heading north after graduating from the Yale architectural school . . . was to get away from New York and what he regarded as its incestuous round of talk about architectural history and criticism. In this he was the archetypal opposite of his classmate Robert A. M. Stern. But they were alike in believing that there was something wrong with the International Style as it was being practiced at the time, and each of them set out to do something about it in his own way.

Sellers, however, carried one of the International Style's last and most dangerous myths along with him to the north. It was the myth of originality, and it reinforced Sellers's own mythology of the pioneer.[209]

Eventually, the "lumbering mountaineers" bought and parceled out some of the land to other like-minded rebels, including Louis Mackall (b. 1941; B.A. 1962, M.Arch 1968) and Sidney Magee (b. 1939), as well as "dozens of students from all over the country," who came up to design and build their own houses (4.52).[210] Inspired by a desire for independence, Sellers displayed a surprisingly keen grasp of business practice. "I'm not interested in economics," Sellers told *P/A*. "I *have* to know it." He continued, asserting what was at the time a particularly bold stance on the nature of architecture: "I think that the architects who don't know how things are paid for, and who won't know why things have got to make money, I think, are irresponsible to their field. Architecture has got to be a profit-making thing, there's no question about it. It's a commodity, it's a saleable item, and it's gotta be made to work for somebody, or else he's not going to spend dough on it. It seems to me the least responsibility you have . . . is to be at least economical and efficient."[211]

Students were excited to be able to build buildings right out of school— some even while they were still in it. "It was a very heady experience. But it soon disintegrated—both figuratively and literally." As Charles Brewer points out, many of the houses "rotted away after the first couple of years because they didn't know anything about waterproofing and that sort of thing." The houses were nonetheless "very imaginative and very exciting."[212] Sellers's reputation as a countercultural trendsetter would soon enough be cemented with a featured article in the March 1967 issue of *Life* magazine.[213]

With the passage of time, Sellers, who continues to practice in Vermont, has softened around the edges, as has his work. So much so that in an article about the design of a log-built Adirondack-style house and boathouse on Lake Winnipesaukee in New Hampshire, he made the surprising point that he was "just trying to create appropriate beauty."[214]

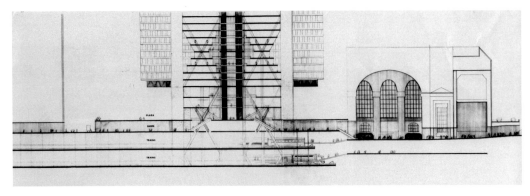

4.53   Peter Gluck (B.A. 1962, M.Arch 1965), A New Pan Am Building, section. Thesis project (1965).

4.54   Robert A. M. Stern's thesis project is presented at the last review Rudolph would attend before his retirement (1965). From left to right: Serge Chermayeff (cut off), Paul Rudolph, Robert Venturi, Henry Cobb, and King-lui Wu (standing).

4.55   Robert A. M. Stern (M.Arch 1965) presenting his thesis, A Design for a New Home for the Whitney Museum of American Art (1965).

At the end of May 1965, the last jury attended by Rudolph in his capacity
as department chair, marked not only the end of an administration but also
a changing of the guard in American architecture. The assembled faculty
and critics included the old guard—Chermayeff—and the new establishment—Rudolph, Cobb, and Scully—as well as the most controversial figure
to challenge them all—Robert Venturi. These figures represented the debate
between heroic form-making of the late International Style and the emerging
semiological architecture, as did the student work. Peter Gluck picked up on
the direction implied by Sellers's department store project with a redesign of
the already-constructed Pan Am Building (1963) in New York, in which Gluck
(4.53) revived the complex geometries of Kahn, especially as manifested in his
tower projects of the early 1950s.[215]

Robert Stern's thesis, also presented at this jury, proposed a new home
of the Whitney Museum of American Art on Seventy-Fifth Street and Madison
Avenue in New York (4.54, 4.55), then under construction. Following the same
program given to the Whitney's architects, Marcel Breuer and Hamilton
Smith (b. 1925; M.Arch 1950), it sought to combine the idea of the museum-as-
monument with that of museum-as-warehouse, proposing three street-facing
figural towers housing the permanent collection, and loft-like galleries for
changing exhibitions accommodated in a back building that was expandable
in two directions. Venturi's criticism was invaluable in shaping the design
and refining the argument. Bold strokes such as the single column in the loft
space and the oversized lettering along the diagonal "street" were the direct
result of his suggestions.

On September 21, 1964, it was publicly announced that Rudolph intended to
step down as chairman effective June 30, 1965, in order to, in his own words,
"devote my complete time to the practice of architecture."[216] The decision did
not come as a surprise to recently appointed university President (1963–77)
Kingman Brewster, Jr. (1919–1988; B.A. 1941), who told the *Yale Daily News* that
"For several years Paul Rudolph has let the administration know that the time
would come when the demands of professional practice would not permit him
to continue as chairman of architecture at Yale. Yale has been fortunate to hold
on to him this long and under his leadership architecture at Yale has gained
an enviable reputation. This professional accomplishment has done much to
make all of Yale a more creative and exciting place."[217] Rudolph's retirement
initiated a search for a successor that, given both his prominence as well as
that of the program he had developed, evoked wide interest among students,
alumni, educators, and professionals.

Even before the public announcement of his decision to step down, in response to Brewster's request, Rudolph, with characteristic candor, drew up an elaborately annotated list of possible successors, characterizing each according to their strengths as administrators or creative talents, identifying those whom he did not know personally and those he felt desirable but who would probably not be available.[218] In most respects, Rudolph's list was predictable: his former Harvard teacher Marcel Breuer, whom he did not think was likely to take the job; Breuer's former student Edward Larrabee Barnes—already known to Brewster for his work at Yale—whom Rudolph deemed both creative and a good administrator. Three other Harvard alumni of Rudolph's generation—Ulrich Franzen, John M. Johansen, both of whom had been successful at Yale as studio critics and jurors, and I. M. Pei—were also listed, although Rudolph questioned Johansen's administrative abilities and Pei's availability. Louis I. Kahn was listed for his creative ability but was deemed not likely to be available. G. Holmes Perkins, then dean at the University of Pennsylvania, and George A. Dudley, dean of the School of Architecture at Rensselaer Polytechnic Institute and chair of the University Council for Architecture, were commended for their administrative skills. Rudolph also included the relatively untested James Stirling, whom he praised as a creative person who could handle administration, and Colin (Sandy) St. John Wilson, whose administrative skill he admired but not his creativity. Finally, Rudolph's list included two more architects whom he did not know personally, but respected for their creativity: the Dutch architect Aldo van Eyck (1918–1999) and the Dane Jørn Utzon (1918–2008), both of whom had dramatically rising reputations.

From the moment it became known that Rudolph intended to leave Yale, architects and alumni also began to offer the president replacement recommendations and advice. August Heckscher (1913–1997; B.A. 1936), author and director of the Twentieth Century Fund, wrote to correct what might have been "a wrong impression" conveyed to the president at a recent meeting: "I said that Ed Barnes," with whom Heckscher had worked closely on the design of buildings at the St. Paul's School in Concord, New Hampshire, and in the design of his summer house at Seal Harbor, Maine, "is too much engaged in an active and growing practice to be thought of in terms of the post." But after reflection and "talking with one or two people . . . I have come to feel that Ed Barnes might very well make an ideal Dean. His architecture is of a type which could inspire young men and not merely encourage them to copy his own style. He is a born teacher (actually he began his career teaching in one of the New England schools [Barnes taught English, art, and architecture at

Milton Academy] after Harvard College) and seeing him in his office one feels he is a man whom younger workers delight to follow."[219] Following meetings with both Rudolph and Heckscher, Peter Blake conveyed to Brewster his "absolutely brilliant idea" for chairman: to wit, Reyner Banham, whom Blake described as "the Thinking Man's Sigfried Giedion."[220] Brewster declined Blake's suggestion, saying that "probably we want an active designer."[221]

On September 29, Associate Professor of Architectural Engineering Herman D. J. Spiegel (1924–2008; M.Eng 1955) wrote to Brewster to recommend Louis Kahn and Kevin Roche (b. 1922), but more significantly he outlined the characteristics he believed a leader of Yale's program should possess—characteristics that, ironically, did not describe Spiegel, who was subsequently to lead the program (1970–76) (see Chapter 6): "Get a great architect to head the school. One who will not come unless he gets the freedom that any good teacher insists on having. Discuss with this man what the format will be, and if within the stretches of reason—then let him perform. My feeling is that a program set up by lesser men will never get a great man to go along with it nor would it command the students' attention."[222]

Sibyl Moholy-Nagy, professor at Pratt Institute and an outspoken critic, wrote to Brewster, not to nominate a candidate, but to assert that Yale's emphasis on "architecture as the art of making buildings" must not be overlooked in the face of "the fate that has befallen architectural education during the last decade [when] our most renowned schools have either become so technology-minded that they are by now semi-competent training centers for civil engineers; or—most frequently—they have abdicated design under the pretext of 'environmental study' meaning city planning." For Moholy-Nagy, Yale "remained one of the few, if not the only school where a gifted student can sharpen his appetite and his skill for creative design through the exceptional coordination of the architectural approach, an unusually brilliant department of architectural history, and the open collaboration between architects and artists."

In the same letter, Moholy-Nagy put forward the qualities she believed a new chairman should have to properly guide Yale's challenging student body: "Since it is implicit in the Yale approach that the students are harder to handle than those docile nonentities seeking refuge under the anonymous cloak of technology or planning, a chairman should be young enough to understand the problems of this harassed group of form-seekers, and mature enough to give them a constructive place in society." Notably, she advised that "'big names' who are compelled by their acknowledged position to devote themselves exclusively to self-realization" not be considered. In concluding the letter, Moholy-Nagy expressed her "ardent hope that Yale will break with the sterile cliché of matching her own reputation with that of her appointees. Yale is old and famous enough to bestow prestige on an unacknowledged talent who brings to the difficult task of saving architecture the unjaded enthusiasm of being a teacher and an architect, and nothing else."[223]

Serge Chermayeff offered Brewster his views in the form of a somewhat pompous memo that began with his observation that "The Architectural Future is critically poised between two poles (complementary activities). First. The shaping of something new by creative, sensitive minds into wholes which transcend the sum total of parts and processes. Second. The Mastery of Technology and recognition of the pressures which increasingly influence directly and indirectly all form making, which may be measured and understood." For Chermayeff, a "crisis [existed] because Architecture still predominantly relies on the former: and overlooks the latter."

To address "the first requirement," Chermayeff argued for a "LEADER-DESIGNER" (Chermayeff's capitalization) who must be "CONTINUOUSLY PRESENT AND INVOLVED to attract and inspire an excellent faculty and the best students." To "fulfill the second requirement," what was needed was a "LEADER-ADMINISTRATOR, who can use all the resources of a great university to support, sustain and enrich the Architectural and City Planning Departments on a much broader front than the current practice." Chermayeff did "not believe that these two tasks can be performed any longer by a single individual," and was convinced that there must be a "creative-doer (chairman)" and a "creative-knower (dean)" to "sustain and stimulate each other, the school and the university." This argument carried with it an implicit suggestion that architecture be reconstituted as a school instead of a department, as well as a thinly veiled criticism of Rudolph's waning commitment to the department during the last semesters of his tenure, which was a source of considerable concern for many. Chermayeff couldn't resist taking a swipe at his art historian critics like Carroll Meeks and Vincent Scully: "It is my belief that we can no longer look to historian-scholarship-criticism as a source for these purposes. The evidence is before us: this leads to HISTORICISM (vide Pevsner's censure) [at the A&A dedication] or worse to the easy expediences [*sic*] of FASHION-MONGERING (culture mongering). The Technologists are equally dangerous: BLIND MEN who mistake the rational-obvious components for the whole of Architecture (vide Berkeley, Cal.)," by which he was presumably referring to the work of Sim Van der Ryn and others.[224]

In October, Carroll Meeks proposed additional names for consideration that "have been given to me by one of the brighter young critics [possibly

Herbert Newman, b. 1934; M.Arch 1959] who works with Ed Barnes": Romaldo Giurgola (b. 1920), then on the faculty of the University of Pennsylvania; Gunnar Birkerts (b. 1925), teaching at the University of Michigan; and Charles Moore (1925–1993), teaching at the University of California, Berkeley, whose name "has come up several times." In the same letter, Meeks echoed Rudolph's mention of Aldo van Eyck, James Stirling, and Sandy Wilson. All in all, he concluded, "The principal merit of this group of men is that they are almost the right age."[225] Indeed, it's clear that the age of the new chairman needed to be considered along with his philosophical and professional position—someone not too old but with experience; someone who was respected in the profession but wouldn't be overly distracted by practice.

A few days after Meeks's letter, with news of Rudolph's intended departure now public, four students representing the department's Student Council wrote to Brewster voicing their concerns and suggestions—Council President Donald Metz (b. 1940; B.A. 1962, M.Arch 1966); his predecessor, David Sellers; John I. Pearce (b. 1939; B.A. 1961, M.Arch 1965); and William Mason Smith III (b. 1939; M.Arch 1965). The students' letter reflected a sense that Rudolph had become distracted by his burgeoning practice, so that "it would be better to have . . . a man who was 'going places' in his own development, as opposed to an established architect who had 'arrived' professionally." The students went on to commend Rudolph's willingness to seek out "the opposing points of view in the critics and jurors that he has invited to the school," but at the same time, reflecting the Socratic pedagogy of Peter Millard, they expressed the concern "that there has been too much emphasis on performance in the department to the detriment of process." Anticipating the mantra that would prevail among students in very many schools during the late 1960s and early 1970s, they called into question "the jury system, [which] . . . places a premium on results."[226]

With so many people feeling invested in the selection process, Kingman Brewster's task was not an easy one. Yet by mid-November he had narrowed the field to three candidates: Robert Venturi, Romaldo Giurgola, and Charles Moore. Venturi, then junior faculty at Pennsylvania, had taught at Yale in 1961 as Rudolph's assistant in the Master's Class studio, but made little to no impression on the department, or for that matter, on Rudolph. But, in 1962, Helen Searing (b. 1933; Ph.D. 1971), then a graduate student in the Department of Art History working under Vincent Scully, had encouraged Robert Stern to visit Venturi in Philadelphia and to consider him for inclusion in his issue of *Perspecta*. Stern took the advice and returned with enthusiastic reports of Venturi's Vanna Venturi House (1964), which he had visited under construction, and excerpts from a text on the history and theory of architecture—sections of which he included in *Perspecta* 9/10, prior to its full publication in 1966 as *Complexity and Contradiction in Architecture.*[227] In large part as a result of Stern's enthusiasm, Venturi's name became increasingly familiar to students in the school.

Stern introduced Venturi's work to Scully, who had completely forgotten that he had published an unrealized Shingle-style house design by Venturi in a 1961 compilation of new talent.[228] Initially, Scully disdained Venturi's other work, but he soon came to celebrate it as an antidote to what he and others increasingly viewed as the overblown heroics of late modernism's New Brutalism and quickly became a strong advocate for the young architect. "I was against it [Venturi's work]," recalls Scully. "But as soon as I saw Guild House [Philadelphia, 1963], I thought it was terrific. . . . It really reminded me of Michelangelo's apses in St. Peter's. Everybody laughs when I say that, but it's like that. So Stern got me very excited about him and I told Kingman that he was the man."[229] At the same time, Venturi was becoming a popular figure among students, who, aware of his theory class at Penn, encouraged Rudolph to invite him to offer it at Yale, which he did in spring 1965, beginning an historically important relationship.

Scully continued to make a case for Venturi in further letters, formally addressing Brewster as "Mr. President" but casually signing them "Vince": "Forgive me for bombarding you yet once again with Venturiana, but I wanted to pass on to you what Kahn said about him the other day: 'Gentle outside, and always gentle in method; but inside relentless—relentless in will and in objective, which is nothing less than the understanding and control of architecture.'" Scully, reporting that Kahn would "much prefer" Venturi to Van Eyck, concluded this letter with his own assessment: "I am more than ever convinced that [Venturi] is our man and that, among all young architects now, he represents the best of the future. His work also brings new parts of the past to life." Referring to Searing's dissertation, he suggested that "his best graduate student," at work on "the splendid city buildings done in Amsterdam during the teens and twenties [but] unappreciated by historians and swamped by the International Style until now," finds herself "constantly forced to refer to Venturi's work."[230]

Others also endorsed Venturi, including the highly respected California-based architecture journalist Esther McCoy (1904–1989), who, in writing to Brewster, referred to her pleasure in discovering "how many of the young architects whose work I elect to write about received their training at Yale."[231] Thomas R. (Tim) Vreeland, Jr., wrote Brewster a long and thoughtful letter in support of Venturi, whom he had gotten to know on the faculty of the University of Pennsylvania.[232] So too did Robert M. Kliment (b. 1933; B.A. 1954, M.Arch 1959), also teaching at Penn.[233] Support was also expressed in writing by Marshall D. Meyers, a close associate of Kahn, and by A. J. (Jack) Diamond (b. 1932), a respected Canadian architect. These endorsements were offset by contravening arguments against Venturi. Said to be vicious in tone and, in part, to be filled with innuendo about presumed homosexuality, these were principally advanced by Chermayeff and Charles Brewer.

Encouraged by the persistence of Scully and others, Brewster had begun to narrow his focus onto Venturi, whom he invited to New Haven to discuss his "dreams and plans for the Yale campus." In his thank-you letter to Brewster, Venturi alluded to his host's "cryptic reflections on the Kennedy Library question," implying that Brewster may have promised to advance the young architect for consideration in connection with one of the era's most prestigious commissions.[234] Venturi's quiet manner seemed to resonate with Brewster, but his insistence that he be promised a building commission proved to be a deal breaker for the president. Although it is said by Scully and many others that Venturi declined the position, the truth is that it was Brewster who decided against him. In a letter dated February 19, 1965, Brewster notified Venturi of his decision, writing, "I have decided that at this stage of your work, thought, and development it would be a mistake to invite you to assume the chairmanship." Nonetheless, Brewster expressed the hope "that you will continue your participation as a visitor who has brought and can continue to bring enormously valuable insights to both our faculty and our students."[235]

As Venturi's candidacy faltered, Brewster, through an intermediary, requested information on the other two candidates from Robert A. M. Stern, whose *Perspecta* 9/10, which was at that point literally on the presses, featured considerable documentation of all three men being considered for the chairmanship. Stern recalls that "someone from the president's office came to see me. . . . And they asked me if I knew someone named 'Gara-gola' or something—they could never pronounce his name correctly. I said, 'Yes, I had that material,' so we went over to the press and got the section and it was sent over to the president's office." The process would be repeated again when Charles Moore became a likely candidate: "They came back to me again and said, 'I understand you have material on Moore.' These architects were largely unknown except for *Perspecta* 9/10."[236]

Romaldo Giurgola, whose potential was first mentioned in Meeks's initial letter to Brewster, became a strong contender for the position, which

Scully acknowledged in a February letter that compared him with Venturi.[237] For Scully, Giurgola's architecture was "more derivative and haphazard." Although stating that he "would not for a moment deprecate Giurgola's promise," Scully, echoing the four students who had written to Brewster, wrote that "it is a better time in Venturi's career to become chairman of a school, since Giurgola, somewhat older [Giurgola was five years older], is already very busy." In concluding his letter, Scully reiterated his belief in Venturi's character with a sentiment similar to Kahn's: "There is iron in there. When he gets onto an architectural subject he focuses like a samurai . . . it is Venturi I tend to see as the methodological innovator."[238]

Peter Millard, seemingly no supporter of Venturi, also failed to be impressed by Giurgola: "He would be an adequate chairman, but not an outstanding one. He is sensitive, intelligent, and articulate as well as being a very humane person. I fear he might be indifferent to the administrative aspects of the chairman's role and, through delegation of responsibility, could create a climate of conflict and suspicion. His thinking is concerned with the impact of new big things on our environment—as is the thinking of most architects today, especially the younger ones: I don't glean any unusual strength or depth of insight from his words or designs but feel they would serve the needs of a departmental figurehead."[239] Millard went on to suggest that Cesar Pelli (b. 1926), known to many faculty from his time as Saarinen's assistant in charge of Yale's Stiles and Morse Colleges, "might also be worth talking with. . . . He is not threatened by the idea of cooperative effort and has a deep understanding of the nature of learning." George Dudley proposed a compromise that addressed Millard's concerns by suggesting that Giurgola and his partner, Ehrman B. Mitchell (1924–2005), be hired together—the former responsible for the artistic direction of the program, the latter for administration.[240]

Getting down to business "at this late hour," Chermayeff listed three names for chair in order of preference: Stirling, Giurgola, and Polish-born architect Jerzy Sołtan (1913–2005), who had worked with Le Corbusier in Paris and was currently professor of architecture and urban design at Harvard; for dean, Chermayeff recommended Joseph Passonneau (1921–2011), who was then dean of the School of Architecture at Washington University in St. Louis. "Neither Wilson, nor [Charles] Moore are, in my opinion, in the same class in either category."[241]

Brewster offered Giurgola the chairmanship. But his offer was not accepted. Instead, Giurgola assumed the chairmanship of the Department of Architecture at Columbia University, citing the location as an important consideration in his decision; while at Columbia he would maintain his office principally in Philadelphia while opening a second office in New York—an arrangement that would satisfy his wife's preference for living in New York over either Philadelphia or New Haven.[242]

Enter Charles Moore, chairman of the Architecture Department in the College of Environmental Design at the University of California, Berkeley, whose name was first suggested to Brewster by Edward Larrabee Barnes. Determined to appoint a new chairman before Rudolph's departure, Brewster pursued Moore vigorously. Moore seemed to Brewster to be a sort of antithesis to Rudolph. In a waspish mood, Moore later recalled that "Kingman was not a patron of the arts or of architects. . . . He is not the sort who tolerates well what he takes to be artistic nonsense, so that the 'Rudolph hysteria' was anathema to him, especially when he was making these little numbers on campus that couldn't be swept or washed. It made him angry."[243] Putting aside Brewster's presumably negative feelings for Rudolph's architecture and, more than likely, his personality, the president may have been attracted to Moore as a candidate whose teaching experience, combined with his youthful promise, was comparable to Rudolph's when he was first appointed to Yale in 1957, promising that the Brewster presidency would make its own distinct mark on campus architecture and architecture education.

5
Architecture or Revolution? 1965–1971

"To the architect falls the satisfaction of seeing the ideas and attitudes of his society take physical form, to become the container for man's activities and the imprint of his society and himself on the face of the earth. In today's period of explosive growth this is a more challenging activity than ever before. Ordering the earth becomes in some respects more difficult and more exciting than arriving at the moon. Providing for the physical needs of more and more people without destroying the individual's relation to the land, maintaining his important sense of having some distinguishable place in the world. . . . The architect, who may once have seen himself standing slightly apart from society, is now wrapped up in some of its central problems."

Bulletin of Yale University, School of Art and Architecture, 1966–67

5.1   Charles Moore, Sea Ranch (1965), California.

5.2   Charles Moore (ca. 1970).

On May 14, 1965, Moore's appointment as chairman of the Department of Architecture, effective July 1, was announced to the public in a press release detailing his biography and achievements, particularly his environmentally sensitive work at Sea Ranch (5.1), a development of vacation houses then under construction in northern California, and his recent article, "You Have to Pay for the Public Life," which had been featured in *Perspecta* 9/10—the very issue that, in some small way, helped him land the job.[1] Moore arrived in New Haven to take charge of the department during the summer. It was a pivotal moment when, as Eve Blau has written, "the critique of modernism shifted from activist challenges to established codes of practice, to cultural radicalism and a focus on representation and cultural signs (images, information, messages), as generators of new forms of society, culture, experience, and subjectivity."[2] For the next five years, in the tumultuous period of American history typically referred to as "the Sixties," the Department of Architecture was transformed, and Moore with it. In the portrait photograph that accompanied the *New York Times* article announcing his appointment, the balding Moore, in thick spectacles, looked more like a conservative engineer than one of the most controversial architects and educators of the decade. Soon enough, though, under the influence of his students and the trends of the times, Moore would adopt muttonchop whiskers that gave him the air of an avant-garde iconoclast (5.2). His academic and professional work combined with his personality to constitute a bright point of optimism—albeit occasionally tinged with biting cynicism. During an era that marked a seismic shift in the American cultural and political landscape, especially among university students, Kingman Brewster's leadership kept Yale remarkably on course, while Moore, who led the architecture program until 1970—first as chairman of the Department of Architecture and then, briefly, as dean of a newly constituted School of Architecture—became the most visible architect-educator in the country.

Charles Willard Moore (1925–1993) was born in Benton Harbor, Michigan. He was an exceptionally bright child with a photographic memory whose talent and natural curiosity were nurtured from an early age by his mother. At the age of sixteen he enrolled in the five-year architecture program at the University of Michigan, where he studied under Roger Bailey, a former Yale instructor (1936–37), whom Moore considered to be a "huge influence."[3] After earning his bachelor of architecture from Michigan in 1947, Moore went to San Francisco, a city that he found "fascinating and challenging," where he interned with several firms, including the offices of Mario Corbett, Joseph Allen Stein, and Clark & Beuttler. By the time of his twenty-third birthday, Moore was a licensed architect. During 1949–50, he traveled through Europe and North Africa on a George Booth Traveling Fellowship from Michigan, using his time to write, take photographs, paint watercolors, and most notably make short films on urban spaces. Upon returning to the States, he was invited to teach at the University of Utah, where his mentor, Bailey, was establishing a new architecture program. Moore taught at Utah for two years before he was drafted into the Army, serving in Korea from 1952 to 1954. After his military service, he decided to continue his education at Princeton with help from the G. I. Bill. Somewhat ironically, given the character of his tenure at Yale, Moore wanted to go to graduate school to pursue a career in teaching because architecture schools "needed, it seemed to me, some discipline, something to hold them together, and I thought that would more properly be architectural history than design as I saw it being taught."[4]

At Princeton, Moore earned his master of fine arts degree in 1956, and his Ph.D. in 1957, after which he stayed on as a postdoctorate fellow and then assistant professor. During this time, he met Paul Rudolph: "I remember the first year I was there, there was a three-way discussion among Paul Rudolph, who was famous, and Bucky Fuller, who was famous, and Lou Kahn, whom I'd never heard of." Rudolph was teaching with Hugh Hardy (b. 1932). Moore remembers struggling through awkward conversations with Rudolph: "He was a hero for that period and would try to say things to be nice, and they would always come out just wrong . . . he would try to say things to be gracious and they would always be just insulting."[5] Meanwhile, Kahn, who came to Princeton to substitute for the school's senior design instructor, Jean Labatut (1899–1986), then on sabbatical leave, would say things to be wise and they would always sound esoteric. During his last year at Princeton, Moore served as Kahn's assistant and found himself often tasked with interpreting the koan-like pronouncements the master offered his students as criticisms. "There were lots and lots of messages," Moore says of Kahn's teaching, "all very complex and intertwined, but I thought the major one was the enormous and thrilling importance of doing things right."[6] The experience would serve Moore well. In the late 1960s, when Kahn was undertaking the ill-fated Church Street Housing Project in New Haven, Moore would once again take on the role of interpreter as he presented Kahn's plans to New Haven's largely hostile and mystified low-income communities. While Moore wanted to be a teacher and academic, toward the end of his life, he claimed that he "didn't have any specific ambitions about being the head of [an architecture school]" but did see himself "shaping architectural education."[7] Though tempted to stay at Princeton to teach and work with Kahn, Moore was also anxious to get back to the Bay Area, and in 1958 accepted an invitation from the University of California at

Berkeley, where he was appointed associate professor, and, in 1962, would become chairman of the Architecture Department.

Three years later, Moore was lured away from Berkeley by Kingman Brewster. When asked why he agreed to what was, in effect, a lateral career move, giving up one chairmanship for another, Moore replied, "In six years at Cal, I've only met [university President] Clark Kerr in a receiving line. Dr. Brewster . . . has been on the phone to me every day, asking what he can do."[8] Ironically, another factor in Moore's decision to leave Berkeley was the very same sort of gossip that surrounded Rudolph and, unjustly, Robert Venturi, whose possible nomination for the position of chairman was met with vicious attacks and rumors started by faculty who were opposed to his appointment. At Berkeley, despite enjoying the support of the dean, Moore was never promoted to full professor, and when he demanded to know the reasons why he had not been promoted despite chairing the department, Moore was informed that "there were rumors around that he was gay."[9] Adding injury to insult, the university had previously assured Moore that they would select his firm, Moore Lyndon Turnbull Whitaker (MLTW), to design their new art museum—a project that Moore said would have kept him in the Bay Area—but instead decided to hold a national competition. Moore's frustration with UC Berkeley is perhaps best reflected in his pronouncement that "the top administration were all fools. At Berkeley, one set of faculty runs the university, and the others get Nobel Prizes. At Yale the same people do both."[10]

Moore was flattered by the attention he received from Yale; Brewster was a "supercharmer." Moore was particularly impressed by the fact that "if you have an important professorial role at Yale," it's assumed "that you must be well educated and the only possibility of being well educated is to have gone to Yale, and so they give you a Master's degree, Honorary, to make you a Yalie."[11] The decision for Moore to accept Brewster's offer also seemed like good business. Moore was encouraged to take the position by Princeton-trained William Turnbull (1935–1997), one of his partners at MLTW, who believed that an administrative position at a prominent Ivy League school would improve the firm's reputation and attract more work. "I was having dinner at my sister Mimi's with Bill Turnbull," Moore told his biographer, David Littlejohn, "and the phone call comes from a Mr. Brewster in San Francisco—the only Brewster I could think of was the President of Yale—and so he said he would like to see me about the chairmanship. And I expected Mimi and Bill to say, 'You don't want to do that! That's terrible! That dirty old place, all that sludge?' But no, that's not what they said at all. 'What a wonderful idea. Go see Kingman! Whoopee! How exciting!'"[12]

William Turnbull confirmed Moore's recollection of the events: "Basically Mimi and I sat down that night at the dinner table and said, 'Hey, look. Look at Rudolph coming out of Florida. And look where he was,'" referring to what seemed a transformation in scope and scale of Rudolph's practice after coming to Yale, despite the fact that Rudolph's first large projects, the Mary Cooper Jewett Arts Center at Wellesley College completed in 1958 and the Blue Cross/Blue Shield office building in Boston, completed in 1960, were well under way before his arrival in New Haven. "'And then,'" Moore recalls Turnbull saying, "'look at what we're doing now. We've had a couple of good buildings, but we're not going anywhere, we're still doing houses. Economically, it's to your advantage to go; professionally it's to your advantage to go. It's the only way to get your name *known* by the New York crowd. Do it, Chuck.'"[13] Turnbull acknowledged that Moore's treatment by the Berkeley faculty played a part in his decision, but ambition for his career was the primary reason. "It was that rational, that cool. It's about the one time I can remember doing any real career strategy. It was a gamble. It was, 'Let's roll the dice for the Big Time!'"[14] The gamble would pay off. After only a few years in New Haven, Moore was, as Littlejohn wrote, "established as a 'celebrity architect.'"[15]

Moore settled into his new role in time for the beginning of the fall semester, quickly establishing a professional office in New Haven and commencing the dramatic renovation of a Greek Revival cottage at the edge of the campus to serve as his residence (5.3).[16] In what would become his typical policy, Moore staffed his office with students and recent graduates. According to Mark Simon (b. 1946; M.Arch 1972), this practice reflected his "fear of conflict"—younger architects weren't going to give him as much grief as established architects. With younger architects he "could avoid conflict and they could be more his acolytes."[17] The peripatetic Moore also retained an office in Berkeley, inaugurating what would become a network of satellite offices orbiting around himself, offices that would eventually evolve into independent entities.[18]

In 1965 New Haven, the turbulence of the Sixties was merely incipient, but what Joan Ockman has described as the "postwar paradigm of the multiuniversity" would soon trigger a major backlash that would shake "architectural education to its foundations" as "architecture students joined their peers throughout the university in protesting against all forms of traditionalism and elitism represented by the establishment, including modernism itself, now received as a false messenger of democratic ideals and social reform."[19] Inheriting a program that, under Rudolph, was one of the most admired by the profession, and perhaps the most closely watched, many wondered, what would Moore do? How would the department change with a chairman who was by all accounts Rudolph's polar opposite? At the beginning, Moore moved cautiously. His first year as chairman was not, "nor was it meant to be," he later acknowledged, "a year of dramatic change." However, careful readers of the architectural section of the school's annual *Bulletin* would almost immediately notice a dramatic shift of emphasis in the school's mission statement, from one of enlightened pragmatism under Rudolph to something decidedly more humanist and philosophical in its view.

In his first report to the university, written in June 1966, after one year's service, Moore backed up this philosophical shift, in which he seemed to dismiss his predecessor's emphasis on high-wire professionalism by alluding to the changes that he would soon implement, such as de-emphasizing the department's traditional "strong tie with the most exciting architectural developments in the New York Metropolitan area," where the profession was "addicted to glamour."[20] Moore would later recall that the "New York offices would come recruiting at Yale for people getting their Master's degrees and I would say, 'Don't you go to Pratt and to Cooper Union and schools around New York?' and they would say, 'We get our draughtsmen from there; we come to Yale for our future partners.'"[21] But Moore wanted something else for the program. Claiming to be "anxious" to see that the department maintained its sterling reputation, he began to take the first steps toward remaking the program into what he thought it should be: "a center for academic and intellectual development on the frontiers of a profession which still seems peculiarly vague about where its frontiers are."[22] Moore, too, seemed "peculiarly vague" about his plans for the school, tactically adopting a laissez-faire administrative style in response to Yale's buttoned-up culture: "I made no attempt to adopt the life-and-death impersonal style of my predecessors," he recalled in the 1980s. "People thought I was afraid to hold faculty meetings. But I made a point of being smarter than I seemed."[23]

Moore's intuitive style of administration seemed, on the whole, to make remarkably good sense as Yale, like most universities, struggled to adapt to an increasingly rebellious era. Against the backdrop of escalation in protests over the Vietnam War and social inequities at home, graduate students in the Drama and Music schools, and especially the School of Art and Architecture, were becoming increasingly vocal about the inadequate financial support for their programs and especially for the glaring lack of financial aid. However, after a year of apparent drift when Moore seemed to accomplish little, students became concerned, and a group met with him to discuss "various aspects

5.3 Charles Moore, New Haven Residence (1966).

5.4 Raymond Kaskey (M.E.D. 1969), *Portlandia* (1985). Portland, Oregon.

of the school's operation." In a two-page, single-spaced typed memo titled "Information and Agitation," the students asked Moore to explain his plans and what they considered to be the "current administrative centralization, or apparent centralization" within the chairman's office. They also demanded that he articulate the "philosophy behind the selection of new faculty members and visiting critics." Overall, the memo suggested that students were concerned that the department was adrift, while faculty and—worse, still—their new chairman weren't taking their responsibilities seriously enough.[24] Students wouldn't have to wait much longer to see dramatic change.

Moore was better prepared to meet the new era than many other architects and architectural educators, having experienced the challenges of the times on the faculty at Berkeley, where the Free Speech Movement began disrupting campus life in 1963.[25] Despite his seemingly "laid-back" manner—or perhaps *because* of it—Moore at first appeared to have successfully addressed student concerns about governance, the war in Vietnam, and the plight of the poor and racial minorities, while also holding on to a measure of studio discipline. As Yale students became increasingly outspoken about elitism, Moore opened the program up to the immediate world outside the studio, encouraging them "to spend a great deal of their time . . . exploring New Haven—its railway and dock yards, urban neighborhoods, factories and industrial edges—as well as the vernacular and monumental public architecture of towns and cities throughout New England, and farther afield. Looking, sketching, painting, photographing, filming, reading widely and making three-dimensional objects of all kinds were considered far more important for the education of the architect than developing expertise in drafting."[26] Social issues were brought to the forefront when Moore initiated the Building Project in 1967, thereby making Yale the only architecture school to actively address the problems of life in the nation's less-advantaged areas with a specific program of design and construction.

In 1967, Moore introduced significant curricular reform when he shortened the four-year first professional program to three and a half years (shortened to three in 1973), leading to a master of architecture degree for those students entering with a nonprofessional bachelor of arts degree.[27] This degree change, which was in keeping with similar moves at peer institutions, was done to make it clear that Yale's was a graduate-level professional program. Dean Danes and Moore situated the change in relation to evolving professional education in the field: "There is every reason to make the change to put our graduates from a seven-and-a-half year curriculum into an appropriate competitive position for teaching and other academic opportunities, as well as to prepare the way for their participation in academic graduate level work which is on the threshold of being developed in our field." Acknowledging that the change "could work against the interests of those students from the last few years who have received the B.Arch for their long Yale careers," they insisted that such "does not seem adequate reason for perpetuating an anomalous situation."[28] A compromise was eventually reached that made it possible for graduates with the proper credentials to apply for a retroactive upgrade from bachelor of architecture to a master of architecture.

Moore claimed that his restructuring of the degree programs was in keeping with the times and with the changing concerns of the profession: "Students and faculty have now become involved to an unprecedented extent with the problems of society—the social issues and human use of the environment as a whole rather than the shape of the objects within it." With the idea of "relevance" becoming a critical issue for students of the 1960s, Moore saw the writing on the wall: "Current design solutions are expected to come at least partly from interaction with the user, rather than from the imposition of an architect's formal preconceptions."[29] He was also concerned about "the character and quality of our one-year M.Arch degree program currently in place," which he saw as little more than an architectural finishing school. Instead, as his first important act, he proposed a two-year, advanced post-professional program, arguing that "the need for real graduate programs at least two years in length and using the academic resources of the University . . . is now acute."[30] The proposed program, leading to a nonprofessional degree, the master of environmental design (M.E.D.), would be "based specifically in design and in aspects of the complex urban environment which would allow for really advanced work at the graduate level in the central problems architects face today."[31]

On January 27, 1967, the Educational Policy Committee of the Yale Corporation approved the decision to initiate a two-year degree program leading to the master of environmental design, a degree that would first be awarded in 1969.[32] The new program, which began accepting students in fall 1967, was intended for architects as well as for others interested in the field and would involve "substantial independent work," with closer ties to other disciplines—"especially to graduate work in Planning," and, Moore hoped, would eventually lead to the establishment of a Ph.D. program. With great prescience, Moore observed that though "the Ph.D. is presently unimportant in schools of architecture . . . with a growing concern for the development of theory, I expect that to change greatly in five years."

Moore hoped the master of environmental design program would attract students who "will do advanced graduate work in areas of their individual interest—the new degree focuses on architecture in relation to other arts, to the sciences, and applied sciences, and on problems of planning and design."[33] But what did that actually mean? Donald Watson (b. 1937; B.A. 1959, M.Arch 1962, M.E.D. 1969), who had just returned from a stint in Africa with the Peace Corps, had been awarded a $25,000 research fellowship and was invited by Moore to do his research at Yale as a member of the first M.E.D. class. Watson recalls the program's beginnings as well-intentioned but vague, with Moore describing the curriculum as "we're gonna do interiors, we're gonna do buildings, we're gonna do landscapes, and we're gonna do cities."[34] Besides Watson, the first M.E.D. students included applicants who had been accepted into the now-terminated, one-year-long, post-professional master of architecture program, and were offered the choice of enrolling in the new three-and-a-half-year master of architecture program or the two-year M.E.D. program. Those choosing to be part of the first M.E.D. cohort included some who would go on to significant careers in practice: Steven Izenour (1940–2001; M.E.D. 1969), longtime partner with Robert Venturi and Denise Scott Brown; urbanist Douglas Southworth (b. 1944; M.E.D. 1969); and Australian architect Peter Corrigan (b. 1941; M.E.D. 1969). It also included sculptor Raymond J. Kaskey (b. 1943; M.E.D. 1969), perhaps best known for his work with Michael Graves on the *Portlandia* statue (5.4), and with Friedrich St. Florian on the National World War II Memorial in Washington D.C.[35]; arts administrator Richard Solomon (1943–2005; M.E.D. 1969); and digital media guru and academic William J. Mitchell (1944–2010; M.E.D. 1969). Amidst the growing clamor on the part of students for independence, the program seemed ideal, especially given that, as Watson has stated, "Charles had no program for them" and promptly handed the baton to Felix Drury (1928–2009), newly appointed, who was asked to figure out "what these people want." As Watson says, "That was Charles."[36] In 1970, Watson was put in charge of the M.E.D. program and formally made director in 1975—a position he held until 1990, when he became dean of the School of Architecture at the Rensselaer Polytechnic Institute. Taking the "master of environmental design" program at face value, Watson's own career focused on sustainable design—particularly the field of solar design.

Felix Drury, who had been teaching at the Carnegie Institute of Technology (renamed Carnegie Mellon University in 1967) before coming to Yale, was one of Moore's first faculty hires. In his first term at Yale (fall 1965), Drury was a visiting critic in the first year, and in the spring semester (1966) was a visiting critic in the third year. Moore had initially encountered Drury at Princeton, where Drury "had master-minded" Moore's Ph.D.[37] Initially Drury proved a hit with Yale students and offered compelling design problems. In fall 1967, early on in Drury's tenure as professor adjunct, he asked his third-year studio to design an addition to the Art and Architecture Building—the first of many studios to be devoted to the "problem" of Rudolph's building. Soon after, however, Drury began to lose favor with students. In an anonymous, undated survey taken in 1967 or 1968, a few students described Drury as a good critic when he applied himself, but most found him evasive, irresponsible, selfish, and usually ambivalent or even vindictive toward his students.[38] Turner Brooks (b. 1943; B.A. 1965, M.Arch 1970) remembers Drury as a "cool" guy in a bomber jacket who, in contrast to Moore's occasionally too-kind guidance, was a harsh but insightful critic: "We all loved him. He was tough and we felt we needed that. . . . Then he came back the next year to give a studio in second year. He wasn't there. The class unraveled and it was a terrible thing. Very sad."[39] Later, Moore reflected on Drury's fall from grace: "That first class of ours . . . they adored Felix. But when the Yale revolution started, student hatred seemed to pour in on him rather than me."[40] At one point, student dissidents interrupted a class taught by Drury and carried him out of the classroom, announcing that "the course has been liberated."[41] The ill will toward Drury followed him to the M.E.D. program, where, although he was ostensibly in charge, he failed to inspire students, many of whom saw his interests as limited to the design of education environments and the use of new building materials. Watson remembers that "two or three or four of the class followed Felix, but most of them said 'no way.'" With Drury unable to supply the leadership the new M.E.D. program needed, Moore turned to Watson and said, as Watson recalls, "'Watson, you're a writer and a researcher. You must know something about research. They gave you this research thing.' So then Charles gave me the baton and said, 'Watson, figure out what to do.'"[42]

William J. Mitchell would become in many ways the best-known and most influential member of the first M.E.D. class. Trained in architecture in his native Australia before coming to Yale, Mitchell would go on from the M.E.D. program to a significant career as a theorist, writer, and educator specializing in digital media. Mitchell was dean of MIT's School of Architecture and Planning from 1992 to 2003, and at the time of his death, head of the Smart Cities group at the MIT Media Lab.[43] For Mitchell, the unrest of the Sixties was not "comfortable or reassuring." He had been attracted to the M.E.D. program because Yale, under Moore, "simply seemed the liveliest, most intellectually exciting place to be—clearly the hot spot for engagement of the issues and debate that were beginning to shake the certainties and platitudes of the architectural world we knew."[44] Mitchell recalled his arrival in New Haven in 1967, "after the ensuing Summer of Love had sourly succumbed to the poison of Vietnam." His first encounter with Moore was at the Duchess Diner, "a particularly squalid eatery, even by New Haven's low standards," where the new chairman was "tucking into a large breakfast, by himself, among the pimps, hookers, and graduate students. . . . If ever there was a lonely hearts club band, the breakfast crowd at the Duchess was it."[45]

Mitchell flourished under the M.E.D. program's lack of a standardized curriculum, which gave students—and still gives students—a license to pursue whatever classes and engage whatever faculty they choose throughout the university:

> Some ended [up] pounding the Las Vegas Strip with Bob Venturi and Denise Scott Brown. Others argued (and argued!) about urban design with Serge Chermayeff. Most of us went to Scully's great theatrical lectures in the Law School auditorium. We showed up when Lou Kahn and Bucky Fuller spoke. We hacked computers. We took courses in forestry, game theory, theatre design, polymer chemistry, whatever. We built weird things out of improbable materials. We drew and talked endlessly and drank imprudent quantities of cheap red wine. We each did what we knew we needed to do, and it changed our lives.
>
> Charles Moore was wise enough and courageous enough just to create a space for all this to happen. God knows there must have been pressure to clean it up and get it organized, but he never seemed very much interested in that. He was interested in our intellectual projects though, and from time to time would engage them with the quick, vivid, and learned mind that he so carefully hid behind a hesitantly amicable manner. And he showed us the wit, generosity, and genuine respect for the passions and convictions of others that made his architecture such a wonder.[46]

Another member of the first M.E.D. class was Richard Solomon, who, though trained as an architect, would go on to a career in arts administration, serving as head of the Graham Foundation for Advanced Studies in the Fine Arts from 1993 until his death in 2005. In 1970, Solomon characterized the M.E.D. program as "The Perfect Mess" in *Novum Organum,* a politically charged, countercultural newsprint broadside published by a group of art and architecture students that made its debut on November 19, 1968. Solomon portrayed the M.E.D. program as "Classical Anarchy, that is, a condition devoid of non-personalized structuring power," concluding his essay with the observation that it had "as much validity as any other description of M.E.D. structure, that is, none."[47]

The freedom granted the M.E.D. students to pursue whatever they wanted yielded an incredibly diverse collection of work. In many ways, Peter Corrigan took the most advantage of the independent, interdisciplinary nature of the new program, so much so that by his own admission he never quite fit in; Corrigan's biographer, Conrad Hamann, reports that the faculty was "puzzled" and "discomfited" by Corrigan's seemingly "out-of-step" interests and argumentative, transgressive behavior: "He took 'wrong positions' in what you'd describe as 'refined situations.' He annoyed Louis Kahn by asking if Kahn ever doubted his own decisions. He annoyed Charles Moore by observing marked affinities between Moore's completed work and the more successful student designs." He had "uneven" relationships with Robert Venturi and Denise Scott Brown, who may have been "too close" to his own nuanced beliefs. Hamann notes: "He wrote a ferocious letter to Denise Scott Brown on one occasion, and when I reminded Robert Venturi of the expatriate Australian he clapped a hand to his head and exclaimed, 'Oh God! Corrigan!'"[48] While still a student, Corrigan worked for the New Haven Redevelopment Agency as a senior planner. The agency's unpopular plan for the Hill neighborhood had led to the city's first race riot in August 1967. As the agency sought to rethink plans for the Hill, Corrigan worked with Kahn, who was preparing designs for a new high school and community center.[49] Corrigan remembers him as "charming, very overcommitted, exhausted, and, in some ways, seemingly carrying American architecture's considerable moral burden."[50]

M.E.D. students worked together to organize a lecture series that introduced ideas from other disciplines they deemed applicable to design, inviting three psychologists, a computer scientist, two architects, the Buckminster Fuller acolyte John McHale, as well as Lionel March, a mathematician from the University of Cambridge, and Buckminster Fuller himself, who cut short a visit in October 1968 because of a disagreement over compensation but returned in January 1969 as a visiting professor.[51] Though their areas of study were diverse, many M.E.D. students shared an interest in teaching. A 1971 report on the program noted that over a quarter of the graduates of the first two M.E.D. classes quickly established themselves as full-time faculty in architecture departments across the country. This interest was evident even in M.E.D. student work, such as Sam Davis's (b. 1946; M.E.D. 1971) thesis, "Study on Architectural Education." Davis, who joined the faculty at UC Berkeley soon after graduating, went on to start a practice focusing on affordable housing.[52]

Given the initial loose structure of the program, many M.E.D. students invented their own projects. One student project was a Plastics Media workshop established and led by John G. Marshall (1932–2009; M.E.D. 1970), with support from various companies, providing training and facilities for the use of plastics for students in architecture and many other departments. Other early M.E.D. projects included designs for inner-city neighborhoods, two schools, and low-income housing, as well as mathematical models for design procedure, and the political implications of architecture and urban design. Ted Landsmark's (b. 1946; M.E.D. 1973, J.D. 1973) thesis, "Design of Correctional Facilities," was indicative of the students' growing social conscience and Landsmark's own concern about the relationship between environment and identity, which was formed during his childhood growing up in public housing in Harlem. But Landsmark had reservations about his future in architecture, a profession that had very few black practitioners, and pursued a law degree simultaneously with his M.E.D. degree. After graduation, he briefly worked in a large law office in Boston before deciding he could do more good as a lawyer for the Contractors' Association. It was in this capacity that in 1976, on his way to a meeting at City Hall, Landsmark was attacked by a group of antibusing protesters. The violent scene of racial hatred was captured in Stanley Forman's Pulitzer Prize–winning photograph, *The Soiling of Old Glory*. The incident only further inspired Landsmark to help minorities succeed in Boston. He eventually entered into politics, working in the mayor's office for nearly a decade as director of Jobs and Community Services and director of the Safe Neighborhoods Project, before returning to architecture and planning. Since 1997, he has served as the president and CEO of Boston Architectural College.[53]

In 1971, to help define its role in the school, then-dean Herman Spiegel appointed an M.E.D. Committee—including Professor Walter DeSalles Harris, Jr. (1924–2007), Assistant Professor of Design Methods Research Robert Frew (b. 1945), and Donald Watson—who worked together to strengthen the program, reorganizing it as a formal two-year research program. Under Watson, the program emerged as a vehicle for research by architects and related professionals, with requirements that every thesis include the word "architecture" in addition to another idea. According to Watson: "That 'something else' could be anything that the university could support. We had architecture and divinity, architecture and computers, architecture and forestry, whatever. And then, if you were interested in forestry, I would introduce you to someone in forestry who could support your topic. And it became, in my mind, one of the first premier independent study programs in any Ivy League School."[54] Gradually, as the emphasis of the M.E.D. program became more

Architecture or Revolution?

257

research-oriented, it drew fewer of its candidates from the professional world of architecture and more from the humanities, such as Blair Kamin (b. 1957; M.E.D. 1984), from Amherst College, who would go on to become the Pulitzer Prize–winning architecture critic of the *Chicago Tribune*.[55] Nonetheless, architects continued to participate. Larry Wayne Richards (b. 1944; M.Arch 1975), who came to Yale after undergraduate studies in architecture at Miami University in Ohio, was attracted by the "wonderful kind of freedom and flexibility" it afforded him. Richards, who would go on to be dean (1997–2004) of the John H. Daniels Faculty of Architecture, Landscape, and Design at the University of Toronto's School of Architecture, did "a third of his studies in architecture, a third in art history, and a third in art." However, because of his broad interests, he found himself to be "much closer to the M.E.D. students because they were generally more mature, more experienced, more experimental," as compared to the master of architecture students, whom he saw as "very conservative." For the most part, Richards sought out "people and opportunities beyond the School of Architecture. The concrete castle was a very internalized world."[56]

In an undated memo written around 1999, Watson estimated that of all the M.E.D. graduates, 50 percent were in practice, 24 percent in academia, and 13 percent serving as deans or program chairs.[57] The program also appealed to international architects such as Eeva-Liisa Pelkonen (b. 1962; M.E.D. 1994), who would develop her thesis on postwar Austrian avant-garde architecture into a book.[58] Pelkonen, now faculty, went on to receive a Ph.D. in architecture from Columbia and would become director of M.E.D. Studies in 2000, reworking its program to emphasize history, theory, and criticism of the built environment.

William Mitchell began his interest in exploring and charting advanced techniques in digital media at Yale despite the fact that most of the faculty, at least according to Dean Danes, tended to regard the computer as little more than a tool for "analyzing, diagnosing, and processing . . . information."[59] However, the decision to ask Murray Milne (b. 1936)—a "systems guy" who had studied mechanical and industrial engineering at the University of Michigan before getting his master of architecture at the University of California, Berkeley—to join the faculty in 1966 (where he would remain until 1969) indicates Moore's growing sense that the computer had an increasingly important role to play in design. Prior to his Yale appointment, Milne was a design engineer for General Motors and a research engineer for North American Aviation, where he worked on the Apollo command and service module. While some students thought building systems and computers were interesting, Milne had a hard time translating his research-based abstract concepts into real-world architectural problems. He was, as Barton Phelps (b. 1946; M.Arch 1972) says, "a guy who struck people the wrong way so powerfully and so quickly that we just stopped going to his class."[60] John Jacobson actually led the revolt. "We were so disgusted with this class and we did not want to take it with this guy that we all decided to not register for the class. We wanted to let them know that this guy was horrible. . . . So the school got the message and got another teacher to come in and teach us. Milne was not around the following year."[61] The passive protest that removed Milne from the school was an early indication of students' desire to have more control over their education.

While the computer was recognized as a critical tool, no one was quite sure how to use it. The first significant sign that Yale might assume a role in digital design innovation came on April 18–20, 1968, when, as many were later surprised to learn, the department hosted the first-ever "Conference on Computer Graphics and Architecture," an event that took place only a few years after the first working computer-aided design system had been demonstrated at MIT's Lincoln Laboratory by Ivan E. Sutherland.[62] Following a seminal meeting on architecture and computers at the Boston Architectural Center—which had been attended by Walter Gropius, Serge Chermayeff, the structural engineer William LeMessurier, and Marvin Minsky, founder of MIT's artificial intelligence lab—Yale's symposium, to a considerable extent shaped by William Mitchell, was convened by Assistant Professor of Architectural Engineering Luis Summers (b. 1939), who, like Milne, had joined the faculty at Moore's invitation in 1966.[63] The roster of speakers included Frank Skinner of IBM; Bruce Graham, partner in the architecture firm Skidmore, Owings & Merrill; Thomas Ellis of the RAND Corporation; Nicholas Negroponte, instructor in computer-aided urban design at MIT; Ralph Warburton, an advisor to the U.S. Department of Housing and Urban Development; Steven A. Coons, professor of mechanical engineering at MIT and at Harvard; and Louis I. Kahn. The proceedings of the event, published by the school as *Computer Graphics in Architecture and Design,* enjoyed wide circulation and influence.[64]

Moore approached the potential of computers in architecture with his characteristic mix of curiosity, skepticism, and insight. In a news release issued in advance of the symposium, he acknowledged that the computer would inevitably play a significant role in architecture, but went on to state that "architects are not trained to program computers, and there is no evidence of any architectural trend in this direction." Drawings and sketches, Moore added, "are the modes of expression natural to architects, not numbers or words." Moore provocatively went on to say that computers could be "a very efficient money-making dead end—the opposite of innovation."[65] However, he backtracked somewhat when interviewed by Joseph G. Herzberg, a reporter for the *New York Times* who covered the symposium, stating that "for architects with souls, the proper use of these machines will be able to release our vision and free us from the constraint of the media we now use."[66] But, as Herzberg reported, Louis I. Kahn, "the most widely known architect at the symposium, was rough on computers, [stating] at breakfast one morning [that] 'what you have here are two things: mind and brain. The computer can do many things better than the brain; it is no substitute for the mind.'"[67]

Luis Summers envisioned the computer as a sort of "super pencil" or "light pen" that could draw on a cathode ray tube—essentially a television screen—speeding up the design process but also changing it in fundamental ways, allowing architects to see their designs evolve in almost motion-picture form. Anticipating theories of digital practice widely advocated a generation later, Summers believed that computer graphics would eliminate the need for working drawings because the final detailed design of a building might be computer controlled.[68] Other symposium participants were also enthralled with the computer's liberating potential, but one speaker, the programmer Nicholas Negroponte, who would occasionally teach at Yale while principally at MIT, confessed that his Urban 5 program, a design system developed jointly by IBM and MIT, would have to be abandoned because it was proving too restrictive and "too limited to human thought."[69] Perhaps the most startling presentation at the symposium came from Warren McCulloch (1898-1969; B.A. 1921), the president of the American Society of Cybernetics and a researcher at MIT. As a Yale undergraduate, McCulloch had been a student of Jay Hambidge's (1867-1924), the artist and historian known for his pioneering research into the ancient Greeks' use of geometry, particularly the use of "sacred" ratios—the golden section, for example—in the design of architecture.[70] Influenced by Hambidge, McCulloch followed an attack on modern architecture with a call for a return to craft—something that surely must have surprised the audience: "Now I think this is one of the big problems of the present moment—that the architect has pulled too far away from dealing with things with his own hands. I'm all for his having to draw. But I'd rather he had to get out and saw wood, lay up stone, bake tiles, make brick, and mix concrete. He'd learn a lot more."[71]

Writing in 2001, William Mitchell recalled that Steven A. Coons, said to be the father of computer graphics, "had some pretty sensational stuff to show—a computer graphics image of a beautiful, rotating, smoothly curved surface." But, Mitchell noted, Coons offered some cautionary advice: "You could pretend . . . that the graphics system used to produce it was 'a magic computerized modeling clay that a sculptor might use, literally, to sculpt some shape.'" But Coons asked whether "architects would like to have a partner that could do things like this?"[72] According to Mitchell, Charles Moore "didn't want a partner *quite* like" the one Coons suggested the computer could be. "He wasn't much interested in blobby curved surfaces—then or later—but he clearly saw where all this was headed. It would enable new architectural languages."[73] In the concluding panel discussion, Moore, after stating with dry wit that "the major change in architects' language thus far in the twentieth century has been the replacement of Chinese ink with India ink," argued that the computer can't create a new language—only architects can do that. And, should they prove successful, they "may find computers saving rather than superseding" them.[74]

Reflecting on the 1968 computer conference in 2001, William Mitchell wrote: "Strictly speaking, this was still science fiction. Coons readily admitted that he wasn't actually showing realtime three-dimensional graphics; his three-minute film had taken eight hours to compute. And this sort of thing could only be done, anyway, on big, costly computers in a very few places. But those constraints were of no real consequence: 'The purpose of this symposium is not to make you think that it is possible, for a large expenditure of money, to make certain facilities available to you now. The purpose is to make you aware that we are only at the beginning. . . . Computers will be different tomorrow. They will be more capable, they will be cheaper, and they will be far more congenial to human beings than they are today.'"[75]

Despite important work in computers by architecture faculty Summers and Milne, Yale was not itself a center of research in the field. As Mitchell recalled, "There was a computer center in the outskirts of the campus [the Watson Center, 1961, designed by Skidmore, Owings & Merrill on Sachem Street between Prospect Street and Hillhouse Avenue] but you couldn't get your hands on the big, blue machines; they blinked and whirred behind a glass wall, and you handed your boxes of punched cards to white-coated attendants. You programmed in Fortran, or a perversely incomprehensible notation called APL, and if you wanted to try anything ambitious you had to go to assembly code. There was the merest, primitive beginning of a network throughout the campus. IBM typewriter terminals were wired to the central computer. We had one of these in the basement of the Art and Architecture building, and I used it to teach some of the first classes, anywhere, in computing for designers."

What was taught, Mitchell recalled, "was never intended to be immediately practical; it was more appropriately understood as technologically supported performance art with a pedagogical agenda of provocation. Because we couldn't do graphics, but also out of conviction, we focused upon the spatial organization of human activities rather than shape and surface."[76] Meanwhile, at many other universities, as Mitchell later pointed out in 2001— particularly Stanford, UCLA, and MIT, the last two of which by then he knew firsthand as faculty—a "powerful alliance of the emerging hacker subculture with sixties counterculture" was taking place. But at Yale "this emerging alliance took on a particular local flavor, since it developed in a milieu of the arts, design, and social and political activism—not, as elsewhere, in engineering laboratories driven by large, militarily funded programs of technology research and development. Interest focused largely upon the appropriation of digital tools for cultural, political, and social purposes and the potentially transformative effects of this: What we saw at Yale, in the late-sixties prehistory of digital culture, was a deep yearning for a more just and less culturally restrictive world, and a search—conducted simultaneously on many fronts— for ways to achieve it." For Mitchell, "and many others of [his] generation, technological innovation became politics by other means."[77]

Mitchell's skepticism notwithstanding, significant early M.E.D. research involving the computer as a design tool did take place, with students forging links to similar work being carried out at MIT, UCLA, and the University of Waterloo in Canada. Raymond J. Matela's (b. 1946; M.E.D. 1974) thesis was titled "An Analysis of the Animals of Architecture: A Complete Enumeration of Polyominoes by Some of Their Architectural Properties"[78]; Hanna Shapira (b. 1947; M.E.D. 1974) offered "A Procedure for Generating Floor Plans: Computer-Aided Design"[79]; and Michael Benedikt (b. 1946; M.E.D. 1975), who would go on to write a number of books on computing as well as architectural theory while teaching at the University of Texas, Austin, studied "The Information Field."[80] Students interested in computers worked with the University of Waterloo-trained Robert Frew, who came to Yale in 1970 as assistant professor of architecture, and by 1972 had carved out a niche for himself as "the computer guy,"[81] so that his title was changed to assistant professor of design methods research and coordinator of the Advanced Methodology Sequence, "concerned with the management of design information and the development of knowledge of the built environment."[82] Frew's Methodology Sequence included the school's first formalized computer courses: "Computation and Quantitative Methods," which introduced students to programming and networks, and "Computer Applications to Architecture," a survey of computer programs that could aid the design process and ultimately required students to solve a design problem by creating a computer program. In 1974, Frew was promoted to associate professor, and his program, renamed Design Research Methodology, offered an expanded roster of courses, including "Introduction to Computer-Aided Design," "Graphics in Computer-Aided Design," and "Modeling in Computer-Aided Design," which Frew taught with William Mitchell.

Moore surprised many by extending Serge Chermayeff's contract for three years. How much the two men had in common is not clear, but they surely shared one thing: an antipathy to the formalism of Rudolph's design approach. However, they disagreed over its antidote, the new sensibility emerging in the mid-1960s that, ten years later, would be characterized by Chermayeff's former Harvard student Charles Jencks as postmodernism[83] and could already be seen in *Perspecta* 9/10 (1965)—the publication of which had displeased Chermayeff, as its editor intended. According to biographer Alan Powers, "Chermayeff took violent exception to the tone of the magazine, with its emphasis on monumentality and the value of history, accusing the editors of complicity in a 'private cabal or conspiracy aiming to promote private power or personal advantage.'"[84] Moore recognized that Chermayeff's concept of research-based studios was perfectly attuned to the discourse of the late 1960s, when there was an abundance of government and foundation resources available, with support coming from the U.S. National Bureau of Standards and the Twentieth Century Fund, "with whose help he [Chermayeff] . . . set up a true multidisciplinary laboratory for research based on computation and systems designed thinking."[85]

Moore tolerated Chermayeff in part because his approach was a distinct alternative to the influential views of the Berkeley-based urban planner and theorist Melvin Webber (1920–2006) and his students, who "took for granted the inevitable liquidation of what they called, oddly, 'cityness' and promoted a chaotic free-wheeling private automobile dominated paradigm."[86] Webber's paradigm would soon enough become one of the dominant themes in the work of Denise Scott Brown and Robert Venturi, with whom Chermayeff visibly and vocally clashed in Yale studios to electrifying effect. Donald Watson recalls hearing them shout arguments across the double-height drafting room: "They'd both be giving their little seminars and then they would turn and shout at each other. . . . I saw what was a very interesting moment when the people Chermayeff had here—John McHale, Bucky Fuller, Christopher Alexander, René DuBos, all the people that were writing in *Ekistics* on world, global, and environmental stuff in the 1960s, Chermayeff had here. So you had a moment when the word 'environment' was used globally," which was seen in contrast with "people like the Venturis saying, 'Architects cannot change the world, should not change the world. We're not sociologists so let's learn about design.'

What a wonderful debate . . . with these characters yelling at each other—cordially yelling at each other."[87]

Despite his objections to the explicit formalism and implicit historicism of the emerging postmodernist sensibility, Chermayeff nonetheless shared its conviction that the technologies and urban premises behind modernism since the 1920s were exhausted and that modernism had degenerated into a style. This can be seen not only in his Yale teaching, but also in the book he wrote with his former student and co-teacher Alexander Tzonis, *Shape of Community: Realization of Human Potential* (1971), which was dismissive of modern architecture as a whole—both modernism and incipient postmodernism—arguing that: "Most of the changes in the last half-century, somewhat speciously described as the period of the 'modern movement' in applied arts, were in the realm of aesthetic form rather than the substance of a great transition in human affairs. With very few honorable exceptions, most of the protagonists in the movement were ignorant of, or indifferent to, the changes in need and potential that were generated during the same period."[88]

According to Chermayeff and Tzonis, the path to responsible environmental decision-making lay in "the methodology of science, particularly in the field of cybernetics with its attention to alternations between contrasting conditions, rather than the earlier scientific model of selecting one of a series of possible choices as 'correct.'"[89] The book's argument was in some ways naïve, even amateurish. For example, in a discussion of the public space of urban squares, Chermayeff and Tzonis proposed commerce-free, climate-controlled, indoor agoras, not much different from the increasingly ubiquitous atria of sprawling shopping malls.[90] The book also lashed out at "pseudo-professionals of all kinds (their number is growing as more and more people jump onto the 'urbanology' band wagon) [who] produce pseudo-realities to deceive innocent men further. Pseudo-plans produce pseudo-reconstruction, urban renewal and, worse, pseudo-critics."[91] But what was the point of such negativism? Not surprisingly, *Shape of Community* failed to resonate with critics or readers and can be said to have had little impact.

After his age-mandated retirement in 1970, Chermayeff continued his affiliation with the university as professor emeritus but had little actual contact with it, especially after 1972, when he sold his once widely discussed but strangely planned Lincoln Street house (1962) (5.5), which had served as a kind of textbook demonstration of the ideas found in *Community and Privacy*.[92] To mark his retirement, Peter C. Papademetriou (b. 1943; M.Arch 1968) and Stuart Wrede (b. 1944; B.A. 1965, M.Arch 1969), editors of *Perspecta* 12, dedicated the issue to Chermayeff, with Tzonis paying tribute to his former teacher's enduring loyalty to the idea of a revolutionary architecture.[93] Chermayeff's fundamental displeasure with Rudolph's Yale was revisited in 1998, when the editors of *Perspecta* 29, which was devoted to the events that took place at Yale and New Haven in the late 1960s and early 1970s, embraced Chermayeff's critique of the school as a criticism of their own experience: "As we know to have been true enough throughout architectural discourse over the last quarter-century, our graduate training was almost totally disengaged from the social and professional dimensions of design. While form and formal theories were analyzed exhaustively, questions of social planning, technological innovation, user participation, and professionalism—concerns that naturally arose in our thoughts and conversations—were largely ignored in the studio and classroom. Missing too was any sense of architecture as a vehicle of opposition to the social and economic directions of the nation as a whole."[94]

Despite his interest in research, Moore was, at heart, committed to basic design education, which he correctly deemed to be lackluster and largely directionless at Yale and most other places. Before implementing a new curriculum, Moore made some changes to the faculty. He relieved T. Gorm Hansen, Paul J. Mitarachi, Peter J. B. Vercelli, and Olav Hammarstrom of their positions, while bringing in new hires who were more sympathetic to his ambitions for the school, including Felix Drury; John Fowler (1934–1975), assistant professor of architectural design; and sculptor Kent Bloomer (b. 1935; B.F.A. 1959, M.F.A. 1961), assistant professor of technical design. In selecting faculty, Moore was guided by a "strong aversion to an individual instructor's tactical withholding of knowledge in order to keep the student's educational development under control."[95]

Moore tasked the English-born John Fowler with bringing rigor to the more advanced studios. Fowler had studied at the London Polytechnic before coming to the United States as a post-professional student at Columbia, where he shared an apartment with fellow classmates Peter Eisenman (b. 1932) and another Englishman, Noel Michael McKinnell. After Columbia, Fowler moved to New Haven to work for Paul Rudolph, and his influence on the design of the Yale Married Student Housing complex, especially on its unrealized first version, was well known.[96] At the time of his faculty appointment, Fowler maintained an independent practice in New Haven. A small house he designed on Mount Desert Island in Maine (1970) would be highly regarded.[97] Less so was the 1970 renovation to the interior of Carrère & Hastings's Commons dining hall, which made extensive use of silver Mylar in a misguided attempt to make the monumental wood-paneled room "hip" (5.6).

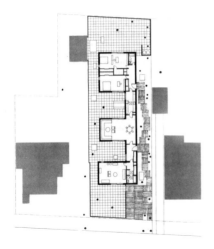

5.5   Serge Chermayeff, Lincoln Street House, New Haven, plan (1962).

5.6   John Fowler, Freshman Commons Dining Hall (1970).

5.7   Charles Moore, Church Street South (1975), New Haven.

Moore's most important appointment was Kent Bloomer, who would become his closest faculty collaborator and Basic Design guru. Bloomer had studied physics and architecture at MIT before pursuing sculpture at Yale. Like Drury, Bloomer was teaching at the Carnegie Institute of Technology when he first encountered Moore, who "came to give his seminal Disneyland lecture" and then visited Bloomer's studio classroom, the walls of which were lined with old sepia photographs of Greek temples and ancient ruins that Bloomer "mixed in" with student projects about "polyhedra, catenaries, and modular structures."[98] A friendship between the two would soon follow and, in the wake of the reorganization of the department's degree programs, they would work together to shape the new curriculum—particularly the first-year curriculum.

The difference between Moore and Rudolph was obvious from the beginning. As one student told the *Yale Daily News:* "When Paul Rudolph was here, the architectural faculty was like a pyramid with Rudolph on top. Professor Moore works much more quietly, within the structure."[99] Unlike Rudolph, who tended to confine his teaching to advanced students, Moore *only* taught first-year design studio along with seminars that were also open to undergraduates. Paul Goldberger (b. 1950; B.A. 1972), who would go on to become a Pulitzer Prize–winning architectural critic for the *New York Times,* enrolled in Moore's seminar on the Bauhaus as an undergraduate. Goldberger remembers the class "as the one where, in a sense, I began my career." Goldberger's paper for the seminar impressed Moore, "and his reaction led me to believe for the first time that I might have some ideas about architecture worth taking seriously. . . . That translated for me into a kind of support like none other—the support that gives you the courage to get started."[100]

Bloomer has stated that some likened Moore's arrival at Yale to a "California breath of fresh air" bringing "humor, wit, and new perspectives. He expected that the school [department] would be easily managed because it was considerably smaller than [the University of] California's College of Environmental Design, and New Haven was quieter than Berkeley, where the free speech movement and the barricades and tear gas were dividing the campus."[101] As Bloomer saw him, Moore was a committed architect-scholar with rigorous, if quirky, standards.[102] For Ray Gindroz (b. 1940), a former student of Bloomer's at the Carnegie Institute of Technology who started teaching at Yale in 1967 as a visiting critic in the first year, the decision to focus on that year was a defining aspect of Moore's tenure: "It was striking to people that as the dean [chairman] he chose to be the faculty member for the first year of the graduate program. He felt it was the most important thing to get right. The Core curriculum, which we did as a team, was Charles as the visionary and the architect. Kent was concerned early on with basic design and later with his interest in ornament and visual design, and me as the urban designer. We saw a direct connection between urban design and ornament because of the role of the details of aspects and how they work and function."[103]

Moore's new curriculum supplanted a rather pedestrian series of first-year design problems offered during the Rudolph years with a carefully calibrated set of exercises. Beginning in fall 1966, a series of basic design problems followed by a series of short architectural problems, of increasing complexity, culminated in the design of a community center in Kentucky.[104] Students were made to realize that there were no absolutes. For example, a design program that called for a trailer grouping was to be executed in two ways: as sleeping quarters for twenty-eight military personnel at a radar post and at the same time, as quarters for twenty-eight members of a private northern camp. The binary program reflected not only Moore's commitment to a multivalent approach, but also to a considerable extent his personal experiences and hang-ups as someone who had done military service and not particularly enjoyed it, and who was concerned about the impact of military operations on the national psyche. Moreover, as a man whose fundamental character was shaped by midwestern values, he was ambivalent, perhaps even a bit hostile, toward Yale's still-dominant upper-class culture. The sleeping quarters problem, therefore, was intended to make a vivid distinction between upper-class "roughing it" and military "toughing it." This pair of problems was followed by another social pairing—a public bathing facility in Tent City, Lowndes County, Alabama, and urban housing for Church Street South in New Haven, a project then under way in Moore's professional office (5.7).[105] Students were then given a brief sketch problem, calling for the design of a marquee and entrance to the University Theatre, home stage of the School of Drama. According to Bloomer, Moore "did not believe in oversimplifying the requirements of an assignment in order to make the problem graspable and explainable. Multiple and complex agendas were to be included in each assignment. He argued that a studio problem should represent a reasonably complete and probable architectural situation to be addressed holistically, rather than reductively."[106]

Although Moore's professional work and studio programs each gave the impression that his principal focus was on small, shack-like structures, he believed that the department needed to strengthen its offerings in urban topics, including city planning and urban design. To this end, the curriculum was broadened "to include 'context' and methodology as well as design, and advanced courses were welcomed from any source and of almost any format, whether faculty or student initiated."[107] For example, Professor Adjunct Herman Fritz Pat Goeters (b. 1929; M.U.S. 1967), who before accepting his 1966 appointment had taught urban design at the University of Notre Dame, offered a class on utopia; Wojciech Grzegorz (Gregory) Leśnikowski (1938–2014), a Polish architect and city planner who previously taught at the École des Beaux-Arts, led a studio on modular housing; David Lewis (b. 1922) and his design partner, Ray Gindroz, led urban design; and Peter Millard taught "Techniques for Qualifying the Physical Environment." Despite the shaky status of the City Planning Department in the school, Moore was adamant that some sort of city planning courses were essential to professional training in architecture: in 1970, as part of his final report as dean, with the planning program being phased out, Moore stated that "the design school, to be useful, must have adjacency to knowledge about cities and the environment." He continued, "This seems especially critical at a juncture when architecture schools across the country in the search for relevance have abdicated their strength in design. The work of our faculty and students offer, I think, impressive current evidence of our health in spite of everything in this critical area; it is worth hanging on to."[108]

As Moore shaped the curriculum, it increasingly became "a kind of subversive apologia for nonmodern architecture" as embodied in Bloomer and Moore's 1977 book, *Body, Memory, and Architecture*.[109] The "subversive apologia" was initially tested on the first-year class that entered in September 1967. Andrus Burr (b. 1944; M.Arch 1970), a graduate of Williams College, was a member of that class. Writing in 1980, he recalled that as the first year proceeded, his class "became increasingly aware that they were being treated in a manner different from the classes ahead of them. Older students were often envious that Charles Moore spent nearly all his teaching time with *First Year*." Some members of the class found Moore's program difficult and the assignments too abstract or vaguely defined. As Burr notes, "The criticism was infuriatingly non-specific," but as some students struggled with the uncertainty, others became motivated to "gain a deep understanding of architectural questions."

For Burr, the "exciting, highly charged atmosphere" of the studio resulted from the loose curriculum and the fact that students—first-year students, no less—were "making very real architecture."[110] The apparent lack of discipline also nurtured an ethos of entrepreneurialism but, as Craig Hodgetts (b. 1937; M.Arch 1969) was to point out, "It wasn't a careerist thing. It was a very individualistic student body. Everyone was searching. There wasn't a follower in the whole place. . . . Under Charles's regime, there was a sense that you are all peers; the faculty and the students are peers. It wasn't hierarchical. Faculty and students would go out and have a beer together at that dungeon next door [the Old Heidelberg]."[111]

Rules and regulations, including traditional academic courses required for licensure, seemed almost trivial to the students, many of whom allegedly never completed the required courses in structures. This was the case not only for those in first year, but also more advanced students. Not only were courses in structures avoided by students, but other traditional fundamentals such as drawing were downplayed. To some students, such as Heather Willson Cass (M.Arch 1972), who entered the department from Holyoke College with virtually no prior training in architecture, this presented something of an "impediment."[112] Cass struggled to learn fundamentals along the way: "You learned how to learn. I think for me this is part of the unheralded genius of Charles Moore, which is that he figured out what you needed to know and what you wanted to know. If you didn't have a class that taught you something you need, you'd go to the library to find a book and then go find somebody who can help you. You also learned in studio. I learned a lot from Jim Stirling about line weight. Pretty much all I needed to know."[113]

From his perspective on the faculty, Ray Gindroz believes most of the students, like Cass, were "very self-motivated," and the school's relaxed approach to academic discipline was, overall, beneficial: "The great continuity was the students." And the students "tended to find their own way through the very rich menu of items that were offered by the school" without "hardcore ideological directions. . . . There were hardcore ideological people who waged war with one another occasionally, but the overall effect was a very catholic and eclectic diet of possibilities. And that to me was the great strength."[114] Others were not so sure. Philip Johnson, for one, came to disdain Moore's approach and his tolerance for student radicalism, to the extent that in 1970, Allan Greenberg, then new on the faculty, was dispatched to meet with him and repair relations.[115] Even one of the more radical students, Stuart Wrede, became convinced that Moore's laid-back approach was not the right one for all: "Moore . . . ran a very laissez-faire operation, especially in the more advanced years, allowing students to more or less choose whatever project they wanted to work on. It both unleashed a lot of creative energy and at the same time caused a good deal of anxiety and questioning among the students."[116] Moore was able to tap into the rebellious mood of the moment when students advised each other not to trust anyone over thirty years of age. He seemed to thrive on the swirling currents of student rebellion, which he celebrated as the motivation for change, transforming the buttoned-up program of Paul Rudolph into, as he boasted to President Brewster in 1968, "an extraordinarily turned-on school, thanks first to the quality of our students and then to the absence of restrictions on their imagination and involvement."[117]

Many students found Moore too kind and too encouraging in his evaluations, and not tough enough in his criticism. Students were also frustrated with his constant absences from the school and concerned about his administrative style. "It is really too bad we don't get more exposure to his criticism," said one anonymous student. "Get this man out of the office and into the drafting rooms."[118] Moore's peripatetic nature increasingly grated on students who, according to Robert Miller (b. 1945; B.A. 1967, M.Arch 1971), "following radio's faux-superhero Chickenman," mocked their chairman with the tagline "He's everywhere!" Perhaps another anonymous student described Moore best: "an excellent teacher who[m] we see very little of."[119]

The Yale Building Project would prove to be not only Moore's most significant contribution to the program, but also perhaps to architectural education as a whole.[120] Although credit for the program as a permanent feature of the curriculum belongs to Moore, the idea that Yale students would undertake their own independent design-build projects had a history extending back to the early 1960s, when David Sellers and others undertook houses for family or friends or cabins targeted to upper-middle-class clients. The Building Project, on the other hand, was a socially motivated collaborative involving an entire class, as well as faculty. It was conceived during Moore's first year as chairman, when he became aware of the independent work of three social activist students: Tom Carey (b. 1943; M.Arch 1970), Steven Edwins (1943–2014; M.Arch 1970), and Robert Swenson (b. 1941; M.Arch 1969). Swenson, a Southern Illinois University undergraduate, had first visited Appalachia as a political organizer in the summer of 1964. Motivated to use their skills to address real social problems, Carey, Edwins, and Swenson spent the summer of 1966 working with the Christian Appalachian Project in a rural community in eastern Kentucky, where they designed and built low-cost housing and community buildings. The following fall, the three students inspired their second-year classmates to get involved, along with newly appointed studio instructor Pat Goeters. Dubbing themselves "Group 9," the students, with Moore's blessing, found a design project—a community center—to work on during the academic year.[121] The interest in Appalachia aligned with a national trend stimulated by the founding of the Volunteers in Service to America (VISTA) and other programs that focused attention on American poverty.[122]

Inspired by the work of the students and the local residents, Moore decided to make the Community Center in New Zion, Kentucky, the topic of the spring 1967 first-year studio, and what would become the first annual Building Project. In his characteristically convoluted way, Moore described to the university how this new program would be integrated into the curriculum: "A number of students about to enter the second year [were] working with Appalachian problems in McKee, Kentucky, building and programming needs of that area in order to work with next year's first year students who are to design simple structures in response to the need described by the students returning from Kentucky and who then, we plan, will themselves go to Kentucky for ten days to build one of the designs."[123]

In an organizational pattern that remains in place to this day, during the spring 1967 term, the thirty first-year students of the class of 1970—the first to experience the full extent of Moore's curricular changes—divided themselves into six design groups with four to nine members, with each group giving itself a name such as "Stud and Skin" or "Land Formation."[124] Near the end of the semester, the faculty selected one design for construction. The winning scheme, by the team named "Group-Group," was a wooden shed-style building that bore more than a passing resemblance to Moore's own Sea Ranch. Then the hard work began, with students working on-site in New Zion, "a genuine backwoods town," where "conditions were primitive, with no local government and not one flush toilet among two hundred inhabitants" (5.8).[125] Poverty and ignorance abounded. John Jacobson remembers it as "a really eye-opening experience":

We lived in people's houses where they only had heat from fireplaces or stoves. And they only had outhouses. There were no bathrooms, no toilets, no showers. I'll never forget visiting one of these people and having to go to the bathroom. Their outhouse was over a creek. So all the waste was going directly into the water. There was no waste left on the property, but I guess it was clean for them, but my god. It was an interesting bonding experience for the class. We all became extremely close.[126]

Although Moore gets and deserves the lion's share of credit for seizing on the Building Project as a critical aspect of his revised curriculum, the project's success was largely dependent on the widespread desire of young people to play an active role in redressing society's deficiencies, especially in regard to the plight of the poor. Restless and impatient with traditional paper projects, students seized on the Building Project and made it a defining part of their Yale experience, a project that mattered, that had the capacity to improve people's lives, and "as a practical matter . . . [was] of a size that was buildable within the time available." Students recognized that large-scale urban problems such as those posed by conditions in Harlem "were inappropriate to the First Year."[127] Mark Ellis (b. 1946; M.Arch 1971), a member of the second Building Project team, expressed the view of most, that being on-site and working with the community was important: "We enjoy the feeling that we have participated constructively in the life of the inhabitants of this timeless region, where people farm the hills for subsistence in much the same way as their ancestors learned from the Indians. By personally handling the entire construction—from dealings with the government and keeping our creditors at bay through actual carpentry—we may have learned even more than our school expected."[128]

Over the years, the selection process for the Building Project has remained consistent, as has the emphasis on collaborative work and, perhaps most importantly, the invaluable lessons about design that can only be learned through hands-on construction experience. However, the project had its critics. To the dismay of experienced architects, "students came to mistrust drawings as a biased representation of architecture, incapable of knowing how one would really experience a building," Burr observes, so that Yale graduates from the Moore era were "somewhat less desirable for positions in large architecture firms where drawing continued to be the important medium. But that fact hardly daunted the class of 1970 who preferred to throw themselves into working on their own rather than selling their souls to the devils of corporate architecture."[129]

The first-year Building Project can be seen as a decisive break with the hermetic studio culture that Yale, perhaps given Rudolph's intensity, espoused. As Richard Hayes (b. 1959; M.Arch 1986) points out, it also "shifted the locus of the architecture student's identification from the *atelier* to the *chantier,* proposing a more engaged definition of the architect,"[130] becoming the most visible manifestation of Moore's determination to shift the program's emphasis from decontextualized shape-elaboration toward a concern for architecture's potential for quotidian usefulness. From the first, he saw it as a significant alternative to traditional methods of architectural education. Moore put this succinctly in 1967: "To teach architecture simply as the composition of shapes is out of the question."[131]

For young architects, the first lesson of New Zion was one of exhilarating power. They didn't have to be old and hoary to build; they could make things now. They also could learn to work collaboratively. The Building Project

5.8   Yale students with Kent Bloomer (third from left) and Charles
Moore (fourth from left) in Jackson County, Kentucky (1967).

5.9   The Building Project featured on the cover of *Progressive
Architecture* (September 1967).

5.10   Peter de Bretteville (B.A. 1963, M.Arch 1968), Craig Hodgetts (M.Arch 1967), and
Eugene Kupper (M.Arch 1967), Mobile Theater Prototype, model (1972).

confronted the uncertainties many of the students had about architecture as a socially viable discipline, although not every student was comfortable with Yale's presence in Kentucky. The premiere issue of the radical broadside *Novum Organum,* an important outlet for student dissent and opinion in the late 1960s and early 1970s, included an unsigned article, "Education for Alienation," which reported that the "deep satisfaction left in us is indicative at some level. It is difficult to deal with architectural abstractions about shape, textures, and scale in the face of concrete needs and unhappiness, which theoretically justify the program but in actuality are victimized by it."[132] Nonetheless, on reflection, most participants in the first Building Project believed, and to this day continue to believe, that it came at a perfect time in their professional training.

The Building Project propelled Yale's architecture program to the forefront of professional attention and continues to attract students to the school to this day. In 1967, the editors of *Progressive Architecture* were inspired to illustrate the New Zion building on the cover of their September 1967 issue (5.9) and to observe that since Moore's appointment as chairman, "things have been taking on a decidedly non–Ivory Tower aspect. . . . Moore's technique . . . seems to be to get the students right out of the New Haven atmosphere and right down to the heady atmosphere of the client argument, the less-than-glamorous activities of figuring budgets and scheduling construction, and the hands-in-the-dirt experience of pouring foundations and putting up siding."[133] *Progressive Architecture* would regularly cover the events at Yale under Moore, especially after the magazine relocated from Manhattan to Stamford, Connecticut, in May 1969 and took advantage of its new proximate location to document the school's approach. Indeed, so frequently was Yale mentioned in its pages that *P/A* soon became referred to, somewhat sarcastically, as "The Yale Alumni Magazine." The annual *P/A* "Design Awards" issue for 1967 awarded a citation to a project by a team of Yale students; the 1969 issue recognized five projects by Yale alumni, including Lester R. Walker (b. 1939; M.Arch 1966) and Craig Hodgetts, who were awarded the magazine's highest honor for a modest though technically innovative design for a rental building. Five years later, Hodgetts, along with fellow alumni Peter de Bretteville (b. 1941; B.A. 1963, M.Arch 1968) and Eugene Kupper (b. 1939; M.Arch 1967), working under the name Works West, won the First Design Award in 1972 for their design for a mobile theater that featured inflatable structural components (5.10).

The Building Project proved a real test for the mostly upper-middle-class students, who had never wielded a hammer. For some, like Turner

Brooks, it would inspire a career as designer of houses and small institutional buildings, including Yale's Gilder Boathouse (2001), which he won in competition against two other firms with Yale ties.[134] Brooks's rejection of big-city professionalism would take place after six months of experience in the New York office of Philip Johnson, a step others of his generation would skip entirely. Peter Woerner (b. 1941; B.A. 1966, M.Arch 1970), who acted as the overall job captain for the first Building Project, also found his métier in Kentucky and went on to a successful career as a residential architect in Connecticut.[135] As the Building Project evolved, it became clear that the students needed an experienced construction supervisor in the field. In 1973, this job was given to Paul Brouard (b. 1930; M.Arch 1957), who joined the Building Project team with fifteen years of professional experience, first in the office of John Johansen and then on his own. Brouard remained connected to the Building Project until his retirement in 2013.[136]

The Building Project inspired similar design-build programs at many other schools, ranging from the Putney School (a Vermont prep school) to the Massachusetts Institute of Technology and Kansas State University. But none of these efforts had the continuity of Yale's, nor its embedded location in the curriculum. Asked to identify his most important accomplishment at Yale, Moore said that he "was most proud of [the Building Project]."[137]

The first class of students to be exposed to Moore's revised curriculum constitutes a remarkable group, many of whom have carried forward his ideas in their own work as practicing architects and educators. But not all: Peter Rose (b. 1943; B.A. 1966, M.Arch 1970), initially an enthusiast, has come to question Moore's approach. "I learned a great deal from Moore," says Rose, "to carefully look at, to see, and be thrilled by buildings (what a great place Yale was for that); to be political, to value history, to be bold, to take risks, and to design thoughtfully. Then began the hard part, finding my own voice as an architect."[138] According to Rose, now a respected architect and adjunct professor of architecture at Harvard, Charles Moore "sort of set things up in such a way that you knew you weren't going to make mistakes for which you'd be judged in some very painful way, in the school. And he also said things—he or Kent [Bloomer] or maybe it was just in the air—but he talked about not knowing what an education was really composed of but that making the analogy of vegetables in a greenhouse, you throw in some design, you throw in some traveling, you throw—I don't know what else—sun and fertilizer . . . [and] you create enough heat and energy in a place, and learning will happen."[139] Rose is at once appreciative of Moore's style and angered by it: "[Moore was] an

incredibly intelligent, well-educated, well-read, well-travelled human being."
But looking back after thirty years, Rose couldn't

> remember being assigned a reading or being told that there was any dis-
> cipline or rigor or that there was any kind of foundation to learning about
> architecture. It was all just conversational. And it was a shock to me to
> learn that there was a profession and there was professionalism and
> there were methods. For all of his love of history, he never taught me a
> thing about history in my recollection. I saw a gazillion buildings with him
> and I remember, also, jokingly saying once among a bunch of us when
> we were looking at a building with him, "Do we like this building, Charlie?"
> . . . We waited to hear what he said and what we liked. And so we were
> kind of dependent upon him and he did not give us a lot of hooks into
> things outside our experience at school that would allow us to continue
> our learning.[140]

Kent Bloomer does not share this view. He believes that Moore "brought
history back. He got us away from the notion that architecture was a contemporary activity with an intellectual history of about 20 years." According
to Bloomer, Moore paired history with a "concept of place, which I think he
really got from J. B. Jackson and others. . . . Those were his two major cam-
paigns—history and place."[141] History, yes, but as a kind of "image gathering"
divorced from program, politics, economics, and other considerations. Urging
students to look at the architecture of the past and not to mimic contemporary
architectural styles, he emphasized the value of starting from a stance that
was already known to work, and expanding from there. This attitude laid the
foundation for the practice of historical allusion that would appear in the later
work of many Yale students from the late 1960s and early 1970s. According
to Andrus Burr, Moore "suggested that if the designer could consciously
control the image of his building and allude to previous architecture, he could
influence a viewer's perceptions and response. Kent Bloomer elaborated on
this idea as memory in the book *Body, Memory, and Architecture*. Once again
this was a thought that ran directly against the grain of 'Brave New World'
Modernism."[142]

Burr has pointed out that Moore advocated an intuitive approach to
design, which encouraged students to assemble "an architectural scheme" as
"a series of vignettes . . . composed to make an orderly but picturesque whole.
Within this process there were no theories—it was essentially empirical."[143]
By 1969, Burr recalls, "it was agreed that one needn't be limited to copying

5.11   Peter Rose (B.A. 1966, M.Arch 1970) and James Volney Righter (M.Arch 1970),
Pavillon Soixante-Dix Ski Resort (1977), Mont Saint-Sauveur, Quebec.

5.12   Daniel Scully (M.Arch 1970), '57 Porsche Monument House,
elevation (1972).

5.13   Daniel Scully and Robert Knight (M.Arch 1970), Yale University Theatre Marquee (1968).

vernacular ideas, one could also 'quote' from architecturally important buildings without jeopardizing the originality of a scheme."[144] This was ironic given
the period's presumed anti-intellectualism and the perception by many in the
profession that Yale's students were a group of near-hippies wandering around
an intellectual desert.

While Peter Rose ultimately rejected the historicizing approach that
Moore espoused, his early work with James Volney Righter (b. 1935; M.Arch
1970) was notably "postmodern"—as in the Pavillon Soixante-Dix ski resort in
Quebec (5.11).[145] Righter, who took up architecture after a few dispiriting years
in advertising, would remain true to Moore's vision, assisting him in studios
at Yale while operating an independent practice specializing in houses. In
1980, Righter was joined by his former student Jacob Albert (b. 1955; B.A. 1977,
M.Arch 1980), whose early work was more influenced by Robert Venturi, and
John Tittmann (b. 1959; M.A. 1981, M.Arch 1986) joined the firm in 1996.[146]

Daniel Scully (b. 1943; M.Arch 1970) also thrived under Moore, but
his early independent work was less historicist and more connected to the
pop-culture enthusiasms of Robert Venturi, as can be seen in his 1972 design
"'57 Porsche Monument House," which proposed to use the shell of an actual
vintage Porsche as an operable skylight (5.12). Within a month of his high
school graduation in 1963, a politically engaged Scully, son of historian
Vincent Scully, had "been beaten by the police and was in jail for three days in
Virginia, incommunicado," so he is very quick to make a distinction between
the social and political revolutions of the 1960s and the "very different" revolution that Moore brought: "He [Moore] was like a flower child from California.
But that was his greatness—the inclusiveness he brought with that. . . . I never
sensed that Charles was obsessed with being a revolutionary, even though
he was certainly making changes."[147] While a student, Scully worked for some
of Yale's most influential faculty, including Kahn, Rudolph, and Venturi, and
during his final year at Yale, he won the Rome Prize. Having established an
independent practice in New Hampshire in 1983, Scully's professional work
embraces both historical context and sustainable design.[148]

Inclusiveness and accommodation were key elements of Moore's professional practice and pedagogical approach. Robert "Buzz" Yudell (b. 1947;
B.A. 1969, M.Arch 1973)—who studied under Moore at Yale before starting the
Los Angeles–based firm Moore Ruble Yudell, with Moore and John Ruble in
1977—remembers the architect as "a disciplined, rigorous designer, wrapped
in a puckish, irreverent personality. He drew clients, friends, colleagues into a
magic realm of collaboration, powered by a sense of wonder about the world
and an unflagging optimism about the ways in which architecture can ennoble

our lives. His commitment to architecture as an inclusive and humanist art was profound and irresistible."[149]

Just as Rudolph was occasionally attracted to oddball candidates like Stanley Tigerman, Moore welcomed Craig T. Hodgetts, who arrived at Yale in 1965 with very sketchy credentials, having "bounced around a lot," from engineering school to drama school to working at General Motors to working as a dramaturge with the San Francisco Actor's Workshop. "But I couldn't make a living," remembers Hodgetts. So, after enjoying helping an architect with a competition model, he decided to enroll in architecture school. Hodgetts went to Berkeley and spoke with then-chairman Moore, who agreed to admit him to the program. Hodgetts soon changed his plans when, studying in the library one day, he came across an issue of *Domus* featuring James Stirling and James Gowan's Engineering Building at Leicester University: "It blew. My. Mind.," says Hodgetts. "I thought this was the greatest thing I had ever seen in my life. . . . The very next day I decided that I have to go see this guy."[150] Leaving Berkeley in the middle of his term, Hodgetts "just showed up at Yale," knowing that Stirling would be teaching there. The newly appointed Charles Moore admitted him on the spot.

Unfortunately, in the wake of the student protests of 1969 and the destructive fire in the Art and Architecture Building, Moore's expanded curriculum seemed to spin out of control. For example, during their second year, students Marc Appleton (b. 1947; M.Arch 1972), Stephen Blatt (b. 1946; M.Arch 1972), Tony Farmer (b. 1945; M.Arch 1971, M.C.P. 1971), and M.E.D. student Sam Davis set up a studio on George Street in order to pursue extracurricular design-build projects as a sort of supplement to their education. Working in what they described as a spirit of democratic collaboration, the group, calling itself Projects, designed and built houses in Colorado, Vermont, and New Mexico.[151] In point of fact, the partners of Projects perceived "deficiencies in Yale's architectural curriculum," notably the "unavailability of detailed considerations in design studios and the absence of a professional dialogue." They believed the studio culture prevented work from being developed "beyond a conceptual stage," with little or no participation of non-architects who could help students translate "conceptual design into workable programs." Working in an atmosphere of "democratic collaboration on design decisions," the criticism the team received from each other was "more valuable than any we experience in school," and this independence encouraged them to "make decisions and take on responsibilities" not demanded of them by academic studios.[152] The formation of the Projects group is significant in that it revealed a commitment to a more professional approach to architecture maintained by some students at Yale, while rebellious students at other schools seemed intent on withdrawing almost entirely from the discipline. However, most Yale students of the late 1960s were not committed to traditional practice. As Burr has written, every student "owned carpentry tools and in varying degrees knew how to use them. The watchword of those days was the rather unsubtle 'get it up.' One didn't talk about architecture, one built it."[153]

While Moore was principally concerned with first-year design, his influence could be seen in the curricular direction of the entire sequence of study, which eschewed the investigation of "masterpiece" structures in favor of "ordinary" buildings such as shopping malls. During the fall 1967 semester, second-year students were assigned a ten-week project for the design of a shopping center for Zayre, a chain of discount retail stores, on a prototypical suburban site. The spring term's work also included a three-week problem for a commercial center to be part of the Church Street South redevelopment, and concluded with a two-week facade project. Encouraged by Robert Brustein (b. 1927), the inspired but controversial dean of Yale's School of Drama, the class also competed for the design of a marquee intended to undercut the staid formality of the Gothic-style University Theatre (1926)— originally designed by Blackall, Clapp & Whittemore and renovated in 1931 by James Gamble Rogers—and "bring the [Drama] School out to the street, out of the recessed shadows . . . [and] give it some signage."[154] Daniel Scully's proposal, a Gothic-inspired, angular arrangement of dark-red metal pipes carrying strings of used car lights and two kiosks fabricated from oil drums, was selected and subsequently realized by Scully during the summer with the help of his classmate Robert Knight (b. 1944; M.Arch 1969), who was so proficient with welding techniques that he was from then on forever known by the nickname "Torch" (5.13). Almost forty years later, Brustein recalled his enthusiasm for Scully's design, describing it as an embodiment of "the spirit of the times."[155] The marquee's great moment of glory came on September 16, 1968, at the end of the opening-night performance of Julian Beck and Judith Malina's Living Theatre staging of *Paradise Now,* when it illuminated assorted cast and audience members as they stripped off their clothes upon leaving the theater to take to the streets, leading to their arrest for indecent exposure.[156] The "temporary" structure lasted for twenty years, "perhaps more than many permanent buildings," notes Scully. "Then one day it was just gone, apparently without drama."[157]

Felix Drury's spring 1968 second-year studio was devoted to the construction of experimental sprayed-foam houses (5.14). The project was

5.14   Inflatable foam house built near the picnic grove of the Yale Golf Course under the direction of Felix Drury (1968).

5.15   *Vogue* spread featuring Yale students building an inflatable foam house (October 15, 1969).

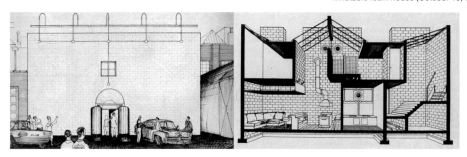

5.16   Arthur Golding (B.A. 1963, M.Arch 1967), Gerard Ives (B.A. 1964, M.Arch 1968), Louis Mackall (B.A. 1962, M.Arch 1968), Douglas Michels (M.Arch 1967), and David Ryan (B.A. 1963, M.Arch 1968), A Youth Recreation Center in New Haven, elevation and section (1966).

5.17   Peter Millard and Earl P. Carlin, New Haven Central Fire Station (1962), New Haven.

actually conceived by William Grover (b. 1938; M.Arch 1969), who worked as an industrial designer with General Motors before attending Yale and who would begin working for Moore in New Haven immediately upon graduation. Grover "was a slightly older student when he went to architecture school," and Turner Brooks remembers him as "a kind of inventor who was always into experimental technology, which appealed to us students a lot." As the story goes, Grover conceived the foam house project after seeing an advertisement from Union Carbide "about inflating a structure and spraying it with Urethane foam." After an in-class competition, three urethane structures were selected to be built on land made available on the Yale Golf Course. Brooks recalls: "We got [$7,500 worth of] Urethane foam donated by Union Carbide in these big fifty gallon drums. . . . It was this horrible gooey-looking stuff that when sprayed from the foam gun immediately expanded to thirty times its liquid volume. . . . We also got a fabric that was made for sandbags destined for Vietnam, a laminated burlap which was the ideal material to use to tailor these huge balloon-like shapes and blow them up and then spray them."[158]

Though innovative, they were derided in the pages of *Novum Organum* by Manfred Ibel (1937–1992; M.Arch 1968), who was one of the most incisive design critics of his Yale generation and would go on to a career practicing in both New York and Key West, Florida. Ibel labeled the foam structures "Experimental Houses for Squirrels." Although the inflatable spray-foam structures could theoretically be used for emergency housing, for the rebellious, outspoken Ibel, they were a useless, self-indulgent experiment that typified the teaching in the architecture department: "three (notorious) prototype urethane structures" built to "further research and experimentation by certain class members after graduation." However, the structures were better received by the popular press, including *Vogue* magazine, which commissioned one that it featured in its October 1969 issue as a manifestation of ultra-modern design along with an accompanying article about "decorating ideas" for "living in foam" (5.15).[159]

Drury's approach, like John Johansen's before him, was innovative and, in light of the advancement of computer-generated designs that emerged in the 1990s, it seems more than reasonable to regard it as a precursor to the "blob" approach advocated by Greg Lynn (b. 1964) and others.[160] According to Drury, "The project, from an educational standpoint . . . [was] to get away from the stick mentality thinking exclusively in terms of post and beam—so that after the graduate students will feel at ease with a material like this and its curved surfaces."[161] Ibel attacked Drury's approach as "naive" because it focused on single-family houses, which he deemed "just another example of architects playing around without any consideration for those who actually use buildings."[162] Moore supported Drury's approach, perhaps because he believed in it, but certainly because he saw it as another way to express his displeasure with Rudolph's A&A Building, as witnessed by the fact that he allowed students to test the spray foam techniques in its monumental spaces. Turner Brooks recalls: "We made these enormous balloons and experimented with blowing them up in the second-floor exhibition space. The one I did in the central area, it went up above the balcony and then looped over into the secretary pool. . . . Anyway, then we transported them out to the golf course and built the real thing on-site."[163]

As Moore's new curriculum began to take hold in the first and second years, advanced students who had entered the department in the Rudolph years found themselves disoriented and dismayed. Mark Simon, who came to Yale after college at Brandeis, recalled that when he arrived, there was "a schism in style of student. . . . The Rudolphians were kind of dressed up and professional and smoked pipes—if I'm going to caricature them. But they were serious. And [Moore's students] were loose and enthusiastic . . . totally different. And who knows whether it was the times or Charles Moore?"[164] Barton Phelps recalls holdovers from the Rudolph era working on massive design projects. "Their saying was 'airport or bigger.' There were these vast projects. . . . I remember thinking, 'Boy, they've been here for a long time.' They were the vestigial remains of the Rudolph thesis, which was apparently quite terrifying. Charles said, 'We're not going to have a thesis.'"[165]

Not all the Rudolph-era holdovers fit Simon's stereotypical view. Some were quite in tune with the new regime. In 1966, five of Peter Millard's students—Doug Michels (1943–2003; M.Arch 1967), Arthur Golding (b. 1942; B.A. 1963, M.Arch 1967), Gerard Ives (B.A. 1964, M.Arch 1968), Louis Mackall, and David Ryan (b. 1943; B.A. 1963, M.Arch 1968)—who were ineligible for the first-year Building Project, decided to find an actual project to take on in studio. Working with a local antipoverty organization as their client, the students designed a recreation facility for neighborhood youths in job-training programs. Their design for an affordable, versatile, and vandal-proof concrete building lit by skylights and two enormous warehouse-like windows (5.16) was never built, but it did earn a citation from *Progressive Architecture*'s annual Design Awards program in 1967, though the jury expressed mixed feelings about the project, with one member describing it as "a manifestation of the depths to which the art world has fallen," calling it "cute" and "tricky," while design jury member Charles Moore, otherwise recusing himself, praised it as "an important manifestation of our century."[166]

Like King-lui Wu and Serge Chermayeff, Peter Millard was a carryover from the Rudolph era. Millard had a considerable following among students, especially after the controversy his and Earl P. Carlin's (1923–2012; B.Arch 1945, M.Arch 1951) design for the monumental New Haven Central Fire Station (1962) **(5.17)** engendered in the *Progressive Architecture* Design Awards jury in 1961, but even more so because of his increasingly in-your-face Socratic teaching style, which forced students to levels of precise verbal expression in describing their work that was generally not typical, even among the more verbally articulate students.[167] Millard's manner—which was parodied by students who would ask each other, "What do you mean by 'mean?'"—refused to tolerate the use of the word "notion" to explain an incubating design idea. "Notions," he would say, "are what you find in a five and dime store." As the Sixties went on, Millard became more Kahn-like in his thought and expression, as exemplified in "Now and Then," an epigrammatic contribution to *Perspecta* 11 that included phrases like "More people are dealing with more information, exercising more choice over more factors of living."[168] Millard advocated a functionalism that would not reject formal brilliance but be integral to the problem at hand. He also lobbied against the hero-architect model that Rudolph embodied: "I am interested," Millard wrote in *Perspecta,* "in finding methods of combining diverse insights in the creative construction of architectural ideas: the hypothesis I'm testing is that more minds are better than fewer, provided that the principle of relevance can be maintained."[169]

Craig Hodgetts remembers enjoying the freedom of Millard's studio, and the lessons that came with it:

> Peter took us out and sat us under an oak tree in the courtyard behind the Kahn art museum and explained to us the routine of the studio. He said, "Ok, I'm going to be in my office. Here's the phone number. Decide on a project you want to pursue. I will see you at X date for the final presentation. Call me if you have any questions." It was kind of fantastic to me to be let loose after Berkeley's prescriptive educational format. "You shall draw on this particular piece of paper," etc. That wasn't appealing to me. So Millard did that. I was happy as a clam; so was everyone else. I found a competition project that I liked. You did what you felt like doing. So I made a presentation that I thought was pretty fantastic, with inlaid aluminum foil and all this stuff. It was up on the wall and during the final review—there had been no contact between me and Peter, zero. [At the final jury, Peter] came up to it and he asked me why I had done the project. I said, "Well it was a competition." He said, "That's not good enough."

And I was stunned. I was speechless. I couldn't summon up another reason for doing it. Another reason never even occurred to me. And he failed me. I thought it was the most incredible lesson I'd ever had in my life. It was like the zen master coming up and saying, "Oh, you've swept this clean? Well I'm going to dump some leaves on it." It was very powerful. It was simple. It was a good lesson. So things righted themselves a bit. I went after things with a different sense of meaning.[170]

After breaking up his partnership with Earl P. Carlin, Millard embarked on a quixotic career as a sole practitioner, a career that would be compromised by his growing cynicism about the profession as a whole. His work, as seen in a series of houses published in *Perspecta* 18, reveals how he moved from the Brutalism of the Central Fire Station to the historicism of the Colonial, Georgian-inspired Prete House in Woodbridge, Connecticut (1973).[171]

Like Millard, Pat Goeters had reservations about the prevailing studio culture, and especially the jury system, which together constituted "a first class patrician attitude" that "tends to habituate the student toward *isolated and proprietary decision-making; decisions based on cult-values: values shared among architects often almost exclusively; treatment of client which alternates between numerical data orientation and evasive competition*" (Goeters's emphasis).[172] Millard and Goeters were influenced by Chris Argyris (1923–2013), Beach Professor of Administrative Science until 1971, when he decamped to the Harvard Business School, and Kai Erikson (b. 1931), professor of sociology and American studies.[173] Goeters quoted Argyris's assessment of university education: "The university has typically assumed that learning (1) is for the individual, (2) occurs when it is given, (3) is tested by contrived examinations of the knowledge acquired, (4) need not be relevant to any immediate problem, (5) should be designed and controlled by the educator to define the problems, develop ways to solve them and define the criteria for evaluating who passes and who doesn't." He then went on to recapitulate an alternative model devised by Argyris: an educational approach that "(1) focuses on individuals in team systems and (2) it occurs where the problem is located, (3) is learned by the use of actual problems and (4) is tested by the effectiveness of the actual results, and (5) is controlled by those participating in the problem (aided by the educator as consultant)."[174]

In 1966, the Charlotte Shepherd Davenport Fund was established through the generosity of Professor Shepherd Stevens.[175] As masterminded by Brewster, the fund, supporting a visiting professorship, would ensure that the visiting critic system would be a permanent part of the program. Brewster was never quite sure about Moore, believing his strength was as an educator rather than as a designer. Moreover, Moore preferred to surround himself with like-minded resident faculty, but Brewster was intent on inviting high-wire visiting design faculty like those Rudolph had attracted to Yale.

In the effort to ensure James Stirling's continued association with Yale, the school invited him to serve as the inaugural occupant of the Davenport Chair and, as such, function as the department's artistic leader, with Moore focusing on administrative duties. In an April 1965 letter written to Stirling while Rudolph was still chairman, but with Moore already appointed as his replacement, Brewster stated that the chair carried "academic obligations similar to those until recently discharged by Paul Rudolph, except that Charles Moore, as chairman . . . would have the responsibility for developing the educational strategy of the school and for dealing with University admin-istration with respect to the human and financial resources to carry it out." Recognizing Stirling's "primary ambition . . . to design and build buildings of significance," Brewster stated his belief that Stirling's "work as an architect would benefit from your role as teacher and critic, just as I think Paul's has." Brewster also offered Stirling some unsolicited professional advice: "The best way to enter intensive practice in the United States with minimum loss of momentum would be to become affiliated in a purely formal way with some existing office." Addressing a popular concern among the practicing architects on Yale's faculty, he added, "One matter I would speak of quite can-didly, although not with negative intent: that is the chance of building at Yale. Obviously we have no flat bar to commissioning a member of our own faculty to build a Yale building. However, I am against making forward commitments to any particular commission until it is upon us." Brewster concluded his letter of invitation with a few words about his ambitions for the school: "Under Paul, who was supported without reservation by my predecessor, we have sustained a momentum of high excitement, and have remained true to a tradition which has emphasized design—architecture as an art. While I real-ize that new technology and new urban demands are posing new problems and possibilities which may draw on other disciplines, I hope that design may remain the focus of Yale's work in architecture." Recognizing Moore's disdain for the New York scene, Brewster hoped that Yale, presumably as a consequence of Stirling's international reputation and continued presence on the faculty, would "remain not only an exciting intellectual annex to the New York profession and clientele, but shall remain a place where new excitement and new younger practitioners will expect to be found."[176]

After giving the invitation "long and conscientious thought; weigh-
ing out all the factors," Stirling replied that he had "decided not to take up
[Brewster's] very generous offer." Conveying his "regards to Charles Moore"
and wishing "him every success in his new position," Stirling went on to
express his willingness to continue his association with the school as a visiting
critic.[177] Months went by with no appointment made to fill the chair, but by
September 10, 1965, Moore had revised Brewster's initial invitation in a way
that would allow Stirling to maintain his active practice by occupying the
Davenport Chair for only part of each academic year, saying: "But I wonder
whether the following arrangements wouldn't be the best procedure: would
you come as Visiting Professor (we could stick a fancy name on that) for say
10 to 12 weeks each year (more if you would like) for the next 5 years (or more
or fewer if you would like) so that we and you could advertise the connection?
If the period were not so long so that it disturbed your existing practice but
long enough so that it gave you the opportunity to nail down the available jobs,
then we would seem to have achieved some modest measure of simultaneous
cake-eating and -having."[178] In January 1966, Gibson Danes and Moore took the
matter of the Davenport Chair one step further, proposing that the position be
split three ways: offering it to Stirling, Venturi, and the Dutch architect Aldo
van Eyck—a rich mix that, according to Moore, had led Ed Barnes to go "so
far as to talk about the New Bauhaus."[179] Ultimately, it was decided to split the
Davenport Chair between Stirling and Venturi, in effect carrying over the most
provocative visiting critics from the Rudolph years. Initially, each architect
occupied the chair for a part of each term, but beginning in 1971, when Venturi
resigned from the position to focus more on his growing professional practice,
Stirling alone occupied the chair in the fall term, permitting a succession of
other notable architects to occupy it during the spring terms. After Stirling
stepped down, a new appointment was made each fall term as well. Recently,
Greg Lynn has occupied a position similar to Stirling's as a semipermanent
fixture at the school, serving as Davenport Professor almost every spring term
since 2000.[180]

In his early visits to Yale under Rudolph, Stirling did not write his own
studio briefs, but participated as a critic with others in various studios and
worked with thesis students. However, during Rudolph's last year, Stirling
was able to determine his own studio briefs, offering two projects, the MAXX
Housing (spring 1965) and the TRACK Housing (fall 1965), revealing a socially
minded approach in keeping with the times. Doug Michels's TRACK house
design utilized a modular, panel-based system that could be adapted to suit the
needs of its occupant (5.18, 5.19). For the MAXX studio, Michels, together with

Arthur Golding and Craig Hodgetts, set out to design a conceptually related "plug-in" development, presented with "flashy and colorful graphics . . . geared toward a project's dissemination in the media."[181] Their proposal was published in *Archigram* 7, which was particularly appropriate because Hodgetts and Michels were greatly influenced by the rebellious group of English architects and their eponymous journal. Inspiration for the MAXX project also came from Hodgetts's own background in automotive engineering and his collaborations with the Sculpture Department, led by Erwin Hauer (b. 1926):

> This plug-in housing thing progressed kind of in tandem with the sculpture studio. The models we made were plaster, and we made them down in the sculpture studio, which was a dark dungeon at that point with a seven-foot-high ceiling.
>
> This was one of those neat times when things fuse together. Hauer, I think, was quite fascinated with vacuum forming [fig. 5.20]. He had never seen that before. I did some vacuum forming experiments, which were kind of double-curved surfaces and Klein Bottle–like intersections. We built our own vacuum forming thing with two-by-fours and a vacuum cleaner. The sculpture studio was very active. There was an incredible energy down there. Anyway, our homemade vacuum former was not powerful enough to draw the deep forms we designed. So we went to a company that does those signs that stick to the sides of cars and that guy made the pieces we used. It was painted very bright colors, and painted with automotive spray paint. The drawings were done with Zip-a-Tone and not hand drawn. At that time, you would stipple things by hand; we were using synthetic overlays. There was one jury when Philip Johnson said, "I'm not going to look at any more of this shit," and walked out. I would say the reception was not very warm. But there were a few, like Stirling, who were exceedingly supportive.[182]

Once Stirling began to occupy the Davenport Chair, the focus of his studios shifted away from individual buildings to a growing emphasis on cities, which were assumed by many to be dying entities in the face of suburban expansion and the rise of home-based entertainment via electronic media. Stirling seemed to accept this, but did not despair, offering a prophetic conception of urbanism: cities "may continue to exist primarily for young people and mainly for entertainment. The whole city is a discotheque."[183] Stirling's grasp of urban issues was intuitive rather than theory-based and reflected his growing disdain for both modernist architecture and urbanism, which he first

5.18 Doug Michels (M.Arch 1967) TRACK Housing, model (fall 1965).

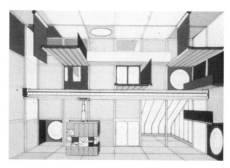

5.19 Doug Michels TRACK Housing, section-
perspective (fall 1965).

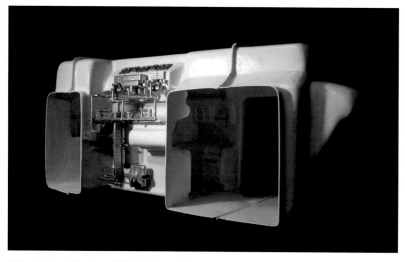

5.20 Arthur Golding (B.A. 1963, M.Arch 1967), Craig Hodgetts (M.Arch 1967), and Doug Michels,
MAXX Housing, vacuum-formed model (spring 1965).

expressed in a 1967 interview in *Perspecta*: "I think it's unfortunate you [the United States] didn't continue skyscraper building after the war unaffected by European modern architecture. Compared with the towers of the 20s and 30s the new buildings are fat regular slabs and the old silhouette is being blocked in by them. More seriously, the effect of the street is being diminished by the 'commercial concession' of positioning the new buildings back from the pavement line and forming plazas, podiums, etc." In the *Perspecta* interview, Stirling goes on to reflect that "it's a pity the traditional Chrysler type wasn't further developed with pedestrian circulation systems forced through and across the block at the lower levels making shopping arcades and internal self-supporting environments of which Grand Central is a primitive prototype." Proclaiming himself "almost 100 percent preservationist, particularly in regard to 19th century towns in England, which are being transformed by 'contemporary' architecture into meaningless, anonymous and inefficient places," Stirling wrote that "even apart from the monuments, almost every 19th century (and earlier) building has more architectural quality than the 'contemporary' architecture which is replacing them."[184]

As Brewster and Stirling had discussed, Stirling's decision to commit to Yale was in large measure a reflection of his desire to establish an architectural practice in the United States. His biographer, Mark Girouard, writes that "It was frustrating for him, constantly shackled as he was to underfunded buildings in England, to observe the potential lavishness of expenditure in America: a good American practice was a chimera which he was to pursue all his life."[185] Within a year of his appointment as Davenport Professor, an opportunity for American professional work arose when his former student Jaquelin T. Robertson, then in the administration of New York Mayor John V. Lindsay, invited him to head a team tasked with studying the West Midtown section of Manhattan, stretching from Eighth Avenue to the Hudson River between Forty-Second and Fifty-Seventh streets.[186] To help prepare the plan, Stirling set up a New York–based team that included M. J. Long, who since leaving Yale in 1964 had been working in England for Sandy Wilson "and had returned to America to escape from a situation which was to end in her marrying Sandy, as his second wife, in 1972,"[187] and Craig Hodgetts, who went straight into the office where Stirling appeared "only sporadically"; once Stirling realized that no building commissions were likely to come his way, he preferred to concentrate on the development of a bird's-eye view of the planning area.

Stirling's studios typically reflected his own professional interests, but Davenport Professor Robert Venturi, working in collaboration with Denise Scott Brown, favored research-intensive studios focusing on situations that were rarely encountered either in practice or in architectural schools at the time. The Venturi–Scott Brown studios—Scott Brown's participation was critical to the success of these studios, though only Venturi was given the title Davenport Visiting Professor—marked a significant shift away from "master-piece" design studios toward thematic platform studios. The Venturi–Scott Brown approach was not unlike Chermayeff's in its emphasis on research and its concern with urban situations, but it was significantly different in its distinctly antimodernist bias, its on-the-ground approach, and its Pop-art–like embrace of commercial culture. Taken together, these studios introduced a new approach to design with conventional scholarship and traditional modes of representation with new media, including film. Though the Venturi–Scott Brown studios were widely regarded as seminal pedagogical events of the 1960s, they were, as Martino Stierli has observed, surprisingly out of step with the typical politicized studios of the day at other schools of architecture: "Venturi and Scott Brown's approach was revolutionary precisely in its renun-ciation of the rhetoric of revolution in favor of focusing architectural thought and action on the here and now. . . . Working with the image of the city, and working *on* the image of the city [Stierli's emphasis], became one of their cen-tral concerns. It is this insistence on the city as it actually is that is the lasting legacy of Learning from Las Vegas."[188]

Venturi's first studio as Davenport Visiting Professor took place during the fall 1967 semester: "The People's Freeway Project" analyzed the Herald Square subway station in New York. The now-iconic studio "Learning from Las Vegas, or Form Analysis as Design Research" followed in fall 1968, and then "Learning from Levittown or Remedial Housing for Architects" in spring 1970.[189] "The People's Freeway Project" (see 5.25) challenged students to consider what Venturi believed to be the new paradigm for civic space: the long, low, artificially illuminated public interior. In preparing for the studio, Venturi and Scott Brown, along with Brewster (Bruce) Adams (1915–1989) and teaching assistant Gregory Matviak (b. 1941; M.Arch 1969), were assisted by members of the New York City Planning Commission's recently founded and Yale-dominated Urban Design Group; the group was led by Jaquelin T. Robertson, Jonathan Barnett, Myles Weintraub (b. 1937; B.A. 1958, M.Arch 1962), and Richard Weinstein (b. 1932), a 1960 graduate of Penn's architecture program who had been driven out of Harvard's first year by Serge Chermayeff because he insisted on working in the tradition of Frank Lloyd Wright. The establishment of the Urban Design Group marked a decisive turning point in New York's planning policies and procedures, adding to the customary con-siderations of demographics, statistics, and land-use a responsibility for the shaping of public space; its work would have a lasting impact, not only on New York, but also on many other American cities that incorporated its strategies into their planning processes.[190]

The emphasis of the People's Freeway Project was on "communication over circulation." Its decidedly antiheroic tone was made clear in the *Perspecta* 12 documentation of the project "Mass Communication on the People Freeway or Piranesi Is Too Easy," in which Venturi wrote that "lighting and the words and symbols of advertising," along with the "assemblages of conventional subway elements such as gum machines," are the tools available to contemporary architects who have "limited control" over infrastructural shapes.[191] Seventeen students enrolled in the "People's Freeway" studio, including six from the Graphic Design Department. The architects included Manfred Ibel, Herbert Short (M.Arch 1969), and Simeon Bruner (M.Arch 1968), who, with Leland Cott, would later form an important Boston-based practice.[192] Scott Brown's program, directing student research toward considerations of lighting and ventilation systems, user behavior, and way-finding graphics, had as its basis the conviction that high construction costs made it infeasible to build new, monumental, Piranesian spaces such as those of Grand Central Station, while the "big low civic space," such as the nearly finished rebuilt Pennsylvania Station in New York (1968), presented a new typology "brought about by urban densities and the costs of air-conditioning."[193]

The seminal "Learning from Las Vegas" studio was held in the fall term of 1968, but juried in January 1969.[194] It was led by Venturi and Scott Brown, with Steven Izenour as teaching assistant. Scott Brown first showed an interest in Las Vegas in 1965; a year later she invited Venturi to join her on an exploratory trip to the desert city, resulting in the publication in March 1968 of their jointly written article, "A Significance for A&P Parking Lots, or Learning from Las Vegas."[195] Venturi's Davenport Professor position provided them with the perfect opportunity to extend their research. But before the work could truly begin, Venturi and Scott Brown were adamant that their students had to experience Las Vegas firsthand. Unfortunately, funds for student travel were almost unheard of at the time. Given the cost of travel for students and faculty, they projected a studio budget of $10,925 (approximately $75,000 in 2015), of which only $2,000 was "in hand."[196] Venturi solicited $5,000 in funds from Howard Hughes, but the reclusive billionaire with extensive business interests in Las Vegas was not forthcoming. Eventually, money was raised from multiple sources, including $1,000 from Philip Johnson, $2,500 from the Edgar Kaufmann, Jr., Foundation, $1,000 from the Nathaniel and Margaret Downing Foundation, $1,000 from Yale, and another $2,000 as a loan.[197] Additionally,

Ray Schaeffer, of the Stardust Hotel, housed and fed students during their ten days in Las Vegas, and Vaughan Cannon of the Young Electric Sign Company made four cars available for student use, while Tim Vreeland, then professor at UCLA's architecture school, arranged for the studio to use a UCLA guesthouse and some cars during the first leg of their trip.[198]

Fourteen students drawn from the third year, as well as from the programs in graphic design and city planning, took part in the studio, which began with a four-day visit to Los Angeles, "to become better acquainted with the unique environment of which Las Vegas is really a satellite"—that is to say, the auto-centric contemporary American city.[199] In Los Angeles, students saw high art and low, visiting the artist Ed Ruscha in his studio, Disneyland, the Sunset Strip, Simon Rodia's Watts Towers, as well as houses by Frank Lloyd Wright, Rudolph Schindler, and the custom car garages of George Barris and Ed "Big Daddy" Roth, which Tom Wolfe had written about in his best-selling collection of essays *The Kandy-Kolored Tangerine-Flake Streamline Baby* (1965). After four days in the City of Angels, the studio headed for the desert to begin their ten-day stay in Las Vegas, during which they attended the opening night of the newest casino on the Strip, Circus Circus.[200]

The subject matter of the studio was startling, with students asked to think critically about the "ordinary" and the "everyday" landscapes of the postindustrial city—sprawl and all—and to give serious consideration to pop-culture iconography. Expectations were high. "Denise in particular," says Peter Hoyt (b. 1944; M.Arch 1970), "really drove us to have the highest standards in our research and documentation."[201] For Ron Filson (b. 1946; M.Arch 1970), "The workload that Denise laid out made it seem that we had just arrived at Paris Island for Marine boot camp. . . . But," he added, "somehow a few of us managed to waste a little time at blackjack."[202] Filson says: "We did a few drawings that only a crazed third-year student with too little sleep could produce. I can't believe the number of hours that I spent slumped over a film-editing machine." Another student in the studio, Charles Korn (M.C.P. 1969), remembers that throughout the entire process, Scott Brown and Venturi "encouraged, demanded, cajoled, and supported us in their unique style."[203] As Daniel Scully recounts: "I remember clearly realizing the great depth of informative analysis Denise, as city planner, organized into the studio; and that Bob, as architect, probably learned all he needed to by a few trips up and down The Strip."[204] The student work was prolific: five thousand slides and three thousand meters of film were produced, as well as pages upon pages of statistical information. Upon their return to New Haven, Venturi and Scott Brown observed that this nearly exhaustive collective of research presented its own set of challenges: "Our problem is to find the graphic means to distinguish our hard knowledge from the [t]remendous variety of subjective, but no less meaningful, knowledge we all brought back from Las Vegas."[205] The studio's highly innovative documentation methods linked scientific research techniques with architectural design, and, as with the "People's Freeway" project, it emphasized collaborative work. Students experimented with new and hybridized documentation and representation techniques, using maps, diagrams, sketches, video, and other nontraditional (for the time) modes of architectural and urban analysis (5.21, 5.22).

The final presentation of the term's work—before a panel of critics that included Vincent Scully, writer Tom Wolfe (b. 1931; Ph.D. 1957), and the Miami-based, professionally derided architect Morris Lapidus (1902–2001)—took place on January 19, 1969, and was advertised with large posters describing the studio as "The Grand Proletarian Cultural Locomotive" (5.23). The studio's findings served as the core of the book *Learning from Las Vegas: The Forgotten Symbolism of Architectural Form* (1972), which was, as Venturi scholar Martino Stierli has written, "both a serious urbanistic study and a rhetorical thunderbolt" that would have a profound influence on architectural culture, history, and theory, forever changing the way architects look at the commercial landscape.[206] *Learning from Las Vegas* became one of the most important texts—arguably *the* most important text—of postmodernism, perhaps rivaled only by Venturi's own *Complexity and Contradiction in Architecture* (1966). The Las Vegas book covers much more than the Yale studio and includes an extensive and devastating critique of New Haven's Paul Rudolph–designed Crawford Manor (1966) apartments that would cause lasting damage to the architect's reputation. However, reviews of the book were mixed. Historian and critic Kenneth Frampton deemed it "ideology in its purest form," a promotion of "the ruthless kitsch of Las Vegas, as an exemplary mask for the concealment of the brutality of our own environment."[207] Moore, whose work is often compared with Venturi's and who described himself as Venturi's "ardent fan," was uncomfortable with the Las Vegas study: "I grow most uneasy because the dialectic seems contrary to that inclusive tolerance of new and old things and of different points of view that illuminates Venturi and [John] Rauch's work, and makes it, in my opinion so extraordinarily important."[208]

Writing about the studio in *Novum Organum,* Donald Watson reported that some students recognized it to be "a carefully edited perception of one aspect of Las Vegas. . . . The LLV production was a limited representation of a limited point of view, an abstraction of an abstraction of an abstraction most eloquently typified by the drawing 'Nolli's Las Vegas.'"

5.21 Students mounting a camera to the hood of their car to document a drive down the Las Vegas Strip (1968).

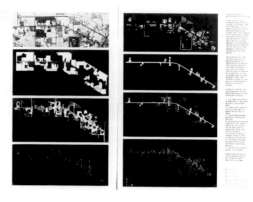

5.22 A page from the first edition of *Learning from Las Vegas* (1972) depicting Nolli-style maps of the Las Vegas strip created by students.

5.23 Poster advertising the final review of the Las Vegas studio (1969).

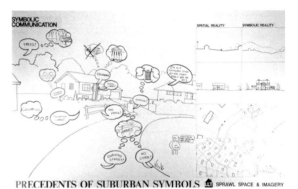

5.24 Robert Miller (B.A. 1967, M.Arch 1971), Precedents of Suburban Symbols (1970).

5.25 Manfred Ibel (M.Arch 1968), The People's Freeway Project, Collage Impressions of the Thirty-Fourth Street-Herald Square Subway Station (1967).

5.26 Robert Miller, preparing to cut into his "Panther Arms" cake project. At right: Denise Scott Brown (1970).

Watson's critique anticipated that of numerous subsequent attacks made on the studio by scholars and historians. But his conclusion differed: "LLV . . . shows us how to perceive the world as the Venturi's [sic] do. And this, for an architectural student, is an invaluable education."[209] In time, the Las Vegas studio would be recognized as a turning point in architectural education that "all but jettisoned the traditional design component of studio instruction," launching "a new 'learning from' paradigm in architecture education and, by deferring design until it could be informed by actual research, [it] also gave new life to formal investigation."[210]

"Learning from Levittown," the last Venturi–Scott Brown studio, was more politically engaged than its predecessors, responding to "the short-comings of urban renewal and the failures of affordable housing."[211] Although the program for the Levittown studio was published in *Venturi Scott Brown and Associates: On Houses and Housing,* Jessica Lautin writes that "it gets lost in the shadow" of the Las Vegas studio, "in part because there was no resulting publication [of the student projects] but also because it is difficult to grasp its conclusions."[212] The Levittown studio also got overlooked because it was offered at the school's nadir, when it was struggling to recover from the cataclysmic events of May and June 1969. The studio "attempted . . . a conversation between artists and audience by asking students to investigate those developments already in place," with the expectation that the "students would then use their knowledge to create designs and policies for suburban homes that lower-income residents could afford."[213] At the studio's outset, students were presented with a thoughtful and provocative, idea-based program statement that was, in effect, an argument—a far cry from the value-free list of program requirements typically handed out to students in the Rudolph era: "The studio is an attempt to relate ourselves as architects more realistically to the problem of housing than we have done in the past. Interest lies more in what people make of their housing than in what the architects intend them to make of it. It is an examination of the field from an action-oriented and architectural point of view, designed to make deeper study of housing more meaningful."[214]

The Levittown studio began with research and culminated "in the design of a suburban area which includes low-income residents in a regional strategy for low income housing in New Haven." Students were expected to design "new roles for architects to fit new ideals and a new situation" to offer "an artistic reinterpretation of suburban residential artifacts."[215] Needless to say, the studio was more concerned with the iconography of ordinary house types—split level, Cape Cod, Ranch—than with "the iconography (or structure) of the Dymaxion House or Falling Water." Early in the term, students traveled to Levittown, Pennsylvania, Washington D.C., and Williamsburg, Virginia. Back in New Haven, there were lots of "rap" sessions, along with lectures and presentations from experts in the social sciences and development, including social scientists Kai Erikson and John Zeisel, as well as planning theorist and social activist Paul Davidoff of the Suburban Action Institute.[216] Vincent Scully lectured on the United States' tendency to destroy rather than conserve.

According to Jessica Lautin, Robert Miller's final project "best illustrated the studio's ambitions and its missing ingredients."[217] Miller, who had been editor of the *Yale Record,* the undergraduate humor magazine, developed precedent drawings that appropriated comic book graphics (5.24). But even more interesting was his model, a large cake that he shaped, baked, and decorated to suggest a Ranch-style suburban house situated amidst more conventional subdivision houses (5.26). Referring to one of the era's best-known protest movements, Miller named his project "Panther Arms" and boldly took on sensitive suburban stereotypes by replacing the all-too-familiar black-faced lawn jockey with a custom-made, red-dyed version whose fist was raised in the Black Panther salute, thereby transforming a racist, elitist image with one of radical race pride. Many critics found Miller's proposal, and the studio itself, a bit too much to take, including Vincent Scully, who thought its focus "too vulgar."[218] Ultimately, there were few connections made between the students' taxonomy of suburban architectural styles and their research into low-income housing, and, as Lautin notes, "the students' work demonstrated only a cursory understanding of those values and lifestyles."[219] Nonetheless, the work was provocative, if somewhat inscrutable and open to interpretation, and ultimately led to a museum exhibition: *Signs of Life,* at the Smithsonian's Renwick Gallery in 1976, which was an attempt by Venturi and Scott Brown "to survey the pluralist aesthetic of the American city and its suburbs, and to understand what the urban landscape means to people, through an analysis of its symbols, their sources, and their antecedents."[220]

In March 1967, Gibson Danes announced his intention to resign as dean in July in order to take the "irresistible" post of dean of visual arts at the newly established Purchase, New York, campus of the State University of New York, where his responsibilities would include planning new buildings, "developing a new curriculum and program and recruiting a new staff." [221] Howard Sayre Weaver (1925–1982; B.A. 1945) took over, first as acting dean, then, in May 1968, as dean. Whereas Danes was an experienced arts administrator before coming to Yale, his successor brought diverse but unusual qualifications to the job. During World War II, Weaver interrupted his undergraduate years at Yale to serve as pilot of a B-25 on low-level bombing and strafing missions in China and Burma. After the war he returned to Yale to complete his education, worked as a press officer in the State Department, then returned to New Haven in 1959 as assistant director of the Yale University Press and, soon afterward, as an assistant to university President Alfred Whitney Griswold and then to Kingman Brewster. As presidential assistant, his duties—official and unofficial—included handling public relations, representing Yale at alumni functions, planning new university programs, and hosting Martin Luther King, Jr., when Yale presented him with an honorary degree in 1964. Although not an artist or architect, Weaver's experiences representing Yale made him seem well suited to the task at hand, particularly as the school and university were increasingly challenged by the New Haven community. On the occasion of Weaver's appointment, Danes assured Brewster that the new dean "will make an excellent Zoo-Keeper and one who can plot many of the inevitable new developments for the future."[222]

In spring 1968, while Yale students and faculty were pondering the role of computers in architecture and building idiosyncratic foam structures in the studio and on the golf course, Columbia's architecture students were joining forces with undergraduates and others to protest an ill-conceived gymnasium proposed for a site in Morningside Park that would have provided separate and unequal facilities for university students and Harlem residents.[223] The crippling student strike that ensued and Columbia University's decision to invite city policemen onto the campus to break it up shocked the nation. At the same time, architecture students in Paris struck out against the École des Beaux-Arts, causing the architecture section of the more than 320-year-old institution to be dissolved. Needless to say, these events were carefully watched by students at Yale, many of whom had witnessed the riots that had taken place in the summer of 1967 in New Haven's black neighborhoods.[224]

It was not until fall 1968 that things began to heat up at Yale, when architecture students became increasingly political and vocal, encouraged in part by the arrival of Harry J. Quintana (1938–2009; M.Arch 1969) and Colin (Topper) Carew (b. 1943; M.Arch 1970). Quintana was born in San Juan, Puerto Rico, and raised in Harlem. He attended Howard University but took a leave from its Department of Architecture and Planning to enter both the master of architecture and master of urban studies programs at Yale. Quintana was an adamant advocate for culturally specific education.[225] In the April 1968 issue of *Jet* magazine, he criticized Howard's curriculum, asking, "Why should our music students break their necks over Bach, when our people identify more readily with James Brown. Soul is just as much a reflection of black people today as Bach was of the Europeans in his time."[226] Consciously employing controversial language, Quintana, writing with Charles Jones, a Howard University architecture student, angrily stated the problem in *Perspecta* 12: "The books were written by whites for the designing of White America, and they conceded either all niggers belong in vertical concentration camps called Public Housing Projects, or whites can let them in a little at a time into their sterile sprawling suburbs. We threw away all those stupid racist books and looked out of the window of our studio, located in the Black inner city of Washington, and asked ourselves—what's wrong with our people's environment? The answer is simple—it was not designed for us and for our life style, and we are not in control of it."[227] In concluding the *Perspecta* article, Quintana and Jones acknowledged authors who influenced their thinking: Malcolm X, Marshall McLuhan, and Robert Venturi and his book *Complexity and Contradiction in Architecture*.

Topper Carew had studied architecture at Howard University but never graduated. "Our senior project," he told an interviewer in 2005, "was to design an executive mansion for the vice president. I wasn't feeling that, and I quit," though he stayed in D.C. as an unlicensed, self-proclaimed "people's architect," working out of a storefront on behalf of those in danger of losing their homes under laws of eminent domain.[228] At the same time, Carew started filming the neighborhood kids who would look curiously through his storefront windows and began to incorporate these videos into his architectural work. When he came to Yale as a student, Carew also taught a course on community activism and the social relevance of architecture. Eventually, he would leave architecture completely to go on to a career in film and television, where he is perhaps best known as the creator of the NAACP Image Award–winning television show *Martin,* which ran from 1992 to 1997.

Egged on by the radicalism of Quintana and Carew, both the school's architecture and city planning programs became increasingly radicalized. Brian Goldstein, in an excellent overview of the roles the Architecture and City Planning departments played in the collapse of what he calls New Haven's "New Deal Spatial Order" of top-down planning and redevelopment, states that Yale students "resisted what they considered an authoritarian mode of urban design that seemed increasingly obsolete both as it was taught and as it was practiced" and, "like their colleagues nationwide . . . demanded peda-gogical changes that would help to foster greater engagement with the people whom architects and planners served." In this story of dramatic change that marked the end of traditional city planning as a discipline at Yale, but more importantly as it set out to become an instrument for positive social change, the university provided "an especially rich context," offering, as Goldstein writes, "at one site the convergence of a leading design school, an active student movement, and the country's most exemplary urban redevelopment program. Design students frustrated with their education had only to look out the window to find inspiration in the social protests of fellow students and increasing unrest among their neighbors in the 'model city.'"[229]

According to Goldstein, it was students in Carew's fall 1968 urban design seminar who "turned the professional critique implicit in [prevailing] alternative design practices into an explicit critique directed against architecture's major professional organization, the AIA."[230] This took place in New Haven at the November 8, 1968, New England Area AIA conference where, encouraged by Carew, students staged a dramatic walkout. The students, many of whom had worked in poor communities, were primed to make a statement and "didn't need much nudging," according to Tom Carey, a leader of the revolt. The disruptive group then held a counter-conference with their own speakers and agenda. Art Hacker (B.A. 1965, M.Arch 1970) reported in the pages of *Novum Organum* that the "statements and subsequent walkout met with applause from the AIA delegates," many of whom, in return, "deserted their own conference for the students'" in an attempt to better understand what unique views the students were advocating."[231] Immediately after the walkout, the protesting students quickly drew up a petition (5.27) stating their intent:

> All people must have the right and power to control their own lives. Like any other profession, architecture is not an end in itself, but part of a political process. Because we believe human values are more important than material values:
> - We will only use our skills as tools for liberating oppressed peoples.
> - The architects [*sic*] only responsibility is to the people who use the environment.
> - We will work for the Equal Distribution of Economic Power.
> - [We will] work against such U.S. Activities as the War in Southeast Asia, or any imperialist and racist exploitation at home and abroad. [We will] work against those who exploit people and land for their own power and profit.[232]

The petition was signed by more than fifty people and included some names that, in retrospect, seem quite surprising, such as that of Edward P. Bass (b.

1945; B.S. 1967, Art.A 1972, M.A.H. 2001), who was from a wealthy Texas family and would go on to become the senior fellow of the Yale Corporation and a major donor to the university. This document and the post-walkout counter-conference led to the formation of The Architects' Resistance (TAR) as a "communications network, research group, and action group" with a presence in several northeastern schools.[233] The group was composed of students as well as planners and practitioners intent on bringing, as they proclaimed, a "moral and social conscience to the practice of architecture."[234] Through demonstrations, events, and by publishing papers on subjects such as architecture and racism, and the Nuclear Arms Race, TAR set out to expose "allegedly unethical practices within the profession."[235]

As Goldstein has written, the walkout in New Haven was "rich with symbolism; not only did students bring the guerrilla tactics of the New Left into the heart of their chosen profession, but in walking out of the conference venue at the Park Plaza hotel, a key component of New Haven's Church Street Redevelopment project, they enacted in physical terms the rejection of the New Deal Spatial Order that they [the students] had just vocalized."[236]

On the heels of the Park Plaza walkout, amidst the increasing rebelliousness of undergraduates and especially graduate architecture students, Vincent Scully emerged as an important cautionary voice, urging students to keep their "revolt professional," to "remember . . . that the easy generalizations of various political groups are generally useless. . . . What goes on between the heart and the head, and getting that down on paper, is professional. Therefore, I take a stand, and I hope you do, against some of the elements of activism in the political organizations on campus in their current hatred of professionalism. If I were you I would honor it. It [takes] hard professional discipline to make of your profession something more than it is at the moment." Scully hoped "that as you continue in your revolt you will continue to see where the fact of your power lies, and you will continue to see what is in fact your weapon and not your enemy. This is what I mean. There were some at that walkout . . . not from Yale, who seem to regard universities as their primary enemy. And I heard some of them say also that the liberals were their major enemy." Reminding his audience of similar statements made in Germany in the early 1930s, Scully expressed his hope "that the architects' revolt has nothing to do with such suicidal, self-destructive intentions. I would hope, in fact, that you'd recognize what any reactionary will tell you, that the university is in fact the shield and spear of human freedom always."[237]

As the academic year progressed, noisy demonstrations on campus were the most visible signs of student activism. Equally unnerving was the growing sense of entitlement characterized as "student power," which centered around a conviction that young people were better equipped than their elders to address the social problems of the day. Emboldened by the slogan "Don't trust anyone over thirty," students began to press for a greater voice in the governance of the Department of Architecture, beginning with the Committee of Eight, formed in October 1968, after seventy-two architecture students signed a petition expressing their dissatisfaction "with our lack of knowledge of the administration of the Department of Architecture," which they believed "has caused considerable mistrust and misunderstanding between faculty and students."[238] The Committee of Eight, consisting of two students from each class, proposed that their members would serve on standing faculty committees, including ones dealing with curriculum, budget, and the selection of visiting critics. Although they proposed to take their new positions without voting privileges, they requested the ability to initiate proposals and to participate in all discussions. Notwithstanding Moore's relaxed, even permissive, administrative style, and the somewhat touchy-feely curricular innovations that he had initiated for advanced students, whereby students could choose "among many diversified studio/seminars, which stimulated experimental and joint projects,"[239] the increasingly politicized students argued that the curriculum was too much a reflection of standardized requirements imposed by the National Architectural Accrediting Board, proposing that "two categories of degrees be offered; an accredited M.Arch and a non-accredited M.Arch." They also called for a more intellectual approach, asking that "a seminar or lecture in the history of architecture be offered within the school" by one of the following: Charles Moore, Robert Venturi, Vincent Scully, or Bernard Rudofsky, as well as an elective course in landscape architecture and "a series of 'gratis' lectures open to all four years," which "would cover a greater range of material in a time period and depth commensurate to the material offered"; the students asked that the lecture series "in the doldrums for the past two years . . . be revitalized."[240] As part of the Committee of Eight's proposal, students in third-year and thesis programs asked that their studios be replaced by three or four semesters of distinct work options or seminars, with some possibly operated out-of-residence. They also asked that the first-year environmental control course "become what was originally proposed—a theoretical introduction to the implications of the perception and control of environments—a course aimed at *what* environmental control is, rather than *how* it is achieved."[241] In a thinly veiled attack on Moore's administrative style, the Committee of Eight suggested hiring a business manager and requested that some measure of regulation be imposed on the studio work areas, the informal partitions of which

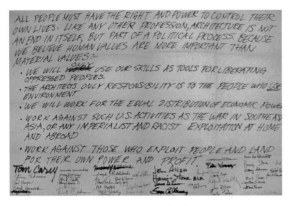

ALL PEOPLE MOST HAVE THE RIGHT AND POWER TO CONTROL THEIR
OWN LIVES. LIKE ANY OTHER PROFESSION, ARCHITECTURE IS NOT
AN END IN ITSELF, BUT PART OF A POLITICAL PROCESS. BECAUSE
WE BELIEVE HUMAN VALUES ARE MORE IMPORTANT THAN
MATERIAL VALUES:–
• WE WILL ~~ONLY~~ USE OUR SKILLS AS TOOLS FOR LIBERATING
   OPPRESSED PEOPLES.
• THE ARCHITECTS ONLY RESPONSIBILITY IS TO THE PEOPLE WHO USE
   ENVIRONMENT
• WE WILL WORK FOR THE EQUAL DISTRIBUTION OF ECONOMIC POWER
• WORK AGAINST SUCH U.S. ACTIVITIES AS THE WAR IN SOUTHEAST
   ASIA, OR ANY IMPERIALIST AND RACIST EXPLOITATION AT HOME
   AND ABROAD
• WORK AGAINST THOSE WHO EXPLOIT PEOPLE AND LAND
   FOR THEIR OWN POWER AND PROFIT

5.27   Petition drawn up after the 1968 AIA walkout.

5.28   Mock funeral organized by A&A students to protest financial aid
(May 8, 1969).

5.29   Students lowering the coffin of the "Unknown
A&A Student" into the sunken sculpture court of
Beineke Library.

5.30   John Jacobson conducts a mock auction at the Yale University Art
Gallery to protest inadequate financial aid (May 9, 1969).

5.31   Kingman Brewster meets with students in the
Art and Architecture, Drama, and Music schools
(May 15, 1969). In the background is a power-fist
symbol created by A&A students for use during
protests.

had formed something like a *favela* on the fourth and fifth floors of the Art and Architecture Building.

Stuart Wrede felt that the committee's meetings with Moore placed the students "in an ambivalent and frustrating situation which none of us like. We are playing Mr. Moore's game on his terms; in retrospect the situation seems to have been cast that way from the outset," with information concerning the budget, visiting critics, and contracts made public "but only as irreversible decisions for the coming year." Wrede believed that Moore used the committee as an "information source" but did not give them a real role in decision-making: "Thus, the two most critical issues, the inadequate commitment on the part of the university to the School and the problem of the school being staffed largely by mediocre faculty (many of them brought here by Mr. Moore himself) cannot be dealt with."[242]

As the spring 1969 term neared its end, everything seemed to spin out of control, beginning with the students' decision to concentrate on one specific issue: the lack of financial aid available to the university's art programs. On April 28, 1969, they petitioned Kingman Brewster to grant students of the arts equal financial support to that given Ph.D. students in the Graduate School of Art and Sciences, where "over ninety percent of the students receive financial aid in the order of full tuition waiver, plus two hundred dollars a month." In their petition, the students also requested that incurred debts for enrolled students be canceled and a policy of need-blind admissions to the school be established. The students concluded with a promise to be at the president's office on May 7 to receive a written reply.[243] In a letter to Brewster, Weaver expressed his support for "efforts to achieve uniform procedures of allocation of financial aid on the basis of need in all schools and, obviously, to increase financial aid available to students in this School." However, in light of the bleak prospects for raising funds to meet their goals, Weaver advised "candor on the part of students," surely meaning to write "on the part of the administration."[244]

At noon on Wednesday, May 7, approximately one hundred students from the various arts divisions—art, architecture, music, and drama—bearing placards and carrying banners advocating financial parity with students in the Graduate School of Arts and Sciences marched on Woodbridge Hall, where they received Brewster's answering letter acknowledging their plight, but offering no expectation for a near-term solution: "The only honest answer to the 'demands' for tuition abatement or greatly increased student aid for next year is that neither is possible."[245] In his letter, Brewster pointed out that government programs as well as gifts to the endowment that helped support the

Graduate School of Arts and Sciences were not available for the various professional art schools. After the letter was read to the amassed students by Henry Stone (b. 1943; Art.A 1973), a smaller contingent marched to the Art Gallery where, denied entrance, they pounded on the locked doors shouting "Art is for the people!" and "More money now!" and then, before dispersing, fastened the doors with bicycle locks and embellished them with posters and palm prints in purple paint. A dozen students then camped out overnight in the Art and Architecture Building.

On the following day, May 8, art and architecture students continued their protest over financial aid. Employing techniques of "guerilla theater," they staged a mock funeral that began with the loading of a coffin labeled "The Unknown A&A Student" into a hearse, which, accompanied by motorcycle escort trailed by elaborately costumed mourners, traveled from the Art and Architecture Building to Beinecke Library, a building considered by many students to be decadent, inefficient, and inhuman (5.28, 5.29). At Beinecke, the coffin was unloaded with great solemnity into the sunken sculpture court, whereupon Tom Carey delivered a eulogy. Vincent Scully, who accompanied the procession, praised "the whole thing" as "a beautiful performance, done with great style. It was like the Living Theatre."[246]

Brewster agreed to meet with the students, but the students kept to their already-formulated plans, including a mock auction of paintings in the Art Gallery to be held later in the day (5.30). Run by auctioneer John Jacobson—"I remember being corralled into being the auctioneer but don't know why," remembers Jacobson, "I must've been to an auction recently"[247]—the protest was intended to demonstrate, according to Stone, "that the University cares more about storing paintings than supporting artists." Nearly one hundred people gathered in the gallery to hear auctioneers Jacobson and Robert Knight pitch Rembrandts and Pollocks to collectors bidding with "bogus Brewster bucks." None of the paintings were actually sold, but when the chief of campus police asked the students to leave at the gallery's closing time, they remained, continuing the auction until Vincent Scully asked them to respect the closing time: "You've made your point, and it's a good point. I advise you to leave now."[248] A short discussion followed, but students did not comply until Dean Weaver formally asked them to leave. According to Roc Caivano (b. 1944; M.Arch 1970), the students "wanted to show we felt strongly enough about the issue to consider a sit-in. But our leaving showed a commitment to reasonable action."[249] Later that evening, art and architecture students culminated their day of protests at the opening of a Yale Repertory Theatre production, where they circulated through the audience begging and selling pencils to dramatize their financial plight. Henry Stone exulted: "We hope to embarrass Brewster and the administration. . . . [Begging] was an attempt to point out the poverty of the arts at Yale."[250]

Whether or not it was a result of the student protests, Brewster and the university agreed to provide additional funding for scholarships in the various arts programs, but the students remained dissatisfied and persisted with their protests, returning to their earlier concerns about the school's pedagogy and administration in a series of large, open meetings with the faculty "to try to get at what is wrong with the educational structure" of the program (5.31).[251] Herbert Newman, who was then working with Edward Larrabee Barnes as campus planning advisor to Brewster, remembers that the student body "would gather together like a French Revolutionary council—150 of the art, architecture, painting, and graphics people . . . encouraged by some of the faculty members." The group became increasingly emboldened to the point where it decided "that instead of degrees, we would have 'The Crown of Creation.' We would put all the art and architecture students together and at the end of three or four years they would get a degree called 'The Crown of Creation.'"[252]

On May 15, Brewster attended a closed-door, three-hour meeting with the architecture faculty to address the growing discontent among the student body and to dissuade it from imposing a moratorium on coursework. Newman remembers the explosive visit:

> Brewster came with Charles Taylor, the provost, to meet the faculty up in the conference room. The students were all gathered in the gallery and were yelling at them as they walked into this private meeting with the faculty. We were all sitting there, the faculty, with [Brewster], and he was sitting at one end of the table and he said, "You know, this is not a democracy. We are accountable to the students and we are accountable to the faculty, but we are not going to give the students votes." . . . And he said, "So that's the way it is. You're the faculty. Do your job. You're in control." Charles Moore was absent, of course. But that was very telling. . . . Meanwhile, the students were up above us, banging on the glass and cursing. Banging and banging. It was very scary. The faculty were mute. But I raised my hand because I thought [Brewster] knows me and I'm his trusted advisor—the young pisser that I was—and so I said, "Mr. President, I can't speak for everyone else but I agree with what you're saying. I just want to make one suggestion: one of us should go out there and tell the students that we are meeting with you and we have a

5.32 Claes Oldenburg, *Lipstick (Ascending) on Caterpillar Tracks,* arriving in Beinecke Plaza (May 15, 1969).

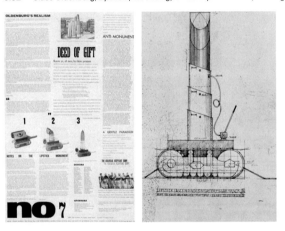

5.33 *Novum Organum* 7 (1969), a special issue dedicated to the *Lipstick*.

5.34 The Directors of the Colossal Keepsake Corporation. From left to right: Gordon Thorne (B.A. 1963, M.F.A. 1966), Charles Brewer, Robert Coombs (M.Arch 1971), John Allen (B.A. 1964, M.Arch 1969), Claes Oldenburg, W. Dennett (Danny) Goodrich (B.A. 1965), Stuart Wrede (B.A. 1965, M.Arch 1969), Vincent Scully (B.A. 1940, M.A. 1947, Ph.D. 1949), Sam Callaway (B.A. 1964, M.Arch 1969). Not pictured: Peter Almond (M.F.A. 1965), Susan Casteras (M.A. 1973, Ph.D. 1977).

right to meet with you and when we are through, we will report back to them about what happened." He had a bulldog jaw and he stuck it out further than I had ever seen it. His eyebrows dropped and he said, "This is just what I'm talking about. We have no obligation to report to anyone about what we are doing. We are in charge. I don't care if they break the windows. I don't care if they come down that stairway and carry me out to Chapel Street and kill me. I don't care. I'm doing my job. Are you going to do yours?" Everyone stood up and roared. He gave us our spine back. Then he left. He walked through the students proudly and they parted like the Red Sea.[253]

According to the *Yale Daily News*, Brewster's purpose at the meeting was "to warn the faculty members against abdicating their academic responsibilities" and, referencing some recent difficulties in the Department of City Planning, to remind them to keep students in check, particularly regarding "the establishment of requirements for the granting of a degree and the appointment of faculty."[254]

Amidst the May protests and meetings, there was one delightfully exuberant moment: the installation of Claes Oldenburg's (b. 1929; B.A. 1950) twenty-four-foot-tall, three-thousand-pound sculpture, *Lipstick (Ascending) on Caterpillar Tracks,* on Beinecke Plaza outside Woodbridge Hall, home of the university administration (5.32). The event had been planned well in advance, and Vincent Scully was largely responsible for attracting a considerable portion of the Yale community to it: "For some weeks beforehand, I ended my lectures in the Law School, just next door, by saying 'Beinecke Plaza, twelve noon, 15 May.'"[255] Additionally, copies of *Novum Organum* 7 (5.33) were distributed to students in the dining halls. At noon, crowds "happily estimated as thousands of people" watched as "a truck came slowly up Wall Street, pushing through the crowd and packed with architecture students and pieces of the Lipstick, with Oldenburg hanging off the running board like a character in an old agitprop movie."[256] Once set in place, the sculpture's crowning feature, a red vinyl lipstick, was inflated, arousing the crowd to applause. President Brewster, returning from lunch during the event, "slunk into his office without saying a word."[257] Oldenburg presented the deed of gift to Reuben Holden (1918–1995; B.A. 1940, M.A. 1948, Ph.D. 1951), secretary of the university, who in accepting it on Brewster's behalf, called the event a "joyous" occasion, while averring that the university "appreciated the thought and idea" of the donors, but made it clear that the Yale Corporation or "other university officials" would decide whether or not to keep it.[258] According to the deed of gift, if the sculpture did not remain on Beinecke Plaza, it would revert to the owners, the Colossal Keepsake Corporation (5.34).[259] Oldenburg made it clear that "Beinecke Plaza is the only place for it here at Yale. I don't want it stuck out on the golf course; monuments should be visible. We expect the University to be gracious," but he added that if it should refuse the gift, it would be given to another university—namely, Harvard.

The *Lipstick* project was the brainchild of Stuart Wrede who, along with a few others, approached Oldenburg in February to realize a design for the sculpture that he had made at the request of the *Yale Alumni Magazine* in 1968.[260] Wrede, "interested in art's culturally and politically subversive power," had interviewed the radical, leftist philosopher and sociologist Herbert Marcuse (1898–1979) "and told him about Oldenberg's then un-built monuments, of which he was unaware. He became quite excited and exclaimed: 'If you could ever imagine this could be done [built] you would have the revolution . . . I would say . . . and I think safely say this society has come to an end . . . there is a way in which this kind of satire, of humor can indeed kill . . . I think it would be one of the most bloodless means to achieve radical change . . . but the trouble is you must already have the radical change in order to get it built and I don't see any evidence of that. But just imagine that it would suddenly be there.'"[261]

Inspired by Marcuse, Wrede "gradually came to the realization that Yale was the perfect place to pull off this 'bloodless' coup. Forget Times Square or Park Avenue, previous sites for Oldenburg's proposed *Banana* and *Good Humor Bar;* these spaces were already a commercial free-for-all. Some of the few sacrosanct spaces in the United States were the well-groomed and conservative university campuses. No better spot existed than Yale University's Hewitt Quadrangle, commonly known as Beinecke Plaza, which was also a war memorial. We could utilize the very mechanism by which the university survived—alumni gifts—to implement our coup. Furthermore, Claes Oldenburg was an alumnus and already one of the most famous artist graduates of the university."[262] Joined by Samuel Callaway (b. 1941; B.A. 1964, M.Arch 1969) and Gordon (Gordie) Thorne (b. 1941; B.A. 1963, M.F.A.P. [painting] 1966), Wrede commissioned Oldenburg, who offered to take no fee to design the *Lipstick* and to help raise money for the fabrication of what would be the artist's first realized monument. Wrede and his committee gathered funds from "sympathetic professors (Vincent Scully and the philosopher Paul Weiss among them) and even got a sizable donation from Philip Johnson, who was an Oldenburg admirer." Later, as he recalled, "we had a larger group of students who were a major help in making the project a reality."[263]

Oldenburg's sculpture provided the bold, antiestablishment statement the students craved, a monument that, according to Björn Springfeldt, former director of the Museum of Modern Art in Stockholm, was a "powerful double exposure of a death-bringing warhead and a tool for erotic excitement."[264] Although the Hewitt Quadrangle was the site of two memorials to World War I, Oldenburg's sculpture was not originally conceived as an antiwar send-up. Vincent Scully, who was involved with the project from the beginning as an advisor, recalls that "there was . . . no intention on any one's part to make fun of the war memorial through this juxtaposition—certainly not on Wrede's and, while I can't speak for Oldenburg, I think certainly not on his either."[265] Susan Casteras (b. 1950; M.A. 1973, M.Phil. 1975, Ph.D. 1977), a member of the Colossal Keepsake Corporation, affirms Scully's recollection, writing in 1974 that "The Lipstick was definitely not a political commission; our intentions had almost nothing to do directly with the war or with military symbolism, although the subject of war was obviously on everyone's mind at the time."[266] In fact, Oldenburg originally intended to create an enormous cigarette balanced over the parapet, visually transforming Beinecke's sunken courtyard into an ashtray. If anything, the *Lipstick* was a further destabilization of architecture at a civic scale in the same way that Project Argus subverted Rudolph's Art and Architecture Building; it was a Dada-like statement, an upside-down, flaccid ionic column alone in a stark plaza, creating some sort of Surrealist landscape.

Oldenburg's sculpture remained in place over the summer, but no official action about its future was taken by the administration. In the fall, when Yale College admitted its first women, some, according to Judith Ann Schiff, chief research archivist at the Sterling Memorial Library, "came to view the sculpture as a female symbol of coeducation [while] others interpreted it as a phallic symbol."[267] Meanwhile, campus unrest increased, with calls for moratoriums to end the war in Vietnam, a student strike at the Law School, the occupation of Wright Hall by the SDS (Students for a Democratic Society), and demonstrations in support of the Black Panthers all taking their toll on the sculpture, whose tank-like base, covered by posters and graffiti, served as a speaker's rostrum. The *Lipstick* began to degrade, and by March 1970 it became necessary to move it to a factory in North Haven for repairs. Led by Vincent Scully, a group of art professors and historians saw to its restoration and return to the university in 1974, when it was accepted by the Art Gallery and placed on indefinite loan to Morse College, where Scully was the master. Scully recalls that the gallery director "wrote a letter to all the masters asking if they would like it in their courtyards. To a man, they thought he was kidding. They thought it was a joke. But of course I said yes. That's how we got it."[268] The renewed, and technically improved, *Lipstick* failed to capture the playfulness of the original, an aspect of design that Oldenburg desired from the first, stating in a leaflet handed out at the unveiling: "The subject is not erotic—a motor car, which it resembles is equally erotic. It also suggests an Ionic column (upside down), a Chicago fire plug, a drain-pipe, or the famous tower of Tatlin for Red Square."[269] Wrede has recently reflected that "In the end, Marcuse was wrong." Although many were offended by the *Lipstick,* "society has probably not changed all that much. Perhaps the art world has changed: the more outrageous the project, the more it is embraced." However, "the event on May 15, 1969, can be regarded as an important socio-political happening."[270]

Although society did not come to an end with the arrival of the *Lipstick,* as Marcuse suggested it might, the school year, and indeed Yale as it had been since World War II, pretty much did. Despite Brewster's objections, on May 15 the school's faculty decided to suspend academics and let the year end with a resounding whimper. A resolution was adopted providing that "regular academic work begun in the term can be completed at a later date according to arrangements between each student and his individual instructors."[271] Even before the tumultuous events of May, the University Council committee responsible for overseeing the school had recognized the unrest among the art and architecture students, placing much of the blame on the faculty, which, it reported, "has taken a free-wheeling approach to programs, giving students lots of choice, requiring a less rigid first year course, and allowing much independent structuring of courses in second and third years," a situation that, in their view, led to the formation of splinter groups, such as the Niagara University Spatial Dynamics Exercise, "an interior environmental space experiment using one system of material (string)"; the Pen Shop, "a socially conscious and politically oriented group of students who conduct their own special programs and publish a student newspaper"; and the Black Workshop, which worked with the New Haven black community. The council had done its homework well, observing that "some students are openly critical of deadwood on the faculty and others are strongly anti-establishment, anti-AIA, anti-organized architecture, and anti-the Paul Rudolph Building," before going on to state that the "new student freedom is causing new problems," including "an apparent weakness of administrative control of splinter groups and 'mini courses,' non-regular critiquing of student work and the desire by many students, on the other hand, for more structure in the design education process."[272]

The extent to which Moore endorsed, and even encouraged, the curricular fragmentation can be measured by the statement of curricular philosophy published in the 1969–70 school *Bulletin:* "In response to changing needs and values in a rapidly changing world, the School has increased the flexibility of its educational program to accommodate a variety of legitimate views on the role of the architect in contemporary society. It promotes no single radical position but attempts rather to provide a range of study options for professional specialization while at the same time providing a solid grounding in the knowledge and skills fundamental to the practice of architecture.... As a responsible professional giving physical expression to the spirit of an historic moment, the architect negotiates a thin line between art and professionalism. The School's curriculum takes cognizance of this difficulty and maintains open doors rather than striving for consensus."[273]

Of the splinter groups, the Black Workshop was the most formidable. It was founded in 1968, with help from a newly radicalized Charles Brewer, who made a trip to Detroit at the behest of William L. Slayton, president of Urban America, Inc. Slayton "had the idea that if you could bring the leadership of the black gangs together with American corporations, you would find that their systems of organization were very much the same," and, as Brewer recalls, "a CEO was the same as the gang leader or warlord or something like that. Anyway, this was an issue he wanted to look into.... I never quite understood why I was asked to be a part of this, but I was asked, and I figured out later that I represented education."[274] Brewer was "made to go to a lot of meetings" with community leaders, planners, and even gang members. Though he entered the situation with some trepidation, he left "impressed": "These guys were interested in getting the credentials. They realized they wanted to be architects, planners, graphic artists, but it was the arts as an engine. They realized that they may have the capability but they would never get the chance to use it if they didn't get the credentials. I agreed with them. I heard all their histories and they were active in lots of areas and neighborhoods in Detroit. And they were mostly legitimate, but they were very, very angry. They said, 'Look, we know you teach at Yale and we want to get in.'"[275] After three days of meetings in Detroit, Brewer wrote to Moore, telling him that he was "convinced" of their "expressed need for self-determination." Brewer went on to state that "in the name of the school and as co-chairman of the Admissions Committee" he had "offered to help any candidates for admission to the architectural curriculum."[276]

Brewer got Moore's blessing to invite the young men to Yale, on the condition that he take responsibility as their faculty advisor. "So there I was, less than a year later, [with] ten recruits standing in the doorway waiting to get in. . . . We worked out programs and the remedial work they had to do and everything started moving forward. They were given the opportunity to see what they could muster."[277] In reflecting on the situation, Brewer may have slightly romanticized the plight of his "recruits." Most had undergraduate degrees or some sort of technical training, and some had professional design experience. The ten black students that came to Yale in September 1968 were John S. Coke (1936–1995; M.E.D. 1969); Ralph Johnson (b. 1943; M.Arch 1969, M.C.P. 1969); Charles Louis (b. 1939; M.U.S. 1969); E. Donald Van Purnell (b. 1941; M.Arch 1969, M.E.D. 1971); Roland Bedford (b. 1938; M.Arch 1970); Richard Dozier (b. 1939; M.Arch 1970); Reginald Jackson (b. 1945; M.F.A. 1970); Joseph Middlebrooks (b. 1941; M.Arch 1970); Mervyn Fernandes (b. 1943; B.A. 1967, M.Arch 1971); and Harry Quintana.

At first, the group tried to work within the standard school curriculum. But they almost immediately discovered that the content of the studios addressed few of their concerns. One of the students, Richard Dozier, who later became dean of the School of Architecture and Construction Science at Tuskegee University, was "an aspiring architect [who] went to Yale to work on my master's . . . [and] kind of backed into the 60s." When Dozier got to Yale, "One of the first problems we were given in studio—and mind you, I already had a lot of professional experience, as did most of the other black students— was the redesign of the Blossom Shop." Needless to say, the one-week Blossom Shop sketch problem, calling for the design of a small New Haven flower shop, was harshly criticized by students as being socially irrelevant in light of larger community issues, such as the planned ring road that was threatening predominantly black communities. As Dozier says, "We were at Yale but we lived in the community, and our homes were being destroyed. For these kinds of reasons we established the Yale Black Workshop."[278]

Brewer worked with the black students to form the Black Workshop, an independent program governed by a self-imposed mandate to go beyond "irrelevant classroom projects" to provide community design and public education projects to New Haven's African American neighborhoods, particularly the Hill area, which was undergoing a wrenching process of "urban renewal."[279] The workshop found space in a run-down storefront at 1086 Chapel Street, which they fixed up over the next year with some small funds provided by the university.

Operating virtually independent of the school, the workshop, after earning the trust of the local community, was able to get involved with various projects in New Haven, including the planning stages for the construction of the Yale Medical Center garage. Herbert Newman, in his capacity as assistant to campus planner Edward Larrabee Barnes, had undertaken to design the garage with retail on the ground level and housing above, as "a bridge between the Hill neighborhood and the university" over the Oak Street Connector, a six-lane highway being constructed to bring cars from two interstate highways into the city's heart.[280] The workshop argued against the garage, and other similar projects, believing that "Yale was not concerned with what is or is not desirable for the community, only what is best for Yale. . . . Yale did not want to inconvenience its personnel, but would not hesitate to inconvenience community personnel."[281] The workshop also sought to influence Louis Kahn's plans for low-income housing in the Hill Central area. Charles Brewer remembers a particularly uncomfortable meeting between Kahn, the workshop, and the residents of the Hill district:

> Lou Kahn was a guy with a big heart who had feelings—he was the right guy. But he did it all wrong. He would come to a meeting and the Black Workshop would say to him, "Who have you talked to in the community?" And Lou would say, "Well, I've only really spoken with the client." And they would say, "Have you ever been to the Hill district?" And he said, "Oh yes, I've been there." "How many times?" "Oh, three or four." "Did you ever get out of the car?" "No." They just destroyed Lou Kahn. I was at the meeting and I'll never forget this: Lou Kahn said, "I'm sympathetic. I'm a poor man. I'm injured. My face is distorted. I'm ugly. And I'm Jewish. I've been through all this and I know what you're feeling." They wouldn't accept that. . . . Lou slumped away and he was hurt. He was injured as deeply as I've ever seen. In the aftermath of all this, he called me up one day and he said, "I know I did that wrong. I know I'm never going to repair the damage that I've done. So I'm going to back off." I said, "These guys who gave you so much grief are not bad people. They have suffered also. Why don't we sit down and talk with the Black Workshop." Lou Kahn said, "I'd love to speak to them." So I gathered up the Black Workshop and all nine of them went down to Kahn's office and we had a whole day with him. They tried to explain what they were trying to do with the community and how what he wanted to do, as wonderful as it might've been architecturally, he had missed the whole point. I've never been to a better meeting than that day watching Lou Kahn eat crow. He was absolutely convinced by them that he had done the wrong thing. And that's when he said he was going to give up the commission.[282]

In an article for the *Yale Graduate Professional,* Christopher Tunnard, chairman of the school's Department of City Planning, recognized the role black professionals were beginning to play in the city planning process, noting that "with the help of the Black Workshop . . . Yale was beginning to become known as a place where city planning education was forward-looking and fruitful."[283] But the workshop's relationship with the university was rife with conflict, especially over financial support. As Dozier reflected on the situation in 1971, "We were setting up something that would benefit the University through improved community relations with real-life experience for students, we felt they should help finance some type of development fund enabling the projects to go beyond planning and design."[284] Additionally, as an off-site studio ostensibly open to all architecture and planning students, the workshop's status was ambiguous: Was it an autonomous operation or a university program? In an April 23, 1969, memo to Charles Brewer, but also copied to faculty members in other departments, Dean Weaver made it clear that the Black Workshop, which hoped to "become an autonomous corporation with its own Board and operating as an independent, non-profit design and planning service for the black community," faced several problems that needed to be addressed by the faculty and not by the dean, including the question of academic credit and the issue of financial support for students. In his memo, Weaver was very clear that "the needs of black students as students and the needs of the Workshop as an entity" were "closely related, but . . . not identical."[285]

A critical bone of contention between the Black Workshop and the university was the group's intention to provide community services as an "outside school within the university," offering an associate's degree in planning, architecture, or graphic design.[286] The insistence on autonomy concerned Weaver, though he acknowledged that some students felt Yale wasn't doing enough to address the problems endemic to black communities and believed that the workshop should be considered "an extension and elaboration of the educational program, not an alternative to it." As he wrote to Provost Taylor, though he was supportive of the Black Workshop, Weaver was not confident that it would succeed without a profound restructuring. "I personally think that the fundamental aspect of the Black Workshop is not mere separation but a range of problems which, because we have been ill-prepared to solve them, require new relevant forms of organization and relationship—that is to say, that we are all in this together."[287]

The spring 1969 term was marked by discussion and argument about the status of the Black Workshop–issued demands—responsibility for recruiting their own students and faculty and additional funding from the university—while the university pledged to recognize the program and support it as much as it could, something that the workshop saw as a halfhearted commitment. In a heated letter to Weaver that was also sent to Brewster, as well as to The Architects' Resistance, anonymous authors insisted that the "Black Workshop is an *outside school* within the university, known on most campuses as an extension school. However," they continued, "it seems most officials of Yale wish to view this as a 'separate school.' This to us and the Black Community of New Haven is a direct refusal by the University to allot the proper proportion of it's [*sic*] resources to the community." By so stating, the workshop was insisting that the "total Black community" of New Haven needed to be served by the university. To accomplish this, they insisted "that Yale must support an external location in the 'Black Community' for the Workshop"—in other words, Yale must provide for the workshop's operating expenses.[288]

Funding was granted on a limited basis in the immediate wake of the city planning department's blowup on June 12, 1969, following a discussion with four members of the Yale Corporation's Educational Policy Committee, who supported the workshop out of "a desire to strengthen Yale's programs in urban design and planning in a way which focuses effectively on the problems of the inner city and its predominantly black neighborhoods."[289] As the group began to get more involved with redevelopment efforts in New Haven, they requested additional operating funds from the university.

After classes resumed in fall 1969, the workshop proposed that Donald Stull (b. 1937), principal of a Boston-based firm, become its leader. With additional time to review the proposal, Provost Taylor wrote to workshop members Donald Van Purnell and Joseph Middlebrooks, with whom he had previously spoken, reporting that Stull did not endorse the workshop's proposal, nor was he confident that it would be acceptable to the university. "As you know," Taylor continued, "the Corporation, the President, and I were relying heavily on Mr. Stull's willingness to accept faculty appointment and to oversee the program of the Workshop."[290] Negotiations regarding the workshop's future and the possibility of Stull's assuming a leadership role continued until March 1970, when Stull declined the position, leaving the workshop, as Moore wrote to its members, "without the direction Yale University has required in order to make the Workshop an integral part of the institution."[291] Stull went on to practice as an architect and urban designer in Boston with his partner, M. David Lee, where they were responsible for creating several notable civic buildings, including the John D. O'Bryant African-American Institute at Northeastern University, Roxbury Community College, and the Ruggles Street Station of the Massachusetts Bay Transportation Authority. In 2006, the firm designed the Hurricane Katrina Memorial in New Orleans's hard-hit Lower Ninth Ward neighborhood.

Unable to achieve the leadership required or to arrive at a mutually agreeable structure of governance and unwilling to fund the program at the level demanded, the university nonetheless provided the workshop with sufficient interim funding to enable the appointment of Arthur Symes (b. 1935) and Ed Cherry for the remainder of the 1969–70 school year as visiting critics.[292] In May 1970, the Black Workshop's fortunes seemed to take a turn for the better when, in a surprising move, Henry Broude (1925–2007), director of academic planning; Charles Moore, now dean of the newly constituted Faculties of Design and Planning; and Joseph Lieberman (b. 1942; B.A. 1964, LL.B 1967), executive associate to the dean, wrote to President Brewster that "Following a very impressive and enlightening review of Workshop projects and activities of the past year, we are convinced that the lack of positive University support for the Workshop is a serious oversight."[293] Two days later, however, Provost Taylor rejected the recommendations of Broude, Moore, and Lieberman.

On June 26, 1970, Moore again endorsed the Black Workshop's bid for further expansion, highlighting three components of its proposed program. First, it should be "a legitimate studio for which students can receive credit in architecture or city planning," noting that with the appointment of architects Cherry and Symes the school had faculty responsible "for evaluating and grading the work of the individual students." Second, the workshop would have "a project component which in some senses coincides with the studio component," that is "the area in which Workshop members work in actual architectural or planning projects in the community. As you know," Moore continued, "this component is altogether consistent with the trend in architectural education away from model-making and toward project-building as a learning experience." Citing the example of the Building Project already undertaken as part of the curriculum, Moore told Brewster that "the Workshop's project component does not present the School with an unprecedented situation." However, he went on to acknowledge that the "request for School funds to support the project component is unique," pointing out that normally such projects are funded "either by the client or some public agency if the client is lacking in resources." Moore supported the workshop's budget proposal as a short-term solution, fully expecting the workshop to become self-sufficient.

Moore described the workshop's third component, a "proposed internship program," as "a very interesting and valuable idea," albeit one that "raises larger questions regarding Yale's relationship to the New Haven community which cannot be answered finally by me." After reiterating his support for the workshop as one of the school's "highest priorities," Moore slyly observed that "to be a high priority of an impoverished school does not mean very much." Consequently, much as he believed in the workshop, he "could not possibly commit any significant part of our operating budget to the Black Workshop without thereby doing damage to the educational opportunities of the rest of our students."[294] All in all, Moore's commitment to the workshop was tentative at best. Once again he proved himself a master of evasion.

Growing increasingly frustrated with the school, Richard Dozier, "sensing that the inability to respond to social needs was somehow built into the structure of the University," began to realize that the best way to effect change was from within.[295] With Dozier as assistant professor in the school, the Black Workshop was brought more fully into the fold of the university and was reconceived as the Black Environmental Studies Team, with Dozier serving as its director (see Chapter 6).

As student protests in the Architecture Department over governance and financial aid were heating up, students and faculty in the Department of City Planning were contemplating unprecedented action regarding admissions and curriculum. The City Planning Department remained a weak program. After a slow start under deans Meeks and Sawyer as a program within the Department of Architecture, in 1961, city planning had become its own fully independent department chaired by Arthur Row, an experienced planner who had served as Edmund Bacon's deputy in Philadelphia, recently completing Philadelphia's Physical Development Plan.[296] Under Row's five-year tenure, the program took on a "technocratic/administrative dimension" that was in its way a perfect reflection of Rudolph's view that planners were bureaucrats. To encourage the development of a higher level of scholarship in the field, an additional, parallel degree was added in 1964, the master of urban studies (M.U.S.), which was much more loosely structured than the master of city planning (M.C.P.) degree, and much more idea-based—a one-year research program designed for students who already have a professional degree in another field. Originally conceived of as a joint program with the Law School, the master of urban studies program soon evolved into an interdepartmental program that eventually settled into the School of Art and Architecture, with an experimental curriculum featuring very few required courses but requiring students to produce a publishable research paper. The program was changed dramatically in 1966, when Row stepped down to go work in India and Christopher Tunnard, the principal faculty member who had directed the program from 1951 to 1960, took over. In 1963, Tunnard was joined by Harry J. Wexler (b. 1936; LL.B. 1962), a socially sensitive attorney who was appointed visiting lecturer.

Encouraged by Wexler, Tunnard quickly shifted the curriculum "toward policy analysis, social change, and clinical experience."[297] Vincent Scully seemed concerned about the shift in emphasis, not because of its increasingly hostile attitude toward New Haven's urban renewal policies, but because he felt it left unaddressed planning's physical consequences, something he felt characterized not only Yale's, but most city planning programs. In a lecture subsequently published as "Visual Art as a Way of Knowing," Scully struggled to reclaim for city planning an involvement with place-making and building, "because the objective of planning must be physical reality." He went on to say: "The statistics, the data which the planner gathers, must in the end be developed into three-dimensional reality by someone—perhaps by the planner himself, if he is trained physically and visually. The end of planning is not planning but architecture. So let us call planners who can design in three dimensions, 'architects,' and let them in fact *be* architects. All others are statisticians; let them have no power over architectural decisions, but let them inform those who do."[298]

As minority empowerment rose to the forefront of planning issues in the late 1960s, Yale's program evolved from "the absolutism of the plan and the authority of its planner to a consideration of the 'conflicting roles' that planners faced."[299] As William Mitchell stated with thirty years' hindsight, for many in the Department of City Planning, "there was a conviction that architects had traditionally served as 'soft cops' (to use a term popular at the time) of the existing order, and that new modes of professional intervention were needed. They embraced grassroots activism, participatory processes, and advocacy planning."[300] This new sense of the department's role as an instrument of social activism was first decisively articulated during the spring 1968 term, when, encouraged by Harry Wexler, then serving as acting chairman of the department while Tunnard was on sabbatical leave, "students began to behave as though they were advocate planners."[301] To beef up the program Wexler required new faculty. Reporting to the president and fellows of the Yale Corporation, he referred to the policy memo Gibson Danes and Charles Moore had transmitted to Provost Charles Taylor two years before, in 1966, which identified "insulation from related programs in other areas of the University and an over-dependency upon a visiting, non-resident faculty" as the City Planning Department's "two principal ills."[302] Wexler reported that since then, the curriculum had been adjusted to allow for greater interdisciplinarity, and the faculty had been strengthened with new hires, including Pat Goeters, associate professor of architecture and city planning, hired in 1967, and Alexander Garvin (b. 1941; B.A. 1962, M.Arch 1967, M.U.S. 1967), instructor in city planning, who in spring 1968, while also working in Philip Johnson's office, offered a seminar on Harlem and the first of his undergraduate courses in city planning, an innovation so unusual that it was reported in the pages of *Progressive Architecture*.[303] Visiting faculty helped expand the menu of available advocacy-oriented classes: advocacy planner Chester Hartman (b. 1936) taught the course "Social Implications of Housing Policy," while Harvard-trained architect and planner C. Richard Hatch, founder of the Architects' Renewal Committee in Harlem, taught "Planners and Clients," and Mortimer Zuckerman (b. 1937)—later a leading property developer as well as a prominent magazine and newspaper publisher—served as visiting critic.

As 1968 gave way to 1969, the City Planning Department became embroiled in its own revolution, when faculty and students voted to constitute themselves as a new administrative body, the City Planning Forum, with full control over a department made wholly independent of the school, including control of budgets, appointments, curriculum, and, perhaps most critically, admissions. This step would ultimately lead to the end of city planning as a separate discipline at Yale. According to the revolutionary group, all members of the City Planning Forum—faculty and students alike—were to have an equal vote, and decisions were to be made by majority rule. Should faculty and students be split on an issue, the vote would be deemed invalid.[304]

The forum, motivated by the desire to dramatically increase the enroll-ment of African American and Hispanic students, assumed full responsibility for admissions, a process hitherto overseen by the dean, who would set class-size targets and issue formal letters of admission to students in all school departments. On April 19, 1969, Provost Charles Taylor, aware that something was afoot, wrote to Dean Weaver, copying President Brewster and City Planning Chair Tunnard, to express his concern about the potential admission of "students whose educational expectations we are unable to meet."[305] Taylor rightly believed that the forum was intending to admit more students than the program's budget allowed, and that standards for admission might be significantly lowered in the case of minority candidates. A month later, Taylor, having read the "Charter of the City Planning Forum," wrote to Weaver to remind him "that for recommendations concerning admissions to be valid they must be endorsed by the Dean, who is expected to act on the basis of recommendations from a committee of the faculty, whose membership and procedures he approves."[306]

Despite repeated warnings from the University Council and the administration, the City Planning Forum, in collusion with the Black Workshop,
recklessly pushed forward with its plan to offer admission to twelve minority
candidates without authorization from Dean Weaver, making it clear, however,
"that the extent of financial aid available in the School of Art and Architecture
has not yet been resolved."[307] They did this despite knowing full well that eight
students, seven white and one black, had already accepted formal admission
offers from the department and that the university only budgeted enough
to support a total of fourteen entering students—a reduction from previous
years, resulting in part from the university's decision to expand financial
aid offerings for students in the arts. With only fourteen students, the size
of the program would be drastically reduced—at its peak in 1965, thirty-one
students had entered the program. Determined to diversify the student
body at any cost, the forum went forward with its rogue plan. In keeping
with the egalitarianism of its recently adopted bylaws, and possibly out of a
fear of retribution, each letter of admission was to be signed by a different
individual—either a student or faculty member—on behalf of the forum.[308]
Architecture students closely monitored the planners' actions. The admissions
debacle, as architecture student Barton Phelps has stated, "was everything we
could have hoped for in terms of an issue. We were all trying to feel as guilty
as we could for being white and upper middle class, so it was just what the
doctor ordered."[309]

On May 26, 1969, with the school's classes suspended, Weaver, alerted
to the forum's plan to admit twelve additional candidates without consent,
but unaware that the unsanctioned acceptance letters had already been sent,
addressed the city planning faculty and students in writing, labeling the letters
of admission "not merely a violation of official procedure but, more importantly . . . a cruel and deceptive subordination to other purposes of the hopes
and aspirations of the applicants." Weaver recounted in detail the sequence of
events that began three days before, on the morning of May 23, when he had
arranged a 2:00 p.m. meeting with planning students and faculty to review
admissions procedures and to make clear his intention to exercise his responsibilities with regard to final decisions concerning candidates. Weaver believed
that the meeting had ended with a clear understanding of his position, and
that a final meeting would take place on Monday morning, May 26, at 9:00 a.m.,
when he would consult with the planning chairman, the Planning Admissions
Committee, and the assistant dean in charge of allocation of financial aid, in
order to complete the process and "dispatch the final letters of admission,
combined with offers of financial aid."[310]

However, after the end of the meeting of May 26, Weaver was informed that letters of acceptance had already been written and sent on Friday, May 23—*before* the 2:00 p.m. meeting. Once made aware of the situation, Weaver informed the provost and met with the city planning chairman and the president, who, "at the conclusion of that discussion . . . accepted the resignation of the Chairman."[311] Weaver then sent telegrams to the twelve recipients of the unauthorized letters, informing them that the letters "in no way constitutes notice of admission" and that their applications were still "under review," pending official communication from him.[312] On May 27, Kingman Brewster sent a severe letter of reprimand to those forum members who signed the unauthorized letters of admission, writing that their action is "at best an extraordinary lapse of responsible judgment, at worst [an act of] deceitful bad faith in relation to both the University and the applicant."[313] On the same day, Brewster also sent the wrongly admitted students what was surely an unusual and difficult, not to mention embarrassing, letter for a Yale president to have to write. His letter began with a harsh exhortation: "As a result of some very recent, unexpected, and unfortunate occurrences here, we strongly advise you not to enroll at Yale next year for the degree in City Planning." Although Brewster went on to say that the university would do its "best to honor [its] commitment of admission," he made it clear that the future of the City Planning Department was uncertain, and a degree could not be guaranteed. With the letter, Brewster enclosed catalogues of various other university schools offering courses that might appeal to perspective planning students, accompanied by the statement that "if the department does not continue in its present form, you will be entitled to fashion a program as you see fit, subject only to the permission of the instructor with respect to enrollment in a particular course."[314] On May 28—less than a week after the unauthorized letters of admission were sent—the university released the full story to the press, including copies of Brewster's letter to the wrongly admitted students, and Weaver's to city planning students and faculty.[315] On the same day, Brewster explained the situation to all university faculty, saying that in addition to Tunnard stepping down from the chairmanship at his request, and Louis DeLuca stepping down as assistant dean at Weaver's request, he had also told Harry Wexler and Pat Goeters that he would not support any request for extensions to their appointments. Brewster emphasized, however, that Tunnard and DeLuca would remain on the faculty—Tunnard in a diminished capacity as director of studies in planning, with responsibility for the curriculum but little else. On May 29, Weaver followed up by rescinding the rogue admission letters:

It is with great regret that I must inform you officially that we cannot admit you to the School of Art and Architecture for next year.

I further regret that you have been subjected to a confusion in communications in this matter, occasioned by recent developments in the administration of the Department of City Planning.

After careful consideration of all factors I must advise that it is unwise for you as well as for us to consider your matriculation at Yale in September.

I send this with respect and all good wishes to you for your future.[316]

Ultimately, it was decided that seven of the twelve candidates invited by the forum, of whom six were black, would be admitted to the school as "special students," largely because they had the prerequisites, particularly the bachelor of architecture degree, which would also qualify them as candidates for admission to the newly established master of environmental design program.[317] As historian Tom McDonough has written, "Their enrollment was promptly used by Yale as evidence of the university's commitment to encouraging African-American matriculation."[318]

City planning students, still angry at Brewster's initial actions, weren't appeased by the limited admission and began meeting to craft their own response. A petition was sent to Brewster in which the forum reiterated its many demands: a call for recognition as the official governing body of the department, financial support for the Black Workshop, the admission of twenty students, the reinstatement of Tunnard as chairman, renewed appointments for Wexler and Goeters, and the rescinding of the administration's threat to withhold the degrees of those students who acted as unlawful signatories. What's more, they demanded the appointment of three additional faculty members for the following year—one black, all to be chosen by the forum. Their pleas were largely ignored. Architecture students were also very vocal about Brewster's decision. The Russian Constructivist–inspired cover graphics for *Novum Organum* 8, a "special graduation issue" edited by Robert Coombs (1934–2001; M.Arch 1971), Jeremy Scott Wood (b. 1941; B.A. 1964, M.Arch 1970), Eleazor Wheelock (false name), J. Aeneas Pilkington-Phutt (false name), and I. Duncan (false name), proclaimed "Kingman Brewster's destruction of the City Planning Department." A flyer was circulated by the City Planning Forum listing Tunnard's impressive credentials from *Who's Who in America,* proclaiming: "Brewster removed this man for being incompetent." Later, 150 students, led by Tom Carey, marched from the A&A Building to Brewster's Hillhouse Avenue residence to hold a Navajo ritual to "counteract the 'evil' actions" of the president.[319]

Faculty from other departments in the university wrote Brewster to express concern about the situation.[320] One letter, from William E. Reifsnyder, professor of forest meteorology and public health in the School of Forestry, did not address issues of governance but instead suggested that the troubles in the Department of City Planning resulted "from its being in a School with which it has little natural affinity. The problems of city planning are hardly architectural although architecture must of course play some role." Reifsnyder went on to suggest that "the University's work in urban and rural planning be organized around an expanded School of Urban and Natural Resources" that "might appropriately include" forestry, city planning, and the Department of Public Health, and would have strong ties to the Department of Sociology and the Law School.[321] Amidst the chaos, Reifsnyder's imaginative proposal fell on deaf ears.

While some of the more radical supporters of the forum believed Brewster's decision was motivated by race, he had no such agenda. In fact, when unrest in the City Planning Department first surfaced, he had sent Weaver a densely argued, six-page position paper expressing what he hoped would be some "useful" words about "the University's attitude and policy about black admissions, black faculty appointments, black programs in general and black arts in particular." Yale, he stated, was "aggressively eager to see barriers to equal educational opportunity removed," and was actively devising programs to overcome obstacles that are financial "but are also an inheritance of generations of discriminating social and educational . . . disadvantage." Nonetheless, the university was unwilling to "admit students whom we do not feel will be able to earn their degrees by normal Yale standards." He also said that the same standards applied to faculty members. Reviewing the various black-oriented programs in the college and the Law School before tackling, in some confusion, the situation in the creative and performing arts and professions, Brewster stated that "while some may argue about the definition and distinctiveness of 'black theatre' or 'black arts' or 'black architecture,' there is undoubtedly a distinctive black style, most widely perceived in dance and music . . . and there are black community audiences and community clients which deserve an artistic experience and tradition of their own, under the direction of their own people." However, Brewster argued that Yale could not afford "to launch a parallel 'black drama' or 'black arts' program in addition to its effort to run a program without ethnic focus, which attempts to develop artistic capacity in all its students, whatever their backgrounds and whatever their particular career objectives." After some more discussion of black programs, and an expression of belief in the value for those with an "urge for identity" to study "in a school which is devoted to a totally black experience," one that was "authentically black, not an appendage to a program which is predominately white," he concluded by stating that "present policies and attitude toward black programs, admissions, and appointments are bound to be rethought. We have done quite a lot, all in quite a short time. As so we should, for there was much long time to be made up for."[322]

Set against the background of other virtually simultaneous events in both the School of Art and Architecture and the city of New Haven, the consequences of the City Planning Forum's actions cannot be underestimated. According to Brewster biographer Geoffrey Kabaservice, the city planning admissions situation presented the president "with a constitutional crisis." When Brewster heard of the Planning Forum's action, he "hit the roof." In early June, still fuming from the events of the previous term, Brewster delivered the commencement address at Johns Hopkins University in which he expressed his belief that "No sentimental egalitarianism, racial or otherwise can be permitted to lower the standards for the relatively few institutions which are capable of really superior intellectual accomplishment."[323]

Word of the crisis spread quickly through the media. *Washington Post* writer Nicholas von Hoffman, in his June 27 column, "Urban Blues," offered a thoughtful, if a bit slanted, account highlighting the fundamental disciplinary dilemma: "City Planning is a mish-mash field . . . an un-field of study, but there are a lot of key jobs in housing, planning, transportation and other aspects vital to city living that you can only get if you're licensed and certified with a city planning degree. Black people need city planning degrees, not simply because the pay is good but because city planners have done more to ruin the black man than any profession you care to name. They're the ones who've supplied bureaucratic and technical double-talk which has rammed the superhighways through the ghettos, which has engineered the urban renewal speculation that's driven black people from neighborhood to neighborhood, which has built the public housing monstrosities."[324]

Reflecting on the situation ten or so years later, Charles Moore put the blame for the city planning crisis on Tunnard, who "had simply caved in to student demands and admitted double his 1969 quota to get in lots of blacks."[325] Charles Brewer has come to see things differently. In his view, it was a return to form for Tunnard, the onetime radical: "During the revolution, Christopher Tunnard became a revolutionary again," says Brewer. "Christopher Tunnard, the most conservative member of the faculty . . . suddenly was on the ramparts again. That defied everything!"[326]

Though an interesting scholar possessed of a "good heart," Tunnard was not a strong leader, a fact that did not escape the notice of the University

Council, who as early as 1966 had suggested that planning education be reorganized as a comprehensive, university-wide program in urban studies—if they could find "the person capable of leading it."[327] It seems that such a leader was never found, and three years later, in April 1969, the month the admissions crisis began, the council once again forcefully expressed its reservations about the city planning program, stating that it did "not adequately fulfill [the] role of bringing together inter-disciplinary resources of related design disciplines on [the] one hand with social, economic, ecological and related disciplines on [the] other hand." The council was so disappointed in the program that they recommended its abolition and advocated for the establishment of a course in urban design "parallel to and closely interlocking with the Department of Architecture," with those parts of the existing program "not dealing with physical design" being absorbed into a planned Center of Urban Studies (which was never realized).[328] But it was too late: not only were there no funds to realize a comprehensive overhaul of the program, but the entire Department of City Planning had become so radicalized that it was deemed by university administration to be completely unmanageable.

The fire in the Art and Architecture Building on June 14 temporarily sidelined the situation in city planning, but on July 3, 1969, Weaver issued a memo to city planning faculty and students, outlining a course of action for the coming year that began by informing them of his intention to serve as chairman of the department as well as dean of the School of Art and Architecture.[329] But by then it was clear that Brewster was intent on shutting down the program and relocating its faculty and their disciplines to various Yale departments. To help facilitate this process and presumably create faculty support, on July 11, Provost Taylor solicited faculty in various departments to serve on a committee chaired by Professor of Economics John Meyer, who was asked to offer suggestions to President Brewster as he prepared his report to the Yale Corporation concerning "how Yale can best pursue study of and training for work on urban problems."[330] The Meyer Committee did not offer its report until February 26, 1970, taking "much longer than expected," so that it was impossible to adopt any of its suggestions, especially as regarded faculty appointments for 1970–71.[331]

Initially the report was given serious consideration, leading Charles Moore to write in the November 1970 issue of *Sensus:* "The Meyer Committee had proposed last spring that separate schools of Architecture and City planning join with Forestry and other schools in a councilium [*sic*] to share appointments of distinguished professors in fields which support our own. A committee to comment on this report had been convened by President

Brewster during the summer; its report, not yet distributed and the report of the Dudley group [the University Council] will be helpful in developing the University's attitude toward the ways in which Planning and Architecture's program can be most effective in the University community."[332] Moore also reported that "the Yale Corporation gave a directive that all schools in the University, particularly the professional ones, be critically reviewed in the light of the financial crisis in which Yale, like many other universities, now finds itself." He noted that "one concomitant of this directive has been the recommendations . . . concerning the future course of studies in City Planning," a statement that sent shivers through the professional schools, especially in the arts, causing everyone "to feel afresh the need to justify all of our professional programs."[333] This directive was seen by students, faculty, and alumni as a signal that Brewster and the Yale Corporation were considering a complete shutdown of not only the Department of City Planning but also of the Department of Architecture.

In January 1970, two months before the release of the Meyer Report, the Department of City Planning expressed unanimous support for Harry Wexler's reappointment, which needed to be made by January 26, 1970, citing his "enviable teaching record."[334] Moore, now dean of the School of Architecture, passed this recommendation on to Provost Taylor without adding his endorsement, "because of the thoroughly uncertain future of City Planning at Yale and the imminence of a new Dean of the school."[335] Although Provost Taylor hoped Moore would talk to Wexler about the decision not to renew his contract, Moore, typically eschewing direct confrontation, elected to write a brief and rather cold letter.[336] When confronted by a reporter from the *Yale Daily News* who knew that Moore had not supported Wexler in what was supposedly a confidential letter to the provost, Moore said that, despite his high academic regard for Wexler, "having a fight over his reappointment would not be in the best interest of the department."[337] Wexler, the *News* reported, believed that Moore was under direct orders from the president and the provost not to renew his appointment, despite a faculty recommendation in his favor. Wexler challenged the nonreappointment notice in a letter to Moore on January 30, stating that under the department policy for appointments of the School of Art and Architecture, faculty with three-year adjunct appointments are entitled to written notice of nonrenewal no less than two semesters before termination.[338] Wexler continued as associate professor adjunct until 1971, when his contract expired. He would go on to a career as a consultant for nonprofit groups interested in community development.

The Meyer Report enumerated the problems of Yale's city planning program, particularly its small size and lack of interdisciplinarity. It drew attention to the lack of university courses in management, such as might be found in a school of business or public administration—the establishment of which it recommended (Yale would establish a School of Management in 1974). It called for the development of linkages that "would require the creation of new institutional and administrative forms that transcend conventional disciplines and departments," the establishment of a "Concilium on the Environment," and a Ph.D. in urban studies. Given the university's increasingly dire fiscal situation, and the restlessness of the student body, the report resulted in no specific new initiatives in city planning, and on March 12, 1970, Kingman Brewster began the process of shutting down the program so that in fall 1970, nine students entered it as the last class admitted, joining the nine in the second year.[339] At the same time, Jorge Hardoy (1926–1993), visiting professor of planning and a specialist in urban design, replaced Tunnard as director of studies. Despite the looming cancellation of the program, Hardoy offered a full curriculum, including several new courses.

By fall 1970, the fate of the city planning program was sealed. In a memorandum to Moore, Hardoy, and Joseph Lieberman, whom Brewster had appointed executive assistant to the dean of design and planning, Brewster stated that he had "told the Corporation that the discussions with the Meyer Committee and the visit of an ad hoc group to review the Meyer Committee recommendations, make me very dubious about the wisdom of concentrating Yale's resources on the study of the City at the Masters level."[340] At the same time, Lieberman, who would go on to a distinguished career in politics, was asked to become director of studies in city planning, replacing Hardoy, who was leaving Yale at the end of January 1971. Lieberman was specifically tasked with the responsibility of phasing out the program so that its official end would come at the conclusion of the spring 1972 semester.[341] As such, Lieberman recalled twenty years later, he "was really something of a trustee in bankruptcy. I mean, I had no illusions. I had come in after it was decided to dissolve the program, and so I was just overseeing the last year or two, trying to keep the mood as decent as I could and work with the people there."[342]

On December 7, 1970, President Brewster shared his intentions for the City Planning Department's future at a meeting with faculty, and again, on the following day, at a meeting with faculty and students. Describing the university's "immediate financial situation" as "one of true crisis" requiring "basic strategic decisions" for the "longer-run prospect," he reported that the Yale Corporation "has requested a special review of certain departments and schools," noting that it imposed "a special burden of persuasion" on the Department of City Planning "because of the awareness of the inadequate resources which had been devoted to the Department." He stated that the Yale Corporation, made aware of these problems by students, faculty, and alumni, were "most particularly . . . impressed by the report of the so-called Meyer Committee," which "urged the continuation of professional work in city planning." However, Brewster "made it quite clear that the present Yale resources and organization and personnel were wholly inadequate to the task of offering a program in city planning which was up to the standards the country has a right to expect of Yale." In so saying, Brewster articulated a strategy similar to that first suggested in April 1966 by the University Council, wherein courses in urbanism would be fielded in "all the appropriate disciplines" and the appropriate schools such as Law, Medicine, Public Health, Forestry, and Divinity as well as Architecture. "So the question is *not* whether to continue work on the study of the city. That is an essential commitment for any modern university."[343]

So ended city planning as an independent discipline at Yale. In his insightful 2011 article on New Haven's urban renewal, historian Brian Goldstein delivered a fitting eulogy to the once-promising program: "In destroying Yale's professional program in city planning, Brewster only pitched the profession into greater turmoil. Students lost not only a center of planning education but a platform too, one from which they had waged a campaign against the New Deal spatial order that resounded in the halls of A&A, in New Haven's neighborhoods, and across the disciplines of architecture and city planning. Brewster, in turn, lost his voice in the discourse of the profession. Once he had dismantled the Department of City Planning, Yale could no longer train future planners. With planning's end, the debate that raged at Yale over the future of the profession came to an abrupt—and unresolved— conclusion."[344] Though the Meyer Report was largely forgotten, in 2012 a new endowment from the Henry Hart Rice Foundation made it possible to hire additional faculty—as of this writing, Associate Professor Elihu Rubin (b. 1977; B.A. 1999)—to offer undergraduate- and graduate-level courses in urbanism and to begin fostering an effective interdisciplinary program in the field.[345]

If Charles Moore didn't hold a grudge against the Art and Architecture Building before coming to Yale, he certainly developed one very quickly. Part of his animus may have been personal—Moore had not liked Rudolph from their first encounter at Princeton, when Moore was a graduate student and Rudolph was teaching. As Moore recalled, "Rudolph and I had had a hard time trying to get along. We weren't trying to be ugly, I can tell you that, but we found ourselves rubbing each other the wrong way every time we talked."[346] In the years between Moore's graduation from Princeton and his arrival in New Haven, the relationship between the two men did not improve. Herbert Newman, a longtime faculty member who had many opportunities to observe both Rudolph and Moore from close range, saw the men as near complete opposites. Whereas Moore was "very shy and insecure and . . . didn't take confrontation well, Rudolph told you what he thought. He told you the way it was and if you didn't like it, you didn't like it. But you knew where you stood. With Charles, the ground was always shaking. You never really knew. He had this fear of engagement."[347] As Moore himself said, "Things were not cozy between me and Rudolph, but I had not gone to Yale thinking I was about to inhabit a disaster."[348]

The "disaster" that he was referring to was the Art and Architecture Building, which Moore quickly came to hold in high contempt for what he believed was its sacrifice of environmental considerations to those of monumental form. Although he admitted that he enjoyed "being in it," Moore objected to the A&A and to the way Rudolph had run the architecture program. "I disapprove of the Art and Architecture Building wholeheartedly," he said, "because it is such a personal manifestation of non-personal use."[349] The ideas that are quite literally embodied in the building were in direct opposition to those espoused by Moore: if Moore had the right ideas for Yale at the right time in the late 1960s, then the Art and Architecture Building could only be understood as the wrong building in which to advance those ideas. Even before Moore arrived at Yale, the Art and Architecture Building had begun to fall from a high place of grace and become, for a new generation, the embodiment of an overweening modernism. By the end of the 1960s, it would fall victim to incendiary rhetoric and then to fire itself.

Prior to taking the position at Yale, Moore only knew the Art and Architecture Building through photographs and the many articles that announced its completion. "I hadn't liked it," he told C. Ray Smith fifteen years later. "Well, in fact I didn't at that point actually dislike it; my attitude toward it, as I told a friend, was that it was like a warehouse in concrete, which was not my bag." Once he arrived in New Haven, he was surprised to find that "for all its great concrete strength it was rather tiny and not the concrete warehouse I had romanticized it to be. There was very little way to make more space in it, because it obtruded so." For Moore, it was "a monument to one way of looking at things."[350] And a monument, he had written in "You Have to Pay for the Public Life," is "an object whose function is to mark a place, either at the place's boundary or at its heart."[351] But a monument is not necessarily a good place to work, and the department's new chairman quickly came to see the building as an impediment to realizing a new pedagogy.[352]

Moore objected in particular to the openness of the chairman's office—"Mr. Rudolph didn't feel the need for privacy that I do"—and the lack of acoustical separation between faculty bathrooms—"I guess some people find the resulting mingling of sounds pleasurable." He also disliked the building's unfortunate lack of air conditioning, saying, "If I don't do anything else at Yale except get air introduced into this masterpiece, I will have left my mark."[353] Moore would certainly leave a mark on the A&A, but he never did get it air-conditioned. Overall, he found Rudolph's building "about as accommodating as Leon Battista Alberti is as a personality. It was its own Albertian perfection. It's there."[354] Settling in as chairman, Moore found it "difficult and frustrating, and ultimately wearing and depressing, to try to accommodate [to the building]—because it did not try to accommodate to me." Moore's major complaint with the building was its unabashed formalism. "It was designed as a piece of sculpture, as a three dimensional object in space. And the details of inhabiting it, things like the way the air felt, the way the light feels, and so forth, weren't considered."[355]

Moore's negative response to the building could be seen in the renovations he made almost as soon as he became chairman. Discovering that the chairman's office, reflecting Rudolph's preference for spatial openness and administrative transparency, had no doors or full-height walls or acoustic privacy, Moore immediately saw to its enclosure, claiming that a suit of clothes had been stolen from it. He also entered into discussions with university administration concerning structural renovations—including the installation of the air conditioning that had been cut from the original project for budgetary reasons: "The building was just intolerable in hot weather; the rooms on the south side . . . would get to be at least one hundred degrees. And it was impossible to heat the rooms on the north side in winter much past fifty-five degrees."[356] Moore's request for air conditioning was denied.

Early on he also replaced the second-floor student lounge, a somewhat ill-defined and austere alcove tucked away at the northwest corner of the exhibition gallery, where coffee, candy, and soda were available from coin-operated machines semiconcealed in a bunker-like enclosure, with a penthouse café in what was originally the principal guest apartment (5.35).[357] While the penthouse café proved quite popular, especially with faculty and students from other departments who enjoyed its commanding view over the campus to the distant East Rock, architecture students felt its remote location and limited daytime hours compromised its utility. On December 5, only a few months into his first term, Moore was forced to respond to the concerns of "some students over changes already made and some planned for the A&A building," and designated Henry Pfisterer as the faculty member who would "receive opinions and suggestions from students" and represent their legitimate concerns as part of ongoing physical planning.[358] In other words, in what would prove to be characteristic fashion, Moore dodged responsibility, encouraging students to interpret this as a carte-blanche invitation to accommodate themselves to the building as they, too, began to adopt Moore's opinion of Rudolph's architecture. "The Art and Architecture Building is truly 'architecture for its own sake,'" wrote Manfred Ibel in *Novum Organum*. "It is certainly not designed for the needs of the architects, painters, sculptors and graphic designers working and studying there. Griswold said, 'They have built monuments,' and I would add, 'to themselves.' What do we need monuments for? To worship in or to be worshipped?"[359]

One anonymous faculty member described the A&A Building as "a teaching program that has been poured in place."[360] Scully had previously compared the building to an opéra bouffe, and now it seemed students were taking on the characteristics of actors in a Greek tragedy. Before the program was shortened to three and a half years, students in the advanced studios were the featured occupants on the lower floor of Rudolph's grandly theatrical double-height drafting room, with the Master's Class typically occupying the elevated platform facing York Street, and the first-, second-, and third-year students arrayed across the platforms on the north, south, and east sides, along with the city planners—an arrangement that mirrored the journey of pedagogical progress toward graduation. Empowered by Moore's hostility to the building, students working in the double-height space began to make changes, sheltering their desks within a sea of makeshift cubicles (5.36) that were illustrated and commented on by Ellen Perry Berkeley, in a widely discussed but not particularly flattering article, "Yale: A Building as a Teacher," published in the July 1967 issue of *Architectural Forum*. Berkeley's article proved highly embarrassing to the university and damaging to both the reputation of the building and its architect, especially given Moore's undiplomatic claim in it that the A&A was "a magnificent building, with fatal flaws," although he was quick to add that such was "much better than a good building with minor flaws."[361]

Berkeley seemed at once shocked and unimpressed by the "architecture settlement" that had replaced the rows of De Stijl–inspired workstations Rudolph had designed for the drafting room. "Today," she wrote, "it is a *favela,*

5.35 Left: Art and Architecture Building penthouse as a guest suite (ca. 1963); right: Art and Architecture penthouse as a coffee shop (ca. 1967).

5.36 Fourth- and fifth-floor studios, Art and Architecture Building (1967).

5.37 Fourth- and fifth-floor studios, Art and Architecture Building (1967).

a spontaneous shanty-town that changes with the years as new students bring their talents and needs to this unassigned design problem." According to Berkeley, the structures of this "settlement" were "flimsy or solid, straightforward or whimsical, modest or grandiose. Last year, a student built a two-story office for himself; next year may see a totally new answer to the special requirements of function (a place to hang your drawings, as well as your hat), of privacy (a place to shut out your neighbors), and of ego (a place to express your own personality)."[362] Rising above the tide of plywood, cardboard, and sheet plastic, the large stone statue of Minerva, Roman goddess of poetry, wisdom, and commerce, could still be found commanding the studio, but now wearing a top hat and brandishing cigarettes, with painted toenails and eyes blanked-out "like Little Orphan Annie"[363] (5.37). As Berkeley saw it, the favela was evidence of student resistance to Rudolph's deterministic geometries: they would defy the building, expressing their personalities, and their discontent. In reality, their self-expression— extending to the stairwells, the hallways, and the raw concrete surfaces in the bathrooms, which were all covered in graffiti—reflected the personal impact that both Rudolph and Moore each had on students. One graffitist asked, "What would Paul Rudolph think?" Another proclaimed, "Moore is less." While Berkeley praised the Art and Architecture Building as "emphatically an educator, for students in and out of school . . . in a time of bland buildings and bland education," her article was widely resented by the university administration and older alumni as a public laundering of private linen. The four-year-old building surely had its limitations, but it was appreciated by many of the students whose seemingly excessive acts of inhabitation were less a reflection of environmental dissatisfaction than an expression of rebellion against authority.

As word spread about the Yale "favela," similar constructions began to proliferate in other schools. In spring 1967, at "a much smaller scale," as Richard Hayes points out, MIT students subdivided their designer studios with a few partitions and constructed mezzanines out of heavy timbers resting on concrete blocks, "encountering a hostile reaction from MIT administration."[364] However, in the fall 1967 term, after Donlyn Lyndon (b. 1936), Moore's former student at Princeton and a partner at MLTW, became head of MIT's Architecture Department, students were permitted to personalize their work areas. Soon afterward, Howard Barnstone's (1923–1987; B.A. 1945, M.Arch 1948) students at the University of Houston, and those of Richard Oliver (1942–1985), a former Moore student at Berkeley, followed suit, but none of these rivaled the individuality characteristic of the Yale studio constructions nor the grandeur of the ensemble as it could be experienced in Rudolph's monumentally scaled drafting studio.

Even in the midst of the countercultural ferment that turned young architects against monumental formalism, the building seemed somehow able to communicate with the students. In a 1978 interview with C. Ray Smith, Doug Michels remembered a project that directly involved the building: Louis Mackall "once presented a project in one of the corner rooms, on the 4th floor on the glass walls, and he drew on the glass and he painted on the glass in transparent inks, and the morning of his presentation I remember the sun was coming in that window and the colors were really alive. It was a transparent, translucent kind of presentation he made, very abstract, and poetic."[365]

The fourth-floor favela, rampant graffiti, and unusual projects were only a few examples of how the students and building had become engaged in a dialogue that rendered almost unrecognizable the pure, didactic space originally documented in the published photographs taken at the time of its completion only four years before. Some of the students' most interesting interventions in the building were the result of specific assignments cooked up by Moore, most notably the fall 1968 supergraphic-inspired elevator project, assigned by San Francisco–based graphic designer Barbara Stauffacher (b. 1932), who had previously garnered acclaim for her "supergraphics" designed for Sea Ranch, where she had been assisted by Doug Michels, who was responsible for executing the bold, environmentally scaled paintings before he came to Yale.[366] In a 1967 interview in *Progressive Architecture,* Michels said that supergraphics "start with a two-dimensional thing that becomes a three-dimensional overlay. . . . These are space trips."[367] Already at Yale when Moore became chairman, Michels decorated Moore's first professional office, painting the "most intricate examples of interwoven painted planes" with red, blue, and green stripes passing over floor, walls, and ceiling. "For a while," he noted self-mockingly, "nobody would step on it because it was Art."[368] Michels also contributed a supergraphic to Moore's New Haven residence—the enormous image of a squatting, suited man that came from a Volkswagen billboard Michels used to spruce up the apartment in anticipation of a *New York Times* photoshoot.[369] In 1968, Michels would cofound the countercultural group Ant Farm, a collection of radical artists and architects who worked in various media, including video, performance, and installation art. Best known for their projects *Media Van* (1971), *House of the Century* (1972), *Cadillac Ranch* (1974), and *Media Burn* (1975), Ant Farm was very much in line with the early 1970s zeitgeist but seems perhaps even more relevant in light of today's media-driven culture. These interests were evident in Michels's Yale work. Bill Grover recalls helping Michels make "a five-minute 16mm movie with an old wind-up camera" for a studio project: "We walked and drove around New Haven at night and filmed the highways and lights and shopping centers of the city. The film was called *Walk Don't Walk*. . . . The background music was the Beatles' 'Good Day Sunshine.' I don't know what happened to the film—but it baffled his final jury."[370] Michels went on to work in Philip Johnson's office (1979–82) and had a career as an educator at various universities, including the University of Houston, where he was director of the FutureLab design studio (1999–2000), dedicating much of his time to working on a speculative project for a space station to be occupied by both humans and dolphins; he died in 2003 as he climbed to an observation point while working as a consultant on a movie about whales.[371]

Stauffacher's studio required students to, as Ada Louise Huxtable reported, "'explode' the dull box of the school elevator[s] with color and pattern." Their painted designs were executed, two a week, until the end of the semester (5.38). "Certainly no one in the building was bored," Huxtable wrote, by designs that ranged from a stars and stripes enhanced "peace elevator" to more abstract, space-expanding experiments with fluorescent "day-glo" paint and pulsating strobe lights that impressed her as "legitimate exploratory exercises as any of the abstract study courses apotheosized by the Bauhaus as the heavenly road to architectural creativity."[372] To others, such interdisciplinary interventions seemed unnecessarily hostile.

Moore's boldest intervention was unveiled on April 28, 1968—an installation formally titled *Project Argus: A Multiple Montage from the Griggs Collection of Classic Film and an Experiment in Light and Sound Environment in and around the Department of Architecture's New Structure in the Exhibition Hall of the Art and Architecture Building* (5.39–5.41). Argus was an aggressive, two-story wooden structure that filled the double-height space of the second-floor gallery. Designed by Moore and Felix Drury, it was constructed as a class project by twenty-two students—including Tom Carey, William Grover, Robert "Torch" Knight, and James Righter, as well as M.E.D. students Steven Izenour and Raymond Kaskey—working alongside the innovative, interdisciplinary research group PULSA, who pioneered an art form they described as "the programmed environment." PULSA's membership included a filmmaker, two painters, a lighting designer, an architect, an engineer, and a photographer. Manipulating the physical and phenomenological qualities of a space with the ultimate purpose of "experientially heightening knowledge of the human environment," PULSA attempted "the dissolution of barriers between different

WAGNER, J.

CHRISTIANSEN, J.

RIGHTER, J.
CALDWELL, J.

5.38 Student designs for the Art and Architecture Building elevators, as seen in *Progressive Architecture* (October 1968). From left to right: Jerome Wagner (M.Arch 1973), John Christiansen (M.Arch 1970), and James Righter (M.Arch 1970) with James Caldwell (M.Arch 1969).

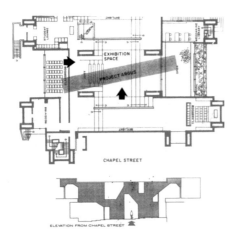

5.39 Project Argus, plan and elevation (1968).

5.40 Students constructing Project Argus in the second-floor gallery of the Art and Architecture Building (April 1968).

5.41 Project Argus, installation in the Art and Architecture Building Gallery (1968). The Mylar surfaces made Argus difficult to photograph.

forms of media and different forms of art through the creation of responsive sound and light installations."[373]

Named after the many-eyed monster of Greek mythology, Project Argus, described as "a panoptic presentation of the art of film, light, sound, and architecture," consisted of a show in two parts: a multiple screening of silent films from an extensive archive donated to Yale in 1968 by the estate of former actor John Griggs, and a dazzling bombardment of light and sound projected and reflected from a massive architectural installation.[374] Seven simultaneously operating projectors screened the films on mirror-like, Mylar-covered surfaces that comprised the sixty-foot-long, thirty-foot-wide, ten-foot-high central structure. Large banks of fluorescent tubes—up to 190 in a single grouping—were programmed to create a flashing effect heightened by intense bursts from strobe lights and electronic sounds from immense floor-to-ceiling electrostatic loudspeakers. Racks of lights were suspended from the ceiling and hung in banks along the sides of the structure, while sheets of reflective Mylar used to clad the structure confused the eye so that its actual shape was difficult to comprehend. The effect was blinding and deafening, with the sound penetrating the entire building and rendering office life on the third floor virtually intolerable. "I think it's very dangerous, like the ultimate weapon," Argus operator and PULSA member Paul Fuge told the *Yale Daily News*. "In the hands of some very unhip people it could do some serious damage."[375]

Argus was a deliberate attack on what Moore believed to be the Art and Architecture Building's conceptual and perceptual "squareness." In the view of historian Eve Blau, "the abstracted 'psychedelic' spaces of Argus were the architectonic correlatives of the radical actions of those who were attempting to 'creatively destroy the system.'"[376] To Ada Louise Huxtable, Project Argus was a "temporary destruction" of the building's major areas, and a "mind-bending esthetic experiment and design *double entendre* that practically told Mr. Rudolph to sit up on the shelf and stay there."[377] In Herbert Newman's view, it "wasn't an exhibition" so much as "a house that was built inside the building" that "transformed" the grand vistas of the gallery into "this tiny little place," and "in so doing he [Moore] sabotaged its spirit."[378] When later asked to reflect on the various interventions he made to the Rudolph building, Moore dryly replied: "It has seemed to me for some time that an architecture school was a place where people were trying to be architects."[379] However, C. Ray Smith, an important chronicler of the emerging postmodernist techniques of supergraphics and light shows, considered Project Argus and PULSA a suitable extension of Rudolph's design. There may be some reason to support this interpretation, as Timothy Rohan has observed, given that "the A&A was already so visually dense and complex that the light show seemed to fulfill the promise of Rudolph's vision and to indicate the direction in which his architecture was now developing."[380]

Parallel to Moore's various assaults on it, Rudolph's building was also the victim of poor maintenance. Windows had not been washed since the building's completion, owing to the university's unwillingness to spend the $2,200 (approximately $6,500 in 2015) needed to do the job properly. Rudolph had intended to use a rope system to give the window washers access, but that method did not work and "cherry pickers" were needed. Moreover, the once-bright, paprika-colored carpets had become dirty and worn out and, in what was perhaps the most visually disruptive change made to the building, Moore replaced them with dull beige yardage, robbing the concrete of its rosy glow. When Ellen Perry Berkeley asked Rudolph about this, he stuck by his choice of color, saying he would select it again but specify a better-quality carpet.

The building's natural and artificial lighting proved problematic as well. The grid pattern of the cargo netting specified by Rudolph to reduce heat gain at the east- and south-facing windows cast distracting and ever-changing shadows on student worktables. If the building was overly bright by day, by night it was cavernously gloomy, with exposed low-wattage lightbulbs delivering an eerie dimness, made worse by the fact that the bulbs were being continuously pilfered by students for use at home. Worst of all, the sprayed asbestos ceilings, intended to provide a measure of acoustic control—particularly necessary in an age when desktop radios reflecting students' varied listening tastes combined with the din of conversation to make the noise level a constant distraction—were continuously crumbling. Lastly, the optimistic openness of the building combined with its dramatically configured, cavernous staircases became a liability as New Haven's crime rate rose, prompting repeated incidents of petty theft.

Moore's hostility was shared by painting and sculpture students and faculty, who were ill-housed on the upper two floors and the subbasement, respectively. Perhaps the least-suitable accommodation was the subbasement sculpture studio, which until spring 1967 was not served by a freight elevator—an important feature that was, along with air conditioning, cut from the original budget—forcing students to confine themselves to small, portable work or to aggregate larger pieces from smaller ones, in order to navigate the building's twisting stairs as they moved their materials to the basement workshops to be transformed into sculptures and then transported as finished work to the second-floor exhibition spaces for judgment and display. In May 1967, just about a month after an article in the *New York Times Magazine* rehashed the art students' protests accompanying the building's completion in 1963,[381] a petition labeling the building's work space "totally inadequate" was signed by forty-nine of the fifty-six graduate art students and four faculty members, with the Beaux-Arts–imbued Deane Keller (1901–1992; B.A. 1923, B.F.A. 1926, M.A.H. 1948), professor of drawing and painting, also joining the protest.[382] In a vitriolic letter to the *Yale Daily News,* Keller, senior faculty member in the Art Department, who had served in World War II as a Monuments, Fine Arts, and Archives officer, described the building as "the worst place in which to try to make paintings and sculpture that I have ever seen anywhere, both here and abroad."[383] Even in the face of this public protest by their fellow art students and faculty, many architecture students remained loyal to Rudolph's concept. In response to the statement of a sculptor that "the building was designed by architects for architects," one architecture student rather smugly remarked, "Oh yeah, I know there are complaints about lack of space. I've got it all." Soon however, disaster would strike, and the architecture students would have none of it.

At 3:58 a.m. on June 14, 1969, a New Haven police officer was alerted to the fact that a Yale building on the corner of York and Chapel was burning.[384] The Art and Architecture Building was ablaze, lighting the summer sky with a fire that stretched through three floors. An officer on the scene reported that "he had halted his patrol car . . . facing the A&A Building when suddenly a terrific explosion blew out the Chapel Street side of the fourth level and the whole area was instantly engulfed in flames."[385] Some witnesses mistakenly believed a bomb had exploded, but it was in fact the pressure from the fire's heat that blew out the building's windows. The New Haven Fire Department arrived less than fifteen minutes after the three-alarm blaze was reported and, having protected the ground-floor library with plastic to prevent water damage, went on to combat the fire in the floors above. At 4:15 a.m., New Haven Fire Marshal Thomas Lyden, Jr., arrived. "As I approached the A&A structure," he reported, "it was observed that the 4th and 5th floors were completely involved with the fire and it appeared that the flames were licking its [*sic*] way up to the 6th floor. Three aerial H_2O towers in operation dispensing close to 2,000 gallons per minute" caused some concern that so much water cascading through the structure would fill the studio pits like swimming pools, and compound the crisis with fears of structural collapse.[386] While the New Haven Fire Department battled the flames, Henry Pfisterer, roused from his bed, rushed to the school from his house in nearby Hamden. Standing on York Street, Pfisterer worked furiously, demonstrating incredible technical savvy, as Robert Miller, then

5.42 Yale School of Architecture, Art and Architecture Building, shortly after the fire (June 14, 1969).

5.43 Yale School of Architecture, Art and Architecture Building, the morning after the fire was extinguished (June 14, 1969).

5.44 Fourth- and fifth-floor studios, Art and Architecture Building, two days after the fire.

a first-year architectural student, remembers: "[He was] coolly watching the blaze next to New Haven's fire chief, working his slide rule to calculate how much water each of the many concrete floors could take before failing."[387]

The fire was contained within the hour, but all the contents on the building's top four floors were destroyed (5.42, 5.43). The double-height space of the architecture studio and the sixth-floor painters' studios were completely burned out. Floor seven was heavily damaged by smoke. Fortunately, the ground-floor library was safe and the other lower floors only experienced slight water damage. Photographs of the building's interiors taken shortly after the fire show a burned-out husk, with the student favelas reduced to piles of ash, a sad irony in light of the fact that the space that students had struggled to restructure and redesign themselves had been returned to its pure state of being, the magnificent ruin Rudolph had once imagined it might eventually become.[388] However, amidst the destruction in the double-height architecture studio, there was one charred beacon of hope for the building's future: rising above the melted carpet, blackened debris, deformed metal, and charred concrete, the statue of Minerva continued to preside, largely unscathed (5.44). As the *New York Times* reported, "The statue, the only object of any consequence on the two floors that survived intact, is now doubly appropriate. Minerva was a goddess who both protected the arts and went to battle."[389] Now she had the scars to show for it.

As Fire Marshal Thomas Lyden noted in his final report on the incident, "No building is more fireproof than its contents, an important factor to be considered regarding the A&A fire." Describing the student favelas in near disbelief, Lyden wrote: "It is almost impossible to visualize the layout of the 4th and 5th floors prior to the fire. However, they had close to 125 students scattered on these floors with each member having his or her own drafting board protected with an enclosure of teakwood or cardboard or other highly combustible material that the students could obtain. . . . Other types of ingredients found were rubber cement, spray paint, varnish, turpentine, lacquer thinner, plastic adhesive, plexiglass, paper, and so many other highly dangerous substances that definitely would contribute to an inferno, be it the Yale A&A Bldg. or any other structure."[390]

Paul Rudolph was traveling in Europe when he was told about the fire. Asked later about his reaction to the news, he said, "I felt as if somebody had died."[391] Charles Moore, with his almost preternatural ability to avoid difficult situations, was also out of town when the fire occurred.[392]

Given the widespread student unrest and the crisis in the City Planning Department, many assumed the fire was an act of arson—the ultimate expression of student frustration. A press release distributed by the university on July 28 announced the conclusion of the six-week investigation into the fire's origins, citing Fire Marshal Lyden's official statement on the matter: "At this point after a thorough investigation, I must rule the cause of this fire 'Undetermined.' . . . With the assistance of the New Haven Police Department, Yale campus Police, and Yale officials at all levels, I have not come forth with evidence that arson was directly involved."[393] An insurance agent's report corroborated Lyden's findings. Lyden, however, also noted that "There is a possibility that a person or persons may have unknowingly contributed to the start of this fire; however, investigation to this point has not brought forth evidence to substantiate this." Although Fire Marshal Lyden found no proof of foul play, New Haven Fire Chief Michael J. Sweeney stated that he strongly suspected arson, telling *Architectural Record* immediately after the fire that he "will consider this fire to be of suspicious origin until we prove differently."[394] In a 1978 interview, Lyden remembers his disagreement with the chief: "Just because we were having unrest at various campuses, the Black Panthers, you name it, what right did anyone have to say this is arson? I don't think that's fair until it falls under approval [*sic*] that it was arson. This is my attitude, so I had to contend with him, which wasn't very pleasant."[395]

Adding fuel to the fire, as it were, was a document distributed around the school only days before the disaster. As reported by Joseph Lelyveld in the *New York Times* on July 29, 1969, "The aroused university community still finds it hard to separate the fire from the unrest that preceded it, partly because of a provocative broadsheet that received wide circulation the week before the fire. 'Why has Yale not gone up in smoke?' it asked. 'See the A and A building,' the broadsheet advised. 'See every building. See them soon.'" The implied conclusion—" . . . while you can"—meant trouble was afoot.[396] While this coincidence made for a good story, Lyden said that any connection between the fire and the broadsheet was "not substantiated."[397] The broadsheet was almost immediately brought to the attention of the fire investigators. One of the five students responsible for its publication "said that they had meant merely to call attention to the deterioration of communications among students, faculty members and administrators on a campus that so far has escaped violent unrest. The fire, said the student . . . was 'an extremely unfortunate coincidence.'"[398] The students also dismissed the claims of arson as implausible, with some saying they would "sooner have set Woodbridge Hall ablaze than their home base."[399] As one of the Black Workshop members recalled: "When that building burned, everyone that I know was in shock. You hated the building; there were all kinds of problems with the architecture school; but that was your building."[400] To

344

this day, some architects and students still speculate on the fire's origins and the true identity of the presumed arsonist. But almost ten years after his initial investigation, Lyden defended his findings, as well as his character and professional ethics: "If you knew me, I will say a spade is a spade, and this they knew, the city knew it, and Yale knew it. I will not conceal anything. I want the facts. . . . I lost out on raises because I didn't go along with politicians."[401] A freak occurrence it may have been, but the fire in the Art and Architecture Building is still seen by some as a symbolic inevitability. For Turner Brooks, then a third-year student, "the building burst into flames out of its own psychic guilt. It was the only solution."[402]

Regardless of how the fire started, Peter Blake, former editor in chief of *Architectural Forum* and in 1969 architecture critic for the recently founded magazine *New York,* believed that the event should be seen as a symbol of problems young architects had with the profession: "The Yale fire did dramatize a state of concern not limited to Yale's architecture students, but found at just about every school of architecture in the U.S. today: a profound uneasiness among students (and some faculty) about the priorities that today govern American architecture and American architectural education." Blake went on to cite incidents at other schools across the country that reflected the general shift from aesthetic to social concerns as students began "questioning the 'relevance' of a profession that devotes most of its efforts to designing buildings for the rich (and for public or private clients that represent the Establishment and/or the 'military-industrial complex') and very few of its efforts to designing for the poor."[403]

Over the summer, tempers seemed to cool somewhat along with the building's ashes, and plans were made for the resumption of fall classes. An "Ad Hoc Committee for Studying and Making Proposals for the Reassessment of the Art and Architecture School" was formed with Charles Moore, Kent Bloomer, and fourth-year students Roger Simmonds (b. 1940; M.C.P. 1970) and Alberto Lau (b. 1945; M.Arch 1970) constituting its Steering Committee, leading to the design of a multilevel "temporary structure" to be erected in the second-floor gallery.[404] The proposal, echoing Project Argus, was rejected for cost reasons and, instead, the so-called "Box" was built, intended to meet "part of the needs, including a wall for exhibition, office spaces, a projection booth, and a physical separation of work space (drafting) from congregating space." Almost immediately this arrangement proved deficient and distasteful: "The box or cube does not fulfill satisfactorily even those parts of the original plan it seeks to implement, and as a monstrosity in scale, appearance, and placement, it is at best minimal and at worst offensive."[405] So unpopular was the Box that it became a popular target "for guerilla warfare, graffiti and stink bombs," with "one art student declaring a personal 'war'" and proceeding to "paint his animosities in vivid red on it. Others have begun to demolish it by kicking holes in its side."[406] Moreover, none of the faculty members for whom it was intended used the Box, and no one seemed ready to claim responsibility for designing or building it. In spring 1970, students, with Charles Moore's blessing (and assistance), transformed the Box into a new lounge. Years later, Barton Phelps remembered it as "insulting to the building" and confesses to having "put the first hammer through the wall."[407]

Moore, in his characteristically arch way, would later report that the 1969 summer meetings to discuss curriculum, restructuring, and governance made it "evident that the serious reformers would come to meetings designated as 'curricular,' the revolutionaries to the ones marked 'governance' and a mixture of the group to the 'restructuring sessions,' since it was not clear what that meant." The more revolutionary students advocated a governance proposal allegedly ghostwritten by Moore that featured "overtones of parliamentary democracy meant, like the Mexican one-party system, to seek leadership from the left and to move it, by the centripetal weight of responsibility, toward center. That system, which put decisions in the hands of a series of faculty (appointed by the Dean)-student (elected) committees, was adopted in the Fall [1969] by the School."[408]

Five days after the fire, Howard Weaver, reporting on plans for the relocation of the staff and students, advised that although the building above the third floor was unusable, the school would reopen in September "with all planned programs underway."[409] Weaver's memo outlined procedures for handling the day-to-day mundanities, as well as new problems needing immediate attention. Damages to the building totaled $925,015 (approximately $6 million in 2015) by the fire marshal's official estimate.[410] Student losses were not covered by the university's insurance policy, leading Weaver and alumnus Earl P. Carlin to solicit alumni and others for emergency funds to assist those who lost personal equipment in the fire.[411] By July 16, regular use of the unaffected lower floors had resumed. By September, the school reopened with partial use of the fire-damaged building, as well as various temporary spaces on and off campus that had been reconfigured into ersatz classrooms and studios. The architecture and planning programs were scattered to the building's second-floor exhibition space and to the upper two floors of a building at 294 Elm Street. Studio space was also set up in nearby buildings at 1082, 1086, and 1164 Chapel Street, as well as 165 York Street, making it possible for *Architectural Record,* in its March 1970 issue, to report that "Yale's graduate courses in architecture are being held in New Haven lofts and storefronts and in the remains of the Art and Architecture Building . . . with many of the students liking things that way, according to Moore."[412]

As the A&A Building was being cleaned and repaired for partial reuse, Moore and Weaver endeavored to reach a long-term solution to the problem of overcrowding by relocating the now-independent Faculties of Design and Planning to the relatively remote Hammond Laboratory, a recently vacated former Engineering School facility at the leafy northern edge of the campus a half mile away.[413] Moore's willingness to leave Rudolph's building not only reflected his personal animus toward it but also his not inconsiderable contempt for inner-city New Haven and gritty cities in general. On March 12, 1970, he informed faculty and students of the proposed relocation, acknowledging that there were "some problems . . . notably the distance to the Art Library and from coffee" but stating that he considered the move to be "the most helpful thing the University has done for us in some time."[414] However, Moore miscalculated student affection for Rudolph's building. The proposal came after "five years of discussions with faculty and students, which had seemed to me almost unanimously in favor of a move to useful space," but the choice of Hammond Hall was not welcomed by the architecture students and faculty. It was, instead, embraced by the Sculpture Department of the Art School, which gradually began to occupy the building in 1971 and continued to do so until 2008.[415]

As part of Moore's postfire negotiations with Weaver, most of the useful and symbolic space in the A&A went to the School of Art, so that when the low-ceiling top floors of the building were reopened in 1970, they became the architecture studios, along with the dimly lit basement and subbasement, as well as various off-site locations, while the painters were given the grand studio on the fourth and fifth floors. This arrangement was regarded by many as a form of revenge for the building's initial neglect of the art students—a sort of punishment against architects for their overweening heroics. Once they commandeered the fourth and fifth floors, the art students promptly constructed their own version of the much-derided favelas, in the form of seemingly innumerable locked cubicles that destroyed all sense of the room's grandeur.

Long before the fire, the Yale-as-Bauhaus idea had run its course, with the ideal of collaboration among the various disciplines no longer seeming achievable or even desirable. Motivated as much by space needs as by pedagogical philosophy, the University Council, as well as the Yale Corporation, had, as early as 1967, begun to advocate splitting the School of Art and Architecture into two separate entities, each with its own dean and its own building, with design (architecture), city planning, graphic design, and proposed programs such as industrial design, space planning and interior design, and landscape architecture retaining the use of the A&A Building.[416]

According to Jim Swiss, writing in the *Yale Daily News* in January 1969, the November 1968 AIA walkout, ostensibly a result of student dissatisfaction with the profession's orientation, was also motivated in part by "the very structure of the School itself," with seemingly autonomous departments beholden to a single dean.[417] That year, Brewster got on board with the split, which he believed to be "highly desirable and even urgent," with architecture, graphics, and urban design housed in the Art and Architecture Building, a building that "can never be satisfactory for the fine arts."[418] With the fire giving impetus to making a decision, on September 15, 1969, Brewster announced the split on a "purely . . . interim" basis "for this year of reappraisal only." Seeking to uncouple the decision from the recent fire, he noted that it was consistent with a 1968 report of the University Council,[419] notwithstanding Brewster's insistence that the changes provided "an opportunity for a balanced and objective, fundamental reappraisal of what Yale should be doing, and how it should do it, in the arts, design and planning."[420] The *New York Times* refused to rule out the fire as a principal motivation for the reorganization, reporting that the split came "apparently in response to last spring's disorders," before going on to state that students regarded "these changes as a reaction to the student activism and a measure to provide greater administration control in the future."[421] The split was made effective September 1969, but the division wasn't officially formalized by the Yale Corporation until 1972.[422]

Moore welcomed the split into two separate faculties, believing that it "improved morale at almost every level, at my own chiefly, by removing budget and administration from the realm of black comedy (It is now, I suppose one could say, laughable.)"[423] Moore, tired of administration, reluctantly agreed to take on the duties of dean of what was initially called the Faculties of Design and Planning, "under three conditions: one, that I reported directly to [Brewster]; two, that I had no chairman under me; and three, that I could trade my two remaining years as chairman for one year as dean."[424] Moore never liked being chairman or dean. "It was not what I was cut out for. I felt I had done my duty, damn it, saved the school. . . . I was still seen as a fascist pig by some of the students, of course, but I wasn't as bad as Brewster or the art school dean [Howard S. Weaver], so I emerged relatively unscathed. I hadn't said or done anything more than usually offensive. I had been against the war from the start of course, in favor of student responsibilities."[425] According to Moore, Brewster "kept on pushing" for him to remain as dean, and he stayed in the post for a year and a half, stepping down at the end of the spring 1971 term, in effect serving for only two semesters and taking a third as a sabbatical leave.

The fire at the Art and Architecture Building came at the end of the most tumultuous year in Yale's history, and the hope for restored calm during the summer break proved illusory. The 1969–70 year would prove to be just as turbulent as the last. Charles Brewer stirred up his own share of controversy and was, according to Gindroz, "the most contentious" member of the faculty. Under Rudolph, Brewer had been entrusted with much of the department's day-to-day management, including membership on the Executive and Admissions Committee, which he chaired from 1962 until 1969. Gindroz recalls that toward the end of Brewer's time as chairman of the Admissions Committee, he "proudly" boasted that "'not a single member of the incoming class stated that they wanted to be an architect.' It was a kind of anti-class."[426] Brewer was also a member of the Rules Committee in 1969, at which time he proposed a plan for departmental governance that gave exceptional power to students, including the right to participate in faculty hiring.[427] As Brewer became increasingly radicalized, his contract was not renewed and he left Yale in 1971, along with mild-mannered Bruce Adams and firebrand Pat Goeters.[428] Brewster also considered terminating Peter Millard and King-lui Wu, but ultimately decided against it. Millard would retire as associate professor adjunct in 1987, and Wu would retire as professor adjunct in 1988.

To help address problems of governance, Moore surprised many by advocating the return of "tenure," which, with his encouragement, the school had abandoned in 1966 "for what seemed to be good reasons." Now Moore thought differently, arguing that tenure would achieve "the depth and continuity of faculty concern we require . . . to keep support people in structures, basic design, environmental controls . . . and probably design methodology; a system of part time tenure appointments for architectural professionals, on the model of the Davenport professorships continues to seem appropriate. I expect soon to deliver a tenure proposal to the Provost."[429] He did not; and tenure as well as multiyear adjunct appointments would not be adopted until the 1980s, as part of Thomas Beeby's administration.

The situation in the school began to heat up again in March 1970, when Weaver informed Brewster that anonymous posters and pamphlets had been put up in the building immediately following spring vacation, suggesting the possibility of more student agitation. "Last year equity—this year survival," one poster read. Another one, "Tyrannicide," was a thinly veiled rant against Moore. There was also a sudden appearance of posters seemingly designed to stir up discontent among students with plans for postfire renovations: "Imagine Sculpture and Painting Studios on the *Third* Floor [the administrative level]."[430]

Tensions peaked on "Panther Weekend" (May 1–2, 1970), when, as William Mitchell has recalled, "several conditions . . . emerging more or less independently [came] together . . . to produce a perfect storm of disaffection. The precipitating event was the transparently political murder trial, in New Haven, of the Black Panther leader Bobby Seale," extensively documented in Paul Bass and Douglas W. Rae's 2006 book *Murder in the Model City: The Black Panthers, Yale, and the Redemption of a Killer.*[431] Mitchell witnessed thousands of protesters converging on the city:

> There were armored military vehicles in the streets; Yale students declared a strike; a series of confrontational public meetings took place—one, in Ingalls Rink, followed by bomb blasts; and academic life did not return to normal for the remainder of the year. Within the University, the School of Art and Architecture was a particularly unruly center of radical activism and one of President Kingman Brewster's biggest headaches. At one contentious meeting with him, representatives of the School came decorated with colored dots on their foreheads, and accompanied by a chicken named Kingman Rooster—a political tactic that was known as a mind fuck.
>
> A large part of it, of course, was about the Vietnam War. Nobody could ignore the escalating disaster, the ongoing protests, and the increasingly violent suppression of dissent—which was to culminate in the Kent State shootings a few days later on May 4, 1970. Then there was the draft, which many graduate students were at Yale to avoid. And there was the latent outrage; on April 30, President Nixon had announced the invasion of Cambodia.

All this, Mitchell remembered, "intersected with an acute consciousness, among the students, of issues of race, class, and social equity."

> Memories of the Kennedy-era Civil Rights Movement, the Freedom Riders and the violence they met, and Martin Luther King were still fresh and very raw. The Panthers were organizing black communities, advocating revolution, and attempting to form alliances with other radical groups.

And New Haven was no idyllic, isolated college town; Yale was, conspicuously to the point of over-the-top caricature, an island of great wealth and privilege set in an economically decrepit former mill town that had been going downhill for as long as anyone could remember, and that included large, desperately poor and under-serviced, alienated black communities. This condition confronted you, and couldn't be forgotten; wander a few blocks from the School into the Hill district, or down Dixwell Avenue, if you dared, and you were suddenly in another world.[432]

Turner Brooks, at the time in his last year as an architecture student, paints a similar picture of Panther Weekend (5.45): "The evening in May [May Day]. . . . There is an incipient revolution in New Haven that's as if it's going to happen but it is miraculously absorbed. . . . There were all these hippies and revolutionary teeny boppers camping out on the Green. All of Yale was going to basically be stormed. The National Guard was surrounding New Haven . . . sealing off York Street along Chapel. They were standing cheek to jowl, bayonets fixed to their rifles, gas masks on. This great surging, unruly mob confronted them on Chapel Street. And this great burned out, gloomy charred hulk of the A&A Building rising up behind them seemed to symbolize everything that was wrong with everything for that moment."[433]

During the events of Panther Weekend, Charles Moore was characteristically absent, Brooks notes. "Moore, as far as I know, didn't deal much with the politics of the revolution at all." He "absconded, disappeared to California and allowed the revolution to sort of burn itself out, and then returned like a triumphant Chinese emperor . . . after the Mongol hordes had been absorbed, and tranquility reigned once again." He had "essentially run away from the School, hating any kind of political ferment. But he returned to give us our diplomas in a very sort of perfunctory way," letting the class of 1970, the first class admitted under his watch, just fizzle out. After constructing an enormous model of a social housing development for New Haven's Hill district as his final project, Brooks was disappointed to find that "there was nobody to look at it. There was no final review. There were no final reviews. I asked a critic to come look at it finally." This was Allan Greenberg, who was very supportive. Greenberg, then working with the New Haven Redevelopment Agency, suggested to Brooks that he show his project to the mayor, but Brooks soon realized that, given the tenor of the times, the mayor would disapprove of its "labyrinthian urbanism" because the design was too defensible from within. "The city was looking for wide 'Haussmannesque' boulevards that could be conveniently controlled by police or military intervention."[434]

Still, the school seemed to maintain much of its academic luster, in part because the visiting critic system continued to function at a high level. Advanced students were enjoying their newfound freedom to choose among Master's Class–like studios taught by visitors, such as James Stirling in fall 1970, and faculty, such as Herbert Newman in the spring. Moore noted that these studios "were far and away the most popular, and that the faculty-student curriculum committee in architecture has developed for next year a highly organized, economical, carefully structured and fairly short list of available courses with strong design emphasis. And once again, as in the years before last year, the architectural students admitted by us have just about unanimously chosen to come here. Our strength, I believe, is that we are still a design school."[435]

At the end of Moore's first term in the dean's office, he sent a confidential letter to Provost Taylor articulating ideas for the school's future and suggesting that the school might most easily balance its budget "by reducing its student population from 150 to 87, and reducing its faculty accordingly." Moore was sure that the faculty and students would be pleased with the plan that he felt represented "a substantial educational improvement in the department, greatly increasing the kind of contact with the most inventive minds in the profession, on which our school's reputation for excellence (as well as its special quality of ebullient 'free-wheelingness') is based. The dissatisfaction of last year," Moore continued, "and the student charges of faculty 'mediocrity' came, I am convinced, not only from dissatisfaction with the profession and society, but also because the school has grown (in a discipline which, as I hear often pointed out, is short on theory and heavily dependent on insight deriving from personal contact) too large for everyone to profit from the important faculty we do have."[436] Moore proposed to cut enrollment by introducing a term's credit for professional work, which would reduce the eight-term master of architecture sequence to seven. The program was reduced to three years in 1972, bringing Yale in line with most of its peers. Moore also called for the termination of the Black Workshop unless outside funds could be secured. Recognizing that the restructuring and the drastic cutbacks might not be popular, and all too anxious to end his deanship, Moore averred that he would lay his resignation on the line "if there is a really violent objection."[437]

Moore's sunny report on the program's status notwithstanding, reports about the university's fiscal problems, figuring so prominently in published accounts of student unrest, not to mention the increasingly negative reputation about New Haven as a place to study and live, caused the newly independent architecture school to suffer, with the University Council in November 1970 reporting "a downturn . . . in number of students choosing Yale."[438] Truth be told, the very future of the school was in jeopardy. On November 3, 1970, Moore struggled to cope with severe budget cuts brought on in part by poor management of Yale's endowment and in part by a severe economic downturn. A year before, in December 1969, his proposal for streamlining the curriculum in the school while enhancing the undergraduate courses in design and planning had not pleased Brewster, who felt that it included insufficient reduction in faculty numbers, an "inordinate" increase in undergraduate offerings, and a failure to address the "'workshop' problem" (a reference to the Black Workshop). In his report to Provost Taylor, Henry Broude, who had attended Moore's presentation, said he believed "that the draft proposal was quite different from what we had expected and," referring to the previous proposal to reduce the seven-term program by turning one term into a term of an apprenticeship in a professional office, "that it left unresolved the basic question of whether certain fundamental skills could— indeed, should—be acquired away from Yale, either through apprenticeship experience in architectural offices or through taking courses elsewhere (in such basic things as mechanical structure, drafting, etc.)." In November 1970, Moore was asked to return with a new proposal that would "rely on non-Yale resources . . . [for] basic tools and skills," with the question "left open as to whether a student would enroll in some other institution for a year and then 'transfer' to Yale or whether a cooperative job program might be set up where selected architectural offices would employ students and, in the course of that employment, train them. It was also left undecided as to whether this segment of a program would be preceded by a short period at Yale—perhaps the summer after a student graduates from college the first fall term thereafter." The new proposal was even more dramatic than that of December 1969: it would use a student's time at Yale to focus on courses in design theory and aesthetics and "might be broken into two periods which would alternate with on-the-job experience, with the expectation that the present three-and-a-half-year-long program would be drastically shortened to two years plus two summers."[439]

The need to make financial cutbacks seemed to pose a distinct threat to the school's future. As word of budget-slashing seeped out to students, faculty, and alumni, Brewster found himself forced, as he put it in a letter to Moore dated November 20, 1970, to express regret for raising "false fears about Yale's intentions in Architecture," and he urged Moore "to reassure . . . colleagues and students there is no intention to abolish, phase out, or otherwise lay siege to professional architectural education at Yale." Brewster then went on to spin the situation: faced with "an inexorable budget squeeze," he wrote, "I want very much to use that circumstance positively rather than negatively." Brewster asked that Moore and his "colleagues . . . engage in a fundamental reappraisal to see whether the content and sequence of professional education of architects could be improved in the process of reducing the demand on University financial resources."[440] Nonetheless, the urgency of the budget situation and the postfire crisis mentality that pervaded the school fueled persistent rumors that the school was doomed. Perhaps it might have been, had it not been for the Davenport Fund, which was of such magnitude as to not only support two visiting professors each year but also other faculty salaries, essentially guaranteeing the school's future. Nonetheless, it was necessary to find ways to save money while also advancing the program.

In April 1970, Moore shared with Brewster a ten-year plan for the school's future, as required by the National Architectural Accrediting Board. Moore chose not to take "any pains to discuss it with . . . faculty."[441] A remarkably prescient document, it regrettably doesn't appear to have been consulted by successive deans. Despite frequent criticism of Moore as an administrator and leader, the plan revealed his brilliance as an educator. In many ways anticipating concerns that would not surface for ten years or more, Moore described the school as a "*laboratory to develop the capacity for intuitive design*" (Moore's emphasis). The plan endorsed the visiting professor format and the decrease in the school's size. But the school also needed to develop "*the student's respect for facts* which often suffers in design schools, where the intuitive leapers skip perfectly useful facts which already exist." The plan also advocated the development of "an understanding of the *natural systems* which affect the environment (ecology). Failure to do this has brought this country, with much of the world, to the point of crisis, but the response so far has been largely rhetorical."[442]

Moore's ten-year plan revealed the depth of his understanding of what needed to happen if architectural pedagogy was to be reinvented for the post-Sixties era, calling for "strengthening the sense of realism and accomplishment in the studio program which is to say in the school. The synthetic action of the design studio has long been the great strength and fascination of architectural education, but . . . it is now apparent across the country that studios which address made-up problems are in disrepute as too simple, but that studios which address real problems without really providing their solutions are in even worse disrepute for falsely raising expectations and playing with peoples' [*sic*] lives."[443]

Moore went on to emphasize the role of direct experience through travel: "*Seeing what exists.* Which, as soon as (or if) the present panic about narrow relevance subsides, an organized independent program of travel should become a required part of the architecture curriculum." This did not become policy until 2000, when an endowment from the Henry Hart Rice Foundation made funds available for teacher-directed student travel in advanced studios. Moore also argued for "*clarifying the vocational base* of architecture, wherein the various technical disciplines related to architecture—structural engineering, environmental controls, acoustics, etc. are better taught," calling for the extension of "knowledge about the field through research. The point is often made that architecture is in about the same primitive state that medicine was in when every doctor was a general practitioner and that architecture, like medicine, must develop and give equal status to a new breed of research." Moore also sought to expand "the frontiers of practice" by "undertaking real work within the full visibility of the student body, for which professional responsibility is taken by interested faculty members."[444] In this he was referring to his two-year-long effort "to found the Yale Design Group, a corporation designed to assume, through faculty members, professional obligation for pioneering design work," something that would become one of the hallmarks of his time at UCLA, where he worked through the Urban Innovations Group, and would eventually bear fruit in part at Yale with the establishment of the Urban Design Workshop in 1992. As Moore would write in the 1970 *Bulletin,* the architect "who may have once seen himself standing slightly apart from society is now wrapped up in some of its central problems."[445] Moore's final goal was the development of opportunities for advanced study and research. Drawing attention to the inauguration in 1967 of the master of environmental design program, Moore, one of few architects to hold a Ph.D., went on to propose interdisciplinary Ph.D.-level work, but perhaps more provocatively, the establishment of a Ph.D. in architecture, which he believed was not presently viable but might be so five years in the future.[446] A Ph.D. in architecture was inaugurated in 2008.[447]

The struggle with the budget and Brewster's general irritation over the contentious behavior of architecture students and faculty significantly influenced Moore's decision to step down as dean, effective June 1, 1971. He remained on the faculty, teaching first-year studio along with Kent Bloomer until 1977 and, afterward, maintained an affiliation with the school as visiting professor until 1984. However, his decision to leave the dean's office and reduce his time at the school was not entirely related to his distaste for administrative responsibility, but also to problems with his professional practice.

5.45 Protesters on the New Haven Green during "Panther Weekend" (May 1–2, 1970).

5.46 Louis Kahn, early design for the Yale Center for British Art featuring a bridge across Chapel Street (1971).

Returning from his sabbatical trip to Mexico in spring 1971, he found that "the sheriff was at the door, and Brewster was still mad at me for leaving. There was the usual 'ex-dean' scene at Yale, with the new dean [Herman D. J. Spiegel] telling everyone they were having a renaissance—by which I presumed he meant that my term must have been the dark ages."[448]

During the late 1960s and early 1970s, despite general unrest and a declining endowment, Yale undertook a number of major building projects with varying degrees of success. Moore participated in the decision-making process surrounding the construction of new buildings, but his voice was not as influential as had been George Howe's and, even more so, Paul Rudolph's. Clearly, Brewster relied on the advice of Edward Larrabee Barnes, who designed the Cross Campus Library and no doubt advocated for Marcel Breuer's selection as architect of the Becton Center (1970). But Moore was, at least initially, involved in architect selection for the British Arts Center, the most significant university building project to be undertaken during his tenure as dean.

On December 9, 1966, the university announced that Paul Mellon (1907–1999; B.A. 1920, L.H.D. 1967) agreed to give the university his collection of British art and books, along with the funds to construct a museum to house it. For tax reasons, Mellon had to make the gift quickly, so that Yale's acquisition of a 255-by-150-foot site facing Chapel Street across from the University Art Gallery was only announced by Brewster and Mayor Richard C. Lee one day before the gift was made public. Despite a prior agreement not to cross Chapel Street, Yale persuaded the city to allow it to build the new facility on the site opposite the Art Gallery—although initially a second site was considered on the northwest corner of Broadway and York Street, facing the back of Sterling Library, a site favored by the university librarian, who wanted to incorporate Mellon's book collection within the library.[449] The Chapel Street site got the nod because it would not only complement the Art Gallery but would also be more visible to the general public. In return for crossing Chapel Street, the university committed to ground-floor retail in the new building. The willingness of New Haven to allow the project to go forward on the Chapel Street site seemed to mark the beginning of a new era in town-and-gown relations.

Five days after the announcement, Moore wrote to Brewster advocating that James Stirling, "whom we all pushed as the best one [architect] extant in Britain, as well, perhaps in the world at large" be given the commission.[450] But Gibson Danes had other ideas, and less than a week later proposed that a "selective invitational competition be set up for ten or fifteen architects." Danes felt that the competition results would make "an exhibition in which architectural students in many parts of the country would be most interested" and that "the results might be of sufficient interest to have them published by the Yale Press."[451] Danes recommended that Ed Barnes, Louis Kahn, Kevin Roche, James Stirling, Robert Venturi, and Charles Moore be asked to compete.

On December 22, Danes, in a follow-up letter to Brewster, reported that after "some extended conversations" with Moore, Moore would "be writing to you to withdraw his earlier proposal that this work be assigned to Jim Stirling." According to Danes, Moore "was quite enthusiastic about the idea of a competition" but felt that "his most effective role would be to administer the handling of this event."[452] Danes and Moore went on to develop a list of potential competitors, while others weighed in: notably, Lloyd Goodrich, director of the Whitney Museum of American Art, who proposed Marcel Breuer, architect of its recently completed building and of Becton Hall at Yale.[453]

Moore's January 10, 1967, letter in support of the competition idea contained the names of nine architects: Stirling, Kahn, Peter Millard, Barnes, Venturi, Giurgola, Aldo van Eyck, Gerhard Kallmann, and Kevin Roche. He also suggested a "jury of educators (Joseph Passonneau, Vincent Scully, perhaps my ex-partner Donlyn Lyndon, who is this week being confirmed as the new Chairman of Architecture at MIT)."[454] A handwritten note by Brewster on the letter asks his assistant to "have me call Moore *pronto*" (Brewster's emphasis). Additionally, the file copy of the letter has the names of four architects crossed out: Millard, Venturi, Van Eyck, and Kallmann.

On January 31, a large number of architecture students petitioned Brewster on Stirling's behalf.[455] Architect selection lagged, and in November 1968, with the endorsement of Walter Cahn, chairman of the Department of Art History, Vincent Scully recommended, in order of preference: Robert Venturi, Louis Kahn, and Philip Johnson, along with "two supplementary candidates [who] also deserve consideration"—James Stirling and Charles Moore.[456] By December, Kahn, favored by Jules Prown (b. 1930), the recently appointed inaugural director of the center, seemed to be the architect most seriously under consideration.[457] But Brewster, who may have had some reluctance to select Kahn, after stating that he wanted to know Paul Mellon's thoughts, reminded Prown that "the decision is ultimately with the President and the Fellows."[458]

On March 8, 1969, Prown attended a meeting with Provost Taylor, and probably President Brewster and Bruce Adams, that was concerned with the new building's relationship to the Yale Art Gallery. Of particular interest was "the use and location of a bridge across Chapel Street" (5.46) (a service tunnel would eventually be built), and "the special possibilities for developing the block" to be shared with the Yale Repertory Theatre that had begun using the former Calvary Baptist Church (1871) at the southeast corner of Chapel and York streets shortly after it was acquired by the university in 1966. Taylor and Prown also discussed the need to be "responsive to non-academic external factors, that is, to social, political and urbanistic considerations," including "the implications of disrupting commercial life along Chapel Street." Prown advanced the idea of an "arts area plan" (something that would not enjoy serious consideration until the 1990s) and the decision to invite Robert Venturi "*to develop a rough block plan that will help to define the external program for the Mellon Center [to] be carried out as an aspect of Mr. Edward Barnes' general university planning*" (Prown's emphasis).[459] Prown's call for an "external program" proved to be prescient.

The process of programming for the new building and architect selection moved slowly and rather secretly. On April 3, 1969, a group calling themselves "Concerned Citizens, Faculty, and Students" wrote to Paul Mellon to express their "concern and confusion over what little we know of the proposed plans for the Mellon Center for British Studies," going on to state that their "concern grows partially out of an increasingly sensitive political climate at Yale and within the city." The letter went on to refer to New Haven's citywide riot in the summer of 1967, and the ongoing challenges raised over "the past 5 years [by] large segments of the black and white communities" in relation to the city's urban renewal policies.[460] Of the sixteen signatories, two were architecture faculty—Charles Brewer and Pat Goeters—and five were architecture students—Samuel R. Callaway, John L. Allen (B.A. 1964, M.Arch 1969), Tom Carey, and Paul Bloom (M.Arch 1970). Two planning students and two art school students also signed. The remaining five signatories were local merchants whose businesses were likely to be dislocated by the project. Mellon's reply on April 30 was evasive, stating that on most of the "Concerned Citizens'" points, he himself had "little information except what I read in the public press and gather from occasional conversations with Mr. Brewster, Mr. Prown, and others," but expressing a willingness to "sit in a meeting" with Brewster and the group, should Brewster "decide that it would be useful or informative."[461]

On May 6, Prown, recently returned from a visit along with Mellon to inspect Kahn's Salk Institute in La Jolla, California, responded to Brewster's request for a recommendation in regard to an architect for the center with an emphatic endorsement for Louis I. Kahn. Prown believed Kahn's selection "would be widely applauded within the Yale community" with "the one major exception to this [being] Vince Scully who is pushing hard for Robert Venturi."

According to Prown, Scully felt that Yale would "make a serious error" if it did not commission an architect "who is what he believes to be the cutting edge of contemporary design."[462]

On May 7, Scully wrote Brewster to "urge Robert Venturi on you as architect for the Mellon Center. Ten years ago," Scully stated, "it would have been a heroic act to employ Kahn. To-day it would have no particular significance, or would even constitute a certain backward step. A great shift toward what I think we must call 'realism' has taken place in American architecture during the past few years, and it has been initiated and led by Venturi. Now, today, he is the best designer in America, the quickest, simplest, most intelligent, most generous, most economical." In a postscript, Scully stated "the students would go mad with joy."[463] Scully's son Dan also wrote to Brewster, stating that "as one who has worked for both men . . . Venturi, not Kahn, is now the teacher." Dan Scully felt that Venturi would design a building that better related to its users, include the public on the street, and would not be overwhelmingly monumental.[464] Over the course of the summer, Kahn was awarded the commission for what came to be known as the Yale Center for British Art.[465] The building was not completed until 1977, three years after Kahn's death.[466]

In October 1969, Moore inserted himself more directly into another Yale project, the addition to Leet Oliver Memorial Hall, a not particularly distinguished 1908 Gothic building designed by Charles C. Haight, home to the Mathematics Department, located on Hillhouse Avenue just south of the sunken cut of the former Farmington Canal. Heralding a strategic sea change for new architect selection at Yale, an open competition was proposed with a brief, clearly bearing Moore's imprimatur, that made clear the university's intention to return to the more integrative approach of the James Gamble Rogers era, rather than the scattering of individual, "iconic" design statements favored in the postwar Griswold era, when the campus came to be known as the "greatest open air museum of modern architecture" on the continent.[467] Reflecting on the competition four years later, Moore stated that though the Griswold era was "still much admired, I think it is accurate to note that nobody, not President Kingman Brewster nor his planner Edward L. Barnes nor the Mathematics Department nor Yale's Office of Building and Grounds Planning nor anyone in the Architecture Department, had any interest years later in the restoration of an era of building individual monuments."[468]

As the competition got under way, Moore served as professional advisor. Charles E. Rickart, chairman of the Mathematics Department, along with Edward Dunn, director of Buildings and Grounds Planning for Yale, and Vincent Scully, the non-architect members of the jury, were joined by four architects: John Christiansen (M.Arch 1970), a Yale architecture student who was already a registered architect; Edward Larrabee Barnes; Kevin Roche; and Romaldo Giurgola. Sixteen hundred architects registered to enter the competition, and by the deadline in January 1970, 468 projects had been submitted. These were then reviewed anonymously by the jury, who selected five finalists for the second stage: Venturi and Rauch; John Fowler, John Paul McGowan Architects; Office of Fitzhugh Scott-Architects, Inc.; Van Slyck, Callison, Nelson Architects; and Verman, Lepere, Petit.

On May 22, 1970, Venturi and Rauch were selected as the winners of the second stage with a scheme that satisfied the Mathematics Department's programmatic requirements and the university's wish for a building, which, as the winners stated, would be "a working, institutional building enhancing rather than upstaging the buildings around it."[469] Paul Goldberger, just finishing his senior year in Yale College but already a nationally published architecture critic, greeted the winning design as "an eloquent application of the Venturi philosophy" that "is more like Yale's Gothic and Georgian structures than its modern ones, for it seeks, as the older buildings do, to create an integrated architectural fabric on campus. The Math Building does not stand out: it blends graciously into the complex row of buildings already on Hillhouse Avenue"[470] (5.47).

However, for some members of the architecture community, the competition was far from over. Within a month's time, Moore was challenged by unsuccessful competitors, some of whom claimed, among other things, that anonymity had been breached. When the competition results—the schemes of the winner and the four runners-up—were published in *Architectural Forum,* the magazine was flooded with letters.[471] Many architects just didn't like the winning design. Sam Carson, in Los Angeles, called it "a piece of junk." Other, slightly cooler, heads, such as James Lamantia and Warren Platner, asked that all the submissions be published despite the fact that the program had stated they would not. Eventually twenty-five projects, in addition to Venturi's winning design, were published in the book *The Yale Mathematics Building Competition: Architecture for a Time of Questioning.*[472]

Sibyl Moholy-Nagy was among the most outraged of the dissenters: "In every boxtop contest employees are banned from participation—not at Yale." Accompanying her letter with an elevation drawing of J. J. P. Oud's 1924 design for the Rotterdam Stock Exchange, Moholy-Nagy, who had extolled Yale's virtues during the Rudolph years, now saw things very differently:

In every architecture school, NEUE SACHLICHKEIT a la '20s is considered 50 years behind the future—not at Yale.

In every architectural competition, specification concerning environmental response must be met by the winner—not at Yale.

Every family affair made respectable by a supporting cast of 479 would treat the losers with gratitude rather than derision—not at Yale, nor even by *The Architectural Forum*.[473]

Moholy-Nagy later revealed to the *Yale Daily News* that her caustic but witty letter was not published in full, as the magazine "could hardly afford a lawsuit from the Venturi gang, which would be surely forthcoming since I accused them of collusion, lies, deception, and—on top—of lousy architectural judgment."[474]

Colin Rowe, on the other hand, offered a nuanced but not exactly supportive assessment of the design that was not published at the time, but was circulated privately among peers and subsequently published in 1976. In a lengthy and characteristically dense essay, Rowe evaluated the building in the context of Venturi's oeuvre and Yale's campus, touching on many of the criticisms, compliments, and controversies that surrounded Venturi during what was at that point his relatively short career. While Rowe believed that the building would only be "satisfactory," he praised it as one that "quashed establishment architecture" and for being "worthy of criticism."[475]

Perhaps the most surprising reaction was that of Serge Chermayeff, who had recently retired: "How refreshing a 'contradiction' to use Robert Venturi's favorite category—to find that the design of Yale's Mathematics Building will now fill a conspicuous gap in her Architectural Collection." Chermayeff, feigning pleasure in Yale choosing a non-monumental building that was "workable" and "economic," and "in fact a good old 'Functionalist Building' (circa 1925)," went on to express delight that "Vincent Scully's ever ready rhetoric still flourishes in spite of stormy weather. So intense and so controlled in its attempt to deal with the program—'a door opening on the future of architecture' [a phrase later attributed by Scully to an unnamed source]. This may be quite a shock to some of his students who have seen him keeping this very door steadfastly closed for a decade or two. In any case even if the key has been in strange hands awhile, it is good to have it open again. Never too late to remember. The model suggests that the new Yale building was designed by Connell Wood [Ward] and Lucas in the '20s, before 'monumentalism' revived by Sigfried Giedion seduced the Scully generation."[476]

Of those who objected to the competition, Knoxville, Tennessee–based architect Joshua Lowenfish (1904–1985) was the most vocal. In his letter of protest, he identified himself as someone who deemed Rudolph's Art & Architecture Building to be "a miserable failure" from its inception. Criticizing the winning design, Lowenfish asserted that it "does not accommodate its users well" (despite enthusiastic approval from the Math Department stating otherwise) and claiming that "certainly, there is something malodorous at Yale"—his belief that professional ethics had been violated when Venturi and others on the Yale faculty were permitted to participate in the competition.[477]

In reply to these statements, Moore began by expressing "a romantic's as well as an historian's pleasure in noting that the . . . competition has achieved, for what I believe is the first time, the agreement of Serge and Sibyl." However, he continued, "Mr. Lowenfish's letter . . . is not so much fun; it would be libelous were it not so inept." But Moore nonetheless proceeded to respond to Lowenfish's points, using wit and sarcasm to deflate his claims before getting to what irritated so many of the other failed competitors—the fact that the jury was composed of many individuals who shared a point of view, "first identified with Philadelphia and based on the insights of Louis Kahn, [and] . . . now much in evidence at the Yale School of Architecture." But, he concluded, "It can then come as no surprise that when this jury found an entry which met the program requirements with unusual felicity and also carried a stylistic message of particular interest to them that they gave it the prize. I could not have predicted that such an entry would be there," Moore somewhat disingenuously continued, "but it seems to me a tribute to this jury's connoisseurship that their prize went to such a simple solution instead of to one of the numerous entries which bore a much larger burden of devices generally associated with Robert Venturi's 'style.'"[478]

Lowenfish refused to give up. On July 16, 1971, he wrote to Senator Hubert Humphrey (Democrat, Minnesota) to protest the competition's methodology, including a page-long statement of "salient facts" as well as a copy of the recently deceased Sibyl Moholy-Nagy's letter.[479] In September, the *Yale Daily News* covered the story in a three-part article, drawing particular attention to Moore's insistence that Yale faculty are not employees of Yale's trustees—an insistence backed by an official amendment to the initial rules.[480] The *Yale Daily News* stories enraged Scully, who was under particular scrutiny because of his close association with Venturi, leading him to write to editorial-page editor Stuart Rosow to protest being misquoted and having his views distorted in an article whose front-page headline boldly declared "Scully Blasts Math Building Critics as 'Despicable Scum'": "As I told the interviewer,

5.47 Venturi and Rauch, Proposal for New Mathematics Building (1969).

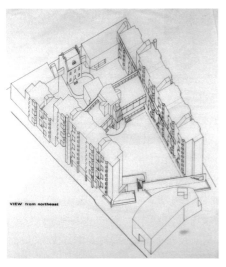

VIEW from northeast

5.49 Patrick Pinnell (B.A. 1971, M.Arch. 1974), Design
for New Residential Colleges, perspective (1973).

CHAPEL STREET

5.48 James Kruhly (M.Arch. 1973), Design for the Mellon Center,
perspective (1972).

I had nothing whatever to do with initiating the competition, framing its requirements, or administering it. I was simply one juror among many. In that capacity I formed the opinion that the design by Venturi and Rauch was the best entry, and I believe that it will make a very beautiful building of which Yale can be proud."[481] Undeterred, Lowenfish persisted with his letter-writing crusade,[482] eventually charging Yale with mail fraud, requiring the university to refute the charges on June 29, 1972, with a twenty-two page reply prepared by John E. Ecklund, university treasurer, drawn in part on a document prepared by Moore dated June 28.[483]

Robert Venturi cogently defended his design, saying that his intent was "to make the Yale Mathematics Building in the tradition of ordinary architecture. Ordinary in the way the eighteenth-century Connecticut Hall at Yale was ordinary—in its construction, program, and appearance: ordinary in the sense that it *is* convention and it *looks* conventional." Venturi criticized the heroic, modernist architecture Yale had become known for in the 1950s and 1960s, saying that "this is not the time, and ours is not the environment, for heroic communication via pure architecture. Every medium has its day, and the statements of our time— civic, commercial, institutional— will come, not from architecture alone, but from combination of media: an impure, eclectic architecture of words, sculpture, and associations, more adaptable to the scale, tempo, and timbre of our cacophonic environments."[484] Unfortunately, the efforts of both sides would be for naught. Despite pursuing funding from many alumni and corporations with intimate connections to the discipline of mathematics, including IBM, the university was unable to fund the building and it became relegated to the ash heap of history's unbuilt masterpieces.

The Mathematics Building wasn't the only significant structure that Yale would attempt but be unable to realize during this time. In 1970, as a result of the decision to admit women to Yale College, undergraduate enrollment increased dramatically, and the Yale Corporation decided to go forward with plans for two new residential colleges housing a total of five hundred male and female students, to be funded by John Hay Whitney (1904–1982; B.A. 1926).[485] Architect selection began in earnest in early summer 1970, with Edward Larrabee Barnes asked to draw up an initial list of five to ten architects in anticipation of a selection to be made in September.[486] On July 28, 1970, Moore submitted a list of possible architects, including several alumni firms: Benjamin Thompson; Norman Fletcher; Giovanni Pasanella; Don Stull Associates; and a collaboration between James Polshek, Topper Carew, and Tunney Lee, dubbed "Combine," which they had formed to seek the commission for the Federal City College in Washington, D.C. Non-Yale architects on the list were Hugh Hardy, Mitchell/Giurgola, and Peter Chermayeff of the Cambridge Seven. Mitchell/Giurgola was selected.

The new residential colleges were to be located on a Yale-owned site at the northwest corner of Grove Street and Whitney Avenue. That the commission should go to Giurgola, one of the three candidates considered for architecture chairman in 1965, was tinged with irony given that Venturi, another candidate for chairman at that time, was the one who inquired about a university commission as a condition of his coming to Yale, and whose proposal for the Mathematics Building was languishing due to lack of funds. Also surprising to many was the decision to bypass James Stirling, then in his sixth year as Davenport Visiting Professor of Architecture, given his appropriate experience with collegiate residential architecture at St. Andrew's University in Scotland (1964–68) and at Queen's College, Oxford (1966–71), the designs of which surely influenced Giurgola on the Yale project.[487] Reflecting his interest in the commission for both the Whitney Colleges and for the British Art Center, Stirling assigned each as studio projects (5.48, 5.49).

As planning proceeded, costs began to escalate, reducing to three hundred the number of students to be housed. In addition, negotiations with the city of New Haven concerning, in particular, the amount of commercial area to be incorporated in the new colleges were protracted and unproductive, despite the intention to provide for street-level shops and second-floor offices that would remain on the city's tax roll, a similar arrangement to the one forged between the city and Yale in 1969 that had allowed construction to proceed on the British Art Center. Drawings of the design for the new colleges were released in November 1972 in the *Yale Alumni Magazine,* leading to some criticism, including a letter expressing concern for "conflicts with its surroundings to the point of violent reaction," jointly written by two 1969 master of environmental design graduates, John S. Coke and James W. People, practicing as a partnership in Columbus, Ohio.[488]

Giurgola's design proposed that the two colleges be housed in a single eight-story structure that wrapped around St. Elmo's (now Rosenthal) Hall to form two landscaped courtyards (5.50). North of the Farmington Canal right-of-way, a two-story commercial block would face Whitney Avenue, in keeping with the university's pledge not to diminish the city's tax yield from commercial property. Students would enjoy single rooms grouped in suites, each with a living room and kitchen. Construction was expected to begin in March 1973, with occupancy scheduled for September 1975.

In April 1973, the city of New Haven refused to grant permission for construction to proceed, using the colleges "as leverage to make Yale pay more money [in lieu of taxes] annually to the city."[489] The battle over payments was exacerbated by the City Planning Commission's negative report "which, in itself was enough to kill the project since under the planned development unit ordinance City Plan approval was required."[490] The stalemate between Yale and the city of New Haven persisted, but, as the *New Haven Journal Courier* reported in February 1975, the project was "scratched as economically unfeasible."[491]

The town-gown controversies of the Mellon building and, especially, the failed attempt to reach an agreement on the new residential colleges proved that Yale had not yet come to terms with the new realities of community participation. To this end, two students, Herbert Short and Manfred Ibel, early in 1969 offered a thoughtful but presumptuous bid for a place at the university's policy-making table, proposing that they be retained by the university to take on physical development oversight, hitherto the responsibility of professional staff and paid outside consultants. Short and Ibel's proposed Yale Planning Forum would "provide channels for student and community participation in the process of physical planning at Yale." In part, it reflected 1968 student protests over university planning at Columbia, but, more importantly, reflected events closer to home—notably, the simultaneous proposed construction of an underground extension of the Sterling Memorial Library beneath the cross-campus mall, which had met with strenuous opposition from both students and faculty, including R. W. B. Lewis, master of Calhoun College who, speaking on behalf of college fellows, objected to plans to pierce the mall with sixteen skylights.[492] Bradley Nitkin (1947–2009; B.A. 1969), a resident of Berkeley College, which would be adversely affected by the proposed design, led the Cross Campus Committee that would subsequently contribute to a revised design.[493]

According to Nitkin, the university had deliberately neglected to maintain the cross-campus greensward so that it "looked like a sandbox" when the corporation met in May to review the proposal and would, therefore, "be more inclined to let the skylights go in."[494] Barnes's proposal threatened to become the same kind of lightning rod for student unrest that Columbia's virtually simultaneous proposal for an underground gymnasium in Morningside Park would be. Hunter Morrison and Hugh Spitzer began their June 1968 analysis of the situation in the *Yale Daily News* by comparing the situation that had just developed at Columbia as a result of the ill-advised gymnasium plan with the Yale protest over the underground library: "There was, however, no seizure

5.50   Mitchell/Giurgola Associates, Proposal for New Residential Colleges (1972).

5.51   The Cross-Campus Library Courtyard (ca. 1980), New Haven.

of building, no closing of the University," in part, they argued, because Yale's "active system of communications" effectively channeled student and faculty demands to the administration.[495]

By March 1969, Barnes had proposed a second scheme, using a less obtrusive "moat" system to let in natural light, which satisfied both the architect, the university, and the students.[496] Although the completed building would be called "womblike" and compared to Kafka's "The Burrow," the Cross Campus Library became one of the most widely used libraries on campus (5.51). However, the facility was plagued with problems—among them an endlessly leaking roof and insufficient space for the growing use of computers—that would frustrate campus facilities personnel, librarians, and students alike. In 2005, Thomas Beeby, of the firm Hammond Beeby Rupert Ainge Architects, was selected to completely redesign the aging facility, which in its new configuration was named in honor of donors Robert Bass (b. 1948; B.A. 1971) and his wife, Anne, who gave substantially toward its renewal.[497]

Short and Ibel took the fracas over the Cross Campus Library as an opportunity to advance their plan. Stating that the "architects . . . chosen in the recent past (except possibly Eero Saarinen), have been fascinated with architectural form itself rather than with designing buildings which respond imaginatively to human use," their proposed Yale Planning Forum "could bridge this gap between the people and architecture for those people." As they saw it, it would be a clearinghouse of opinions and ideas that "would eliminate the duplicated time of many students individually approaching administrators or the architect-in-charge (as during the Cross Campus Controversy) and would counteract the frustration students and architects feel in their search for information." The two students envisioned the forum as a nonpartisan "workshop for criticizing and developing ideas and images, for suggesting and testing with models known guidelines for campus development."[498] As Brian Goldstein notes, Short and Ibel "linked the university's approach to the authoritarianism of the New Deal Spatial Order [which] became abundantly clear in the comments they circulated" before a meeting with Edward Larrabee Barnes, during which they argued that "Yale's feudal approach to the administration cannot solve today's problems," a claim echoed by various students who complained of Yale's secrecy about expansion plans.[499]

Asked by Provost Charles H. Taylor, Jr., to comment on Ibel and Short's proposal, E. W. Y. Dunn, director of Buildings and Grounds Planning, argued that "The Forum idea is not good. It could develop a lot of unchanneled student ideas all of which would be separate from the actual process and much of which would be far from reality. It could easily develop into an outlet for irresponsible criticism instead of constructive suggestion."[500] The architecture faculty, also less supportive of the idea, countered by proposing a workshop course on campus and town planning to provide students with a more productive outlet to address socially relevant projects that directly impact the school and campus. The faculty-initiated workshop, formally announced on February 3, 1969, would address "the actual problems that Yale University and the City of New Haven face as the University develops."[501] According to Dean Weaver, it would provide a "new kind of educational opportunity . . . for students, incorporating a chance to cope not with simulated problems but with real situations in the company of professionals."[502] The course, open to graduate students and a limited number of undergraduates, was taught by Herbert Newman and Charles Brewer, as well as city planning faculty members Louis DeLuca, Pat Goeters, and Ralph Tucker. Additionally, Edward Barnes was expected to participate as a visiting professor, along with other representatives from both Yale and the New Haven community. Despite the school's efforts to address their concerns through the curriculum, Short and Ibel persisted in requesting a meeting with Brewster to discuss the Planning Forum proposal. Brewster eventually agreed to see them, and a meeting was finally scheduled for early April 1969, at which time the president promptly rejected the proposal.[503]

Moore was on sabbatical leave during his last term as dean (spring 1971), although, as previously indicated, he maintained ties to the faculty for fourteen more years. Asked in the early 1980s by biographer David Littlejohn to reflect on why he left Yale to go to UCLA, Moore replied: "Oh, you know—palm trees . . . happy memories of childhood. Actually, I was asked to come by Tim Vreeland, for whom I had considerable respect—perhaps more than I have now. And by former M.E.D. student Bill Mitchell who was chairman and whom I'm fond of and listen to. He made it seem reasonable."[504] Part of Moore's decision to go to California can be attributed to his inability to put down roots and, Littlejohn suggests, "his growing fatigue, even boredom with the Essex-New Haven scene, in which he felt increasingly out of place."[505] With the economy stagnant and a dearth of commissions in his Essex, Connecticut, office, the time Moore spent to merely keep his business afloat began to wear on him: "I would spend the morning at my office, then drive the frantic forty minutes to New Haven and deal with my class or whatever, and then jump in my car and grab some dinner on the way, and go back to the office at the end of the evening, and finally go to bed. I was just getting bored."[506] Above all, Moore had come to regard New Haven as "the awfulest, ugliest town in the United States."[507] He objected to its weather, the run-down condition of many

370

of its neighborhoods, and the presumed corruption of its government. But ultimately, it appears that Moore would question if not outright regret his decision to leave Yale. When, in the early 1980s, Moore was asked to identify "the best architectural school in the country *today*," he replied, "Oh, Yale, of course. It may not be as good as it used to be, but it's still number one."[508] Ruefully, he observed: "Yale did everything right; UCLA does everything wrong. When I told Kingman Brewster of my decision, he said, 'You made a *terrible* choice.'"[509]

6
Back to Basics
1971–1977

"The teaching of architecture at Yale had at its inception, and continues to have, design at its core because the rational manipulation of spatial elements for specified purposes is the quintessence of architecture, both as an art and as a profession. . . . In response to changing needs and values in a rapidly changing world, the School has increased the flexibility of its educational program to accommodate a variety of legitimate views on the role of the architect in contemporary society."

Bulletin of the Yale School of Architecture, 1972

After any revolution, there is a bit of confusion as one form of government gives way to the next, new laws are implemented, and the old guard is exiled. Unfortunately, in 1970, Yale had few resources to accommodate a regime change—just one consequence of the severe budget problems that began a few years earlier. The university's financial mire was the result of a heady cocktail that mixed rapid physical expansion with the initiation of new academic programs at a time when alumni gifts were plummeting in reaction to a number of issues, ranging from the abatement of preferential admissions for the sons of Yale College alumni to the decision to admit women to the college—not to mention displeasure with the increasingly liberal views of both President Kingman Brewster and the student body. What's more, the fuel crisis of the early 1970s plagued the university with an unprecedented increase in operating costs, while an economic recession and a dramatic drop in the stock market resulted in the poor performance of its endowment.[1] Despite taking drastic measures, including a reduction in the number of new faculty appointments, the university reported a deficit of $3.5 million (approximately $21 million in 2014) in the 1970–71 academic year.[2]

The unrest of the late 1960s initially pointed to a reexamination of the prevailing pedagogy in architecture, as students advocated for a shift in focus toward research and interdisciplinarity that would enlist various faculties in the university to address "relevant" problems of the built environment. At Yale, as at most other radicalized architecture schools, these pedagogical reforms were never really implemented, not only as a result of the economic crisis but also because the young radicals who called for political and social reform had graduated or moved on to other pursuits, while a new generation turned its attention to the limitations of the discipline, questioning modernist ideas and architectural language in light of failed urban renewal and social housing projects. During this period of relative calm and disciplinary reflection, the newly independent Yale School of Architecture settled back into what, in comparison to its immediate past, was a standard academic routine and, as early as 1971, the University Council Committee on Art and Architecture was able to report "a much improved climate," noting that: "After a period which can in the mildest terms be called one of 'turmoil,' if not virtual revolution and certainly very broad breakdown in communication, there has begun to emerge in most of the Departments of the Schools [of Art and Architecture] a spirit of self-examination and determination to return to the basic tasks of the kind of education which a university such as Yale should be capable of providing."[3]

In the School of Architecture, "self-examination" began with the search for a new dean to succeed Moore, who, depending on one's perspective, may or may not be credited with successfully steering the school through the stormy seas of student rebellion. Though it was now clear that the most serious storms had passed, the waters were still unsettled. The search for a new dean hinged on the question: What kind of person could keep the ship steady? "Whoever that person is," wrote University Council Committee member Jonathan Barnett, "he is going to have a tough assignment. The students are demanding a much more clearly structured curriculum—a refreshing change from three years ago when all they wanted was freedom."[4] These student demands came through their elected representatives on the Dean Search Committee, an acknowledgment by the administration that concerns about the top-down management expressed by the Committee of Eight and other organizations had not fallen on deaf ears, and a small victory for former student revolutionaries who got to see a few of their ideas adopted as permanent policy.

Though it was clear that the business of architectural education needed to be reexamined, the University Council realized that due to fiscal constraints, any curricular changes might take years. Moreover, any incoming dean would have to struggle with more than the budget in order to accomplish change; he would also have to deal with existing faculty, toward whom many students still harbored resentment. As a result, the council recommended that Brewster wait for a year before making an appointment and allow Herman Spiegel, appointed acting dean for the spring 1971 term, to continue running the school so that "the new man would thus have an opportunity to look around for new faculty without being the target for student discontent over the lack of change. Ordinarily, such a lame duck period is bad practice; but, in the case of Yale, everything that could happen has happened already."[5]

Herman D. J. Spiegel, an architectural engineer with an active professional practice based in New Haven, had been teaching in the department since 1955 (6.1). Spiegel saw his role as acting dean as that of a manager and a communicator, not only with students but also with university officers and administrators as well as alumni. Although Spiegel would eventually not-so-subtly portray himself as the school's savior—something Moore was to resent deeply—he did acknowledge that the school's recuperation had less to do with his own skills than with the changing temper of the times.

At the time of his appointment as acting dean, Spiegel was highly regarded as one of the most effective and good-natured faculty members in the school. Students appreciated his ability to clearly and concisely explain the principles of structural engineering in the classroom and on field trips. As one student charmingly put it, using the parlance of the times, Spiegel and Henry Pfisterer were "the beautiful stardust twins of our architectural experience."[6] Students respected Spiegel's no-nonsense approach. Barton Phelps remembers: "He could criticize Lou Kahn and get away with it. He could attack the holy of holies. He could be pretty charismatic when he wanted to be. He'd say, 'Lou! Lou talks about concrete but he doesn't really understand concrete.'"[7] Spiegel's view of his students was equally generous. Conveniently overlooking the fact that 1968 student rebellions at Columbia and the École des Beaux-Arts preceded those at Yale by a year, he wrote that Yale students, "having been one of the first to question many of the hang-ups of the past, were therefore one of the first to begin to come out of the doldrums." According to Spiegel, students were "ready, indeed eager and hungry for real architectural involvement," which as he defined it meant "not only design from a sculptural or three dimensional spatial manipulation point of view, but all of that including other technical, social, economic, legal, etc. realities that lend credence to the design process."[8]

Acknowledging that his good nature and pragmatic sensibilities did not necessarily equip him to provide the vigorous design leadership needed to counteract the lingering sense of gloom among students and alumni after the controversies and disasters of the last few years, Spiegel recognized that the program needed a prominent designer to help kick-start the school's resurgence. Though his funds were limited, he had one ace-in-the-hole: the recently established Davenport Chair, for which no appointment had been made for the spring 1971 semester after Robert Venturi had decided to step down from teaching. The Davenport Chair was, in Spiegel's view, the "only chance to show the students that we meant to provide a healthy and active educational environment."[9] Spiegel worked with the Curriculum Committee—amazingly comprising three faculty members and *four* students—to develop a list of architects qualified to fill the chair and, "by a stroke of good luck," was able to bring in Moshe Safdie (b. 1938), architect of Habitat, the celebrated, high-density experimental residential compound that had been built in 1967 as part of Montreal's Expo.[10]

The choice of Safdie proved to be astute. He was "an extremely involved and sensitive teacher," asking students to develop a program and a design for an urban kibbutz in downtown Manhattan, which seemed just the right kind of assignment.[11] In tune with the late Sixties' "vibe," Safdie was willing to "rap" with the students, as Roger Yee (b. 1947; B.A. 1969, M.Arch 1972), a student in his studio, reported to alumni:

Noontime Monday or Tuesday, a dozen or so students gather for *Lunch with Moshe.* The menu is simple: bread, cheese, and wine.

The conversation not surprisingly begins with architecture; and may close on matters of child care, sheepdogs, or the cultural differences between Canadians and Americans. . . . [Safdie] leaves few stones unturned in the effort to define what makes man tick, and how to build for him.

Moshe, as he prefers, has brought a fresh, down-to-earth viewpoint to Yale. For children in the age of operational systems analysis it is a pleasant surprise to discuss design criteria based on kids, playgrounds, and sunshine. To be sure, there is a Safdie methodology which assembles everything in a thorough professional way. But as he points out, it is *his* way and not necessarily anyone else's.[12]

After his term at Yale, during the summer break, Safdie took students from his studio to Montreal, where they spent three weeks working together on an entry to the Plateau Beaubourg Cultural Center competition (6.2).[13] Safdie's entry was awarded one of the thirty second prizes, but the winning scheme for the building that we now know as the Centre Pompidou was awarded to Yale graduate Richard Rogers in partnership with Renzo Piano. Heather Willson Cass (b. 1947; M.Arch 1972) was one of the students in Safdie's studio who worked on the Beaubourg competition over the summer: "The deal was that if we won we'd all get jobs in Paris in his office. And if we were runners up, he'd split the prize money among us after expenses," says Cass. "We didn't end up with a lot of money, just a few hundred dollars, but it was a wonderful experience. It was, you know, the sort of thing that seemed to happen to students all the time in those days."[14]

As Spiegel settled in to what was supposed to be a temporary position as acting dean, he began to indiscreetly undermine Moore, attributing many of the school's recent problems to his predecessor's laissez-faire style and criticizing Moore's preference for a like-minded faculty despite his espousal of an "inclusive" approach. Claiming that it wasn't constructive "to dwell very long on happenings of the past," he nonetheless expressed the concern that students were not getting the education they needed and faculty were just "hovering around the fringes . . . not quite knowing what to do or what actions were expected of them or indeed not knowing if they had the power or inclination to do anything anyway."[15] Growing bolder and more confident at the end of his semester as acting dean, Spiegel began to imply that his leadership would be critical to the school's future success: "As pompous as it may sound, we do intend to become the best school of architecture in the world. The next few years will tell the tale."[16]

While Spiegel concentrated on getting the school back into working order, the search for a new dean proceeded with faculty members, alumni, and others contacting Brewster to suggest names of potential candidates. King-lui Wu's top choice was Harvard-educated Henry (Harry) Cobb, a partner of I. M. Pei and a frequent visiting studio teacher during the Rudolph years. According to Wu, Cobb was a designer of large-scale projects who was "also known as a superb administrator. . . . He is quiet, thoughtful, but firm and always to the point." Wu's second recommendation was alumnus James Stewart Polshek, a rising design talent with a developing practice in New York, someone "concerned with the total environment, dynamic and methodical" who "attracts the young." Although Polshek was not seriously considered for the Yale job, within a year he would be appointed dean of the Graduate School of Architecture, Planning, and Preservation at Columbia, a post he held for fifteen years, during which time he rebuilt a program that had been moribund since the late 1930s and was virtually destroyed by the student unrest of the late 1960s.[17] Wu's third choice was another Yale graduate, Jaquelin T. Robertson, who followed his time at Yale College with a year studying at Oxford as a Rhodes Scholar before returning for graduate work in the Department of Architecture, followed by professional work with Sir Leslie Martin (1908–2000) in England and Edward Larrabee Barnes in New York. In 1966, Robertson joined the administration of the recently elected, charismatic mayor of the city of New York, John V. Lindsay (1921–2000; B.A. 1944 [graduated 1948]), where he cofounded the Urban Design Group. Though Robertson was the youngest of Wu's candidates, Wu believed that his considerable public persona, his teaching experience at Columbia, and the "keen intellect [that] lies behind his charm and energy" more than compensated for his youth.[18] Wu concluded his letter with the names of two senior figures who would be "short-term candidates (three years perhaps)": Philip Johnson, who through his outside contacts "can put our school into economic health," and Sir Leslie Martin, head of the School of Architecture at the University of Cambridge. "In Britain," Wu wrote, Martin "is perhaps still the most influential man in architecture and planning. Sir Leslie could attract men of talent into Yale. He is modest, considerate and civilized."[19]

While on sabbatical, in a letter dated February 23, Charles Moore gave Brewster an "exhaustive" list of possible successors. Moore's first choice was alumnus Thomas R. (Tim) Vreeland, currently head of the recently established Department of Architecture at UCLA. Moore was full of praise for Vreeland. Later, after joining the UCLA faculty, he would come to see Vreeland in a less favorable light, but in 1971 he respected Vreeland's talent as a designer and found him to be thoughtful, exciting, and smart on the public platform, as well as being "distinguished (read 'a gentleman' or whatever post-revolutionary equivalent is acceptable) in ways which would please our Alumni and greatly benefit the School." Moore went on to report that Vreeland has gathered "considerable support from our faculty (except, I think, from his old friend Denise Venturi, who has lately cooled to his ideas) and some from students. His new school at UCLA has leaned heavily on design methodology (about which, as you know, I have reservations) but his vision of what Yale's School might be is quite different in what I think is [a] pretty accurate cognizance of its strengths and potential."[20]

Moore's second choice was Joseph Passonneau (1921–2011), longtime dean of architecture (1956–67) at Washington University in St. Louis, whose response to Brewster's question—"What can architecture do for Yale?"—was less than inspiring, stating that a school should "teach conventional skills, . . . give professional training in very large scale project programming and design," and contribute to "regional location theory."[21] Moore also drew the president's attention to Don Stull, who was known to Brewster for his connection to the Black Workshop, although Moore was inclined to Brewster's "earlier judgment that he [Stull] might be most effective heading a specific program." Noting that Stull's "own goals seem to conflict with his coping with the Deanship," Moore believed "his capabilities put him high on the list." In other words, Stull, as a black architect, had a place at the school, but, it would seem, that the place was with other black architects and planners.

Moore also advanced the name of Robert Harris (b. 1935), chairman at Oregon, and Denise Venturi's candidate, Charles Burchard (1913–1990), whose thoughtfulness Moore respected, despite some difficulty "reconciling his folksey [sic] salesman's ardor with our school's famous responses ('Have the piranhas got you yet?' I was asked with chilling regularity when I first came)."[22] He also brought up Donlyn Lyndon (b. 1936), his sometime professional partner who was then chairman of architecture at MIT. Moore deemed Lyndon "a fine designer, an experienced school head (at Oregon before MIT, though he is still 35) and the most brilliant architectural theoretician I know of."[23]

Lastly, Moore felt obliged to include the young New York practitioners who maintained contact with the school, "and who will appear in the recommendations of Ed Barnes and others. Personality here figures heavily, since they are all talented and increasingly important architects." From this group Moore favored Polshek or Giovanni Pasanella, over Charles Gwathmey or Robertson. But he refused to give any of them his full endorsement because, seeming to forget his own marginal professional status when he came to Yale in 1965, he told the president that "the job is by now much too special and demanding to serve as a boost to a young architect on the way up, and in turn to be served by him."[24]

Vincent Scully also weighed in with a letter to Brewster in which he wrote that "since nobody has asked my opinion on the architecture deanship," he was "all the more eager to give it." Scully was concerned with some of the suggested names circulating through the school, so he provided pithy assessments of the rumored candidates: Jaquelin Robertson—"Yes. A former student of mine. Urbane, class. OK"; Bob Stern—"Yes. A former student of mine. Young, smart, semi-OK"; Tim Vreeland—"No. A former student of mine. Dumb, authoritarian. N.G."; Shadrach Woods (1923–1973)—"No. Perhaps you haven't heard this name. If so, forget it. Disaster gulch; That Dean in St. Louis whatever his name is [Joseph Passonneau]—No. A step backward for Yale; that Dean at VPI [Charles Burchard at the Virginia Polytechnic Institute] beloved by the Venturis. Don't know him. No opinion; Ed Barnes. No. I haven't heard his name but knowing you like him I list it, No; Philip Johnson. I guess not really. He did ask once to be considered at about this stage in his life. Students probably hostile. Could do worse." Finally, Scully came to Allan Greenberg, who was then teaching at Yale: "I would say that he is my surprise candidate. Another tough, dedicated South African like Denise Venturi who would be very good, but I believe, wouldn't do it. This man Greenberg has great qualities of a political no less than a cultural kind. I worked closely with him in the anti-redevelopment wars. He has earned the gratitude of the community. He is young and might arouse some resentment at first, but I suspect he has thought more creatively about architectural education than any of the others."[25]

Denise Scott Brown, still signing business letters as "Mrs. Robert Venturi," wrote to Brewster on two separate occasions to advocate Charles Burchard, as Scully surmised she would (Venturi and Rauch were designing a new library for VPI), as well as Greenberg, whose scholarship she praised along with his "strong social concern which has involved him in community work in New Haven and which he translates ably into architectural and education terms."[26] Scott Brown believed Greenberg's combination of social awareness and intellectual and professional rigor made him an ideal candidate for the job of dean. "I respect him further," she wrote to Brewster, "because he is one of the few architectural educators I know who has a strong interest in and his own philosophy of pedagogy. . . . His appointment would be in line with our feeling (shared by other members of the architecture department) that the School needs full-time, dedicated architectural educators of outstanding ability in its highest administrative positions, rather than big name architectural practitioners."[27] Still apparently under the impression that both a dean and a chairman were being sought, Scott Brown concluded her letter to Brewster by offering support for the team of Burchard as dean and Greenberg as chair, but stated that if Burchard were unavailable, Greenberg would do very well in the top job. On April 5, Vincent Scully wrote Brewster again to say that the school needed "a clean sweep of dead wood and a truly systematic intelligent dean." Scully once again advocated Greenberg, who "has a plan for the reassessment and redirection of the School which seems to me the most natural and dignified proposal for it that I have seen in my twenty-five years or so of close association with it."[28]

After receiving his master of architecture degree from Yale in 1965, South African–born Greenberg remained in New Haven working for the city's redevelopment agency, where he witnessed the destruction of neighborhoods to make way for what was, for a time, considered to be the nation's "Model City." Angered by the sacrifices imposed on the poor whose "dwellings were characterized as 'units,' abstractions to be tabulated like beads on an abacus" and by the elitist attitude of planning officials whose proffered explanation to citizens was "you are too ignorant to understand what is best for you," Greenberg gradually withdrew from the fray, seeing it as similar to the one he had left South Africa to avoid.[29]

Craving something "solid and coherent" on which he could focus his attention, Greenberg returned to a paper he had begun to write while working in Sweden during his pre-Yale years, comparing the architecture of the English Classicist Sir Edwin Lutyens (1869–1944), whose work had been introduced to him while a student in South Africa, and Le Corbusier, expanding it to also include Frank Lloyd Wright. The paper, "Lutyens's Architecture Restudied," was published in Stuart Wrede and Peter Papademetriou's *Perspecta* 12 (1969), the most politically radical issue in the journal's history.[30] Greenberg's juxtaposition of the three seemingly antipathetic architects, combined with his penetrating analysis of their work, especially their handling of architectural space, was to have a profound influence on a young generation of architects anxious to heal the polemically charged split between traditionalism and modernism that was coming to be perceived as a dead end.

Greenberg was first invited by Charles Moore to join the faculty as a visiting critic in 1968.[31] Amidst the period's "intense questioning rather than rigorous reflection," Greenberg assigned "challenging problems involving additions to important old buildings or projects set in historic parts of cities," developing exercises to show students that most Classical and Gothic buildings were not, as many modernists insisted, simply copied from the past.[32] Greenberg was respected by students and able to elicit unusual amounts of

6.1   Herman D. J. Spiegel (1978).

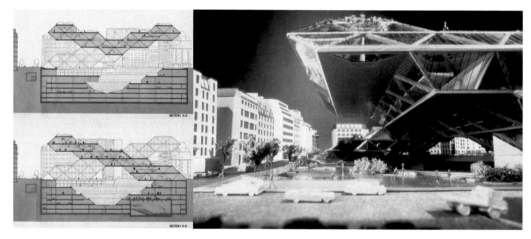

6.2   Moshe Safdie and Yale students, Plateau Beaubourg Cultural Center, sections and model (1971).

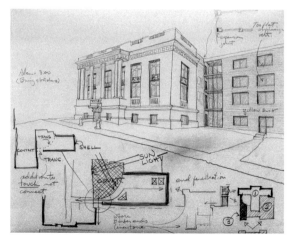

6.3   Marc Appleton (M.Arch 1972), Addition to the Hartford County Courthouse. Allan Greenberg studio (ca. 1970).

work from them, asking that they make models of rarely considered buildings that no longer existed or had never been built, such as Alvar Aalto's demolished Finnish Pavilion at the New York World's Fair of 1939 or Hannes Meyer's unrealized Petersschule in Basel of 1926–27. By 1971, Greenberg's was an important voice in the school. His student Marc Appleton reported to alumni that Greenberg's spring 1971 studio, "Architectural Theory and Analysis," was "based on the premise that skills in analysis of existing works are one essential part of architectural education, needed not only to better understand the achievements of architecture in the past, but in evaluating day-to-day work over the drawing board." Appleton continued: "Such a studio has been sorely missed in the curriculum of the School; until now, these skills have been only implicit in both design studios and architectural history courses."[33] Writing in *Sensus,* a new but short-lived publication, Appleton stated that the structure of Greenberg's studio involved "a kind of sequential case study approach with students working individually and in groups to analyze buildings for form, content, and context, writing papers as well as producing drawings and models. Each of the exercises is two to three weeks long. For some sixteen students this spring, the studio has been the source of intensive research and study, the development of new perceptual skills, and a more profound appreciation of architectural history as it speaks to the conscience of the profession today" (6.3).[34] Greenberg's approach would continue to influence Appleton who, after graduating, worked in several firms, including three years in the office of Frank Gehry, before embarking on independent practice in his native California, where he specializes in regionally based, traditional design.[35]

Deliberately echoing a 1950s studio assignment given by Philip Johnson, Greenberg asked students to design houses in the style of great architects in order to further understand the work of the masters. Each year Greenberg's studio visited Johnson at his Glass House in New Canaan—reviving a pilgrimage Yale students had not been making since the Rudolph era—where its owner "always showed the students around the estate, diligently answered their questions, and patiently reviewed their designs."[36] Johnson, always interested in school gossip, would occasionally get students to answer a few of his own questions as well, as Barton Phelps recalls:

> Philip took about five of us into the guesthouse and we sat on the floor, on the shag carpet of the guesthouse, which you know, has no windows. So he starts playing with the lights and is ostensibly giving us a didactic discussion on light levels. So he'd say, "This is good for a group about this size." Then he'd turn it down and say, "This is better for three or four

people." Then he turned it down until it was very, very dim and said, "I'd have wonderful conversations with just one person at this level." Then he turned the lights out all together and quickly said, "Would Mr. Greenberg make a good dean?" Everyone answered at once: "Yes, no, maybe, yes, I don't know!" Then Philip said, "We thought Charlie was the right guy. Guess he wasn't."[37]

Greenberg's plan for the school was substantive. Concerned with its increasing isolation from the discourse of the university as a whole, he argued that the school should deemphasize subjects more readily learned in a professional environment *after* graduation, and instead go beyond building design into the world of policy-making. He articulated a specific set of objectives that would equip graduates with the necessary knowledge to not just design buildings, but also to participate in the decision-making process at all levels of government, in areas that will influence the role of architecture in society: "Design as embodied in zoning and public health ordinance has a far more crucial effect on an environmental scale than the design of a building." Under his program, students would "undertake original research into the theoretical bases of architecture . . . undertake original research into architecture's relationship to other disciplines," and "become leaders in their fields, constantly striving to expand the scope of the profession."[38] In essence, he believed that the school should prepare students to participate "in the decision-making process at all levels of government, in areas which will influence the use society will make of architecture." As Greenberg saw it, Yale graduates should be able to "determine policy" and "implement policy."[39]

On February 25, 1971, Acting Dean Spiegel sent a memo to the faculty and visiting critics soliciting their views about who the new dean might be, asking them to narrow the choice of candidates to three, to be selected from the six most commonly mentioned names: Burchard; Cobb; Passonneau; Robertson; the German architect O. M. Ungers (1926–2007), chairman of architecture at Cornell; and Vreeland. Significantly, Greenberg's name was not on Spiegel's list, but faculty were encouraged to add other names in anticipation of a vote that was to take place on March 3.[40] On March 9, Spiegel sent Brewster the results of the faculty poll. Of twenty-two ballots sent, nineteen were completed and returned. The top three choices were, in order, Vreeland, Ungers, and Robertson—Spiegel, who was not among the six, received one vote.[41] On the same day, Spiegel wrote Brewster a letter that, in retrospect, appears to have been a thinly veiled act of self-nomination, stating that he wished to reiterate his "serious concern as to whether most of the candidates can really show a positive enough future direction to our school. Architecture is really at a crossroads," he continued, "and the time is ripe for a positive move in a somewhat different direction. This new direction will not only include all that we have done well over the past years here at Yale but will take on many more realistic approaches to better serve the architectural needs of our times." But lest he appear too self-serving, Spiegel went on to express support for "an architect like Moshe Safdie [who] seems to encompass the full gamut of intellectual thought and realistic application which is what I have always thought architecture was to be all about." Promising to arrange a meeting between Safdie and Brewster, he also promised to report back to the president "as to whether I am still willing to back Jaquelin Robertson or not."[42] From this, it would appear that Robertson was the president's choice.

Art School Dean Howard Weaver, sounding like someone returning a collegial favor, expressed the interest and willingness of his faculty to help with the search. Weaver let the president know "how impressive the administration of the Architecture faculty has appeared to be during the current term under the direction of Herman Spiegel and with Moshe Safdie as a distinguished visitor." He claimed this observation as his own but stated that it was also the belief of "many with far more familiarity than I with years of developments and personalities in both Art and Architecture. Nor is there a suggestion in this of a criticism of Charles Moore, who has certainly been always our friend and admired fellow-sufferer."[43]

Students had their opinions as well, and there seemed almost no end of petitions on behalf of various candidates, with many students signing more than one. On March 5, a large group of students, emphasizing their commitment to the "classic orientation" of the school as a design school, with an emphasis on visiting critics over standing faculty, asked the president to appoint a full-time administrator and educator who had his own point of view but was open to others. This group of students endorsed Greenberg and Safdie, who tied with eleven votes. Shadrach Woods had seven votes, but also had the endorsement of a second faction of students, led by Gabriela Goldschmidt (b. 1942; M.Arch 1971).[44] Woods had taught at Yale in 1962 and again in 1969 while practicing in France. Recently relocated to the United States, where he was in partnership in New York with alumnus Myles Weintraub, he was seen as a socially responsible antihero in direct opposition to such establishment figures as Philip Johnson, Kevin Roche, and Paul Rudolph, who had together been the subject of a recent exhibition (October 1, 1970–January 3, 1971) at the Museum of Modern Art that had led Ada Louise Huxtable, improbably caught up in the era's heady counterculturalism, to publicly chastise the exhibit's curator, Arthur Drexler, director of the museum's Department of Architecture, for selecting "a threesome . . . scorned by the current crop of architectural graduates."[45]

There were a lot of opinions among the students, but not much consensus, as illustrated by a petition from yet another group of students who demanded that Safdie's name be removed from consideration. Although Safdie's tenure as Davenport Visiting Professor was making a positive impression on upper-level administrators, it seems that he was not universally beloved by the students. "I think people thought he was kind of a poseur," recalls Barton Phelps, "that he was overly supported by the press and the reputation he earned just from doing Habitat."[46] On March 11, yet another group of students—nineteen in total—sent Brewster a letter outlining in more detail the qualities they believed to be "most needed in a new dean" while also informing the president of their general preference for Allan Greenberg. In their letter, the students called for a "broadening and intensification of the educational process," not only in design, but in "areas which must be given more than lip service . . . programming, theory, history, and methodology to name a few." They also called for "connections outside the traditional grounds of architecture. . . . We cannot operate in a vacuum."[47]

Brewster asked Spiegel to sound out James Stirling about the job; Stirling declined but expressed support for Ungers.[48] In April, Tim Vreeland met with Brewster and toured the school, and he was pleased to see the situation improved since his previous visit in September. In a follow-up letter, Vreeland wrote of his distinct "impression that the faculty and the students were eagerly awaiting strong direction from the new dean and, if he were the right man, could count on considerable support from them in building a new program." Vreeland went on to share his opinion that the school "could benefit from a more diversified faculty and a more balanced mix of specializations—a mix in which architectural design remains paramount but many more specialized subjects which support design are taught." Vreeland, like Greenberg, stressed the need for teacher-researchers who could reach out to other disciplines within the university, and expressed the belief that "students in the M.Arch. program could benefit from a more structured curriculum." Significantly, Vreeland emphasized urbanism as part of the design curriculum: "[There is a] need for more teaching at the scale of the city beginning with the First Year. . . . With only three years in which to prepare architects, the School must place the student in his principal area of action from the start."[49] Vreeland gently expressed reservations about Brewster's pet idea for cost-cutting: internships in professional offices in lieu of a term spent in residence.

Encouraged by members of the Yale Corporation and influential Yale College alumni, Brewster offered the job to Jaquelin T. Robertson, who was then seriously considering a return to private practice. "I came directly out of Ed Barnes's office when I got my license and went to work for [New York City Mayor John V.] Lindsay. And I wanted to go back to practice. I told John [Lindsay] when I was going to leave and he said, 'No, no, you can't leave now. I want you to become the chairman of the Planning Commission.' I said, 'John, I can't do it. I have to go back.' He said, 'OK, OK, OK, I got it.'" At the time Lindsay began to talk with Robertson about the Planning Commission post, Robertson was also in conversation with Sir Richard Llewelyn Davies (1912–1981), a top English architect-planner who "wanted me to run his English office. For a variety of reasons, at that time I didn't want to do that. So I came back and I said, 'Thanks a lot but no thanks.' I then got a call from Kingman Brewster . . . [who] said, 'Jaque, you've been recommended to me by a number of people: Scully, Johnson, John Lindsay [then a member of the Yale Corporation], and I'd like to come to New York and talk to you about becoming the new dean.'"[50]

Brewster came into New York, staying with John Hay (Jock) Whitney (1904–1982; B.A. 1926), an influential member of the Yale Corporation. Robertson's office was on the top floor of 220 West Forty-Second Street, a building that was not only home to the office of Midtown Planning and Development, which he directed, but also "where the vice cops and everyone hung out. It was a pretty exciting place." Robertson recalls:

The day [Brewster] was supposed to come, he didn't arrive and we were worried. I finally got the call and he said, "Jaque tell me where your office is? Oh my god, we went to East Forty-Second Street. It's on West Forty-Second Street. I thought that was right but the chauffeur said it couldn't possibly be. That's the porno district." . . . Anyway, we went out and had lunch at the Century [Association] and he said, "This is what we want you to do. I was told that some years ago you came to Yale for a jury and were not happy." I said it wasn't that I was not happy. It's that there was nothing there to be happy or unhappy about. You had people writing huge letters on yellow trace about what was wrong with the world. . . . It was hopeless. I got up in front of the jury and I said, "This is a waste of everyone's time." And I said to the students, "If this is what you're going to do, you might as well leave now and save the money and do something else. Because you're not doing architecture." This was probably '69. I was so depressed. . . . And there was no leadership in the school. Moore was an incredibly bright guy and a very interesting architect but he didn't work out as a dean. Maybe it would have been bad for anyone.

At the end of their first meeting, the president told Robertson to make a list of things he would change and send them to his office. "So I did that and he called me up about two weeks later and he said, 'OK. I don't have a problem with any of these. You're probably going to get some of the faculty bent out of shape but I don't care about that.'" Brewster offered him the deanship. "I said, 'This wasn't a faculty decision, was it?' He said, 'Of course it wasn't a faculty decision. It's the decision I made after talking to half a dozen people.'"[51]

Robertson accepted the offer, and it was announced that he was going to come to New Haven the following spring. But that would never happen. Shortly after taking the position, Robertson realized that he had made a very public mistake:

I went to a cottage I have in East Hampton with my wife and walked around for a couple days and said, "I don't want to do this. Why did I do this?" I walked around and said, "OK, I'm doing this. I'm going back to New Haven. I've already spent eight years in New Haven and I've been away from my practice [working for the city of New York] and I don't want to spend more time in an institution." Working for the city was really just a different kind of academia. "I don't mind teaching but I really don't want to be dean now. Why did I accept?" It was very simple. Part of it was ego. And part of it was my concern for Yale.

So on a Sunday morning, I called up Kingman and told him that I had made a terrible mistake and I didn't want to do it. And there was a deadly silence. . . . The first thing he said was, "I bet this was a tough telephone call to make." That gives you the quality of the person in that one sentence. I said, "The worst in my life." I said, "I have done something that was immature and I deeply regret it." He said, "Yeah, it is immature." So we talked and he asked me more about why I didn't want to do it and why I said that I would do it. I told him, and he said, "OK, Jaque. I understand. These things happen. But you will never make this kind of mistake ever again, will you?" I said, "No, I won't."[52]

Many were surprised and disappointed by Robertson's decision. Robertson says that Philip Johnson called to tell him, "You let me down. Why did you do this?" and Vincent Scully had a similar message, telling him, "'I don't understand it but someday you'll tell me." Both of them said, "It's our loss," and Johnson said, "and it'll be your loss." Robertson further recalls: "So then I called [Mayor] Lindsay and he said, 'I just heard about it. Tell me.' So I told him and at the end he said, 'Jackie, you made the right decision. You made it a little too late, but you made the right decision and I support you in it. I know Kingman really well and he'll deal with it.' And he did."[53]

Robertson's decision propelled Brewster into quick action. After the perceived antics of the Moore era, as well as the embarrassment over Robertson's withdrawal, he turned to Spiegel, appointing him to a five-year term as dean of the Faculty of Design and Planning, as the newly independent school was briefly designated, and director of studies in architecture. The appointment, announced to students on September 3 and to the public on September 12, 1971, was made effective immediately.[54] Brewster's decision to turn to Spiegel was viewed as surprising by many—an *engineer* at the helm of the Yale School of Architecture? Professionals and academics regarded the decision as expedient and a reflection of what many felt was Brewster's low regard for the school. On the most basic level, the appointment was an easy out for Brewster, who clearly was not comfortable with the other candidates who had been proposed. Spiegel's insider status as a faculty member was a way to show that the corporation was prepared to move on and put the Architecture School problem behind it. In its December 1971 visit to the newly established independent schools of Art and Architecture, the University Council concentrated its attention on the School of Architecture. In what was a "personal review," University Council Chairman George Dudley characterized Spiegel's year at the helm—a term as acting dean, then almost a term as dean—as one of "re-grouping, a year to 'let the new set-up take time to develop' or, as another faculty member put it, a year which in many ways both Schools constituted a 'start-up program.'"[55]

Herman D. J. Spiegel was born in the Roxbury section of Boston. After three years in the Army in the European and Pacific theaters during World War II, he graduated from the Rhode Island School of Design with a bachelor of science in architecture degree in 1953 and, two years later, received a master of engineering degree from Yale. He began his teaching career in the School of Engineering, but soon transitioned into the School of Architecture, offering basic courses in structural engineering, occasionally leading seminars, and participating in studios that "explored the relationship between structures and 'design-oriented' architecture."[56] While teaching, Spiegel also maintained an active private practice, most notably in the office he founded in 1964, Spiegel & Zamecnik, Inc. (formerly Associated Engineering).

In the official news release announcing his appointment, Spiegel surprised many by expressing strong opinions about the state of American architecture, and the need for architectural education to refocus on the design of buildings after its recent detour into social pamphleteering. In this he appeared to echo Robertson's concerns: "Very recently . . . the visual language, [as] opposed to verbal language, seems to have been going out of style in some schools. Students seem to prefer promises to visual realities. I intend, not to divorce ourselves from the verbal world, but nonetheless to stress production in the visual one—because that is where we all live."[57]

Following his appointment, Spiegel wrote to Provost Charles H. Taylor to express his appreciation for the administration's confidence in his leadership and to outline certain strategies for the deployment of endowments and other present and future resources that were intended to at once put the school on sound financial footing while also strengthening its curricular offerings. Spiegel recognized that the school "still had a pall of gloom about it, because of the wide-spread feeling held over from the fall semester, that our school would be eliminated, and because of the lack of permanent leadership which is what it takes to provide direction."[58]

Additionally, as a report by George Dudley made clear, the school was seriously underfunded, though no longer threatened with extinction. As incoming dean, Spiegel "was accorded certain forms of increased financial support for the School," but, Dudley stated, "it continues with one of the lowest budgets per student in the Ivy League Schools." Dudley also pointed out that the traditional disparity in financial support between Yale College and the various professional and graduate schools had an especially negative effect on architectural education and "as the broadened concept of the architect's role in our society has been developing, as the needs for interdisciplinary research and teaching are so rapidly growing, this disparity deserves to be corrected."[59] Despite best intentions, it would be decades before the school had anything like the financial support it needed.

Alexander Purves (b. 1935; B.A. 1958, M.Arch 1965), who had been practicing in New York as part of the office of Davis, Brody & Associates when he returned to Yale at Spiegel's invitation to serve as visiting critic in 1973 and associate professor adjunct in 1975, remembers that "Herman was asked by Brewster to take charge of a very messy situation and he did. And he did it well. Some people were not very helpful because they thought he was just a bean counter. He wasn't."[60] Indeed, Spiegel initially proved to be more than up to the job, finding ways to get the school back on its feet despite inadequate financial resources. Unable to afford new multiyear hires, he increased teaching loads for remaining faculty. He also reformed admissions policies and procedures, seeking candidates whose career trajectory pointed toward professional success. To further the school's professional focus, he strengthened the Core curriculum in the first three terms. Perhaps most significantly, Spiegel proved himself an effective communicator with alumni—something that had not particularly interested Moore. To this end, he began to publish a quarterly calendar that included photographs, drawings, articles, and essays highlighting events at the school, work of alumni, and what would prove to be the first of numerous reassessments of the Art and Architecture Building (6.4).

Despite the deplorable postfire state of the building, and the minimal renovation that enabled its renewed occupation in 1971, students began to once again appreciate Rudolph's masterwork. Arriving in New Haven in fall 1971, just as the A&A was being reinhabited, James Oleg Kruhly (b. 1947; M.Arch 1973) was immediately drawn to its qualities. Forty years later he recalled: "People said it wasn't efficient and you couldn't find your way around. But . . . if you're an architecture student why do you look for efficiency? You look for wonder, for adventure. That building, no matter how long I was in it, it still contained surprises."[61] Quick to sense this sea change in respect to the building, Spiegel saw to it that the inaugural calendar included a passionate editorial by its student editor, Henry Wollman (M.Arch 1973), who called for the restoration of the building to the architectural pantheon:

> Burnt, closed, walled-off, in tumult, A&A carried a legacy of confusion and overwhelming sadness during the restoration process. But not even the holocaust of fire could in any ultimate way tear the heart from this monument of American architecture, this presence on the Yale campus. The terrifying, ferocious nobility and grandeur that are so much the fabric of this building remain.
>
> It is, for these reasons, not an easy building to live with. Physically, it is often uncomfortable. Fundamentally, however, it is the emotional demands of the building that are the most difficult. In this sense the cliché "the building is too strong" rings true: too difficult to live the humdrum student life; too aware of itself; too much concerned with an idea; not concerned enough with the reality of everyday.
>
> Yet somehow we manage to live with it. We are aware that we are in confrontation with more than structure, more than function. We are aware of the fact that we are in confrontation with the heart of monumental architecture, a statement of human spirit and a material manifestation of an ideal of human culture.[62]

Alerted to Wollman's editorial and to Edwin William de Cossy's renovations, Ada Louise Huxtable, the influential architecture critic of the *New York Times,* said she learned of the renovations from "of all things, a calendar published and distributed several times a year by the Yale School of Architecture." Huxtable took the opportunity to inform her readers about "The Building You Love to Hate"—a play on the description given to Austrian actor Erich von Stroheim, who frequently played sinister characters in Hollywood films—writing that "it was generally assumed that either an act of God or an act of man had destroyed, with uncanny prescience for the moment and the mood, a monument that embodied the despised Establishment standards and values that the radical young men were rejecting on moral and social grounds."[63]

Huxtable allowed herself a small pat on the back for the prescience of her observation in her enthusiastic but not unqualified 1963 review of the then-new building: "If the students responded to the challenge of their environment they should never think, or see, quite the same again."[64] But in her 1971 review, she came down rather hard on the rebellious late 1960s students who, in her view, "reviled" the building for reasons beyond its (admitted) litany of functional faults. "In the oversimplification and slick superficiality of revolutionary rhetoric, it became the archetype of the imposition of a false value system by an architect on an anti-people ego trip." Not uncharacteristically carried away with her own rhetoric, Huxtable reminded her readers that the building was "a symbol in the revolution of the consciousness of man" that had become, after the fire, "a super symbol." And, as happens with symbols, the A&A "had become an object of hate." Huxtable rather shockingly saw the fire as "proof" of the building's "wrongheadedness," arguing that the ruined building, a shadow of its former self, stood as "a lesson to those architects lacking in consciousness, who would finesse their deeper social responsibilities to impose their vanity on man."[65]

In April 1974, two and a half years after Huxtable's reassessment, Paul Goldberger, her precocious successor as the *Times'* architecture critic, belatedly marked the building's tenth anniversary, writing that reaction toward it had "mellowed somewhat, a result, many at Yale believe, of the calmer state of the university in general and of an increasing willingness on the part of students to view it more as an architectural problem than as a symbol of modern architecture's overbearance." Goldberger's article reported that Rudolph, who had refused all invitations to visit Yale since he stepped down as chairman in 1965, had returned in early April to give a lecture, during which he discussed his work but assiduously avoided any mention of the building.[66]

The school's early calendars tracked the rapid changes that were taking place as Moore's program gave way to Spiegel's. They illustrated alumni work, reported on programs such as the Building Project, and explained the Yale Corporation's vote on June 10, 1972, to replace the bachelor of architecture with the master of architecture degree. The March to May 1973 calendar reported on the May 6, 1972, vote of the corporation to redesignate the "Faculty in Architecture and Design" as the "School of Architecture." The same calendar also highlighted historic preservation as an important professional concern, a rare instance for a school that has largely rejected the topic in its curriculum, although many of its graduates, such as James Polshek and Frederick Bland (b. 1945; b.a. 1968, M.Arch 1972), have made important contributions to the field. According to Stephen R. Hagan (b. 1951; b.a. 1973, M.Arch 1977) and James Kruhly, editors of the calendar, a group "affiliated with the School of Architecture," organizing itself as "the Student Community Housing Corporation," "has become a driving force in the preservation and rehabilitation of existing housing around the Yale and New Haven area." Hagan and Kruhly also reported that President Brewster, in response to student petitions, "has agreed to establish a university committee to review the architectural heritage on the Yale campus and ensure that no wanton demolitions occur without a full review process."[67] As things stabilized in the school, Spiegel-era calendars were often focused on issues at the forefront of the profession's concerns. Subsequent calendars' topics, printed under Spiegel's successor, Cesar Pelli, included "Academic Buildings" (December 1975–February 1976), "Monuments, Memorials, and Public Spaces" (October–December 1976), and "Places for Work" (October–December 1978).

Spiegel adroitly used the calendars to reassure alumni that, under his leadership, the school was returning to glory. For example, the calendar for September–November 1974, citing various favorable admissions statistics, revealed the dean at his most blustery: "One measure of judging the success of any product is its market value," Spiegel stated, before reporting that Yale's "stock has climbed way above that of all our competitors." He attributed the school's reclaimed success to the appeal of "our way of teaching architecture, our pluralistic approach which encompasses more than one concept or aspect of architecture." However, instead of articulating pluralism as an enduring principle at the school, he chose to see it as the approach most suited to the moment: "Students today seem to favor our pluralism which allows them the freedom to follow the road of their own choice after exposure to many."[68]

Although some tended to dismiss Spiegel's pride in the school's pluralism as an expression of an engineer's insecurity, many observers who had

braced themselves for the worst with the announcement of Spiegel's appointment saw his approach as a necessary response to the chaotic situation of
1969. Spiegel was proving to be not so much a strong leader as a good listener.
Despite Spiegel's tendency to sound a bit hard-nosed about the more speculative aspects of design, under his leadership the school retained its character
as a community of individuals dedicated to the art of architecture. Sometime
after graduating, Kruhly, reflecting on a conversation he had as a student with
Gerald Allen (b. 1942; B.A. 1964, M.Phil. 1968, M.Arch 1972), who was closely
allied with Charles Moore, remembers Allen making the point that the school
"wasn't training architects, but was instead training principals for a firm."
Kruhly thought about Allen's observation "for a long time after that conversation" and realized that the school wasn't "just giving you skills to be useful
and productive in a firm," but was "really suggesting in so many different and
subtle ways that the real art of architecture is being the principal in a firm."[69]
In other words, as opposed to Moore's emphasis on individual expression and
countercultural practice, under Spiegel, the school resumed its focus on a
disciplined approach to educating professional leaders.

One of Spiegel's biggest curricular challenges was posed by the Black
Environmental Studies Team (BEST), which had been allowed to evolve out of
the Black Workshop into an officially sanctioned "graduate program sponsored by the Yale Corporation within the School of Architecture," intended to
provide black students "with a means towards developing creative approaches
in solving problems of the Black and thus larger community."[70] Led by Thelma
Rucker, assistant professor of environmental design, with Richard Dozier and
Edward Cherry serving as assistant professors of architecture, BEST set out to
examine the role of the black architect in a changing urban society by emphasizing "psycho-social approaches . . . to explain locational decisions of various
sorts by various actors, as it is these decisions that preform the pattern of
human life and its relationship to the architecturally created environment and
its thereby changed ecology."[71] In 1972, Spiegel secured funds from the university to continue the program for three years, noting that the school is "unique
to date in having secured this kind of institutional support for programs in
the BEST category." There may still have been concerns about the program,
though, because as Spiegel told Dozier, "The future of the BEST option within
the School of Architecture now depends on its education excellence and on
its success in attracting the qualified students whom its program is designed
to serve."[72] Unfortunately, by 1974 the program, though initially promising, was
"doing poorly," and Spiegel expressed his intention to reorganize it after its

initial funding ran out the following year.[73] Beginning in 1976, BEST would be disbanded in favor of an elective advanced study area run by Cherry that was more clearly integrated into the school's curriculum, a change that, according to Spiegel, was "a means to bring specific minority interests into a closer relationship with the basic program of the School and of establishing the means whereby the School and its policies might more directly and effectively reflect, on an ongoing basis, the culturally and ethnically diverse interests which identify contemporary American society."[74] Cherry's curriculum offered two courses, in addition to independent course work: "The Urban Form," an advanced seminar presenting problems in contemporary cities, with visiting lecturers including local planning professionals and city legislators, and "Introduction to Community Involvement," which explored the needs of local residents through case studies and discussions with neighborhood representatives. These courses were designed to provide students with an awareness of and sensitivity to the "preferences and lifestyles of minority groups,"[75] while also teaching them how to successfully maneuver through civic bureaucracies. The program ended in 1979 during the tenure of Spiegel's successor, Cesar Pelli.

Ray Gindroz, whose time on the faculty extended from the Moore through the Spiegel eras, remembers one aspect of Spiegel's way of avoiding the double standard for whites and minorities that was characteristic of academic politics in the late 1960s and early 1970s: "In those days, it was the politically correct thing to go overboard in accommodating minority students." When the request for financial aid for failing minority students was being considered, "Herman, in a very clear way, said, 'This is simply wrong.'"

He said, "Never in the history of the University had a scholarship been awarded to someone who had failed to meet all his requirements. Why should we do it now? Why should we break precedent for this one person?" And it was the first time I had heard someone stand up to that reality. And he did stand up to it and there was no outcry. Everyone thought this was the correct reaction. And it calmed down that whole situation. Now, others may have a very different view of it but that's how I saw it. And it demonstrated Herman's clarity of thought, his integrity, and his ability to see things through.[76]

Despite the terrible state of the school's facilities and its perceived near-death in 1970, top students continued to apply for admission. James Kruhly arrived in fall 1971 with advanced standing as a second-year student, having

6.4   Yale School of Architecture Calendar. Above, June–August 1975; below,
December 1975–February 1976.

6.5   Duany Plater-Zyberk & Company, Seaside (1980), Florida.

studied architecture as an undergraduate at the University of Pennsylvania. "There was a freedom [at Yale] that I thought was extraordinary. If you were doing something, building something, that was OK."[77] Kruhly found his classmates to be intelligent and diverse. "Everyone had a different story; there was no homogeneity. We were a wide cross section of people with different interests and beliefs. It was . . . an intellectual free-for-all."[78]

Elizabeth Plater-Zyberk (b. 1950; M.Arch 1974) and Andrés Duany (b. 1949; M.Arch 1974) came to Yale with sophisticated backgrounds in modernist architecture from their undergraduate years at Princeton. Looking back on her time under Spiegel, Plater-Zyberk remembers the school as a place with "an aversion to theory," which she, along with Duany, fought against, insisting "that the act of thinking is always attached to the act of building. We learned that we would always be conscious of our predecessors. Vincent Scully's History of Architecture course influenced by [Harold] Bloom's *The Anxiety of Influence* brought that home to us very clearly and made us very conscious of the past as well as the transition into the future."[79] While students at Yale, Duany and Plater-Zyberk began down the path that would lead to their eventual careers as architect urbanists by documenting and analyzing New Haven's neighborhoods. From this they would not only evolve a clear understanding of what went wrong with contemporary city planning, but also develop a set of methodologies and codes known as the New Urbanism that aimed to adapt the admirable features of traditional urbanism to modern life.

In Vincent Scully's view, New Urbanism "is the climax of everything that has happened underneath the culture of the Yale School [of Architecture]. . . . That's New Haven and Yale. New Urbanism, the study of it, the fighting against redevelopment, all those things. It changed the language, it changed the intelligence, it changed the direction, it changed the objective. And Moore's a part of it. Certainly Venturi's a part of it. And I think it culminates with Duany Plater-Zyberk."[80] Herbert Newman agrees. According to Newman, what became New Urbanism, as exemplified by the new town of Seaside, Florida (6.5), sprang directly from the contextualism and urbanism that Moore advocated during his tenure as dean: "The idea of New Urbanism, the ideas of Andrés and Elizabeth who were in school a few years after, those ideas that Moore and Venturi and Gindroz, and in a small way myself, were espousing, those ideas were introduced in courses in urban design that we taught students during the first and second year. . . . We used to talk about, and still believe, that the city is the architecture. From a hyperbolic point of view, we can say that the city is the architecture and the buildings sublimate themselves to serve the architecture, which is the city."[81]

Patrick Pinnell (b. 1949; B.A. 1971, M.Arch 1974), a classmate of Duany and Plater-Zyberk, remembers that "the two of them added some very interesting chemistry, besides their Princeton undergraduate education, to the class. Liz was so interested already in planning and the systems behind planning that she became known as Liz Planning-Zoning within about two weeks of the fall semester."[82] Pinnell remembers that Duany and Plater-Zyberk helped organize their passionate but shambolic fellow students: "The two of them immediately injected some different aspects of rigor to a class that was already very aware of the issues of urban design and urban renewal," largely as a result of the impact Ray Gindroz and David Lewis, his partner in Urban Design Associates, were having on the first-year Core curriculum. "We had been told, basically . . . that we should be emulating things like [the A&A] and the Knights of Columbus Building and the Coliseum. And out of whatever reflex resistance to that, our class was already tending not to do that." Pinnell recalls that he and some of his fellow students were instead "looking toward the Dwight-Edgewood neighborhood where a lot of [architecture] students were living, and [its] wonderful mix of houses . . . and the streets and block systems and understanding that there was a kind of richness to those places."[83]

Despite Spiegel's efforts to counteract the school's presumed permissiveness in the Moore era, it was difficult for him to overcome faculty who tended to support individualist candidates as new students. David Schwarz (b. 1952; M.Arch 1974) remembers himself and many of his classmates as independent-minded with their own goals and agendas, recalling that "nobody wanted anybody to tell us what to do. We wanted to do what we wanted to do. We wanted to find our vision and have the teachers help us refine our vision. We didn't like requirements."[84] Schwarz claims to have "viewed architecture school as being a kindergarten for adults. When I was there [1971–74], there was an extraordinary lack of rigor. And that's both good and bad. . . . I had to learn rigor on my own. . . . But my time at Yale helped me refine my world view."[85] Schwarz, who had read the classics at St. John's College in Maryland, remembers doubting the dominant pedagogy of the time: "I think that in school, our professors told us what worked. And to varying degrees we believed them. But somewhere in the back of our minds, there was this notion that 'I'm not sure this really works.' So as we started walking around New Haven, we started becoming more and more convinced that the gospel of the day was not leading to places we liked. It became obvious: Kevin Roche's Knights of Columbus Building and Coliseum . . . was built while we were there to great fanfare, but if you looked at the place it made, the place it made was terrible. Whether or not the architecture was good was not the question. The place was terrible."[86]

Schwarz recalls Moore and Scully as "the two strongest influences on me at Yale. I had an independent study with Charlie and Vince, which was probably one of the best things I did. . . . Getting together with them once a week for three hours and listening to them fight with each other . . . was interesting. . . . And I learned a lot from it."[87]

William McDonough (b. 1951; M.Arch 1976), who would become a pioneer of sustainable design and the "Green Dean" (1980–88) of the University of Virginia's School of Architecture, chose Yale in part because "I saw so many of these schools that were putting people through drills. The drills of learning the profession." These schools "looked like the equivalent of the USS *Missouri*. Shoving off for three years and doing drills on the deck. You get technically proficient and then you land in port and move on to your next station." Yale seemed different to McDonough, especially because Moore, though no longer captain of Yale's ship, still very much had his hand on the tiller of the first-year curriculum, which, as McDonough recalls, had "more in common with the Good Ship Lollipop than the USS *Missouri*. [Moore] was still teaching first year. That's what I loved about him, that he would want to teach us coming in." According to McDonough, despite Spiegel's efforts to rein it in, the program was still very much Charles Moore's:

> When I talk about the projects that would go on, and the diversity of students—from what I saw, it just seemed so exciting. I would be in a class with dancers and actors and artists. It wasn't a professional program.
>
> It was about meaning. And the various charms of studying things at a molecular level or an emotional level. Or a technical level, but in terms of engaging with society and culture in a creative way—a way that was playful as well. Cheerful. Optimistic. It just fit with my nature much more, to be free and open.

Moore's first design assignment was, as McDonough recalls:

> a Center for your Ego in the Universe. "Because we might as well get it over with." Isn't that fantastic? It's genius. Genius! We're all sitting there looking at each other, and everybody's measuring each other up. All alpha dogs. And we're about to put our egos on display. Just get it over with. It's so brilliant. So we each had to build a model of this thing in the first week. We had people doing little Corbusian villas out of Plexiglass and plaster—they had already been to Harvard [presumably for Harvard's "career discovery program"] and had been training to be architects and

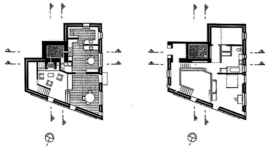

SAVE RESIDENCE   PLANS ▬▬ ▬▬ 1/8"   W.A.McDONOUGH   1975

6.6 William McDonough (M.Arch 1976), Neave House, photograph
and plans (1977), Shanagarry, Ireland.

6.7 James Stirling (ca. 1975).

knew what they were doing. And then you had dancers who were trying to put spaces in clay and open them around complex shapes. And then you had one person, she wanted to live in a pinecone.[88]

McDonough remembers one memorable encounter with Richard Meier, Bishop Visiting Professor in spring 1975. McDonough was not in Meier's studio, but the architect "came over to my desk and said, 'What are you doing?' I said I was designing a solar house in Ireland that I'm going to build myself starting this summer. He just came out straight up and said, 'Solar energy has nothing to do with architecture.' And I said I didn't understand." Meier's "houses at the time were featured in GE lighting ads. Giant west-facing houses with lots of lightbulbs everywhere. And I just didn't understand that. I read Vitruvius and I thought some of it was still applicable. Orientation matters."[89]

McDonough took studios with Stirling and Harry Cobb, Davenport Visiting Professor in spring 1975, and did his final project under visiting critic Hans Hollein (1934–2014), with whom he became good friends. It was a diverse education shaped by contemporary architectural culture. "When I came into first year, it was the Whites versus the Grays. That was the dialogue. Eisenman, Meier, and then you had Venturi and Moore and the Gray stuff. At the time Stern was just coming into a kind of residential, postmodernist phase. And then Stirling, the very singular, modern mind. Hollein, the jeweler working at a larger scale. Cobb, the corporate modernist."[90]

Along the way, McDonough built his solar house in Ireland (6.6) and remembers that after finishing it, "I came out of it humble. Then I went to New York to apprentice. I was Alec Purves's teaching assistant at Yale and he had introduced me to Davis, Brody because I wanted to do public housing. So I got hired at Davis, Brody immediately, though [Lewis] Davis [who, with Samuel Brody, had been Davenport Visiting Professor in spring 1974] said he'd never hire somebody from Yale, they can't draw." But, "When they heard Alec was my reference, they said, 'Hire him.' But I never got to do public housing because they went into corporate work. It was a recession. So I just did competitions for Davis, Brody and we were very successful. And then I started my own firm. I started my own firm the day after I got licensed."[91]

While at Yale, McDonough would also have his first encounter with Jaquelin Robertson, whom he would eventually succeed as dean at the University of Virginia's School of Architecture. Robertson was offering a seminar at Morse College. He had just gotten the commission for Shahestan Pahlavi, the new center of Tehran, Iran. Curious about it, McDonough asked Robertson "to come early next time and have dinner with me in my little garret apartment on Dwight Street. He said sure. When I look back on it, he was a man in the news, in the *New York Times,* and he's got this huge commission, and he said sure. A week later, he shows up before class" and has "dinner with me before going to teach his class. I just thought that was normal. An instructor takes time to talk to a student. It didn't occur to me until I was a hyperactive professional that it's really hard to do. If students called me up and said, 'You're coming to teach at Stanford, would you come a few hours early and have lunch?,' the answer is yes. Because that's how I learned to behave. That's what it was like at Yale. That's what [Hans] Hollein was like. I hosted Hollein when he came to New Haven. He had nothing else to do and he would come to dinner at our house every night."[92]

Perhaps as an antidote to the cramped conditions in the rapidly deteriorating Art and Architecture Building, and because visitors from abroad such as Stirling and Hollein tended to stay in New Haven for many days at a time, students frequently entertained at dinners and evening parties to cultivate an atmosphere of collegiality. "My father was the president of Seagram," recalls McDonough. "He was in their international wine and spirits business. He had done something rather clever, I thought. He had found out what the various professors liked, as was his business. He knew what they liked and he sent it all up to our house in Hamden. There were six of us architecture students living there—Turks and Americans. We had great Turkish food and I took care of the wine cellar. And we had fabulous dinners every night. There were ten at the table. We had Charles Moore there, Vincent Scully, Stirling, Hollein, all the visiting professors, because they didn't have anything to do. We were the spot. Every night we would talk about architecture. . . . It was a great time." McDonough remembers a dinner conversation with Scully, Stirling, and a few students. When in New Haven, Stirling stayed in the guest apartment atop the A&A Building. At this dinner, the British architect, who "was usually kind of quiet, said, 'I want to know what everybody at this table thinks of the A&A Building. *Really.*'" Much to McDonough's chagrin, Stirling complained that Rudolph "had put that corduroy concrete wall in the shower," causing Stirling to scrape his back when he slipped on a bar of soap—"and I have the scars to prove it."[93] Like McDonough, David Schwarz believed that "the best way to learn from your teachers was to invite them to dinner. Cesar [Pelli], when you ask him still, if we run into somebody he'll introduce me as 'This is David Schwarz, he makes the best chocolate soufflé.' I've gotten to the point where I wish he'd mention some of my buildings but it's still about the chocolate soufflé."[94] After graduating, Schwarz went to work for Paul Rudolph, whom he contrasted with Moore: "Both of them were totally accessible. You could ask questions and have conversations with them. Rudolph was much less success-ful at conversation. Charlie was far less opinionated than Rudolph. Rudolph was very opinionated. Charlie was not. I always have the feeling that Rudolph knew the truth. And I always had the feeling that Charlie was looking for it."[95]

Interestingly, according to Schwarz, despite the fact that his class (1974)—the first to be admitted after the school's independence from the Art Department—is notable for its number of high-profile graduates, including Andrés Duany and Elizabeth Plater-Zyberk, Spiegel did not think much of the class as a whole: "Herman at our graduation said to us, in effect, 'I can't wait to see you guys gone. You're the worst class Yale has had in ten years.'"[96] In so saying, Schwarz believes Spiegel was sincere. "We were the last class admitted by Felix Drury," recalls Schwarz. Which is to say that the class of 1974 was essentially made up of holdovers from the Moore era: "Felix Drury admitted one sort of people and the people after Felix admitted another. I had the nick-name 'the last of the magicians' because I was the last person that Felix had admitted. The very last. The people that Felix admitted looked like they fucked around all the time but they showed up with great projects."[97]

As if to counteract the looseness of the Moore-influenced Core, Spiegel saw to it that the advanced studios were taught by experienced professionals, many of them partners in large practices. The appointment of visiting professors was and remains solely the responsibility of the dean and, following Moore's lead, Spiegel and then Pelli saw to it that Stirling occupied the Davenport Chair each fall until 1983. After Safdie's term as Davenport Chair, Spiegel appointed Cesar Pelli in spring 1972; then Lewis Davis and Samuel Brody in spring 1974; Henry N. Cobb in spring 1975; and Hugh Hardy in spring 1976. While the veritable merry-go-round of spring Davenport appointees helped keep the advanced studios fresh, it was Stirling's continuing presence that gave them a compensating gravitas, with many alumni, students, and prospec-tive students regarding Stirling's presence as the essence of Yale's Advanced Design pedagogy (6.7). During his time at Yale, Stirling's work moved from Le Corbusier–influenced modernism to a decidedly more eclectic approach. The March to May 1975 school calendar included an excerpt from his fall 1974 lecture that was indicative of an incipient change in his approach to architecture. It began with a characteristic provocation: "I consider 99% of modern architecture to be boring, banal, and barren and usually disruptive and unharmonious when placed in older cities." Going on to elaborate, Stirling was outspoken in his rejection of orthodox modernism in favor of a more contextual approach: "I believe that the shapes of a building should indicate—perhaps display the usage and way of life of its occupants, and it is therefore likely to be rich and varied in its appearance, and its expression is likely to be simple. The collection (in a building) of forms and shapes which the everyday public can *associate* with and be *familiar* with—and *identify* with— seems to be essential. . . . The particular way in which functional-symbolic elements are put together may be the 'art' in the architecture."[98]

In his talk, Stirling, always an adept and nimble student of history, articulated both a refutation of fellow Brit Reyner Banham's technocratic views on architecture and a tempering of Charles Moore's "image collecting." The lecture, prescient in its advocacy of what would soon come to be known as postmodernism, was delivered a year before Charles Jencks first used the term in his 1975 essay "The Rise of Post-Modern Architecture."[99] It also anticipated the changing views toward architectural history that would characterize Yale beginning in the late 1970s and place it once again in the center of architectural discourse.

As a teacher, Emmanuel Petit has written, Stirling pushed students to combine "the iconicity of 'authoritative' architectural form with a witty play with fragmentation and recombination."[100] Stirling "functioned more by inspiration than by instruction. . . . He appeared quite pragmatic and intuitive in studio, and was never interested in supplying a socio-political or theoretical 'libretto' to accompany the projects. In his mind, all architecture materialized as a particular instantiation of the spatial organization of the program and circulation of a building."[101] Stirling did not have an overarching theoretical strategy for his studios. Instead, he ran them pretty much as he did his London office. Seizing upon the freedom that the Davenport professorship afforded, he offered studio projects that were of personal and professional interest to him. For example, while working on the Derby Civic Centre competition in 1970, Stirling had his students doing the same; in fall 1972, students developed alternative designs for the Mellon Center (now the Yale Center for British Art) (see 5.48), then under construction, a commission Stirling had coveted. In 1973, he assigned a low-cost housing problem in Runcorn, England, a project that he himself had worked on in 1967. When Mitchell/Giurgola were designing new residential colleges for Whitney Avenue, Stirling's students did the same (see 5.49). During the fall 1975 term, Stirling's students were asked to design an art gallery in Düsseldorf, Germany, a competition program he was also at work on. According to Stirling's studio brief, the Düsseldorf project, as Petit summarizes it, "thematized the integration of the existing, neighboring buildings in the schemes, and defined sequences of public pathways through the exterior spaces of the museum"[102] (6.8). Stirling was engaged "in an intense dialogue between the old and the new in the city—a dialogue that became crucial to the students' projects."[103] The fall 1976 semester saw students develop a Museum of Science and Technology in Tehran—another failed proposal from Stirling's office (6.9). One of Stirling's most celebrated projects was the Staatsgalerie in Stuttgart (1984), a project that he assigned students in fall 1978—a year into the actual project's construction (6.10).

In the five years before he left Yale in 1983, Stirling would assign cultural buildings that were either projects in his office such as the Fogg Museum extension (now known as the Arthur M. Sackler Museum) in Cambridge (fall 1979; 6.11) and the Tate Gallery Addition (now known as the Clore Gallery) in London (fall 1981; 6.12), or ones he was competing for such as the Hood Museum at Dartmouth (fall 1980; 6.13) (which ultimately was awarded to Charles Moore). In 1982, Stirling skipped a year at Yale, but upon his return, for his last Yale studio, he chose the Performing Arts Center for Cornell University in Ithaca, New York (fall 1983),[104] for which many students produced strong designs (6.14), particularly Marion Weiss (b. 1957; M.Arch 1984) (6.15, 6.16). Weiss recalls having

two sets of drawings: one was a full charcoal set and then the obligation in the Stirling studio was to do exquisite ink-on-Mylar Choisy up-views, pulled-apart axonometrics, etc. He was very demanding about any drawing having that level of rigor in what you'd share with him. I struggled with this high level of completion as a strategy moving through the semester and came up with a completely detailed scheme—plan, section, elevation, axonometric—for about six different schemes. None of which felt satisfying. I could do them; I was capable of doing them at a high level, but none of them were satisfying. It was a massive frustration. I felt that I was much more fluid in my thinking in charcoal. I had been given a notice at mid-semester, as a few people were, that I was failing. Rob Livesey was the co-teacher with Stirling and told me that I was failing, in part due to the high turnover on my schemes. So I broke away for a moment from the teleological journey with all these detailed drawings and just started drawing in charcoal—plans, sections, perspectives, all of it I designed in charcoal. It moved very fast and it made a lot of sense. I nailed it in charcoal, then I went from that to the other drawings. It remained a smart scheme but it was still unsatisfying. I hadn't had the time. So I presented, at the final review, both sets of drawings. This *horrified* Stirling. I remember Stirling being appalled at the mess of charcoal adjacent to the pristine drawings. I think we had Michael Graves, Bob Stern, maybe

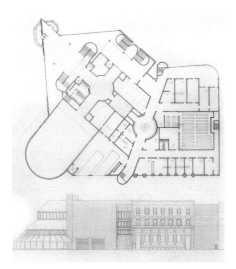

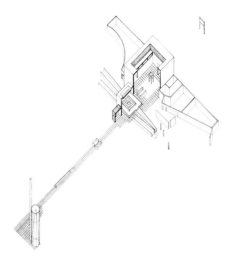

6.8 Carl Pucci (B.A. 1973, M.Arch 1976), Düsseldorf Museum of Modern Art, plan and elevation. Stirling studio (fall 1975).

6.9 Louise Braverman (M.Arch 1977), Museum of Science and Technoloy in Tehran, axonometric. Stirling studio (fall 1976).

6.10 Richard Clarke (M.Arch 1979), Staatsgalerie Stuttgart, elevation. Stirling studio (fall 1978).

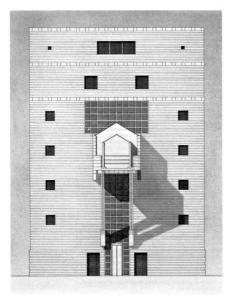

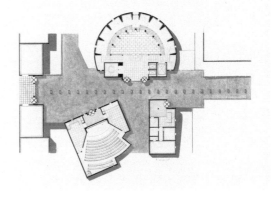

6.12 Brian Healy (M.Arch 1981), Hood Museum of Art at Dartmouth, plan. Stirling studio (fall 1980).

6.11 Robert Kahn (M.Arch 1980), Fogg Museum in Cambridge, elevation. Stirling studio (fall 1979).

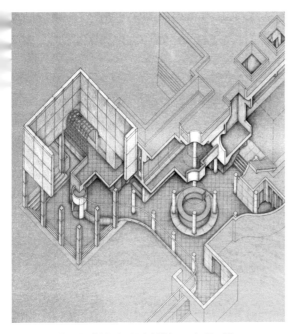

6.13 John Boecker (M.Arch 1982), Addition to the Tate Museum, axonometric. Stirling studio (fall 1981).

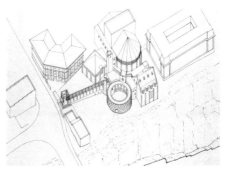

6.14 Tim Lenahan (B.A. 1980, M.Arch 1984), Cornell Performing Arts Center, axonometric. Stirling studio (fall 1983).

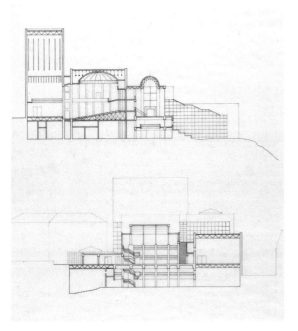

6.15 Marion Weiss (M.Arch 1984), Cornell Performing Arts Center, section. Stirling studio (fall 1983).

6.16 Marion Weiss, Cornell Performing Arts Center, charcoal sketch. Stirling studio (fall 1983).

even Richard Meier—it was an all-star lineup for the final review. Since people were really responding to the charcoal drawings and almost ignoring the ink line drawings, Jim started asking about the legitimacy of this as a design. He was not very favorable toward the charcoal. Michael Graves stood up and defended the design as embedded in the charcoal drawings.[105]

Stirling's star power as an architect extended to his studio teaching: "Jim took his responsibilities seriously," Cesar Pelli has written, "not so much to the institution—that probably didn't count for much—but his responsibilities toward the students were extremely important to him."[106] Stirling expected his students to faithfully adhere to the program and to time schedules, and to represent their ideas completely with plans, sections, elevations, and details. As Robert Kahn (b. 1950; M.Arch 1980), Stirling's student in 1978, put it: "He just showed up, and because one had so much respect for him, you produced a lot of work, and he would make very direct and astute comments about the project: 'You could do this and you could do that,' and then move on. Near the end of the semester, for some people, he would start to draw things that actually looked like images, or make concrete suggestions about how to change something, but not until near the end."[107]

Stirling appears to have adjusted his approach to best meet the needs of each student. Alexander Gorlin (b. 1955; M.Arch 1980) felt that Stirling's "critiques . . . involved inversions, or taking something that was familiar, and turning it around, or shifting it in some way that would pull it together, but in a very unexpected way."[108] Gorlin's classmate, Ulrike Wilke (b. 1955; M.Arch 1980), who went on to work for Stirling, "liked the fact that he didn't talk much." Wilke's recollections differ from Kahn's: "He sat beside you at the drawing board, took the pen and drew. I learnt from him to reduce an idea to the bare essence, and then experiment with that. He didn't hesitate to sketch what he would do; he started from what you were presenting him, but he would almost say, by drawing it, 'Look, how about that? What do you think about this?'"[109]

Stirling's star-studded juries were the high point of each school year, although Mark Girouard, Stirling's biographer, has dismissed them as "more entertainment than useful events—entertainments at least, for Jim, though the architects did not always see it that way. It was Jim as people player"[110] (6.17). Stirling loved to gather, as Audrey Matlock (b. 1951; M.Arch 1979) recalls, "the biggest powerhouses on his jury . . . and he'd have a roomful of these people, and he'd sit back. He would never criticize his students' schemes in front of anyone. He was always, if anything, defensive, or supportive. But he knew these people probably as well as they knew themselves. He would know exactly what comment to make, or what conversation to start, which would bring up a particular issue that would get someone fired up. And he'd just sit back there, this half smile on his face, and watch it happen."[111] At semester's end, after the final jury, Stirling would single out a few projects, presenting one of his neckties or a pair of his signature bright-purple socks to the student whose scheme he liked best, or to the one whose scheme was most like the one he was working on in his office. To Alexander Gorlin, Stirling "was a kind of gentle giant. Physically you would think he would be very intimidating, but he wasn't. He never pulled rank. He was very kind as a teacher, and really elicited the best from the students."[112]

Under Spiegel and Pelli, Stirling was not the wild man he'd been in the 1960s—to the disappointment of the students who seemed to know all the stories. But he did continue to eat and drink with them in the Old Heidelberg, a popular restaurant around the corner from the school, where Ulrike Wilke remembers how "he used to like his onion rings, three plates of onion rings. . . . We had good times there. He loved talking about people. He liked—I wouldn't call it gossip—but he wanted to know what was going on."[113] Audrey Matlock, who today has an international practice based in New York, has observed that Stirling was constantly probing the students for their takes on the faculty and the current heroes. "He'd get a lot out of us. 'What do you think of this? What do you think of that? How did you find Peter Eisenman on the jury?' And then he'd sit there, and his eyes would twinkle. But he never bad-mouthed anybody or gossiped himself. He'd make jokes about people but they weren't below the belt. He was careful about that. He was very cautious, actually."[114]

In spring 1973, a second endowed visiting professorship, the William Henry Bishop (1847–1928; B.A. 1867) Chair, was initiated by designating the use of a 1928 bequest that had increased in value over time.[115] This new chair served to further strengthen the visiting critic system, and in so doing further diminished the role of resident design faculty, many of whom resented the reduction in opportunities to teach advanced studios. The first Bishop Visiting Professor was Henry N. Cobb.[116] The University Council admired Spiegel's use of the visiting critic system to give the school "a 'Pluralistic' approach rather than the 'Discipline' approach of working under one great 'Form Giver.' Thus the student develops a free approach and has the opportunity to arrive at an independent philosophy."[117]

Although Spiegel was successful in redirecting the first professional program toward a greater emphasis on "responsibility and feasibility" in architectural design, he admitted to less success with the master of environmental design (M.E.D.) program initiated in 1967, which suffered because it lacked a director and even more so because there were few "students motivated and equipped to undertake advanced, independent professional and scholarly research in the broad field of environmental design." In the 1972 University Council report to President Brewster, George Dudley called attention to the program's weakness, arguing that it should be strengthened with increased support as a "program . . . for the development of architecture and urban environmental research."[118]

Spiegel was also confronted with the need to dramatically rethink the undergraduate major, which was in danger of being removed from the curriculum by Yale College due to a perceived lack of academic rigor. Moore's permissive first-year Core studio for graduate students, in which all undergraduate students majoring in architecture were also required to enroll, did not sit well with college administrators, who, according to Allan Greenberg, likened its inclusive approach to "collecting leaves in Autumn."[119] In spring 1973, Spiegel asked Greenberg to serve as director of Undergraduate Studies. Under Greenberg's leadership, the number of course offerings in Yale College was doubled but, more importantly, as Spiegel reported in 1973, "a philosophic base [was] established to guide the program's future growth, backed by a belief in architecture as a vital liberal arts vehicle."[120] Greenberg's revised curriculum began with a very popular introductory course that attracted more than twice the number of students of Moore's course. Greenberg said:

> I knew exactly what I had to do. I divided this course into two lectures a week and three projects. And I used M.Arch students as T.A.s for these three projects. The first year, I had eighty-four students, which was up from Charles Moore's thirty-five. The first day, I handed out a reading list. This was a lifetime's worth of reading. It was twelve pages. I got a 100 percent turnover of students. The first lecture, I gave everybody a pencil and paper and I said draw twelve pyramids. And of course everybody could draw a pure pyramid but then I showed them all the Aztec and Maya pyramids which have different shapes and massing and different ideas about staircases.[121]

Initially, Spiegel lauded the success of Greenberg's program, but as it grew in popularity, it became the focus of intense resentment by the faculty, some of whom believed it diverted too much of the school's already-limited human and financial resources to Yale College, others of whom, especially Moore appointees, saw it as a repudiation of their approach. Things got so bad that the University Council was moved to note that the undergraduate program provoked "sometimes traumatic inner-faculty discussion," adding "it should be basically a liberal arts program and not primarily a form of pre-architecture concentration."[122] Soon, Greenberg found himself "under siege from attacks by the full-time faculty in the architecture school" who took exception to his increasing emphasis on history—both in his professional work and in his pedagogy. Greenberg was "convinced that the faculty, even though part of a great university, would not enter into a serious dialogue related to the limitations of modernism and the architectural approach [I] advocated." As a result, Greenberg's tenure as director of Undergraduate Studies would be brief:

> I came back the next semester, the fall semester [1973], and was told that I had 430 students in my class. I went to see Herman Spiegel and I said, "Herman, I've got a problem. It would be the height of stupidity to turn these students away. These Yale College students are going to grow up and be our . . . clients. This major has to be an introduction to architecture for discerning students. It doesn't have to be a stepping stone to a career in architecture. Everybody who studies art history isn't going to be an art historian. It has to be about the discipline of architecture. I'm going to need a huge number of T.A.s and a much bigger budget."

Greenberg had "worked very closely with the Course of Study Committee [of Yale College]," in particular its chairman of the committee at that time, the economist Ray Powell.[123] Greenberg said the committee was "elated with the change that I brought about," and he reported their pleasure to Spiegel. According to Greenberg, Spiegel looked at him and said, "Allan, I'm not going to increase your salary. I'm not going to give you more T.A.s. In fact, I might even give you fewer T.A.s. And you're just going to have to figure out how to live with that." In response, Greenberg said, "Herman, I'm out of here. Good luck. Good health. God bless you. I'm out of here."[124] Greenberg's resignation from the School of Architecture took effect on June 30, 1974, but he continued at Yale in the capacity of visiting faculty at the Law School, where "the zeal and confidence with which fundamental questions, often at odds with current legal practice, were debated by law students and faculty" in a way that was not paralleled in the School of Architecture.[125]

Spiegel ended his 1973 report with a bit of self-service, as he was being reviewed for an extension for two more years in the dean's office:

> A number of top architects and many alumni have heartened me with favorable comments about the School's present activities and direction in which our program is moving. Overall I have gained a strong impression that our star is once again in the ascendancy and although today a number of different approaches to architectural education may be justified, I feel certain that on our chosen path we are leading the pack.
>
> The above may sound like "puffery," but most of it stems from an honest feeling which seems to be shared by some others.[126]

Despite Spiegel's perceived "ascendancy," the bottom line was that the school was very much still in crisis. While its programs were regaining some of their pre-1965 rigor, the severe shortage of funds—a problem that was to plague the school for another ten to fifteen years—was hampering real progress in developing a comprehensive curriculum that would provide the rich mix of courses needed to meet the expectations of the rapidly expanding character of professional practice and, even more to the point, the increasingly serious hunger for courses in history, theory, and other scholarly topics on the part of student applicants, the lack of which led many to select Harvard, Columbia, Princeton, or Pennsylvania over Yale.

From the day it opened in 1963, the A&A Building has been the physical embodiment of the school. As designed, it was a tribute to Rudolph's struggle to enrich modernism. But it was also seen by many, especially by Charles Moore, as a monument to the potential of architecture to impose, for better and worse, a single man's pedagogy in perpetuity. Moore's disposition toward an ad hoc approach to form clashed with the unforgiving structure. Caught up in the rebelliousness of the late 1960s and predisposed to a more accommodating architecture, Moore regarded the building as emblematic of an architectural establishment whose beliefs were no longer relevant. Through Moore's actions (and inaction), Rudolph's spaces became the students' spaces—the simultaneous headquarters for and target of the student revolutionaries who occupied the building. During Spiegel's tenure, as the school's curriculum slowly recovered from the events of the late 1960s, the design studios, once the focus of all attention in the grand double-height room at the building's heart, were banished to the building's least attractive spaces, including the low-ceiling, stygian subbasement. Making matters worse for both the

Art and the Architecture schools were university-imposed financial restrictions drastically curtailing maintenance. All Spiegel could do—all he was asked to do, really—was keep things together with the meager means available.

Postfire repairs had taken place in 1970 during the transition from Moore's deanship to Spiegel's, and a few changes were made to mitigate some of the building's more glaring flaws. Responsibility for the basic physical reconstruction was put in the hands of the firm of Orr, de Cossy, Winder & Associates, led by Rudolph's former student Edwin William de Cossy, who was assumed by many to know more about Rudolph's work than anyone else. Out of deference to his mentor, de Cossy wanted to adhere closely to the original vision for the building. When asked why Rudolph himself wasn't hired to undertake the renovations, he replied that the university "made it very clear that they weren't about to have him do a damned thing for Yale anymore." De Cossy did meet with Rudolph to discuss the renovations, but there was hardly a sense of collaboration: "I asked for his input which he just informally gave me. I showed him some of my ideas and he commented about them and then I went on from there."[127]

The most controversial change to the building made by de Cossy was the highly visible addition of exterior sunscreens, replacing the cargo netting originally specified to combat the glare and heat gain caused by the extensive south- and east-facing, untinted, single-pane windows (6.18). De Cossy and Rudolph "discussed the sunscreens" and Rudolph, apparently, thought them a good idea. It's likely that they were modeled after the similar screens Rudolph used on the Jewett Arts Center at Wellesley College (1958). De Cossy "thought they'd look well on the building. One of the things that I felt about that building was that the glass was altogether too apparent and that it read under most light conditions as being so solid that it detracted from the anatomy of the building."[128] Many others were not so sure, believing that the sunscreens scarred the building worse than the fire. While the sunscreens may have helped with heat gain, they ultimately proved to be a maintenance problem when the fastenings devised to attach them to the building developed problems.

Elizabeth Plater-Zyberk, Andrés Duany, and David Schwarz believe that theirs was the first class to re-appreciate the building. According to Duany, "The class before us [who entered in fall 1970, when the building was still a shambles] was ideologically against Rudolph. . . . It was our class that said, 'This is really pretty cool.'"[129] Duany believes that his class "was really either non-ideological architecturally, or multi-ideological," loving "Charles Moore's stuff" and Roche-Dinkeloo's New Haven Coliseum. "It wasn't just,

'Well, ideologically, I accept everything.' It wasn't that. It was, we were terribly excited about everything."[130] David Schwarz's appreciation for the building was instant: "I think the first thing that made me interested in Yale was the building. The Rudolph Building, which I adored then and still adore. . . . I think it is a tour-de-force of architecture. Far and away, Rudolph's best building."[131] After graduating, Schwarz would work for Rudolph in New York before relocating to Washington, D.C., to embark on a successful career specializing in traditional architecture.[132]

Despite the renovations, Schwarz believed that the building was "extraordinarily good at resisting attempts to deface it. And even as bad as it was during the time I was there, with closing up the holes [i.e., closing the light monitors to create additional floor space] and doing this, that, and the other thing, the building still always reads through."[133] Like others from his generation of students, William McDonough remembers the Art and Architecture Building fondly, but not without reservations. He remembers "brushing asbestos off your drawings and getting your cornea scratched . . . and going to the hospital screaming in terror and pain and wanting to roll up on the ground and not be able to move from the terror and the pain."[134] Despite the building's capacity to inflict physical harm, it did have an admirable "heroic aspect." Although architecture students began to re-appreciate the building, the art students continued to resent its aggressive mass and what they believed to be its inappropriate spaces—even after the double-height studio celebrating the community of the architectural studio was given over to them, which they elected to divide up into locked private cubicles. Nor did the art historians have much use for the building, finding the library ill-suited to concentrated study.

Plagued by graffiti, as well as an indifference to reasonable house-keeping on the part of the students, the building was a challenge for the beleaguered maintenance staff. Following a 1972 visit, an architect from Columbus, Georgia, wrote to Spiegel to express his dismay about its physical condition: "The most touted of buildings of the past decade was a filthy mess. What went wrong? What does Yale intend to do about it?"[135] In his reply, Spiegel revealed his own ambivalent attitude toward the building: "Be assured that yours is not the first communication made to me on this subject," he wrote, before promptly placing blame on the building's design—"such as the choice of materials for floors, wall, and ceilings which precipitate dusts of one kind or another and lack of adequate storage space"—and what he referred to as "the do-nothing maintenance crew defended by a strong local union." He also derided changes supposedly made without his knowledge,

414

including the addition of a sprinkler system with exposed pipes in the exhibition hall, and changes made to adapt the building to the needs of the Art School, "which are painful for an architect to contemplate." Spiegel pointed to "some interim measures for modest improvement, including the remodeling of the corner of the third floor for my offices and the cleaning and painting of parts of the building this summer by a student work-crew."[136] Spiegel copied his letter to high-level administrators Henry Broude, George Langdon, and John. F. Embersits, director of University Operations, who lost little time in blasting back to the dean, whom he addressed as "Herm": "Your charge that part of the problem" lay with a "do-nothing maintenance crew defended by a strong local union is pure, unadulterated bullshit." Embersits, who had six years behind him dealing with the "recurring and extensive problems" in the building, stated that the university had spent "well in excess of $1,000,000 [approximately $5.7 million in 2015] in capital costs and hundreds of thousands in operating cost to try to prove the theory that a few sane, hardworking individuals can offset the trashing tendencies of a building full of budding geniuses. Regrettably, we have failed and will continue to fail." After outlining the pressures being placed on the university to install equipment and to initiate procedures that, had they been in place, might have prevented the 1969 fire, Embersits promised to establish a regular maintenance schedule, provided the school could undertake to "exercise a discipline over its constituencies."[137]

Further difficulties with the building arose in 1974, when Robert C. Kaufmann, arts librarian, reported eye irritation that was quickly attributed to flaking particles of asbestos, the material Rudolph had specified to enclose the building's ceiling plenums. Kaufmann's complaint precipitated a new crisis that would further damage the building's reputation. Doctors from the Medical School, called in to investigate the problem, enlisted several students to wear "small machines on their belts with battery operated pumps sucking air through snorkel tubes clipped to their shirt collars and incorporating airborne particulate counters to monitor . . . exposure to asbestos fallout."[138] After two months of study, a safe method for removing the seventy thousand square feet of asbestos ceilings was developed, reducing the building to little more than a shell. Orr, de Cossy, Winder were once again retained to heal the wounds, but Roger T. Jones (b. 1950; M.Arch 1977), who served on a committee formed to consult on post-asbestos renovations, was not impressed with their proposals. Jones remembered the "look of horror and sickness" on the face of "respected and somewhat feared" faculty member John Fowler when Orr, de Cossy, Winder presented their proposal to seal up all the light wells with new floor slabs, in an effort to provide more usable space. Fowler had "worked on

6.17 Stirling jury (fall 1978). Bill Mead (M.Arch 1978), Will Paxon (M.Arch 1978), and Wendell Wickerham (M.Arch 1978) stand behind a seated Cesar Pelli. Seated front row (from left to right): Fred Clarke, Robert A. M. Stern, George Ranalli, unidentified, Giancarlo de Carlo, Henry Cobb, and Fred Koetter. Middle row: unidentified, Shao Ling Chen (standing, M.Arch 1978), Jeff Goldberg (M.Arch 1979), and James Stirling. Top row (standing): three unidentified men, John Kuipers (M.Arch 1978), unidentified, and Paul Lytle (M.Arch 1978). Mac Ball (M.Arch 1978) is on the floor with his back to camera.

6.18 Exterior sunscreens added to the Art and Architecture Building (ca. 1970).

6.19 Fluorescent lighting installed in the Art and Architecture Building studios (ca. 1997).

the A&A in Rudolph's office before joining the School, and . . . felt especially strong[ly] about it."[139] Yet despite his protest, the university moved forward with the renovation, although the new floor insertions were done in such a way that they could be reversed in the future, as was the case after the Art School moved out in 2000. After the asbestos removal and the space-gaining renovations, the building was no longer a health hazard, but the absence of hung ceilings, revealing exposed piping and concrete slabs never meant to be seen, and the introduction of evenly distributed, industrial-strength fluorescent lighting in place of Rudolph's incandescent bulb-strips in light coves eliminated virtually any sense of dramatic mystery that the building's interiors once had (6.19).

The asbestos problem had one positive side effect: it led to a somewhat more equitable distribution of space between the Art and Architecture schools. After the fire, the architecture students, assigned ten thousand square feet less space than in 1963, were scattered throughout the building, with two upper years occupying most, but not all, of the sixth floor, and the first year ensconced in the basement and subbasement. Prior to the asbestos crisis, the University Council expressed a concern that "the *space* problem is still vastly unworthy of Yale," citing as a particular instance the inability to find a place to accommodate a donated computer, around which the school could build a subcenter devoted to computer graphics. The space crunch was "badly blunting the new momentum of the School toward its proper future mix of teaching and research."[140]

Architecture students aired their concerns about overcrowding, petitioning Spiegel, Art School Dean William Bailey, and Provost Hanna Holborn Gray for use of the seventh-floor studio then being used for undergraduate painting classes, in order to liberate the first year from the subbasement. The students' petition had originally been Spiegel's idea. In Machiavellian style, he concocted a story of potential student rebelliousness, holding out the possibility that they might demonstrate at a reception for all incoming graduate and professional students scheduled to be held at the president's house. As far as Roger Jones knew, "no one had even thought" of a protest, "except Herman, of course. But the days of student revolt and craziness were so fresh in everyone's memory that it may not have sounded too implausible," so that in fall 1975 the school got the use of the seventh floor—and the undergraduates were banished to the recently abandoned Fence Club.[141]

By the late 1970s, even the Moore-era alumni who had reviled the building began to appreciate it. In a 1978 interview, Doug Michels, who as a student under Moore had been "all for whatever was going on that was permissive and

. . . against [the A&A]" had come to the conclusion that he and his classmates were wrong: "We had misinterpreted it, and we could have learned a lot more . . . about the essence of reality and nature and the things we should have been studying there, rather than going around and painting paint on wall[s], and floors and ceilings—not that that wasn't good fun and that we didn't learn from it." Michels, by 1978, believed that the building "was blamed unfairly . . . [for] being the cause of many things [when] in fact it was the victim."[142]

Spiegel was to serve only one term as dean. Unquestionably, he had done much to restore the school's reputation. Certainly, he proved himself an effective administrator. While many alumni resented the fact that he wasn't an architect, most had to admit that he had done a good job righting the ship, but thought it was time to have a new dean who would be a practicing architect with a strong point of view, someone who would provide a focus for the freewheeling program. Ray Gindroz found Spiegel to be at once the opposite of Charles Moore and "the same in other ways. He had the same intellectual openness. . . . But he was very disciplined and organized, which Charles was not. And he drew lines in the sand to establish frameworks within which this flexibility would operate. So out of the chaos of the end of the '60s, [and the] beginning of the '70s, Herman, without diminishing any of the diversity, introduced order into the school."[143] Gindroz's recent assessment is similar to that of the 1977 University Council Report of the Committee on Architecture, submitted by its new chairman, Atlanta-based architect Cecil A. Alexander (1918–2013; B.A. 1940), who noted that Spiegel "took over a school in disarray with even its continuation in doubt" but "leaves it functioning well, accepted and supported by the administration."[144]

In his September 30, 1975, letter of "Personal Commentary" written to President Brewster, Spiegel gave no indication that he was nearing the end of his term as dean—perhaps because he had not been so informed. Instead he expressed appreciation for an increased budget and for improvements to the "space problems, which have given me constant anxiety since I became Dean four years ago."[145] But Spiegel's September 1976 annual report made clear that it would be his last as dean. In it, he volunteered his services to help raise the school's endowment, which Spiegel believed was the lowest among the university's graduate and professional schools, as part of the larger "Campaign for Yale," though regrettably his efforts did not meet with much success.[146] He also responded to alumni grumblings that he was responsible for the school's seeming lack of direction and that he did not provide the strong core of belief needed in a program that deliberately embraced a diverse approach to architecture, writing somewhat defensively that he was concluding his term "with a clear conscience." Taking pride in the "monumental strides" the school made under his watch that led to "international recognition and acceptance of Yale's pluralistic and humanistic approach to the teaching of architecture," he drew particular attention to the visit of the National Architectural Accrediting Board in December 1975, which "suggested to me that other schools of architecture could very well consider the Yale School of Architecture as a model of where architectural education should be going today."[147]

7

A Brand-New School 1977–1984

"The task of architecture is the creation of human environments. It is both an expression of human values and a context for human activity. Through the design process, architecture addresses the interrelated environmental, behavioral, and cultural issues that underlie the organization of built form. The student of architecture is called upon to direct sensitivity, imagination, and intellect to the physical significance of these fundamental issues in designing a coherent environment for people. Architectural design as a comprehensive creative process is the focus of the Yale School of Architecture.

"The objectives of the School of Architecture reflect the view that architecture is an intellectual discipline, both an art and a profession."

Bulletin of Yale University, School of Architecture, 1977–78

It is not clear whether Herman Spiegel was asked to step down or whether, as some have claimed, recognizing his limitations, he did so voluntarily. In either case, the search process for a successor was nowhere near as long or complicated as some had been in the past. Cesar Pelli very quickly emerged as a leading candidate for the job. Indeed, it was Spiegel himself who proposed that Pelli, who had a successful term as Davenport Visiting Professor in spring 1972 and as Bishop Visiting Professor in fall 1974, succeed him.[1] "I think you'll be the only appropriate replacement," Spiegel told Pelli.[2] President Brewster agreed. "I love Yale," Pelli remembers. "And I knew Yale. I knew how Yale was run, how independent the dean at Yale is, and how much support the dean got from Mother Yale."[3]

Cesar Pelli (7.1) served as the third dean of the Yale School of Architecture from January 1, 1977, until June 30, 1984.[4] Initially, his appointment raised eyebrows. His close association with Eero Saarinen, then not held in particularly high esteem by the academy, seemed problematic to some, and even more so, his corporate architectural practice; in Los Angeles he had been director of design at Daniel, Mann, Johnson & Mendenhall (DMJM, known colloquially as Dim Jim) and partner for design at Gruen Associates. Nonetheless, at the time of his appointment, though not exactly part of the East Coast scene, Pelli was generally admired by important people connected with Yale, especially J. Irwin Miller (1909–2004; B.A. 1931), a member of the Yale Corporation, who had first encountered him when he was a key associate in Saarinen's office.

Plunging into the job with enthusiasm, Pelli saw the school as an institution primed for positive change.[5] Commenting on his predecessors, the normally circumspect Pelli has allowed, in retrospect, that Charles Moore had "lost control of the school. It went to hell." Then, under Spiegel, "it took years just to get the machine in working shape again. But there was no architecture being created or discussed. So this was like a brand-new school."[6]

Born in Argentina in 1926, Cesar Pelli grew up in a family who cultivated an awareness of the world beyond their home country—a cosmopolitanism that was at the time atypical for an Argentine household. After graduating from the School of Architecture at the Universidad Nacional de Tucumán in 1950, Pelli came to the United States, earning a master's degree from the University of Illinois, then staying on to teach for a year before accepting an offer to join Saarinen's Bloomfield Hills, Michigan, office in 1954. Pelli and his wife, the historian and landscape designer Diana Balmori, quickly adapted to their new environment. "Before we knew it," he says, "we were Americans."[7] He remained in the Saarinen office for ten years, moving with the firm to Connecticut in 1961 to serve as project designer for Stiles and Morse Residential Colleges at Yale, which were designed by Saarinen in 1959 but not completed until 1963, two years after his death.[8]

Pelli left Eero Saarinen & Associates in 1964 and embarked on a career as a designer in large corporate firms, but unlike many designers in corporate practice, he was able to develop a distinct individual approach that spoke to two separate, sometimes even opposing constituencies: the public-at-large and "a thoroughly enlightened select group of architects and critics . . . who are really interested in subtle issues of architecture."[9] Pelli earned the respect of the academic architectural community, not only with teaching stints at Yale but also by taking an active role in the effort to bring together disparate Los Angeles architects as part of the "Silvers" group, formed along with Saarinen office alumni Anthony Lumsden (1928–2011) and Paul Kennon (1934–1990), and Yale-trained Los Angeles architects including Tim Vreeland, Eugene Kupper (b. 1939; M.Arch 1967), and Craig Hodgetts. The formation of the group was triggered as a response to the "Whites" and "Grays" then rising in prominence on the East Coast. The name "Silvers" was chosen to reflect the preference of some of its members for high-tech, slick-surfaced architecture.[10] The new group, formed to host a conference at UCLA alternately referred to as "Four Days in May" or "White and Gray Meet Silver," presented a decidedly ahistorical, commercial, and techno-centric counterpoint to the more formalist and historicist agendas of their White and Gray guests, illustrating an early difference between East Coast and West Coast architects that largely continues to this day.[11] Charles Jencks, then teaching for part of each year at UCLA, summarized the position of the Silvers: "A tough-minded pragmatism which treats each job as an opportunity to develop and celebrate economic forces no matter what they are: a commitment to organizational orders which emphasize linear circulation, the extruded section, and isotropic warehouse space: the covering of this space with flat membranes of an homogeneous material whether glass, nylon or brick: the tendency for polished surfaces whether these are brown, blue or, most appropriately silver."[12] The Silvers disbanded their loose affiliation in 1976 but, as architect Todd Gannon has written, they "made a lasting impact on architectural discourse in Los Angeles by generating significant architectural debate—and whetting an appetite for further conversation—in a city that previously simply hadn't had any."[13] Though Pelli was known in academic circles as a Silver, professionally he was most associated with another color—blue. When completed in 1975, his Pacific Design Center in Los Angeles, an enormous structure sheathed in blue-tinted glass with the "purity, grandeur, and brute force of an ocean liner," became an instant

7.1   Cesar Pelli (ca. 1973).

7.2   Cesar Pelli with Gruen Associates, Pacific Design Center, Los Angeles (1975).

7.3   Cesar Pelli with Gruen Associates, Music Center for Yale University (1975).

landmark in its otherwise nondescript West Hollywood neighborhood.[14] At the time of his Yale appointment, the building, affectionately known as the "Blue Whale," was the architect's most acclaimed work (7.2).[15]

Pelli's departure from Los Angeles was viewed as a loss to local prestige. According to *Los Angeles Times* writer John Dreyfuss, Pelli, "a magnetic force in attracting long-sparse recognition to Southern California building design," was valued by the architectural community "as a man of exceptional charm, poise, tact and discretion, a man who disagrees without being disagreeable, one who takes firm stands without offending."[16] Thomas Hines, a professor of history at UCLA specializing in architecture and planning, concurred: "Cesar is not a big talker. He's a listener and a doer, but when he does talk people listen. He makes strong statements without hurting people."[17] He was perceived to have few enemies, "a rarity in the captious world of architects."[18] Asked to comment on this, Pelli smiled "benignly" as he explained that "we architects are very polite about our cut-throat competition."[19]

Though based in Los Angeles for more than ten years prior to his return to New Haven, Pelli had kept up with the Yale scene. Besides serving as visiting professor, he was also commissioned by the university, on the strength of his Saarinen connections and friendship with Irwin Miller, to prepare designs for a new building opposite Silliman College on a midblock site between Cross Campus and Wall Street (7.3).[20] As proposed, the unrealized, one-hundred-thousand-square-foot Yale University Music Center would have gathered into one structure all of Yale's disparate music-related programs, providing classroom space, a music library, practice space, recording studios, and a performance hall. The project fell victim to the financial crisis that would affect most university initiatives in the early 1980s; the crisis also roughly spanned the period of Pelli's deanship.[21]

Asked at the time of his appointment to explain his decision to accept the position of dean and relocate to New Haven, Pelli stated that he found the architecture community in the East to be denser, more critical, better informed, and more secure in its ideas than that of the West. In the East, "as your ideas and thoughts develop, they are being examined. I feel that this, at this moment in my life, just may add another level of pressure, of excitement of intellectual discipline that would be quite good."[22] Pelli's decision to come east was also pragmatic. He realized that the big, prestige projects he coveted typically went to East Coast architects, particularly those in New York or New Haven, where his friends and former Saarinen colleagues Kevin Roche (b. 1922; D.F.A.H. 1995), and John Dinkeloo were located. To this point, Pelli probably also based his decision on a hunch that were he located in New

Haven, he would improve his chances at being hired for the overhaul and significant expansion of the Museum of Modern Art in New York, a project for which he was being considered along with I. M. Pei and Romaldo Giurgola. The move paid off, and on January 27, 1977, less than a month after taking over the dean's office, Pelli was awarded the commission, "one of the most sought-after in the country."[23]

Philip Johnson, who had previously petitioned Pelli to lead Harvard's Graduate School of Design when José Luis Sert stepped down as dean in 1964, was ecstatic about his appointment to Yale: "His wit, his brilliance, his design, his intellect all combine to make him a leader."[24] Charles Moore, who was teaching at both Yale and UCLA, seemed a bit less enthusiastic, deeming Pelli "my favorite of the big shape modern architects."[25]

From the first, Pelli surprised the students by proving himself to be more than a "corporate architect." Once he was installed in the dean's office, few were willing to deny his effectiveness in the job, which he conducted in a "strict, business-like manner," delegating "authority with awesome efficiency."[26] Heather Willson Cass had him as her thesis advisor in 1974. "It was a wonderful experience," she remembers. "He's a superb critic and a kind and thoughtful person. It was particularly interesting because the scale of work that he was doing was like nothing that any of us had ever seen."[27] James Kruhly, enrolled in Pelli's spring 1972 studio, saw his approach as an example of one of Yale's great strengths: "People looked at what you accomplished in terms of where you started, not in terms of some prescription and some standard that was given. They looked at the distance you traveled." Pelli's studio project called for the design of a new library facing the New Haven Green, replacing Cass Gilbert's existing 1911 structure. Kruhly "got completely fascinated with the idea of the facade on the Green, [but] in the end" designed "a mediocre building [with] a really beautiful, interesting facade" (7.4). Kruhly remembers telling Pelli that he was "really falling behind on the building," to which Pelli replied, "Keep going. If you don't have a building at the end, fine." At the final review, Kruhly remembers one juror saying, "I like your facade but in the back it looks like a VA hospital."[28]

When Pelli arrived, the university was tackling serious problems: unchecked crime was rampant in its nearly ungovernable host city, the local economy was in a downward tailspin, and the faltering endowment continued to generate insufficient income.[29] Like Spiegel before him, Pelli would have few resources to implement curricular reform. In fact, he was asked to reduce the school's operating budget a little more each year during his tenure.[30] Not only did this mean that no new permanent faculty could be added to the school, it also meant that Pelli had to cut the budget for visiting critics—one of its largest expenses. Although he did his best to strike a balance between visiting instructors and the resentful resident faculty, his real interest lay in the visitors and their studios, leaning on professionals who, flattered to be invited to teach at Yale as visitors, accepted minimal compensation. Pelli's charm and Yale's reputation proved to be effective bargaining chips and, in his own view, he "got the very best people in the world."[31]

To students, and especially to the faculty, Pelli's management style was a lesson in itself. According to Fred Clarke (b. 1947), who became Pelli's professional partner in 1977, Pelli had a "unique way of doing architecture by delegating vast amounts of responsibility. He's in control, though he doesn't think he has to do it all."[32] Pelli's management style served him equally well in the dean's office as in his professional office. He was decisive, capable of multitasking, and also a keen observer of people. When Ray Gindroz first met Pelli, the new dean told him right away: "Look, this is a school with a great tradition and a very dynamic program. I'm not going to change anything for the first year, I want to see how it works because it seems to work very well!" After a full year on the job, however, as Pelli would tell Gindroz, "This is a school for thoroughbreds . . . and we need to refine what it is."[33]

Like Rudolph, and for a brief time Moore, Pelli established a professional office in New Haven. Consequently, he was very much around, and students appreciated his presence in the school, where he was able to exert a strong influence as its gravitating force. Students quickly sensed that the new dean was a very different type of practitioner-academic than Moore. "Pelli's magnetic power," the *Yale Daily News* reported, "derives from his professional background. He is not the independent, academic, 'crazy architect type' like Charles W. Moore. . . . He is more the 'high-tech, corporate employed architect' with many professional connections."[34] In short, he seemed to be an "enigmatic combination of a warm, honest humanitarian and a tough-as-nails, exacting dictator. Cesar Pelli runs a tight ship."[35] Indeed, John Kaliski (b. 1956; B.A. 1978, M.Arch 1982) found it "nearly impossible to disagree with him."[36]

Pelli also proved effective with alumni and the profession-at-large. More than any of the school's leaders since George Howe, Pelli took seriously the need to generate and disseminate knowledge beyond the school itself, by using the seminar room, the lecture hall, publications, and exhibitions to ratchet up the discourse. Assisted by King-lui Wu, he invited a diverse roster of speakers to the school, in 1979–80 alone fielding twenty-six public lectures. Speakers included architects Frank Gehry, Jaquelin Robertson,

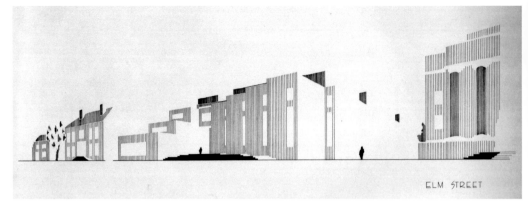

7.4 James Oleg Kruhly (M.Arch 1973), A New Haven Library, Pelli Studio (spring 1972).

7.5 Left: Carpenter's Company shield; right: Yale School of Architecture Shield.

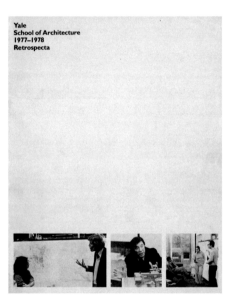

Yale
School of Architecture
1977–1978
Retrospecta

7.7 The premiere issue of *Retrospecta* (1978).

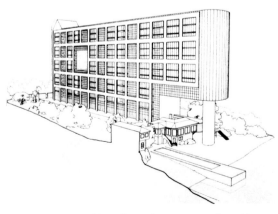

7.6 Arquitectonica, Atlantis Condominiums, published in the Yale School of Architecture Calendar (fall 1979).

Stanley Tigerman, James Polshek, Allan Greenberg, and Clovis Heimsath (b. 1930; B.A. 1952, M.Arch 1957), as well as historians Gavin Stamp, David Watkin, Barbara Miller Lane, and Vincent Scully.[37] The school also hosted evening conversations.

Gavin Macrae-Gibson (b. 1955; M.Arch 1979), a native of England and graduate of the University of Cambridge who would teach design and theory at the school for ten years while establishing an independent practice in New York, feels "very lucky to have been there right at that moment because everything was breaking open." According to Macrae-Gibson, Pelli encouraged people "to really break out in all directions. That's what we felt. You had a lecture by Eisenman one day, Colin Rowe the next, then Bob [Stern] would come up, and then I had Giancarlo de Carlo who is the most totally ideological modernist you could ever imagine. And that was a perfectly acceptable point of view as well. So you had a very challenging intellectual environment."[38]

The public lectures were a boon to the school's reputation as a center of discourse, but Pelli's most enduring contribution to the school's claim to once again be living up to its reputation as a force in architectural culture was the reorganization and revitalization of *Perspecta,* the languishing student-edited journal that had only published two issues in the 1970s. For all intents and purposes, Pelli recalls, "*Perspecta* was dead."[39] There wasn't even a single issue of the journal in the dean's office. Pelli quickly rectified the situation, soliciting funds and restructuring its editorial board. The result of his efforts was the reemergence of the magazine as it had been in its prefire heyday—a widely acknowledged barometer of contemporary architectural thinking.[40]

To enhance the image of the school within the university and to bolster the self-esteem of the students and faculty, Pelli also redesigned the school's coat-of-arms, with a design inspired by that of the Carpenter's Company in Philadelphia (7.5). This may sound trivial, but it was much appreciated by students participating in the university's elaborate commencement exercises. More importantly, Pelli forged links with other university programs, notably implementing in 1980–81 a joint program between the school and the newly instituted School of Organization and Management, enabling students to receive both a master's degree in public and private management (M.P.P.M.) and a master of architecture in four years' time. Given his background in corporate architecture, it's surprising that the joint program was not Pelli's idea, but rather, as he recalls, one "brought to me by some students. . . . I thought it was a great idea so I talked with the dean of the School of Management who also thought it was a great idea."[41] The joint program continues to this day.

Pelli refocused the series of thematic calendars featuring the work of graduates begun by Spiegel, broadening their content to include not only alumni work, but also the work of current students interspersed with occasional mini-essays such as Vincent Scully's on Louis I. Kahn in the April–June 1979 calendar devoted to the "Architecture of the Spirit."[42] The presentations of alumni work in the calendars provide invaluable snapshots of the shift in emphasis in the profession from Charles Moore–inspired shack-like informality to more disciplined formalism and an incipient Classicism, as well as an interest in environmental sustainability.[43] The calendar's student editors were attuned to what was new and interesting among alumni work. For example, the fall 1979 calendar featured drawings for the Atlantis Condominiums designed by the newly formed Miami-based firm Arquitectonica (7.6), in which three of the five partners held Yale degrees: Andrés Duany, Elizabeth Plater-Zyberk, and Hervin A. R. Romney (b. 1941; M.E.D. 1975). Significantly, these calendars listed Pelli as both dean and director of studies, making it clear that he was the school's administrative head as well as the architect of its curriculum. In 1977, Pelli augmented the calendar mailings with a new publication, *Retrospecta,* a student-produced annual highlighting some of each year's accomplishments. What began as a modest, seven-page pamphlet (7.7) over the years has developed in scope and size to become a comprehensive record of student work and of the diversity of viewpoints represented in the studios and classrooms. Initial editions tended to emphasize the studios taught by visiting critics, although studios led by resident faculty were also represented. The calendar series was discontinued in 1985.

In 1977, the same year that Pelli became dean, George Ranalli (b. 1946), who had initially been hired by Herman Spiegel, began an exhibitions program in the second-floor gallery—the use of which was severely limited for the Architecture School, in keeping with an agreement with the Art School made by Moore and Weaver. In addition to highlighting the work of faculty, alumni, and students, Ranalli's exhibitions also presented other important contemporary work, frequently accompanied by modest but meticulously designed catalogues. For his inaugural show, Ranalli curated an exhibition of Paul Rudolph's drawings, including many of the original drawings for the A&A. "I called Paul and said, 'I know you have bad feelings about this but would you be willing to have a show?'" remembers Ranalli. "He said, 'Well, alright. I might be willing to do it. But I don't know if I'll be willing to go.' I knew I'd have to work on him. He was a bristly guy. He was tough as nails. But we put a show together."[44] Rudolph himself designed the installation, which saw the gallery completely covered in drawings mounted on double-sided dividers hung in space to display more drawings. "It was a bit excessive," says Ranalli, "but that was Paul."[45] Though Rudolph could indeed be "tough as nails," when opening night came around, he revealed a more sensitive side. "Paul had tears streaming down his face" when he saw the A&A.[46] "Look what they did to my building," he lamented. "It's a mess."[47] His building may have been defaced, but he was warmly welcomed by the students, and the show was a success.

Pelli gave Ranalli considerable curatorial latitude as, for example, in the January 14–February 1, 1980, exhibition of twenty-one young architects who, in the words of *Yale Daily News* writer Julie Peters, constituted a group emerging "out of the fumbling confusion of post-Modernist architecture." The exhibit included Susana Torre, Robert Livesey, Mark Rosenstein, Coy Howard, and Frank Israel, among others. As Peters noted, the architects "have nothing in common. If ever placed in a room together they would probably fling streams of architectural jargon at each other, dissecting and destroying (as architects usually do)."[48] Ranalli also organized an exhibition (November 1–December 3, 1982) of the work of the high-style, high-tech corporate modernist Helmut Jahn (b. 1940), who would serve as Davenport Visiting Professor in spring 1983, as well as a show (October 31–December 2, 1983) of the work of Jahn's design opposite, the Italian architect and furniture designer Gaetano Pesce (b. 1939).[49] Ranalli's exhibition program also included a show (October 26–December 4, 1981) dedicated to the work of Raimund Abraham (1933–2010), best known for his evocative drawings, and the first display in the United States (October 22–November 23, 1984) of Carlo Scarpa's (1906–1978) drawings of the Brion Cemetery.[50] Students also organized exhibits, such as the fall 1981 show, *An Ideology for Making Architecture,* curated by four members of the class of 1982—Joseph Chadwick (b. 1955), J. Peter Devereaux (b. 1956), Thomas Kligerman (b. 1957), and Theodore Mahl (b. 1955). This exhibit examined the work of six architects or firms influenced by Louis I. Kahn: Roy Vollmer; Levinson, Zaprauskis Associates; C. William Fox Associates; Peter Millard; Roth & Moore Architects (Harold Roth, b. 1934, M.Arch 1957; William Moore, b. 1941, B.A. 1963, M.Arch 1966); and Marshall D. Meyers.[51]

Ever the diplomat, Pelli managed to be in tune with the post-heroic spirit of the late 1960s and early 1970s, while at the same time favoring stricter discipline rooted in an enlightened pragmatism, helping students to move from an intuitive formalism toward a learned approach to the discipline. As the editors of *Perspecta* 16—the first issue published after Pelli's reorganization—put it: "While one can invent form, one cannot totally invent meaning. Meaning accumulates through time."[52] Although Pelli exhibited a surprising (to some) tolerance for academic discourse, he never embraced it as a substitute for disciplinary skill, telling students that "When artistic impulse is supported by, rather than runs counter to, the other realities of your problem, you will be developing an architecture that will last."[53] For someone perceived to be a committed modernist, Pelli embraced precedent as a key to creativity. In an interview published in *Perspecta* 19, Pelli made his position explicit: "In a way, all architecture depends on collective contribution. No architect invents architecture. Learning from immediate precedent is critical, because that is our tie with our past and with our near contemporaries. In this manner we become part of a historical continuum. When we design a building to be as fresh and new as possible, all we have really done is reinterpret ideas, thoughts, formal devices, and solutions that others, including, perhaps, ourselves, have used before. We give them a new twist or add a few new things, but most of that design comes from the past. Nobody can invent all that we need to solve the simplest design problem in one lifetime."[54]

Elizabeth Burns Gamard (b. 1958; M.Arch 1984) remembers it becoming "clear early on that you needed to be able to quote history to have any credibility."[55] Pelli encouraged the students' growing engagement with history and, to a lesser extent, theory in seminars that brought prominent members of the younger generation to the school, eventually collecting transcriptions of the proceedings into two volumes.[56] Invited speakers included Kenneth Frampton, Michael Graves, Charles Jencks, Robert A. M. Stern, Stanley Tigerman, Robert Venturi, Richard Weinstein, Peter Eisenman, Allan Greenberg, John Hejduk, Charles Moore, and Elia Zenghelis, with each giving a public lecture the night before the seminar in order to lay the groundwork for discussion.

Building on the success of these seminars, Pelli initiated a course in architectural theory taught by Patrick Pinnell, then located in Washington, D.C., and practicing in partnership with Heather Cass. Pinnell believes his selection was a politically astute move by Pelli, who chose him because, as a recent Yale graduate, he was "somebody who knew the secret handshakes . . . and was sympathetic about the place," but was also someone who "had been consorting with Peter [Eisenman] and Kenneth Frampton and Colin Rowe" at the Institute for Architecture and Urban Studies (IAUS), a New York–based think tank with strong connections to Europe. As a result, Pinnell "was regarded as somebody who might know about this stuff but still be safe."[57] In 1982, the following year, the recently graduated Gavin Macrae-Gibson was also invited to teach theory.

Coming from a rather academic background at Cambridge [England], I found that the supporting classes were not good—especially the more academic ones like history and theory. And I said the school needs a theory survey class, so I suggested doing a survey of great books from Laugier to the present. And that's what I did. I developed that course, which subsequently became a larger course that had three or four people teaching it. But I actually started it. And the amazing thing was, I was right. The school was completely starved for theory, for an under-standing of theory from a historical point of view. The first day it was oversubscribed. We had to turn people away. We could've had twice as many people in the class.[58]

Pelli took particular pride in the school's high-level engagement with theory, and wisely used it to impress Yale's scholarly new president (1978–86), A. Bartlett Giamatti (1938–1989; B.A. 1960, Ph.D. 1964), with the knowledge that "the interest of our students at this moment is taking a strong turn toward intellectual analysis and logical constructs for evaluating esthetic attitudes in architecture. This is something that has grown to form a major component of our students' self-perceived needs; it was almost non-existent when I took over this office."[59]

Pelli took a direct interest in admissions, leading to what Macrae-Gibson, an Admissions Committee member under Pelli, recalls as a "very diverse entrance policy," inviting students the likes of whom hadn't been seen since the heady days of Charles Moore. "What struck you was that these were not just architects," recalls Macrae-Gibson. "You had dancers and filmmakers, and people with MBAS."[60] Nonetheless, even the dancers and film-makers had to submit portfolios, although they were often a bit unorthodox. "This portfolio had to set you apart from the others," says Macrae-Gibson. "If you were a dancer, there had to be something about the dance that was very spatial, maybe very organized in some particular way that had to do with making space or suggesting space. On the Admissions Committee that was what we looked for. There was a lot of discussion about, 'Does this have any architectural merit despite the fact that it is an excellent portfolio?' So it was very diverse."[61]

Not all the new students came from outside traditional fields. Many had been immersed in architecture as undergraduates and had come to Yale because they were sure to find interesting visiting faculty. Robert Kahn, a graduate of Washington University of St. Louis, where he had begun to study architecture, told a reporter from the *Yale Daily News:* "I can't think of one architect I'd like to study under who hasn't been here or isn't coming soon."[62] Marion Weiss, who had studied architecture as an undergraduate at the University of Virginia, went about deciding where to get her professional education in a deliberate manner. Weiss—now Graham Chair Professor of Architecture at the University of Pennsylvania and partner in the firm Weiss/Manfredi, notable for such significant projects as the Olympic Sculpture Park in Seattle and student centers at Smith and Barnard colleges—considered Harvard, Columbia, Princeton, Penn, and Rice in addition to Yale.

> I visited all the schools. I felt a bit of a chill at Harvard, not just physically, not quite knowing where the "there" there was. At Penn, where I [now] teach, I had challenges with the building, which I still have challenges teaching in because it's a building that throws the energy to the periphery rather than to the center, although its model, if you were to cut it in section, shares some relationship to the A&A Building. . . . Then I went to Princeton, where I ran into Alan Plattus, who was a student there. I asked what he thought of Princeton and he said that I should go to Yale. Then I went to Columbia and still couldn't locate the "there" there. Visiting Yale, there was something wonderful about the mess and personal identity that seemed to be legible in all the studios that were littered around the trays. You could see them, there was an intimacy to the space, the spatiality and debris of it. . . . Yale seemed to be the most catholic in the things it would embrace pedagogically. There didn't seem to be the adamance that one position was the only position. You could argue that schools that had certain pedagogical identities that became so streamlined and narrow seemed less compelling.[63]

Pelli enthusiastically embraced Yale's "old and excellent tradition of inviting distinguished architects to teach" by bringing in designers who were not only practitioners, as he stated, "but also thinkers or educators." He pretty much gave the visiting critics free rein to organize their studios as they each saw fit, so that "they can transmit their individual understanding of architecture in the best possible way to our students."[64] Under Pelli, the intensity of the advanced studio culture of the Rudolph era returned, but with each studio far more highly focused on a building type or setting, or occasionally an abstract idea. As in the Rudolph years, visiting professors were typically assisted by regular faculty, but there was no pretense of equality. The assistants were expected to carry out the visitor's ideas as best he or she could in the master's absence. Shortly after the end of his tenure, Pelli emphasized the importance of bringing students into "direct contract with the individuals who are chang-ing the way architecture is made and the way we think about architecture"[65] (7.8). The range of advanced studio offerings was dazzling. Macrae-Gibson remembers Giancarlo de Carlo, who served as Davenport Professor in spring 1978, as a particularly passionate instructor who was "very interested in the effect of space on cities."

> What I remember most about Giancarlo is not so much his criticism, because it could be extremely inscrutable—you didn't quite know what he was saying. But really, the point was not what he said but how he said it. Because he so clearly believed, so deeply, in what he was saying, that there was a huge sense of mastery of his ideas.
>
> You can't explain it, you have to experience that. Knowing that there are architects who have a tremendous intensity about what they do is tre-mendously helpful as a student, because it gives you a sense of mission, that this is a vocation. And you need to have that sense, I think, because architecture is so difficult. His studio was really great from that point of view. He was sort of master artisan giving you these pearls of wisdom every so often.[66]

Pelli also brought in as visiting professors recent graduates such as Jaquelin Robertson, David Sellers, Charles Gwathmey, Robert A. M. Stern, and Stanley Tigerman to teach side by side with important American corporate-practitioners such as Henry Cobb, Helmut Jahn, Paul Kennon, and theorist-practitioners such as Peter Eisenman and John Hejduk (7.9–7.12). Stern's studio took on urban housing in the fall 1978 semester. His project "Toward an Urban Suburbia: A Development Alternative for the South Bronx" asked students to propose a garden suburb for the notorious, rubble-strewn Charlotte Street site in the South Bronx—an unconventional undertaking for the time. The student projects varied in their expression, from Macrae-Gibson's inventive reimagining of the pre–World War I English garden suburb to Alexander Gorlin's more abstract, almost sculptural proposal (7.13). The studio was an early exemplar of the methodologies and social attitudes that have become central to the New Urbanism movement, possibly inspiring Edward Logue (1921–2000; B.A. 1942, LL.B 1947), who as president of the New York State Urban Development Corporation constructed single-family, "Ranch-style" houses on the site in the mid-1980s.[67]

The appointment of David Sellers in particular represented an example of Pelli's inclusiveness. In spring 1978, Sellers's studio focused on design for

7.8   Studio coordinators for spring 1980. From left to right: Myles Weintraub, Fred Clarke, Peter Eisenman, Mark Simon, George Ranalli, Charles Moore, Jaquelin Robertson, and King-lui Wu.

7.9   Charles Dilworth (B.A. 1979, M.Arch 1983), Mixed-Use Development in Chicago, perspective. Jahn studio (spring 1983).

7.10   Eisenman studio jury (spring 1980). Front row: James Stirling, William Gass, Peter Eisenman, Mario Gandelsonas, Elyse Grinstein, and Robert Livesey. Top-left corner: Tom Patch and Robert Kahn.

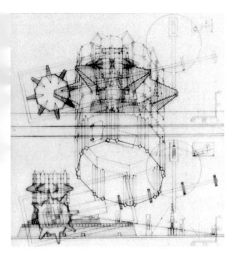

7.11 Margot Alofsin (M.Arch 1982), House for a Mapmaker, composite views. Hejduk studio (spring 1982).

7.12 Students wearing masks they made John Hejduk at the New Haven Railroad Station (spring 1982).

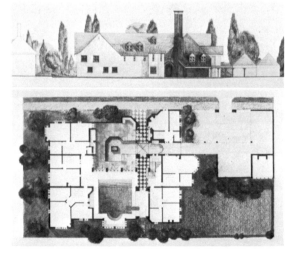

7.14 David Carter (M.Arch 1980), Native American School, plan and section. Sellers studio (spring 1978).

7.13 Gavin Macrae-Gibson (M.Arch. 1979), A Development Alternative for the South Bronx, elevation and plan. Stern studio (fall 1978).

7.15 Jacob Albert (M.Arch 1980), A Condominium in Manhattan, elevation. Moore studio (spring 1980).

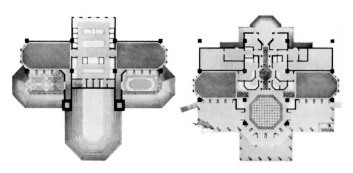

7.16 Paul Chiasson (M.Arch 1981), A Complex of Four Restaurants. Moore studio (spring 1981).

7.17 Pelli studio review (fall 1979). From left to right: Cesar Pelli, Frank Gehry, Stanley Tigerman (gesturing), Charles Moore (behind), unidentified (standing), and Jaquelin Robertson in the lower corner.

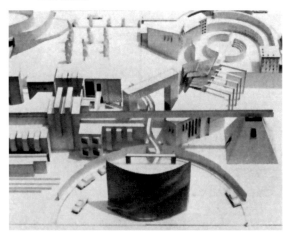

7.18 Kari Nordstrom (M.Arch 1980), American Embassy in Damascus, Syria. Gehry studio (fall 1979).

climate and energy efficiency rather than a specific building type (7.14). In spring 1979, Sellers, long ensconced in rural Vermont as a virtual guru of the design-build approach, surprised students with multiple design problems in multiple cities, with the aim of developing their understanding of materials, energy, and mechanical systems. Charles Moore continued to teach, offering advanced studios in spring 1980 and in spring 1981, asking students to address issues of taste and style in their designs for a condominium and a complex of four restaurants, respectively (7.15, 7.16).

In fall 1979, students had the choice of Pelli's studio on the American skyscraper, which asked students to design a corporate headquarters for Rolls Royce facing Manhattan's Grand Army Plaza—a type of building and client virtually unconsidered as a possible topic since Rudolph's day (7.17); James Stirling's studio calling for the design of a new building for the Fogg Museum at Cambridge, Massachusetts, a project then on the master's drawing board; and Bishop Visiting Professor Frank Gehry's first studio at Yale, in which he asked the students to design an American Embassy in Damascus, Syria, challenging them to consider their "design's quality as a future ruin" (7.18). In fall 1982, Gehry returned as Davenport Chair, replacing Stirling, who had taken a leave of absence. Gehry had his students enter the Soling Competition, competing with seven other architecture schools in the design of a multiuse skyscraper in Manhattan.[68] Peter Eisenman, as Davenport Professor in spring 1980, asked students to design "A Monument to Palladio," focusing their efforts "on the process of design" with "objects" that "were real works as well as serving as notes on the process"[69] (7.19). This was Eisenman's first time teaching a studio at Yale. He would not teach again at the school until spring 1999, during Robert A. M. Stern's first year as dean, when he was invited to serve as Philip Johnson's "teaching assistant." In dramatic contrast to Eisenman's highly abstract problem, his then professional partner, Jaquelin Robertson, as Bishop Visiting Professor in the same term, challenged students to tackle "The Architecture of Real Estate: Art and Commerce" by designing a luxury apartment building for Manhattan.

Aldo Rossi was Davenport Chair during spring 1981, asking students to design "an idealized college campus" in Lowell, Massachusetts, the quintessential nineteenth-century American mill town (7.20). He stressed typology and urban morphology, providing a provocative counterpoint to the rising tide of stylistic postmodernism, which, as Mary McLeod has observed, was "part of a broader social and cultural discussion of the 'postmodern condition' and postmodernity."[70] Pelli's embrace of various points of view was not at the expense of his own opinions, which could be very ideological, particularly

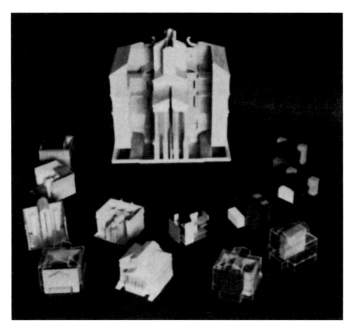

7.19 Jay Tackett (M.Arch 1980), A Monument to Palladio, models.
Eisenman studio (spring 1980).

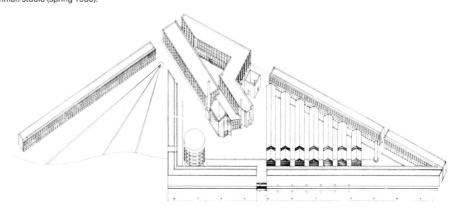

7.20 Frances Humphreys (M.Arch. 1981), College Campus in Lowell, Massachusetts, axonometric.
Rossi studio (spring 1981).

7.21 Marti Cowan (M.Arch 1984), Abattoir, model. Tigerman studio (spring 1984).

toward the use of materials and building systems, and were often expressed during reviews. "I remember one famous occasion when somehow the issue of renovating the British Art Center came up and Bob [Stern] happened to be on [the jury]," remembers Macrae-Gibson. "Bob was saying, 'We could make these rooms like eighteenth-century drawing rooms.' And Cesar said, 'Absolutely not! I've never heard such a load of nonsense. You could never do that! It's got nothing to do with the architecture whatsoever.' And I have to say that Bob was a little bit cowed at that moment because, you know, Cesar was the dean and he was older and so forth. But he got his revenge."[71]

Some visiting critics pushed Pelli's tolerance almost to the breaking point, but on the whole he took things in stride. For example, when Stanley Tigerman proposed to offer a design studio "about the architectural implications of the abattoir," Pelli, reflecting on his Argentinian background, "thought it a wonderful idea insofar as his own parents had told him that 'if you consume something, you need to know whence it came, and how it got to the table'"[72] (7.21). Tigerman believed the abattoir to be a "perfect" design problem "because architecture is made of materials that were once alive. Did the students get it? I'm not so sure."[73]

In 1984, the school benefited from a third endowed chair for visiting architects. Honoring Eero Saarinen, this was jointly established by Kevin Roche who donated his Pritzker Prize money, and by Saarinen's patron and friend J. Irwin Miller. According to Pelli, "Roche set some stipulations and one was that it would be for an architect who had made a mark not only as a teacher or theoretician, but also as a practitioner of the art of architecture."[74] Roche also requested that as a tribute to Saarinen's intense curiosity, there be an annual Saarinen lecture delivered by someone from outside the profession but related to it. The lecture series was inaugurated in 2000, with Anthony Williams (b. 1951; B.A. 1979), then mayor of Washington, D.C., delivering the first talk.

Kazuo Shinohara (1925–2006) was the inaugural Saarinen Professor in fall 1984, choosing for his studio topic "An Architectural Complex in Shibuya," a dense urban node in Tokyo, a problem he had previously offered to his Japanese students (7.22, 7.23). In an interview about his time as Saarinen Professor, Shinohara said that the "word 'anarchy' became very popular at Yale. Its significance became more similar to my own design method, which is to make and destroy, make and destroy repeatedly without making any progress."[75] The studio's final jury took place over two days, with Pelli, Charles Gwathmey, and Los Angeles–based Coy Howard sitting in on the second day's proceedings. Shinohara found it "interesting that Gwathmey and Howard criticized several of the projects on the grounds that they were only

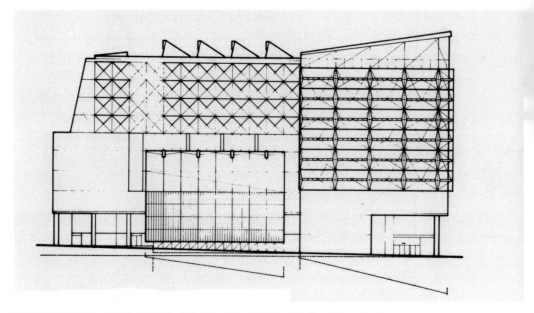

7.22 Chariss McAfee (M.Arch 1985), Mixed-Use Complex in the Shibuya District of Tokyo, elevation.
Shinohara studio (fall 1984).

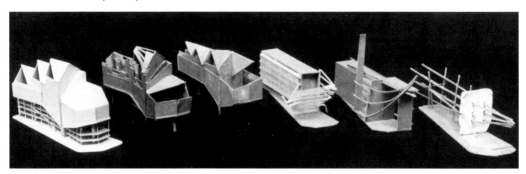

7.23 Olivia Emery (M.Arch 1985), Mixed-Use Complex in the Shibuya district of Tokyo, models.
Shinohara studio (fall 1984).

two-dimensional, and that the only thing which stood out was the elevation; in other words, they said, there was 'no volume.'" Reflecting on this, he concluded that "Japanese students are more conceptual and American students are more practical," but went on to state that "he received objections from some Americans regarding this latter term 'practical.'" He went on to say: "There were some occasions when it seemed that the term 'resolute' would be the most applicable expression to describe the students' images of space and form. There were several students who would cling to some strange or unique image which had nothing at all to do with today's architectural scene, and they wouldn't abandon it, all the way to the end. This was very much in contrast with young Japanese students, who are very aware of and responsive to the foreign situation which is brought to them through journalism." To this observation, Shinohara added something of a footnote: "In addition to this particular tendency among my American students, it was extremely interesting to see that Modernism—which has so far lasted over a half century—and also the European traditions which lay behind it, could be observed in the students' everyday small tasks, sometimes quite obviously, sometimes concealed."[76]

Although Pelli chose to concentrate his own efforts on enriching the advanced studios, which for most students represented the last half of the six-term program, he did not ignore the Core, working with the full-time faculty to change its curriculum—which still pretty much reflected the one Moore and Bloomer had established in 1966 and, with the exception of Alexander Purves, was largely taught by carryovers from the Moore era, including, to a limited extent, Moore himself. But as Moore shifted his emphasis to UCLA, his influence among graduate students was waning. Gavin Macrae-Gibson recalls that while he "had certainly opened up vistas into the past," Moore was "an echo but not a presence."[77] Although Pelli believes that the students at the time of his appointment "were almost 100 percent postmodernists,"[78] their attitudes toward Moore were at best ambivalent, particularly after his Piazza d'Italia (1978) design in New Orleans seemed to suggest an increasingly frivolous approach. Elizabeth Gamard recalls: "Charlie Moore tried to give a talk to our class, but we walked out half-way through, making up excuses along the way. We were just not interested in him. . . . He seemed a sad reminder of a time when things were crazy and perhaps more psychedelic. Alumni from that time would wander into our studio. They all seemed slightly out of it, zoned perhaps."[79]

With Moore still teaching in the first term and the Building Project dominating the second term, change was most easily introduced in the third term, which was strengthened under the leadership of Alec Purves. Additionally, Moore-era design faculty were replaced with George Buchanan, James Jarrett, Robert Livesey (who frequently also helped Stirling with his studios), Harold Roth, Giuseppe Zambonini (1942–1990), and Andrea Leers (b. 1942), who would continue to teach at the school until 1989. Under Pelli, the third term of the Core permitted individual faculty to choose their studio topics. Typical examples included studios focusing on typological studies focused on building over theory, such as libraries and industrial buildings favored by Leers. Like M. J. Long, who began as faculty in 1972, Leers, founder of Leers Weinzapfel Associates, was an important role model for female students.[80] Marion Weiss remembers her as "a stellar example of someone who takes both practice and academia very seriously" and who "demanded the clarity of the diagram to be at the underpinning of all the formal implications of architecture."[81]

To help reshape the Core, Pelli appointed Purves and George Ranalli as coordinators in 1982. The two men, working with critics Jarrett and Zambonini, committed themselves to design fundamentals. Jarrett, one of Yale's most talented students in the early 1950s and a disciple of Johnson and Kahn, brought a sense of Classical discipline to the studio, which was reflected in his own work of the time, such as his palazzo-like 1980 annex to New York's Park Avenue Synagogue, a building that, as Paul Goldberger wrote, "underscores with particular eloquence the extent to which talented architects have abandoned the modernist mode."[82] Jarrett remained on the faculty until 1987 and set the stage for renewed student interest in Classical design, as exemplified in the work of Scott Merrill (b. 1956; M.Arch 1984), John Tittmann (b. 1959; B.A. 1981, M.Arch 1986), Duncan Stroik (b. 1962; M.Arch 1987), and others. Though Purves and Ranalli did not always see eye to eye, they shared an emphasis on craft "to give students the capability to think through their hands."[83]

Ranalli, a decidedly street-smart New York native with something of an edge, reflected in his preference for sharply tailored black suits, stood out amidst the prevailing Yale faculty, whose tastes ran to J. Press tweeds. A graduate of Pratt Institute and Harvard, he describes his appointment at Yale as "an absolute fluke" that resulted from a brief meeting with Vincent Scully at the Institute for Architecture and Urban Studies, during which the young architect impressed the historian with his knowledge of Kahn's work. "Vince said, 'Why don't you come up and see me at Yale. If you're interested in a Ph.D. program, come see my program at Yale.' So the next week I went up and talked with him and he looked through my portfolio and said, 'You should be teaching here.' I was twenty-nine years old. I said, 'Have you been drinking? I can't teach at Yale.' But he called over to the Architecture School and I met with Spiegel. Herman said to me, 'There are three hundred people who have applied for this job and there are two positions available. I don't think there's much chance for you but give me your résumé.' The next thing I know, I got a call telling me I was short-listed. Eventually I went out for an interview and got the appointment."[84]

In fall 1976, Ranalli joined the faculty as assistant professor. In 1982, he was promoted to associate professor adjunct. He became associate professor in 1991, and full professor in 1995. A brilliant teacher, he was also a demanding one who frequently clashed with other faculty members and chafed under a system that encouraged all critics in the Core to work with a shared pedagogy, insisting instead that even Core studios be built on the individual point of view of each critic. Ranalli's insistence on independence in the Core reflected, in part, his concern that other faculty failed to impart basic techniques and values to beginning students. Scott Merrill, who graduated from the University of Virginia with a bachelor's degree in English, "struggled with drawing" but was particularly inspired by both Ranalli and Zambonini, "who were very much taken with craft and materials, and with drawing, and drawing correctly and evocatively." Influenced by Carlo Scarpa and Raimund Abraham, they conveyed "a certain seriousness and ambition that may have been lacking in other work at that time. They were very influential."[85]

Ranalli was determined to make his studios "explorative, disciplined and directed toward an idea about synthesis and a return to the craft of architecture."[86] While clearly a repudiation of Moore and Bloomer's more laissez-faire approach, it came to be regarded by some as a personal attack. In fact, contrary to what many people believe, Moore and Ranalli in particular got along quite well: "Teaching with Charlie was one of the best experiences of my life," he says. Despite their ostensible differences—Ranalli's education was, in his words, "much more abstract"—he found it "intoxicating" to talk to Moore, with the two men finding common ground in their shared love of architectural history. At Pratt, Ranalli had studied with Sibyl Moholy-Nagy, who taught him the importance of a building's place—both in space and in time, that a building was an historic act. When Ranalli joined the faculty, Moore had just published *The Place of Houses* (1974), and his work was focusing on very similar issues.[87] "We'd have these very long discussions in front of students about a lot of these issues. 'What does it mean? What does it represent?' A whole array of issues about roofs and walls and cities and landscapes. It was very comprehensive. Charlie was brilliant. He was a brilliant, brilliant person. . . . It was a great experience."[88]

Unlike Eugene Nalle's tectonically based Core curriculum, the Purves/ Ranalli Core was deeply humanistic, with a focus on the role precedent played in design.[89] Ranalli noticed that there were some students who just weren't making progress and wondered, "Why wasn't the whole studio operating at a higher level?" To help these students, Ranalli began to change the way he taught, looking all the way back to the École des Beaux-Arts, where, he says, "students were asked to make a little sketch in the beginning and they weren't allowed to change it. They spent six months developing that idea. That's a very interesting methodology." Ranalli, intent on having students be more productive, changed the organization of the studio to help keep students on track: "Externalizing work is a very hard process. Unless you commit to putting stuff down, you're always left just thinking about it," says Ranalli. "Buildings are too complicated for that. You can't just *think* about it. . . . If you have an idea, finish drawing it and don't stop until you're done. . . . That's the process. And I started getting very adamant about teaching it that way, that this is a process. You can't teach people to have ideas but you can frame the experience. These were very well-educated people. I gave all types of programs and they brought all their intellectual capability to them."[90]

Ranalli and Pelli shared a belief that the program was being held back by the low level of presentation skills. "When I got there, the place was in shambles," Ranalli says. "I can only describe it as ad hoc. There were no formal vehicles for representation. Students drew on anything—paper bags, ripped pieces of trace. It was very casual. The standards were not high." To help get things back on track, Ranalli, at Pelli's behest, offered to teach a course in "Descriptive Geometry," combining techniques of the Beaux-Arts with those of Albers to benefit students who hadn't mastered the basics of architectural representation or, for that matter, composition: "If it's an isometric system, what are the properties of an isometric system that would allow you to expand it? What different design understanding would using a perspective give you? What would the perspective facilitate? So it was a way of showing them that these projection systems had different sensitivities and benefits. They allow you to see different things."[91]

In keeping with the school's pluralistic approach, Ranalli's emphasis on precise drawing was counterbalanced by that of Philip Grausman (b. 1935), a sculptor whose drawing course concentrated on freehand perspective, which Grausman referred to as "picture making" (7.24). Grausman believed that architectural plans and photographs, as well as film and television—the signs and symbols that dominated culture—were representations of two-dimensional thinking: "Since we no longer depend on or deliberately use three-dimensional perception, our ability to understand a space, mass, form, or volume *intuitively* has atrophied." Interviewed in 1985 by his student teaching assistant Mark Rylander (b. 1957; M.Arch 1985), Grausman described his course as an attempt "to reestablish the connection between physical activity and three-dimensional perception through the act of freehand drawing."[92]

Pelli also attended to the architecture major in Yale College, increasing Purves's presence there while also keeping him busy in the Core. After the Greenberg-Spiegel debacle, Purves took over the introductory course for undergraduates, which gave them the opportunity to study architectural principles and actually get involved in the design process. Purves, now emeritus professor, continues to offer the course to this day. "I love teaching undergraduates," he says. He adds, only somewhat in jest: "You have to be a little careful because, at least initially, they'll believe whatever you tell them."[93] Though different from Greenberg's in detail, Purves's class was clearly intended, as Pelli stated, to "be neither professional nor pre-professional but be a branch of the humanities," an approach designed for undergraduates who expect to go on to a wide variety of advanced programs and careers.[94] At the same time, it would be "unique because it offers non-architecture majors the opportunity to experience the studio environment which is a key element in the graduate program."[95] Pelli also persuaded Karsten Harries (b. 1937; B.A. 1958, Ph.D. 1962), chairman of the Philosophy Department, to offer undergraduates a required course, "The Philosophy of Architecture," that, according to Kent Bloomer, was the "only example in the United States of a Philosophy Department offering a Core requirement in an architecture major."[96]

Purves offered the key undergraduate class, but the college program remained in the hands of Bloomer, who led studios with former Moore student James Volney Righter, ensuring that Moore's influence continued to be felt. Although Moore's approach no longer seemed the right one for graduate students, it found a perfect audience among undergraduates, who relished the opportunities for direct experience of architecture on field trips organized by Righter, typically to New York, Hartford, Newport, Boston, and North Easton, Massachusetts. Bloomer's undergraduate studio, "Fundamentals of Form," stressed geometry and organizational systems "employed in the design of products from baskets to street systems . . . [giving] the students the opportunity to design some contrivances of their own (such as a paper dome for one person)."[97] Added to these were Scully's lecture course on "Modern Architecture" as well as various other offerings in the history of art, all in all combining to make a rich undergraduate experience, but one that was not as

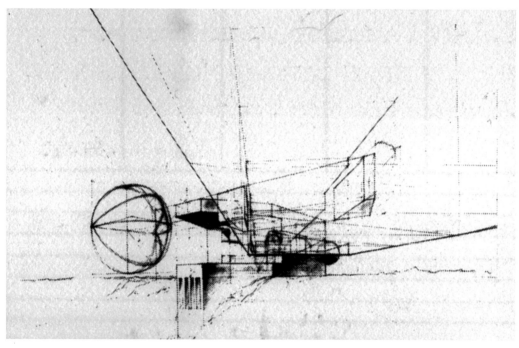

7.24 David Harlan (M.Arch 1986), A Lunar Station, drawing for Philip Grausman's class (fall 1983).

skill-based as those offered students at peer institutions. This did not seem to be a problem for one Yale undergraduate, Maya Lin (b. 1959; B.A. 1981, M.Arch 1986), who would electrify the profession and public alike with a project that would have a lasting effect on the American landscape.

In 1981, Lin, then a senior in Yale College, won the open competition for the Vietnam Veterans Memorial to be built on the Mall in Washington, D.C. The competition brief called for a design honoring the 57,692 Americans killed in Vietnam without making a political statement. Lin's entry was a simple pastel drawing of the now-famous black granite "V" cut into a gently rolling landscape and carved with names of all the fallen soldiers (7.25). The memorial design, Lin's senior design project, had its origins in a seminar in funerary architecture taught by former Moore student Andrus Burr. During the course, Lin and her classmates learned about the competition through a notice posted at the school and, as a class, decided to use it for their final design project. This fact, according to Lin, proved integral to her success: "I think the most important aspect of the design . . . was that I had originally designed it for a class I was taking at Yale and not for the competition. In that sense, I had designed it for me—or, more exactly, for what I believed it should be. I never tried to second-guess a jury. And it wasn't until after I had completed the design that I decided to enter it in the competition."[98] Lin's design was selected from a field of nearly fifteen hundred entries that included proposals from amateurs and professionals alike. The contest officials praised her scheme as "very much a memorial of our own times, one that could not have been achieved in another time or place."[99]

Lin's design was partly inspired by Yale's Memorial Rotunda (Carrère and Hastings, 1901), where walls are carved with the names of all alumni killed in wars. "I had never been able to resist touching the names cut into these marble walls," Lin remembers, "and no matter how busy or crowded the place is, a sense of quiet, a reverence, always surrounds those names. Throughout my freshman and sophomore years, the stonecutters were carving in by hand the names of those killed in the Vietnam War, and I think it left a lasting impression on me . . . the sense of the power of a name."[100] Lin was also inspired by Sir Edwin Lutyens's memorial to the missing soldiers from the Battle of the Somme at Thiepval, France (1928–32), which Vincent Scully had discussed in his history course. "Professor Scully described one's experience of that piece as a passage or journey through a yawning archway. . . . It was a journey to an awareness of immeasurable loss, with the names of the missing carved on every surface of this immense archway." Lin learned her lessons well. Her bold, historically influenced design has become the memorial to which all others are now compared.

A Brand-New School

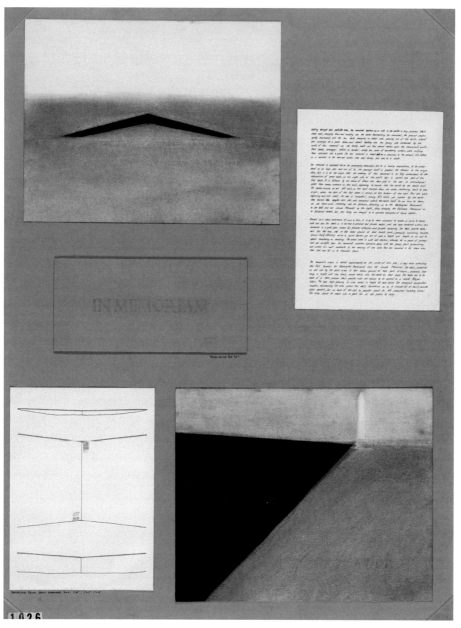

7.25 Maya Lin (B.A. 1981, M.Arch 1986), original submission to the Vietnam Veterans Memorial competition (1981).

Some undergraduates regretted the lack of an undergraduate program such as those at Princeton and Columbia, where greater effort was being made to introduce a measure of professional discipline. Students coming from such programs frequently eschewed Yale's graduate program because they confused the permissive approach in the college with the increasingly rigorous graduate curriculum. The school still "suffered" from the perception that its students were "arty," individualistic, and rambunctious—qualities that became less dominant over the course of Pelli's tenure, as a result of the fact that many incoming "students have taken architecture courses and have developed good architectural skills before entering school here. The students of the 1980s reflect a new professionalism which appears to be a growing trend among many architectural schools."[101]

One thing, however, did not change under Pelli: the state of the Art and Architecture Building, where the writing was literally on the wall, with graffiti covering virtually all available surfaces and stairwells full of noxious fumes from undisciplined model-makers using various spray adhesives and paints. All in all, the building remained the "anarchic environment" it had been since the late 1960s. Moreover, it was seriously overcrowded, and the Art School's decision to give each student a private locked cubicle and to restrict access to the fourth and fifth floors only to its students and faculty meant that there was almost no interaction between the two disciplines, nor did students, faculty, or administrators have any real sense of the grand double-height space that had constituted the building's principal feature. Rather than becoming the socially and programmatically interconnected workshops of the arts that Albers and Sawyer had hoped for, and that Rudolph had tried so hard to realize in built form, the Art and Architecture Building had become "a layer cake of separated things," where students from other disciplines met only in the elevator, if at all.[102] Nonetheless, despite all its shortcomings, for most of the students, if not for the faculty, and certainly not for members of the central administration, the building was inspiring; despite being confined to cramped spaces on the building's top floors, architecture students made the best of it, building out the space as previous generations did, but not necessarily as act of aggression against the building as it had been in the late 1960s, but more as a sort of organic community building.

After three and a half years on the job, Pelli wrote to President Giamatti, telling him, "[Were I] to assess my primary contribution to the School, it would be perhaps, in the excitement with architecture that I have tried to bring to the studios, courses, and public programs such as lectures and exhibitions."[103] Taking pleasure in the school's renewed vitality, Pelli also enjoyed managing university demands and expectations. At the same time he was building up his own practice, where he employed students part-time, as well as recent graduates—some of whom went on to become his longtime associates and partners, such as Mariko Masuoka (b. 1956; B.A. 1978, M.Arch 1980), Mitchell Hirsch (b. 1954; M.Arch 1981), and Phillip Bernstein (b. 1957; B.A. 1979, M.Arch 1983).

At the end of his five-year term, as was customary, Pelli's accomplishments were reviewed. His appointment was renewed but, shortly thereafter, swamped with new professional work, including the massive office buildings of the New York World Financial Center, he suddenly realized that he no longer enjoyed the challenges of running an architecture school. "At the beginning, whenever we had a crisis, and we had several, I loved it. Because a crisis is the best opportunity to make changes. Because there is a crisis, you will get almost total support to make a change to solve the crisis. But if you use it with some higher-range intention, that allows you to shape a school. So I used to love all the crises. But one day we had a crisis and I thought, 'Oh my god, that's the last thing I need.' I watched myself from the outside and thought you should not be dean anymore. You need somebody who will come and enjoy all the crises again."[104]

On November 16, 1983, Pelli announced his intention to step down as dean, effective June 30, 1984.[105] By all reasonable standards, his time in the office had been a success. Seemingly miraculously, despite continuous financial challenge, he was able to accomplish a lot with a very little. Near the end of his tenure, Pelli reflected on the school's difficulties in a January 1983 letter to President Giamatti. Although he proudly reported that there was "a sizable group of students, professionals and critics who feel this School to be the best there is," he pointed out that its resources were inadequate, marred by a continual reduction of budgets and expenditures. For Pelli, the quality of education was too dependent on "the willingness of a few individuals to be stretched to the maximum—and occasionally beyond it."[106] Yale paid less than comparable universities, justifying this on an assumption that architecture professors would supplement their income with their own practices, but this was not the case with some key faculty who were needed to keep the enterprise in good operational order on a day-to-day basis. Reluctant to advance design faculty to tenure, he did see to it that Martin Gehner (b. 1932), a University of Michigan graduate, was tenured as professor of architectural engineering, to take the place of Henry Pfisterer, who had died in 1972.

Though Pelli's contributions as dean were crucial in restoring the identity of the school as a center of high-wire design and discourse, in the end the pressures of practice rendered him a somewhat remote figure. Students have short memories. A *Yale Daily News* article published the day after he announced his resignation reported that "some students in the School of Architecture have questioned the extent to which Pelli has tangibly influenced the School," quoting a student's claim that "It was as if we didn't have a Dean."[107]

Despite student carping, there could be no doubt that Pelli returned Yale's status among its peers to a level that it had not enjoyed for quite some time. One sure sign of this was the consistently high rate of enrollment in the M.Arch I program. In 1981, 302 applied for admission to first year. Forty-seven were accepted and, of these, forty elected to study at Yale—a remarkable statistic. After news of Pelli's resignation was made public, the number of overall applicants slipped to 277, and of the sixty students admitted, only thirty-nine chose to accept Yale's offer.[108] Clearly, the value of Pelli's leadership was widely sensed and appreciated, if not by students in the school, then at least by the profession and those seeking to take their first steps toward preparing for it.

8

Rappel à l'Ordre 1985–1992

"The Yale School of Architecture has a long tradition that each student is taught as an individual rather than as part of a focused program of training. This tradition is grounded in the belief that true education requires free inquiry. The advanced studios reinforce this faith, for the major creative thinkers in architecture come as visiting critics, offering a rich and complex mix of theoretical positions to the students. Historically, these advanced studios have been the heart of the educational experience at Yale for here is where master confronts student across the drawing board. However, the first three Core Curriculum studios at the School are critical to the student's education; only the rigor and intensity of the Core studios prepare the student for the freedom of the advanced studios.

"The last twenty years have seen a major upheaval of values within the architectural profession forced by a continuing reassessment of the very nature of the discipline. . . . As a result, the curriculum in a school such as Yale has grown more and more diffuse reflecting this pluralistic critical atmosphere."

Thomas Beeby, *Retrospecta 1985–1986*

Cesar Pelli's decision to step down with little prior notice meant that the school had to once again have interim leadership. This time the task fell to Associate Dean Martin Gehner (b. 1932), who served as acting dean from July 1, 1984, until December 20, 1985, when the appointment of Chicago-based architect Thomas Beeby went into effect. During those three interim semesters, which once again saw an engineer leading the cash-strapped school, there was a growing concern over Yale's ability to uphold its reputation. Prospective students, alumni, and others with a vested interest in the school worried that it would be difficult to attract a dean who could match Pelli's qualities as practitioner and educator, someone who could keep the school on course against a rising tide of literature-derived theory that threatened to dislodge a pedagogy traditionally rooted in high-wire form-making.

In early 1984, a Search Committee consisting of Herman D. J. Spiegel (chairman), Kent Bloomer, Walter DeS. Harris, Jr., Herbert Newman, and King-lui Wu was just beginning its work. Reading Vincent Scully's letter to the president, one gets the impression that the Pelli years had been nothing short of a disaster. For example, Scully, making it quite clear that he felt no remorse over Pelli's departure, expressed his preference for someone "of international stature who will *also* run, and *lead,* the School," which in Scully's view was suffering after "close to a generation of near-mediocrity," barely managing to coast along "on the momentum Rudolph gave it and because of other factors special to Yale." Likely fearing that his assessment of the school's recent history would come off as dismissive, Scully backpedaled somewhat: "I do not mean to criticize Cesar. He was the best of the group, and I like him, but he did have certain limitations which should not be perpetuated now." Scully expressed support for the school's pluralist approach and visiting critic system and urged the appointment of a "wholly first-class architect and intellectual" who could ensure these traditions continue successfully.[1] He gave his primary endorsement to Robert A. M. Stern, who "comes closest to filling [the] difficult bill" to lead the school, noting, "He is tough (though wholly non-paranoid) and disliked by some, [but] distinctly respected by others. Many of his early detractors have become his firmest friends and admirers. . . . He surely has the broadest, most rational approach to architecture and teaching of anyone I know at this time."[2] Scully also listed other possible candidates, including many alumni who had been previously considered for the deanship: Jaquelin Robertson, recently appointed dean of the University of Virginia School of Architecture; Allan Greenberg, whose focus on Classical architecture Scully saw as both a strength and possible weakness; Tom Beeby, "a wholly liberated intellect . . . whose work still shows the effect of Mies' wonderful discipline, his classicizing language of form"; and Stanley Tigerman, "a man of wit and, I think, considerable gentleness," who "cares a lot about Yale." After running through a few other names, Scully concluded his letter by reprising his lament for the school's unfulfilled potential, given its initial role in the breakup of modernism's hegemony over architecture and urbanism: "The great revolution in architecture—perhaps counterrevolution is a more accurate word—which has been taking place over the past twenty years has been made largely in America and in New Haven not least of all, although not primarily in the Architecture School itself. In fact, I have not concealed from you my feeling that the School has sometimes been a bit of an embarrassment, often a disappointment, considering what it could and ought to be as part of Yale. . . . 'Pluralism' itself, without at least one profound stiffening in every generation, can end in nothing."[3]

Peter Millard, writing to Search Committee Chair Herman Spiegel, echoed Scully's concerns about the "pluralistic nature of the faculty," noting that its shortcomings were most evident in the Core curriculum, "where debate is often personality conflict and discussion a dog fight." Millard didn't proffer any specific recommendations—yet—but advocated for a dean of steadfast character. Recalling his own student days, he believed that the new dean "will enter a situation not unlike the one George Howe found," when the school faced "an uncertain future" requiring a "confident, competent restate-ment of architecture's fundamental capacity and continual need to achieve a unified result capable of reflecting widely varied and diverse perceptions." Millard called for "a person whose attitudes are tempered by experience, whose words derive from educated intellectual rigor, and whose judgments reflect a comprehensive understanding of the Art of Architecture." Only under such leadership, Millard concluded, could the school successfully respond to emerging student interests, lead the way in professional methods and social concerns, and develop "more effective ways to pursue the integration of pro-fessional training with architectural education."[4]

After six months, the Search Committee had little to show for its work. Second-year students were fed up with what they saw as inefficient bureaucracy; many believed the committee represented neither the school nor its students and should not influence its future. But the composition of the committee stood, and by September 1984, it was able to narrow down the list of candidates from sixty-eight names to three, all alumni: Thomas Beeby, Stanley Tigerman, and Charles Gwathmey. Beeby made the short list despite his expressed reluctance to be considered for the position.[5] Three alternates were also listed: Harry Cobb, M. J. Long, and Jaquelin T. Robertson, who quickly found support among the student body.[6] With the field narrowed, each of the three candidates on the short list made formal presentations to the students and faculty and met with their chosen representatives in smaller groups.

Kent Bloomer, a member of the Search Committee, submitted an independent opinion strongly advocating Beeby, then serving as director of the School of Architecture at the University of Illinois at Chicago and running his own office as partner of the prominent Chicago firm Hammond, Beeby & Babka. For Bloomer, Beeby was a talented practitioner and an experienced academic administrator with "a personal character and balance commensurate with his accomplishments."[7] Bloomer recognized that the tendency in Beeby's work toward an abstract Classicism deeply imbued with a Miesian rigor could provide the stiffening that Scully felt the school needed. According to Bloomer, Beeby was someone who had "the finest understanding of our School's uniqueness, which is that Yale has a tradition of *diversity* rather than singularity of method; leadership rather than 'bandwagon'; and decorum rather than hustle. . . . We have a solid record of Deans who have expanded our genetic pool. We have never had one who has tried to impose their personal standpoints and accomplishments."[8]

Vincent Scully was also concerned about the imposition of personal ideologies, especially with regard to Charles Gwathmey, whose views on architecture "have crystallized rather than tempered" since his student days. Gwathmey, as Scully wrote to President Giamatti, seemed less concerned with "what students do than with 'how moral you are.'" This moralistic fervor resonated with students and catered to the "naïve expectations of the faculty." Despite his surprisingly strong appeal to the students, Scully believed Gwathmey was "the least likely among the three candidates to achieve the things that students need and most likely to frustrate more than their excited expectations."[9]

Peter Millard and King-lui Wu had completely opposing views about who was best suited for the job. Wu was one of the few on the faculty to champion Gwathmey, describing him to President Giamatti as a passionate, loyal alumnus who "knows well the traditional concept of graduate education at our school" and could "rebuild our school into the quality that we once enjoyed." As Wu saw it, the school needed a strong leader to put it "back on the international arena."[10]

Peter Millard, however, saw Gwathmey as someone accustomed to running an office but who would be less effective in a school. In a letter to Spiegel, he described Gwathmey's "suggestion that raising standards and levels of performance [could] be achieved through discussion with faculty and students" as inconsistent with the candidate's previously exhibited tendency to dominate the conversation: "The net result, more often than not, is that people stop talking with each other apparently because the only discussion that matters is the one with Charley." Echoing student concerns about some faculty members "winging it," Millard noted that Gwathmey "makes it up—when he shows up—as he goes along."[11]

John Hejduk and Robert Stern endorsed Stanley Tigerman, who impressed Hejduk with his "agile mind, and acerbic wit, and an ability to attract well known visitors."[12] Although, like Beeby, deeply imbued with Miesian discipline, Tigerman, who combined practice with teaching and had considerable academic administrative experience, was nonetheless a vocal critic of the near-worship of the late master's formal language and of the undue influence his legacy exerted on Chicago practice. Tigerman's 1978 collage, *The Titanic,* depicting Mies's Crown Hall sinking into Lake Michigan, was a brilliant expression of his belief that Chicago architects needed to move beyond Mies, who had died nine years before. The collage became a symbol of postmodernism.[13] In contrast to Gwathmey, when interviewed by the Search Committee and at a presentation to the students, Tigerman made specific proposals, advocating frequent design reviews in all Core and advanced studios, to which he would invite critics with opposing views in order to provoke discussion and debate.[14]

Like Scully, Millard was not convinced that the school needed to engage in a "great debate," contending that Tigerman's call for increased diversity of expression was a nostalgic holdover from his student days that would do more harm than good, coming "not only from a lifelong personal involvement with the kind of anxieties that go with it, but also from his memories of coming to Yale as a student when Paul Rudolph did something similar." Arguing that the school, and architectural education in general, had changed in the intervening years, Millard questioned Tigerman's conflict-centric approach: "The Rudolph era was a much simpler ideological climate," he wrote, "with more coherence and focus of student aspirations, and narrower and fewer alternative views to be found in and around the profession."[15] Beyond provoking anxieties, Millard was concerned that Tigerman's proposal would replace one-on-one desk-side criticism with massive formal reviews that, in many cases, would be less beneficial for the students. Concluding his analysis, Millard stated that Tigerman's "interest in pursuing 'the question' has an immediate, on-going and—for the School—very pertinent aspect" but did not offer "a clear answer to the students' persistent and anxious question: 'How can I best become an architect?'"[16]

Millard's view of Thomas Beeby was more conflicted. Beeby conveyed an "impression of a calm, confident, and reasonable man" who, like Tigerman, expressed his belief that the Core program needed to be stronger. However, Beeby made no solid proposal to change the Core, and his vague suggestions were delivered without the passion exhibited by the other candidates, leading Millard to see it "as a sign of lassitude, or simply dullness" that, along with Beeby's avowed interest in history and theory and "the fashionable thrust of his published work," suggested "a lack of design strength and intellectual substance."[17] Summing up the three, Millard wrote that each candidate seemed to be reacting to the "uncertainties born of the Vietnam years—and the architectural confusion of theory and style that have grown out of them—with the common desire to revert to what made sense to them when they were in school." Millard, like Scully, was convinced that the next dean, whoever he might be, must implement a renewed focus on fundamental design skills. In Millard's view, it wasn't necessary "to make the School more dazzling or fascinating or profound," but "to find better ways to prepare students to make better use of what it already offers."[18] In essence, Millard's position was essentially conservative, calling for a return to techniques of training that had existed when he was a student. Noting that there was already something of an effort being made by Core faculty toward tightening standards, Millard argued that a truly rigorous program would never emerge solely from faculty initiatives or student discussions: "We need a Dean who can and will direct and lead the School in that direction," and "Tom Beeby seems most likely to do so."[19]

For students, the choice was clearly between Beeby and Gwathmey. In November 1984, nine representatives of the student body forwarded to President Giamatti a summary of a school-wide survey that elucidated student concerns and summarized their opinions of the candidates. Students felt that Beeby was the most approachable and believed that he was the most likely to successfully help them articulate nascent ideas and unspoken concerns. They were also impressed by Beeby's desire to encourage and facilitate communication between students, faculty, and administration. However, although they appreciated Beeby's "ability to synthesize divergent issues within his own work," they were, as Millard feared, apprehensive about his perceived lack of energy; the students saw Beeby as a poor motivator and a weak administrator. There was also concern that, in his presentation to the student body, Beeby had failed to articulate "a clear understanding of the current situation of the School" and lacked "a clear vision of its future."[20]

Gwathmey, however, was admired by students for his "forceful critique of the current situation and his energetic and relatively specific vision of what needs to be done." On the other hand, they noted that his "strength of will is feared by many students as involving inflexibility and a want of responsiveness." While they believed willfulness might very well make Gwathmey a skillful administrator, the students were not confident that they could comfortably approach him with problems and ideas, "particularly if they are not well-defined."[21]

The student representatives did not have kind words for Stanley Tigerman. Although they respected him as an academician and theoretician, and appreciated his enthusiasm, they found him to be "more interested in intellectual exploration than in architecture as such." Echoing Millard's concerns, they commented that "his built work, in addition to being perverse and apparently frivolous, is taken as indicative of an inability to effectively translate intellectual notions into built form. And although Mr. Tigerman understands and subscribes to the values and ends of a pluralistic education, his ability to implement a discipline's pluralism are [sic] seriously questioned."[22]

Ultimately, the new dean would be selected by President Giamatti, who interviewed each of the candidates. Tigerman recalls that during his interview, the president asked him "to explain who I was innately in one word. Without any thought and in a nanosecond I blurted out, 'Action.'" Later, Tigerman jokingly suggested to Beeby that when asked the same question, "he probably waited a half minute or so before carefully replying, 'Contemplation.' Typically, Beeby smiled knowingly but didn't react directly; needless to say, Beeby got the post."[23]

On January 28, 1985, Thomas H. Beeby's appointment was publicly announced, though it wouldn't go into effect until the end of the year (8.1).[24] In the announcement, Giamatti, perhaps alluding to Beeby's initial reluctance to take the job, said, "Yale is indeed fortunate to have been able to persuade Mr. Beeby to leave Chicago for this extremely critical post at the University."[25] Beeby's Chicago roots ran deep. He was born in Oak Park, a suburb closely associated with Frank Lloyd Wright's early career, and was raised in an 1868 Queen Anne–style house in the adjoining suburb, River Forest, where from his bedroom window he could see Wright's J. Kibben Ingalls House. So, from an early age, he had an eye—quite literally—on a work of architecture that was modern but steeped in tradition. Beeby earned his undergraduate degree in architecture at Cornell, where he was "exposed to a comparative analytical method that carefully scrutinized Classical architecture looking for precedent but did not allow the drawing of historical detail as part of the design process."[26] After Cornell, Beeby enrolled in Paul Rudolph's master's program at Yale (see Chapter 4). At Yale, he began to understand that "all architecture is transformed from past architecture."[27] After graduating, he returned to Chicago and began working at C. F. Murphy Architects, a large corporate firm where the young architect learned how to design Miesian buildings "that are well built, that are serious buildings that represent civic architecture" and how to connect Miesian modernism with Classicism: "When I first began to work at C. F. Murphy, I couldn't evaluate Classical buildings," Beeby told *Progressive Architecture* in 1990. "I had no critical faculty for seeing them. But after working for around six months on Miesian projects, I suddenly could see buildings as planar surfaces, as problems of shallow relief on facades, as compositional problems dealing with repetition. Mies opened my eyes to Classicism."[28]

It was this ability to synthesize ostensibly disparate influences that first attracted the Dean Search Committee to Beeby, whom they saw as a well-established, open-minded practitioner-teacher ideally suited to tempering Yale's pluralism with some much-needed skill-based rigor. His academic credentials included serving as director of the University of Illinois at Chicago School of Architecture from 1985 to 1991 and, before that, teaching at IIT from 1973 to 1980, where students were challenged to produce things "that were really perfect, not just conceptually perfect but physically perfect"—an idea that Beeby "closely tied to the notion of the Beaux-Arts way of teaching, where you had to master technique exactly."[29]

Tigerman and Gwathmey were both disappointed about not getting the Yale appointment; each took the president's decision quite personally. "That was something that each of us wanted to do," Tigerman has said, "probably more than Tom."[30] Gwathmey in particular did not take his rejection gladly. Notorious for acrimonious letters written to those he perceived had wronged him, he expressed his disappointment accordingly, writing to Giamatti that he had "obviously made the conservative choice, maintaining the status quo of the 'visiting/working dean' and acknowledging the credibility of a self-indulgent and protective faculty."[31] Tigerman largely agreed with Gwathmey's sentiment that Giamatti was looking to maintain the direction established by Pelli, and did not want "another Paul Rudolph . . . who came in with guns blazing."[32] However, Search Committee member Herbert Newman says Beeby was selected because the others "were not thought of at the time, by myself and others on the selection committee, to be inclusive and egalitarian in their approach to architecture."[33] It was a view that the committee believed to be crucial to the success of the school. "We didn't want to give that up," says Newman. "We saw it as something that expanded our horizon of what architecture was about."[34]

The belief that Beeby would stay the course was both right and wrong. Beeby was committed to change, but he was not one to explicitly state his strategy for going forward. In fact, he outwardly chafed at the idea of the strong dean, finding it "institutionally irresponsible because it puts too much emphasis on individuals."[35] But his stance was to some extent a ploy, a cover for what proved to be a canny strategist who during his seven years as dean would dramatically reshape the school's curriculum and rebuild his faculty to support his own ideas.

Beeby believed that the program he found in place in 1985 was eerily similar to the one he had encountered as a student under Rudolph twenty years earlier:

> The sense of the School hadn't really changed. As Colin Rowe [his teacher at Cornell] once said about Yale, "Places don't change, people do." In a way, Yale has a kind of persona that remains unchanged by anything. It's always been undisciplined, open to free discourse, open to all sorts of influences from outside. It has never attempted to become an academy of any kind. It has always been interested in inquiry. The work is highly individualistic and diverse and people are on their own. . . . It has very good students—not too many of them—and it has enough money to be quite idiosyncratic and pursue what's interesting.[36]

While "the sense of the school" may have been similar to the Rudolph era, its governance reflected the freewheeling participatory character of the Moore era. Beeby believed that some changes were necessary. Concerned that the Curriculum Committee was disproportionately influenced by student members, he achieved stronger faculty control. "Who's running the School?" he asked, adding that it was "structurally impossible to function [by consensus] because the students cannot actually dictate the curriculum of the School. That's against University rules."[37] Although he publically endorsed the school's seemingly nonideological stance, he set out to increase the permanent faculty in order to mitigate the overreliance on visiting critics in the first-year Core, which was the principal focus of his attention, instead hiring young teacher-practitioners to take on significant responsibility. In so doing, he was forced to face the same problem that Yale's deans had faced since the time of Everett Meeks: "How do you keep [a school] focused on practice and primarily run by practitioners if they're going to be out and about practicing?"[38] To stabilize the school while holding on to teacher-practitioners, Beeby introduced mul-tiyear adjunct appointments that allowed practitioners "to have a significant involvement in the School—up to 80% full time," while also providing them flexibility when they got busy with work.[39]

Beeby's first important hire was Alan Plattus (b. 1953; B.A. 1976). While an undergraduate at Yale, Plattus had taken a year's leave of absence to study at the Institute for Architecture and Urban Studies in New York, where he worked with Peter Eisenman while sharing an office with Rem Koolhaas, then busily researching and writing his book *Delirious New York* (1978). After graduating, Plattus went on to earn his master's degree in architecture from Princeton, remaining on its faculty there until Beeby invited him back to Yale in 1986 as a lecturer and critic.[40] Although Plattus had no direct Cornell connections, he identified himself "as a theorist and historian interested in Renaissance architecture and modern architecture, a very conventional Colin Rowe–like mix of stuff."[41] Plattus became the cornerstone of a faculty that Beeby would largely populate with former Rowe students, including Barbara Littenberg (b. 1949), copartner of Peterson Littenberg Architecture & Urban Design, who was appointed visiting critic in spring 1986 and, after 1991, associate professor adjunct, and Judith DiMaio (b. 1950), appointed critic in architectural design in 1988, who in 2001 would become dean of the School of Architecture at the New York Institute of Technology. Littenberg had worked with Richard Meier, and DiMaio had worked in the office of Kohn Pedersen Fox.

Beeby would also invite former Rowe students to serve as visiting critics, thereby shifting some of the emphasis of the advanced studios away from high-wire practice to a more conservative academicism: J. (Jon) Michael Schwarting served as visiting critic (fall 1986); Werner Seligmann as Bishop Visiting Professor (spring 1988); and Michael Dennis as Eero Saarinen Visiting Professor (fall 1988). In Rowe's former students, Beeby saw a group of studio-theorists who were still involved in practice but whose principal interest was in formal composition.

The changes in the faculty were not received favorably by everyone. Beeby acknowledged that some students, faculty, and alumni feared that, given Rowe's distinct pedagogy as articulated in the book *Collage City* (1978), which he coauthored with Alfred (Fred) Koetter (b. 1938), it might be "an attempt to brainwash people and force them into some kind of channel."[42] But Beeby was convinced that things would inevitably be different at Yale: rather than pursuing careers in teaching or theorizing, as many students at Cornell or Princeton would do, students came to Yale to learn how to build buildings. "I think that there has been a tendency here to see architecture as something in which the final test is in the real world—in other words, buildings are built. The highly theoretical, speculative work hasn't been the main thrust here."[43]

Beeby's agenda for the school was best articulated in a special issue of *Rap Sheets,* an independent, pamphlet-sized student publication begun in 1986 and principally edited by Mark Linder (b. 1960; M.Arch 1986, M.E.D. 1988) and Oscar Mertz (b. 1956; M.Arch 1988). Inspired in part by a conversation with Peter Eisenman and Jaquelin Robertson, who had recently established an ideologically improbable professional partnership, Linder and Mertz initiated the journal to repair a perceived flaw in the studio system of the time, which, according to Linder, was failing "to foster sophisticated and constructive discourse among students."[44] Challenging their classmates to take on a more critical voice, *Rap Sheets* invited students to submit proposals and take on editorial responsibilities. In contrast to *Retrospecta,* which emanated from the dean's office, or *Perspecta,* which was student-edited but did not typically contain student writing, *Rap Sheets* was an outlet for students themselves to opine on the debates that were taking place in the studios, and to publish responses and rebuttals from members of the faculty.[45]

Two years into Beeby's tenure, Hans Baldauf (b. 1959; B.A. 1981, M.Arch 1987) and Gilbert Schafer (b. 1961; M.Arch 1988) conducted extensive interviews with the dean for a special two-volume edition of *Rap Sheets.* They suggested that at Yale, where the dean "traditionally defines the direction of the School," it was important to learn more about Beeby, who despite being "consistently accessible and particularly personable," was "an enigma to many" and had "never formally articulated his vision for the School."[46]

In his *Rap Sheets* interview, Beeby expressed reservations about the rise of literary theory as part of studio curricula and architects who "are proving theories with their work rather than having to build in a responsible way."[47] Although he enriched the menu of offerings with courses in history and theory, they remained distinct from and uncoupled to studios, to avoid the "dark side of theory," which constitutes a "replacement of a synthetic process in favor of analysis." In lieu of abstract theory and the interdisciplinary dialectics largely derived from linguistic studies that were dominant in peer architecture programs, Beeby insisted that students consider social issues and the psychological perception of space: "There is a kind of responsibility that the School has that it can't throw to the winds," he told the editors of *Rap Sheets.* "It's very easy to want to demand high profile positions and brilliant discourse on architecture, the highest level live in the areas that are currently considered to be interesting, but how about the basic stuff that actually allows you to be an architect?"[48]

8.1   Thomas H. Beeby (1988).

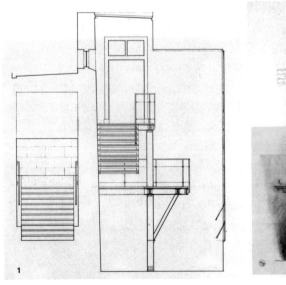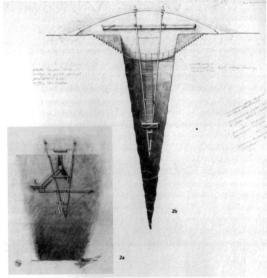

8.2   Left: Frieda Menzer (M.Arch 1990), Stair Problem (1987). Right: Liza Lockard (M.Arch 1994), Bridge Problem (1992).

Despite the characteristically fierce resistance of the typical Yale student to design "rules," Beeby was personally determined to increase curricular
discipline in the Core. While Paul Rudolph and Cesar Pelli chose to work
with advanced students, Beeby, like Moore, preferred to teach in the first year,
where he was quite specific in emphasizing an approach rooted in design fundamentals. "Before you finish the Core," Beeby said, "you ought to be able to
understand how buildings are made to the degree that what you draw is based
on some kind of reality."[49]

Acknowledging that the student body included "incredibly gifted
people . . . pursuing their own agendas," Beeby felt a responsibility to all students, including those unfamiliar with the basic tenets of the profession, many
of whom, in his view, "were getting no education at all."[50] In what might seem
a contradiction, despite his intention to tighten the Core, Beeby shared the
conviction of many of the faculty that the program should continue to admit
significant numbers of students who had little or no previous preparation for
architecture. In 1989, the ratio between admitted M.Arch I students who had
pre-architecture backgrounds and those who did not was reversed, so that 60
percent of each incoming class came with no prior preparation. As a result, the
school became populated by "more academically and intellectually prepared
students with less developed graphic skills and technical backgrounds." The
decision came about, in part, as a reaction to the proliferation of relatively rigorous, pre-professional undergraduate programs in architecture in the 1970s,
such as at Pennsylvania, Virginia, Columbia, and other feeder schools where
students were encouraged to demonstrate what "appeared to be artistic virtuosity" in portfolios submitted as part of their applications, but were "actually
the result of intense training rather than innate potential."[51]

While Beeby did appoint Cornell-trained faculty, he also added faculty
with other points of view to teach "the basic stuff" in the Core. Deborah Berke
(b. 1954) and Steven Harris (b. 1950), for example, were made adjunct faculty
in 1988, and Turner Brooks in 1991. Berke had received B.F.A. and her bachelor
of architecture at the Rhode Island School of Design and her master of urban
planning in urban design at the City University of New York, where she studied
under Jonathan Barnett. Now professor adjunct and a prominent independent
practitioner known for a severe version of mid-century modernism, Berke was
at the time of her appointment emerging from a partnership that specialized
in small, vernacular houses, many built at the new town of Seaside.[52] Steven
Harris, a disciple of Michael Graves, with whom he studied at Princeton before
joining his office and then teaching at Harvard, was also just embarking on
independent practice in New York. Harris shared an interest with Berke in

vernacular building, leading to their collaboration on the book *Architecture of the Everyday* (1997).[53] Turner Brooks had followed his student days at Yale with a stint in Philip Johnson's office before establishing his own practice in Vermont, where he realized a series of idiosyncratic houses.[54] Berke remembers that "Beeby made a very firm move to hire Alan, Steven, Turner, and me as adjunct, younger people who were going to stir things up a bit and come into the school with some new ideas." She noted that "It was an adjunct position but it felt full time. We were in New Haven three days a week. It was killer. You could barely have a practice."[55]

Beeby also saw to it that the largely male resident faculty were joined by women—Littenberg, DiMaio, Berke—and also invited women to occupy prestigious visiting professorships. Bishop Chair female appointees include Diana Agrest (fall 1983), Ada Karmi-Melamede (fall 1985), and Elizabeth Plater-Zyberk, with her partner Andrés Duany (spring 1987); that same term, Denise Scott Brown and Robert Venturi shared the Saarinen Chair, which Henry Smith-Miller and Laurie Hawkinson jointly occupied a few years later (fall 1990); but the prestigious Davenport Chair wasn't occupied by a woman until Beeby's appointment of sculptor Mary Miss (fall 1991). Beeby also actively sought to increase visibility of women students in the school, encouraging Debra Coleman (b. 1959; M.E.D. 1990), Elizabeth Danze (b. 1956; M.Arch 1990), and Carol Henderson (b. 1962; M.Arch 1989) to found the *Yale Journal of Architecture and Feminism* "to advance a feminist perspective in architectural scholarship, criticism, and practice."[56] Beeby's successor, Fred Koetter, continued to support the project, with Deborah Berke serving as faculty advisor. The first issue, the result of an open call for papers that received more than one hundred submissions, was published in 1992; the journal eventually led to a book, *Architecture and Feminism* (1996).[57]

Initially, women encountered difficulties gaining acceptance among some of the old guard on the faculty. Berke recalls one particularly revealing meeting with Herman Spiegel: "I get to Yale and nobody knew who I was but I was assigned to a bunch of committees by Tom. I remember being on this one with Herman and we all sat down and he looked across the table at me and said, 'Go get us coffee.' Maybe it was because I was the youngest but I think it was probably because I was the only woman in the room. So that sits with me forever. That was my first year at Yale. And I don't want to pick on Herman because I ended up becoming very fond of him. He came from a different era."[58]

In 1987, Berke and Harris began teaching in the Core with Alec Purves, who had been coordinating the first-year, first-term studio since 1982—initially with Ranalli, then Bloomer, then a rotating cast of other critics. Reflecting Beeby's bias, Purves increased the focus on the act of building, a perspective that was becoming increasingly unpopular in peer institutions. The Purves-Berke-Harris partnership proved to be a success. Their studios typically began with a small design problem—usually for a stair or a bridge—that challenged students to address issues of material, structure, scale, and proportion (8.2). Successive problems introduced issues of program, landscape, and type. Each year the curriculum was tweaked and refined, and although the three critics had their differences, they shared "the belief that architecture was [about] building," says Purves. "That we didn't discuss. That's just the way it was. Deborah and Steven are fanatics when it comes to detailing and material choices and things like that. They're much more experienced even than I am, but we all shared that."[59] Purves, Berke, and Harris brought building rigor to the Core, but not at the expense of creativity. "We weren't trying to stamp out imagination," says Purves, "but to give students a little more feeling that when they talked about a brick wall, they were confident that they knew what a brick wall was."[60]

The Core continually evolved by trial and error, and at times it seemed almost contradictory, encouraging students to focus on "the basics" of architecture as well as contemporary issues in architecture.[61] However, Beeby held the line, concerned that the changing nature of architectural education at other schools, in which the design process was increasingly dependent on criteria borrowed from sociology, advanced technology, and literary criticism "fractured the theoretical consensus of architecture."[62] While most of the new faculty cooperated with Beeby's efforts to reshape the school's Core curriculum into a collective, cogent series of problems undertaken by all students in the class, George Ranalli resented the requirement that he teach collaboratively, so that, according to Martin Gehner, he was "removed from the team of faculty teaching the first required design studio" and "given the opportunity to teach his self-contained doctrine without the constraints of cooperation with other faculty," although he "chose to condemn the decision because he wanted to be in charge of that faculty group."[63]

In order to retain Ranalli, Beeby asked him to teach in the advanced studios, where he could set his own agenda. In this setting he proved to be an inspiring teacher, one whose passion for history undergirded each of his demanding studio assignments. Realizing that the typical student understood architectural history as a series of dates when key monuments were built, but didn't really know the buildings physically, "didn't understand the plans, the sections, the intimacy of the architecture," he dedicated the first two weeks of

8.3   Philips Exeter Academy Library, model. Ranalli studio (fall 1988).

8.4   Left: Hammond, Beeby & Babka, Harold Washington Library (1991), Chicago. Right: Kent Bloomer Studio, ornament detail, Washington Library (1991).

8.5   Timothy Steele (M.Arch 1987), Graphic Reconstruction of the Arsenal of Philo at Piraeus, interior perspective. Smith studio (spring 1986).

each advanced studio to a thorough investigation of key modern monuments, requiring students, working in teams sized proportionately to the complexity of their assigned buildings, to know them through drawings and beautifully crafted models, many of which are now displayed throughout Rudolph Hall (8.3). Ranalli adopted this strategy in part to "relieve the students of the burden of having to be creative" by facilitating "the process of just working. You could get into production mode without needing a big idea or a great idea. . . . You could lavish all this energy on these prototypes, these other buildings. You'd come to an understanding of the building but also of how to make things."[64] Looking back on what he called "the whole political thing" surrounding his refusal to team-teach, Ranalli, who in 1999 left Yale to become dean of the School of Architecture at the City College of New York, actually seemed to agree with Gehner's assessment that it was all for the better: "Things aren't always as smooth as they can be with some people," he reflected. "I was happy to focus on other things. So it was a good time to focus on bigger projects and getting students to understand a methodology that would allow them to externalize their ideas."[65]

Though Beeby may not have intended to, as Macrae-Gibson put it, "mold the school into a Classical academy,"[66] he did feel that pluralism, if unchecked, would result in a detrimental "grab-bag," where "everyone is a visitor, and things are added, things are taken out."[67] As a result, Macrae-Gibson, who served on the faculty under both Pelli and Beeby, observed a shift that occurred in the school, from a "very free-flowing" place toward a more rigorous, compartmentalized environment where party lines were being drawn among the students "so that people who were doing historical work became more historical, and people that were doing modernist work said, 'We want nothing to do with that. We're going to be modernists.'"[68]

As Beeby's own work took on a distinctly Classical turn, as evident in his work on Chicago's Sulzer Library (1985) and Harold Washington Library (1991), for which Kent Bloomer provided the ornament (8.4), he encouraged the study of Classicism: "I think to study the orders is an activity that has equal consequence to studying modernism," Beeby told students in 1992. "I think that it would be difficult to refute the reality of the impact of the classical system in architecture. . . . I think that to remove any piece of information that is significant is something the School shouldn't get into."[69] To this end, Beeby advised students to study with George Hersey (1927–2007; G.R.D. 1954) in the History of Art Department and invited "New Classicist" Thomas Gordon Smith (b. 1948) to offer an advanced studio as visiting assistant professor in 1986. Smith would then go on to the University of Notre Dame, where, with the

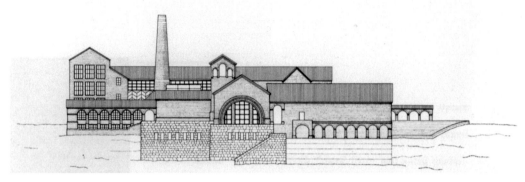

8.6   Mary Cerrone (M.Arch 1990), An Arts Institute, elevation. Porphyrios studio (spring 1989).

8.7   H. Randall Goya (M.Arch 1991), Reconstruction of the House of the Faun, Pompeii, into an Institute for the Study of Pompeiian Archaeology, History, and Architecture, elevation and section. Porphyrios and Krier studio (spring 1991).

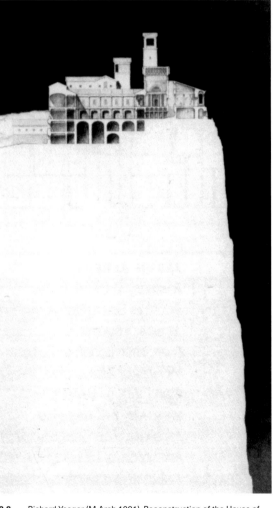

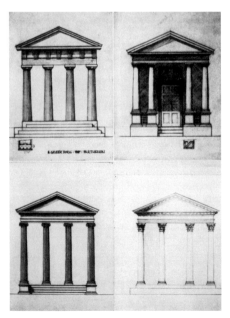

8.8   Richard Yeager (M.Arch 1991), Reconstruction of the House of the Faun, Pompeii, into an Institute for the Study of Pompeiian Archaeology, History, and Architecture, section. Porphyrios and Krier studio (spring 1991).

8.9   Aari Ludvigsen (M.Arch 1989), Temple Elevations. Jarrett studio (fall 1987).

support of the architect John Burgee, he transformed an uninspired modernist pedagogy into a strong curriculum stylistically and ideologically bound to the revival of Classical design. Smith's Yale students were asked to design three projects: two brief archeological projects (8.5) and the third, an addition to the 1894 Richardson Romanesque-style building housing the Yale Collection of Musical Instruments.

Beeby also invited Andrés Duany and Elizabeth Plater-Zyberk, now leaders in the New Urbanism movement, to return to Yale as Bishop Professors in spring 1987, and lead a studio focusing on suburban redevelopment with an emphasis on the analysis of historic precedent and comparative studies of housing densities. Demetri Porphyrios (b. 1949), a Princeton-trained Classicist, was also invited to lead advanced studios. During his first term as the Davenport Professor in spring 1989, Porphyrios, assisted by Harold Roth, gave students a fragment of a plan by Letarouilly, which they were asked to use as the basis of a design for an Arts Institute, "initially drawing on the room typologies of the fragment and its compositional significance"[70] (8.6). In spring 1991, Porphyrios returned to share the Davenport Professorship with the outspoken Classicist Léon Krier (b. 1946). Their studio, focused on adaptive reconstruction, asked students to transform the House of the Faun in Pompeii into an Institute for the Study of Pompeiian Archaeology, History, and Architecture (8.7, 8.8).

In addition to its presence in studios, encouraged by Beeby, Classicism was also introduced into new history and theory courses, such as "Classical Romanticism," taught by Visiting Professor Francesco Dal Co (b. 1945); "Theories of Architectural Order," taught by Patrick Pinnell; and James Jarrett's "The Architect's Use of Architectural History." Jarrett, who as a Yale student had discovered Classicism by way of Philip Johnson and Louis Kahn, taught design and theory from 1981 to 1992 (8.9). In 1990, Beeby told *Progressive Architecture* that he was concerned about the problems posed by the need to build in a society that was constantly changing: "How do you keep architecture from being an endless carnival of styles, one after another?" Classicism was one answer to that question, and it was crucial for him that students have some familiarity with its language. Interviewed by Ross Miller, Beeby offered an ironical view of Classicism: "One of the things that is interesting about Classicism is that not only is it a complete language, but it's a complete galaxy of languages. It offers a way to layer meaning where a person who is uninformed can appreciate it in terms of space and form, and a person who understands more can see its intellectual content and a person who really knows architecture can understand the irony of its misappropriation or deformation. The argument now is that no one

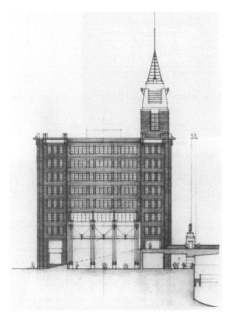

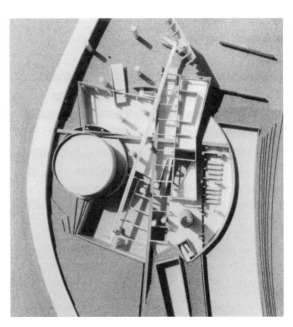

8.10 Gilbert Schafer (M.Arch 1988), A New Building for the Boston Institute of Contemporary Art, elevation. Venturi and Scott Brown studio (spring 1987).

8.11 Gilbert Schafer, An Urban Park with Planetarium, model. Tschumi studio (spring 1988).

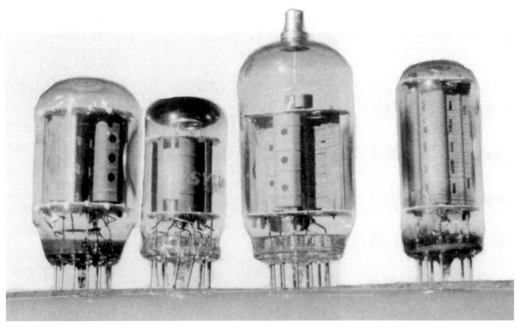

8.12 Vicki Smith (M.Arch 1990), Model. Gehry studio (fall 1988).

understands Classical Architecture anymore, but my sense is that no one ever really understood it."[71]

Stimulated by the emphasis on Classicism in both studios and classrooms, many students went on to become leaders in a new generation of Classical and traditional architects. These include John Tittmann, who as an undergraduate was introduced to Classicism by George Hersey and in an advanced studio led by Thomas Gordon Smith. In 1996, Tittmann joined fellow alumni James Volney Righter and Jacob Albert, bringing Classical discipline to their more freewheeling, Moore-inspired practice, which was renamed Albert, Righter & Tittmann Architects.[72] Duncan Stroik had already been imbued with Classical values as an undergraduate at the University of Virginia during Jaquelin Robertson's term as dean. At Yale, he studied with Thomas Gordon Smith and worked in Allan Greenberg's office, eventually following Smith to the University of Notre Dame faculty and a career specializing in church design.[73] Students who studied Classicism at Notre Dame were, in turn, attracted to Yale to pursue postprofessional degrees, such as James Tinson (b. 1969; M.Arch 1994) and Melissa DelVecchio (b. 1971; M.Arch 1998).

Gilbert Schafer (M.Arch 1988), who had studied "Growth and Structure of Cities" as an undergraduate at Haverford College, came to Classicism by a different path. Inspired by "a love of architecture and its history," Schafer decided to follow in his grandfather's footsteps to pursue architecture and "enroll as a graduate student in architecture at Yale." However, once he arrived at the school in 1985, it became clear to him that the architectural environment he grew up in and the example of the work of his grandfather, a prominent traditional architect in Ohio, "weren't as valued in the academy. There, the principles of modernism and expressing, architecturally, the spirit of the modern age were at odds with a reverence for tradition and the aesthetic pursuit of something that was 'charming.'"[74] Schafer did not pursue Classicism at Yale, though he did study under Venturi who, deeply embroiled in the competition for the National Gallery extension in London, was largely absent from the school (8.10). When Venturi's scheme for the National Gallery was selected, Schafer remembers sending him "a congratulatory telegram from the studio, telling him that Nelson finally had a reason to turn around."[75] Schafer was also a top student in Davenport Visiting Professor Bernard Tschumi's (b. 1944) advanced studio in spring 1988, winning the H. I. Feldman Prize for the best solution to an architectural problem in the advanced studios (8.11). Assisted by the theorist and historian Joan Ockman, Tschumi had asked students to design an "urban park on the site of previous World's Fairs in New York. Each individual project explored issues of simultaneity, permutation and disjunction through the superimposition of five different architectural structures. Students designed a planetarium complex on one of four sites in Flushing Meadows, combined with one of the following: roller coaster, aviary, swimming pool, or stadium sized wide screen."[76] After graduation, Schafer went to work in Tschumi's office. Then he had a change of heart: "With my modernist credentials in hand and the beginnings of a career in pursuit of the avant-garde underway, I began to realize that I had lost touch with the things that had drawn me to architecture originally. In truth, I was much more interested in making places that spoke to my own memories and experiences, places with a more explicit connection to architectural history, than in the abstract theories of design championed by my formal education."[77] Schafer left Tschumi's studio to work for a firm specializing in traditional houses. He then devoted his time to the Institute of Classical Architecture, where he served as president and later as chairman before establishing an independent practice in 2002. Given that he did not take a single studio or class having to do with Classicism, Schafer still doesn't see his time studying under Venturi, Gehry, Josef Paul Kleihues, and Tschumi as wasted: "The great thing about a Yale education is that it teaches you to think and to solve problems. Language is not what's important, it's the way you think about solving problems, and the rigor, and the way you think through a solution. . . . I think I got a great education but I didn't learn to be a Classicist at Yale."[78]

Despite Beeby's own commitment to helping beginning students develop necessary skills, he recognized that the advanced studios were, as mentioned earlier, the "heart of the educational experience at Yale for here is where master confronts student across the drawing board."[79] As if to counter-act the perception of some that by inviting former Rowe students and modern Classicists such as Krier and Porphyrios to teach advanced studios, Beeby was a crypto-Classicist intent on overthrowing modernism, he also invited some of the most provocative avant-garde design talents of the day to the school. Beeby supported Frank Gehry, who had returned in fall 1985 as Davenport Visiting Professor, and again in 1987, as visiting critic, when he offered the seminar "Discussions on Art and Architecture," with a select group of art and architecture students working collaboratively on the design of an eighty-story New York skyscraper. Though it wasn't a formal studio, the course was a design-intensive elective that revisited the idea of the collaborative problem last offered by Kahn and Albers. Again, as in the 1950s, the studio was not a complete success, with the artists and architects struggling to produce a cohe-sive union of the arts. Gilbert Schafer remembers that "it was very difficult." Paired with a Japanese sculpture student who "didn't speak a word of English,"

Schafer's final project was not well resolved, although he notes that "others worked really well."[80] The following fall, Gehry returned as Davenport Visiting Professor to pursue collaborative work, but in a studio requiring teams of art and architecture students to develop a single project for a specific site in New Haven (8.12). The projects, which were intended to mix metaphor with architectural pragmatics, included Pizza Pie Opera House: Chiasmus and Emanation; TV Decodings: Urban Sprawl as Fields, Lines, Points; Theater of Rupture: Distance of Artifice and Nature; and Camera Obscura Habitation.[81] Perhaps unsurprisingly, the resulting projects were more sculptural than architectural. Gehry led a similar collaborative studio during his fall 1989 term as Davenport Professor. To ensure more compatible teammates, each student in the studio selected "a literary quotation on the subject of the city," and then teams were created based on "a mutual philosophical approach" and everyone was given the same program-less project: the "super block" site of the Old City Hall on the New Haven Green.[82]

Japanese architect Tadao Ando (b. 1941) served as Davenport Visiting Professor in fall 1987. Ando spoke little English and was assisted in the studio by George T. Kunihiro (b. 1951), who also acted as his translator. Reflecting the ongoing preoccupation of faculty and students with the Art and Architecture Building, Ando asked students to transform it into an architecture museum (8.13, 8.14), an assignment he deemed "an exercise for a radical study of modern architecture" that would force students to find their own positions: "Did they see the A&A Building within the context of the entire spectrum of architectural history or simply within the modern movement?"[83] Ando pulled no punches in assessing his students, who were, as he wrote in a book published to document the studio, "unquestionably superior to some [Japanese students] . . . of the same generation," but less disciplined, leading him to express a concern about the training students were receiving, which he believed placed too much focus on "their form-making ability." Echoing Shinohara, he said: "Perhaps that is why the students had a very difficult time dealing with conceptual operations. While there were some interesting projects among their submissions, I observed that not one of them was able to make a clear, logical presentation of the polemical position of their work. For example, for my whys, there were only 'because I wanted to' answers."[84] By the time Ando assigned it, tackling the future of the Art and Architecture Building was already a recurrent advanced studio project, beginning in fall 1967, when Charles Moore asked third-year students to design an addition to the building. In spring 1974, George Turnbull (b. 1944; M.Arch 1974), working on his thesis under the direction of James Stirling, undertook the design of a Yale University Cultural

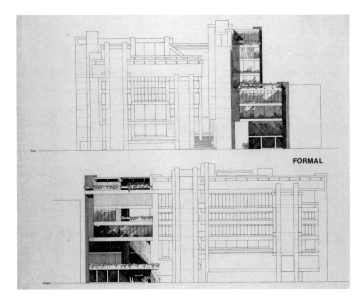

8.15 George Turnbull (M.Arch 1974), Yale University Cultural Arts Center, elevations. Thesis project under James Stirling (spring 1974).

8.14 Kevin Gannon (M.Arch 1988), A Museum for Modern Architecture, model. Ando studio (fall 1987).

8.13 John Butterworth (M.Arch 1988), A Museum for Modern Architecture, model. Ando studio (fall 1987).

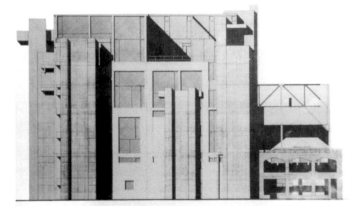

8.16 Adam Anuszkiewicz (M.Arch 1990), An Addition to the Yale Art and Architecture Building, elevation. Independent studio (spring 1990).

Arts Center as an addition to the A&A (8.15). The Ando studio rekindled interest in the A&A problem, and in spring 1990, Adam Anuskiewicz (b. 1962; M.Arch 1990) designed an addition as an independent project (8.16). In fall 1990, Bishop Visiting Professor Mario Gandelsonas asked students to redesign the building as a means to examine the future of architecture. In fall 1994, Lebbeus Woods (1940–2012) asked postprofessional students to focus "on the conditions in Paul Rudolph's master work" as part of an installation intended for publication in the series *Pamphlet Architecture*.[85] In spring 1999, Philip Johnson and Peter Eisenman asked students to design a new architecture building replacing Rudolph's A&A (8.17, 8.18); four years later, students in Turner Brooks's advanced studio designed a new Art History Building adjacent to Rudolph's building, on the same site that would soon be occupied by the Gwathmey-designed Loria Center (8.19, 8.20).

Parallel to his efforts to reshape the Core curriculum, Beeby continued Pelli's commitment to making the school an important force in architectural culture with lectures and a broad array of exhibitions that featured excellent accompanying catalogues. In October 1987, Gavin Macrae-Gibson mounted a show featuring the recent work of thirty-two faculty. In his catalogue introduction, Macrae-Gibson echoed Beeby's doubts about the efficacy of the school's inclusivism, stating that "the diversity of the work can be seen as testament to the School's vitality, what is less obvious is where all this energy is being channeled, what the faculty's goals are, and how they presently affect or may in the future affect the School as an academic institution. Is there sufficient common ground anywhere among the exhibitors that we may speak of a general faculty agenda, or of a dialogue within it, or of some less cohesive but still tangible unity?"[86]

In November 1987, the school exhibited the largest collection of Frank Lloyd Wright chairs ever assembled. Curated by alumnus Alexander Gorlin, then teaching history courses in the school, the show included thirty-six chairs, mixing originals and contemporary reproductions (8.21). The highlight of the exhibition program under Beeby was the student-initiated and curated show *Paul Rudolph: Drawings of the Art and Architecture Building at Yale, 1959–1963*, which was on view from October 31 to November 19, 1988 (8.22). With Rudolph's input, sixty drawings of the twenty-five-year-old building were selected for exhibition by Roberto de Alba (b. 1957; M.Arch 1988), Aubrey Carter (b. 1953; M.Arch 1988), Bennett Cho (b. 1964; M.Arch 1990), Dale Cohen (b. 1961; M.Arch 1989), Alan Organschi (b. 1961; M.Arch 1988), Gilbert Schafer, Randy Wilmot (b. 1960; M.Arch 1989), and Robert Young (b. 1962; M.Arch 1988),

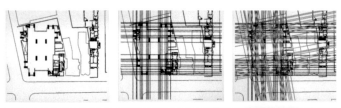

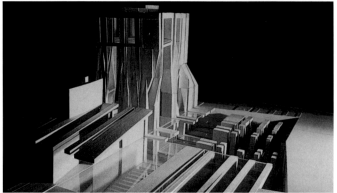

8.17 Tetsuo Tsuchiya (M.Arch 1999), A New Art and Architecture Building for Yale, diagrams and model. Johnson and Eisenman studio (spring 1999).

8.18 Lori Pavese (M.Arch 1999), A New Art and Architecture Building for Yale, model. Johnson and Eisenman studio (spring 1999).

8.19 Yat Ng (M.Arch 2003), A New Art History Building, rendering. Brooks studio (spring 2003).

8.20 Tracy Desrosiers (M.Arch 2003), A New Art History Building, photo collage. Brooks studio (spring 2003).

with Schafer and Young editing the catalogue.[87] The student organizers visited Rudolph at his New York apartment and talked with him about the building—a topic the architect had generally avoided since the fire. Schafer remembers that "He came out of his shell a little because we were genuinely appreciative of the building and interested. So he talked a lot about it. He explained the evolution of the design."[88]

Vincent Scully, who had not been completely won over by the A&A at the time of completion, but by the 1980s had begun to reconsider his position, wrote in *Perspecta* 22 (1986) that "with every passing year one is more and more pleased that Rudolph fought it out as he did," transforming his early, Le Corbusier–influenced designs into the spatial and tectonic grandeur he drew from Frank Lloyd Wright's Unity Temple and Larkin Building. In Scully's view, the "pallid criticisms" of the A&A's detractors had come to "seem less and less germane. . . . There his building stands, as indestructible as he could make it—a weathered mountain, an irredeemable ruin—one of the enduring monuments to the marvelous irrationality of art and to the blessed restlessness of the human spirit. It will be there for a long time, our perennial scapegoat, bashed, battered, trashed and burned, still challenging us to get along with it somehow, and with ourselves."[89] The significance of the student-curated Rudolph exhibit was, as art historian and Rudolph scholar Tim Rohan points out, "exceptional. Beyond Yale, the A&A was derided as an example of mid-1960s establishment mentality, carelessly lumped together with corporate modernism, the very architecture it criticized, or else seen as further evidence of modernism in its final, most alienating and decadent stage. Although Rudolph had for the most part disappeared from contemporary discussions, his A&A had become homiletic—a handy example of the canonical other, the anti-canon."[90]

The character of the double-height exhibition hall had been virtually erased by the Art School, which insisted that its concrete piers and walls, as well as the glass wall that overlooked the Arts Library, be covered with Homasote to simulate the "white box" environment of commercial art galleries. However, the student curators convinced the Art School to let them take down the Homasote, permitting visitors to the exhibition to experience the gallery's interlocking spaces. Because it wasn't feasible to take down the Homasote covering the gallery's concrete piers, the students "painted them the color of the concrete so you could have an impression of what that space was like with the piers coming down. . . . We were trying to get people to remember the building as it was and get excited about it. We really got to understand the building."[91] The Rudolph show came as a revelation.

8.21 *The Chairs of Frank Lloyd Wright,* installation, Yale School of Architecture Gallery (fall 1987).

8.22 Paul Rudolph (center) with student organizers (1988). From left to right: Dale Cohen (M.Arch 1989), Alan Organschi (M.Arch 1988), Rudolph, Roberto de Alba (M.Arch 1988), Randy Wilmot (M.Arch 1989), Robert Young (M.Arch 1988), Aubrey Carter (M.Arch 1988), Gilbert Schafer (M.Arch 1988), and Bennett Cho (M.Arch 1990).

Paul Goldberger, alerted to the student exhibition of Rudolph's drawings, reported on the "startling, if small, transformation in the building itself" brought about by the removal of the Homasote. "Suddenly," he wrote in the *New York Times*, "there is, once again, a sense of transparency; it is possible to see through layers of space, which was what Mr. Rudolph wanted us to experience in this building."[92] Goldberger then went on to explain why, despite its deplorable physical state, the building was beloved by so many Yale architecture students, who venerated it as an heroic gesture realized during a time of American optimism, and as a survivor of intervening decades of unfulfilled promises and disappointment. They are "thus less inclined than their predecessors to see Mr. Rudolph's assertive spaces as a case of excessive architectural hubris. They are not so suspicious of architectural heroism, and many of them rather like it. Even among those who are less enamored of the idea of the architect as assertive, heroic figure, the Rudolph building seems now to be admired as a powerful, even noble set of forms." Goldberger ended his article with what was in effect a mission statement that would not be fulfilled for another twenty years: "to restore the building to what it once was, not because they share Mr. Rudolph's views of architecture, but because they know what respect a great work of art has the right to command."[93] Unfortunately, any appreciation for the reopened space was surpassed by the Art School's hostility to its character. According to Schafer, "We thought everybody would love it and they'd never put [the Homasote] back but the Art School said it had to go back. . . . So the wall went back up and I remember we were all really upset about it."[94]

Beeby contributed a powerful preface to the catalogue for the Rudolph show:

Sometimes I think that I can remember what the Art and Architecture Building was *before,* but it is a fugitive vision from a past now so distant. We came to Yale because of this building and what we thought it represented. We came to study with Paul Rudolph. It was a window of time that was singular and brief. . . . Here was a temple of creation that could rival the temple of work (that was the Larkin Building); a heroic structure, optimistic, unquestioning, forming a self-referential idiom that was a powerful language of its own.

The war in Vietnam ended the condition that created the Art and Architecture Building. Literally consumed by the incendiary times, the building became one of the many casualties of social unrest that questioned the very nature of this country and its institutions. As a result, the structure was not restored; instead it was subverted at every level.

After decades of disregard the building still speaks to those who wish to listen but with a muffled voice, for it has been bound and gagged. I am certain that there is still fear in some who would rather not reveal the architecture in all its power once more. However, they should see that the war is over and it is time to release the prisoners.[95]

Two years prior to the exhibition, with a gift of endowment from Claire and Maurits Edersheim, friends and clients of Rudolph, a lecture series honoring the architect had been established. Appropriately, Rudolph delivered the first Paul Rudolph Lecture on October 17, 1986. Although he refused to speak about the building in his lecture, he did agree to discuss it in an interview with Michael J. Crosbie, published in 1988, as the drawing show was on view in the school's gallery. When asked about the building, Rudolph said, "I almost never talk about it. It's a very painful subject for me. I talk quite freely about many of my buildings when asked, but I *never* talk about this building. It's partially because I don't think I can look very objectively at it."[96] Asked about the sequence of early designs for the building, Rudolph averred that "the Yale Corporation thought the very first proposal was the most awful thing they'd ever seen. Maybe they were right. I guess it's fair to say that there were a lot of people interested in the design at that point. There were a lot of people who had a lot of looks."[97] Rudolph also reflected on the building's pedagogical mission:

To start with the architects, I thought it was important that first-year architecture students be very aware of what their elders, the older students, were thinking and doing. To that end, the drafting rooms were a multileveled affair, so you couldn't help but see and be quite aware of what other people were doing. . . .

I also thought, perhaps quite mistakenly, that the jury system would be of some interest to other than architecture students. To that end I suggested that the jury [space] be in the middle of the exhibition space, and that people could come and listen if they wanted. I believe that you learn about things in mysterious ways, and that the chance encounter can be as important as the formal lecture. I quite mistakenly thought the department of art might be interested in the discussions, . . . not just the architects. But that, perhaps, is too public a position, even for architects. Too much like throwing people into the lion's den—too much exhibition, if you will.

Asked about possible additions, Rudolph said that "there were doodles," and that the elevator core was placed on the north edge to encourage an addition perhaps forming a courtyard.[98]

Leading up to the Rudolph exhibition, a group of second-year students had successfully proposed an elective course dedicated to "the intensive investigation of a single building of central importance for the development of modern architecture." Taught by Alan Plattus, "Critical Monuments of Modern Architecture" was kicked off in 1987 with a study of the A&A. "To us, the [A&A] building was a playground," says Roberto de Alba. "We were finding new spaces all the time." The ambition for the seminar and resulting exhibition was "to bring the building back to people's attention."[99]

Beeby not only advanced the program of exhibitions, he also helped convene a number of symposia—a kind of discourse that had not taken place at the school since the 1950s and 1960s, when the Yale Arts Association, in effect the school's alumni group, would occasionally sponsor such events. To celebrate the twenty-fifth issue of *Perspecta,* a two-day symposium was held on September 15–16, 1989.[100] While the exhibition program and the *Perspecta* symposium valorized aesthetics, theory, and historical research, the school's public outreach was not unmindful of the social issues that were a growing concern to the profession. On February 6–7, 1987, the school sponsored a symposium, "Developing the American City: Society and Architecture in the Regional City," that was attended by over four hundred people.[101] The event was organized by six students—Hans Baldauf, Cary Bernstein (b. 1962; M.Arch 1988), Mary Buttrick (b. 1960; M.Arch 1987), Carey Feierabend (b. 1960; M.Arch 1986), Baker Goodwin (b. 1955; M.Arch 1987), and Li Wen (b. 1961; M.Arch 1988)—who brought together a wide-ranging group of speakers from architecture, real estate, and local government to examine the various artistic, political, and cultural forces affecting cities and explore how architecture could respond to them, using beleaguered New Haven, only a generation before lauded as a "model city" for rebuilding America, as a point of reference. A month prior to the symposium, the six student organizers published an issue of *Rap Sheets* to clarify their plans for the event, noting that "By using New Haven as a reference point, we see the discussion moving between the specific issues pertaining to New Haven to a more national view of middle-sized cities."[102] According to the organizers, the symposium was an opportunity to address complex questions such as "Are the criteria of development and architectural design mutually exclusive?" and "What are the urban implications of the growing underclass?"[103] On January 30–31, 1988, the school and the Connecticut Society of Architects sponsored the symposium "Search for

8.23   First-Year Building Project, An Affordable House Built with Habitat for Humanity (1989), New Haven.

Shelter," as part of a national program focusing on the problems of housing the homeless in the United States. During the proceedings, four design teams formed to work on housing plans for sites in Bridgeport and New Haven.[104]

On November 9, 1991, during Beeby's final term as dean, the school hosted a symposium, "People of Color in Architecture," coinciding with the display in the gallery of the exhibition *African American Architects and Buildings: A Historical Overview,* curated by Auburn University architecture librarian Vinson McKenzie.[105] The one-day event was organized by J. C. Calderón (b. 1965; M.Arch 1992), who was intent on offering Yale an opportunity to encourage a new dialogue about diversity in architecture.[106] It was the outgrowth of a protest by over 70 percent of the student body who, in an April 1990 petition to President (1986–92) Benno Schmidt, Jr. (b. 1942; B.A. 1963, LL.B. 1966) and Dean Beeby, expressed outrage that not one black student had been admitted into the school in the 1989–90 academic year. "People of Color in Architecture" included speakers and panelists such as J. Max Bond, Jr., partner of the New York firm Davis Brody & Associates; M. David Lee of the Boston-based Stull & Lee; Luis Aponte-Parés of City College of New York; Mui Ho of the University of California at Berkeley; Richard Dozier of Florida A&M; and *Progressive Architecture* editor John Morris Dixon. The event sparked contentious debate stimulated by the surprisingly divisive presentation of Harvard-trained Bond, then chairman of the architecture division at Columbia, who, echoing the 1960s Black Workshop, claimed that African American architects, whom he regarded as separate from the professional mainstream, were "in a better position to deal with real-world problems [than white architects]."[107]

During the 1970s and 1980s, the Building Project, absent the federal funding that had supported its early socially conscious efforts, was forced to take on projects such as small structures in summer camps, shore-front pavilions, and, in 1987, an ambitious concert band shell for the city of Bridgeport, Connecticut. But in 1989, amidst the school's renewed commitment to social outreach, the Building Project was dedicated for the first time since the early 1970s to the problems of the economically disadvantaged.[108] This time it was not the citizens of rural Appalachia whose needs were to be addressed, but those in New Haven's poorest neighborhoods, where students, working in conjunction with the local branch of Habitat for Humanity, designed an affordable house (8.23). The shift away from cabins and park pavilions occurred as the result of a suggestion by Kari Nordstrom (M.Arch 1980), who was serving on the charity's board.[109] The Building Project's new direction was embraced by both faculty and students. Not only did the renewed focus on affordable housing reintroduce a sense of social urgency to the Core curriculum, it also provided students with a more comprehensive experience of construction and community collaboration than had been typical in the Building Projects of the 1980s. Moreover, the educational value of designing and building a house further reinforced the sense that the Core studios had to have a pragmatic basis. As Paul Brouard (b. 1929; M.Arch 1961), whose association with the Building Project began in 1971 and who served as its director from 1973 until 2006, stated: "The idea of having to complete a building that was not just a structure, but also had all of the mechanical and other amenities that you need in a residential building, is fantastically comprehensive for the students. As learning experiences, the pavilions were great structural and expressive exercises. But I think that it's much more challenging to start your education by designing and constructing a building that has a full program and also has the personal aspect of being a house built for a real family in a local neighborhood."[110]

As the program evolved, it became clear that the structures could not be completed during the period of approximately one month required of all first-year students after the end of the spring semester. As a result, interested students from the first year, as well as some from advanced classes, were given the option to continue on as paid interns, working throughout the summer until classes resumed. Since 1995, this summer work has been supported by the Charles W. Moore Building Program Fund, an endowment established by Moore's friends, students, colleagues, and his former partners at Centerbrook Architects. Additional support has come from Tai Soo Kim (b. 1936; M.Arch 1962), a prominent Hartford, Connecticut, architect, and from Marshall Ruben (b. 1960; B.A. 1982) and Carolyn Greenspan. More recently, a parallel course was developed that was not only intended to make the students' introduction to principles of wood construction more systematic, but also to require each team to produce a set of working drawings and cost estimates. Additionally, a minicourse in group dynamics has been added through the support of the New Practice Paradigms Lectureship Fund established in 2007 by Phillip Bernstein and Nancy Alexander (b. 1959; B.A. 1979, M.B.A. 1984). Thus the Moore years' emphasis on collaboration has if anything been intensified. And despite the selection of a single design, an improvisational aspect remains, with the students adding details and embellishments while building it in the field, with the entire class working in teams. As Brouard gradually limited his involvement, he was joined by Adam Hopfner (b. 1971; M.Arch 1999). Hopfner is currently director of what is now officially known as the Jim Vlock Building Project, so named in 2008, when the school received a significant endowment from Vlock's son Michael and Michael's wife, Karen Pritzker, to honor a man long associated with social causes in New Haven who had worked closely with

Charles Moore on Tower One (1971), part of the Church Street South Housing complex that Moore had master-planned and designed.[111]

In May 1991, Beeby privately decided to resign from the deanship, effective January 1, 1992, but his decision wasn't announced publicly until October. President Benno Schmidt, Jr., unsuccessfully tried to persuade the dean to complete his second term, or at least to delay his departure until the end of the academic year, but Beeby was adamant about his need to concentrate on architectural practice.[112] The decision was inevitable; in some ways, Beeby never fully settled into the job. While he had chosen to live near New Haven—in Guilford, Connecticut, where he maintained a small studio—his professional office remained in Chicago, creating "a major commuting situation." Plus, he believed that a six-year term was a "healthy positive and within the nature of the School." As he told a *Yale Daily News* reporter: "I have implemented some changes and I feel fairly good about them. Now it's time to move on."[113] Beeby, however, remains closely connected to Yale as consulting architect to the Yale Corporation's Committee on Buildings and Grounds and to the school as professor adjunct, leading a studio and seminar every other spring term.

At the conclusion of his time as dean, Beeby prepared a "Strategic Plan for the School," the first, it would seem, since Moore's ten-year plan of 1970. Like Moore's, Beeby's plan was thoughtful; like Moore's, it does not appear to have been circulated among faculty, alumni, or students; and like Moore's, it drew attention to problems that it would take the school years to address. One of its principal concerns was the role of computing in the school's curriculum. As dean, Beeby had seen to it that students had begun to incorporate computers "into the Core studio as a tool that can increase the designer's capability to envision and evaluate complex three-dimensional form."[114] Indeed, by the end of his tenure, students had access to AutoCAD and AES (Architecture Engineering System) software, which was then being tested in the school, but the computers were located in a special basement classroom. In his ten-year plan, he noted that the "dramatic increase in computer literacy and interest in computers on the part of students entering the School" had to be satisfied with new equipment and teaching initiatives. Beeby, in his plan, wrote that "even if it does not choose to become a center for the cutting edge of research in this field it [the computer] has a responsibility to support the needs and interests of students and faculty which will, in certain cases, inevitably extend to whatever constitutes the cutting edge." At the very least, Beeby pointed out, the computer would need to be "integrated into the mainstream of the School's work, in the design studios and courses, with ease of access and availability, as in modern offices where it is on the desk along with conventional drafting equipment, and not relegated to the basement."[115] The truth of the matter was that, despite the best efforts of the administration and the faculty, with regard to computing, the school was woefully behind its competitors. As a keystone of his program, Bernard Tschumi, appointed dean at Columbia in 1988, pushed the use of computers, introducing a so-called "paperless studio" in 1994 with the intention of replacing all previous means of design conceptualization and production. Yale's computer capacity was nowhere near that point, nor did the faculty embrace Tschumi's approach.

Reviewing the evolution of architectural discourse in the schools and the profession since 1965, especially the attack on the authority of modern architecture "on all fronts: social, political, and aesthetic," Beeby stated in his "Strategic Plan" that "the proliferation of competing ideologies" in the schools had "made the 1980s a time of both exhilarating theoretical debate, and petty competition for the hearts and minds of students," a trend he believed would continue "with no single position capable of reestablishing a consensus within the Schools, much less between the Schools and the profession."[116] The Yale School of Architecture, Beeby contended, was not immune from these trends and, in some cases, "had been where they originated." However, Yale's traditional pluralism made the school better able to cope with the times because it "has never depended upon its connection to a particular fashionable theoretical or polemical position for its strength and energy."[117]

In his plan, Beeby touched on many other issues, including the condition of the Art and Architecture Building, which should be "considered to be a major landmark for its period of design" and treated accordingly.[118] Reviewing the school's various programs, he reported that "the possibility of a post-professional degree program emphasizing a collaborative model of environmental design" was being considered by the schools of Architecture and Forestry—something that would eventually be adopted with mixed success in 2006.[119] Beeby, like Moore, drew attention to "the merits and problems of . . . Ph.D. programs in architecture. Should these degrees become standard at competing institutions, Yale would have to consider a major shift or commitment of new resources."[120] A Ph.D. program would be inaugurated in 2008.[121] Beeby also reported that the school, having "instituted required core courses" taught by faculty in the history and theory of architecture, was "considering consolidating numerous visiting slots in favor of distinguished yearly visitors on the model of the visiting professorships in design."[122] To be properly realized, his proposal required an endowed professorship, which wouldn't happen until 2003, when the Vincent Scully Visiting Professorship of Architectural History was funded, with Kurt Forster as its inaugural occupant.[123]

All in all, Beeby left the school in better shape than it had been for quite some time. His focus on the art and practice of architecture and his resistance to theory-based design set the school apart from its peers. Beeby said: "One of my concerns is that architecture is becoming more and more academic. I'm concerned that the rift that exists between practice and the Schools is going to get worse and worse." Beeby feared that "architecture could be taught like law where the faculty never has to prove itself in the field" and worried about a climate where architecture as it "exists in the Schools is in a world of its own. I think that would really be a tragedy, particularly in respect to this school which has this long tradition of being tied to the idea of architectural practice."[124]

9
Toward Urbanism
1993–1998

"Our continuing dedication to the importance of the urban condition
has informed many elective course and studio offerings and
has given increasing presence to our Urban Design Workshop."

Fred Koetter, *Retrospecta 1994–1995*

With Thomas Beeby's resignation, effective January 1, 1992, Alexander Purves assumed the responsibilities of leadership as acting dean, serving until January 1, 1993, when the appointment of Alfred Koetter took effect. As Alan Plattus recalls, having Purves as acting dean "felt a bit like a throwback. Alec is wonderful but he's one of these people that doesn't want to say no to anybody."[1] Purves himself has said as much and has acknowledged his personal reluctance to make difficult decisions that affect others. Unfortunately, he was forced to say no quite a lot while acting dean when the university, in reaction to the collapsed stock market of the late 1980s and early 1990s, once again mandated significant cuts to the school's budget. Unable to cut salaries, Purves says he "had to let some [faculty] go. It wasn't a happy experience. Staff were cut, too. There wasn't any money to do anything that was fun."[2]

Meanwhile, Purves was also serving as chair of the Search Committee to find Beeby's successor. The committee consisted of Art History Professor Richard M. Barnhart, Music School Professor of Composition Ezra Laderman, and architecture faculty members Deborah Berke, Barbara Littenberg, George J. Ranalli, and Herman D. J. Spiegel.[3] Early in the process, the committee expressed an interest in reconnecting with Robert Venturi, who declined to be considered for "professional reasons"; Venturi did, however, write a letter of support on behalf of Alan Chimacoff (b. 1942)—a Cornell student of Colin Rowe's, a former Princeton University professor, and currently director of design at the Hillier Group—whom Venturi believed to be "a *perfect* choice."[4] As was typical of previous searches, professionals and alumni wrote to opine on the selection of the next dean, with nominations running the full gamut from traditionalists to radicals. Philip Johnson suggested the Austrian Deconstructivist Wolf Prix, while Craig Whitaker suggested Robert A. M. Stern, who would eventually be interviewed by the committee but ultimately rejected due to the nature of his practice.[5] "The sticking point didn't have to do with Stern's capacity to run the school," Purves remembers, "but it had everything to do with his work. People weren't happy with the kind of work he was doing then—the Shingle-style houses and so forth."[6] Steven Holl wrote to President Schmidt with a late suggestion that the university should seek out a candidate like Bernard Tschumi, who when appointed dean at Columbia "had not constructed large buildings" but was nonetheless proving to be an excellent choice, exhibiting "outstanding . . . intellectual achievement and teaching commitment."[7]

Surprisingly, one of the most controversial figures to be proposed was an insider—something no previous dean or chairman, with the exception of Herman Spiegel, had ever been. George Ranalli was recommended by Thomas

Mayne, Stanley Tigerman, Henry Smith-Miller, and Frank Gehry, who noted that Ranalli "has certainly given his all to the School and many students have reaped the benefits."[8] However, the outspoken teacher was not without his detractors. Gavin Macrae-Gibson believes that Ranalli liked "to think of himself as an *enfant terrible*. . . . He was more interested in saying why [the school] was wrong, because it didn't adhere to what he felt were [his own] clearly superior points of view. In that sense, he was not very 'Yale.'"[9] While many did not see Ranalli as particularly open-minded, one of his former students, Audrey Matlock, did, writing that he "both understands and has always supported the pluralistic education that Yale has always provided" and "has a long history as an educator of Yale students."[10]

All in all, the names of more than 140 individuals were considered. Eventually the committee reduced the pool to two candidates: Alan Chimacoff, Tom Beeby's classmate at Cornell, and Fred Koetter, Harvard Graduate School of Design professor and principal of the Boston-based architecture and urban design firm Koetter Kim & Associates.[11] As Purves remembers, "We gave Benno those two names, unranked. I was told that he had a very impressive meeting with Fred and never met with Alan. He was sold."[12] On May 7, 1992, Koetter's selection was announced, though he would not take up the position until January 1993.[13] According to Purves, much like the Search Committee that selected Beeby, the committee was looking for someone with "an inclusive attitude about architecture" who would "maintain our pluralistic approach toward design." They were also impressed with Koetter's background as an architect whose practice included urban design, which they took to mean an understanding of "architecture as part of a group effort." While there was some justifiable concern that an increasingly busy architect might be "torn between his practice and the School," the committee was encouraged by Koetter's assurance that he would move both his family and his firm to New Haven—something that only partially came to pass, when Koetter and his wife and partner, Susie Kim, relocated their family but chose to keep the offices of Koetter Kim & Associates in Boston.[14]

Raised in Great Falls, Montana, Alfred Koetter (9.1) studied architecture at Montana State University for one year before transferring to the University of Oregon, where he received his bachelor of architecture in 1964. He then went on to Cornell, where he earned his master of architecture in 1966 and, after graduation, joined the faculty, closely aligning himself with Colin Rowe, with whom he collaborated on the book *Collage City,* an attempt to synthesize traditional and modernist approaches to urban design.[15] Koetter joined the Yale faculty in 1975 as associate professor of architectural design, but after

9.1   Fred Koetter (1992).

9.2   Daryl Haughn (M.Arch 1994), The Museum and the Street. Peterson studio (fall 1993).

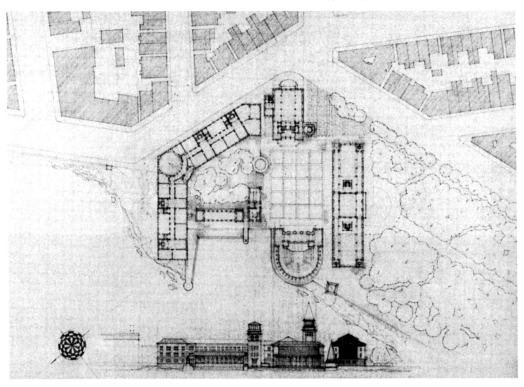

9.3   A. James Tinson (M.Arch 1994), A Science Center for Long Island City. Post-professional studio (ca. 1994).

three years, he accepted a position at Harvard's Graduate School of Design and, upon making the move north, established an active Boston-based architecture and urban design practice.[16] During the fall 1984 semester, Koetter returned to Yale to serve as Bishop Visiting Professor, but otherwise remained at Harvard until accepting the deanship.

Although Alan Plattus was closely allied with Chimacoff, with whom he had taught at Princeton and collaborated professionally, he welcomed the appointment of Koetter, "one of the smartest people" he had ever met, who was "as sharp a critic as any. Speculative, open, curious . . . and he had an amazing hand. He was one of the most facile designers I've known." As a critic on juries, Koetter "was never a bully. He listened. He was perceptive. [There was] nobody you'd rather teach with or work with on a project." However, there is another aspect to being a dean, one that involves managing complex university bureaucracies, strong personalities, and of course, school finances. In this administrative regard, as Plattus notes, Koetter would ultimately prove "not up to what Yale needed at that time."[17]

The ramifications of Koetter's laid-back disposition would soon be felt, but in the immediate wake of the 1980s boom, when leading architects had begun to be cultivated—and to cultivate themselves—as personalities, it seemed refreshing. Describing the new dean in a profile written for the *Yale Alumni Magazine,* Mark Alden Branch contrasted Koetter with "the 'high-design' stars of the 1980s" who were "mere stylists divorced from both the mechanics of building and the concerns of society," and welcomed the appointment as a sign that Yale would continue to focus on training practitioners over theorists. To some extent, Koetter echoed Beeby's belief that the decline of the architect's cultural relevance could be traced back to many schools of architecture, where, as Branch put it, "theorists have been mining literary criticism and philosophy for ideas" rather than concentrating on architecture's own discourse.[18]

Koetter's appointment closely coincided with the abrupt resignation of President Benno Schmidt, Jr., on May 26, 1992.[19] Though Schmidt's tenure as president had been somewhat rocky, he enjoyed wide alumni support, was a prodigious fund-raiser, and was passionate about the university's physical plant, initiating massive renovation and construction projects. Schmidt stepped down at about the same time the economy took a dramatic downward turn, leading the university to scale back its plans for renovations and new buildings and initiate cuts in academic programs.[20] As a search was conducted for Schmidt's successor, Howard Lamar (b. 1923; Ph.D. 1951) served as interim president until the somewhat surprising appointment of Graduate

School Dean Richard C. Levin (b. 1947; Ph.D. 1974) as president (1993–2013); Levin inherited a largely demoralized faculty, a decaying campus, and frosty relations between town and gown.[21] Although Schmidt had made early strides toward improving Yale's relationship with the city of New Haven by committing the university to making payments in lieu of taxes, tensions between the two entities had been exacerbated after the 1991 murder of Yale College student Christian Prince in the very heart of campus on the steps of St. Mary's Church on Hillhouse Avenue.[22] But change was on the horizon. Along with Levin's appointment, the election of Mayor John DeStefano, Jr. (b. 1955), in 1994 held the promise of a new town-gown partnership.

Koetter assumed his new responsibilities just in time to attend a symposium at the school, the "Yale Conference on Housing" (January 29–30, 1993) organized by students Louise Harpman (b. 1964; M.Arch 1993) and Evan Supcoff (b. 1966; M.Arch 1993), who were editing an issue of *Perspecta* that would document much of the event's proceedings.[23] The conference, which helped set the tone for Koetter's tenure, was attended by more than three hundred people. It provided "a forum for architecture students, practicing architects, housing developers, local and national housing officials, and housing specialists" in an effort "to realign the architecture and housing development communities and to reestablish architects as advocates of quality dwellings."[24] Speakers included Vincent Lane, chairman of the Chicago Housing Authority, and Felice Michetti, commissioner of the New York City Department of Housing Preservation and Development. In conjunction with the symposium, the school mounted two exhibitions: an overview of four affordable houses built by Yale students as part of the first-year Building Project and an exhibition of innovative housing schemes by students, practitioners, and planners.

Supported by Associate Dean Alan Plattus, Koetter began to shift the school's curricular emphasis toward urbanism. This agenda very quickly became clear to students, some of whom were fully supportive. "We think he has everything to gain by sticking with urban planning," Clemon Andre Johnson (b. 1968; M.Arch 1995) told the *Yale Daily News*. "This program is concerned with interacting with the environment and being realistic on an urban level."[25] Koetter's agenda was made explicit in his annual letters published in the beginning of each issue of *Retrospecta,* in which he often cited the school's "continuing dedication" to the importance of the city and, more generally, "the urban condition."[26]

While Beeby had concentrated on the Core, Koetter would attempt to redirect Yale's program principally through a reorganization of the post-professional curriculum, which was having problems attracting students—partially because of its relatively long two-year duration (a comparable program at Harvard was for one and a half years, while Columbia's took only a year, including a summer term). Koetter, recognizing that the program had no focus of its own, attempted to position it as a distinct urban track within the school that he would personally oversee (9.2, 9.3). In so doing, he was building upon a coyly titled 1994 student-edited publication, *Suspecta: Advanced Studies: The Post-Professional Program at the School of Architecture*, in which students past and present made clear that the program suffered from a sense of isolation in the school. In a transcript of a roundtable discussion between post-professional students Charlie Stott (b. 1961; M.Arch 1993) and Michael Haverland (b. 1967; M.Arch 1994), as well as Tom Beeby and Fred Koetter, Beeby, empathizing with the current group of post-professionals, recounted his own experience as a post-professional student in 1964–65: "Nobody in the rest of the School talked to us; we had a terrible faculty and were totally isolated."[27] According to Beeby, when he came back as dean, nothing much seemed to have changed: students "were at that point, concerned about not being part of the School, that they were left out of the group. They felt that they wanted to be more integrated; they were concerned that they didn't have enough contact with the rest of the students." To help integrate the post-professional students, Beeby, during his tenure as dean, provided them with funding to initiate their own programs "with the idea that you can't do something like this for yourselves, you have to do something for the whole school."[28] These programs included a lecture series, film series, and, in spring 1990, a symposium featuring architects and writers Peter Carl, John Hejduk, and Jeffrey Kipnis. Koetter's strategy was to teach an introductory studio exclusively for the post-professionals, as well as a seminar, "Issues in Architecture," intended to lift the discourse and establish a "dialogue and cohesion among these students."[29]

Koetter's predilection toward urbanism and social activism was evident in his invitation to architects and architect-planners to serve as visiting professors: Ray Huff (b. 1948), for example, led a studio analyzing public space in Charleston, South Carolina, while questioning how architecture can change the perception of a city (fall 1994); Bishop Professor Steven Izenour, partner of Robert Venturi and Denise Scott Brown, offered the studio "Relearning from Las Vegas," reexamining the desert city in light of its efforts to reposition itself as a family entertainment destination; and Izenour, returning in spring 1998, worked with Michael Haverland to revive the spirit of the original Las Vegas studio with "Learning from the Wildwoods," focused on the New Jersey shore resort, notable for its "vivid '50s imagery, rich palette of color, decoration, lights, plastic and glitz, while not freeze-drying the past." The work produced by the studio was exhibited at Penn and Kent State, but to many it seemed more nostalgic than provocative.[30] Samuel Mockbee, founder of the Rural Studio in Alabama, served as Davenport Professor during the spring 1997 semester and asked students to consider the "broader circumstances of economics, political, and environmental forces that make up the cultural landscape."[31] Bishop Professor (fall 1997) José Antonio Acebillo had served as the director of the Institute for Urban Development in Barcelona from 1988 to 1994, during which time he led the city's physical reconstruction in anticipation of the 1992 Summer Olympic Games. At Yale, he asked students to redesign a portion of the Barcelona waterfront. Continuing Beeby's emphasis on Colin Rowe–inspired formalism in the studios, Koetter invited yet another Cornell-trained architect, Steven Peterson, Barbara Littenberg's life and professional partner, to serve as Bishop Visiting Professor in fall 1993. Peterson's studio on the architecture of the street also reflected what was becoming the program's prevailing emphasis on urbanism.

The focus on urbanism and social outreach gained significant traction when Davenport Visiting Professor (fall 1993) Stanley Tigerman, who had been invited by Beeby, used his studio as a "dry run" for Archeworks, the Chicago-based independent school that he was in the process of establishing with designer Eva Maddox as an "experiment in alternative architectural education," where students working in multidisciplinary teams would partner with nonprofit organizations to create socially and environmentally aware products.[32] Tigerman's Yale studio, "ArchitectuRE-works," proposed to build relationships between design students and community programs. The studio began by investigating abandoned buildings and vacant storefronts in New Haven, and created an outreach initiative to connect with existing community programs. During the second half of the studio, students developed individual programs and projects in response to needs in the community (9.4). Two students, Matthew Bremer (b. 1967; M.Arch 1995) and Andy Reeder (b. 1965; M.Arch 1994), actually realized their design for an advanced care room in an existing transitional housing facility run by the Connecticut AIDS Residence Program, which ran halfway houses for people who were HIV-positive at a time before drugs had been developed to address this urgent health emergency.[33] Bremer, along with John Woell (b. 1963; M.Arch 1995) and Tom Zook (b. 1965; M.Arch 1995), also organized an exhibition, *AIDS and Housing,* that combined local statistical data with student design projects to encourage architects to become involved with a critical health care issue.

Tigerman's studio culminated in a one-day symposium on December 4, 1993, entitled "Collaboration '93," organized by Michael Haverland and Kate Iverson (b. 1963; M.Arch 1994) to engage a broad audience with the studio's generating premise—namely, how architecture and planning might improve Yale's relationship with New Haven (9.5). Representatives from Yale's Law, Nursing, and Forestry schools were invited to the conference to discuss how they might constructively work together with the School of Architecture to achieve more effective solutions to town-and-gown problems. The day consisted of a series of interdisciplinary workshops, followed by a public forum attended by Koetter, School of Management Professor Douglas Rae, University President Richard Levin, University Secretary Linda Lorimer, New Haven Ward 1 Alderman Stefan Pryor, and New Haven Mayor John DeStefano, who told the attendees, "If any city in the U.S. can set an example of collaborative partnership and solving urban problems, this city can."[34] The dialogue between the city and the university, not to mention the new president and the new mayor, was productive. Looking back on the studio after fifteen years, Tigerman noted, "The very fact that several parties responsible for Yale's and New Haven's joint and several destinies came together signaled that perhaps subsequent dialogues might be beneficial to both institutions."[35]

In 1992, preceding the "ArchitectuRE-works" studio and conference, university funds had been made available to help establish the Yale Urban Design Workshop (UDW) and Center for Urban Design Research under the leadership of Alan Plattus, who was assisted from 1995 to 2005 by Michael Haverland, and since then by Andrei Harwell (b. 1975; M.Arch 2006). The workshop's initial mandate was ambitious: according to Koetter, it was to provide "a venue within the School of Architecture for work and discussion which extends the Core curriculum and educational experience of the School into the field of urbanism."[36] Though the UDW did not become the forum for discourse on urban theory that many hoped it would, it did succeed as a community-oriented planning consultancy, providing research and design services for communities across Connecticut, as well as undertaking actual design projects, such as a transit-oriented plan for Bloomfield, Connecticut, and master plans for Wassaic, New York, and Winsted, Connecticut (9.6).

The establishment of the UDW was a reflection of Yale's growing concern that its location in New Haven, which had an exceptionally high crime rate, was adversely affecting its ability to attract students and faculty. According to Plattus, when Levin was being considered for the presidency, he underwent numerous interviews, and in each one, the most important question was "What are you going to do about New Haven?" It was made explicitly clear that New

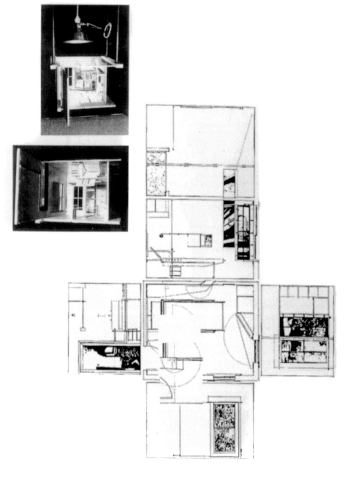

9.4   Matt Bremer (M.Arch 1995) and Andy Reeder (M.Arch 1994), examples of work.
Tigerman's ArchtectuRE-works studio (fall 1993).

9.5   A panel of speakers at the "Collaboration '93" forum. From left to right: Douglas Rae,
Linda Lorimer, President Levin, Mayor DeStefano, and Fred Koetter.

Haven was to be front and center on the new president's agenda, which fortuitously coincided with Koetter's own interests in urban design and planning. With the publication of an extensive two-part article in the *New Yorker* on New Haven's plight, the dire state of things was no longer just local news.[37] To address the situation, the Yale Corporation formed a committee chaired by Oklahoma Senator David Boren (b. 1941; B.A. 1963). Plattus was on the committee, along with Lee Adler, a highly respected preservationist from Savannah, Georgia, and Bruce Alexander (b. 1943; B.A. 1965), an experienced developer long associated with the Rouse Company, who would become Yale's vice president for New Haven and State Affairs in 1998. The committee structured a general approach to improving conditions in New Haven, in which the UDW would figure prominently.

The specific event that led to the UDW's founding was more a result of happenstance than of intention. It started when Andrew Meyers (b. 1963; M.E.D. 1993), researching charrettes with Alan Plattus, struck up a conversation with a man on an airplane about public design workshops and architects who work with local communities. The man was the political and social activist Ralph Nader, and he told Meyers, "We could use something like that in my hometown, Winsted, Connecticut."[38] So, as Plattus recalls, "Through Ralph, Meyers got me hooked up with Winsted. Winsted said yes."[39] Plattus put together a team that included landscape designer Diana Balmori, Kent Bloomer, Peter de Bretteville (appointed critic in 1990), architect and educator Ann Tate, and Doug Rae from the School of Management, who had been chief administrative officer of the city of New Haven under the John Daniels administration (1990–93) (9.6).

The Winsted charrette would be the nascent UDW's first project, staffed by graduate and undergraduate students who spent four days in the town, where they were "put up in local B&Bs and people's houses." The UDW next turned its attention to New Haven, undertaking a Neighborhood Discovery Program, a student-run initiative that taught design-thinking and basic urbanism to elementary school kids through the auspices of the Dwight-Edgewood Design Collaborative, which provided assistance to community leaders and organizations and volunteered members' skills to help design parks, playgrounds, maps, and models of the area. Recognizing the growing interest in urban design and community engagement, as well as the urgency of the situation in New Haven, the university agreed to provide initial funding for the UDW. Later, it was supported by the federal government during the first Clinton administration, which, under the leadership of Henry Cisneros, secretary of Housing and Urban Development (1993–97), established a program of community outreach partnership grants set up to fund university-city initiatives "on the theory that universities should partner with their communities to help them revitalize the area."[40] The New Haven project would be a hallmark of Levin's presidency—a sign of positive change in town-gown relations that came not a moment too soon. But, as federal and central university funds dried up in the second half of the 1990s, Koetter could provide little more than moral support. According to Plattus, "He obviously approved of what we were doing but he didn't give us anything in the way of resources." He did, however, appoint Haverland to the faculty, making it possible for him to stay on at the workshop and teach at the school.[41] Subsequently, Haverland, under the auspices of the UDW, would undertake the design of a significant addition to the Timothy Dwight Elementary School in the troubled Edgewood neighborhood (9.7).[42]

Community engagement at the school was at levels that hadn't been seen since the late 1960s, but without the previous era's anger or its macho bravura. Plattus and Doug Rae inaugurated a lecture course "designed to introduce Yale undergraduates to the history and current affairs of the City of New Haven." Additionally, Patrick Pinnell and Peter de Bretteville taught a course on the history of Yale's campus planning in fall 1994, and Koetter led a course called "New Haven and Conditions of the Periphery," which "utilized the findings of these studies in the formation of conceptual studies for the possible future(s) of the city."[43]

Koetter continued Beeby's policy of making sure that women were well represented among the visiting critics: Mary-Ann Ray and Robert Mangurian served as Davenport Visiting Professors (spring 1996); Peggy Deamer (spring 1992), Homa Fardjadi (fall 1992), and Merrill Elam (fall 1996) were appointed Bishop Visiting Professors; Toshiko Mori (fall 1992), Ada Karmi-Melamede (fall 1993), Karen Bausman (spring 1994), and Homa Fardjadi (fall 1995) served as Saarinen Visiting Professors; and Deamer became associate professor of architectural design and theory in 1995.

Koetter capitalized on the interest in Classical architecture that Beeby had encouraged by initiating a three-week summer workshop in Rome—at the students' request, it was extended to four weeks in 2005. The Rome seminar, designed to provide a broad overview of that city's major architectural sites, topography, and systems of urban organization, emerged from a class taught by two new faculty members whom Koetter had brought in from Harvard: T. Kelly Wilson, appointed critic in architectural design in 1993, and Jeff Klug, appointed critic in architectural design in 1994. "I brought those two guys in," remembers Koetter, "and then some of their students came into my office and said, 'We would like the school to have a Rome studio.' . . . [Wilson and Klug] had experience doing Rome programs, so they knew people there."[44] Koetter approved the trip, but students were responsible for finding their own funds for travel and accommodations. Unlike typical Rome studios fielded by architecture schools, this was not a design studio, but instead it was a seminar requiring students to keep sketchbooks as the primary way to improve their drawing skills and their capacity for observation, with the buildings, streets, landscapes, and gardens of Rome providing a rich textbook of historical continuity and change over its long history—the strategy continues to this day (9.8). When the Rome studio hit something of a bumpy patch in 2001, as the result of the turn-over of key faculty, Alec Purves, now emeritus professor, was asked to take over. "I said, 'What the hell. It might be interesting,'" remembers Purves. "I said I'd do it on one condition—that I can do it with Stephen Harby [b. 1954; B.A. 1976, M.Arch 1980]," who had studied with Purves as both an undergraduate and graduate student.[45] The program was restricted to twenty-four students entering their final year, attracting about half of the second year and some post-professional students. But the cost of travel and the loss of possible income from summer employment prevented a number of students from participating. In 2010, with gifts from alumni, the program was grown to thirty students and an additional faculty member was added. In 2010, when budget restrictions threatened the seminar's cancellation, Frannie and Gordon Burns (b. 1953; B.A. 1975) and Edward Bass generously provided enough funding to waive tuition and cover all travel expenses for the foreseeable future.

Koetter's emphasis on urbanism, admirable though it was, failed to resonate with a great many prospective students. As part of an effort to reclaim some of its fading prestige as a program that trained design leaders, in fall 1995, the School of Architecture mounted *Ten Years Out,* which appears to have been its first-ever alumni exhibition. Showcasing work completed within the first ten years after graduation, the exhibition included the work of established practitioners such as Hugh Newell Jacobsen (b. 1929; M.Arch 1955), Norman Foster, and Charles Gwathmey, as well as more recent alumni such as Brian Healy (b. 1956; M.Arch 1981), Daniel Rowen (1953–2009; M.Arch 1981), Terry Dwan (b. 1957; M.Arch 1984), Scott Merrill, and Maya Lin. After its run in New Haven, the exhibition traveled to Italy, where it was installed at the 1996 Milan Triennale.

Immediately upon settling into the dean's office, Koetter was made aware of the shaky state of the undergraduate major. The program was poorly housed in the near-derelict former headquarters of the Fence Club, a facility the

9.6   Urban Design Workshop, Plan for Winsted, Connecticut (1993).

9.7   Urban Design Workshop, Addition to the Timothy Dwight Elementary School, New Haven (2001).

9.8   Student sketches from Rome seminar. Left: Daniel Markiewicz (M.Arch 2011), Piazza del Popolo (2010). Right: Eleanor Measham (M.Arch 2014), Galleria Borghese, Piazza Navona, Cappella Chigi (2013).

university acquired in 1979, when fraternities were banished from the campus. The building was, as the *Yale Daily News* reported in 1993, downright dangerous: "Students have found homeless people upstairs and syringes strewn around the floor."[46] The undergraduates were resentful of the isolation and what they deemed second-class status: "Not only were we in our own building, but we were very much a marginal presence in the school," remembers (Michael) Surry Schlabs (b. 1976; B.A. 1999, M.Arch 2003, Ph.D. forthcoming). "We rarely attended lectures. We were, in some cases, actively discouraged from attending lectures. So there was something of a tense relationship between the architecture major and the school. We didn't feel particularly welcome there."[47] The separation from the main building did have its perks, though. As Schlabs notes, "We did whatever we wanted to. There was absolutely no oversight at the building. We were pouring resin, spray-painting the floor, playing loud music, building partitions, and installing sculptures. There is a little courtyard there, which was full of these aborted sculptures and model projects."[48]

Writing to Provost Judith Rodin in February 1993, Koetter, basing his observations about the Yale College major on a report prepared by Kent Bloomer, Director of Undergraduate Studies, painted a sunny picture that was not necessarily shared by Yale College administrators or undergraduates, as evidenced by the declining numbers of students choosing to major in architecture. Koetter, channeling Bloomer, tried to put a good spin on the enrollment situation by stating that although the applicants to the major had "leveled off and even decreased," 450 students a year were availing themselves of course offerings fielded by the school, suggesting "that many Yale College students seem to place value upon visual literacy, spatial problem-solving and issues related to the man-made environment, especially the urban environ-ments."[49] As Koetter saw it, the inadequately funded undergraduate program was the victim of the school's overall budget crisis, leading him to make two suggestions: eliminate or significantly reduce the scope of the undergraduate program and its corresponding faculty, or increase graduate school enroll-ment and maintain current faculty. Though both options would alleviate the budget crunch, Koetter made it clear to Provost Rodin that, in his opinion, "When I think of the big picture—when I think of the role of a program of this kind within the University at large—its elimination or near elimination" is "a bad idea, a genuinely lousy idea." Koetter supported his argument with a quote from Bloomer, who noted that Yale's undergraduate program is the only one within the university "that is primarily dedicated to *spatial* (as compared to verbal or numerical) problem solving," and as such "is the only undergraduate program offering a curriculum in the theory, analysis and design of the *manmade environment,* as compared to the analysis and 'control' of the 'natural' environment,"[50] leading Koetter to defend the major as "a model of how a graduate school can positively serve the educational interest of the University's academic center—its undergraduate college."[51]

In his letter to Provost Rodin, Koetter neglected to mention that college administrators and many students thought the major lacked rigor and that drawings and design exercises were not strong compared with the work produced at peer colleges—something that was made apparent by the portfolios of each year's applicants to the graduate program. In 1994, Koetter replaced Bloomer with Judy DiMaio as director of Undergraduate Studies. According to Plattus, DiMaio "really whipped it into shape. There was a lot of resistance to that at the time because she was seen, quite rightly, as a Cornell, Colin Rowe type." DiMaio introduced "a much less phenomenological approach" to design than had previously been the case, promoting a "rigorous sort of analytically, historically grounded approach to teaching architecture." The changes bordered on the pre-professional without becoming *too* technical. DiMaio was also an ardent advocate for the undergraduates. "When we were initially booted from a Philip Johnson lecture, Judy DiMaio fought to allow us to sit in the back row," remembers Schlabs.[52]

Koetter was also confronted with an even more serious problem in the professional program: a precipitous decline in applicants. In 1993, Deborah Berke, a member of the Admissions Committee since her faculty appointment and currently its chair, reported that the total number of applicants to all three of the school's graduate programs had dropped from 719 in 1990 to 576 in 1992, with a further drop to 530 or less anticipated in the current year—"a dramatic decline" that she found alarming. Even more alarming was the decline in the number of acceptances by the ten to fifteen students targeted each year as the most qualified, who receive financial incentives apart from normal financial aid. While eight of the fifteen targeted students selected Yale in 1991, only two of the ten targeted chose Yale in 1992. Sidestepping the possibility that the school's shifting focus from architecture to urbanism may have contributed to the problem, Berke went on to state that the "single biggest problem is money for financial aid," noting that it was not only Princeton, with its famously generous financial aid packages, but also Harvard and Columbia that were offering more support. Berke was direct: "I need money for scholarships so we can continue to accept 'need blind'; I need money for merit scholarships to 'sweeten the pot' for the best students and to get them to Yale and away from Harvard and Columbia; and I need money for minority scholarships."[53]

Berke drew attention to another glaring problem: the condition of the A&A Building, which was "in an advanced state of disrepair" with completely inadequate facilities, especially when compared to other schools. "Our studios are overcrowded and our pin-up and classroom space is severely limited. Our library is also in terrible shape. . . . Students selecting among Yale, Harvard, and Columbia do visit the Schools . . . and we just don't look very good." She concluded her report with the admonition that "the past reputation of the School . . . alone will not attract the best students and will not retain the best faculty."[54]

What Berke did not say was that prospective students and many alumni regarded the school as sleepy and perhaps even moribund. For example, Larry Wayne Richards (b. 1944; M.Arch 1975), dean of the John H. Daniels Faculty of Architecture, Landscape, and Design at the University of Toronto from 1997 to 2004, had the "impression [in 1994] that the School has been in a rather weak phase for more than a decade. Although, from a distance, one gathers that a high level of professional competence and social responsibility have been maintained, there is also the sense that . . . [it] has not been at the center of critical discourse" as compared with Columbia, Harvard, and Princeton. "Why is it that there is this worrisome sense that the Yale School of Architecture has lost momentum, lost its edge?"

Reporting to Provost Rodin, Koetter put the issue of admissions and recruiting at the top of his list of "gravest concerns." As he saw it, the school's 26.3 percent drop in applicants over four years could not be attributed "to a general condition of the profession or the economy," nor was he willing to put blame on the basic academic program, which he believed was "at least on a par with those of our competing institutions." Koetter, echoing Berke, argued that Yale was losing applicants due to its meager financial aid offerings and the generally dismal condition of its facilities. He believed that in order to turn things around for the school, the university needed to act on three key issues: the restoration of merit-based and minority-based student aid supplements, which had been in effect during Beeby's term but had been allowed to lapse; the repair of the Art and Architecture Building; and, finally, something needed to be done about the "dangerous urban environment" of New Haven.[55]

Although the A&A's reputation was rising among architecture students and faculty, the general public—not to mention prospective students—continued to disdain the building. In part, this can be attributed to the cyclical trends of taste that made it seem so very dated, but also to the building's deplorable physical state, which certainly did not help it win over any hearts and minds. The poor state of the building was attributable to the brutalizing renovations after the 1969 fire and the asbestos problem of 1974. But it was also attributable to the perilous state of Yale's finances and the resulting policy of "deferred maintenance" that continued until the mid-1990s. Who could blame university faculty, administrative officers, and trustees, as well as students outside architecture, for hating the building? Timothy Rohan remembers Vincent Scully's "magisterial lectures" in which the historian "showed beautiful slides of the building in its original condition and insightfully described its downfall amid the sociopolitical crises of the late '60s," concluding "that the A&A was part of the 'tragic drama' of the '60s, and that such buildings had no place in what was now the 'age of irony.' Evidently, this was a lesson in what *not* to do."[56]

Koetter's assessment of the physical condition of the Art and Architecture Building was particularly detailed and to the point. In order to address the problem of the building's shortcomings, a renovation program "utilizing presently available funds" was needed to repair the building envelope and prevent further exterior deterioration "before the costs of the work become completely untenable." Although it would also be necessary to do some work on the building's mechanical systems, Koetter noted that "aside from an increase in energy use efficiency and possible enhancement of air quality and temperature control within the building, this program [would] do little to improve the interior working environment and nothing to improve our basic space needs nor address fundamental facilities issues such as the increasingly marginal condition of the library."[57] Like Spiegel before him, Koetter blamed the university for inadequate custodial support, stating that the lack of a building custodian or assigned maintenance person placed the responsibility for maintenance in the hands of the faculty and support staff in both the School of Architecture and School of Art— "an extremely expensive, inefficient and notably ineffective way of getting the job done. In these times of budgetary constraints this is nonsense, and with respect to the resultant condition of the facilities, counter-productive."[58]

Koetter also reminded the provost that the A&A Building, "sited at the outer edge of the campus in a condition of more or less direct interface with its surrounding urban context," was highly vulnerable to random crime. Student impressions of the building were, "to put it mildly," he wrote, "less than positive—they involve uncertainty and fear."[59] Acknowledging that there was a positive aspect to "the real world" character of the building's context, he went on to observe that the "actual security of our building (along with its sense of security)" was "less than adequate and . . . has become a negative condition on the daily life of the School and a deterrent to attracting prospective students." Taken together, the building's dilapidated condition and the lack of adequate security "constitutes, in a very real sense, a tragedy waiting to happen," leading to "a real and growing possibility that our poorly maintained building and its inadequate security systems could lead to an incident involving bodily harm or worse."[60]

In July 1993, the school was reaccredited by the National Architectural Accrediting Board (NAAB) for a full five-year period. But the report raised serious questions about the school's future; in particular, it was concerned about the building. Pointing out that it had previously expressed those same concerns in its 1988 report, the NAAB stated that the "specific environment of the School of Architecture" was "significantly damaged" by its physical facilities that were "having a significant negative impact on the quality" of its academic environment, which in some instances did not meet the minimal standards required for accreditation.[61]

A few years earlier, in 1991, President Schmidt had shocked faculty and alumni with the news that $1 billion would be needed to repair Yale's existing buildings, and placed the arts buildings at the top of the list of facilities in need of attention: the two museums, the University Theatre, and the Art and Architecture Building.[62] Schmidt's successor, Rick Levin, had little choice but to carry out the barely initiated program of rebuilding Yale. Mort Engstrom, university director of Capital Management, was particularly concerned about the Art and Architecture Building, which was ranked eighth worst among 129 university buildings included in a 1990 report to the Yale Corporation. The building was in perilous condition: its crumbling concrete was exposing iron reinforcing bars to weather; windows and mechanical ventilation systems were failing; and the Arts Library, lacking air conditioning, was unable to safeguard its collections on-site. The *Yale Daily News* reported that students were suffering from "a rash of health problems ranging from head colds and nose bleeds to fainting, nausea and allergy attacks," possibly resulting from the use of toxic resins and paints in poorly ventilated spaces.[63] According to Engstrom, approximately $5 million in gifts (approximately $8.6 million in 2015) were in hand to help fund renovations, with the largest coming from Josephine and Walter B. Ford II (1920–1991; B.A. 1943) and George Caulkins (1921–2005; B.A. 1943), as well as from the bequest of H. (Herbert) Gordon Smith (1917–2001; B.A. 1941).

In 1993, Engstrom reported to newly appointed President Richard Levin that "because of the change in the cast of players in Facilities Planning and the Architecture Dean's Office," progress had stalled, but Koetter, with the concurrence of the dean of the School of Art, had begun to work with Facilities Planning "to develop a realistic approach to the building."[64] By the end of the summer, an expedient strategy was developed, motivated to

9.9 Sketches by Paul Rudolph for new Art and Architecture Building glazing (ca. 1993).

9.10 Yale School of Architecture, showing window patterns devised by Fred Bland and Paul Rudolph (photo 2006).

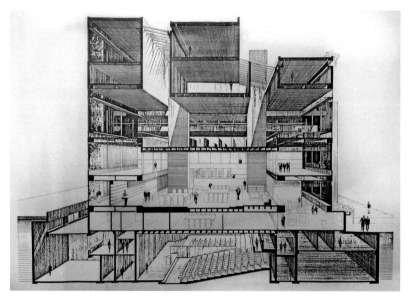

9.11 James Polshek, proposed renovation of the Art and Architecture Building, section-perspective based on Paul Rudolph drawing (ca. 1996).

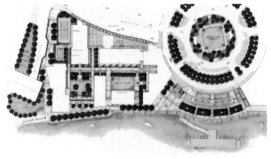

9.12 Koetter | Kim & Associates, Inc., Urban Design Study for Canary Wharf, London.

a considerable extent by the A&A's enormous energy bills attributable to its single-pane windows. Frederick Bland, partner in the New York firm Beyer Blinder Belle, specialists in preservation work on historic buildings, was asked by Archibald Currie III, university director of Project Management and Design, to undertake basic renovations.[65] Work proceeded in 1994. In response to health concerns, the building's ducts were cleaned and new fans were installed to provide improved air circulation. Because double glazing could not be obtained in the large-sized panes originally used, Bland asked Paul Rudolph to informally propose a new fenestration pattern using smaller-sized panes, which he did in a series of sketches made at a meeting in Bland's New York office (9.9).[66] At the same time, Edwin William de Cossy's sunscreens were removed.[67] The problem of exposed metalwork in the concrete was remedied by the introduction of precast concrete cover plates that further coarsened the building's proportions. The renovation took much longer than planned, forcing students to work alongside construction workers. Koetter made the best of the situation with a seminar on construction and renovation, in which the building served as "a very good learning device." When it was finally completed in November 1994, the renovation had modestly improved its internal environment, but at the expense of a dramatically altered outward appearance (9.10). The renovations were generally regarded as, at best, a stopgap, and served to make clear that a much more comprehensive program of rehabilitation was essential.

Similar problems faced the Art Gallery, leading the provost to create an Arts Advisory Committee made up of the various art school deans and museum directors who worked with architect James Stewart Polshek to create an overall plan for the university's Arts Area that was formally adopted in 1996.[68] The Arts Area Plan was primarily focused on addressing the "severe physical deterioration of buildings, lack of space, and dispersion of programs and resources" in the Art and Architecture schools as well as the Art Gallery and the Arts Library. As part of his effort, Polshek drew up some plans for how the A&A might be renovated to better accommodate its various programs; his design dramatically altered Rudolph's interior spaces by expanding the library into the second-floor gallery (9.11) and enclosing behind glass the third-floor trays where administration and faculty offices were located. The plan was not received favorably by architecture faculty.

The school's apparent loss of traction could not only be attributed to a lack of sufficient financial aid or to the dilapidated state of its building, or even to an increasing programmatic emphasis away from building design to large-scale urbanism, but also to its failure to take sufficient note of what Stanley Allen, dean (2002–12) of Princeton's School of Architecture, has characterized as "an emerging sense among younger architects and educators" in the early 1990s that there was "a new virtuosity" among those who "borrowed software and digital technologies from the film and aviation industries. The computer made the generation of complex form easy, and designers were fascinated by the new plasticity enabled by fluid modeling."[69] Compared to its peers, especially Columbia and to the upstart Southern California Institute of Architecture (SCI-Arc), Yale was neither equipped to follow these trends, nor did its faculty seem particularly interested in them. Indeed, the entire university was lagging behind in the use of computers. The glaring lack of sophisticated digital equipment led to the formation of a student-faculty committee, chaired by Professor of Computer-Aided Design Robert Frew and Alexander Aptekar (b. 1968; M.Arch 1996), who wrote to President Levin about the poor condition of the school's computer facilities.[70] Once aware of the magnitude and urgency of the problem, the university supported the school in the purchase of ten new computers, but this was little more than a drop in the bucket in relationship to the lack of sufficient equipment and a proper strategy for reshaping the curriculum for the dawning of the digital age. A more formal committee on computing was established in 1997 that reflected Yale's interdisciplinary tradition in the arts, leading, in 1998, to the opening of a Digital Media Center for the Arts, which was intended to provide equipment and expertise for various divisional programs and to encourage and enable "cross-disciplinary interaction, discovery, and creation within the Arts Area community in the field of electronic media" while also investigating "how new information technologies fit into established educational systems in the Arts."[71] However, the Digital Media Center, though a step in the right direction, quickly proved inadequate for the school's purposes, as noted in the February 1998 report of the Visiting Committee of NAAB, which was considerably more critical of the school than the previous report.[72]

The NAAB put on top of its list of problems the school's insufficient building, its insufficient financial resources, and its insufficient attempts to come to grips with the digital revolution, the school was also losing ground in areas that had, since the 1970s, been ranked among its great strengths, especially its ability to communicate its activities to alumni, the wider university, and the public. For example, no catalogue was produced for the 1996 exhibition *The Student Work of the James Stirling Studio.* Moreover, the public lecture series had become largely invisible as a result of the decision to let architecture students design the posters and flyers, which they did, sometimes after a term's series was completed—leading Steven Harris to complain that "for a place with a world-class graphic design department, what comes out of Yale looks like shit. Yale has done less than anyone else to publicize what we do. It's our own bloody fault."[73]

As the economy picked up in the mid-1990s, Koetter began to encounter a problem that had plagued many of the school's former leaders: a surge in his professional practice increasingly kept him away from the school as he split his time between his Boston office and a branch office located in London. Koetter himself admitted to the difficulty he was having in balancing his responsibilities, telling *Metropolis* magazine in 1998, that "Up until about a year and a half ago it was manageable, but then our practice took off in a big way."[74] Looking back on this, Koetter remembers, "I had many many things to do at Canary Wharf [London; 9.12]. I was running a lot of projects. We were designing a lot of stuff over there and I was going back and forth across the Atlantic a lot. I was going a week at a time or something like that." As a result, Koetter admitted, "there was a vacuum at Yale."[75] With the dean away, there was, as Deborah Berke has stated, a diminution of faculty commitment: "He didn't really check in on faculty performance. Nobody came to faculty meetings. It was pretty loosey-goosey."[76]

In Koetter's absence, other faculty were forced to pick up the slack. Koetter began to delegate administrative responsibilities to Alan Plattus, associate dean for Academic Affairs, and John Jacobson, who was made associate dean of Business Affairs. Plattus considers the Koetter situation to be a replay of what happened under Beeby: "Fred became, pretty quickly, a focus of frustration because of the kind of loose administrative stuff. I was getting more and more involved with the Urban Design Workshop and less and less interested in being dean. Fred, left to his own devices, would just dump everything on me. And I did the best I could but it wasn't that much fun."[77] Until Jacobson took on his new role in spring 1997, the "budget was still a big problem. . . . The way the money was managed and the way the business end of the school was run was a real mess." Parallel to his teaching, Jacobson had run a successful business and seemed up to the task. As Plattus says, "Neither Fred nor I had the time or inclination to sort it out but it clearly needed to be done. It was a disaster."[78]

It came as little surprise when, on May 6, 1997, President Levin informed the Yale community of Koetter's request that he not be considered for a second term. In his announcement, Levin drew attention to Koetter's work overseeing "the first phase of improvements in the Art and Architecture Building," and his leadership in planning for an expansion of the School of

Architecture's presence in the building, which was slated to take place in 2000, when the School of Art would move across Chapel Street to new facilities (Holcombe T. Green, Jr., Hall, Deborah Berke, 2000), as well as "his good advice and counsel on our overall plans to renew the Yale campus."[79] As a consequence of Koetter's decision, on the next day, May 7, 1997, Plattus called Rick Levin to shed some light on the state of the program. Levin was traveling, so Plattus expressed his concerns to Nina Glickson, Levin's assistant: "Things at the School of Architecture are a mess. Something practical needs to be done at the School next year, even if Fred is still the Dean in title. Even in the short term." Glickson reported to the president that Plattus "does not want things to slip further," as "the School has taken a big hit this year in admissions" and "the word seems to be out that things at the School are bad."[80]

Soon enough, Levin began to receive letters concerning the selection of a new dean. But, unlike such letters at other times of transition, these went beyond the typical litany of proposed names to, in some cases, carefully thought out and candid assessments of the situation and what the school needed to do to get back on track. Notable among these letters was one from New York City Planning Commissioner, alumnus, and planning instructor at Yale College Alexander Garvin, who drew attention to the school's "disgraceful physical plant, outdated equipment," and an "instructional program that no longer adequately prepares its students for future employment." Although he praised the Building Project, Garvin bemoaned its lack of permanent financing, charging any new dean with the primary responsibility "to provide a permanent income stream to pay for this program." Garvin went on to call for involving the visiting design professionals in the rest of the curriculum and to criticize the lack of a structured system of student advising, the lack of "career advisory or placement programs," and a fund-raising approach that was "still being carried on as it was prior to World War II."

Garvin acknowledged that the school had dramatically increased its urban design emphasis under Koetter, but found its curriculum severely lacking in courses to support his ambitions. It did not include landscape architecture, environmental analysis, or commercial development, and, in Garvin's view, "does not reflect major changes in professional practice that have taken place over the last two decades." He also lamented the isolation of "most students and faculty . . . from the rest of the university" and the consequent fact that "few of its courses attract students from outside the School." Garvin went on to cite the school's failure to place itself at the center of contemporary discourse and its inability to bring "to Yale the leading figures in fields that intersect with architecture, sponsor workshops on the future of the profession, and schedule programs that will make clear that Yale is where people should come if they wish to be at the forefront of the profession." Lastly, he urged the president to find a new dean who would be both "a skilled administrator" and "a skilled ambassador" as well as someone committed to making "Yale the place to which everybody interested in architecture is attracted."[81]

Dolores Hayden (b. 1945), professor of architecture and urbanism, also wrote candidly to Levin, reporting that the "draft" self-assessment being prepared for the accreditation review scheduled for 1997–98 was "largely a booster document that does not mention recent decline in student acceptance of offers of admission or low faculty morale." Hayden admired Koetter as "a good studio critic . . . [who] worked on a lot of planning committees for the University," but, as the victim of circumstances, having "inherited a school where previous deans had gotten by without addressing some basic issues of financial viability and faculty accountability," he "didn't choose to tackle" the school's more serious issues.[82] Hayden continued: "I think we have come to a low point because this term [spring 1997] there has been very little administrative presence on a day to day basis. The dean travels constantly. We have two associate deans—John Jacobson is new this term and is still working out of his home trying to figure out the numbers in the School's budget." The problem wasn't helped by Plattus's growing involvement with the Urban Design Workshop, which, as Hayden noted, had become "a major extracurricular activity in the School." Additionally, Koetter "also let all of the other tenured faculty go on leave for part of this year, so there have been big gaps in committee approvals and procedures."[83]

Hayden bemoaned the condition of the Art and Architecture Building, stating that "no potential dean should take the job without guarantees of prompt renovation and/or expanded space elsewhere." But the school's problems, she stated, were "bigger than a bad building." Like Garvin, she found that the "roots of the current problem lie in architecture's isolation from other departments and schools that might have balanced its lonely and anarchic tendencies." Hayden, who spent a good deal of her time in the American Studies program, was antipathetic to the school's studio-driven culture, which she deemed an outmoded approach founded on the Beaux-Arts model, with its emphasis on "a 'master' who runs an atelier and gathers his apprentices around him." According to Hayden, Yale was "the only American architecture school I know of still carrying a lot of this educational style into the late twentieth century." Citing the rise of corporate practice, she characterized Yale's approach as out of step. But while Garvin called for a broadening of the curriculum, Hayden wanted the school to change its nature completely:

Yale has tended to romanticize itself as the last bastion of the independent artist-architect. . . . In addition, Yale and perhaps the profession at large have tended to idealize the Dean's job here as the "last master in the last atelier"—so it has attracted ambitious designers who have hoped to establish (Pelli) or expand a personal design practice (Moore, Beeby, Koetter) and distribute patronage such as our "visiting" chairs. But it seems we have run the atelier model into the ground with a globally busy current incumbent who touches down to be dean between flights.

Meanwhile other schools such as Harvard or MIT, which have included departments of urban planning, have developed into large entities with many sub-specializations. Here at Yale, the urban and social contexts of architecture have been emphasized in the 1990s as electives or extra-curricular activities, the environmental contexts ("sustainable design") are not very available, and there's not much about computers beyond the basics.[84]

Levin also received letters from alumni. Stanley Tigerman wrote to state "that the lustrous sheen that once gleamed on that school has been tarnished of late. Its recently resigned dean . . . has for some time been an absentee dean and faculty appointments over the past ten years (and more) have generally fallen into what can be judiciously referred to as conservative to say the least. . . . Princeton and Columbia have cornered the market on theory, Harvard on professionalism, SCI-Arc on cutting edge work—in a word, Yale is no longer as sought after as it once was."[85] Charles Gwathmey wrote to the president, asking him to consider Pelli, Jaquelin Robertson, Robert Stern, and himself as members of the Search Committee.[86]

On August 18, 1997, President Levin, failing to heed Gwathmey's suggestion, and failing to understand that what was required was bold leadership and greater professionalism, announced a Search Committee lacking in any strong outside voices: Peter Brooks, professor of comparative literature and brother of faculty member Turner Brooks; Sheila de Bretteville, chair of the Department of Graphic Design in the School of Art and wife of Peter de Bretteville, critic on the architecture faculty; Diana Kleiner, professor of art history and deputy provost for the arts; Martin Gehner; Steven Harris; Dolores Hayden; Alan Plattus; and Tom Beeby as chairman.[87] Soon enough, the committee began to receive expressions of support for candidates, beginning on November 3, 1997, when twenty-two students proposed a list of seventeen architects, including recent visiting professors such as Tod Williams, Billie Tsien, Frank Gehry, and Samuel Mockbee, as well as rising stars in the professional world such as Rem Koolhaas, Jacques Herzog, and Pierre de Meuron.[88]

The process dragged on with little apparent progress through the fall—Koetter's final semester in the dean's office before taking a sabbatical leave. In November, President Levin met over lunch with students. Levin was well prepared, suggesting that he was becoming concerned about the Search Committee's hesitancy to advocate for the strong professionalism that had traditionally been the hallmark of the school's leaders. According to notes made by his assistant, Nina Glickson, he began by talking about some of the school's traditions that must be maintained, including his belief in the necessity of a curriculum that trains students to actually build buildings. Levin also indicated that it was important to avoid making the school the "atelier" of the dean, although Search Committee members were somewhat divided on whether the dean should be a major figure in the field or someone who would be principally an administrator.[89] The students in turn expressed the desire for a visible dean "on-campus as much as possible," and for greater efforts to project the school's "image and some fundamental aspects of what the architecture program should be about." Students were concerned that "the administration feels that the School does not need to sell itself." They felt there was "a lack of vision at the top," so that "some great ideas have gone nowhere," and that the school was being surpassed by Columbia and MIT with regard to computers, among other issues, deeming the recent acquisition of some new equipment as "an interim measure." Moreover, the students confessed to not using the equipment as much as might be expected in part because the faculty and dean did not seem to "know how to use computers for architecture," or at least "know how to manage the use of the computer. It was agreed that computers are important and need to be woven into the program." The students also wanted the school to have a stronger relationship with faculty and visiting professors who "have a regular connection to the School over a longer period of time." Perhaps most significantly, the students felt that "faculty should know more about what is going on at other schools. They are not involved in the profession as much as they should be."[90]

With Koetter on leave during spring 1998, news of the Search Committee's choices began to circulate through the architecture rumor mill, leading Tigerman to once again write to Levin to express concern about "the (presumed) short list . . . i.e. Dana Cuff, Harrison Fraker, and Mark Robbins"—"a list that is more normally seen at schools such as Ohio State, University of Kansas, ad nauseum, more normally assembled for purposes of maintaining a status quo at schools who have neither the ambition nor possibility of providing leadership." Tigerman then went on to recommend a list of daring young talents, including Thom Mayne, Eric Owen Moss, Will Bruder, Wes Jones, Enric Miralles, and Chicago-based alumnus Doug Garofalo (1958–2011; M.Arch 1987), a noted teacher at both the University of Illinois–Chicago and Archeworks, and a practicing architect best known for his collaboration with Greg Lynn and Michael McInturf on the design of the Korean Presbyterian Church of New York, which was one of the earliest projects conceived and executed using digital media, as well as a series of idiosyncratic houses.[91]

For a long time, the committee seemed unwilling to consider a practicing architect, leading Diana Kleiner to report that the search was "like no other I have ever experienced and, as you know, there are times that I have despaired that nothing good would ever come of it." Kleiner and Levin "encouraged the Committee to broaden its search to include some practitioners," which it did, leading Kleiner to write to Levin that she thought the search had "finally turned a corner. . . . I think the two latest additions—[Marilyn] Taylor and [Stephen] Kieran—have real possibilities."[92] Stephen Kieran (b. 1951; B.A. 1973), a rising young architect based in Philadelphia, had received his professional training at the University of Pennsylvania; Marilyn Taylor was a senior partner at the corporate firm of Skidmore, Owings & Merrill specializing in large-scale planning and management. In April, the committee then forwarded the names of four candidates to the president: Kieran and Taylor, plus two who were not architects—Dana Cuff, a sociologist on the faculty of the University of California, Berkeley, whose specialty was the study of architectural practice, and Mark Robbins, an architectural curator at the Wexner Center for the Arts at the Ohio State University. While the candidates were all certainly accomplished in their various ways, it was a short list that seemed borne out of compromise rather than clear conviction. And although encouraged that an appropriate candidate might soon be selected, Kleiner was also concerned that no one would be able to take on the job by the first of July or even by the beginning of the fall semester.

In early May, Marilyn Taylor seemed to be the favored candidate, but a curiously argued letter from David Childs (b. 1941; B.A. 1963, M.Arch 1967), her partner at Skidmore, Owings & Merrill, written a few days after Taylor visited with Levin, may have undermined her chances. After describing Taylor as "the most brilliant strategic thinker I have ever met, and . . . arguably the most important female urban designer practicing in the United States," Childs went on to say that the partners at Skidmore, Owings & Merrill "strongly support" her candidacy and that her "success in the position would not only accrue to

Yale's benefit, but also to her own professional growth, and thus eventually to our firm's future as well."[93] Taylor's case was also not helped by Cesar Pelli, who wrote to President Levin that he had "never encountered as much concern with the appointment of a new dean at Yale as I do now with the replacement for Fred Koetter," with "many alumni . . . disappointed in not finding a noted designer among the four finalists." However, Pelli, ever genial but always to the point, did go on to say that Taylor, though "not a designer," was "well respected in the profession" and had "what it takes to be a very good Dean."[94]

Of course, students offered opinions on the finalists as well. Theodore Whitten (b. 1968; M.Arch 2000) found himself positively surprised by Dana Cuff's potential for the job, but less impressed by Mark Robbins, who, though "smooth" with "a great sense of how to promote the School through publications, symposia, and exhibitions," did not seem committed to Yale. Whitten found Marilyn Taylor impressive as a manager, "but she is not Yale. Yale is not a place that produces corporate architects (for the most part)—that's Harvard. I would have gone there if that were what I wanted." Whitten was least taken with Stephen Kieran, who "couldn't find one positive thing to say about Yale as a school. Our Dean should believe in the Yale tradition, not want to 'fix' it."[95]

Raphael Sperry (b. 1973; M.Arch 1999), who did not get to meet with Mark Robbins, was also not impressed with Marilyn Taylor, who "seemed full of energy" but lacking "in vision for the School's future. She seemed to think of herself as a problem-solver." However, Sperry was more taken with Kieran, who "seemed to embrace ideas for the School that I felt compelling," including "a commitment to architecture as building, for example—but I worried that he would be uninterested in other forums of work that I learn a lot from." Sperry was not troubled by the fact that Cuff was a non-architect, although he personally intended "to leave school and become a practitioner." In fact, Sperry's support of Cuff would prove to be in character: he would go on to pursue a career in social activism.[96] Overall, there was no outstanding support among students for any of the candidates, although Marilyn Taylor did seem to enjoy a slight margin of approval.

In June, sensing that no nominee was right for the job, Search Committee Chairman Tom Beeby prepared a list of additional names for consideration by the president: James Cutler, an architect from Seattle; Julie Eizenberg of Los Angeles; Steven Holl of New York; Patricia Patkau (b. 1950; M.Arch 1978) of Vancouver, who "refused to be a candidate, although she was in our top ten list. She has the perfect profile for a rising presence in the field"; and Tod Williams and Billie Tsien, who had been successful as visiting professors.[97] As the search dragged on, Alexander Cooper offered four more names:

Alex Krieger, an urban designer on the Harvard faculty; Daniel Solomon, a California-based practitioner on the Berkeley faculty; former Davenport Visiting Professor Demetri Porphyrios; and Elizabeth Plater-Zyberk, recently appointed dean of the University of Miami's School of Architecture.[98]

Despite the suggestions, the president still had before him the roster of four candidates proposed by the Search Committee, a roster that seemed uncharacteristic of Yale, as Marc Wortman noted in an embarrassing article revealing the school's inner politics, published in the October issue of the magazine *Metropolis,* a widely read monthly catering to designers, architects, and the interested public. Wortman characterized the credentials of the succession of Yale architecture chairmen and deans as a "combination of star power and commitment to designing and building, not just to theorizing and writing." They were, in his view, people who "brought a wealth of personal connections to Yale—connections that could lure major figures to New Haven and help find graduates spots in the most creative firms" and "embodied Yale's educational philosophy, which has long emphasized the practical aspects of design as much as or more than the theoretical and the stylistic (the School has always favored pluralism over a single stylistic vision)." Wortman had a very clear sense that "beyond the basic tasks of educating students, provoking and moderating discussion, raising money, recruiting faculty, and lobbying for the school's interests," the dean must also serve "as the human—and also very public—face of the School's ideals."[99]

Researched and written during the spring and summer of 1998, when no appointment had yet been made and when it was becoming increasingly clear to Levin that the Search Committee's recommendations were not what was needed, the *Metropolis* article quoted students and faculty who pulled no punches. It reported students' unhappiness over the school's run-down facilities and disengaged faculty. "I had a professor," one student said, "who came in to our last class and said, 'School's out,' with no formal crit or anything." According to another student, Cara Cragan (b. 1972; M.Arch 1999), "The definition of what Yale is about is missing."[100] Wortman reported that "enrollment has fallen off so much that in the past two years the School failed to meet its goal for entering master-level class size, even after exhausting its waiting list."[101] Faculty like Steven Harris and Deborah Berke spoke openly about the school's decline, but it was George Ranalli who, with twenty-two years on the faculty behind him, put it most succinctly: "Yale needs help."[102] The *Metropolis* article made public just how contentious the dean search was, reporting that after a year's work, the Search Committee's list of four possibilities had "hit the A&A's concrete slab floor with a resounding thud."[103] For many, Koetter's involvement with university planning combined with his frequent absences from the school was too high a price to pay. As Meaghan Lloyd (b. 1974; M.Arch 2000), who after graduating would go on to become Frank Gehry's chief of staff, put it: "We're working our brains out. We want to know there's a leader who's out there pushing as hard as we are."[104]

Surprisingly, Vincent Scully, who had always supported the idea of a strong dean, seemed to share the bias of the Search Committee against practitioner-educators: "Yale operated in the hero-architect theme. Now the School needs a solid education in the construction of the city as a whole, and in the creation and stabilization of communities and neighborhoods."[105] Scully pointed to the success of Elizabeth Plater-Zyberk at the University of Miami, where he was teaching one term each year. But Wortman countered with the observation that Plater-Zyberk's professional prominence as a successful architect and town planner put her into "the hero-architect model," whose "success as an academic leader may still have a great deal to do with stardom and personal vision."[106]

Robert A. M. Stern, then teaching at Columbia and in no way involved with the search, also weighed in, telling Wortman that none of the four candidates lived up to "Yale's tradition of leadership by a strong practicing architect with an artistic vision who is willing to put ideas into competition. . . . Some are too professionally involved, some not enough. My reaction in toto to the four candidates was surprise and dismay. . . . If a school doesn't have forceful, controversial leadership, why bother?" Stern asked. "Shaking up the status quo is part of the vitality of a school."[107] Stern's dean at Columbia, Bernard Tschumi, echoed this sentiment: "If a good dean is defined as someone who takes risks, then a good university must also be willing to take risks."[108] George Ranalli agreed: "People are terrified now. We're at the end of a cycle. The culture feels confined, and weaker people don't want to be guided or compelled into the next century. Appointing someone who has a very clear idea forces everyone to confront their own issues."[109]

Before the *Metropolis* article went to press, President Levin, alerted to the concerns expressed by alumni and others, elected to conduct his own search. Things then moved very quickly.

10

Personal Reflections on a New Century by Robert A. M. Stern 1998–2016

"This school must be a crossroads of ideas. Yale should be a place where poetics and pragmatics rub together, where the past and the present intersect, where the abstract and the concrete coexist. . . . Yale must be more open, and more stimulating in its diversity, than any other architecture school. That is Yale's legacy from the past and its gift to the future."

Robert A. M. Stern, remarks to the students and faculty, September 3, 1998

In writing this history to help celebrate the school's centennial, I would be remiss to ignore my years as dean, though writing about them necessarily blurs the line between history and autobiography. Nonetheless, with Jimmy Stamp's invaluable assistance, I doff my historian's hat and don my dean's cap to describe my sense of what has been accomplished since 1998 to secure the school's future.

My appointment as the sixth dean was formally announced on September 3, 1998 (10.1). It was effective immediately and was just as quickly fraught with controversy. As the *New York Times* reported, the announcement "came as a surprise to some members of the architectural community who had received a letter from Yale President Richard C. Levin in July stating that the search for a new dean would not be completed until early fall."[1] The surprise and accompanying anger largely resulted from what many students, faculty, and outside observers perceived as a complete deviation from the traditional selection process. But in my view, a view shared by many of my fellow alumni, that process had failed the school. After a search period that began a year prior with a list of more than four hundred names, no candidate had earned the overwhelming support of the Selection Committee, students, or the administration. Whatever the rationale behind their selection, none of the four short-listed candidates was seen as the right person to provide the type of energetic, comprehensive, and, dare I say, even controversial leadership the School of Architecture desperately needed.

Like many alumni, I was frustrated by the looming prospect of compromise; the school needed to be jolted out of its complacency. Early in the summer, I voiced concerns to Tom Beeby, chair of the Search Committee, who suggested that I speak with Rick Levin. I called the president, whom I had never met, and he listened patiently as I expressed my views over the course of a long conversation, but he didn't say much in reply. I thought that was the end of it, but then a few weeks later, he asked to meet with me in New York. I suggested a lunch at the Century Club but he said it was too public, so we met in my professional office and discussed the issues I had raised during our telephone conversation. In this, and in a subsequent meeting in New Haven, I made some suggestions about what might be done. It seems that my views struck a chord with the president, because in mid-August he called to formally offer me the position of dean.

Despite the fact that overriding the recommendations of the Search Committee was not unprecedented for Levin, who had taken similar action at the School of Forestry and Environmental Studies, the reaction to my appointment was, as the *New York Times* later described it, "shock mixed with disdainful indignation."[2] Some students protested the lack of transparency leading to my appointment, with one student telling the *Yale Daily News,* "It's all about the students not having any involvement. It's not about him or his style of architecture, at least not for me. We were introduced to four candidates and we didn't get to choose them."[3] But I think many more students were upset about what they perceived to be my style, concerned that I might transform Yale into a "retroguard home for historicism."[4] As one student commented, "We're the Yale Architecture School. We could have anyone we wanted and we fell back on the default, who's not even the tried and true default."[5]

Criticism came from the greater architecture community as well. *Architecture* magazine editor and Yale College alumnus Reed Kroloff (b. 1960; B.A. 1982) wrote a mean-spirited editorial describing me as a "suede-loafered sultan of suburban retrotecture, Disney party boy and notorious academic curmudgeon."[6] It's worth noting that Kroloff, after a brief, contentious stint as dean of the Tulane School of Architecture (2004–7), would rescind those words, writing that "Bob Stern may be the best school of architecture dean in the United States."[7] I received angry letters from alumni and one satirical sketch suggesting that I would physically transform the Art and Architecture Building into a work of postmodern Classicism (10.2). They should have known that I would have more respect for it and its architect. It seemed to me that many people had made up their minds before even hearing anything I had to say. But if anyone bothered to listen to what I actually did say at the formal announcement of my appointment on September 3, 1998, they would have heard me make it clear that I never intended to impose my own stylistic predilections on my alma mater. If I may quote myself at the time: "Unlike Louis XIV, Yale is not me."[8]

I will always be grateful to Vincent Scully for publicly voicing his support during this time. "Of all the many distinguished graduates of the Yale School of Architecture," he wrote, "[Stern] best understands its history and values its special traditions." His confidence in me was prompted by more than our long friendship, as he believed that my career track record, "with its unique integration of architectural design, historical scholarship, executive ability, and devoted academic service, especially fits him to be our new dean. The School can confidently expect a fresh and powerful burst of creative energy under his direction. . . . This is exactly the right appointment."[9] I did not know until conducting the research for this book that Vince had proposed my name in several previous dean searches. Bernard Tschumi, who was dean at Columbia (1988–2003)—where, before coming to Yale, I had been on the faculty—agreed, saying that "Bob has his ideological preferences but at the end of

10.1 Robert A. M. Stern (fall 1998).

BEFORE   AFTER

10.2 Anonymous sketch sent to Stern (ca. fall 1998).

10.3 Philip Johnson and Peter Eisenman on the cover of the first issue of *Constructs* (spring 1999).

the day he will cast them aside for the greater good of the institution."[10] That is exactly what I intended to do.

In this book, Jimmy Stamp and I have examined the early lives of many previous deans and chairmen, so in fairness, let me share a little about my own formative years. I was born in Brooklyn, New York, in 1939. From a young age I wanted to get out of Brooklyn and across the river into Manhattan, whose skyline inspired me to be an architect. After receiving a bachelor of arts from Columbia University in 1960, majoring in history, I went on to the Yale School of Art and Architecture, graduating in 1965—significantly, the last year that Paul Rudolph served as chairman of the department. After graduation, at the behest of Philip Johnson, I joined the Architectural League of New York for a one-year term as its first J. Clawson Mills Fellow, reporting to a committee consisting of Johnson and two other architects, SOM partner Robert Cutler and Robert Allan Jacobs of the firm Kahn & Jacobs, who had been charged with revitalizing what had become a moribund institution. After a year at the league, my public programs culminated in the exhibition *Forty under Forty* (1966), which introduced a prominent group of up-and-coming architects.[11] Then, I interned for a short time in the office of Richard Meier, where, admittedly, my ambitions distracted me from my work. As Meier remembers, I "was always out of the office. What was clear was that he was interested in doing many things, not just being a practitioner."[12] These outside interests led me to the New York Housing and Development Administration, where I worked for two years (1967–69) during the first term of John V. Lindsay's tenure as New York's mayor, and then, in 1969, to founding a practice with fellow Yale alumnus John Hagmann (b. 1938; M.Arch 1966) that was soon staffed with ambitious students from Columbia, where I was also teaching. My penchant for talent-scouting and social networking, honed under the guidance of Philip Johnson, began to make a mark with clients, many of whom were met through my 1967 marriage to Lynn Solinger, a socially connected photographer. The firm's early work consisted largely of apartment renovations in New York and the occasional house, the most famous of which, the Lang Residence in Washington, Connecticut (1974), reflected the influence of Robert Venturi, who first made an impression on me during my student days at Yale.[13] In 1976, the firm was dissolved, and a successor office, Robert A. M. Stern Architects (RAMSA), took its place.

When RAMSA opened its doors, postmodernism was gaining momentum, and with one foot firmly planted in professional practice and the other in academia, I embraced its ethos as first defined by Charles Jencks in 1975: "one half Modern and one half something else (usually traditional building)."[14] As the practice became more focused on the continuity of tradition, so too did my pedagogy. In 1986, I also hosted *Pride of Place: Building the American Dream,* an eight-part television series on PBS. Part documentary and part opinion piece, *Pride of Place* examined American architecture "from the ghettos of the South Bronx to the gaudy, stage-set splendors of San Simeon" and was accompanied by a publication of the same name, which I authored with assistance from Thomas Mellins and Raymond Gastil (b. 1958; B.A. 1980).[15]

By the time of my Yale appointment, RAMSA had become a successful 150-person architecture firm. With partners assuming more responsibility, I was able to focus a lot of my time and attention on the school, which was good because, as I soon learned, I would need all the extra seconds I could get. Taking over as dean, I found a school that bore little resemblance to the one from which I had graduated in 1965. Confident in what needed to be done, undeterred by the criticism surrounding my appointment, and with the support of President Levin, I set out to return the school to the prominence it enjoyed when I was a student.

As always, but more so in the course of the failed search, there was concern among some faculty and students about the "strong dean" model that I represented. However, the model had worked well since the time of Everett Victor Meeks and, without such a leader in the 1990s, the school had lost its way. So I plunged in and took charge, not only with faculty appointments that would bring both fresh and mature talents to the school, but also with a schedule of public lectures and events that would help spread the word that the school was once again a vital center of architectural culture.

The first challenge waiting on my desk the first day I walked into the dean's office was the recently issued, harshly critical report of the National Architectural Accrediting Board (NAAB), threatening to revoke the school's accreditation unless the university repaired the Art and Architecture Building:

> The university administration has promised repeatedly for 10 years, through three team visits, to improve these appalling conditions. The latest promises, to integrate refurbishing the building with a new master plan for the Fine Arts and Digital Media and the acquisition of an existing building across York Street, are certainly more exciting than any made in the past.
>
> The team believes that the university administration is sincere in this, but provosts and presidents come and go, adequate funds have not been irrevocably allocated, and still the School of Architecture languishes in an environment that is utterly unworthy, not only of an institution

of international stature, but of any school aspiring to professional recognition.[16]

The report was exactly the kind of mandate needed to get the university's attention. To work toward rescuing a program that had clearly become a liability, the university opened up an array of resources—financial and otherwise. On the day my appointment was announced, President Levin announced a significant increase in the school's financial aid budget, as well as a commitment to invest in new computer equipment, software, and support staff. Funds were also made available to hire new faculty and bring in additional visiting critics. I wasted no time in using these resources to begin reshaping and promoting the program.

Although wary of trends masquerading as ideas, I nonetheless took great pains to reaffirm Yale's traditional pluralism by inviting visiting faculty who represented a broad range of viewpoints. To do this, I had to move quickly and lean on professional relationships developed over a long career, beginning with ninety-two-year-old Philip Johnson, who was coaxed into serving as Eero Saarinen Visiting Professor in the spring 1999 term with Peter Eisenman working as his "teaching assistant" (10.3). The appointment of Johnson, who was by then a legitimate historical figure in architecture, was widely debated. As noted in *New York* magazine, "students feared an onslaught of old boys."[17] But for me, the appointments of Johnson and Eisenman, pedagogical opposites, were intended to make clear that Yale would recapture its position as the most provocative and least ideologically blinkered of all architecture schools. It was the first time Johnson had taught at Yale since 1964 and the first time Eisenman had been invited back as visiting faculty since Cesar Pelli was dean. In *Constructs*—a twice-yearly newspaper I initiated in spring 1999, with the help of its editor, Nina Rappaport—Johnson described his studio as a conversation, casting himself in the role of moderator or provocateur. "Teaching is telling someone something. These kids are way beyond that," Johnson said. "I think that you can inspire and scold. I don't believe in teaching. . . . I am not a teacher . . . I am a rabble rouser and personal exciter-upper. I enjoy the conversation; it is food and drink to me."[18]

Johnson and Eisenman asked students to redesign or expand Rudolph's A&A, reviving what had proved a fascinating studio topic over the years and that, with the building's restoration now virtually guaranteed, took on new relevance. "We chose the Art & Architecture Building because it raises many issues that are important now, particularly to Yale and to architectural education," said Eisenman. "How do you address history? Certainly there is a history

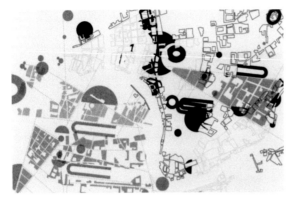

10.4 Brian Spring (M.Arch 2011), "Piranesi/Nolli," "Introduction to Visual Studies" (fall 2008).

10.5 Jonah Gamblin (M.Arch 2005) and Noah Riley (M.Arch 2005), Proposal for an Extension to the Whitney Museum in New York, axonometric drawings and model. Eisenman studio (fall 2004).

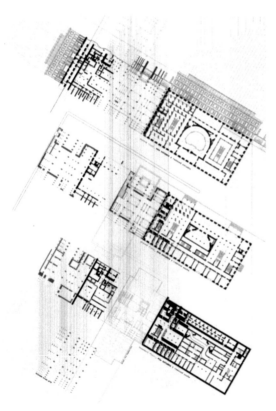

10.6 Cody Davis (M.Arch 2009) and Daniel Yoder (M.Arch 2009), Räume Ohne Eigenschaften NS-Dokumentationszentrum, München, axonometric. Eisenman studio (fall 2008).

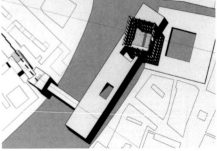

10.7 Aidan Doyle (M.Arch 2010) and Palmyra Geraki (B.A. 2006, M.Arch 2010), Venice Project I, renderings and site plan. Eisenman studio (fall 2009).

in the Paul Rudolph building. If one is making a new building, how much should be retained of the old? How much of the spirit of Rudolph should be there? Should his ghost and traces of the existing building be evident? How do you address a building that no longer functions, but is an icon? . . . We are also commenting on the Stern tenure."[19]

During the Johnson/Eisenman studio's final review, students presented a dramatic variety of proposals (see 8.17, 8.18), reflecting the opposing opinions of their instructors: whereas Eisenman advocated renovating the existing building for use by the school, Johnson favored a *tabula rasa* approach. An impressive roster of critics reviewed the student work: David Childs, Cynthia Davidson, Jeffrey Kipnis, Sanford Kwinter, Greg Lynn, Richard Meier, and Mark Wigley. Little agreement was reached that day, but the diverse and talented roster of critics was a shot across the bow of those who imagined that I would attempt to impose a narrow set of stylistic constraints. Eisenman would go on to play an important and expanded role at Yale, eventually teaching a required, rigorous first-year course in formal analysis (10.4), as well as an annual advanced studio and seminar. Since 2010, he has served as the inaugural Charles Gwathmey Professor in Practice (10.5–10.7). Many students come to Yale because of Peter.

The invitations to Johnson and Eisenman were quickly followed up with invitations to a diverse roster of visitors with strong viewpoints, many of whom shared a deep affection for the school. In fall 1999, Cesar Pelli was persuaded to teach once again, offering as a problem a high-rise tower for a New York site, and Charles Gwathmey, as Davenport Professor, co-taught a studio with Deborah Berke in the same term. These appointments were necessarily made on short notice and were welcomed by students as strong signals that the school was getting back on track. Wherever possible, visiting faculty were appointed to chairs that honored similarly minded architects. For example, it seemed appropriate to ask Daniel Libeskind to serve as inaugural Louis I. Kahn Visiting Professor in fall 1999, a position established through the generosity of Kahn's friends and admirers in recognition of the architect's long association with the school and university. Libeskind had once before taught at Yale, serving as Bishop Visiting Professor in fall 1992, when he was a little-known theorist with a strong interest in music, something he shared with Kahn. And like Kahn in the 1950s, when first appointed, Libeskind was searching for an appropriate direction to take as an architect, but by 1998, with his Jewish Museum in Berlin nearing completion, he seemed to have found his way. Libeskind challenged students with a conceptual design project in the heart of Berlin, calling for "a new idea of building that is neither rebuilding,

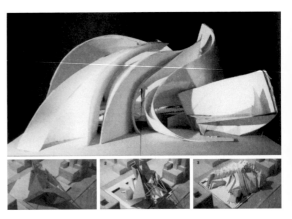

10.8 Nizam O. Kizilsencer (M.Arch 2000), Twilight Dawn, rendering. Libeskind studio (fall 1999).

10.9 Anand Devarajan (M.Arch 2000), A Cathedral in Los Angeles, final model and model iterations. Gehry studio (fall 1999).

10.10 Meaghan Lloyd (M.Arch 2000), A Cathedral in Los Angeles, final model. Gehry studio (fall 1999).

10.11 Anand Devarajan, Jason Hwang (M.Arch 2000), and Qu H. Kim (M.Arch 2000), Design for a Contemporary Art Center, rendering. Hadid studio (spring 2000).

deconstructing, nor fictionalizing the past, but [is] instead the creation of a direct connection to the future."[20] The abstract nature of the studio was proposed to encourage students "to become radically involved in thinking about their own role in the world of architecture and about how to maintain their commitment to the things they believe in"[21] (10.8). Libeskind's appointment coincided with the exhibition *Two Museums and a Garden* in the school's gallery, presenting drawings of his Jewish Museum in Berlin and re-creating a nearly full-scale reproduction of the massive column grid he had designed for its E. T. A. Hoffmann Garden.[22]

Frank Gehry, who like Pelli and Libeskind had not taught at Yale for a long time, returned at my invitation as the Davenport Visiting Professor in the same fall 1999 semester. Gehry asked students to design a Roman Catholic cathedral in downtown Los Angeles—an intended critique of Rafael Moneo's design for the Cathedral of Our Lady of the Angels, with Gehry encouraging students to develop their designs through the iteration of sketch drawings and models (10.9). The jury discourse was pointed and witty: when Philip Johnson asked a student, Meaghan Lloyd (10.10), "Is there supposed to be a roof over the center?" Gehry jumped in with a quick retort, "They don't know how to do roofs yet"—prompting me to jokingly ask, "Do they have to take another course with you on that?"[23] Lloyd is now a partner at Gehry Partners, LLP. Regarding the sudden influx of prominent visitors, Eric Clough (b. 1972; M.Arch 1999), a student at the time of my appointment, told the *New York Times* that "Half the class was concerned with it being a gimmick, while the other half was taking advantage of these amazing people."[24]

Another emerging leader among architects at the end of the last century was the Iraqi-born, London-based Zaha Hadid, who was just beginning to realize her ideas as actual buildings when she came to Yale for the first time. The decision to appoint Hadid as the Eero Saarinen Visiting Professor in spring 2000 was calculated to reflect the commitment to sculpturally dazzling form that she and Saarinen shared. Hadid's studio investigated new forms of public space in relation to the open-ended nature of the "contemporary art center" (10.11), using a program that paralleled her own Lois and Richard Rosenthal Center for Contemporary Art (2003) in Cincinnati, Ohio, the architect's first American building. A book documenting the studio was published in 2001 (10.12).[25] Beyond just depicting student work, it included commentary from Hadid, as well as transcriptions of the final reviews in which architects, critics, and museum professionals discussed specific student projects alongside larger issues such as the changing nature of art museums. Not since Tadao Ando's visit in 1987 had the school published a studio's work. The Hadid book marked

10.12 Douglas Grieco, Wendy Ing, and Nina Rappaport, eds., *CAC Hadid Studio Yale* (New York: Monacelli, 2001).

10.13 Cover images of recent books published by the Yale School of Architecture.

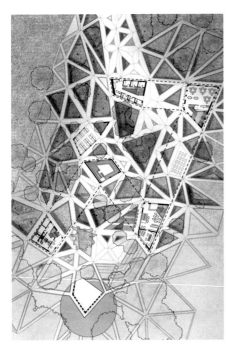

10.14 Elijah Porter (M.Arch 2011), "Terrestrial Veil," Design for a Women's College. Balmori and Sanders studio (fall 2010).

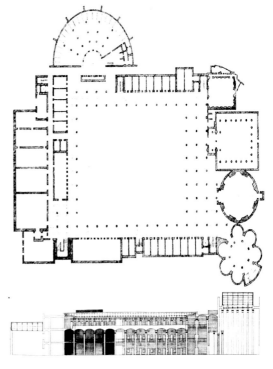

10.15 Donald W. Johnson (M.Arch 2000), "Inventive Rebuilding," plan and section. Porphyrios studio (1999).

the debut of an expanded publication program documenting the work of advanced research studios, thereby broadening the school's impact on other schools and the profession by creating and disseminating new knowledge and new ideas (10.13). Equally provocative advanced studios were also offered by resident and adjunct faculty (10.14).

The commitment to an open dialogue among diverse points of view also required that leading proponents of traditional architecture be part of the program. In spring 1999, Demetri Porphyrios and Léon Krier were invited to each offer studios in an effort to counterbalance the general drift of discourse toward destabilized digital design. The two had previously taught together as Davenport Visiting Professors in spring 1991, and they provided important voices on behalf of traditional design. Many students grumbled about their approach, which stressed hand-drawing and precedent-based design, but, after taking the studios or seeing the work accomplished by fellow students, they began to recognize the value of the traditional approach. Porphyrios's fall 1999 studio, requiring students to design a business school based on a fragment of an antique building at Pergamon, reflected a conviction that "architecture speaks of tradition always in a modern voice"[26] (10.15). To further ramp up the discourse between traditional design and modernism, in November 2002, a symposium was convened focusing on Krier and Eisenman, the school's most celebrated visiting faculty who, as "frenemies" representing opposing viewpoints about design, shared a disdain for run-of-the-mill practice. An exhibition of Krier's conceptual Atlantis project (1986–88) and Eisenman's unbuilt House IV (1970–75) accompanied the symposium that was documented in a subsequent book, *Eisenman/Krier: Two Ideologies* (2005).[27] Over the course of two days, the event featured seventeen speakers, including Vincent Scully, Phyllis Lambert, and Anthony Vidler, each of whom used the occasion to situate contemporary architecture in relationship to history, language, urbanism, and politics. Ultimately, the symposium revealed that architects were not divided by polar oppositions, as John McMorrough noted in his review of the event for *Constructs:* "The two architects and their ideologies in fact give way to the 17 ideologies of the speakers—perhaps even more were one to follow each presenter's allusions."[28]

At the same time, the school took an important step toward helping in the university's effort to rekindle its historic relationship with China, which included the significant architectural contribution of Henry Killam Murphy, a member of the Yale College Class of 1899. A New Haven native, Murphy began studying architecture during his senior year at Yale, after which he went to New York for one year, enrolling in the Atelier Masqueray, and then working

10.16 Henry Killam Murphy, Yale-in-China College and Hospital in Hunan, China (1916).

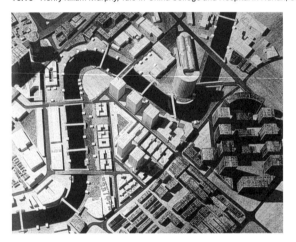

10.17 Jason Hwang (M.Arch 2000), Suzhou Creek Urban Development, Shanghai. Plattus China studio (fall 1999).

10.18 The China studio visits Beijing (fall 2012).

10.19 Adam Ruedig (M.Arch 2001), Millennium House, rendering. Deamer studio (2001).

for some prominent New York offices.[29] In 1906, Murphy took a year-long tour of Europe before establishing an independent practice that rapidly prospered, leading to the decision to enter into partnership with Richard Dana, who would soon be hired to teach at Yale (see Chapter 1); the two had met in the office of Delano & Aldrich. Their reputation quickly grew throughout New York and Connecticut and, in 1914, Yale commissioned Murphy to design a medical school in Changsha (Hunan province), China, as part of the university's Yale-in-China program (10.16). The commission led to many other jobs in China, which were carried out by Murphy's "Oriental Department" staffed by several young, American-trained Chinese architects such as Lu Yanzhi (1894–1929) and Robert Fan (Fan Wenzhao) (1893–1979). Murphy's other significant campus plans and buildings in China include Fudan University in Shanghai, Tsinghua (Quinghua) University in Beijing, Yenching University (today's Peking University), and Ginling College for Girls (today's Nanjing Shifan Daxue).[30]

In 1999, Alan Plattus was contacted by Leslie Lu (b. 1951; M.Arch 1977), chairman of the Architecture Department at Hong Kong University (HKU), who proposed a three-way studio partnership between Yale, HKU, and Tongji University in Shanghai. Plattus and I traveled to Hong Kong and Shanghai in May 1999 to meet key people, check out the scene, and establish curricular objectives. Plattus remembers that "Shanghai was a happening place. It was the Wild West. It seemed like one big construction site."[31] I was totally sold on the idea of the joint studio, and President Levin, delighted with the school's proposed collaboration with China, promised his "enthusiastic report" for the program but provided only a onetime grant of funds.[32]

The first China studio took place in the fall 1999 semester. The initial studio trip to China proved very well timed, not only because American architects were beginning to be commissioned for work there, but also because students, who were asked to propose strategies for urban development and revitalization along Suzhou Creek, felt that they were part of an important moment as China "took a new attitude toward the global economy." As Thomas Morbitzer (b. 1974; M.Arch 2000) and Irene Shum (b. 1971; M.Arch 2000) reported in *Constructs,* "It was only once we were immersed in the diverse texture, scale, and pace of Chinese life with its unique sensory and material qualities that we were able to recognize the limitations of our preconceived notions and engage with the design issues directly. . . . The wild range in the city—from the colonial long-tan houses of the early twentieth century, to the traditional gardens of the imperial era, to the surrealism of the post-Maoist new development area at Pudong—underscored what it means to be building in China at this fast-paced point in history"[33] (10.17, 10.18). The China studio has evolved over the years in response to both changes in the quickly developing country and new partnerships; the school now works only with Tsinghua University in Beijing, whose students and faculty come to New Haven to present their parallel projects at a final review. Since 2007, Plattus has been assisted by Andrei Harwell, with whom he also collaborates at the Urban Design Workshop.

The China studio has since become a fixture of the curriculum, setting the model for virtually all future advanced studios in which two or three weeks of research in New Haven are followed by a week-long site visit by students and their teachers, after which students return to Yale to complete their designs. With the exception of a onetime grant for the inaugural China studio, the school had no endowments to support international travel until 2000, when the Henry Hart Rice Family Foundation generously provided support for term-time, teacher-directed studio travel, with the expectation that students would benefit from the opportunity to travel with their teachers to visit sites and meet with local officials, in order to broaden their understanding of the interrelationships between architecture, urbanism, and the political processes that influence development.

The visiting critic system enabled the advanced studios to ensure that ideologically diverse points of view were always represented. While short-term appointments of visiting critics helped keep the school's advanced studios fresh and varied, a certain degree of continuity was also welcome. For this reason, certain visitors representing distinct points of view have been repeatedly asked to return, such as Greg Lynn, a rising talent specializing in digital design who has been appointed Davenport Professor for each spring term since spring 2000, echoing the long tenure of James Stirling. But certain values had to be uniformly established for beginning students in the Core, no matter who the teachers were. Some new hires, such as Audrey Matlock, Alan Organschi, Louise Harpman, and Mark Gage (b. 1973; M.Arch 2001), were alumni who, beyond their talents as architects, brought insight into the school's history and traditions. Others, such as Martin Finio (b. 1963), a Cooper Union graduate who was just entering independent practice after nine years in the office of Williams & Tsien, and Joel Sanders (b. 1956), a Columbia graduate, brought fresh perspectives from outside.

Regular faculty were also asked to participate in the advanced studio. Peggy Deamer, for example, led a seminar in preparation for her advanced studio, "The Millennium House," in spring 2001, a studio that grew out of her fall 2000 seminar examining domestic architecture at the beginning of the new century. In 2004, the work of the seminar and studio was published as the second book in the series documenting advanced studios (10.19).[34]

As the NAAB's 1998 report made clear, the school's digital curriculum was in need of attention. Although I am not a computer person—in fact, to the shock of virtually everyone, I had the computer removed from the dean's office shortly after my appointment—I was not unmindful of the important role digital media were to play in the future of the school and the profession. However, I believed then and continue to believe that it would be a mistake to go the way of other schools, where digital design replaced traditional sketching and drawing and physical model-making. As I wrote in the first *Retrospecta* of my tenure: "Architecture's relationship to the wider world it serves continually evolves but always there is at its core an unchanging belief that the act of building is in and of itself a great and evolving undertaking. In too many schools students and teachers now seem disinterested in building, distracted by cyberspace and a search for ways to transform the art of building into something else. Architecture is not a branch of information science; it is not a kind of electronics."[35]

Nonetheless, the need to incorporate digital design and fabrication into the curriculum was critical, and less than two months into my tenure as dean, at the suggestion of Rick Levin, I assembled a committee of experts to quantify the magnitude of the problem and suggest a plan to not only bring the school up to date with its peers but also to establish itself as a leader. The committee consisted of both outside advisors and Yale faculty: William J. Mitchell, dean of the School of Architecture and Planning at MIT and committee chairman, who, as an M.E.D. student, had been instrumental in organizing Yale's pioneering symposium on computers and architecture (see Chapter 5); Michael Browne, architecture and production designer with the Walt Disney Company; Associate Dean John Jacobson; Martin Schultz, chairman of the Computer Science Department at Yale; Daniel Updegrove, Yale's director of Information Technology Services; Eden Muir, director of Computer Science and assistant professor (adjunct) at Columbia, then the recognized leader in the field among architecture schools; and Greg Lynn, also a pioneer in the use of computers to generate architectural form.

The committee worked quickly, submitting a report on November 28, 1998, which confirmed that, with regard to digital design, we were nowhere. The committee "strongly" recommended that the school develop a digital infrastructure to "enhance its teaching of computer-related topics, its studio computing facilities, and its general IT support for faculty," noting that "sophisticated computer and digital telecommunication facilities are now a fundamental and growing part of everyday architectural practice." The report went into great detail about several elements that would be necessary to bring the school's technological capabilities up to levels that are "fully competitive with those at other leading schools of architecture" and stressed the importance of computers to the future of architecture. "Many of the best prospective students consider the availability of cutting-edge computation teaching and facilities in their choice of schools, employers look for computer skills in recent graduates, and the accreditation teams now regard adequate curricular coverage and facilities as mandatory. Yale cannot afford to be left behind."[36] In a letter to Deputy Provost for the Arts Diana Kleiner accompanying the committee's findings, I didn't mince words: "Immediate action on this is critical for the future of the School. We cannot continue to run a professional school that is not only vastly inferior in this area to our competition at Columbia and Harvard but also to every architectural office of consequence. There is no way that the action plan can be delayed. Failure to move along will do irreparable damage to the School."[37]

The university largely agreed with the committee's assessment, as well as the plan of implementation proposed by John Jacobson, which called for incrementally improving computer systems over a period of four years. However, computers are useless without expensive architecture software. To this end, Autodesk—at the behest of alumnus Phillip Bernstein, a lecturer who after twenty years as associate principal at Pelli Clarke Pelli had joined the software company—generously donated enough licenses to the school to ensure that all students had the opportunity to learn the industry-standard AutoCAD program. Over the years, Autodesk has made many other software programs available to our students. Also desperately needed was digitally directed fabrication equipment, so that the school's commitment to architecture as a physical discipline—as the art of building   could continue even in the digital era. Generous support from Gordon Burns made it possible for Yale to quickly become not only competitive with peer institutions but also a leader in digital fabrication by acquiring a vast array of equipment that was made available to both graduate and undergraduate students.

The impact of sophisticated computerization on student work was rapid. Very quickly, as can be seen in the pages of *Retrospecta,* computer-generated drawings replaced traditional hand drawings, not only in the advanced studios, as might be expected, but also in the Core, where each class of incoming students was more familiar with digital technology and software than the last. As the school's digital offerings became increasingly sophisticated, it became increasingly important to me that hand-drawing and model-making remain a part of studio design methodologies. There is no better way to understand a building than to draw, and there is no better way to understand a student than to see him or her at work drawing. Some curricular infrastructure was already in place to combat the explosive power of digital programs, in particular the summer Rome seminar. But this was an elective. To make sure that all beginning students were instructed in hand-drawing, in 2009, with the support of Gilbert Maurer, director of the Hearst Foundation, the William Randolph Hearst Endowment Fund was established to perpetuate the teaching and study of hand-drawing at the school, leading the faculty to establish a four-term sequence of required courses in visualization that balances traditional hand-drawing with computer-generated techniques. Following up on the Hearst endowment, two young faculty members who offer drawing courses, Victor Agran (b. 1967; M.Arch 1997) and George Knight (b. 1968; M.Arch 1995), organized the symposium "Is Drawing Dead?" in spring 2012, attracting a huge audience and inspiring widespread public discussion about the importance of hand-drawing in the age of computer-aided design.[38]

Shortly after becoming dean, I was asked to sign off on the Arts Area Plan, which determined that, with the departure of the Art School, the school would have full use of the Art and Architecture Building, excepting the space allocated to the Arts Library. With the departure of the Art School from the Art and Architecture Building in summer 2000, we were able to reclaim the soaring, double-height studio for the architecture program. But how to use it? Clearly it was not to be as in Rudolph's time, when classes were hierarchically arrayed on the trays and graduating students were ennobled in the center. Instead, the center was kept free for pin-ups, juries, and class discussions—a much freer and friendlier arrangement. The departure of the Art School also allowed us to strip the gallery of the white-painted Sheetrock and Homasote that had covered the concrete walls and also the panels that had covered the glass wall between it and the Arts Library, which not only restored the spatial transparency of Rudolph's design, but also provided the school with the setting for major exhibitions and receptions that would allow it to become an active participant in Yale's community of arts institutions. An expanded exhibition program presented the school with new budgetary challenges, which were in part met with generous support from donors, including Elise Jaffe and Jeffrey Brown, Henry Kibel, Walter (b. 1941; B.A. 1963, M.Arch 1967) and Judy Hunt, Bradley Nitkin, and the estate of James Wilder Green (1927–2005; B.Arch 1952). The fall 2000 exhibition *Cesar Pelli: Building Designs, 1965–2000,* the first to be able to take full advantage of the 4,500-square-foot gallery, later traveled to the National Building Museum in Washington, D.C., as well as other venues.[39]

It soon became apparent that the increased amount of space would permit an increase in enrollment. In 1998, the average enrollment had been 152.6, which typically translated to forty students in each M.Arch I class, plus fifteen post-professional students, and six to eight M.E.D.s.[40] By 2001, with the Art School gone from the building, it was possible to increase enrollment in the M.Arch I program to fifty students per year, significantly enlivening the atmosphere by allowing for a richer mix of students, faculty, and supplementary course offerings.

Until Deborah Berke, who still regularly teaches studio (10.20), reduced her administrative commitment to focus more on practice, she and I closely collaborated on admissions while engaging in ongoing discussions about class mix. I agreed with Berke, who supported "a healthy mixture of non-architects—what I used to call 'soft architects,' meaning coming out of Columbia versus hard architects coming out of Michigan." Yale needed to maintain its traditional mix of students with architectural experience alongside, as Berke says, "political science and dance majors and fine arts majors, the people who weren't looking at architecture as an undergrad." Although Berke says she believes that we now have "too few of the non-architects in the mix," she acknowledges that "the distinctions between the undergraduate pre-professional programs and the undergraduate liberal arts architecture program . . . have diminished within the schools we typically draw from."[41] My main concern was that students coming from different educational backgrounds who had little or no prior background in architecture would not be able to quickly catch up with their "pre-architecture" colleagues entering in first year. To this end, in 2007, the school significantly beefed up its summer preparation course required for admitted non-architects. Emphasizing hand-drawing, basic design, and computer techniques as well as a compressed overview of architectural history, not only does the summer program equip students with little or no background in architecture with the skills they need, but it also strengthens the Core program so that the "non-architects" can quickly start exploring more complex architectural problems on an equal footing to those who majored in architecture as undergraduates.

At the heart of my concern about admissions was the issue of standards and to convey a greater sense of our commitment to art-based professionalism to applicants, many of whom tended to regard the school as "arty" but not rigorous. Entrance requirements were tightened, as measured in standardized tests, including English for foreigners, but there was some trick to this.

Students needed to be intelligent and talented. As Pelli and Beeby had recognized before me, many sensed that Yale had never fully recovered the ground lost in the tumultuous late 1960s, and that as a place for "Thoroughbreds," as Pelli had observed, it was intimidating to many candidates who feared they wouldn't measure up to expectations or who didn't see themselves as potential leaders. Lots of recent college graduates were also concerned that our pass-fail system was too permissive. My effort to regain lost ground failed in one respect: an attempt to reintroduce a grading system to the graduate curriculum in an effort to encourage excellence resulted in many letters from concerned students already in the school and a split faculty vote. As the *New York Times* reported, "The students fought it, then admired Stern for listening—and backing down."[42]

Before returning as dean, I remember sitting on a jury of second-year students and being appalled by the sloppy, inchoate, amateurish way they presented their work—not only in terms of drawings but also verbal presentations of their ideas. Lagging admissions standards may have been to blame, but the real problem was that the Core was simply not rigorous enough. In 2001, the University Council Committee on the School of Art and Architecture, as part of a comprehensive assessment of the school, suggested that the Core curriculum be reexamined.[43] To "toughen" the Core, a renewed sense of urgency had to be introduced into the pedagogy. To do this, the policy first established by Beeby, but then seemingly only intermittently honored, was reintroduced so that in any given term all students would pursue the same design problem and variety would be the result of the various ways each critic would approach it, but with the same set of end-of-term deliverables expected in all studio sections. While this might have led to conflict with George Ranalli, who consistently chafed at conforming to a shared studio curriculum, the problem never came up: in 1999 Ranalli accepted the deanship at the City College of New York.[44]

Additionally the Core was extended to four terms and, working with the faculty, I established overarching themes for each of the terms. First-term students would begin with an investigation into the basic components of architecture, such as the wall or skin and the landscape or field; during the first half of their second term, the focus would be on residential design in preparation for the Jim Vlock Building Project that occupied the second half of the term; in the third term, students developed a public building such as a museum or library while considering issues of daylighting and environmental sustainability. As the culmination of the expanded Core curriculum, the fourth term would concern itself with urbanism, undertaking large development

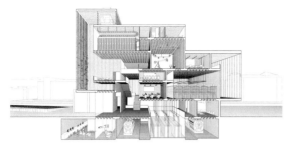

10.20 Katie Stranix (M.Arch 2014), The OPNA Institute, section perspective and exterior perspective. Deborah Berke studio (spring 2014).

10.21 The 2013 Jim Vlock Building Project at 116 Greenwood Street in New Haven.

10.22 Michael Bierut, Yale School of Architecture event posters.

projects in major American cities such as New York—for a number of years, the urbanism studio was prescient in its ongoing analysis of Brooklyn waterfront sites recommended by Alexander Garvin, then a member of New York's Planning Commission—as well as waterfront sites in Stamford, Connecticut, Providence, Rhode Island, and Boston. Each term would have a faculty coordinator responsible for developing specific studio briefs and for bringing in relevant outside experts. To meet growing concerns about the absence of a high-level discourse on landscape design, Alexander Felson (b. 1971), a landscape architect specializing in urban hydrology, was added to the faculty in 2010 with a joint appointment with the School of Forestry and Environmental Studies and has made important contributions to the urbanism studio.

Some faculty approached me early on to suggest that the Building Project had outlived its value, given the digital age, and that it might be a reason why admissions had declined. I did and do not agree. The Jim Vlock Building Project is more important than ever (10.21). I think it's important for social and ethical reasons, but also because it gives students experience with actual construction. Student architects need field experience, which they frequently are denied after graduation when they work in design-oriented offices, many of which do not provide sufficient opportunities for them to engage with actual construction. The Vlock Building Project may be the one chance for students to know what it's like to actually build something with their own hands. Because I believe that it is an invaluable part of the curriculum to be experienced by all first professional degree students, I eliminated advanced placement, at the risk of losing talented students from some feeder schools with intensive undergraduate majors who might not choose three years at Yale, when they could shave off a term or two at other schools. But I believe my decision was the correct one. For example, for Surry Schlabs, the Jim Vlock Building Project was essential to Yale's identity: "If you talk to students about why they came to Yale, the Building Project was a huge part of it. Even in my class, which looking back was kind of a transitional period, early in Bob's tenure, during the transition—both in schools and in offices—into the digital era. The Jim Vlock Building Project—getting your hands dirty and actually doing things, and doing it in the service of some kind of public ideal, was a big part of why people came to school here."[45]

The Jim Vlock Building Project offers students an opportunity to develop and realize a building on a small scale; it was also enriched with workshops and courses to help students with their verbal presentations and to work together on teams without losing a sense of their contributions as individuals. In this we were helped by Phillip Bernstein and Nancy Alexander's endowment, the New Practice Paradigms Lectureship Fund. Furthering the connection between design and realization, a new approach was developed with Martin Finio, consisting of an integrated workshop and lecture series enabling teams of students to develop the technical systems and corresponding drawings for design developed by one team member in the third semester of the Core. Finio's "systems integration" course mirrored professional practice to some extent, bringing together students and consulting engineers and architects to work together to develop technical drawings for projects designed in the previous term, thereby making vivid the tectonic consequences of formal speculation. The course allows for the introduction of Building Information Modeling (BIM) as a technical tool rather than a design tool. When BIM software was introduced, some faculty questioned whether such professionalism was appropriate, but the experience with BIM has proven helpful to students seeking employment in offices, while it in no way compromised the school's commitment to architecture as an art.[46]

Not only was it important to strengthen the school's curriculum, it was also critical that its internal culture be reinvigorated. Taking seriously Steven Harris's complaint about the school's loss of graphic identity, I dug into the archives to find early calendars, posters, and other printed ephemera dating back to the 1970s, which were then framed and prominently displayed in public hallways, faculty offices, and even lavatories. This proved eye-opening for both faculty and students, who were especially interested in the work of alumni from the 1970s and 1980s, many of whom went on to significant careers, including teaching at Yale.

To help the school take on its history as an ongoing process, faculty were asked to pay greater attention to archiving student work and events.[47] As a result, a policy was initiated to film all public lectures and symposia, and to photograph juries and public events. To ensure that the school's outreach efforts were as professional as possible, Michael Bierut, senior partner in the design firm Pentagram and senior critic in the Art School's Graphic Design Department, was asked to take charge of the school's visual identity, which he has done with a continuing series of bold, black-and-white, poster-sized event calendars that draw upon the precedent of Norman Ives's work in the 1950s and 1960s (10.22). Bierut also designed posters for symposia and designed the new publication *Constructs,* while regularly consulting on the student-edited and student-designed *Retrospecta.*[48] *Constructs* was initiated in spring 1999 as a twice-yearly, tabloid-type newspaper highlighting activities and events at the school, as well as interviews with resident and visiting faculty and articles on issues relevant to what was being analyzed and discussed in the design studios.

With help from an augmented gift fund in 2000 and an endowment from Austin Church III (b. 1936; B.A. 1960, ArtA 1963) in 2005, the school was for the first time able to put *Perspecta,* its most prominent publication, on a sure financial footing.[49] A symposium, "Practice and Theory: *Perspecta* and the Fate of Architectural Discourse," held on February 11–12, 2001, to celebrate the journal's fiftieth anniversary, gathered architects, critics, historians, and theorists together to discuss the magazine's history and influence.[50] Subsequently, Alan Plattus, Peggy Deamer, and I were able to realize a long-cherished dream of *Perspecta* editors and enthusiasts: the publication of an annotated collection of the journal's most interesting and influential articles. *[Re]Reading Perspecta* (2004) also included the proceedings of the 2001 symposium.[51]

Even more disturbing than the somewhat erratic publication of *Perspecta*—only twenty-six issues of what had been intended as an annual journal were published between 1952 and 1999—was the diminished size and visual impact of *Retrospecta*. When Cesar Pelli founded it in 1978, *Retrospecta* was the only annual published by an American architecture school. As budgets waxed and waned, *Retrospecta* alternately grew and shrank in size, so that by the mid-1990s it was vastly outclassed by Columbia's *Abstract* and publications at other schools. So, to serve as a better marketing tool in the increasingly competitive world of architecture school admissions, *Retrospecta* was comprehensively redesigned in 1998 with a larger format and many more pages that not only documented student work in detail, but also jury discussions, elective classes, student trips, symposia, lectures, and other events that collectively define the school. In addition to *Retrospecta,* alumni were kept informed by the traditional annual dean's letter that outlined, in what many deem excruciating detail, the school's accomplishments in the previous year and its objectives for the near future.

Unlike previous deans, I chose not to offer a studio, preferring to confine my teaching to a single seminar each year in order to leave time for administrative duties—and time to drop in on studio reviews to stir the pot. My initial seminar was offered in preparation for the William C. DeVane Lecture series "Ideals without Ideologies: Yale's Contribution to Modern Architecture," which I was asked to deliver in 2001, Yale's tercentennial year. Sensing that the school had lost its institutional memory, I used the occasion of the DeVane lectures to combine my own thoughts with those of distinguished alumni—James Polshek, Norman Foster, Alexander Tzonis, David Sellers, Andrés Duany, Elizabeth Plater-Zyberk, and Maya Lin—who reflected on the impact their time at Yale had on their subsequent careers, hoping to inspire students and faculty alike to a greater sense of the school's unique history and importance.[52] The lectures served as the initial inspiration for this text.

Along with the DeVane lectures, the school helped celebrate the university's tercentennial with an exhibition of alumni work, *New Blue: Work of Recent Graduates of the Yale School of Architecture, 1978–1998,* on display September 5–October 19, 2001. Curated by Aaron Betsky (b. 1958; B.A. 1979, M.Arch 1983), it was an opportunity to demonstrate the school's success in fostering diverse perspectives. Collaborating with Michael Bierut, Betsky organized the work of nearly fifty alumni into six loose stylistic categories.[53] The exhibition was accompanied by a symposium, "White, Gray and Blue: Evaluating the Work of Yale Graduates since 1978," held on September 14–15—just days after the September 11, 2001, attack on the World Trade Center in New York, in the wake of which deans were given the opportunity to cancel planned events. I decided to go forward with the symposium, which attracted a large audience, including many recent graduates living and working in Lower Manhattan who saw it as an opportunity to escape the devastation, to socialize with peers, and to discuss the future of architecture in an environment celebrating its history and their place in it.[54]

Complementing the DeVane lectures and the *New Blue* show, *Architecture or Revolution: Charles Moore and Architecture at Yale in the Late 1960s,* an exhibition on view from late October to late December 2001, was intended to burnish the school's reputation for social engagement by focusing on one of the most exciting and controversial moments of its recent past.[55] Based on two years of research by curator Eve Blau (b. 1951; M.A. 1974, Ph.D. 1978), the exhibit, designed by Director of Exhibitions Dean Sakamoto (b. 1961; M.E.D. 1998), captured combined extensive wall text, bold supergraphics, and a partial reconstruction of Project Argus to supplement displays of student-produced propaganda, projects, and publications (10.23).[56]

As a result of *Architecture or Revolution,* President Levin and I agreed that the records of the many talented alumni and faculty needed to be systematically collected, leading to the development of an architectural archive, which, with much help from Richard Szary, Carrie S. Beinecke Director of Manuscripts and Archives, was formally established in 2002. The archive, housed in Sterling Memorial Library, is devoted to drawings and materials related to the buildings of Yale and the work of their architects; work of distinguished Yale alumni, whether graduates of the school or college; work of faculty; and work of important Connecticut architects.[57] Significant early acquisitions to the archive include the drawings and papers of Eero Saarinen; Kevin Roche; pioneering modernist lighting designer Richard Kelly; Cesar Pelli; and Charles Moore's work with his Centerbrook partners. The collection continues to grow, and its contents have proven invaluable to this text and will surely inform and enlighten future generations of scholars and architects.[58]

At the time of my appointment, the public lecture program was in dis-array. Lectures were poorly attended, especially by faculty. Visiting lecturers would come up the steps into the school and encounter the faculty leaving. The reasons for this were surely multiple, but perhaps Alec Purves put it most succinctly: "People were apathetic."[59] Determined to break the culture of apathy, faculty were informed that their attendance at public lectures was mandatory and they were expected to set an example for students by their participation in school-wide discourse. Although many faculty members chafed at this pronouncement, which was probably unenforceable, most soon realized that it would reflect badly on them not to show up at events. Moreover, a new policy of dinners honoring lecturers to which faculty and some students were invited proved an effective strategy to ensure faculty attendance. Purves remembers that I was "vigorous in getting people to go to lectures," although he notes that I "overdid it for a few years. He overdid a lot of things."[60] That may be true, but it was also necessary.

It was particularly dismaying, not to mention disheartening, to see that the lecture schedule previously arranged for fall 1998, my first term as dean, was devoted to "Unconventional Practices," featuring alumni who had gone on to pursue careers on the fringes of, and sometimes completely apart from, the profession. While open to suggestions from students and faculty, I set out to orchestrate the lecture program as a further iteration of pluralism, and a means to provide a heightened sense of the value of architecture as a discipline and a career. I began the spring 1999 lecture series with Bernard Tschumi's Paul Rudolph lecture.[61] My choice of Tschumi as inaugural lecturer was both personal and professional. Bernard had been very supportive of me at Columbia, and I thought it was not only a nice gesture, but also a strategic move to address some of my detractors by bringing in somebody who was very much my opposite.

Low attendance, a lack of strong publicity, and a somewhat downbeat point of view weren't the only problems with the lecture series. Although Fred Koetter had seen to it that there was a reception after each lecture, these were catered by the Central University Food Services. The catering consisted of a mound of cubed cheese and beer and wine served in little plastic cups that looked like those used for urine samples in doctors' offices. After the lecture,

10.23 *Architecture or Revolution,* exhibition, Yale School of Architecture (fall 2001).

10.24 Post–final review dinner in Stern's Chapel Street loft (April 29, 2004).

10.25 Post-lecture reception in the second-floor Art Gallery of Paul Rudolph Hall (2013).

the students would rush in, gobble up the cheese, wash it down with some wine or beer, and leave. They seemed to never talk to the lecturer, or even fellow students; it was just a free meal. This had to change. When I had left New Haven, martinis were being served! I asked myself: how can we prepare students for professional life when we don't treat them like professionals? Told by Associate Dean John Jacobson that martini receptions weren't in the school's budget, my reply was simple: "*Figure it out.*" It was one of the first times I would push the limits of the budget, not to mention the patience of the university administration. But of course, it was "figured out," and the School of Architecture has become renowned for its receptions (at which white wine, martinis, water, and passed hors d'oeuvres are also served) and the sense of community they foster. Many people in the university regarded the martini receptions as excessive, but to faculty and students they were positive signs of a changing school culture. "When I was a grad student here people arrived at the school wearing overalls and left wearing black turtlenecks," remembers Surry Schlabs, who graduated at the end of my fifth year as dean and later returned to pursue a Ph.D. "But now the students arrive wearing black turtle-necks and leave wearing bow ties."[62]

In order to further extend the conversation among students and faculty beyond the studio and classroom, I needed a place to stay during my three-day-per-week stints at the school. My two predecessor deans lived away from the school—Beeby in Guilford and Koetter on Trumbull Street, a twenty-minute walk not conducive to post-lecture events. Remembering parties at Paul Rudolph's High Street townhouse, I sought out a place that was large enough for substantial entertaining and within walking distance from the school. By the end of my first year, I was ensconced in a Chapel Street loft overlooking the New Haven Green, where my post-lecture, post-review din-ners soon became "go-to" events for resident faculty, visiting architects, and students (10.24, 10.25).[63] Of course, some members of the faculty and especially the university administration thought the loft was decadent, but Rudolph's High Street apartment had been similarly regarded. However, to me, the loft was critical to the culture of the school, helping to develop an esprit de corps. And unlike the exclusive meetings of George Howe's "Digressionist Club," the loft events, though by invitation only, were not exclusive, with every student offered the opportunity in his or her graduating year to sign up for at least one dinner with faculty and guest lecturers.

Like Cesar Pelli, I took seriously both administration and curricular policy. My hands-on administrative style came as a shock to many of the faculty, who were accustomed to greater independence. Initially, faculty members felt they were being treated like children or, at best, the subjects of a benevolent dictator. This feeling hasn't completely dissipated. Perhaps even more upsetting for some people in the school was that my method worked. "We were outraged about how he took control of the lectures and exhibitions," says Professor Peggy Deamer. "But he totally raised the stakes. We can be cynical of how controlling Bob is but his control let us know how much it mattered. And the fact that it mattered made the school matter more. And that made our teaching matter more. That was a good thing. We were all held accountable."[64]

It wasn't just the culture within the school that needed to be developed, but its relationship to the greater university. One of my earliest efforts to assert the school's role in university life came in April 1999, when, supported by President Levin, I convened a three-day symposium, "Yale Constructs: Planning and Building for the University's Fourth Century," to discuss the past and future of Yale's campus. Topics included long-range campus development, as well as specific plans for building renovations and new construction. The symposium began on Friday evening with Vincent Scully delivering the keynote address, situating Yale's campus within the context of the city of New Haven. On Saturday morning, Catherine Lynn (b. 1942; M.A. 1978, Ph.D. 1981) offered a detailed history of Yale's nineteenth-century expansion. Scully's and Lynn's talks would form the nucleus of a book, *Yale in New Haven: Architecture and Urbanism* (2004).[65] The symposium, which took place in the Law School's auditorium, was exceptionally well attended by architecture alumni, some presenting their ongoing work for the university and others hoping to learn how to position themselves for future projects. Looking at larger campus planning issues, Alexander Cooper presented Cooper Robertson's Campus Framework Plan, and James Polshek presented the Arts Area Plan and plans for renovating the Yale University Art Gallery.[66] From the administration, Bruce Alexander, vice-president and director of the Office of New Haven and State Affairs, spoke, followed by President Levin.

The "Yale Constructs" symposium made public the school's renewed commitment to architecture as an art-based profession. As city planner and educator Raymond Gastil, writing for *Constructs,* stated: "Refreshingly professional, the symposium offered an opportunity to see architects in the context of what they do more than in the liberal arts context of what they say. The message was hammered home: whatever else it is, the School of Architecture remains a professional program that will continue to produce professionals and play a leading role in shaping the university's buildings." But Gastil, a skeptic, asked, "Can a school function as a 'community of architecture' across generations without a more critical edge?"[67]

The symposium offered no specific answers to that question, but it did encourage productive discussion not only on the future of the campus but also on the stewardship required for its important collection of buildings. Regarding this, one situation struck a particularly discordant note: the future of the Sterling Divinity School (Delano & Aldrich, 1932). In 1996, when the university announced plans to demolish four Divinity School buildings, which accounted for almost half the complex, the displeasure of alumni and neighbors was reported in the *New York Times*.[68] At the symposium, the Divinity School plan was presented by Robert Kliment (b. 1933; B.A. 1954, M.Arch 1959) of the firm Kliment & Halsband. It was met with criticism, the most damning of which came from Vincent Scully. Asking that he be allowed to speak from the platform at the end of the conference, with President Levin seated in the front row, Scully, Yale's beloved teacher for over fifty years, stated: "If the Divinity School were rebuilt according to the present plan, I'd have to rethink my future in this institution. Loyalty can only be stretched so far."[69] I remember the color draining from Rick Levin's face. This was not what he wanted to happen. Scully continued, "I don't like making threats, but from the very beginning I've never understood the University's plans for the Divinity School. The plans show no respect for the character of [the quadrangle] or for the architect. . . . Throughout history fine architecture has always been used for purposes for which it wasn't intended. There's no reason to destroy the buildings because the Divinity School population is getting smaller."[70] Kliment, a former student of Scully's, like most in the audience, was shocked by the declaration, and only commented that he would abide by the wishes of the client. President Levin, in his closing address, seemed momentarily stunned by Scully's remarks but remained firm in his belief that the university was taking the right course of action:

> As for the Divinity School, I understand the passion of those preservationists who are deeply concerned about these buildings and are fighting to preserve them. After long thought and considered discussion of every aspect of this situation, including the historical preservation issues, the aesthetic plan, and the needs of the Divinity School and the University— the dean, the provost, the committee and I believe we are making the right decision. We have listened attentively to the community about this, and I have heard what Vince and others have had to say. In the end, this is our decision.

We are striving to be the very best stewards we can be. It is in our own interest, as well as in the interests of posterity to be faithful wardens of our treasures. But it is also true that the general needs of the University and our community are tremendous, our resources are not unlimited, and we sometimes must make hard—but we hope sensible and sensitive—choices.[71]

The next day, Scully's threat was front-page news in the *Yale Daily News,* whose headline proclaimed, "Scully Says He Could Leave If Yale Destroys Divinity Quad," and in the *New Haven Register,* which shouted, "Art Expert Threatens to Cut Yale Ties."[72] Protests over the university's decision had already taken a decisive turn when a group of Divinity School faculty and alumni, along with Sterling family heiress Cynthia Sterling Russell, filed a lawsuit against the university to halt the demolition. Although an appellate court had previously dismissed the case on the grounds that the filing parties did not have legal standing as plaintiffs, the decision remained under appeal at the time of the symposium.[73] The *Yale Alumni Magazine* also briefly addressed the controversy in its May issue, and letters began to pour in from concerned friends of the school and Divinity School alumni.[74]

The collective efforts of the concerned Yale community seemed to have made a difference. By September 14, the administration had changed its mind, announcing that it was rescinding its proposal to demolish the four threatened Divinity School buildings, and instead moving forward with a new plan to make structural repairs and use one as a library while mothballing the remaining three. The revisions were not solely the result of a change of heart, but a concern that litigation would indefinitely hold up the much-needed renovation of the Divinity Quad's remaining buildings. "I'm very relieved that I don't have to stop teaching," Scully told the *Yale Daily News.* "I was really getting myself fortified to do so."[75]

Symposia proved a particularly effective way for the school to address important issues, from the preservation of modernist architecture to environmentalism to the nature of sacred space to new digital technologies. Faculty and multi-term visitors were encouraged to propose and undertake symposia related to their particular interests. To name just a few: in fall 2003, Peggy Deamer organized "Psychoanalysis and Architecture," bringing together analysts, theorists, and architects to explore the relationship between various schools of psychoanalytic thought, architectural form, and the creation of space; in fall 2007, Karla Britton, interested in the relationship between religion and modern architecture, organized the symposium

"Constructing the Ineffable: Contemporary Sacred Architecture"; in April 2008, Michelle Addington convened "Sustainable Architecture, Today and Tomorrow: Reframing the Discourse," inviting prominent expert speakers from a vast array of disciplines, including neurobiology, public policy, and fluid mechanics, to discuss the possibilities of sustainable design; in spring 2010, Vincent Scully Visiting Professor (2010–14) Stanislaus von Moos organized "Architecture after Las Vegas" to examine the cultural impact of the 1968 Las Vegas studio led by Robert Venturi and Denise Scott Brown (10.26); and in spring 2014, Scully Visiting Professor (2011–14) Mario Carpo gathered architects and theorists to examine "Digital Post-Modernities: From Calculus to Computation."

In 2010, both Barbara Littenberg and Judy DiMaio resigned from the faculty—Littenberg to concentrate on professional practice, and DiMaio to become dean of the School of Architecture at the New York Institute of Technology. The departure of two female faculty led to some concern that I was creating an inhospitable atmosphere for women—particularly in relation to the productive strides made by my predecessors. However, I don't think this gained much traction, given the appointment of several women as junior faculty and the promotion to tenure of Peggy Deamer, Eeva-Liisa Pelkonen, Keller Easterling (10.27), and Michelle Addington. Whether it was the result of any perceived unfairness or just a result of the changing times, an ongoing discussion about gender and the profession began in January 2002, when a panel was convened to discuss "Women, Family, and the Practice of Architecture," featuring Peggy Deamer, Deborah Berke, Lise Anne Couture (b. 1959; M.Arch 1986), Audrey Matlock, Susan Rodriguez, and Alan Plattus. The conversation centered on the fair treatment for women in the workplace and the difficulties—for men and women—of raising a family while simultaneously building a professional practice. The issue came to the forefront again in spring 2005, when the advanced studio offerings did not include a single offering by a female critic, clearly a misstep on my part. In light of this, a new student group was formed, Yale Women in Architecture (YWA), to offer a support network and critical forum for the examination of gender in architectural education and practice. As one of its first events, the group hosted a panel discussion with faculty and alumni, drawing a large crowd to the fourth-floor pit to hear Deamer, Pelkonen, Carol Burns (b. 1954; B.A. 1980, M.Arch 1983), Phillip Bernstein, Kevin Rotheroe, and Joel Sanders share their experiences and offer advice. "You have to be smarter to be considered as smart," Burns, a respected Boston-based architect and educator, told the gathered students. "You have to work harder to be considered

10.26 Denise Scott Brown and Robert Venturi meet with students for a more casual conversation in the fourth-floor studio following the "Architecture after Las Vegas" symposium (2010). At left: Jimmy Stamp moderates the discussion.

10.27 Caitlin Gucker-Kanter (M.Arch 2013) and Amy Mielke (M.Arch 2013), "Poreform," site plan. Keller Easterling studio (spring 2013).

10.28 Women alumni on the steps of Rudolph Hall, assembled for the "Yale Women in Architecture" symposium (December 2012).

as hardworking. You just have to be ready to struggle more." Deamer reminded attendees of the earlier discussion that "it's not about instant progress—it's a daily battle."[76]

The battle for professional advancement and recognition continued in December 2012, when many women graduates gathered together as a group at the school for the first "Yale Women in Architecture" symposium. The event was at once a reunion and a celebration of the thirtieth anniversary of the Sonia Albert Schimberg (1925–1981; M.Arch 1950) Award, given annually to a high-achieving female architecture student in honor of one of the school's first women graduates. Organized by Claire Weisz (b. 1960; M.Arch 1989), the event afforded an opportunity to discuss the lingering prejudices and other obstacles facing women in architecture. "I think it's worth talking about how people operate in the field [and] why there aren't more women in charge," alumna and panelist Lisa Gray (b. 1960; M.Arch 1987) told the *Yale Daily News*. "[It is] a step toward encouraging talented women to stay in the profession"[77] (10.28). The impressive accomplishments of Yale's women graduates were showcased to great advantage, and various speakers, such as Maya Lin, furthered the sense that though much more needed to be done to level the gender playing field, much had also been accomplished.

With its profile on the rise, the cost of running the school inevitably increased, demanding greater levels of support from central administration, who were constantly frustrated with what they saw as "excessive expenditures," "entertainment extravaganzas," and an overall unwillingness on my part to work within budgets, which I regarded as seriously deficient despite the fact that they had been increased considerably at the time of my appointment—largely through discretionary funds. Admittedly, I frequently moved forward with plans that were neither budgeted nor funded, confident that the money would come from somewhere. As Deputy Provost for the Arts Diana Kleiner reported to President Levin, "Bob has continually said to me . . . that no matter what the President has indicated that he will pick up the tab."[78] I may have been testing the limits of the president's support, but, thankfully, new initiatives proved to be effective in attracting increased support from alumni and friends of the school. And they did not go unnoticed outside of the school. I realized that things were really starting to improve when I learned that students at Harvard, seeking a new dean in 2004, said they wanted someone like me.

Increasing the endowment was and is fundamental to the school's long-term success. With the collaboration of the school's director of development, Monica Robinson, the level of support needed to put the school on a healthy financial basis was formalized as part of the university's $3 billion capital campaign, known as "Yale Tomorrow." Besides raising enough money to finance a much-needed renovation of the Art and Architecture Building, great emphasis was put on developing specific endowments necessary to permanently shore up fundamental needs such as financial aid and to institutionalize curricular objectives such as hand-drawing, student travel, exhibitions, and symposia. With great support from President Levin, who helped direct potential donors to the architecture program, the school, by the end of the campaign in 2010, had raised more than $60 million—$10 million beyond its goal.[79]

Another important development in building support for the school was the establishment, at President Levin's suggestion, of a Dean's Council, as a way to strengthen the relationship between the school and the outside world. The council, comprising philanthropically minded individuals interested in architecture, was formed without the expectation that its members would contribute any "advice," but instead, would gather together to enjoy, as Robinson says, "what I call 'insider opportunities'—opportunities to see and do things they wouldn't have otherwise. Opportunities to be together as a group with people they might not otherwise meet."[80] When the time came to find a chairman for the council, I contacted David Schwarz, who turned me down. "I said no chance," Schwarz recalls. "[But then] he had Rick [Levin] call me up and Rick asked me. And I said, 'I'm sorry, Mr. President, but I'm too busy.'" But that wasn't the end of the story:

> Rick then called Ed Bass [Schwarz's longtime client] up and asked him to ask me to do it. At that point I said, "OK, I don't have much choice here. I'll do it." Bob wanted me to do it as a fund-raising mechanism. I said no. I said, "I'll do this if it's fun, if the students are involved, and if it's a serious outreach trying to get the world at large to understand the school better and the school to understand the world at large better. So we need a more broad-based council than just Yale architects, and a much more broad-based group of involvements." So once a year we go somewhere a lot of fun, talk to whatever Yale students happen to be there. Berlin, L. A., Cuba, London, Rome, and once a year we meet in New Haven, which is mostly about the students. It's been highly successful. . . . I think that architects tend to live in a little rarified world. I don't think architects living in a rarified world is useful. We spend far too much time talking to ourselves and our critics and not enough time talking to the people.[81]

In 2000, the School of Architecture began a relationship with the School of Forestry and Environmental Studies, offering a joint course, "Issues in Environment and Design," which was first proposed by graduate students and ultimately organized by Associate Professor Jim Axley, Assistant Professor Adjunct Victor Body-Lawson, School of Forestry Professor Stephen Kellert, and Advanced Design Critic Diana Balmori. Initially, it recalled the old art and architecture collaborative studios, with teams consisting of an equal number of students from both programs initially tasked with preparing a sustainable master plan for Isla Vista, California, a small college town near the UC Santa Barbara campus. These designs were informed by the work of invited guest speakers, architects, ecologists, and researchers, who shared their approach with students, discussed the practice, and sat on reviews of student work. But in 2006, in response to a growing awareness that a shared strategy for addressing environmental issues was needed, the relationship between the two schools was formalized with a new joint degree program—a collaboration intended to benefit both disciplines. Regarding its importance, Jim Axley wrote in *Constructs* that "Environmentalists are ... struggling desperately to shape a new direction of tangible action through design without the expertise to do so," while architects are struggling "to address the biological and societal dimensions of sustainable design with rigor and sophistication."[82]

Historically, the school's technology faculty has been notably small and involved in practice rather than research. But this began to change in 2006, when Michelle Addington joined the faculty. With James Axley's impending retirement, Addington added a welcome new energy to the school's technology curriculum. Originally educated as a nuclear and mechanical engineer, Addington began her career with NASA, where she was a structural analyst designing components for satellites and rockets. She later worked in the chemical industry for many years in various capacities before deciding to pursue a professional degree in architecture, and she went on to earn multiple degrees, including a Ph.D. from Harvard, for which her dissertation focused on "Boundary Layer Control of Heat Transfer in Buildings." Two years later, in 2008, Gerald Hines's gift of endowment enabled Addington to become Hines Professor of Sustainable Architectural Design, with responsibility for a research fund.[83] In 2008, Kyoung Sun Moon, an architect with a Ph.D. in engineering from MIT, joined the faculty, teaching required courses in structural engineering as well as seminars in the design of super-tall skyscrapers. Like Addington, Moon also offers a popular course in Yale College.

Thanks to the dramatic increase in the university endowment, the Levin years were characterized by an expansion of academic programs. While the principal purpose of the Yale School of Architecture remains training for practice, research has been important to the program since the late 1960s. With the renovation of the Art and Architecture Building, M.E.D. students who had been housed in a nasty room located off a stair landing were relocated to the design studio, helping to reintegrate the program with the overall school culture, as had been the case in its early years. Additionally, some faculty began to press for the introduction of a Ph.D. program, which had first been discussed in the era of Charles Moore. Mindful that peer schools such as Columbia and MIT, having started their programs in the 1970s, were very well-established leaders, I felt that, given the strong M.E.D. program, a Ph.D. program was not needed. Most significantly, I was influenced in my resistance to a Ph.D. program by Vincent Scully, who feared the corrupting influence of practitioners eager for critical recognition and believed that architecture historians should not be in the Architecture School, but with other art historians. However, with Scully's retirement and the dramatic reduction of offerings in architectural history by the Art History Department, as well as the increasing demand on the part of faculty with advanced degrees, there was some urgency to establish our own Ph.D. program. As Peter Eisenman told the *Yale Daily News,* "In the past, architecture focused on its mission of creating professionals. What is happening in architecture now is that in order to be influential in academia you need to have an advanced degree. All European Union schools require a doctorate and many more Europeans are applying to us now. We were missing out on this."[84]

In 2008, the new Ph.D. program was launched, directed by Kurt Forster, inaugural Vincent Scully Visiting Professor of Architectural History. To distinguish the program from one in art history, the school requires candidates to be trained architects with at least two years of professional experience. This gives their theoretical and historical work a practical basis so they can teach in studios and in the classrooms. As Forster told the *Yale Daily News:* "The profession is no longer going to run on the standard track of mere commentary. Instead of teaching only things that are remote, our Ph.D. students will be able to look at the involvement of architecture in the life of society at large."[85] Like M.E.D. students, Ph.D. students were given desk space in the studios, where their presence was more than welcomed by the design students. As the program continues to evolve, Ph.D. students are reaching out to architecture and art history faculty and elsewhere in the university community, organizing informal, high-level "dialogues" that are well attended by master of architecture students. They are teaching sections in various lecture courses, assisting in Yale design studios, and playing a substantial part in organizing scholarly events such as the October 2012 symposium "The Sound of Architecture," organized by Joseph Clarke (b. 1981; Ph.D. 2015), as well as the exhibition and symposium marking the school's centennial in 2016.[86]

The explosive growth of the university's endowment enabled a building boom the likes of which hadn't been seen since the presidency of Alfred Whitney Griswold. Between 1998 and 2012, every residential college was thoroughly renovated—none more dramatically than the Saarinen-designed Morse and Stiles Colleges, which the partnership of Stephen Kieran and James Timberlake transformed to better reflect arrangements typical of the other residential colleges.[87] Many of the new buildings that made up the massive campus expansion were designed by alumni or school faculty, beginning with the Art School's new home, Deborah Berke's Holcombe T. Green, Jr., Hall (2000), and soon followed by the Class of 1954 Environmental Science Center (2001) designed by David M. Schwarz Architectural Services, Inc.; Robert Venturi finally realized a Yale commission with the Anlyan Center at the Medical School (2003); former dean Tom Beeby was charged with transforming the inhospitable underground Cross Campus Library into the Bass Library (2005); the Malone Engineering Center (2005) was designed by Pelli Clarke Pelli Architects; the Rose Center (2006), housing both the Yale Police Department headquarters and the Dixwell-Yale Community Learning Center, was designed by William Rawn (b. 1943; B.A. 1965); the Sculpture Building (2007) was the work of Kieran Timberlake Associates; Kroon Hall for the School of Forestry and Environmental Studies was the collaborative project of Sir Michael Hopkins in partnership with Mark Simon of Centerbrook (2009); Koetter Kim were given responsibility for Rosenkranz Hall (2009); and the renovation and expansion of the Yale University Art Gallery (2012) was the work of the Polshek Partnership team led by Polshek, Richard Olcott, and Duncan Hazard (b. 1949; B.A. 1971).

In discussing my responsibilities as dean with President Levin, I asked to have a voice in university building policy, as Paul Rudolph had done in the 1960s. Already, Tom Beeby was playing an important role as consultant to the Buildings and Grounds Planning Committee of the Yale Corporation. Levin's response was to form a three-person committee—made up of Beeby, Pelli, and myself—to advise the president on campus construction, with input in architect selection and actual designs. The committee was quickly dubbed "The Three Amigos" by facilities staff who were amazed at, and sometimes frustrated by, its general unanimity of opinion.

The rehabilitation of the Art and Architecture Building, critical to the school's future, presented the greatest challenge to the university's program of physical renewal. As someone who observed the progress of its construction from ground-breaking and a member of the first group of students to study in Rudolph's building when it opened in 1963, I gave tours of the building to the very many important architects, journalists, and academic administrators who came to New Haven specifically to see it for themselves. Even after its functional limitations became obvious, and its physical state a shambles as a result of the fire and the asbestos crisis, I remained the steadfast apologist for Rudolph's beleaguered masterpiece, which the university, especially after the 1969 fire, regarded as a thorn in its side that it would happily tear down were it not too expensive to do so. Despite its deplorable condition, graduates continued to respect the building and clamored for its restoration.

Getting university support for the building's renovation was one thing, but much more difficult to obtain was a commitment for the building's restoration. Few people in the central administration were able to see its true nature beneath the catastrophes it had endured and the renovations that had been inflicted on it over the years. To help turn the tide in its favor, I mounted a modest exhibition (September 1–17, 1999) of Ezra Stoller's 1963 photographs in the gallery. Then, in 2000, Sid R. Bass (b. 1942; B.A. 1965), former senior fellow of the Yale Corporation, committed $20 million for the building's "comprehensive restoration."[88] Bass shared my admiration for the building and for Paul Rudolph's work. Upon making the gift, he said, "As an undergraduate, I was deeply moved by the bold innovations of Paul Rudolph's Art and Architecture Building. This led to a long working relationship with Paul, who completed for me a residence in the early '70s and two office buildings in the early '80s. I am delighted to provide support for this historically significant building."[89]

The Art School's relocation in 2000 was a bittersweet moment for the Yale's tradition of arts education, marking as it did the end of the idea that had inspired the founding of the Yale School of the Fine Arts in 1869: interdisciplinary collaboration and union of the arts under one roof. Deborah Berke, designer of the new Art School building, acknowledged as much: "The loss of the artists in the building was a loss for the Architecture School. It's not that there was that much overlap, but I remember after studio going down to the painting studios and there would be crazy parties going on. I think the influence of a very different way of being visually inventive and creative was positive."[90] Not only were the art students' hijinks to be missed, but also their freewheeling creativity: "With the art students gone the graffiti in the bathrooms wasn't really that good."[91]

Once the art students vacated the building, the school was able to undertake interim renovations overseen by John Jacobson working with s/l/a/m architects, including necessary safety updates such as the installation of a sprinkler system, but also more profound changes, such as the removal of the "temporary" artists' cubicles on the fourth and fifth floors and of sky-light-blocking concrete slabs that had been introduced to create additional floor space. This work took place over the summer so that students and faculty returning for the fall 2000 term were greeted by a long-hidden, double-height studio washed in natural light streaming down from skylights and to a double-height exhibition gallery overlooking the library and Kahn's Art Gallery beyond. Another happy effect of the recapturing of space was that undergraduate architecture students could be brought into the fold from the dilapidated former Fence Club. In remarks made at the opening of the partially restored gallery, where an exhibition of Cesar Pelli's work was being previewed, I welcomed all students, faculty, and President Levin to a space seen in its entirety for the first time since 1969 and gained the president's public commitment to not just renovate but to *restore* Rudolph's masterpiece. Having secured the necessary funds, the university moved forward with plans that included the construction on the adjacent property of a new building, Jeffrey Loria Hall (2008), to house the art history program as well as an expanded Arts Library. The construction of Loria Hall was crucial to the restoration project, providing mechanical equipment, new elevators, and restrooms that could not be accommodated in Rudolph's original building, but also, by allowing the Art History Department to give up its offices in the Swartwout building and Street Hall, permitting a dramatic restoration of all three Art Gallery buildings.

During the early phase of the Arts Area Plan, Polshek had been retained by the university as the architect both for the renovation of the A&A and the design of the addition for which he produced a set of sketch plans (see 9.11). However, his contract for the A&A was terminated so that he could concentrate on the Art Gallery project. After that, David Schwarz was briefly considered as architect for the A&A restoration, but the assignment was ultimately given to David Childs, senior design partner and chairman of Skidmore, Owings & Merrill, who was also selected to serve as executive architect for whoever was to design Loria Hall. Initially, as one might expect, Childs seemed a bit overwhelmed with what needed to be done. In an interview with the *Yale Daily News,* he described the litany of basic mechanical problems and accessibility issues that had to be addressed, telling the paper that the most challenging aspect of the design would be "to find a way to come into the building and make it float free from all that. We're doing a

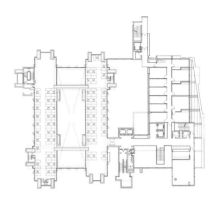

10.29 Richard Meier, Proposed Design for Jeffrey Loria Hall, York Street elevation (2001).

10.30 Richard Meier, Proposed Design for Jeffrey Loria Hall, plan showing connections between Art and Architecture Building (2001).

10.31 Left: Kieran Timberlake, Sculpture Building and Gallery, Yale School of Art (2007), New Haven. Right: Architecture students work in the Sculpture Building during the 2007–8 "swing" year.

10.32 *Model City: Buildings and Projects by Paul Rudolph for New Haven and Yale,* exhibition, Yale School of Architecture (fall 2008).

massive study to figure it all out, no preconception of design things, because the architectural resolutions will come from . . . what the problems are."[92] As for the addition, an invited competition was initially considered, with Norman Foster, Renzo Piano, and Daniel Libeskind as potential participants. The administration then considered both Norman Foster and Richard Meier, on the grounds that their typically clean modernism would provide an appropriate contrast to Rudolph's Brutalism. Jeffrey Loria (b. 1940; b.a. 1962), an art dealer and baseball team owner who was providing funds for the expansion, preferred Meier, whose selection was announced on February 2, 2001.[93] Construction was to be completed by 2004. However, as his design began to take shape, Meier came into conflict with university staff—especially the librarians, who deemed his design for their space to be unworkable (10.29, 10.30). Meier also balked at my request that the new building would not block the view from the A&A's north-facing penthouse windows.

As Meier proceeded with his work on Loria, I concentrated on making sure that Rudolph's building was restored and not merely renovated. This distinction was crucial. As Diana Kleiner informed President Levin, "It was clear from Meeting one that my dear Bob Stern will be a handful for all involved."[94] In her letter to Levin, Kleiner quotes me as telling the Building Committee, "This is not a routine job! The world will be watching. We have to do it right or we shouldn't do it at all!"[95] John Jacobson, chair of the Building Committee, remembers running a meeting and "suddenly realizing that this thing was out of control because Bob was insisting that this was going to be a restoration. That essentially shut down the meetings for a year or more . . . because the University didn't have the funds to make it a restoration. They wanted it to be a renovation."[96] All problems would become moot, however, when Sid Bass announced in 2001 that he would have to delay his promised donation due to an economic downturn. The once fast-tracked project was now indefinitely delayed. Meier's design was never released by the university, but the architect published the scheme in 2004.[97]

By the time Bass was able to honor his pledge in 2005, the university had cut ties with both Meier and Childs and set out to select a new architect who would be responsible for the complete project. I suggested Charles Gwathmey, who had long sought a commission from his alma mater. The university agreed. Charles and his partner, Robert Siegel, were interviewed, but they didn't realize that they were the only ones being interviewed. They were asked to sit out in the hall, and then Rick Levin went out fifteen minutes later and said, "Congratulations! You have the job. But you have to do it in eighteen months." Many asked, "Why Charlie?" My answer: He was very professional and experienced with additions to high-profile buildings such as the Guggenheim and Fogg museums. He understood the problem, and he loved Yale and had been very disappointed not to be considered for the renovation of the Art Gallery.[98]

Key to the project's success was the ability to find a temporary home for the school. Initially, the university suggested a relocation plan that would keep students out of the A&A for two years, but the grueling schedule imposed on the project came at my behest: because Rudolph's "poured-in-place peda-gogy" was just as much a part of a Yale architectural education as the pluralist curriculum, it seemed to me that every student who studied architecture at Yale should have the opportunity to work in the building. Fortunately, around the same time that Gwathmey was selected, the university also selected Kieran Timberlake to design a new building for the Art School's sculpture program, which was scheduled to be relocated from remote Hammond Hall to the newly defined "Arts Area." The Sculpture Building, designed and completed in record time, served as a "swing space" for architecture students during the 2007–8 academic year, while work was under way on the A&A (10.31).[99]

Undaunted by the programmatic complexities and compressed time frame, Gwathmey rejoiced in the commission: "Working on a project as important as the renovation and restoration of Paul Rudolph's iconic Art & Architecture Building is a privilege—one that carries with it enormous respon-sibility, not only to the building itself and the people who will use it, but also to its rich history and its architect's vision."[100]

On November 8, 2008, after eighteen months of construction and almost exactly forty-five years from the day of its dedication, the completion of the restored Art and Architecture Building, renamed Paul Rudolph Hall at the bequest of Sid Bass, and the new Loria Center for the History of Art was formally celebrated by over six hundred guests of the university. The event was marked with a lecture by Rudolph scholar Timothy Rohan as well as an exhibition, also by Rohan, *Model City: Buildings and Projects by Paul Rudolph for New Haven and Yale* (10.32).[101] At the rededication, President Levin stated that "by honoring Paul Rudolph's genius after years of neglecting, even abusing his iconic building, we are atoning for past mistakes. And by a combination of faithful restoration, imaginative reprogramming, and creative expansion, we have produced a compelling environment in which the study and practice of the arts can flourish."[102] Sadly, Rudolph did not live long enough to see his building brought back to life; he died in 1997.[103]

The restoration was comprehensive. Rudolph Hall was stripped to its concrete shell. The too-small windows, recently installed in 1994, were replaced by newly available large sheets of high-performance glass that were virtually the same size as the originals. Sophisticated custom lighting was devised to echo the character of Rudolph's and Richard Kelly's original scheme of bulb-strips, while also improving light levels and energy efficiency. The building's original "paprika"-colored carpet that gave the cold concrete a warm glow was also restored; the new carpet's color was matched to a small, miraculously preserved patch of the original discovered over the course of the work. While the building was restored to its original state in almost every significant way, it was necessary to make some changes in order to bring it up to full compliance with the Americans with Disabilities Act. Ramps were installed to access many but not all of the original structure's thirty-seven levels; and in the Architecture Gallery, a removable wood floor was installed over its multiple levels so that future scholars could, like archaeologists, "excavate" down to the original.

As a culminating gesture of rebirth, a plaster cast of Minerva, the original having been returned to the Art Gallery after the 1969 fire, once again watched over architecture students on the fourth floor (10.33). Initially, there were no plans to bring Minerva back from the Art Gallery, but John Jacobson "kept pushing and pushing and insisting that she be brought back." Jacobson "thought that if you're trying to restore this place, to bring back the feeling of what this building was like, of what the space was like—down to the lightbulbs—why would you not bring Minerva back? She was such an important part of the culture. So I kept insisting. I got Bob on board, I got Gwathmey on board, and I finally convinced the university that it was a worthwhile endeavor. So I'm personally going to take responsibility for bringing her back."[104] The process revealed a hitherto unknown aspect of Minerva: she had the wrong head. Jacobson remembers that "the caster said he had a cast of the head that belongs on the statue and he said, 'Do you want that?' I thought about it for ten seconds and I said no. I want the original. I want the one Rudolph had."[105]

Gwathmey stated that his goal "was to make the Loria Center recessive but articulate—not imitative." He believed the design represented "an expansion and enrichment of the organizing principle of the Art & Architecture Building, while at the same time establishing a separate and unique identity for the new Jeffrey Loria Center for the History of Art."[106] Critics, however, largely disagreed. Léon Krier offered, with mock seriousness, alternate designs (10.34). Many found the design unable to stand up to Rudolph's imposing structure. Vincent Scully, perhaps remembering Meier's original design and the possible selection of Norman Foster, believed "It should have been

10.33 An architecture review in the fourth-floor "pit" (2008).

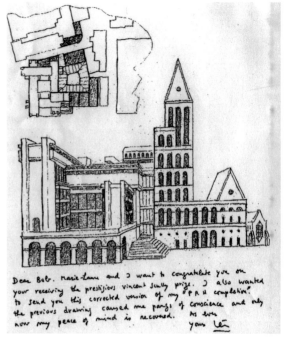

Dear Bob. Marie-Laure and I want to congratulate you on your receiving the prestigious Vincent Scully prize. I also wanted to send you this corrected version of my "P R H completion." the previous drawing caused me pangs of conscience and only now my peace of mind is recovered. As ever yours Léon

10.34 Léon Krier, Proposed Art and Architecture Building addition sent to Robert A. M. Stern, plan and perspective (ca. 2008).

10.35 Gwathmey Siegel, Rudolph Hall and the Loria Center for the History of Art (2008), New Haven.

simpler—maybe all glass." He commented that "Gwathmey tried very hard to dance with Rudolph's building, but there are too many small things in and out, up and down, too many changes of material."[107] Paul Goldberger, however, acknowledged the magnitude of Gwathmey's task, telling the *Yale Daily News* that "Rudolph's building is a powerful work of art that stands on its own. It is difficult to use and aesthetically challenging to add to"[108] (10.35).

Happy to be back, students recognized the importance of their restored home:

> This year we reoccupied Paul Rudolph's Art and Architecture Building—rededicated as Rudolph Hall—and ever since it has preoccupied us. The building is an integral part of the architectural education at Yale, providing the students and faculty who work within it lessons in mass, volume, texture, and affect. To attend the Yale School of Architecture is to gradually discover the building's myriad spaces and surfaces. From its stairwells to its orange carpets to its collection of reliefs and sculptures, it is a vivid argument against the banal. . . . The building at once enforces a hierarchy of students and undermines it. Space flows within and between studios, fostering the dissemination of diverse ideas and agendas. It is this exchange that constitutes the legacy of the School and places it at the forefront of the discipline.[109]

The restoration, following on the heels of the meticulous 2006 restoration of Louis Kahn's Art Gallery extension, was significant in turning the tide of opinion toward a greater appreciation of the works of mid-twentieth-century American modernism. Writing for the *Chicago Tribune,* Blair Kamin (b. 1957; M.E.D. 1984) remembered the A&A of his student days as "a place of transcendent gloom . . . a prime example of soaring architectural ambition that tramped on the simple everyday needs of users. It was an anti-model, not something to emulate." But what he found upon returning to it in 2008 was "a triumph," an incredibly optimistic achievement, and a model: "The project sends the broader message that even the most severely troubled landmarks of mid-twentieth century modernism can be made livable again—and our culture would be poorer without them."[110]

Since 1998, it's been my privilege to lead the Yale School of Architecture. In so doing, it has been my goal to balance old and new methods and ideas. The Yale School of Architecture has never favored one particular ideology of form or content. Pluralism—the idea that many ideas can flourish at once—is its governing ideal. As this is being written, many schools of architecture seem more occupied with related fields of inquiry than with providing disciplinary instruction. Many are trying to leap into the future but are neglecting the here and now, neglecting especially the necessary basics of architecture education that will empower future professional leaders. For this reason, it might be claimed that the Yale School of Architecture is the last architecture school that actually teaches architecture. That's an exaggeration to be sure, but by emphasizing the importance of the fundamental principles as the core experience of architecture education, while also opening itself to many diverse ideas and disciplines, the Yale School of Architecture continues to honor its historic commitment to training for the practice of architecture as the art of building.

Notes

Introduction

Epigraph. *Blueprint for Leadership: Yale School of Architecture* (New Haven: Campaign for Yale, 1976), 24.

1

Beginnings

Epigraph. *The Yale School of the Fine Arts, A Department of Yale College: A Brief Statement on Its Objects and Course of Instruction* (New Haven: Tuttle, Morehouse, and Taylor, 1875), 4.

1. For general overviews of architectural education in the United States, see Arthur Clason Weatherhead, "The History of Collegiate Education in Architecture in the United States" (Ph.D. thesis, Columbia University, 1941); "Patterns of Education for the Practice of Architecture," in *The Architect at Mid-Century: Evolution and Achievement*, ed. Turpin C. Bannister (New York: Reinhold, 1954), 81–127; Joan Ockman, ed., *Architecture School: Three Centuries of Educating Architects in North America* (Washington, D.C.: Association of Collegiate Schools of Architecture; Cambridge, Mass.: MIT Press, 2012); and Michael J. Lewis, "The Battle Between Polytechnic and Beaux-Arts in the American University," in Ockman, *Architecture School*, 74. For more information on MIT, see Mark Jarzombek, *Designing MIT: Bosworth's New Tech* (Boston: Northeastern University Press, 2004); and Julius A. Stratton and Loretta H. Mannix, *Mind and Hand: The Birth of MIT* (Cambridge, Mass.: MIT Press, 2005); for Cornell, see Morris Bishop, *A History of Cornell* (Ithaca, N.Y.: Cornell University Press, 1962), 156–61, 239–40, 246, 398–99; for Illinois, see Lillian Hoddeson, ed., *No Boundaries: University of Illinois Vignettes* (Urbana: University of Illinois Press, 2004); for Columbia, see Richard Oliver, ed., *The Making of an Architect, 1881–1981: Columbia University in the City of New York* (New York: Rizzoli, 1981); for Harvard, see Anthony Alofsin, *The Struggle for Modernism: Architecture, Landscape Architecture, and City Planning at Harvard* (New York: W. W. Norton, 2002); for the

University of Pennsylvania, see the Architectural Alumni Society, eds., *Book of the School, Department of Architecture, University of Pennsylvania, 1874–1934* (Philadelphia: University of Pennsylvania Press, 1934).

2. J. Ferguson Weir, "Memories of a Professor, 1869–1913," pt. V (n.d.), 1–2, John Ferguson Weir Papers, MS-550, ser. II, box 9, Yale University Manuscripts and Archives, New Haven.

3. Ibid., 6.

4. Faculty Meeting Minutes, 1913, 145, School of Art and Architecture Records, RU-189, accn. 1973-A-001, box 2, Yale University Manuscripts and Archives, New Haven. See also *Directory of Yale University*, no. 24 (1948), 837.

5. "Art School Commencement," *Yale Alumni Weekly*, May 27, 1897, quoted in Betsy Fahlman, *John Ferguson Weir: The Labor of Art* (Newark: University of Delaware Press, 1997), 193–94n64.

6. Weir, "Memories," 16–17.

7. "The School of the Fine Arts," in *Yale College in 1871* (1871), 18.

8. For Lindsey's appointment, see *Yale College in 1879: Some Statements Respecting the Late Progress and Present Condition of the Various Departments of the University, For the Information of Its Graduates, Friends, and Benefactors* (June 1879) (New Haven: Tuttle, Morehouse, and Taylor, 1879), 12, Y31-A11–1879, Yale University Manuscripts and Archives, New Haven. The Ph.B. designation is assigned to recipients of a bachelor of philosophy. See *Historical Register of Yale University, 1927–1968* (New Haven: Yale University, 1968).

9. Harrison Wheeler Lindsley, Report of Instructor in Architecture, n.d., School of Art and Architecture Records, RU-189, accn. 1973-A-001, box 1, folder 1, Yale University Manuscripts and Archives, New Haven.

10. Report, Yale School of the Fine Arts, n.d. [c. 1879], 6–7, Yale University Manuscripts and Archives, New Haven.

11. Sibley did not graduate, and no records can be found for Jewett.

12. *Yale Daily News*, April 15, 1889; see also *Yale Daily News*, January 30, 1889; and *Yale Daily News*, April 15, 1889.

13. *Catalogue of Yale University, 1892* (New Haven: Yale University, 1892), 48, cited in Bannister, *Architect at Mid-Century*, 95.

14. See Paul Kruty, "Nathan Clifford Ricker: Establishing Architecture at the University of Illinois," in Hoddeson, *No Boundaries*, 3–14.

15. Lewis, "Battle Between Polytechnic and Beaux-Arts," 78.

16. Catherine Lynn, "Building Yale and Razing It: The Early Twentieth Century," in Vincent J. Scully, Catherine Lynn, Eric Vogt, and Paul Goldberger, *Yale in New Haven: Architecture and Urbanism* (New Haven: Yale University Press, 2004), 199; James M. Hoppin, *The Early Renaissance and Other Essays on Art History* (Boston: Houghton Mifflin, 1892); James M. Hoppin, *Greek Art on Greek Soil* (Boston: Houghton Mifflin, 1897); James M. Hoppin, *Great Epochs in Art History* (Boston: Houghton Mifflin, 1901).

17. John F. Weir to President Arthur Twining Hadley, 18 November 1899, in Records of Arthur Twining Hadley, President of Yale University, RU-25, ser. I, box 90, folder 1766, Yale University Manuscripts and Archives, New Haven.

18. "A Program for Expansion, School of the Fine Arts," c. 1917, School of Art and Architecture Records, RU-189 accn. 1973-A-001, box U, Yale University Manuscripts and Archives, New Haven.

19. Lewis, "Battle Between Polytechnic and Beaux-Arts," 78.

20. John F. Weir, Report of Professor John F. Weir, Dean, in *Report of the President of Yale University in the Academic Year 1899–1900* (New Haven: Yale University, 1900), 68–69.

21. "A Program for Expansion, School of the Fine Arts"; see also John Ferguson Weir, "Notes on a Program in Architecture," n.d., John Ferguson Weir Papers, MS-550, ser. II, box 9, Yale University Manuscripts and Archives, New Haven.

22. Historian Catherine Lynn has suggested that the sudden growth of undergraduate interest in architecture is related to the influence of President Dwight, Yale's last minister-president, who was himself interested in architecture's symbolic capacities. According to Lynn, Dwight exposed students to "sermonizing about the powerful role architecture could play in influencing the very souls of men." Lynn, "Building Yale," 199.

23. The situation regarding architecture was basically also the case for sculpture. While basic instruction in sculpture had been taught at the school since its inception, the sculpture program did not begin in earnest until 1908, with the appointment of Instructor in Modeling Lee Oscar Lawrie (1877–1963), who would go on to a career as one of the most prominent architectural sculptors in America, best known for adorning the Nebraska State Capitol and the bronze statue of Atlas outside Rockefeller Center in New York. See John F. Weir, Report of Professor John F. Weir, Director, in *Bulletin of Yale University: Report*

of the President, 1906 5th ser.,
no. 7 (June 1906).

24. Ibid., 160–61.

25. Ibid.

26. In 1906, Columbia attempted to establish a faculty of fine arts comprising its existing program in architecture and new programs in music and design (painting). To do this, Columbia would establish affiliations with the National Academy of Design, then located on Morningside Heights, near the university, and the Metropolitan Museum of Art. William Woodward, "Art Education in the Colleges," in *Art Education in the Public Schools in the United States*, ed. James Parton Haney (New York: American Art Annual, 1908), 304.

27. John F. Weir, Report of Professor John F. Weir, Director, in *Bulletin of Yale University: Report of the President, 1903–1904* (1904), 169–70.

28. Weir, "Notes on a Program."

29. Weir, Report (1906), quoted in Lynn, "Building Yale," 200.

30. "Professorship Established," *Yale Daily News*, November 24, 1906. Inexplicably, it was not until the appointment of Paul Rudolph as chairman of the Department of Architecture (1958–65) that the title J. M. Hoppin Professor was conferred; it was not conferred on his successors until Robert A. M. Stern requested that it be restored upon his appointment.

31. Weir, Report of Professor John F. Weir, Director, in *Bulletin of Yale University: Report of the President, 1908* 4th ser., no. 7 (June 1908), 160–61.

32. "Art School Elective Pamphlet: R. H. Dana to Give New Course in Architecture," *Yale Daily News*, April 9, 1908; John F. Weir to President Hadley, 19 March 1908, in Records of Arthur Twining Hadley, President of Yale

University, RU-25, ser. I, box 90, folder 1767, Yale University Manuscripts and Archives, New Haven; Richard H. Dana, Jr., *Richard Henry Dana (1879–1933): Architect* (New York: R. H. Dana, 1965).

33. Richard H. Dana, Jr., Report on Class in Architecture, 21 June 1909, John Ferguson Weir Papers, MS-550, ser. II, box 10, folder 5, Yale University Manuscripts and Archives, New Haven.

34. Course descriptions quoted in Lynn, "Building Yale," 199–201.

35. Course descriptions quoted in ibid.

36. Dana, Report on Class in Architecture.

37. John Frederick Kelly, *Early Connecticut Architecture* (New York: W. Helburn, 1924); John Frederick Kelly, *Early Domestic Architecture of Connecticut* (New Haven: Yale University Press, 1933); Theodore Sizer, *J. Frederick Kelly, A. I. A.: 1888–1947* (New York, 1947).

38. John F. Weir, Report of Professor John F. Weir, Director, in *Bulletin of Yale University: Report of the President, 1911–1912* 8th ser., no. 8 (June 1912), 236.

39. John F. Weir, Report of Professor John F. Weir, Director, in *Bulletin of Yale University: Report of the President, 1908–1909* 5th ser., no. 7 (June 1909).

40. Richard C. Carroll, *Buildings and Grounds of Yale University* (New Haven: Yale University, 1979), 36.

41. William Sergeant Kendall, Report of William Sergeant Kendall, Director, in *Bulletin of Yale University: Report of the President, 1917–1918* 14th ser., no. 11 (August 1918), 189.

42. John F. Weir, Report of Professor John F. Weir, Director, in *Bulletin of Yale University: Report of the President, 1909–1910* 6th ser., no. 8 (June 1910).

43. Weir, Report (1911–1912), 132.

44. John F. Weir, "The Art School," *Yale Daily News*, April 9, 1910.

45. Arthur Twining Hadley to William Sergeant Kendall, 20 May 1913, in Records of Arthur Twining Hadley, President of Yale University, RU-25, ser. I, box 59, Yale University Manuscripts and Archives, New Haven.

2

An American Beaux-Arts

Epigraph. *Bulletin of Yale University, School of the Fine Arts, Department of Architecture, 1916–1917*, 9.

1. *Bulletin of Yale University: Report of the President, 1914–1915* 11th ser. no. 11 (August 1915), 61.

2. William Sergeant Kendall, Report of William Sergeant Kendall, Director, in *Bulletin of Yale University: Report of the President, 1913–1914* 11th ser., no. 2 (November 1914).

3. Courses of Instruction for 1914–15, Yale School of the Fine Arts, 1914, 25; "Art School Courses Improved," *Yale Daily News*, December 10, 1914.

4. While there are some images of Douglass's work, such as his aquatints for the Methodist National Cathedral (1927) and Arcady (1929), most of his drawings were lost in a fire. In later years, he would have a second career as a mystery writer, publishing several stories and novels, including *Rebecca's Pride* (1956), which earned him the Edgar Allan Poe Award for Best First Novel in 1957.

5. Secretary's Report, in *Bulletin of Yale University: Report of the President, 1914–1915* 11th ser., no. 11 (August 1915), 60.

6. Ibid.
7. William Sergeant Kendall, Report of William Sergeant Kendall, Director, in *Bulletin of Yale University: Report of the President, 1915–1916* 12th ser., no. 10 (July 1916), 322.
8. Rebecca Williamson, "Degree Nomenclature," in Joan Ockman, ed., *Architecture School: Three Centuries of Educating Architects in North America* (Washington, D.C.: Association of Collegiate Schools of Architecture; Cambridge, Mass.: MIT Press, 2012), 274. In 1968, Harvard replaced the Department of Architectural Sciences with the Department of Visual and Environmental Studies, effectively ending the undergraduate major as a pre-professional program and replacing it with an "undergraduate concentration in architecture studies" jointly administered by the Faculty of Arts and Sciences and the GSD.
9. William Sergeant Kendall, Report of William Sergeant Kendall, Director, in *Bulletin of Yale University: Report of the President, 1914–1915* 11th ser., no. 11 (August 1915), 331; "Rich in Possibilities: Director Kendall Makes First Report on Work of Art School," *Yale Daily News*, June 10, 1914.
10. Fikret K. Yegül, *Gentlemen of Instinct and Breeding: Architecture at the American Academy in Rome, 1894–1940* (New York: Oxford University Press, 1991), 39.
11. *School of Fine Arts, Department of Architecture 1915–1916* (New Haven: Yale University, 1916). Probably because of the nomenclature change from "correlated" to "collaborative," Anthony Alofsin misattributes the likely origin of the collaborative problem to Meeks in 1919; see "American Modernism's Challenge to the Beaux-Arts," in Ockman,

Architecture School, 96. We are indebted to Neil Levine, who placed the origin of the correlated project at the American Academy in Rome.
12. Kendall, Report (1915–1916), 322.
13. Everett V. Meeks to President Arthur T. Hadley, 31 March 1917, in Records of Arthur Twining Hadley, President of Yale University, RU-25, ser. I, box 59, Yale University Manuscripts and Archives, New Haven; see also Everett V. Meeks to William Sergeant Kendall, 20 December 1916, in ibid.
14. See Elisabeth Hodermarsky, *A Moment Ongoing: The Legacy of Everett V. Meeks* (New Haven: Yale University Art Gallery, 2001); for Meeks's project at the Beaux-Arts, see *Les Concours d'architecture de L'année Scolaire, École Nationale Supérieure des Beaux-Arts* (1909): 12–15.
15. See Vincent J. Scully, Catherine Lynn, Eric Vogt, and Paul Goldberger, *Yale in New Haven: Architecture and Urbanism* (New Haven: Yale University Press, 2004), 201; see also Patrick Pinnell, *Yale University: An Architectural Tour* (New York: Princeton Architectural Press, 2013), 141–44.
16. Everett V. Meeks to President Arthur T. Hadley, 30 December 1918, in Records of Arthur Twining Hadley, President of Yale University, RU-25, ser. I, box 59, Yale University Manuscripts and Archives, New Haven.
17. Ibid.
18. Anson Phelps Stokes to William Sergeant Kendall, 31 December 1918, in ibid.; see also Arthur T. Hadley to William Sergeant Kendall, 11 January 1919, in ibid.
19. William Sergeant Kendall to President Arthur T. Hadley, 16 January 1919; and Everett V. Meeks to William Sergeant

Kendall, 16 January 1919, both in ibid.
20. William Sergeant Kendall to Anson Phelps Stokes, 27 December 1918, in ibid.
21. William Sergeant Kendall to President Arthur T. Hadley, 7 January 1919, in ibid.
22. Ibid.
23. "Professorship Awarded by Corporation to E. V. Meeks," *Yale Daily News,* January 25, 1919.
24. Franklin Jasper Walls to William Sergeant Kendall, 1 March 1920, in School of Art and Architecture Records, RU-189, accn. 1973-A-001, box 12, Yale University Manuscripts and Archives, New Haven.
25. Unsigned letter likely from Everett V. Meeks to Thomas W. Farnam, 9 March 1920, in ibid; Everett V. Meeks to President Arthur T. Hadley, 21 January 1920, in Records of Arthur Twining Hadley, President of Yale University, RU-25, ser. I, box 59, Yale University Manuscripts and Archives, New Haven; for details of the Davenport gift, see Chapter 5.
26. A. Kingsley Porter, "New School of Architecture Offers Excellent Training," *Yale Daily News,* January 25, 1917. For Porter, see Arthur Kingsley Porter, *Beyond Architecture* (Boston: Marshall Jones, 1918); Arthur Kingsley Porter, *The Seven Who Slept* (Boston: Marshall Jones, 1919); Arthur Kingsley Porter, *Romanesque Sculpture of the Pilgrimage Roads* (Boston: Marshall Jones, 1923); and Arthur Kingsley Porter, *Spanish Romanesque Sculpture* (Florence: Pantheon Casa Editrice, 1928).
27. William Sergeant Kendall, Director of the School of Fine Arts, Report to the President, *Bulletin of Yale University 1917–1918* 14th ser., no. 11 (August 1918), 187–88.
28. Everett V. Meeks, "Complete

Architecture Course Now Offered by Art School," *Yale Daily News,* June 18, 1918.

29. Kendall, Report (1917–1918), 187–89.

30. Meeks, "Complete Architecture Course"; "School of Fine Arts May Be Visited by Graduates," *Yale Daily News,* February 23, 1920.

31. Princeton University School of Architecture, "History of the School," http://soa.princeton.edu/zone/introduction-school#4 (accessed February 27, 2015); David Van Zanten, "The 'Princeton System' and the Founding of the School of Architecture, 1915–20," in *The Architecture of Robert Venturi,* ed. Christopher Mead (Albuquerque: University of New Mexico Press, 1989), 39–44.

32. "A Program for Expansion, School of the Fine Arts," c. mid-1917, School of Art and Architecture Records, RU-189, accn. 1973-A-001, box 11, Yale University Manuscripts and Archives, New Haven.

33. William Sergeant Kendall, Report of William Sergeant Kendall, Director, in *Bulletin of Yale University: Report of the President, 1918–1919* 16th ser., no. 1 (October 1919), 236.

34. Carroll L. V. Meeks, "Notes on the History of the School of the Fine Arts" (passed on as a result of a conversation with George Langzettel, January 10, 1945), 22 January 1945, School of Art and Architecture Records, RU-189, accn. 1989-A-049, box 1, Yale University Manuscripts and Archives, New Haven; Langzettel (1864–1953; B.F.A. 1898) worked as a wood-engraver before coming to Yale to earn his bachelor of fine arts. After graduating, he stayed at Yale to teach drawing and work as a librarian and as secretary of the School of the Fine Arts until his retirement in 1932. The Yale University Art Gallery contains several drawings and etchings by Langzettel.

35. J. P. Noffsinger, "The Influence of the École des Beaux-Arts on the Architects of the United States," quoted in Steven M. Bedford and Susan M. Strauss, "History II: 1891–1912," in *The Making of an Architect, 1881–1981,* ed. Richard Oliver (New York: Rizzoli, 1981), 38; for a recent discussion of the Beaux-Arts Institute of Design, see Jacques Lucan, *Composition, Non-Composition: Architecture and Theory in the Nineteenth and Twentieth Centuries* (New York: Routledge, 2012), 220–22.

36. National Institute of Architectural Education (NIAE), *Winning Designs 1904–1913: Paris Prize in Architecture* (New York: NIAE, 1964).

37. A. Kingsley Porter, "New School of Architecture Offers Excellent Training," *Yale Daily News,* January 25, 1917.

38. For more on the Beaux-Arts system as it was adopted in American schools, see John F. Harbeson, *The Study of Architectural Design, with Special Reference to the Program of the Beaux-Arts Institute of Design* (New York: Pencil Points, 1926).

39. Van Alen Institute, "Van Alen Institute—History," http://www.vanalen.org/about/history (accessed October 5, 2012).

40. Rosemarie Haag Bletter, "Modernism Rears Its Head—The Twenties and Thirties," in Oliver, *Making of an Architect,* 103–18.

41. R. Randall Vosbeck, with Tony P. Wrenn and Andrew Brodie Smith, *A Legacy of Leadership: The Presidents of the American Institute of Architects: 1857–2007* (Washington, D.C.: The American Institute of Architects, 2008), 82–84.

42. Joyce Zaitlin, *Gilbert Stanley Underwood: His Rustic, Art Deco, and Federal Architecture* (Malibu, Calif.: Pangloss, 1989).

43. For a list of Feldman Prize winners, see the *Bulletin of the Yale School of Architecture, 2013–2014* ser. 109, no. 4 (June 30, 2013).

44. Kendall, Report (1917–1918), 189.

45. Everett V. Meeks quoted in Patricia E. Kane, "Egerton Swartwout's Gallery of Fine Arts at Yale University," *Yale University Art Gallery Bulletin* (2000), 70.

46. Timothy Dwight quoted in Catherine Lynn, "Building Yale and Razing It: The Early Twentieth Century," in Vincent J. Scully, Catherine Lynn, Eric Vogt, and Paul Goldberger, *Yale in New Haven: Architecture and Urbanism* (New Haven: Yale University, 2004), 213.

47. Susan B. Matheson, *Art for Yale: A History of the Yale University Art Gallery* (New Haven: Yale University Art Gallery, 2001).

48. Everett V. Meeks to William Sergeant Kendall, 16 July 1920, in School of Art and Architecture Records, RU-189, accn. 1973-A-001, box 10, folder 65, Yale University Manuscripts and Archives, New Haven.

49. Ibid.

50. John. V. Farwell to William Sergeant Kendall, 23 July 1920, in School of Art and Architecture Records, RU-189, accn. 1973-A-001, box 12, Yale University Manuscripts and Archives, New Haven.

51. Shepherd Stevens to "Auntie" (Charlotte Stevens Davenport), 14 March 1924, in Shepherd Stevens Papers, MS-865, box 48, Yale University Manuscripts and Archives, New Haven; Shepherd Stevens to "Auntie" (Charlotte Stevens Davenport), 27 September 1924, in ibid.

52. Lynn, "Building Yale," 229.

53. Everett V. Meeks, Report of Everett V. Meeks, Dean, in *Bulletin of Yale University: Reports to the President of Yale University, 1924–1925* 21st ser., no. 24 (September 1, 1925), 102, Y31-A13, Yale University Manuscripts and Archives, New Haven; Lynn, "Building Yale," 229.

54. "New Building to House Architecture School," *Yale Daily News,* September 24, 1924; John H. Niemeyer, *Bulletin of the Associates in Fine Arts at Yale* 1 (January 1926), 26–27.

55. Everett Meeks, Preliminary Report on the Yale Gallery of the Fine Arts, 7 February 1939, Yale Corporation Records, Manuscripts and Archives, Yale University Library, in Kane, "Egerton Swartwout's Gallery," 68–86.

56. Everett V. Meeks to President James Rowland Angell, 5 February 1922, in Records of James Rowland Angell, President of Yale University, RU-24, accn. 1937-A-004, ser. I, box 20, Yale University Manuscripts and Archives, New Haven; see also William Sergeant Kendall, Report to the President (1921–22); and "Sergeant Kendall Out as Yale Art School Dean," *Hartford Courant,* March 24, 1922.

57. Kendall, Report (1921–22); "Sergeant Kendall Out," 1; Chester H. Aldrich to Everett V. Meeks, 10 January 1924, in School of Art and Architecture Records, RU-189, accn. 1973-A-001, box 12, Yale University Manuscripts and Archives, New Haven; "Gold Medal Is Presented to School of Fine Arts," *Yale Daily News,* March 4, 1924.

58. Aaron Betsky, *James Gamble Rogers and the Architecture of Pragmatism* (Cambridge, Mass.: MIT Press, 1994), 106.

59. Paul Schweikher, memo to Dean Charles H. Sawyer, 15 November 1954, RU-22, box 25, Yale University Manuscripts and Archives, New Haven.

60. Paul Schweikher, interview by Betty Blum, 1984, "Oral History of Paul Schweikher," 48–50, the Chicago Architects Oral History Project, Ernest R. Graham Study Center for Architectural Drawings, Department of Architecture, the Art Institute of Chicago; for Schweikher's design, see the *Bulletin of the Beaux-Arts Institute of Design* 2, no. 1 (1925).

61. Paul Schweikher, interview by Betty Blum.

62. Julian H. Whittlesey to Thomas Beeby, 16 November 1986, in Yale University, Records of the Dean of the School of Architecture, RU-843, accn. 2002-A-082, box 11, Yale University Manuscripts and Archives, New Haven.

63. George Nelson, interview by Stanley Rosner and Lawrence E. Abt, in *The Creative Experience,* ed. Stanley Rosner and Lawrence E. Abt (New York: Grossman, 1970), 267; quoted in Stanley Abercrombie, *George Nelson: The Design of Modern Design* (Cambridge, Mass.: MIT Press, 2000), 4.

64. Richard Buckminster Fuller, Jr., to George Nelson, 14 December 1976, quoted in Abercrombie, *Design of Modern Design,* 4.

65. "Otto Faelten, 61, Architect 30 Years," *New York Times,* April 25, 1945, 23.

66. Joseph Esherick, "Architecture Education in the Thirties and Seventies: A Personal View," in *The Architect: Chapters in the History of the Profession,* ed. Spiro Kostof (New York: Oxford University Press, 1977), 272.

67. "Merry Meeks," *Time,* June 17, 1929, 66.

68. "More Yale Students in Fine Arts Courses," *New York Times,* April 5, 1926, 11.

69. For Park's resignation, see Everett V. Meeks, Report of Everett V. Meeks, Dean, in *Bulletin of Yale University: Reports to the President of Yale University, 1928–1929* (January 1, 1930), Y31-A13, Yale University Manuscripts and Archives, New Haven; Park's book, *New Backgrounds for a New Age* (New York: Harcourt, Brace, 1927), offered a pioneering look at modernist design as part of a wider presentation of decorative arts and ornament.

70. Arthur Clason Weatherhead, "The History of Collegiate Education in Architecture in the United States" (Ph.D. thesis, Columbia University, 1941), 126.

71. Everett Meeks, "Art School Secures Henry Davenport for Architecture," *Yale Daily News,* May 21, 1919.

72. Everett V. Meeks, Report of Everett V. Meeks, Dean, *Bulletin of Yale University: Reports to the President of Yale University 1927–1928* (January 1929), 124, Y31-A13, Yale University Manuscripts and Archives, New Haven.

73. William Sergeant Kendall, Dean of the School of Fine Arts, Report of William Sergeant Kendall, Dean, in *Bulletin of Yale University: Report of the President of Yale University, 1920* 16th ser., no. 20 (September 1920), 346, Y31-A13, Yale University Manuscripts and Archives, New Haven.

74. Everett V. Meeks, Report of Everett V. Meeks, Dean, *Bulletin of Yale University: Reports Made to the President and Fellows by the Deans and Directors of the Several Schools and Departments for the Academic Year 1929–1930* 27th ser., no. 8 (January 1, 1931), 180–81, Y31-A13, Yale University Manuscripts and Archives, New Haven.

Crane would publish several books on structural design and engineering; see Theodore Crane, *Concrete Building Construction* (New York: J. Wiley, 1927); and Theodore Crane, *Architectural Construction: The Choice of Structural Design* (New York: J. Wiley, 1952).

75. George Nelson quoted in Abercrombie, *Design of Modern Design,* 3

76. Ibid.

77. In 1930, shortly after finishing Yale College, a selection of Nelson's pencil drawings was published in *Architecture* magazine. In 1930, *Pencil Points* published his lithograph of St. Étienne-du-Mont, Paris, with the editors describing him as "one of our coming young men in the field of graphic arts." See "Pencil Drawings by George Nelson," *Architecture* 62, no. 6 (December 1930): 35; "St. Étienne-du-Mont, Paris, a Lithograph," *Pencil Points* (December 1930): 975; and Jochen Eisenbrand, ed., *George Nelson: Architect, Writer, Designer, Teacher* (Weil am Rhein, Ger.: Vitra Design Museum, 2008), 20–22.

78. Rosner and Abt, *Creative Experience,* quoted in Abercrombie, *Design of Modern Design,* 6.

79. Ibid.

80. For Douglas, see Wilmarth Sheldon Lewis, ed., *History of the Class of 1918 Yale College, Forty Years On* (New Haven: Yale University, 1954). Douglas practiced architecture with Douglas Orr from 1929 to 1942 before becoming a museum director. For Johnson, see "Merry Meeks," *Time,* 66; and Meeks, Report (1928–1929), 592–93.

81. George Nelson quoted in Abercrombie, *Design of Modern Design,* 7.

82. "T. H. Locraft Wins Architectural Prize,"

Washington Post, June 24, 1928, 2.

83. "Yale School Scores Another Victory in Prix de Rome Competition," *Art Digest* (May 1932): 32; in 1934, Richard Ayers (1910–1995; B.F.A. 1932, M.F.A. 1934) would also win the Rome Prize; see "Finalists' Drawings for the Paris Prize," *Bulletin of the Beaux-Arts Institute of Design* (August 1932); and "Drawings for Rome Prize—An Auditorium Building in New England," *Pencil Points* (June 1932): 428–32. Nelson's unsuccessful submission for the Paris Prize competition was published in *Bulletin of the Beaux-Arts Institute of Design* 6, no. 4 (February 1930).

84. Nelson's essays were republished in George Nelson, *Building a New Europe: Portraits of Modern Architects: Essays by George Nelson, 1935–1946,* introduction by Kurt Forster, forward by Robert A. M. Stern (New Haven: Yale University Press, 2007), 69–80.

85. For a list of students who have been awarded the George Nelson Scholarship between 1988 and 2000, see Yale University, School of Architecture, Endowment and Term Funds, http://www.yale.edu/printer/bulletin/htmlfiles/architecture/endowment-and-term-funds.html (accessed February 27, 2015).

86. Julian H. Whittlesey to Thomas Beeby, 16 November 1986, in Yale University, Records of the Dean of the School of Architecture, RU-843, accn. 2002-A-082, box 11, Yale University Manuscripts and Archives, New Haven. For Whittlesey, see J. Michael Elliot, "Julian Whittlesey, Archeologist And Architect, 89," *New York Times,* May 23, 1995, B11.

87. "Standish Meacham," Architectural Foundation

of Cincinnati, http://www.architecturecincy.org/programs/biographical-dictionary-of-cincinnati-architects/m/ (accessed February 27, 2015); "Standish Meacham, Kin of Early Settler," *New York Times,* January 4, 1949, 40.

88. For the Tribune Tower competition, see Katherine Solomonson, *The Chicago Tribune Tower Competition: Skyscraper Design and Cultural Change in the 1920s* (Chicago: University of Chicago Press, 2001).

89. "Meeks Speech Explains Modern Building Trend," *Yale Daily News,* February 22, 1924; for Eliel Saarinen and Cranbrook, see Robert J. Clark, *Design in America: The Cranbrook Vision, 1925–1950* (New York: Abrams, in association with the Detroit Institute of Arts and the Metropolitan Museum of Art, 1983).

90. Everett V. Meeks, "Foreign Influences on Architectural Education in America," *Octagon: Journal of the American Institute of Architects* 9 (July 1937): 36–42; see also Bletter, "Modernism Rears Its Head," 114.

91. Paul Schweikher, memo to Dean Charles H. Sawyer, 15 November 1954, RU-22, box 25, Yale University Manuscripts and Archives, New Haven.

92. Carroll L. V. Meeks, "Yale and the Ivy League Tradition," in *The Modern Architecture Symposia, 1962–1966: A Critical Edition,* ed. Rosemarie Haag Bletter and Joan Ockman, with Nancy Eklund Later (New York: Temple Hoyne Buell Center for the Study of American Architecture, 2014), 187.

93. "Sees a New Architecture," *New York Times,* August 10, 1930, N4.

94. Everett V. Meeks quoted

in "Architects' League Has Golden Jubilee," *New York Times,* April 25, 1931, 7.

95. Everett V. Meeks quoted in "Yale's Method," *Art Digest* (August 1935): 24.

96. Everett V. Meeks, "The Fine Arts in Education" (lecture, Brown University, Providence, R.I., November 11, 1932). Thanks to Dietrich Neumann, Royce Professor of History of Art and Architecture at Brown, for drawing my attention to this talk and for providing a copy of the text.

97. Walter Kilham, *Raymond Hood, Architect* (New York: Architectural, 1973); Robert A. M. Stern with Thomas P. Catalano, *Raymond Hood* (New York: Institute for Architecture and Urban Studies and Rizzoli, 1982), 126; Robert A. M. Stern, Gregory F. Gilmartin, and Thomas Mellins, *New York 1930: Architecture and Urbanism between the Two World Wars* (New York: Rizzoli, 1987), 575–85, 616–71.

98. Alfred H. Barr, Jr., Henry Russell Hitchcock, Jr., Philip Johnson, and Lewis Mumford, *Modern Architects,* exh. cat. (New York: Museum of Modern Art; W. W. Norton, 1932).

99. Everett V. Meeks quoted in "Raymond Hood Says That Modern Architecture Should Be Representative of Our Own Age," *Yale Daily News,* February 28, 1925, 1, 4.

100. Everett V. Meeks, Report of Everett V. Meeks, Dean, in *Bulletin of Yale University: Reports Made to the President and Fellows by the Deans and Directors of the Several Schools and Departments for the Academic Year 1932–1933* 31st ser., no. 8 (January 1935), 162, Y31-A13, Yale University Manuscripts and Archives, New Haven.

101. Ibid., 161–62.

102. Everett V. Meeks, Report of Everett V. Meeks, Dean, in *Bulletin of Yale University: Reports Made to the President and Fellows by the Deans and Directors of the Several Schools and Departments for the Academic Year 1930–1931* 28th ser., no. 8 (January 1932), 200, Y31-A13, Yale University Manuscripts and Archives, New Haven.

103. Ibid.

104. *Bulletin of Yale University, School of the Fine Arts, for the Academic Year 1931–1932* 27th ser., no. 21 (New Haven: Yale University, 1931), 11.

105. See Mark Coir, "The Cranbrook Factor," in *Eero Saarinen: Shaping the Future,* ed. Eeva-Liisa Pelkonen and Donald Albrecht (New Haven: Yale University Press, 2006), 29–44.

106. "Chronology," compiled by Eeva-Liisa Pelkonen, in ibid., 325.

107. For more on Oenslager, see Dietrich Neumann, ed., *The Structure of Light: Richard Kelly and the Illumination of Modern Architecture* (New Haven: Yale University Press, 2010), 14, 16, 37.

108. Sandy Isenstadt, "Eero Saarinen's Theater of Form," in Pelkonen and Albrecht, *Shaping the Future,* 102; Neumann, *Structure of Light,* 12–14.

109. For Saarinen's work with McCandless, see Pelkonen and Albrecht, *Shaping the Future,* 101–6.

110. Donal McLaughlin quoted in ibid., 325.

111. Yale University News Bureau, "Yale Wins Architecture Medal for Third Time," press release, January 12, 1934.

112. Pelkonen and Albrecht, *Shaping the Future,* 326.

113. Lauren Wiseman, "Donal McLaughlin Jr., Dies at 102; Helped Design U.N. Logo," *Washington Post,* October 2, 2009; see Michael Bierut, "Donal McLaughlin's Little Button," *Design Observer,* July 25, 2007, http://observatory. designobserver.com/entry. html?entry=5357 (accessed February 25, 2015); see also Michael Bierut, "The Lapel Pin That Changed the World," *Yale Alumni Magazine,* May/June 2007.

114. Mark Coir, "The Cranbrook Factor," in Pelkonen and Albrecht, *Shaping the Future,* 38, 43n32; Mina Marefat, "Washington DC, USA—Revealed: Eero Saarinen's Secret Wartime Role in the White House," *Architectural Review,* October 25, 2010, 22–26.

115. Harold Rome quoted in Glenn Collins, "Harold Rome, 85, Writer of Socially Pointed Songs," *New York Times,* October 27, 1993, D23; "Biographical Sketch," Register to the Harold Rome Papers, MSS-49, Yale University Manuscripts and Archives, New Haven.

116. Haber would go on to a career as an architect, industrial designer, and painter. In 1940, he started teaching painting and drawing at the College of William and Mary and also working on the restoration of colonial Williamsburg. He also served as an adviser to the Metropolitan Museum of Art in New York on the selection of paintings and was one of the first television set designers working at the Magnavox Corporation; "Leonard V. Haber, 80, An Industrial Designer," *New York Times,* June 11, 1992, D23. Barger became known for large, monumental sculptures, perhaps most notably his *The Goddess of Perfection,* which stood atop the Heinz dome at the 1939 New York World's Fair.

117. Parke Rouse, Jr., *Living by Design: Leslie Cheek and the Arts* (Williamsburg, Va.: College of William and Mary,

1985), 53; K. Richmond Temple, *Designing for the Arts: Environments by Leslie Cheek* (Williamsburg, Va.: Society of the Alumni of the College of William and Mary, 1990), 232–37; see also "Three Teams Tied for Rome Art Honors," *New York Times,* January 20, 1934, 17.

118. McCandless quoted in Rouse, *Living by Design,* 57.

119. Though there may be some debate as to who the first apprentice was, Wright gave Liang a signed copy of his autobiography, addressing Liang as "first to accomplish the Taliesin Fellowship." See "Yen Liang," in *Frank Lloyd Wright: Recollections by Those Who Knew Him,* ed. Edgar Tafel (Mineola, N.Y.: Courier Dover, 2001), 128.

120. "In Passing . . . ," *Taliesin Fellows Newsletter,* April 15, 2001, 5; "Yen Liang," in Tafel, *Recollections,* 127–32; Liang's children's books include *Tommy and Dee-Dee* (New York: Oxford University Press, 1953); and *The Skyscraper* (New York: Lippincott, 1958).

121. Glenn Fowler, "John Graham, Architect, 82 Dies; Designed Space Needle for Seattle," *New York Times,* February 1, 1991, A19.

122. "Max O. Urbahn Is Dead at 83; Designed Vast NASA Building," *New York Times,* July 13, 1995, B12.

123. Yale University News Bureau, "Two Lecture Series Announced by Yale School of Fine Arts," press release, September 23, 1935; Mardges Bacon, *Le Corbusier in America: Travels in the Land of the Timid* (Cambridge, Mass.: MIT Press, 2001), 93.

124. Reginald Isaacs, *Gropius: An Illustrated Biography of the Creator of the Bauhaus* (Boston: Bulfinch, 1991), 216.

125. Everett V. Meeks to Dean William Emerson, 3 October 1935, in Yale University School of Fine Arts, Administrative Records, YRG 16-E, RU-189, Manuscripts and Archives, Yale University Library, quoted in Bacon, *Le Corbusier in America,* 93

126. "Wright Decries Lack of American Culture," *Yale Daily News,* October 17, 1935; Bacon, *Le Corbusier in America,* 93–94, 324nn61–62; Betsky, *James Gamble Rogers,* 58–59.

127. "Famous Architect Will Lecture Here," *Yale Daily News,* October 30, 1935, 1.

128. Bacon, *Le Corbusier in America,* 280.

129. George Nelson, "Architects of Europe Today 5—Le Corbusier, France," *Pencil Points* 16 (July 1935): 368–74, reprinted in Nelson, *Building a New Europe,* 69–80.

130. "A Group Plan for a Small Community in a Large City" by R. G. Hartshorne, Jr. (Yale University), Second Medal for Class A Project, Beaux-Arts Institute of Design (1936). From *Bulletin of the Beaux-Arts Institute of Design* 12, no. 9 (August 1936), in Ockman, *Architecture School,* 26, fig. 148.

131. Everett V. Meeks quoted in "Everett V. Meeks, Educator, 75, Dies," *New York Times,* October 28, 1954, 35.

132. Yale University News Bureau, "Yale Department of Architecture Honored for Outstanding Accomplishment," press release, December 9, 1937, Charles Seymour, President of Yale University, Records, RU-23, box 17, folder 144, Yale University Manuscripts and Archives, New Haven.

133. For Hudnut's time at Columbia, see Bletter, "Modernism Rears Its Head," 103–18; and Judith Oberlander, "History IV: 1933–1935," in Oliver, *Making of an Architect,* 119–26. For his time at Harvard, see Anthony Alofsin, "The Crusade for Modernism, 1936–1944," in *The Struggle for Modernism: Architecture, Landscape Architecture, and City Planning at Harvard* (New York: W. W. Norton, 2002), 138–195; see also Jill Pearlman, *Inventing American Modernism* (Charlottesville: University of Virginia Press, 2007).

134. Turpin C. Bannister, ed., *The Architect at Mid-Century: Evolution and Achievement* (New York: Reinhold, 1954), ix, which was volume 1 of the report of the Commission for the Survey of Education and Registration of the American Institute of Architects, quoted in Ockman, *Architecture School,* 22.

135. Bruno Zevi, "An Opinion on Architecture" (May 1941), originally titled "Preface to *A Call,*" Breuer Papers, GARL, quoted in Pearlman, *Inventing American Modernism,* 176.

136. Ibid.

137. Donald Drew Egbert, "The Education of the Modern Architect," *The Octagon: Journal of the American Institute of Architects* 13 (March 1941): 4–12.

138. Ibid.

139. Harry Weese quoted in Robert Bruegmann, *The Architecture of Harry Weese* (New York: W. W. Norton, 2010), 17.

140. Ibid., 18–19.

141. George Dudley, "Oscar Nitzchke in America—A Personal Perspective," in *Oscar Nitzchke Architect,* ed. Gus Dudley (New York: The Cooper Union for the Advancement of Science and Art, 1985), 57.

142. Everett V. Meeks quoted in Yale University News Bureau, "Plans for an American System of Architectural Education Announced by Yale," press release, June 17, 1938.

143. Wallace K. Harrison quoted in Hebert Warren Wind, "Architect II–The Square That Became a Center," *New Yorker,*

November 27, 1954, 70.

144. For the Rockefeller Apartments, see Stern, Gilmartin, and Mellins, *New York 1930*, 421, 424.

145. Wallace K. Harrison quoted in Hebert Warren Wind, "Architect III–A Taxi to the U.N.," *New Yorker,* December 4, 1954, 55.

146. Everett V. Meeks quoted in Yale University News Bureau, "Plans for an American System."

147. Meeks, "Yale and the Ivy League Tradition," 187; for Abramovitz, see John Harwood and Janet Parks, *The Troubled Search: The Work of Max Abramovitz* (New York: Miriam and Ira D. Wallach Art Gallery, Columbia University, 2004).

148. For a brief discussion of Nelson's CBS proposal, see Judith Applegate, "Paul Nelson: An Interview," *Perspecta: The Yale Architectural Journal* 13/14 (1971): 89; see also Stern, Gilmartin, and Mellins, *New York 1930,* 266–69; for Nitzchke, see Dudley, "Oscar Nitzchke in America," 57.

149. "Reminiscences of Hugh Moore," School of Architecture, Yale University, Memorabilia RU-925, accn. 2004-A-120, Yale University Manuscripts and Archives, New Haven.

150. Porter A. McCray, interview by Paul Cummings, September 17–October 4, 1977, oral history project, Archives of American Art, Smithsonian Institution, Washington, D.C.

151. Dudley, "Oscar Nitzchke in America," 58.

152. Ibid., 57.

153. Ibid., 58.

154. Ibid.

155. Porter A. McCray, interview by Paul Cummings.

156. Ibid.

157. Ibid.

158. "Reminiscences of Hugh Moore."

159. Dudley, "Oscar Nitzchke in America," 58–59.

160. See Matheson, *Art for Yale.*

161. *Modern Exhibition—Painting and Architecture,* exh. cat. (New Haven: Yale University, 1943), Yale University Manuscripts and Archives, School of Art and Architecture Records, RU-189, accn. 2002-A-038, box 1, Yale University Manuscripts and Archives, New Haven; see also "Novel Exhibits Installed in Yale Gallery," *New Haven Evening Register,* October 22, 1943. Kibel, a successful architect-developer of high-rise residential buildings in New York, would go on to form the Kibel Foundation, providing support for the School of Architecture's exhibition and publication program.

162. For Kelly, see Neumann, *Structure of Light.*

163. Dudley, "Oscar Nitzchke in America," 59.

164. Henry Kibel quoted in ibid.

165. "Reminiscences of Hugh Moore."

166. Porter A. McCray, interview by Paul Cummings.

167. *Historical Register of Yale University, 1937–1951* (New Haven: Yale University, 1952).

168. Benjamin Thompson quoted in "The Talk of the Town: New Store," *New Yorker,* December 18, 1963, 26; Walter Gropius, ed., *The Architects' Collaborative, 1945–1965* (New York: Architectural, 1966).

169. Charles Seymour, *Bulletin of Yale University: Report of the President, 1937–1938* 35th ser., no. 3 (October 1938), 30–31, Y31-A13, Yale University Manuscripts and Archives, New Haven.

170. Everett V. Meeks quoted in Yale University News Bureau, "Plans."

171. Dudley, "Oscar Nitzchke in America," 58–59.

172. For the Bridgeport study, see George A. Dudley, William S. Evans, Wallace R. Lee, Jr., Maynard Meyer, and James L. Murphy, Jr., *Bridgeport: An Analysis of Urbanism and the Planning for It by the Yale Graduate Group in Architecture, 1929–40* (New Haven: Yale University Department of Architecture, 1940).

173. Abercrombie, *Design of Modern Design,* 152.

174. "Speakers Discuss Low-Cost Housing," *Yale Daily News,* February 1, 1939; for Parkchester, see Stern, Gilmartin, and Mellins, *New York 1930,* 496–500; for Luce, see Alan Brinkley, *The Publisher: Henry Luce and His American Century* (New York: Knopf, 2010).

175. "Yale Plans Research for City Design," *Hartford Courant,* June 13, 1941.

176. Dudley, "Oscar Nitzchke in America," 59.

177. Rico Cedro, *Modern Visions: Twentieth Century Urban Design in New Haven* (New Haven: Yale University, 1988), 14; the exhibit was displayed at City Arts Gallery from June 9 to July 8, 1988, and at the Yale Art and Architecture Gallery from November 7 to November 18, 1988; see also Vincent Scully, *Modern Architecture* (New York: Braziller, 1974), 50–51; and Carola Hein, "Maurice Rotival: French Planning on a World-Scale (Part 1)," *Planning Perspectives* 17 (2002): 247–65.

178. "Reminiscences of Hugh Moore."

179. "Refresher Course on Planning Gets Underway Sept. 7," *Yale News Digest,* August 19, 1943; see also "Meeks Sees Great Need of Planners," *Hartford Courant,* August 7, 1944, 13.

180. Everett V. Meeks to Provost Edgar S. Furniss, 6 May 1941, Charles Seymour, President of Yale University, Records, RU-23, box 17, folder 144, Yale University Manuscripts and Archives, New Haven.

181. *Bulletin of Yale University, School of the Fine Arts, 1943–1944* ser. 39, no. 16 (August 15, 1943).

182. Everett V. Meeks quoted in Yale University News Bureau, press release, March 22, 1942.

183. "Dean Meeks Hits At Credit System, Yearly Courses," *Hartford Courant,* June 3, 1937.

184. Everett V. Meeks quoted in Yale University News Bureau, press release, March 22, 1942.

185. Everett V. Meeks quoted in "Meeks Announces Speed-Up Course for Architects," *Yale Daily News,* March 30, 1942; "Yale Architecture Divided in Studies," *New York Times,* March 22, 1942, D5.

186. Everett V. Meeks, graduation address, quoted in Yale University News Bureau, press release no. 170, January 30, 1943.

187. "Yale Architecture Divided in Studies"; Pearlman, *Inventing American Modernism,* 201.

188. For a complete list of students who have been awarded the Sonia Albert Schimberg Prize, see Yale School of Architecture, "Awards," http://architecture.yale.edu/student-life/awards (accessed February 27, 2015).

189. In Vincent Scully's view, Bennett's brand of modernism, which was indicative of American modernism in the 1940s, was "still as fundamentally pictorial as it had been earlier in the American Beaux Arts." See Vincent Scully, Jr., "Doldrums in the Suburbs," *Journal of the Society of Architectural Historians* 24, no. 1 (March 1965): 37–39. See also Everett V. Meeks, memo to Charles Seymour, "Memorandum to Accompany Nomination of Richard Marsh Bennett for Faculty Appointment," 9 November 1944, Charles Seymour, President of Yale University, Records, RU-23, box 17, folder 144, Yale University

Manuscripts and Archives, New Haven.

190. Ibid.

191. Ibid.

192. Ibid.

193. Ibid. For more on European émigré architects, see William H. Jordy, "The Aftermath of the Bauhaus in America: Gropius, Mies, and Breuer," in *The Intellectual Migration: Europe and America, 1930–1960,* ed. Donald Fleming and Bernard Bailyn (London: Oxford University Press, 1968), 485–515.

194. For the Bennett appointment, see Yale University News Bureau, press release no. 138, December 26, 1944; *Historical Register of Yale University, 1937–1951* (New Haven: Yale University, 1952); "Richard Bennett, Noted Architect, Named Professor," *Yale News Digest,* December 29, 1944.

195. Everett V. Meeks to Provost Edgar S. Furniss, accompanied by "Program in Architecture, Painting and Sculpture," 3 May 1946, Charles Seymour, President of Yale University, Records, RU-23, box 17, folder 144, Yale University Manuscripts and Archives, New Haven.

196. "Sawyer, Charles H.," *New York Times,* March 3, 2005; see also Charles Henry Sawyer, interview, January 25, 1977, oral history project, Archives of American Art, Smithsonian Institution, Washington, D.C.

197. Charles H. Sawyer, "Preliminary Observations on the Yale School of Fine Arts," 22 February 1946, Charles Seymour, President of Yale University, Records, RU-23, box 17, Yale University Manuscripts and Archives, New Haven.

198. "C. H. Sawyer Appointed Arts Division Director and Fine Arts School Dean," *New York Times,* March 3, 1947, 23; "Charles Sawyer Succeeds Meeks as Dean of School of

Fine Arts," *Yale Daily News,* March 3, 1947; Yale University News Bureau, press release no. 393, March 3, 1947; "Appointments," *Architectural Forum* 86 (April 1947): 62; Yale University News Bureau, press release no. 393, March 3, 1947; "Sawyer Revises Existing School of Architecture," *Yale Daily News,* October 29, 1947; see also Charles Sawyer, Report of the Director of the Arts, Dean of the School of Fine Arts, 1 August 1948, School of Art and Architecture Records, RU-189, accn. 1991-A-007, box 1, folder 4, Yale University Manuscripts and Archives, New Haven.

199. Everett Meeks, quoted in Charles Seymour to Charles H. Sawyer, 22 February 1947, Charles Seymour, President of Yale University, Records, RU-23, box 17, Yale University Manuscripts and Archives, New Haven.

200. Yale University News Bureau, press release no. 166, October 27, 1954; "Everett V. Meeks, Educator, 75, Dies," *New York Times,* October 28, 1954, 35; "Excerpts from Resolution Passed at the Trustees Meeting of the Associates in Fine Arts," 12 November 1954, School of Art and Architecture Records, RU-189, accn. 2202-A-099, box 8, Yale University Manuscripts and Archives, New Haven.

3

An American Bauhaus?

Epigraph. Mission statement of the School of Architecture and Design, as first articulated in the *Bulletin of Yale University, Division of the Arts, 1953* ser. 49, no. 2 (January 15, 1953).

1. Hauf's appointment was announced on October 29, 1947; see Yale University News Bureau, press release no. 147, October 20, 1947, Y91+A2 1947, Yale University Manuscripts and Archives, New Haven.

2. Charles H. Sawyer to President Charles Seymour, 24 May 1947, School of Art and Architecture Records, RU-189, accn. 1991-A-007, box 1, Yale University Manuscripts and Archives, New Haven.

3. For Perkins at Penn, see Ann Strong, "G. Holmes Perkins: Architect of the School's Renaissance," in *The Book of the School,* ed. Ann Strong and George E. Thomas (Philadelphia: The Graduate School of Fine Arts, the University of Pennsylvania, 1990), 131–49.

4. "Commander Hauf Receives Citation," *Yale News Digest,* March 29, 1946.

5. For Hauf appointments, see *Historic Register of Yale University, 1937–1951* (New Haven: Yale University, 1952); Yale University News Bureau, press release no. 147, October 29, 1947, Y91+A2 1947, Yale University Manuscripts and Archives, New Haven; and "Yale Revamps Division of Architecture: Noted Architects Are Appointed Visiting Critics in Residence," *Hartford Courant,* October 29, 1947.

6. Peter Millard quoted in "Reminiscences and Memorabilia of Students in Classes 1948–1958," as compiled by Estelle Thompson Margolis and Walfredo Toscanini, RU-961, Yale University Manuscripts and Archives, New Haven.

7. Charles H. Sawyer to President Charles Seymour, 24 May 1947, School of Art and Architecture Records, RU-189, accn. 1991-A-007, box 1, Yale University Manuscripts

and Archives, New Haven.

8. University Council, administrative document, April 1948, School of Art and Architecture Records, RU-189, accn. 1996-A-018, box 4, Yale University Manuscripts and Archives, New Haven.

9. Ibid.

10. Charles H. Sawyer to President Charles Seymour, 24 May 1947, Charles Seymour, President of Yale University, Records, RU-23, box 17, Yale University Manuscripts and Archives, New Haven.

11. Yale University News Bureau, press release no. 393, March 3, 1947.

12. "Sawyer Revises"; Stone writes of his tenure at Yale in his autobiography, *The Evolution of an Architect* (New York: Horizon, 1962), 36–37.

13. See Hicks Stone, *Edward Durell Stone: A Son's Untold Story of a Legendary Architect* (New York: Rizzoli, 2011), 70; and Mary Anne Hunting, *Edward Durell Stone: Modernism's Populist Architect* (New York: W. W. Norton, 2013).

14. R. Paige Donhauser, interview, June 12, 2010, quoted in Stone, *Son's Untold Story,* 111, 309n74; see also Hunting, *Modernism's Populist Architect.*

15. Edward Lloyd Flood to Edward D. Stone, 12 March 1958, quoted in Stone, *Son's Untold Story,* 114, 310n76.

16. Ibid., 123.

17. Vincent Scully, "Doldrums in the Suburbs," *Perspecta: The Yale Architectural Journal* 9/10 (1965): 281–90.

18. Harold D. Hauf, acting chairman, Report to the Dean on the Activities of the Department of Architecture: Academic Year 1946–1947, 3 June 1947, School of Art and Architecture Records, RU-189, accn. 1991-A-007, box 1, folder 4, Yale University Manuscripts and Archives, New Haven.

19. Robert A. M. Stern, Thomas Mellins, and David Fishman, *New York 1960: Architecture and Urbanism between the Second World War and the Bicentennial* (New York: Monacelli, 1995), 396; see also "The Record Report," *Architectural Record* 102 (December 1947): 132; the idea was to persist, and a version was eventually realized as the "XYZ" towers of Rockefeller Center. See Stern, Mellins, and Fishman, *New York 1960,* 410–11, 413–15.

20. Stone, *Son's Untold Story,* 122–23.

21. "U.S. Bars Architect as a Brazilian Red," *New York Times,* January 15, 1948, 3; "U.S. Bars Architect as Red," *Washington Post,* January 15, 1948, 6; "Niemeyer Denied U.S. Admittance," *Yale Daily News,* January 16, 1948; Neal Stanford, "Communist Visitors to U.S. Hit by Visas," *Christian Science Monitor,* January 26, 1948, 16; "The Niemeyer Case Illustrates the Debit Side," *Sun,* April 23, 1948, 18.

22. For the Red Scare, see Albert Fried, *McCarthyism: The Great American Red Scare: A Documentary History* (Oxford: Oxford University Press, 1997); and Ted Morgan, *Reds: McCarthyism in Twentieth-Century America* (New York: Random House, 2004).

23. Victor Christ-Janer (1915–2008; B.F.A. 1940, B.Arch 1947); Henry Kibel; Brooks Parker (B.A. 1942, B.Arch 1948); James A. Kingsland (B.Arch 1948); George Dudley; E. T. Glass, Jr. (B.A. 1942, B.Arch 1944); John D. Caproni (B.Arch 1947); E. Lloyd Flood (M.Arch 1947); Theodore Hood (B.Arch 1948); and Porter A. McCray (B.F.A. 1941) to President Seymour, 5 March 1948, Charles Seymour, President of Yale University, Records, RU-23, box 17, folder 148, Yale

University Manuscripts and Archives, New Haven.

24. Charles H. Sawyer to Victor Christ-Janer, 16 March 1948, Charles Seymour, President of Yale University, Records, RU-23, box 17, folder 148, Yale University Manuscripts and Archives, New Haven; see also Charles H. Sawyer to President Charles Seymour, 18 March 1948, in ibid.

25. William Huff, "Kahn and Yale," *Journal of Architectural Education* 35, no. 3 (spring 1982): 23.

26. See Carter Wiseman, *Louis I. Kahn: Beyond Time and Style: A Life in Architecture* (New York: W. W. Norton, 2007), 56.

27. Harold D. Hauf, Report to the Dean on the Activities of the Department of Architecture: Academic Year 1947–1948, 15 July 1948, School of Art and Architecture Records, RU-189, accn. 1991-A-007, box 1, folder 4, Yale University Manuscripts and Archives, New Haven.

28. *Historical Register of Yale University, 1927–1968* (New Haven: Yale University, 1968), 563.

29. Harold D. Hauf, Report to the Dean on the Activities of the Department of Architecture: Academic Year 1948–1949, 29 June 1949, School of Art and Architecture Records, RU-189, accn. 1991-A-007, box 1, folder 4, Yale University Manuscripts and Archives, New Haven.

30. Charles H. Sawyer, Report of the Director of the Division of the Arts, Dean of the Yale School of Fine Arts, 1 August 1948, School of Art and Architecture Records, RU-189, accn. 1991-A-007, box 1, folder 4, Yale University Manuscripts and Archives, New Haven.

31. Sarah Williams Goldhagen, *Louis Kahn's Situated Modernism* (New Haven: Yale University Press, 2001), 50.

32. Yegül, *Gentlemen of Instinct and Breeding*, 100–102.

33. Harold Hauf, Annual Report for the Academic Year 1948–1949, 29 June 1949, Yale University, Records of the Dean of the School of Architecture, RU-843, accn. 2002-A-082, box 11, Yale University Manuscripts and Archives, New Haven.

34. Goldhagen, *Louis Kahn's Situated Modernism*, 50.

35. Team 7, "Student Architects, Painters, Sculptors Design Together," *Progressive Architecture* (April 1949): 14, 16, 18.

36. Goldhagen, *Louis Kahn's Situated Modernism*, 51; see also Kahn's sketchbook pages in "Yale University, 1948–1949," box 60, "Yale Professor-1950," and "Yale University-Professorship," box 61, Louis I. Kahn Collection, University of Pennsylvania and Pennsylvania Historical Commission, Philadelphia, cited in ibid.

37. Kahn had been assigned to the studio after its original instructor, Matthew Nowicki (1910–1950), the Polish-born architect and sometime colleague of Eero Saarinen, was killed in a plane crash on his way back from India where he, in partnership with engineer, architect, and planner Albert Mayer (1897–1981), was at work on a master plan for the new capital city of Chandigarh. See "Yale University—Division of the Arts. Proposal for Collaborative Problem to be Discussed at Meeting Saturday, July 9, 1949," Louis I. Kahn Collection, 030.11.A.61.27, quoted in Eeva-Liisa Pelkonen, "Toward Cognitive Architecture," in *Louis Kahn: The Power of Architecture*, exh. cat. ed. Mateo Kries, Jochen Eisenbrand, and Stanislaus von Moos (Weil am Rhein, Ger.: Vitra Design Museum, 2012), 139.

38. "Yale University—Division of the Arts. Proposal for Collaborative Problem to be Discussed at Meeting Saturday, July 9, 1949," Louis I. Kahn Collection, 030.11.A.61.27.

39. Pelkonen, "Toward Cognitive Architecture," 139.

40. Edward Nelson to Brenda Danilowitz, 6 July 2004, quoted in Brenda Danilowitz, "Teaching Design: A Short History of Josef Albers," in *Josef Albers: To Open Eyes*, by Frederick A. Horowitz and Brenda Danilowitz (New York: Phaidon, 2006), 45.

41. Ibid., 46.

42. Pelkonen, "Toward Cognitive Architecture," 139.

43. Ibid., 138; see also Goldhagen, *Louis Kahn's Situated Modernism*, 47.

44. Josef Albers, "The Educational Value of Manual Work and Handicraft in Relation to Architecture," in *New Architecture and City Planning: A Symposium*, ed. Paul Zucker (New York: Philosophical Library, 1944), 688, quoted in Pelkonen, "Toward Cognitive Architecture," 138.

45. Pelkonen, "Toward Cognitive Architecture," 138.

46. R. Buckminster Fuller, "The Cardboard House," *Perspecta: The Yale Architectural Journal* 2 (1953): 31.

47. Roy Harrover quoted in "Reminiscences and Memorabilia of Students in Classes 1948–1958"; see also Fuller, "Cardboard House," 28–35.

48. Alofsin, *Struggle for Modernism*, 11–12.

49. For Breuer's house, see "Manhattan's Museum of Modern Art Presents House Designed by Architect," *Architectural Forum* 90 (May 1949): 96–101.

50. University Council, Report, 24–25 April 1948; council members: Leslie Cheek, Jr., chairman; Josef Albers; Phillip O. Elliot; George

Kratina; George Nelson; McKim Norton; Robert Osborn; Eero Saarinen; and Francis Stanton. Nelson and Osborn did not participate in the April meetings.

51.   Charles Sawyer, Report of the Director of the Division of the Arts, 1 August 1948, School of Art and Architecture Records, RU-189, accn. 1991-A-007, box 1, folder 4, Yale University Manuscripts and Archives, New Haven.

52.   Charles Sawyer to President Charles Seymour, 29 September 1947, quoted in Horowitz and Danilowitz, *To Open Eyes*, 44, 257n191.

53.   William S. Huff to his parents, September 1947, quoted in Danilowitz, "Teaching Design," 44.

54.   Paul Rudolph, "Walter Gropius et Son École," *L'Architecture d'aujourd'hui* 20 (February 1950).

55.   Pearlman, *Inventing American Modernism*, 115.

56.   University Council, Report of the Committee of the Division of Arts (Architecture, Sculpture and Painting), 13 June 1949, School of Art and Architecture Records, RU-189, accn. 1996-A-018, box 4, Yale University Manuscripts and Archives, New Haven; council members: Leslie Cheek, Jr., chairman; George Nelson; Eero Saarinen; Robert Osborn; Phillip O. Elliot; Francis R. Stanton; George Kratina; C. McKim Norton; and Josef Albers.

57.   Yale University News Bureau, press release no. 33, August 28, 1949.

58.   Owen Johnson, *Stover at Yale* (New York: Frederick A. Stokes, 1912), tells the story of Dink Stover's undergraduate life at Yale during the early twentieth century and his struggles navigating the university's social hierarchies.

59.   Portions of this chapter were originally published in

Robert A. M. Stern, *George Howe: Toward a Modern American Architecture* (New Haven: Yale University Press, 1975); and Robert A. M. Stern, "Rationalism and Romanticism in the Domestic Architecture of George Howe," a paper presented at the Annual Meeting of the Society of Architectural Historians, Baltimore, Md., January 28, 1963, published in Robert A. M. Stern, *Tradition and Invention: Essays on Architecture*, ed. Cynthia Davidson (New Haven: Yale University Press, 2011), 117–23.

60.   Denise R. Costanzo, "Architectural Amnesia: George Howe, Mario De Renzi, and the U.S. Consulate in Naples," *Memoirs of the American Academy in Rome* LVI/LVII (2011/2012): 354–55.

61.   George Howe to Helen Howe West, in Helen West, *George Howe Architect, 1886–1955: Recollections of My Beloved Father* (Philadelphia: W. Nunn, 1973), quoted in Costanzo, "Architectural Amnesia," 353.

62.   George Howe to Charles Sawyer, 31 August 1949, quoted in Stern, *Toward a Modern American Architecture*, 210.

63.   Edward D. Stone to George Howe, 19 August 1949, quoted in Hicks Stone, *Edward Durell Stone: A Son's Untold Story of a Legendary Architect* (New York: Rizzoli, 2011), 123.

64.   George Howe to Helen Howe West, quoted in Costanzo, "Architectural Amnesia," 354–55.

65.   Charles Sawyer, Report to the President [Charles Seymour], 15 July 1950, School of Art and Architecture Records, RU-189, accn. 1991-A-007, box 1, Yale University Manuscripts and Archives, New Haven.

66.   High Hollow was widely admired and given extensive coverage in *Architectural Record*, including a flattering

essay written by Paul Cret, "A Hillside House, The Property of George Howe, Esq., Chestnut Hill, Philadelphia," *Architectural Record* (August 1920): 82–106.

67.   George Howe, "Some Experiences and Observations of an Elderly Architect," *Perspecta: The Yale Architectural Journal* 2 (1953): 4.

68.   William Jordy quoted in Stern, "Rationalism and Romanticism," 117–23.

69.   Everett Meeks in "Reminisces of Hugh Moore," School of Architecture, Yale University, Memorabilia RU-925, accn. 2004-A-120, Yale University Manuscripts and Archives, New Haven.

70.   Joseph Esherick, "Architectural Education in the Thirties and Seventies: A Personal View," in *The Architect: Chapters in the History of the Profession,* ed. Spiro Kostof (New York: Oxford University Press, 1977), 272.

71.   Kahn may have been the first to mention Howe, but Sawyer also consulted Stone, Harold Hauf, and, in all likelihood, Carroll Meeks, Henry Pfisterer, Eero Saarinen, and Philip Johnson. Howe had previously established a close friendship with Saarinen and Johnson while he was serving in Washington, D.C., where all three were stationed during World War II. Charles Sawyer to Robert A. M. Stern, 9 February 1974, George Howe Papers, Dept. of Drawings and Archives, Avery Architectural and Fine Arts Library, Columbia University, New York, N.Y.; see also Robert A. M. Stern, "Introduction," in *[Re]Reading Perspecta: The First Fifty Years of the Yale Architectural Journal* (Cambridge, Mass.: MIT Press, 2004), xiv–xvii; Kazys Varnelis, ed., *The Philip Johnson Tapes: Interviews with Robert A. M. Stern* (New York:

Monacelli, 2008), 128–33; and Stone, *Son's Untold Story,* 123.

72. For Kahn's appointment, see Yale University News Bureau, press release no. 79, September 23, 1948; and Yale University News Bureau, press release, October 15, 1949; see also Carter Wiseman, *Louis I. Kahn: Beyond Time and Style, A Life in Architecture* (New York: W. W. Norton, 2007), 56; and Vincent Scully, "Louis I. Kahn and the Ruins of Rome," *MoMA: The Members Quarterly of the Museum of Modern Art,* no. 12 (summer 1992): 1–13, republished in *Modern Architecture and Other Essays,* ed. Neil Levine (Princeton, N.J.: Princeton University Press, 2003).

73. Paul Goldberger, "Yale and the Promise of the Modern" (lecture, Yale University Art Gallery, New Haven, December 9, 2006).

74. See *Architectural Record* 107 (April 1950): 186.

75. Jill Pearlman, *Inventing American Modernism* (Charlottesville: University of Virginia Press, 2007), 207.

76. Ibid., 205.

77. Brenda Danilowitz, "Teaching Design: A Short History of Josef Albers," in *Josef Albers: To Open Eyes,* by Frederick A. Horowitz and Brenda Danilowitz (New York: Phaidon, 2006), 43.

78. Leslie Cheek, Jr., University Council Report of the Chairman of the Committee on the Division of the Arts (Architecture, Sculpture and Painting), 25 April 1948, School of Art and Architecture, Yale University, Records RU-189, accn. 2002-A-099, box 8, Yale University Manuscripts and Archives, New Haven; Eeva-Liisa Pelkonen, "Toward Cognitive Architecture," in *Louis Kahn: The Power of Architecture,* ed. Mateo Kries, Jochen Eisenbrand, and Stanislaus

von Moos, exh. cat. (Weil am Rhein, Ger.: Vitra Design Museum, 2012), 138.

79. Cheek, University Council Report, 25 April 1948.

80. Jaquelin T. Robertson, interview by Jimmy Stamp, July 21, 2011.

81. Jaquelin T. Robertson to Robert A. M. Stern, 1974, quoted in Robert A. M. Stern, "Yale 1950–1965," *Oppositions* 4 (October 1974): 45.

82. Jaquelin T. Robertson, interview by Jimmy Stamp.

83. George Howe, Report to the President by the Retiring Chairman, July 1954, School of Art and Architecture Records, RU-189, accn. 1991-A-007, box 1, Yale University Manuscripts and Archives, New Haven.

84. George Howe, Annual Report of the Chairman, 1950–1951, 18 June 1951, School of Art and Architecture Records, RU-189, accn. 1991-A-007, box 1, Yale University Manuscripts and Archives, New Haven.

85. Alfred N. Whitehead, *The Aims of Education and Other Essays* (New York: Macmillan, 1929).

86. George Howe, "Training for the Practice of Architecture," address to the assembled student body of the department, September 20, 1951, School of Architecture Records, RU-1048, accn. 2008-A-159, box 1, Yale University Manuscripts and Archives, New Haven.

87. George Howe, untitled lecture, quoted in Yale University News Bureau, press release no. 479, February 22, 1950.

88. George Howe, Annual Report of the Chairman, 1949–1950, School of Art and Architecture Records, RU-189, accn. 1991-A-007, box 1, Yale University Manuscripts and Archives, New Haven.

89. Ibid.

90. George Howe, memo to Dean Sawyer, 4 November 1954, in

ibid.

91. Charles Herbert Moore, "Training for the Practice of Architecture," *Architectural Record* 49 (January 1921): 56–61.

92. Howe, "Training" (address). A version of this talk was published in the first issue of *Perspecta.* See George Howe, "Training for the Practice of Architecture," *Perspecta: The Yale Architectural Journal* 1 (1952): 2–7.

93. "Significant form" was a term Howe adopted from the English art critic Clive Bell, who in his book *Art* had defined the practice of architecture as "the occupation, with intent to create significant form, of producing designs for and procuring the execution of, any and every sort of work constructed for the use of man." See Clive Bell, *Art* (New York: Stokes, 1924).

94. Howe, "Training" (address).

95. George Howe, "What Is This Modern Architecture Trying to Express?" *American Architect* 137 (May 1930): 22–25, 106–8.

96. Oswald Spengler, *Decline of the West: Form and Actuality* (London: George Allen and Unwin, 1918), quoted in Howe, "Training," *Perspecta,* 5.

97. Howe, "Training" (address).

98. Ibid.

99. Howe, Annual Report (1949–1950).

100. Ibid.

101. Yale-in-China, known today as the Yale-China Association, was founded in 1901 by Yale alumni to establish a mission based in the city of Changsha. It soon began to focus more on an educational rather than an evangelical mission and grew to include a major medical clinic, preparatory school, and college. In 1934, it was reincorporated as a purely secular organization. See Nancy E. Chapman with Jessica C. Plumb, *The Yale-*

China Association: A Centennial History (Hong Kong: Chinese University Press, 2001).

102. King-lui Wu quoted in "Yale Architect Designs Experimental House," *New Haven Sunday Register,* March 20, 1955, 1.

103. "Obituary: King-lui Wu," *Yale University News,* August 16, 2002; David Dunlap, "King-lui Wu, 84, Architect And Longtime Yale Professor," *New York Times,* August 25, 2002, 31; "King-lui Wu," excerpts from eulogies at his memorial (October 25, 2002), in *Constructs* (spring 2003): 12–13; Wu's work is illustrated in King-lui Wu, "Notes on Architecture Today," *Perspecta: The Yale Architectural Journal* 5 (1959): 26–27, 29–35.

104. Alexander Purves, interview by Jimmy Stamp, January 18, 2013.

105. Ibid.

106. Ibid.

107. Charles Gwathmey quoted in Dunlap, "King-lui Wu," 31.

108. See Dieter Bogner and Peter Noever, eds., *Frederick J. Kiesler; Endless Space* (Ostfildern-Ruit, Ger.: Hatje Cantz, 2001), 89.

109. John L. Field, "Unruly and Irreverent Memories of Yale Architecture: 1951–1955," in "Reminiscences and Memorabilia of Students in Classes 1948–1958," as compiled by Estelle Thompson Margolis and Walfredo Toscanini, RU-961, ser. 1, box 1, Yale University Manuscripts and Archives, New Haven.

110. See Franz Schulze, *Philip Johnson: Life and Work* (New York: Knopf, 1994), 164–65, 167; and Varnelis, *Philip Johnson Tapes,* 133.

111. Philip Johnson quoted in Varnelis, *Philip Johnson Tapes,* 47, 131.

112. Ralph H. Comey in "Reminiscences and Memorabilia of Students in Classes 1948–1958."

113. Vincent J. Scully, "Doldrums in the Suburbs," *Perspecta: The Yale Architectural Journal* 9/10 (1965): 289–90, republished in Levine, *Modern Architecture,* 132; see also Peter Eisenman and Robert A. M. Stern, eds., *Philip Johnson: Writings* (New York: Oxford University Press, 1979), 84–97.

114. Louis Kahn to Anne Tyng, 30 January 1954, in *Louis Kahn to Anne Tyng: The Rome Letters, 1953–1954,* ed. Anne Tyng (New York: Rizzoli, 1997), 64.

115. Vincent Scully, interview by Geoff Kabaservice, May 6, 1991, Griswold-Brewster Oral History Project, RU-217, box 10, Yale University Manuscripts and Archives, New Haven.

116. Scully would once again make his opinions on campus construction known when, along with some of his colleagues in the Department of Art History, he supported Saarinen's then-highly controversial design for the Ingalls Hockey Rink. See Vincent J. Scully, Jr. "Ingalls Rink. It's a bird, it's a plane, it's . . . ," Yale/Harvard Hockey Program, February 1974. He also served on the jury for the Yale Mathematics Building competition (see Chapter 5).

117. Vincent Scully, interview by Geoff Kabaservice.

118. Varnelis, *Philip Johnson Tapes,* 169.

119. Herbert McLaughlin, Jr., "The Style of Education," *Progressive Architecture* 39 (July 1958): 11–12.

120. Philip Johnson quoted in Varnelis, *Philip Johnson Tapes,* 134–35.

121. R. Edward Harter in "Reminiscences and Memorabilia of Students in Classes 1948–1958."

122. Philip Johnson quoted in "The Next Fifty Years," *Architectural Forum* 94 (June 1951): 165–70.

123. Marshall D. Meyers, interview

by Alessandra Latour, March 19, 1983, in *Louis I. Kahn: L'uomo, il maestro,* ed. Alessandra Latour (Rome: Edizioni Kappa, 1986), 75.

124. Vincent Scully, interview by Alessandra Latour, September 15, 1982, in ibid., 155.

125. See Elizabeth Mock, ed., *Built in USA: 1932–1944* (New York: Museum of Modern Art, 1944), 66–67.

126. Louis I. Kahn, "Monumentality," in *New Architecture and City Planning,* ed. Paul Zucker (New York: Philosophical Library, 1944), reprinted in *Architectural Culture 1943–1968,* ed. Joan Ockman (New York: Rizzoli, 1993), 48–53; see also Kenneth Frampton, "Louis Kahn and the French Connection," *Oppositions* 22 (fall 1980): 34–36.

127. Scully, "Ruins of Rome," 1–13, republished in Levine, *Modern Architecture,* 298–319.

128. See Russell T. Scott, "Frank Edward Brown, 1908–1988," *American Journal of Archaeology* 92, no. 4 (October 1988): 577–79.

129. Scully, "Ruins of Rome."

130. Vincent Scully, interview by Alessandra Latour.

131. Estelle Thompson Margolis in "Reminiscences and Memorabilia of Students in Classes 1948–1958."

132. William Huff, "Kahn and Yale," *Journal of Architectural Education* 35, no. 3 (spring 1982): 23.

133. See Peter Blake, *Philip Johnson* (Basel: Brikhauser Verlag, 1996), 81.

134. Vincent Scully, interview by Alessandra Latour.

135. Jaquelin Robertson to Robert A. M. Stern, n.d. [1974], quoted in Stern, "Yale 1950–1965," 45; for Irving Colburn, see Jay Pridmore, *I. W. Colburn: Emotion in Modern Architecture* (Lake Forest, Ill.: Lake Forest College Press, 2015).

136. James Stewart Polshek,

Context and Responsibility (New York: Rizzoli, 1988), 22–23.

137. Eugene Nalle, interview by Walfredo Toscanini, Estelle Margolis, and Leona (Annenberg) Nalle, June 10, 2003, transcription edited by Eugene and Leona Nalle, School of Architecture, Yale University, "Reminiscences and Memorabilia of Students in Classes 1948–1958."

138. Howe, Annual Report (1950–1951).

139. Howe, Report by the Retiring Chairman.

140. James Stewart Polshek, "Eugene Nalle, 1916–2008: A Tribute," Constructs (fall 2008): 27.

141. Eugene Nalle, interview by Walfredo Toscanini, Estelle Thompson Margolis, and Leona (Annenberg) Nalle.

142. Scully, "Doldrums in the Suburbs," Perspecta, 284; Levine, Modern Architecture, 132.

143. Eugene Nalle, interview by Walfredo Toscanini, Estelle Thompson Margolis, and Leona (Annenberg) Nalle.

144. Howe, Report by the Retiring Chairman.

145. Eugene Nalle, interview by Walfredo Toscanini, Estelle Margolis, and Leona (Annenberg) Nalle.

146. Howe, Annual Report (1950–1951).

147. Ibid.

148. George Howe, Annual Report of the Chairman, 1951–52, 30 June 1952, School of Art and Architecture Records, RU-189, accn. 1991-A-007, box 1, Yale University Manuscripts and Archives, New Haven.

149. George Howe, "Talk to Third Year Students," October 1953. This talk was closely echoed by Philip Johnson in his "Whence and Whither: The Processional Element in Architecture," Perspecta: The Yale Architectural Journal 9/10 (1965): 167–78.

150. See Stern, Toward a Modern American Architecture, 162–69.

151. Howe, Annual Report (1951–52).

152. Harold Fredenburgh to Robert A. M. Stern, 13 March 1974; see also James Stewart Polshek to Robert A. M. Stern, 15 March 1974, both in Stern, "Yale 1950–1965," 35–62.

153. See Esther McCoy, "Young Architects in the U.S.," Zodiac 8 (1961): 166–85; see also Cory Buckner, Looking through the Lyman House: Drawing, Building, Dwelling (unpublished manuscript, 2010).

154. James Stewart Polshek, "The History of the Future: Connections and Transformations" (William C. DeVane Lecture, Yale School of Architecture New Haven, September 24, 2001), Guide to the Yale School of Architecture Lectures and Presentations, RU-880, accn. 2002-A-151, box 9, Yale University Manuscripts and Archives, New Haven.

155. As Polshek neared graduation, he designed a psychiatric hospital, a program of his own choosing, reflecting his interests "as a pre-medical student before I discovered architecture." Then, as a thesis he undertook a hotel for New Haven, a studio project that would recur a number of times throughout the 1950s and early 1960s until one, the Park Plaza (1966), was actually realized as part of the Chapel Square Mall Redevelopment. Philip Johnson was a member of Polshek's jury, and Polshek remembers his reaction to Johnson's comments, saying: "I didn't think I would graduate. He called it a 'second-hand Erich Mendelsohn.' And when I heard that I thought it was flattering. I don't think he intended it that way"; Polshek, "History of the Future."

156. Prentice would go on to become a practicing architect, founding the office of Prentice & Chan in 1965, but would largely retire from the profession in the 1970s to embark on a career in kinetic sculpture. His work has been installed in many public places and corporate headquarters. See Jane Ingram Allen, "Working with the Wind: A Conversation with Tim Prentice," Sculpture Magazine, March 2012, 46–51.

157. John L. Field, "Unruly and Irreverent Memories of Yale Architecture: 1951–1955," in "Reminiscences and Memorabilia of Students in Classes 1948–1958."

158. Polshek, Context and Responsibility, 21–22.

159. Memo, 11 June 1952, revision of introductory statement, under "Architecture" in the "Undergraduate Courses of Study," Bulletin of Yale University, Division of the Arts, 1952–1953 (1953), 60.

160. Ibid. Vincent Scully, interview by Jimmy Stamp, September 30, 2010.

161. See "One-Room House Gives up Privacy and Slick Finishes, Gains Spaciousness and Flexibility," Architectural Forum 94 (June 1951): 162–64.

162. Vincent Scully, interview by Jimmy Stamp.

163. Polshek, Context and Responsibility, 21–22.

164. Ralph H. Comey, in "Reminiscences and Memorabilia of Students in Classes 1948–1958."

165. Polshek, "History of the Future."

166. Polshek, Context and Responsibility, 21–22.

167. Polshek, "History of the Future."

168. Mark Hardenbergh in "Reminiscences and Memorabilia of Students in Classes 1948–1958."

169. Howe, Annual Report (1951–52).

170. Charles H. Sawyer to A.

Whitney Griswold, 1 August 1954, Yale University, Records of the Dean of the School of Architecture, RU-843, accn. 2007-A-193, box 13, Yale University Manuscripts and Archives, New Haven.

171. Howe, Report by the Retiring Chairman. For a student's view of Yale during the term following Howe's retirement, but just before the dam burst, see Edwin A. Kent, "Graduate Schools: V. School of Fine Arts; New Trends," *Yale Daily News,* October 31, 1954.

172. Howe, Report by the Retiring Chairman.

173. Charles H. Sawyer to A. Whitney Griswold, 18 April 1955, Records of A. Whitney Griswold, President 1950–1963, RU-22, box 25, folder 227, Yale University Manuscripts and Archives, New Haven.

174. Eugene Nalle, "Whole Design," *Perspecta: The Yale Architectural Journal* 1 (1952): 6–7.

175. Kathryn H. Anthony, "Studio Culture and Student Life," in *Architecture School: Three Centuries of Educating Architects in North America,* ed. Joan Ockman (Washington, D.C.: Association of Collegiate Schools of Architecture; Cambridge, Mass.: MIT Press, 2012), 399.

176. George Howe, "Preface," *Perspecta: The Yale Architectural Journal* 1 (1952): 1.

177. See Norman Carver, *Italian Hilltowns* (Kalamazoo, Mich.: Documan, 1979); Norman Carver, *Iberian Villages: Portugal and Spain* (Kalamazoo, Mich.: Documan, 1981); Norman Carver, *North African Villages* (Kalamazoo, Mich.: Documan, 1989); and Norman Carver, *Japanese Folkhouses* (Kalamazoo, Mich.: Documan, 2003).

178. Alvin Eisenman, "The Founding of Perspecta," in Deamer, Plattus, and Stern,

[Re]Reading Perspecta, 797.

179. Ibid.

180. Howe, "Preface," 1.

181. Colin St. John Wilson quoted in Sarah Menin and Stephen Kite, *An Architecture of Invitation: Colin St. John Wilson* (Aldershot, Eng.: Ashgate, 2005), 97.

182. Edwin Gilbert, *Native Stone* (Garden City, N.Y.: Doubleday, 1956), 22; Gilbert's other novels include *Silver Spoon* (1957), *The New Ambassadors* (1961), *Newport* (1971), and *Season in Monte Carlo* (1976).

183. Huff, "Kahn and Yale," 22–31; see also William Huff, "Kahn e Yale," *Rassegna* 7 (March 1985): 74–79.

184. Huff, "Kahn and Yale," 22–31.

185. Gilbert, *Native Stone,* 60.

186. Huff, "Kahn and Yale," 22–31.

187. Howe, Report by the Retiring Chairman.

188. Paul Schweikher, interview by Betty Blum, 1984, "Oral History of Paul Schweikher," the Chicago Architects Oral History Project, Ernest R. Graham Study Center for Architectural Drawings, Department of Architecture, the Art Institute of Chicago; "Recent Work by the Office of Paul Schweikher and Theodore Warren Lamb Associated Architects," *Architectural Forum* 71 (November 1939): 351–66.

189. Meyric R. Rogers, *The Work of Schweikher and Elting, Architects,* exh. cat. (Chicago: The Society, 1949), for a show from March 21–April 14, 1949, at the Renaissance Society at the University of Chicago.

190. Charles Sawyer to Robert A. M. Stern, 9 February 1974, quoted in Stern, *Toward a Modern Architecture,* 223n77, George Howe Papers.

191. Richard Nininger in "Reminiscences and Memorabilia of Students in Classes 1948–1958."

192. Charles Sawyer to Robert A. M. Stern, 9 February 1974,

quoted in Stern, *Toward a Modern Architecture,* 223n77, George Howe Papers.

193. Huff, "Kahn and Yale," 22–31.

194. Lee Mogel in "Reminiscences and Memorabilia of Students in Classes 1948–1958."

195. Walter Kaplan, "Communication Student Indicts Architecture Policy," *Yale Daily News,* February 25, 1955, 2.

196. Paul Schweikher, Annual Report of the Chairman, 1954–1955, 23 June 1955, School of Art and Architecture Records, RU-189, accn. 1991-A-007, box 1, Yale University Manuscripts and Archives, New Haven.

197. George Howe, memo to Dean Sawyer, 4 November 1954, School of Art and Architecture Records, RU-189, accn. 1991-A-007, box 1, Yale University Manuscripts and Archives, New Haven.

198. Paul Schweikher, memo to Dean Charles H. Sawyer, 15 November 1954, Records of A. Whitney Griswold, President 1950–1963, RU-22, box 25, Yale University Manuscripts and Archives, New Haven; see also Charles Sawyer to Paul Schweikher, 15 November 1954, in ibid.

199. Charles Sawyer to A. Whitney Griswold, 18 April 1955, Records of A. Whitney Griswold, President 1950–1963, RU-22, box 25, folder 227, Yale University Manuscripts and Archives, New Haven.

200. Louis I. Kahn quoted in Calvin M. Trillin, "Architecture: Yale's Latest Controversy," *Yale Daily News,* March 3, 1955.

201. Calvin M. Trillin, "Students, Faculty, Hit Architectural School," *Yale Daily News,* February 18, 1955, 1, 4.

202. Paul Schweikher, interview by Betty Blum, 1984.

203. Carroll L. V. Meeks quoted in Trillin, "Architecture, Yale's Latest Controversy."

204. Charles Sawyer to Robert A.

M. Stern, 9 February 1974, George Howe Papers.

205. Carroll L. V. Meeks, *The Railroad Station: An Architectural History* (New Haven: Yale University Press, 1956); Buell's railroad station was also briefly described in Vincent Scully, Jr., "Doldrums in the Suburbs," *Journal of the Society of Architectural Historians* 24, no. 1 (March 1965): 45. See also John M. Johansen, *John M. Johansen: A Life in the Continuum of Modern Architecture* (Milan: L'Arca Edizioni, 1995), 30–35; and John MacLane Johansen, ed., *Nanoarchitecture: A New Species of Architecture* (New York: Princeton Architectural Press, 2002), 11; see also Ian McCallum, *Architecture U.S.A.* (New York: Reinhold, 1959), 187–90.

206. McLaughlin, "Style of Education," 11, 13.

207. Thomas K. Fitzpatrick to A. Whitney Griswold, 20 June 1955, Records of A. Whitney Griswold, President 1950–1963, RU-22, box 25, folder 227, Yale University Manuscripts and Archives, New Haven.

208. Ibid. In addition to Fitzpatrick, director of the School of Architecture at the University of Virginia, the committee consisted of Morris Ketchum, Jr., Walter H. Kilham, Jr., and Hugh Stubbins, Jr., all practicing architects with experience in architecture education.

209. "Architectural School Listed by Accrediting Board on Provisional Basis, 56–57," *New York Times,* January 6, 1957, 73.

210. Charles Sawyer to A. Whitney Griswold, 18 April 1955, Records of A. Whitney Griswold, President 1950–1963, RU-22, box 25, folder 227, Yale University Manuscripts and Archives, New Haven.

211. Richard Nininger in

"Reminiscences and Memorabilia of Students in Classes 1948–1958."

212. William S. Huff to A. Whitney Griswold, 19 June 1955, Records of A. Whitney Griswold, President 1950–1963, RU-22, box 25, folder 226, Yale University Manuscripts and Archives, New Haven.

213. Edgar Furniss in "Regimented Approach? Controversy Sweeps Architecture School," unsigned editorial, *Yale Daily News,* February 22,1955, 2; Trillin, "Architecture, Yale's Latest Controversy"; Calvin M. Trillin, "Architecture Students Win Grading Reforms," *Yale Daily News,* March 25, 1955, 1.

214. Paul Schweiker to A. Whitney Griswold, 6 February 1956, Records of A. Whitney Griswold, President 1950–1963, RU-22, box 25, folder 233, Yale University Manuscripts and Archives, New Haven; A. Whitney Griswold to Paul Schweikher, 21 February 1956, in ibid.

215. Paul Schweikher, interview by Betty Blum, 1984.

216. Charles H. Sawyer to A. Whitney Griswold, 18 April 1955, Records of A. Whitney Griswold, President 1950–1963, RU-22, box 25, folder 227, Yale University Manuscripts and Archives, New Haven.

217. Paul Schweikher to Charles Sawyer, 6 June 1956, School of Art and Architecture Records, RU-189, accn. 2002-A-099, box 8, Yale University Manuscripts and Archives, New Haven.

218. Louis Kahn to Anne Tyng, 24 December 1953, in Tyng, *Louis Kahn to Anne Tyng,* 81; see also ibid., 86, 128.

219. Louis Kahn to Anne Tyng, Thurs., Fri., Sat., last day of May 1954, in Tyng, *Louis Kahn to Anne Tyng,* 138–39.

220. Charles Sawyer to Robert

Osborn, 8 February 1956, School of Art and Architecture Records, RU-189, accn. 2002-A-099, box 8, Yale University Manuscripts and Archives, New Haven.

221. Charles Sawyer to Robert Osborn, 14 February 1956, in ibid.

222. Charles H. Sawyer to A. Whitney Griswold, 19 March 1956, Records of A. Whitney Griswold, President 1950–1963, RU-22, box 25, folder 225, Yale University Manuscripts and Archives, New Haven.

223. See Sawyer's "Draft of Proposed Letter to Mr. Louis I. Kahn, from President W. Whitney Griswold," 19 March 1956, in ibid.

224. Vincent Scully, interview by Geoff Kabaservice, May 6, 1991.

225. Vincent Scully, interview by Alessandra Latour, September 15, 1982, 151.

226. Yale University News Bureau, press release no. 696, June 1, 1956.

227. Charles Sawyer to Louis I. Kahn, 3 May 1956, School of Art and Architecture Records, RU-189, accn. 2002-A-099, box 8, Yale University Manuscripts and Archives, New Haven.

228. Charles Sawyer to A. Whitney Griswold, 13 April 1956, Records of A. Whitney Griswold, President 1950–1963, RU-22, box 25, folder 225, Yale University Manuscripts and Archives, New Haven.

229. Ibid.

230. George Hinds, *Damaged Flight, However the Lark Is Still Ascending* (Charleston, S.C.: CreateSpace, 2014).

231. John Field in "Reminiscences and Memorabilia of Students in Classes 1948–1958."

232. Walfredo Toscanini in ibid.

233. "Appointments," *Architectural Forum* 86 (April 1947): 62; "C. H. Sawyer Appointed Arts

Division Director and Fine Arts School Dean," *New York Times,* March 3, 1947, 23.

234. See "New Exhibition Gallery," *Yale Associates Bulletin* 8 (June 1937): 27–29; "Art Gallery Extension," *Yale Associates Bulletin* 10 (December 1941): 1–3; and "Plans Addition to Art Gallery," *Museum News* 19 (January 15, 1942): 2. In 1950, the gallery expansion project was revived, keeping the scheme first prepared by Philip Goodwin in 1941. See "To Add to Its Building," *Museum News* 28 (May 1950): 1; "Plans to Add a Three Story Wing," *Interiors* 109 (July 1950): 10; "Yale Plans Addition to Art Gallery Building," *Architectural Record* 107 (July 1950): 196; and "To Erect a New Three Story Addition to Its Present Art Gallery," *College Art Journal* 9 (1950): 423–24.

235. Louis I. Kahn quoted in George Sanderson, "Extension: University Art Gallery and Design Center," *Progressive Architecture* 35 (May 1954): 88–92. See also *Yale Daily News Dedication Issue,* November 6, 1953.

236. Huff, "Kahn and Yale," 22–31.

237. Sanderson, "Extension," 88–92.

238. Unidentified student and A. Whitney Griswold quoted in Walter McQuade, "Building Years of a Yale Man," *Architectural Forum* (June 1963): 88–93.

239. "Proposal for a Curriculum in the Department of Architecture Leading to the Degree of Master of City Planning," unsigned, likely by Tunnard, 30 November 1949, School of Art and Architecture, Yale University, Records RU-189, accn. 2002-A-099, box 8, Yale University Manuscripts and Archives, New Haven; Leslie Cheek, Jr., University Council Report of the Chairman of the Committee on the Division

of the Arts (Architecture, Sculpture and Painting), 25 April 1948, in ibid.

240. "Proposal for a Curriculum," unsigned, likely by Tunnard; "Howe Announces Graduate Course," *Yale Daily News,* February 27, 1950, 1.

241. "House Near Halland, Sussex," *Architectural Review* 85, no. 2 (February 1939): 63–78.

242. Christopher Tunnard, *Gardens in the Modern Landscape* (London: Architectural Press, 1938).

243. Philip Johnson quoted in Varnelis, *Philip Johnson Tapes,* 79.

244. David Jacques and Jan Woudstra, *Landscape Modernism Renounced: The Career of Christopher Tunnard (1910–1979)* (London: Routledge, 2009), 59.

245. Bruce Weber, "Henry Hope Reed, 97, Historian, Is Dead," *New York Times,* May 3, 2013, B17.

246. Jacques and Woudstra, *Landscape Modernism Renounced,* 59.

247. Yale University News Bureau, press release no. 481, February 25, 1950; *American City* 65 (April 1950): 5.

248. Charles Brewer, interview by Jimmy Stamp, August 10, 2012.

249. Pearlman, *Inventing American Modernism,* 103.

250. Christopher Tunnard quoted in Jacques and Woudstra, *Landscape Modernism Renounced,* 63.

251. Yale University News Bureau, press release no. 344, April 22, 1952.

252. "Architecture Is Deplored by Belluschi: Modern Construction Called 'Mirrors of Utilitarian Society,'" *Hartford Courant,* April 25, 1952, 23A.

253. Christopher Tunnard and Henry Hope Reed, *American Skyline: The Growth and Form of Our Cities and Towns* (Boston: Houghton Mifflin, 1955);

paperback edition published by New American Library in 1956.

254. Henry Hope Reed, "Monumental Architecture–or the Art of Pleasing in Civic Design," *Perspecta: The Yale Architectural Journal* 1 (1952): 50–54, 56.

255. Henry Hope Reed, "For the 'Superfluous' in Buildings," *New York Times Magazine,* March 4, 1956, VI: 26–27, 47–48.

256. Henry Hope Reed, *The Golden City* (New York: Doubleday, 1959).

257. Charles Sawyer to A. Whitney Griswold, 18 April 1955, Records of A. Whitney Griswold, President 1950–1963, RU-22, box 25, Yale University Manuscripts and Archives, New Haven.

258. Scott Sullivan, "Wright Reasserts 'New' Architecture, Religion," *Yale Daily News,* September 21, 1955, 1, 4.

259. Vincent Scully, "Frank Lloyd Wright and Philip Johnson at Yale," *Architectural Digest* (March 1986): 90, 94.

260. Vincent Scully, "Frank Lloyd Wright vs. the International Style," *Art News* (March 1954): 32–35, 64–66.

261. Philip Johnson made that remark about Wright in an informal talk to students at Harvard (December 1954), published as Philip Johnson, "The Seven Crutches of Modern Architecture," *Perspecta: The Yale Architectural Journal* 3 (1955): 40–45.

262. Scully, "Wright and Johnson at Yale," 90, 94.

263. David Gebhard, *Tulsa Art Deco: An Architectural Era, 1925–1942* (Tulsa, Okla.: Junior League of Tulsa, 1980).

264. Ibid.

265. Scully, "Wright and Johnson at Yale," 90, 94.

266. Ralph H. Comey in "Reminiscences and Memorabilia of Students in Classes 1948–1958."

267. Frank Lloyd Wright quoted in Sullivan, "Wright Reasserts 'New' Architecture," 4.

268. Ibid.

269. Ralph H. Comey in "Reminiscences and Memorabilia of Students in Classes 1948–1958."

270. Perry B. Johnson to A. Whitney Griswold, 15 May 1957, Records of A. Whitney Griswold, President 1950–1963, RU-22, box 25, folder 225, Yale University Manuscripts and Archives, New Haven.

271. Eero Saarinen to Robert Osborn, copied to A. Whitney Griswold, 29 August 1956, Records of A. Whitney Griswold, President 1950–1963, RU-22, box 25, folder 231, Yale University Manuscripts and Archives, New Haven.

272. Ibid.

273. Ibid.

274. Boyd M. Smith to Eero Saarinen, 7 March 1957, in ibid.; Smith was appointed acting dean of the school on October 30, 1956. See Yale University News Bureau, press release no. 216, November 29, 1956.

275. Eero Saarinen to Boyd Smith, 11 March 1957, Records of A. Whitney Griswold, President 1950–1963, RU-22, box 25, folder 231, Yale University Manuscripts and Archives, New Haven.

276. John Knox Shear to A. Whitney Griswold, 18 March 1957, in ibid.

277. Eero Saarinen to A. Whitney Griswold, 12 April 1957; Harold Hauf to Boyd Smith, 12 April 1957; and Boyd Smith to Harold Hauf, 15 April 1957, all in ibid.; for the IIT offer to Rudolph, see Chapter 4.

278. Vincent Scully, interview by Geoff Kabaservice, May 6, 1991.

279. Vincent Scully, interview by Jimmy Stamp, August 23, 2010.

280. Thomas K. Fitzpatrick to A. Whitney Griswold, 18 June 1957, Records of A. Whitney Griswold, President 1950–1963, RU-22, box 25, folder 225, Yale University Manuscripts and Archives, New Haven.

4

A Time of Heroics

Epigraph. Mission statement of the Department of Architecture, in the *Bulletin of Yale University, School of Art and Architecture, 1961–62*, ser. 58, no. 1 (January 1962).

1. Yale University News Bureau, press release no. 720, June 12, 1957; A. Whitney Griswold to Paul Rudolph, 3 June 1957, RU-22, box 25, folder 232, Yale University Manuscripts and Archives, New Haven.

2. Charles Brewer, interview by Jimmy Stamp, August 10, 2012.

3. Rudolph's early years were briefly described in Robert A. M. Stern's forward to Paul Rudolph, *Writing Architecture* (New Haven: Yale University School of Architecture, 2008), 6–7; see also Robert A. M. Stern, "Secrets of Paul Rudolph: His First Twenty-Five Years" (1965), republished in *Architecture on the Edge of Postmodernism: Collected Essays 1964–1988* (New Haven: Yale University Press, 2009), 5–20. See also Sibyl Moholy-Nagy, *The Architecture of Paul Rudolph* (New York: Praeger, 1970), 7–31; and Timothy M. Rohan, *The Architecture of Paul Rudolph* (New Haven: Yale University Press, 2014), 1–33.

4. Paul Rudolph, "Three New Directions," *Perspecta: The Yale Architectural Journal* 1 (1952): 18–22.

5. Ibid.

6. Paul Rudolph, interview by Robert Bruegmann, 1986, "Oral History of Paul Rudolph," the Chicago Architects Oral History Project, Ernest R. Graham Study Center for Architectural Drawings, Department of Architecture, the Art Institute of Chicago; in 1986, Rudolph visited the reconstructed Barcelona Pavilion (Mies van der Rohe, 1929), and an account of his impressions, along with analytical drawings, was published in Roberto de Alba, ed., *Paul Rudolph: The Late Work* (New York: Princeton Architectural Press, 2003), 202–17.

7. See Mildred Schmertz, "Architectural Drawing for Printing Processes," *Architectural Record* 133 (February 1963): 137–44.

8. Charles Brewer, interview by Jimmy Stamp, August 11, 2012.

9. Paul Rudolph to his parents, 12 April 1955, courtesy Paul Rudolph Foundation.

10. Paul Rudolph, interview by C. Ray Smith, December 28, 1977, C. Ray Smith Manuscript and Research Files on the Yale Art and Architecture Building by Paul Rudolph, MS-1948, box 1, Yale University Manuscripts and Archives, New Haven.

11. Paul Rudolph, "Walter Gropius et Son École," *L'architecture d'Aujourd'hui*, no. 28 (February 1950).

12. Paul Rudolph quoted in "Adolescent Architecture," *Architectural Forum* 109 (September 1958): 177, as quoted in Moholy-Nagy, *Architecture of Paul Rudolph*, 11.

13. In 1963, eleven second-year students at Columbia's School of Architecture, dissatisfied with their program and faculty—especially the newly appointed dean, Charles Colbert—applied for admission to the Yale

program. In response, Rudolph wrote what must have been a difficult letter to Grayson Kirk, Columbia's president. See Richard Oliver, "History VI: 1959–1968," in *The Making of an Architect: 1881–1981,* ed. Richard Oliver (New York: Rizzoli, 1981), 175.

14. Paul Rudolph, interview by C. Ray Smith, March 29, 1979, C. Ray Smith Manuscript and Research Files; see also William Grindereng, interview by Bruce Barnes, June 28, 2006, Claire T. Carney Library, University of Massachusetts Dartmouth North Dartmouth, Mass.

15. Charles Brewer, interview by Jimmy Stamp, August 11, 2012.

16. Paul Rudolph, interview by C. Ray Smith, December 28, 1977.

17. John Jacobson, interview by Jimmy Stamp, April 18, 2013.

18. Paul Rudolph, interview by C. Ray Smith, February 15, 1978, C. Ray Smith Manuscript and Research Files.

19. Ibid.

20. See Vincent Scully, "Carroll Louis Vanderslice Meeks, 1907–1966," *Eye: Magazine of the Yale Arts Association,* no. 1 (1967): 5; and George Kubler, "A Personal Memoir," *Eye: Magazine of the Yale Arts Association,* no. 1 (1967): 6–7. See also Spiro Kostof, "The Shape of Time at Yale, Circa 1960," in *The History of History in American Schools of Architecture 1865–1975,* ed. Gwendolyn Wright and Janet Parks (New York: Princeton Architectural Press, 1990), 131.

21. Vincent Scully, *The Earth, the Temple, and the Gods* (New Haven: Yale University Press, 1962).

22. Stanley Tigerman, *Designing Bridges to Burn: Architectural Memoirs by Stanley Tigerman* (Singapore: Oro, 2011), 102.

23. Kostof, "Shape of Time," 132.

24. Etel Thea Kramer, "Notes on the Yale School of Architecture, 1960–63,"

March 1974, Reminiscences and Documentation of Yale University Architecture Students Collected by Robert A. M. Stern, 1970–1974, RU-1001, box 2, folder 50, Yale University Manuscripts and Archives, New Haven.

25. Kostof, "Shape of Time," 134.

26. David McCullough. "Architectural Spellbinder," *Architectural Forum* 111 (September 1959): 136–37, 191, 202; Vincent Scully, *The Shingle Style: Architectural Theory and Design from Richardson to the Origins of Wright* (New Haven: Yale University Press, 1955); Vincent Scully, *The Shingle Style Today, or the Historian's Revenge* (New York: Braziller, 1974).

27. Norman Foster, "Pritzker Prize Address," quoted in Deyan Sudjic's introduction to *On Foster—Foster On,* ed. David Jenkins (Munich: Prestel, 2000).

28. Scully, *Earth, Temple, Gods.*

29. George Kubler, *The Shape of Time: Remarks on the History of Things* (New Haven: Yale University Press, 1962); C. A. Burland, "The Shape of Time by George Kubler," *The Burlington Magazine* 105, no. 724 (July 1963): 336.

30. George Kubler, "What Can Historians Do for Architects?" *Perspecta: The Yale Architectural Journal* 9/10 (1965): 299–302; see also George Kubler, "The Shape of Time, Reconsidered," *Perspecta: The Yale Architectural Journal* 19 (1982): 112–21.

31. Charles Brewer, interview by Jimmy Stamp, August 11, 2012.

32. Tigerman, *Designing Bridges to Burn,* 53.

33. Allan Greenberg, interview by Jimmy Stamp, November 15, 2011.

34. "Architecture Board Restores Approval to Graduate School," *Yale Daily News,* September 22, 1959.

35. Paul Rudolph, "Résumé for the Academic Year 1958–1959," 30 July 1959, Alfred Whitney Griswold, President of Yale University, Records, RU-22, accn. 1963-A-002, box 25, folder 225, Yale University Manuscripts and Archives, New Haven.

36. Ibid.

37. Charles Brewer, interview by Jimmy Stamp, August 11, 2012.

38. "Student Questionnaire Concerning the Curriculum for the Year 1957–58 in the Architectural School," 17 April 1958, School of Art and Architecture Records, RU-189, accn. 2002-A-099, box 8, Yale University Manuscripts and Archives, New Haven.

39. Rudolph, "Résumé for 1958–1959."

40. Ibid.

41. Ibid.

42. Paul Rudolph, introduction to *Perspecta: The Yale Architectural Journal* 5 (1959): 3.

43. Paul Rudolph, "The Architectural Education in U.S.A.," *Zodiac* 8 (1961): 162–65; see also Russell Bourne, "Yale's Paul Rudolph," *Architectural Forum* 108 (April 1958): 128–29, 192; and Rudolph's "Six Determinants of Architectural Form," *Architectural Record* 120 (October 1956): 183–90, in which Rudolph castigated the "early theory of modern architecture" for its limited ambitions. See also Paul Rudolph, "Changing Philosophy of Architecture," *American Institute of Architects Journal* 22 (August 1954): 65–70; and also Rudolph, "Regionalism in Architecture," *Perspecta: The Yale Architectural Journal* 4 (1957): 12–19. For varying assessments of Rudolph as an educator, see Peter Collins, "Whither Paul Rudolph?" *Progressive Architecture* 42 (August 1960): 130–33; and Henry Russell Hitchcock, "The Rise to World

Prominence of American Architecture," *Zodiac* 8 (1960): 1–5. See also *Architectural Record* 131 (January 1962) for an interview between Rudolph and architecture student Jonathan Barnett (b. 1937; B.A. 1958, M.Arch 1963).

44. Craig Whitaker, "Reflections on the Yale School of Architecture," c. February 1974, Reminiscences and Documentation of Architecture Students Collected by Robert A. M. Stern, RU-1001, accn. 2006-A-147, box 4, Yale University Manuscripts and Archives, New Haven.

45. Thomas Beeby, interview by Betty Blum, 1998, "Oral History of Thomas Beeby," the Chicago Architects Oral History Project, Ernest R. Graham Study Center for Architectural Drawings, Department of Architecture, the Art Institute of Chicago, 18.

46. John Winter, "John Winter in Conversation with Adrian Forty and Thomas Weaver," *AA Files*, no. 63 (2011): 21.

47. Norman Foster, "Exploring the City" (William C. DeVane Lecture, Yale School of Architecture, New Haven, October 8, 2001), Guide to the Yale School of Architecture Lectures and Presentations, RU-880, accn. 2002-A-151, box 11, Yale University Manuscripts and Archives, New Haven.

48. Thomas Beeby, interview by Betty Blum, 1998, 15.

49. Allan Greenberg, interview by Jimmy Stamp, November 15, 2011.

50. Allan Greenberg, "Introduction: Fragment of an Autobiography," *Architecture of Democracy* (New York: Rizzoli, 2006), 14–15.

51. Ibid., 18; Jane Jacobs, *The Death and Life of Great American Cities* (New York: Random House, 1961).

52. Paul Rudolph quoted in

53. Greenberg, "Introduction," 18.

54. Tigerman, *Designing Bridges to Burn*, 105.

54. Ibid., 95.

55. Paul Rudolph quoted in Tigerman, *Designing Bridges to Burn*, 94.

56. Ibid., 95–96.

57. Paul Rudolph, interview by Robert Bruegmann, 1986, "Oral History of Paul Rudolph," the Chicago Architects Oral History Project, Ernest R. Graham Study Center for Architectural Drawings, Department of Architecture, the Art Institute of Chicago.

58. Tigerman, *Designing Bridges to Burn*, 97.

59. Norman Foster quoted in Deyan Sudjic, *Norman Foster: A Life in Architecture* (New York: Overlook, 2010), 71.

60. Tigerman, *Designing Bridges to Burn*, 109.

61. Ibid., 105, 107.

62. Ibid., 100; Tigerman's project was published in "Travaux d'élèves à l'université de Yale," *L'Architecture d'Aujourd'hui* 35 (September 1965): LVI.

63. John Hejduk, "Afterword," *Stanley Tigerman: Buildings and Projects*, ed. Sarah Mollman Underhill (New York: Rizzoli, 1989), 256.

64. Stanley Tigerman, interview by Betty Blum, 2003, "Oral History of Stanley Tigerman," the Chicago Architects Oral History Project, Ernest R. Graham Study Center for Architectural Drawings, Department of Architecture, the Art Institute of Chicago, 14.

65. Tigerman, *Designing Bridges to Burn*, 110.

66. Stanley Tigerman, interview by Betty Blum, 14.

67. Foster, "Exploring the City."

68. The Pritzker Architectural Prize, "Norman Foster: Pritzker Laureate Architecture Prize Acceptance Speech," 1999, http://www.pritzkerprize.com/1999/ceremony_speech1 (accessed February 27, 2015).

69. Norman Foster, "Exploring the City."

70. Foster, "Pritzker Prize Address."

71. M. J. Long quoted in Mark Girouard, *Big Jim: The Life and Work of James Stirling* (London: Pimlico, 2000), 116–17.

72. Paul Rudolph quoted in Stanley Tigerman, interview by Betty Blum, 2003, 52.

73. M. J. Long quoted in Girouard, *Big Jim*, 116–17.

74. Norman Foster quoted in Sudjic, *Norman Foster: A Life*, 74–75.

75. Tigerman, interview by Betty Blum, 2003, 36.

76. For Tigerman's paintings, see Emmanuel Petit, "Nine Clouds of Architecture," in *Ceci n'est pas une reverie: The Architecture of Stanley Tigerman*, exh. cat. (New Haven: Yale School of Architecture, 2011).

77. Anthony C. Antoniades, *On the Way to Archituth* (Athens: Free Press, 2012), 108.

78. Anthony Vidler, *James Frazer Stirling: Notes from the Archive* (New Haven: Yale University Press for the Canadian Centre for Architecture and Yale Center for British Art, 2010), 85, 87–90.

79. See Sir Nikolaus Pevsner, John Harris, and Nicholas Antram, *The Buildings of England: Lincolnshire*, vol. 27 (New Haven: Yale University Press, 1989), 86.

80. Richard Rogers quoted in Girouard, *Big Jim*, 100.

81. Norman Foster, "Learning from . . . ," *Architecture Today* 217 (April 2011): 2.

82. Foster, "Exploring the City"; see also Robert A. M. Stern, "The Impact of Yale," in *Norman Foster Works I*, ed. David Jenkins (Munich: Prestel, 2002).

83. "Yale Students from Britain: Their First Look at U.S.," *New Haven Register Magazine*, November 5, 1961, cited in

Bryan Appleyard, *Richard Rogers* (London: Faber and Faber, 1986), 93–94.

84. Appleyard, *Richard Rogers,* 94.

85. Ibid., 96.

86. Paul Rudolph, studio program, quoted in Appleyard, *Richard Rogers,* 97; for Pierson-Sage, see Catherine Lynn, "Building Yale and Razing It," in *Yale in New Haven: Architecture and Urbanism,* ed. Vincent J. Scully, Catherine Lynn, Eric Vogt, and Paul Goldberger (New Haven: Yale University Press, 2004), 187; see also Vincent Scully, "Modern Architecture at Yale: A Memoir," in Scully et al., *Yale in New Haven,* 323–25.

87. See John Howey, ed., *The Sarasota School of Architecture: 1941–1966* (Cambridge, Mass.: MIT Press, 1995); see also Carl Abbott, *In/formed by the Land: The Architecture of Carl Abbott* (San Francisco: Oro, 2013).

88. Richard Rogers, "Team 4," in *Norman Foster: Team 4 and Foster Associates, Building and Projects,* vol. 1, *1964–1973* (London: Watermark, 1991), 14–15.

89. See Reyner Banham, *The New Brutalism: Ethic or Aesthetic?* (New York: Reinhold, 1966).

90. Sudjic, *Norman Foster: A Life,* 73.

91. Appleyard, *Richard Rogers,* 97.

92. See Peter Arnell and Ted Bickford, eds., *Charles Gwathmey and Robert Siegel: Buildings and Projects 1964–1985* (New York: Harper and Row, 1984), 46–49.

93. George O'Brien, "Homework on a Stable," *New York Times Magazine,* October 22, 1961, SM70.

94. For Gwathmey's Fire Island house, see "Design Secures a Beachhead," *Progressive Architecture* (November 1965): 130–33; for his Amagansett house, see "Innovation at the Beach," *House Beautiful* 10 (July 1966): 6, 54–59; "Geometry by the Sea," *Architectural Forum* 124 (April 1966): 52–55; and "Replicated Residence," *Architectural Forum* 126 (January 1967): 81; see also *Five Architects* (New York: Museum of Modern Art; Wittenborn, 1972).

95. Sudjic, *Norman Foster: A Life, Architectural Forum* 74.

96. For Islam, see Zainab Faruqui Ali, *Muzharul Islam, Architect* (Bangladesh: Bangla Academy, 2011).

97. Reyner Banham, "The History of the Immediate Future," *RIBA Journal* 68 (May 1961): 252–57.

98. Reyner Banham, "Morse and Stiles," *New Statesman* (July 13, 1962), reprinted in *Architectural Forum* 117 (December 1962): 110.

99. Ibid.

100. Ian McCallum, *Architecture U.S.A.* (New York: Reinhold, 1959).

101. Rudolph, "Résumé for 1958–1959," July 30, 1959; King-lui Wu to Paul Rudolph, 15 August 1959; and Paul Rudolph to King-lui Wu, 25 August 1959, both in School of Art and Architecture Records, RU-189, accn. 2002-A-099, box 8, Yale University Manuscripts and Archives, New Haven.

102. Phyllis Lambert, interview by Liane Lefaivre, "Phyllis Lambert, Advocacy Planner in the Late 1960s," *Harvard Design Magazine* (spring/summer 2004): 83–86.

103. Phyllis Lambert quoted in ibid., 84.

104. Tigerman, *Designing Bridges to Burn,* 99.

105. Ibid.

106. M. J. Long, interview by Jimmy Stamp, November 9, 2012.

107. Ibid.

108. James Stirling, "'The Functional Tradition' and Expression," *Perspecta: The Yale Architectural Journal* 6 (1960): 88–97.

109. James Stirling, "Conversations with Students," *Perspecta: The Yale Architectural Journal* 11 (1967): 92.

110. Vincent Scully quoted in Girouard, *Big Jim,* 117.

111. George Buchanan quoted in ibid., 119.

112. Ibid., 123.

113. Barbara Chase quoted in ibid., 120

114. Ibid., 119.

115. Barbara Chase quoted in ibid., 122.

116. George Buchanan quoted in ibid., 123.

117. Richard Rogers quoted in ibid., 124–25.

118. Ibid., 125.

119. Yale University News Bureau, press release no. 269, February 5, 1959.

120. For example, see Finkle's design for a country house in "Citation: Residential Design," *Progressive Architecture* (January 1962): 150–51.

121. M. J. Long, interview by Jimmy Stamp, November 9, 2012. For a discussion of Long's immediate postgraduate years, including her voyage of architectural discovery enabled by winning the National Institute of Architectural Education's Annual Thesis Prize in 1964, her decision to work in England for Richard Llewellyn-Davies during a three-month break in her travels, her visit to Cambridge to see Wilson's work, and her decision to join Wilson's office as an employee, leading, ultimately, to their marriage in 1972 and professional partnership, see Sarah Menin and Stephen Kite, *An Architecture of Invitation: Colin St. John Wilson* (Aldershot, Eng.: Ashgate, 2005), 109–11, 165, 166.

122. Paul Rudolph quoted in Moholy-Nagy, *Architecture of Paul Rudolph,* 17.

123. Paul Rudolph, "Alumni Day Speech: Yale School of Architecture. February 1958," *Oppositions* 14 (October 1974):

141–43.

124. John M. Johansen, *John M. Johansen: A Life in the Continuum of Modern Architecture* (Milan: L'Arca Edizioni, 1995), 19.

125. Stanley Tigerman, interview by Betty Blum, 2003, 15.

126. Vincent Scully, interview by Geoff Kabaservice, May 6, 1991, RU-2-17, Griswold-Brewster History Project, Yale University, Yale University Manuscripts and Archives, New Haven.

127. William Huff to Robert A. M. Stern, 26 February 1974, Reminiscences and Documentation of Yale University Architecture Students Collected by Robert A. M. Stern, 1970–1974, RU-1001, box 1, folder 41, Yale University Manuscripts and Archives, New Haven; see also William Huff, "Kahn and Yale," *Journal of Architectural Education* 35, no. 3 (spring 1982); and William Huff, "Kahn e Yale," *Rassegna* 7 (March 1985): 74–79.

128. Paul Rudolph quoted in Huff, "Kahn and Yale."

129. Charles Brewer, interview by Jimmy Stamp, August 10, 2012; see also Charles Brewer, "Arts and Preservation in New Haven," *Journal of Architectural Education* (November 1976): 22–25.

130. Tigerman, *Designing Bridges to Burn,* 126–49; see also Carter Wiseman, *Louis I. Kahn: Beyond Time and Style* (New York: W. W. Norton, 2007): 151–54; and Zainab Faruqui Ali and Fuad H. Mallick, eds., *Muzharul Islam Architect* (Dhaka 1000, Bangladesh: University Press, 2012).

131. Tigerman, *Designing Bridges to Burn,* 142.

132. Paul Rudolph quoted in Moholy-Nagy, *Architecture of Paul Rudolph,* 16.

133. "Paul Rudolph: Young Mover, Changing the Look of American Architecture,"

Vogue, January 15, 1963, 84–91, 106; Sudjic, *Norman Foster: A Life,* 67–68.

134. For detailed accounts of Chermayeff's career, see Richard Plunz, ed., *Design and the Public Good: Selected Writings 1930–1980 by Serge Chermayeff* (Cambridge, Mass.: MIT Press, 1982); and Alan Powers, *Serge Chermayeff: Designer, Architect, Teacher* (London: RIBA, 2001).

135. See Donald Pilcher, "Recreation at the Seaside," *Architectural Review* 84 (December 1938): 305–10.

136. Alexander Tzonis, "The Struggle over the City Idea" (William C. DeVane Lecture, Yale School of Architecture, New Haven, October 22, 2001), Guide to the Yale School of Architecture Lectures and Presentations, RU-880, accn. 2002-A-151, box 12, Yale University Manuscripts and Archives, New Haven.

137. William Grindereng, interview by Bruce Barnes, June 28, 2006.

138. Kenneth Frampton and Alessandra Latour, "Notes on American Architectural Education, from the End of the Nineteenth Century until the 1970s," *Lotus* 27, no. 2 (1980): 5–39.

139. The result of Chermayeff's studio were published as Serge Chermayeff with Peter Leal Floyd, *Search for a New Urbanity* (New Haven: Department of Architecture, Yale University, 1962).

140. Tzonis, "Struggle over the City Idea"; Bakonowsky was cofounder in 1962 of Cambridge Seven, along with Chermayeff's sons Peter and Ivan, Alden B. Christie, Paul E. Dietrich, Thomas Geismar, and Terry Rankine. Later, Ivan and Tom Geismar broke away to found the graphic design firm Chermayeff/Geismar.

141. Tzonis, "Struggle over the City

Idea"; see also Powers, *Serge Chermayeff,* 208.

142. Anthony Alofson, *The Struggle for Modernism: Architecture, Landscape Architecture, and City Planning at Harvard* (New York: W. W. Norton, 2002), 50, 299.

143. Paul Rudolph quoted in Victoria Milne, "Nothing Trivial" (1994–1996), 49, cited in Powers, *Serge Chermayeff,* 208. "Nothing Trivial" is based on interviews with Chermayeff commissioned by his sons, who made them available to Powers.

144. Paul Rudolph quoted in ibid.

145. Powers, *Serge Chermayeff,* 209.

146. Serge Chermayeff to Paul Rudolph, August 1964, Columbia University Avery Library, New York, N.Y., quoted in ibid.

147. Serge Chermayeff, interview by Betty Blum, 1986, "Oral History of Serge Chermayeff," the Chicago Architects Oral History Project, Ernest R. Graham Study Center for Architectural Drawings, Department of Architecture, the Art Institute of Chicago, 9.

148. Powers, *Serge Chermayeff,* 209.

149. Vincent Scully, interviewed by Jimmy Stamp, August 23, 2010.

150. Tigerman, interview by Betty Blum, 2003, 15; see also Tigerman, *Designing Bridges to Burn,* 100–101.

151. Jaquelin Robertson, interview by Jimmy Stamp, July 21, 2011.

152. Thomas Beeby, interview by Betty Blum, 1998, 17.

153. Robert A. M. Stern, "Architectural Education at Yale, 1958–1965," unpublished article written for *L'architecture d'aujourd'hui* (1965), Robert A. M. Stern Architects Records, MS-1859, accn. 2006-M-102, box 35, Yale University Manuscripts and Archives, New Haven.

154. Foster, "Learning from . . . ," 2.

155. Foster, "Pritzker Prize Address"; Norman Foster, "Royal Gold Medal Address," quoted in Sudjic, *On Foster,* 485.

156. Richard Rogers quoted in Kenneth Powell, *Richard Rogers, Complete Works,* vol. 1 (London: Phaidon, 1999), 11, cited in Powers, *Serge Chermayeff,* 209–10.

157. Richard Rogers and Norman Foster to Serge Chermayeff, 2 September 1964, Avery Library, Columbia University, New York, N.Y., quoted in Powers, *Serge Chermayeff,* 210.

158. Norman Foster to Serge Chermayeff, 22 March 1966, Avery Library, Columbia University, New York, N.Y., quoted in ibid.

159. Tzonis, "Struggle over the City Idea."

160. Serge Chermayeff and Alexander Tzonis, *Shape of Community: Realization of Human Potential* (Harmondsworth, Eng.: Penguin, 1971).

161. Plunz, *Design and the Public Good,* xxviii.

162. Powers, *Serge Chermayeff,* 210–11.

163. Paul Rudolph, interview by C. Ray Smith, December 29, 1977, C. Ray Smith Manuscript and Research Files.

164. Gordon Bunshaft, interview, 1990, "Oral History of Gordon Bunshaft," the Chicago Architects Oral History Project, Ernest R. Graham Study Center for Architectural Drawings, Department of Architecture, the Art Institute of Chicago, 211; it is not likely that Saarinen was considered. He had just finished the Ingalls Rink, which was overbudget, he was working on the university's master plan, and he had probably already been awarded the commission for two new residential colleges.

165. Ibid.

166. Often considered to be one of the first true general contractors, the George A. Fuller Construction Company was founded in Chicago in 1882 by George Fuller after the dissolution of his previous company, Clark & Fuller. During the 1890s, the company opened an office in New York and proceeded to build some of the most notable structures in the city, including the New York Times Building and the Flatiron Building (briefly known as the Fuller Building). Though Fuller died in 1900, the company continued under his name, building in New York and Chicago into the 1970s. Mark R. Wilson, "Entries: Fuller (George A.) Co.," *Electronic Encyclopedia of Chicago* (Chicago: Newberry Library, 2005).

167. Vincent Scully, "RIBAM Discourse 1969: A Search for Principle between Two Wars," *RIBA Journal: The Journal of the Royal Institute of British Architects* 76 (June 1969): 240–47; for the debate between Scully and Norman Mailer, see Norman Mailer, "The Big Bite," *Esquire,* May 1963, 37, 40; Norman Mailer, "The Big Bite," *Esquire,* August 1963, 16, 18, 21, 24; "Mailer vs. Scully," *Architectural Forum* 120 (April 1964): 96–97; and Neil Levine, "Vincent Scully: A Biographical Sketch," in *Modern Architecture and Other Essays,* ed. Vincent Scully (Princeton, N.J.: Princeton University Press, 2003), 20–33.

168. Gordon Bunshaft, interview, 1990, 225–26.

169. The decision to go forward with the construction of the Art and Architecture Building was officially announced on June 18, 1960; Yale University News Bureau, press release no 515, June 18, 1960. The Beinecke Library was announced at the same time.

170. Rohan, *Architecture of Paul Rudolph,* 84.

171. Rudolph, "Résumé for 1958–1959."

172. Paul Rudolph, interview by C. Ray Smith, December 29, 1977.

173. Vincent Scully, "Louis I. Kahn and the Ruins of Rome," *MoMA: The Members Quarterly of the Museum of Modern Art,* no. 12 (summer 1992): 1–13, republished in *Modern Architecture and Other Essays* (Princeton, N.J.: Princeton University Press, 2003), 319.

174. Timothy M. Rohan, "Canon and Anti-Canon: On the Fall and Rise of the A&A," *Harvard Design Magazine* 14 (June 2001): 24–32; see also Paul Rudolph, quoted in Paul Heyer, *Architects on Architecture* (New York: Walker, 1966), 295.

175. Paul Rudolph quoted in John Cook and Heinrich Klotz, *Conversations with Architects* (New York: Praeger, 1973), 99.

176. Paul Rudolph quoted in Cook and Klotz, *Conversations with Architects,* 99.

177. Vincent Scully, "Art and Architecture Building, Yale University," *Architectural Review* 135 (May 1964): 332, quoted in Rohan, "Canon and Anti-Canon," 24.

178. Paul Rudolph, "Enigmas of Architecture," *A+U* 80 (1977): 318, cited in Timothy Rohan, "Rendering the Surface: Paul Rudolph's Art and Architecture Building at Yale," *Grey Room* 1 (fall 2000): 84–107.

179. This similarity was first noted by Reyner Banham, who wrote, "It is one of the very few buildings I know which, when photographed, was exactly like a drawing, with all the shadings on the outside coming out as if it were ruled in with a very soft pencil"; Reyner Banham, "Convenient Benches and Handy Hooks: Functional Considerations in the Criticism of the Art of Architecture," in *The History, Theory and Criticism of Architecture, Papers from the 1964 AIA-ACSA Teacher Seminar* (Cambridge, Mass.: MIT Press, 1965), 102, cited

in Rohan, "Rendering the Surface," 87.

180. Scully, "Art and Architecture Building," 326.

181. Paul Rudolph quoted in "A&A, Yale School of Art and Architecture," *Progressive Architecture* 45 (February 1964): 113.

182. Paul Rudolph, interview by C. Ray Smith, February 27, 1978, C. Ray Smith Manuscript and Research Files.

183. Charles Jencks, "Esprit Nouveau est Mort à New Haven or Meaningless Architecture," *Connection* (January 24, 1964): 15–20.

184. Robert A. M. Stern quoted in Victoria Partridge, Sarah Lavery, and Jessica Russell, eds., *Retrospecta 2000–2001* (New Haven: Yale School of Architecture, 2001), 148.

185. Rohan, "Canon and Anti-Canon," 24–32.

186. Phyllis Rosenblatt quoted in "Painters, Sculptors Find New Building Lacks Functionally," *Yale Daily News,* November 9, 1963.

187. Paul Rudolph, interview by C. Ray Smith, February 27, 1978.

188. Sasha M. Newman, "The Yale School of Art: Tradition Reconstituted," in *Yale Collects Yale,* ed. Sasha M. Newman and Lesley K. Baier (New Haven: Yale University Art Gallery, 1993), 65.

189. Paul Rudolph quoted in Mark W. Foster, "Paul M. Rudolph: Brushing Teeth," *Yale Daily News,* November 8, 1963, 7–8.

190. Ada Louise Huxtable, "Winner at Yale: The New Art and Architecture Building Lives Up to Great Expectations," *New York Times,* November 10, 1963, X19; Ada Louise Huxtable, "Yale to Dedicate 3D New Building," *New York Times,* November 9, 1963, 15; Leon Messier, "Art, Architecture Center Dedicated Today by Yale," *Hartford Courant,* November 9, 1963, 9C.

191. Peter Blake quoted in "Critical Comments on A&A," *Yale Daily News,* November 8, 1963.

192. Jan C. Rowan, "Editorial," *Progressive Architecture* 45 (February 1964): 107, quoted by Tom McDonough, "The Surface as Stake: A Postscript to Timothy M. Rohan's 'Rendering the Surface,'" *Grey Room* 5 (Autumn 2001): 102–11.

193. Scully, "Art and Architecture Building," 324–32.

194. Paul Rudolph, interview by C. Ray Smith, February 27, 1978.

195. Nikolaus Pevsner, "Address Given by Nikolaus Pevsner at the Inauguration of the New Art and Architecture Building of Yale University, 9 November 1963," *Journal of the Society of Architectural Historians* 26 (March 1967): 4–7.

196. Ibid.

197. M. J. Long quoted in Girouard, *Big Jim,* 126.

198. Vincent Scully, interview by Jimmy Stamp, August 23, 2010.

199. Robert Mittelstadt to Robert A. M. Stern, 28 March 1974, Reminiscences and Documentation of Yale University Architecture Students Collected by Robert A. M. Stern, 1970–1974, RU-1001, box 2, folder 58, Yale University Manuscripts and Archives, New Haven.

200. For the Fremont Civic Center, see Robert A. M. Stern, "Some Notes on the New '40 under 40,'" in "40 under 40" (special issue), *A+U: Architecture and Urbanism* 73 (January 1977): 49–69, republished in Stern, *Architecture on the Edge,* 86–87.

201. M. J. Long, interview by Jimmy Stamp, November 9, 2012.

202. M. J. Long to Richard Hayes, in Richard W. Hayes, *The Yale Building Project: The First 40 Years* (New Haven: Yale School of Architecture, with Yale University Press, 2007), 28n22.

203. Peter J. Hoppner quoted in Stern, "Notes on the New," 55.

204. "Op, Pop, and Color," *Progressive Architecture* (November 1965): 143–48.

205. Charles Brewer, interview by Jimmy Stamp, August 10, 2012. David Sellers, "Architecture as Culture and Counterculture" (William C. DeVane Lecture, Yale School of Architecture, New Haven, November 5, 2001), Guide to the Yale School of Architecture Lectures and Presentations, RU-880, accn. 2002-A-151, box 14, Yale University Manuscripts and Archives, New Haven.

206. David Sellers to Robert A. M. Stern, March 1974, Reminiscences and Documentation of Yale University Architecture Students Collected by Robert A. M. Stern, 1970–1974, RU-1001, box 3, folder 83, Yale University Manuscripts and Archives, New Haven. Chris Argyris, a professor of industrial administration at Yale, studied the studio teaching and jury review process from the point of view of social interaction and conditioning before going on to a distinguished career on the faculty of the Harvard Business School; William H. Woody, Jr. (1936–1988; B.A. 1958, M.A. 1960), was a charismatic art-history graduate student intensely involved in contemporary art. The interior of his highly idiosyncratic New Haven apartment was featured in the *New York Times* writer Barbara Plumb's book *Young Designs in Living* (Worthing, West Sussex, Eng.: Littlehampton, 1969).

207. Sellers, "Architecture as Culture."

208. David Sellers to Robert A. M. Stern, March 1974, Reminiscences and Documentation of Yale University Architecture Students Collected by Robert A. M. Stern, 1970–1974, RU-1001, box 3, folder 83, Yale

University Manuscripts and Archives, New Haven.

209. Vincent Scully, "Architecture: David Sellers," *Architectural Digest* (June 1987): 149–51, 220, 222.

210. For more on the Prickly Mountain houses, see "2 Architects Put Plans into Action," *New York Times,* January 30, 1966, R1; C. Ray Smith, "Architecture Swings, Like a Pendulum Do," *Progressive Architecture* (May 1966): 150–57; and "Three Houses, Three Generations," *Progressive Architecture* (November 1967): 104, 106–11; for Magee, see Sidney Magee, *Pickens* (Eugene, Ore., 2013).

211. David Sellers quoted in Smith, "Architecture Swings," 150.

212. Charles Brewer, interview by Jimmy Stamp, August 10, 2012.

213. F. Kapler, "Tree-House, Ski House," *Life,* March 24, 1967, 84–87.

214. David Sellers quoted in Scully, "Architecture: David Sellers," 149–51, 220, 222.

215. For Gluck's project, see Robert A. M. Stern, Thomas Mellins, and David Fishman, eds., *New York 1960: Architecture and Urbanism between the Second World War and the Bicentennial* (New York: Monacelli, 1995); for more on Gluck, see Kirkpatrick MacDonald, ed., *Yale University Class of 1962, 25th Yearbook* (New Haven: Yale University, 1987); see also Oscar Riera Ojeda, ed., *Peter L. Gluck and Partners: The Modern Impulse* (San Rafael, Calif.: Oro, 2008).

216. Paul Rudolph quoted in James Adams, "Head Architect to Leave Yale for Own Firm," *Yale Daily News,* September 21, 1964.

217. Kingman Brewster quoted in ibid.

218. Paul Rudolph to Kingman Brewster, 30 July 1964, Kingman Brewster Jr. Presidential Records, ser. 1, RU-11, box 25, folder 2, Yale University Manuscripts and

Archives, New Haven.

219. August Heckscher to Kingman Brewster, 24 September 1964, in ibid.

220. Peter Blake to Kingman Brewster, 30 September 1964, in ibid.

221. Kingman Brewster to Peter Blake, 10 October 1964, in ibid.

222. Herman D. J. Spiegel to Kingman Brewster, 29 September 1964, in ibid.

223. Sibyl Moholy-Nagy to Kingman Brewster, 16 November 1964, in ibid.

224. Serge Chermayeff, memo to Kingman Brewster, 2 April 1965, in ibid.; for Passonneau, see his personal memoir in Eric Mumford, ed., *Modern Architecture in St. Louis: Washington University and Postwar American Architecture, 1948–1973* (St. Louis: Washington University School of Architecture, 2004), 71–79.

225. Carroll L. V. Meeks to Kingman Brewster, 16 October 1964, Kingman Brewster Jr. Presidential Records, ser. 1, RU-11, box 25, folder 2, Yale University Manuscripts and Archives, New Haven.

226. Donald Metz, David Sellers, John I. Pearce, and William Mason Smith III to Brewster, 19 October 1964, in ibid.

227. Robert Venturi, "Complexity and Contradiction in Architecture: Selections from a Forthcoming Book," *Perspecta: The Yale Architectural Journal* 9/10 (1965): 17–56; Robert Venturi, *Complexity and Contradiction in Architecture* (New York: Museum of Modern Art and Graham Foundation, 1966).

228. See Vincent Scully, "New Talent USA: Architecture," *Art in America* 49 (1961): 63.

229. Vincent Scully, interview by Jimmy Stamp, August 23, 2010.

230. Vincent Scully to Kingman Brewster, 5 January 1965, Kingman Brewster Jr.

Presidential Records, ser. 1, RU-11, box 25, folder 3, Yale University Manuscripts and Archives, New Haven; Scully was referring to a talk based on Searing's Ph.D. dissertation, "Housing in Holland and the Amsterdam School" (1971), that she was slated to give at the annual meeting of the College Art Association, to be held in Los Angeles.

231. Esther McCoy to Kingman Brewster, 18 December 1964, Kingman Brewster Jr. Presidential Records, ser. 1, RU-11, box 25, folder 3, Yale University Manuscripts and Archives, New Haven.

232. Thomas R. Vreeland, Jr., to Kingman Brewster, 20 December 1964, in ibid.

233. Robert M. Kliment to Kingman Brewster, 9 January 1965, in ibid.

234. Robert Venturi to Kingman Brewster, 27 November 1964, in ibid.

235. Kingman Brewster to Robert Venturi, 19 February 1965, in ibid. Denise Scott Brown recalls the events slightly differently and mixes up the date. "I believe it was in 1966 that Bob turned down an invitation to be Dean at Yale. He felt he could not divide his time between practice and academe and do well by either"; Denise Scott Brown to Jimmy Stamp, 30 July 2010.

236. Robert A. M. Stern, interview by Jimmy Stamp, June 1, 2010.

237. Before leaving for an extended trip to Jamaica, an ailing Carroll Meeks called Brewster to express his revised views, which did not include Giurgola: "Barnes—splendid; Venturi—question mark; Smithson—no; Christ-Janer—terrible; Franzen—possible." Carroll Meeks, memo of telephone conversation forwarded to Kingman Brewster, 14 January 1965, Kingman Brewster Jr.

Presidential Records, ser. 1, RU-11, box 25, Yale University Manuscripts and Archives, New Haven.

238. Vincent Scully to Kingman Brewster, 8 February 1965, Kingman Brewster Jr. Presidential Records, ser. 1, RU-11, box 25, folder 3, Yale University Manuscripts and Archives, New Haven.

239. Peter Millard, undated memo to Kingman Brewster (received by president's office 23 February 1965), in ibid.

240. George A. Dudley to Kingman Brewster, 10 March 1965, in ibid.

241. Serge Chermayeff, memo to Kingman Brewster, 2 April 1965, Kingman Brewster Jr. Presidential Records, ser. 1, RU-11, box 25, folder 2, Yale University Manuscripts and Archives, New Haven; for Pevsner's censure, see his article, "Modern Architecture and the Historian or the Return of Historicism," *JRIBA* 68, no. 6 (April 1961): 230–40; for Passonneau, see his personal memoir in Mumford, *Modern Architecture in St. Louis,* 71–79.

242. For Giurgola's impact at Columbia, see Oliver, "History VI," 11.

243. Charles Moore, unpublished interview by C. Ray Smith, May 11, 1980, C. Ray Smith Manuscript and Research Files.

5

Architecture or Revolution?

Epigraph. *Bulletin of Yale University,* School of Art and Architecture, 1966–67 ser. 63, no. 1 (January 1, 1967), 19.

1. Charles Moore, "You Have to Pay for the Public Life," *Perspecta: The Yale Architectural Journal* 9/10 (1965): 57–97.

2. Eve Blau, "Architecture or Revolution: Charles Moore and Yale in the Late 1960s," in *Architecture or Revolution: Charles Moore and Yale in the Late 1960s,* exh. cat. (New Haven: Yale School of Architecture, 2000).

3. Charles Moore, interview by Sally Woodbridge, December 28, 1984, 10, California History Project, Archives of American Art, Smithsonian Institution.

4. Ibid., 36.

5. Ibid., 40.

6. Ibid., 44.

7. Ibid., 10.

8. Herb Caen, "Big Wide Wonderful Whirl," *San Francisco Chronicle,* July 1, 1965; see also Charles Moore, interview by Sally Woodbridge, December 28, 1984, 59.

9. David Littlejohn, *Architect: The Life and Work of Charles W. Moore* (New York: Holt, Rinehart, and Winston, 1984), 149.

10. Charles Moore quoted in ibid.

11. Charles Moore, interview by Sally Woodbridge, December 28, 1984, 59; since 1902, the master of arts degree has been awarded privatim to tenured faculty, university officers, and Yale Corporation fellows who do not already hold a master of arts or Ph.D. degree from Yale.

12. Charles Moore quoted in Littlejohn, *Architect,* 95.

13. William Turnbull quoted by Charles Moore in ibid., 95–96.

14. Turnbull quoted in ibid., 96.

15. Ibid., 231.

16. For Moore's New Haven residence, see "The Designers," *Progressive Architecture* (May 1967): 158–60; Robert A. M. Stern, *New Directions in American Architecture* (New York: Braziller, 1969), 76–77; "New Haven Haven," *Playboy,* October 1969, 126–29; "Moore House (Renovation), New Haven, Connecticut, 1966," *Architecture and Urbanism* 5 (1978): 298–99, 306–11; Charles Willard Moore, Gerald Allen, and Donlyn Lyndon, eds., *The Place of Houses* (New York: Holt, Rinehart, and Winston, 1974), 61–63; and Jorge Otero-Pailos, *Architecture's Historical Turn: Phenomenology and the Rise of the Postmodern* (Minneapolis: University of Minnesota Press, 2010), 129–31.

17. Mark Simon, William C. DeVane seminar, Yale School of Architecture, New Haven, October 30, 2001, School of Architecture, Yale University, lectures and presentations, RU-880, accn. 2002-A-151, Manuscripts and Archives, Yale University, New Haven.

18. Moore Lyndon Turnbull Whitaker (MLTW) eventually became Turnbull Griffin Haesloop Architects. While in New Haven and, subsequently, Centerbrook, Connecticut, Moore's office changed names several times, from MLTW to Moore/Turnbull to Charles W. Moore Associates to Moore Grover Harper, ultimately becoming Centerbrook Architects once Moore left Yale. When Moore settled in Los Angeles as a member of the UCLA faculty, he began working with the Urban Innovations Group and also started a new practice, Moore Ruble Yudell. In 1984, Moore relocated to Austin, Texas, where he started Moore/Andersson Architects, known today as Andersson-Wise.

19. Joan Ockman, "Introduction," in *Architecture School: Three Centuries of Educating Architects in North America,* ed. Joan Ockman (Washington, D.C.: Association of Collegiate Schools of Architecture; Cambridge, Mass.: MIT Press,

2012), 94.

20. Charles Moore, "Personal Commentary," 30 June 1966, appended to the dean's Annual Report, 1965–1966, Records of the Dean of the School of Architecture, RU-843, accn. 2007-A-193, box 13, Yale University Manuscripts and Archives, New Haven.

21. Charles Moore, interview by Sally Woodbridge, December 28, 1984, 61–62.

22. Moore, "Personal Commentary."

23. Charles Moore quoted in Littlejohn, *Architect*, 151.

24. "Information and Agitation. November 16, 1966. A Meeting between Students and Faculty," 16 November 1966, King-lui Wu Archives, MS-1842, box 1, Yale University Manuscripts and Archives, New Haven.

25. Robert Cohen and Reginald E. Zelnik, eds., *The Free Speech Movement: Reflections on Berkeley in the 1960s* (Berkeley: University of California Press, 2002).

26. Blau, "Architecture or Revolution."

27. Yale University News Bureau, press release no. 61, September 26, 1967, Yale University News Releases, Y91+A2, vol. 1967/68, Yale University Manuscripts and Archives, New Haven.

28. Gibson A. Danes and Charles Moore to Provost Charles Taylor, 23 May 1966, Kingman Brewster Jr. Presidential Records, ser. 1, RU-11, box 25, folder 1, Yale University Manuscripts and Archives, New Haven.

29. Charles Moore quoted in Yale University News Bureau, press release, September 27, 1967.

30. Gibson A. Danes and Charles Moore to Provost Charles Taylor, 23 May 1966, Kingman Brewster Jr. Presidential Records, ser. 1, RU-11, box 25, folder 1, Yale University Manuscripts and Archives,

New Haven.

31. Ibid.

32. Yale University News Bureau, press release no. 61, September 26, 1967, Yale University News Releases, Y91+A2, vol. 1967/68, Yale University Manuscripts and Archives, New Haven. Yale's embrace of environmental studies and the reconfiguration of its degree programs reflected similar changes at UCLA, where George Dudley was serving as the founding dean (1965–68) of the School of Architecture and Urban Planning. See Ada Louise Huxtable, "Revamping Architectural Education Being Pressed in Nation," *New York Times*, February 20, 1966, 77.

33. Moore quoted in Yale University News Bureau, press release, September 27, 1967.

34. Don Watson, interview by Jimmy Stamp, November 12, 2010.

35. For Kaskey, see Gideon Bosker, "Long-Awaited Portlandia in Place on Portland Building," *Architecture: The AIA Journal* 74 (December 1985): 20, 22; Stephen R. Brown, *World War II Memorial: Jewel of the Mall* (self-published, 1985); and Sam Lubell, "National World War II Memorial Opens in Washington, *Architectural Record* (June 2004): 56.

36. Donald Watson, interview by Jimmy Stamp, November 12, 2010.

37. Charles Moore quoted in Littlejohn, *Architect*, 150.

38. Yale Faculty Evaluations, Collection D: Yale University, 1959–1984, undated, box C7, the Charles W. Moore Archives: Faculty Papers, Alexander Architectural Archive, University of Texas Libraries, the University of Texas at Austin.

39. Turner Brooks, interview by Jimmy Stamp, July 21, 2010.

40. Charles Moore quoted in Littlejohn, *Architect*, 152.

41. An unidentified contributor to *Novum Organum*, quoted in Kevin Keim and Charles Moore, *An Architectural Life: Memoirs and Memories of Charles Moore* (Boston: Little, Brown, 1996), 112.

42. Donald Watson, interview by Jimmy Stamp, November 12, 2010.

43. Mitchell's books on digital media include *City of Bits* (Cambridge, Mass.: MIT Press, 1995), *Me++: The Cyborg and the Networked City* (Cambridge, Mass.: MIT Press, 2003), and *Placing Words: Symbols, Space, and the City* (Cambridge, Mass.: MIT Press, 2005).

44. William Mitchell quoted in Keim and Moore, *Architectural Life*, 120–21.

45. William Mitchell, "Imagining Digital Culture" (unpublished lecture delivered during the Yale symposium "Architecture or Revolution: Charles Moore and Yale in the late 1960s" [2001], New Haven), School of Architecture Records Concerning Events and Exhibitions, RU-886, Yale University Manuscripts and Archives, New Haven.

46. William Mitchell quoted in Keim and Moore, *Architectural Life*, 120–21.

47. "New Organ," *Yale Daily News*, November 19, 1968; Richard Solomon, "The Perfect Mess," *Novum Organum* 5 (1969).

48. Conrad Hamann, with Michael Anderson and Winsome Callister, *Cities of Hope: Australian Architecture and Design by Edmond and Corrigan, 1962* (Oxford: Oxford University Press, 1993), 31.

49. The sketches are reproduced in *The Louis I. Kahn Archive*, vol. 6 (New York: Garland, 1987).

50. Hamann, Anderson, and Callister, *Cities of Hope*, 33.

51. Paul Taylor, "Famed Innovator R. Buckminster Fuller Arrives Here Today," *Yale Daily*

News, October 21, 1968; Tom Andersen, "Buckminster Fuller Returns," *Yale Daily News,* January 29, 1969.

52. See Sam Davis, *The Architecture of Affordable Housing* (Berkeley: University of California Press, 1995); Sam Davis, *Designing for the Homeless: Architecture That Works* (Berkeley: University of California Press, 2004).

53. For Landmark and the infamous photograph, see Louis P. Masur, *The Soiling of Old Glory: The Story of a Photograph That Shocked America* (New York: Bloomsbury, 2008).

54. Donald Watson, interview by Jimmy Stamp, November 12, 2010, in New Haven; master of environmental design theses can be found in the Yale University Manuscripts and Archives under Art, Architecture, and Art History Theses and Projects, Yale University, RU-259, Yale University Manuscripts and Archives, New Haven.

55. See Blair Kamin, *Terror and Wonder: Architecture in a Tumultuous Age* (Chicago: University of Chicago Press, 2010).

56. Larry Wayne Richards quoted in *Suspecta: Advanced Studies* (New Haven: Yale School of Architecture, 1994), 19.

57. Donald Watson, "History of the M.E.D. Program," n.d. [c. 1999], courtesy Donald Watson.

58. Eeva-Liisa Pelkonen, *Achtung Architektur!: Image and Phantasm in Contemporary Austrian Architecture* (Cambridge, Mass.: MIT Press, 1996).

59. Gibson A. Danes, "A Report from the Dean," *Eye: Magazine of the Yale Arts Association,* no. 1 (1967): 26–27.

60. Barton Phelps, interview by Jimmy Stamp, April 17, 2013.

61. John Jacobson, interview by Jimmy Stamp, April 18, 2013.

62. For an account of the early

history of the field, see William J. Mitchell, *Computer-Aided Architectural Design* (New York: Van Nostrand Reinhold, 1977).

63. Witold Rybczynski, "Lost Amid the Algorithms," *Architect* (June 2013): 150, 152, 154, 156, 158.

64. Murray Milne, ed., *Computer Graphics in Architecture and Design* (New Haven: Yale School of Art and Architecture, 1969), the proceedings of the "Yale Conference on Computer Graphics in Architecture."

65. Charles Moore quoted in Yale University News Bureau, press release, March 13, 1968.

66. Charles Moore quoted in Joseph G. Herzberg, "Architects Open Computer Dialog," *New York Times,* April 28, 1968, R1.

67. Louis I. Kahn quoted in ibid.

68. Luis Summers's ideas are restated in Yale University News Bureau, press release, March 14, 1968.

69. Nicholas Negroponte quoted in Herzberg, "Architects Open Computer Dialog."

70. See Jay Hambidge, *The Parthenon and Other Greek Temples: Their Dynamic Symmetry* (New Haven: Yale University Press, 1924).

71. Warren McCulloch, "Panel Discussion: The Past and the Future of Design by Computer," in Milne, *Computer Graphics,* 101–3.

72. Mitchell, "Imagining Digital Culture"; Mitchell quotes Steven Coons in Milne, *Computer Graphics,* 100.

73. Mitchell, "Imagining Digital Culture."

74. Charles Moore, "Panel Discussion: The Past and the Future of Design by Computer," in Milne, *Computer Graphics,* 97.

75. Mitchell, "Imagining Digital Culture"; Steven A. Coons, "Panel Discussion: The Past and the Future of Design by

Computer," in Milne, *Computer Graphics,* 100.

76. Mitchell, "Imagining Digital Culture."

77. Ibid.

78. Raymond J. Matela, "An Analysis of the Animals of Architecture: A Complete Enumeration of Polyominoes by Some of Their Architectural Properties" (master's thesis, Yale School of Architecture, 1974), Yale University Art, Architecture, and Art History Theses and Projects, RU-259, ser. III, box 11, folder 178–180, Yale University Manuscripts and Archives, New Haven.

79. Hanna Shapira, "A Procedure for Generating Floor Plans: Computer-Aided Design" (master's thesis, Yale School of Architecture, 1974), Yale University Art, Architecture, and Art History Theses and Projects, RU-259, ser. IV, box 1, folder 3, Yale University Manuscripts and Archives, New Haven; see also Hanna Shapira and Robert S. Frew, "A Procedure for Generating Floor Plans: Computer-Aided Design," in *Proceedings of the 11th Design Automation Workshop* (Piscataway, N.J.: IEEE, 1974), 229–36.

80. Michael Benedikt, "The Information Field: A Theoretical and Empirical Approach to the Distribution and Transfer of Information in the Physical Environment" (master's thesis, Yale School of Architecture, 1975), Yale University Art, Architecture, and Art History Theses and Projects, RU-259, ser. III, box 3, folder 11, Yale University Manuscripts and Archives, New Haven; see also, Michael Benedikt, *For an Architecture of Reality* (Santa Fe: Lumen, 1987); and Michael Benedikt, *Cyberspace: First Steps* (Cambridge, Mass.: MIT Press, 1992).

81. Donald Watson, interview by Jimmy Stamp, November 12,

2010, New Haven.

82. *Bulletin of Yale University, School of Art and Architecture, 1972–73* ser. 68, no. 10 (May 15, 1972), 29–30.

83. Charles Jencks, *The Language of Post-Modern Architecture*, 1st ed. (New York: Rizzoli, 1977). In 1967, Chermayeff offered a proposal on how the school should move forward during a period of transition that was occurring during Moore's tenure. See Serge Chermayeff, "Collage of Concern," *Eye: Magazine of the Yale Arts Association*, no. 1 (1967): 20.

84. Serge Chermayeff, "Open Letter to the Editors," May 5, 1965, Avery Library, Columbia University, New York, N.Y., quoted in Alan Powers, *Serge Chermayeff: Designer, Architect, Teacher* (London: RIBA, 2001), 213.

85. See Chermayeff, "Collage of Concern," 20–24; and Alexander Tzonis, "Serge Chermayeff, Humanist," *Spazio e Società* 79 (July/September, 1997): 21, quoted in Powers, *Serge Chermayeff*, 210.

86. Tzonis, "Serge Chermayeff, Humanist," 23, quoted in Powers, *Serge Chermayeff*, 210; for Webber, see his influential paper, "The Urban Place and the Non-Place Urban Realm," in *Explorations into Urban Structure*, ed. Melvin Webber (Philadelphia: University of Pennsylvania Press, June 1964); Melvin Webber, "A Different Paradigm for Planning," in *Planning Theory in the 1980s: A Search for Future Directions*, ed. Robert Burchell and George Sternlieb (New Brunswick, N.J.: Center for Urban Policy Research, Rutgers University, 1978); and Melvin Webber, "The Joys of Automobility," in *The Car and the City*, ed. Margaret Crawford and Martin Wachs (Ann Arbor: University of Michigan Press, 1991).

87. Donald Watson, interview by Jimmy Stamp, November 12, 2010; John McHale (1922–1978) was an artist, sociologist, and founding member of the Independent Group, the collection of artists, architects, writers, and scholars who are considered by many to be the founders of Pop art. Other key members were Alison and Peter Smithson, Reyner Banham, and Richard Hamilton. René DuBos (1901–1982) was a French-born microbiologist whose pioneering work in the 1940s paved the way for antibiotics. DuBos was also an early champion of environmentalism and is perhaps best known for popularizing the phrase "Think globally, act locally."

88. Serge Chermayeff and Alexander Tzonis, *Shape of Community: Realization of Human Potential* (Harmondsworth, Eng.: Penguin, 1971), quoted in Powers, *Serge Chermayeff*, 213.

89. Ibid.

90. Chermayeff and Tzonis, *Shape of Community*.

91. Chermayeff and Tzonis, *Shape of Community*, 177, quoted in Powers, *Serge Chermayeff*, 215.

92. George O'Brien, "Designed for Privacy," *New York Times Magazine*, September 13, 1964, 116–19.

93. Alexander Tzonis, dedication, *Perspecta: The Yale Architectural Journal* 12 (1969): 5; one of Chermayeff's final lectures, in which he expressed the hope that students would continue his work, was published as "Serge Chermayeff: Urban Commitments," *Novum Organum* 3 (January 6, 1969).

94. William Deresiewicz, Garrett Finney (B.A. 1986, M.Arch 1990), Sam Kirby (b. 1961; M.Arch 1990), Clay Miller (M.Arch 1990), David Comberg (M.F.A. 1994), and Thomas Starr (M.F.A.1994), "Into the Fire," *Perspecta: The Yale Architectural Journal* 29 (1998): xiii.

95. Kent Bloomer quoted in Keim and Moore, *Architectural Life*, 117.

96. Sibyl Moholy-Nagy, ed., *The Architecture of Paul Rudolph*, with comments from Paul Rudolph (New York: Praeger, 1970), 16.

97. "Award: Vacation House on the Coast of Maine Is Poised Lightly on Its Rocky Setting," *Progressive Architecture* (January 1969): 121–22; for the Mount Desert Island house, see "Klema Residence: Habidu at Seal Harbor," *Progressive Architecture* (May 1971): 72–75; for the Commons Dining Hall, see "Record Interiors of 1971," *Architectural Record* 149 (January 1971): 100–101.

98. Kent Bloomer quoted in Keim and Moore, *Architectural Life*, 117.

99. Unnamed student quoted in Alberto Lau, "Venturi, Stirling Appointed Professors of Architecture," *Yale Daily News*, March 16, 1966.

100. Paul Goldberger quoted in Keim and Moore, *Architectural Life*, 116.

101. Kent Bloomer quoted in ibid., 111–12.

102. Ibid., 118.

103. Ray Gindroz, interview by Jimmy Stamp, July 10, 2012.

104. Charles Moore, "Chairman's Report," *Eye: Magazine of the Yale Arts Association*, no. 1 (1967): 29.

105. For Moore's Church Street South, see "Low-Moderate Baroque," *Progressive Architecture* (May 1972): 74–83.

106. Kent Bloomer quoted in Keim and Moore, *Architectural Life*, 117.

107. Charles Moore, A Report on the Faculties of Design and Planning, 1969–1970, 1970, Records of the Dean of the School of Architecture, RU-843, accn. 2007-A-193, box 13, Yale University Manuscripts and Archives, New Haven.

108. Ibid.
109. Kent Bloomer and Charles Moore, *Body, Memory, and Architecture* (New Haven: Yale University Press, 1977); Charles Moore quoted in Littlejohn, *Architect*, 154.
110. F. Andrus Burr, "Learning under Moore," *GA Houses: Charles Moore and Company*, no. 7 (1980): 173–79.
111. Craig Hodgetts, interview by Jimmy Stamp, October 6, 2012.
112. Heather Willson Cass, interview by Jimmy Stamp, December 17, 2012.
113. Ibid.
114. Ray Gindroz, interview by Jimmy Stamp, July 10, 2012.
115. Jen Renzi, "Modern à la Mode," *Wall Street Journal*, August 3–4, 2013, D9.
116. Stuart Wrede, "Revisiting 1968–69: On *Novum Organum* and *Lipstick (Ascending on Caterpillar Tracks)*," *Perspecta; The Yale Architectural Journal* 44 (2011): 128–35.
117. Charles Moore, Annual Report of the Faculties of Design and Planning: To the President and Fellows of Yale University for the Academic Year 1967–1968, 1968, RU-843, accn. 2007-A-193, box 13, Yale University Manuscripts and Archives, New Haven.
118. Yale Faculty Evaluations, Collection D: Yale University, 1959–1984, undated, box C7, the Charles W. Moore Archives.
119. Ibid.
120. For the history of the Building Project, see Richard W. Hayes, *The Yale Building Project: The First 40 Years* (New Haven: Yale School of Architecture, with Yale University Press, 2007).
121. Group 9 included Carey, Edwins, and Swenson, along with Peter Hentschel (M.Arch 1969), Bob Kurzon (M.Arch 1969), Bill Richardson (M.Arch 1969), Paul Thompson (M.Arch 1969), Larry White (M.Arch 1970), and Dave Hoeffner.
122. Hayes, *Yale Building Project*, 17.
123. Moore, "Personal Commentary."
124. Alberto Lau, "New Zion Community Center: A New Experience in Architectural Education," *Progressive Architecture* 48 (September 1967): 167, quoted in Hayes, *Yale Building Project*, 18.
125. Burr, "Learning under Moore," 173–79.
126. John Jacobson, interview by Jimmy Stamp, April 18, 2013.
127. Tom Carey quoted in Keim and Moore, *Architectural Life*, 117, cited in Hayes, *Yale Building Project*, 16.
128. Mark Ellis, "Yale Goes to Kentucky: An Account of the Lower Grassy Trace Branch Community Center Project," *Interiors* (December 1968): 137, quoted in Hayes, *Yale Building Project*, 22.
129. Burr, "Learning under Moore," 173–79.
130. Hayes, *Yale Building Project*, 23.
131. Charles W. Moore, "The Project at New Zion: Interaction and Building," *Eye: Magazine of the Yale Arts Association*, no. 2 (1967): 19.
132. "Education for Alienation," *Novum Organum* 1 (November 14, 1968): 1; Rob Hamnell, "Empirical Efficiency Analysis of a Typical Workday in Lower Grassy, Kentucky," *Novum Organum* 2 (December 3, 1968).
133. "Out of the Atelier and into Reality," *Progressive Architecture* (September 1967): 166–69.
134. Turner Brooks, *Turner Brooks: Work* (New York: Princeton Architectural Press, 1995); Mark Alden Branch, "Racing by Design," *Yale Alumni Magazine*, April 2001.
135. Peter Woerner, *Peter Kurt Woerner, Architect+Builder: Buildings+Projects, 1968–2004* (New Haven: 9 Square, 2004).
136. "Paul Brouard Retires," *Constructs* (fall 2014): 13.
137. Charles Moore quoted in Keim and Moore, *Architectural Life*, 122.
138. Peter Rose quoted in William Morgan, ed., *Peter Rose: Houses* (New York: Princeton Architectural Press, 2010), 12.
139. Peter Rose, William C. DeVane seminar, Yale School of Architecture, New Haven, October 30, 2001, School of Architecture, Yale University, lectures and presentations, RU-880, accn. 2002-A-151, Manuscripts and Archives, Yale University, New Haven.
140. Ibid.; for Rose's professional work, see Lauren Nelson-Packard, ed., *Peter Rose: Houses* (New York: Princeton Architectural Press, 2010).
141. Kent Bloomer, William C. DeVane seminar, Yale School of Architecture, New Haven, October 30, 2001, School of Architecture, Yale University, lectures and presentations, RU-880, accn. 2002-A-151, Manuscripts and Archives, Yale University, New Haven; J. B. Jackson (1909–1996) was an essayist, cultural geographer, and founder and editor of the journal *Landscape*. As an advocate for and theorist of the American landscape and built environment, he is credited with popularizing the term "cultural landscape." See J. B. Jackson, *Discovering the Vernacular Landscape* (New Haven: Yale University Press, 1984); J. B. Jackson, *The Essential Landscape: The New Mexico Photographic Survey* (Albuquerque: University of New Mexico Press, 1985); and J. B. Jackson, *A Sense of Place, a Sense of Time* (New Haven: Yale University Press, 1994).
142. Burr, "Learning under Moore," 176.
143. Ibid.
144. Ibid.
145. See "Nostalgie du chateau: Pavillon Soixante-dix, St. Sauveur, Quebec, Canada," *Progressive Architecture* (March 1979): 70–75.
146. Dan Cooper, ed., *New Classic American Houses: The*

Architecture of Albert, Righter and Tittmann (New York: Vendome, 2009).

147. Daniel Scully, William C. DeVane seminar, Yale School of Architecture, New Haven, October 30, 2001, School of Architecture, Yale University, lectures and presentations, RU-880, accn. 2002-A-151, Manuscripts and Archives, Yale University, New Haven.

148. See "Cook House, Ticonderoga, New York," *GA Houses* 7 (1980): 218–21; "Scully House, Dublin, New Hampshire," *GA Houses* (July 1990): 144–47.

149. Robert Yudell quoted in Alexandra Lange, "Why Charles Moore (Still) Matters," *Metropolis* (May 2014): 90.

150. Craig Hodgetts, interview by Jimmy Stamp, October 6, 2012.

151. Hayes, *Yale Building Project*, 36; Gerald Allen, "Editorial Statement," *Sensus* 1 (December 1970); "Projects," *Sensus* 1 (December 1970); see also David Gibson, "Vacation House in Colorado," *Sensus* 1 (November 1970).

152. "Projects Statement," *Sensus* 1 (December 1970).

153. Burr, "Learning under Moore," 173–79.

154. Daniel Scully, e-mail message to Jimmy Stamp, May 18, 2014; for the original University Theatre building, see Patrick Pinnell, *The Campus Guide: Yale University* (New York: Princeton Architectural Press, 1999), 53–54.

155. Robert Brustein quoted in Hayes, *Yale Building Project*, 26.

156. See Robert Brustein, *Making Scenes: A Personal History of the Turbulent Years at Yale 1966–1979* (New York: Random House, 1981), 70, cited in Hayes, *Yale Building Project*, 112.

157. Daniel Scully, e-mail message to Jimmy Stamp, May 14, 2014.

158. Turner Brooks, interview by Jimmy Stamp, July 21, 2010.

159. Manfred Ibel, "Experimental Houses for Squirrels," *Novum Organum* (November 14, 1968); "Blow Me a House in Two Days," *Vogue*, October 15, 1969, 139–43. In *Sensus*, 1 (November 1970), Susan St. John and Jeremiah Whitney reported on a 2,200-square-foot foam weekend house realized for a couple with the children in Newfane, Vermont; Felix Drury would continue to work with the material in his professional practice, notably building a guest house for the West Point-Pepperell corporate headquarters in Langdale, Alabama; see "Foam Home," *Progressive Architecture* (May 1971): 100–103.

160. Greg Lynn and Mark Rappolt, eds., *Greg Lynn FORM* (New York: Rizzoli, 2008).

161. Felix Drury quoted in "The Free-Form World of Foam," *Yale Alumni Magazine*, October 1968, 54–57.

162. Ibel, "Experimental Houses for Squirrels." See also Herbert Short, "Post-Script," *Novum Organum* 2 (December 3, 1968).

163. Turner Brooks, interview by Jimmy Stamp, July 21, 2010.

164. Mark Simon, William C. DeVane seminar, Yale School of Architecture, New Haven, October 30, 2001, School of Architecture, Yale University, lectures and presentations, RU-880, accn. 2002-A-151, Manuscripts and Archives, Yale University, New Haven.

165. Barton Phelps, interview by Jimmy Stamp, April 17, 2013.

166. "Citation," *Progressive Architecture* (January 1967): 130–34.

167. For the New Haven Central Fire Station, see "P/A Eight Annual Design Awards," *Progressive Architecture* (July 1961): 132–35; for Millard and Carlin's design for the Whitney Avenue Fire Station, see "The Firehouse Next Door," *Progressive Architecture* (March 1964): 126–31; for a sense of Millard's approach, see Peter Millard, "Some Remarks on Architecture," *Perspecta: The Yale Architectural Journal* 9/10 (1965): 179–82.

168. Peter Millard, "Now and Then," *Perspecta: The Yale Architectural Journal* 11 (1967): 21.

169. Ibid.

170. Craig Hodgetts, interview by Jimmy Stamp, October 6, 2012.

171. Peter Millard, "Notes on Design," *Perspecta: The Yale Architectural Journal* 18 (1979): 196–203.

172. Pat Goeters, "The Patrician Hangup," *Perspecta: The Yale Architectural Journal* 12 (1969): 45–48.

173. Chris Argyris, "Interpersonal Barriers to Decision-Making," *Harvard Business Review* (March–April, 1966); Kai T. Erikson, *Wayward Puritans: A Study in the Sociology of Deviance* (New York: Wiley, 1966).

174. Argyris, "Interpersonal Barriers," quoted in Goeters, "Patrician Hangup," 45–48.

175. Yale University News Bureau, press release, May 14, 1965, Kingman Brewster Jr. Presidential Records, ser. 1, RU-11, box 25, folder 3, Yale University Manuscripts and Archives, New Haven.

176. Kingman Brewster to James Stirling, 19 April 1965, Kingman Brewster Jr. Presidential Records, ser. 1, RU-11, box 25, folder 1, Yale University Manuscripts and Archives, New Haven.

177. James Stirling to Kingman Brewster, 3 May 1965, in ibid.

178. Charles Moore quoted in Mark Girouard, *Big Jim: The Life and Work of James Stirling* (London: Pimlico, 2000), 127.

179. Charles Moore to Kingman Brewster, 11 January 1966, Kingman Brewster Jr. Presidential Records, ser. 1, RU-11, box 25, folder 10, Yale University Manuscripts and Archives, New Haven.

180. In 2004, Léon Krier was

Davenport Chair during the spring term, while Lynn served during the fall 2003 term.

181. Emmanuel Petit, *An Architect's Legacy: James Stirling's Students at Yale, 1959–1983* (New Haven: Yale School of Architecture, 2010).

182. Craig Hodgetts, interview by Jimmy Stamp, October 6, 2012; for Hauer, see Erwin Hauer, *Erwin Hauer: Continua– Architectural Screens and Walls* (New York: Princeton Architectural Press, 2004).

183. James Stirling, "Conversations with Students," *Perspecta: The Yale Architectural Journal* 11 (1967): 91–93, quoted in Petit, *Architect's Legacy.*

184. Stirling, "Conversation with Students," 91–93.

185. Girouard, *Big Jim,* 127.

186. Ibid., 27; for the West Midtown study, see Robert A. M. Stern, Thomas Mellins, and David Fishman, *New York 1960: Architecture and Urbanism between the Second World War and the Bicentennial* (New York: Monacelli, 1995), 313, 320.

187. Girouard, *Big Jim,* 27.

188. Martino Stierli, "Las Vegas Studio," in *Las Vegas Studio: Images from the Archives of Robert Venturi and Denise Scott Brown,* ed. Hilar Stadler and Martino Stierli (Zurich: Museum im Bellpark, Kriens, 2008), 30–31; for more on the legacy and interpretation of *Learning from Las Vegas,* see Aron Vinegar, *I Am a Monument: On Learning from Las Vegas* (Cambridge, Mass.: MIT Press, 2008).

189. Robert Venturi, Bruce Adams, and Denise Scott Brown, "Mass Communication on the People Freeway or Piranesi Is Too Easy," *Perspecta: The Yale Architectural Journal* 12 (1969): 49–56; Robert Venturi, Denise Scott Brown, and Steven Izenour, *Learning from Las Vegas: The Forgotten Symbolism of Architectural Form* (Cambridge, Mass.: MIT

Press, 1972). The Los Angeles– Las Vegas trip occurred in October 1968, but because the Las Vegas studio presentation and exhibition opening were held on January 10, 1969, the studio is frequently listed incorrectly as a spring studio.

190. See Eugenie L. Birch, "From CIAM to CNU: The Roots of Urban Design," in *Urban Design Companion,* ed. T. Banerjee, and A. Loukaitou- Sideris (London: Routledge: 2011), 21; see also Jonathan Barnett, *Urban Design as Public Policy: Practical Methods for Improving Cities* (New York: Architectural Record, 1974).

191. Robert Venturi, "Opening Statement," in Venturi, Adams, and Scott Brown, "Mass Communication," 49–56.

192. The other architects were: James Caldwell (B.A. 1964, M.Arch 1969), James Gage (M.Arch 1969), David Hoeffner, David Lessig (M.Arch 1969), Ali Ramazani (M.Arch 1969), Robert Swenson (M.Arch 1969), Paul Thompson (M.Arch 1969), and Lawrence White (B.A. 1965, M.Arch 1969).

193. Denise Scott Brown, "Program Extracts: Introduction and First Phase," in Venturi, Adams, and Brown, "Mass Communication," 50–51.

194. Denise Scott Brown, "Preface to the First Edition," in Venturi, Scott Brown, and Izenour, *Learning from Las Vegas,* xi; see also Donald Watson, "LLV, LLV:? VVV," *Novum Organum* 5 (1969).

195. Robert Venturi and Denise Scott Brown, "A Significance for A&P Parking Lots, or Learning from Las Vegas," *Architectural Forum* (March 1968): 37–43.

196. Robert Venturi to Las Vegas Mayor Oran K. Gragson, 20 August 1968, School of Art and Architecture, Yale University, Records RU-189,

accn. 2002-A-009, box 19, Yale University Manuscripts and Archives, New Haven.

197. Robert Venturi to Charles Moore, 22 October 1968, in ibid.

198. Ibid.

199. The students of the Las Vegas studio were: Doug Southworth (M.E.D. 1969), Peter Schlaifer (B.F.A.G. [Graphic Design] 1969), Martha Wagner (B.F.A.G. 1969), Charles Korn (M.Arch 1969), Ralph Carlson (M.Arch 1970), Ron Filson (B.Arch 1970), Glen Hodges (M.Arch 1970), Peter Hoyt (M.Arch 1970), John Kranz (M.Arch 1970), Peter Schmitt (M.Arch 1970), Dan Scully (M.Arch 1970), Tony Zunino (M.Arch 1970), Tony Farmer (M.C.P. 1971), and Harry Teague (M.Arch 1972).

200. Peter Hoyt, "£earning from £a$ Vega$," *Yale Graduate Professional* (November 1, 1968).

201. Peter Hoyt quoted in Stephanie Salomon and Steve Kroeter, "The 1968 Learning from Las Vegas Studio Revisited," *Designers and Books,* December 19, 2013, http:// www.designersandbooks. com/blog/1968-learning- las-vegas-studio-revisited (accessed February 27, 2015).

202. Ron Filson quoted in ibid.

203. Charles Korn quoted in ibid.

204. Daniel Scully quoted in ibid.

205. Robert Venturi, Denise Scott Brown, and Steven Izenour, "Studio LLV: Research Topics. Phase I, Tooling Up. Phase II, Library Research and Preparation," in *Studio LLV: Learning from Las Vegas, or Form Analysis as Design Research, Third Year Studio,* ed. Venturi et al. (New Haven: Yale University, Department of Architecture, 1968), quoted in Stierli, "Las Vegas Studio," 15.

206. Stierli, "Las Vegas Studio," 13.

207. Kenneth Frampton, *Modern Architecture: A Critical History* (New York: Oxford University Press, 1980), 289–90.

208. Charles Moore, "Learning from Adam's House," *Architectural Record* (August 1973): 43.

209. Watson, "LLV, LLV:? VVV."

210. Brendan Moran, "Research," in Ockman, *Architecture School,* 170.

211. Jessica Lautin, "More than Ticky Tacky: Venturi, Scott Brown, and the Learning from Levittown Studio," in *Second Suburb: Levittown, Pennsylvania,* ed. Dianne Harris (Pittsburgh: University of Pittsburgh Press, 2010), 317–18.

212. Robert Venturi and Denise Scott Brown, *Venturi Scott Brown and Associates: On Houses and Housing* (London: Academy, 1992); Lautin, "More than Ticky Tacky," 314–39.

213. Lautin, "More than Ticky Tacky," 317–18.

214. "Learning from Levittown Studio Program Statement," quoted in ibid.

215. Ibid.

216. Erikson's research and teaching interests include American communities, human disasters, and ethno-national conflict; Zeissel's work involves using design to help treat dementia and other illnesses; Davidoff was a planning theorist who worked as an advocate for minority and lower-income communities.

217. Lautin, "More than Ticky Tacky," 331.

218. Ibid., 332.

219. Ibid.

220. Venturi and Scott Brown, *On Houses and Housing,* 58.

221. "Dean Danes Leaves Art and Architecture," *Yale Daily News,* March 10, 1967.

222. Gibson Danes to Kingman Brewster, 6 June 1968, Kingman Brewster Jr. Presidential Records, ser. 1, RU-11, box 28, folder 1, Yale University Manuscripts and Archives, New Haven.

223. See Stern, Mellins, and Fishman, *New York 1960,* 42, 740, 742–45; and Marta Gutman and Richard Plunz, "Anatomy of Insurrection," in *The Making of an Architect 1881–1981,* ed. Richard Oliver (New York: Rizzoli, 1981), 183–210.

224. Paul Bass and Douglas W. Rae, *Murder in the Model City: The Black Panthers, Yale, and the Redemption of a Killer* (New York: Basic, 2006), esp. 51–52.

225. Melvin Mitchell, Casey Mann, Robert Jayson, and Harry Quintana, "Black Architects for Black Communities," *Liberator* (February 1968): 14.

226. "Students Take over Howard U.; Want 'Black University' Concept," *Jet,* April 4, 1968, 52–54.

227. Harry Quintana and Charles Jones, "Black Commune in Focus," *Perspecta: The Yale Architectural Journal* 12 (1969): 39–42.

228. Topper Carew quoted in Scott Douglas, "Making a Buck in Maine: A Talk with Topper Carew," *The Bollard,* November 1, 2005, http://thebollard.com/2005/11/01/making-a-buck-in-maine-2/ (accessed February 27, 2015).

229. Brian Goldstein, "Planning's End? Urban Renewal in New Haven, the Yale School of Art and Architecture, and the Fall of the New Deal Spatial Order," *Journal of Urban History* 37 (2011): 402.

230. Ibid., 407.

231. Art Hacker, "The AIA Conference and Counter Conference," *Novum Organum* 2 (December 3, 1968).

232. "Undated Student Petition," Yale University School of Architecture, exhibit materials from *Architecture or Revolution: Charles Moore and Architecture at Yale in the 1960s,* RU-906, accn. 2004-A-044, box 2, Yale University Manuscripts and Archives, New Haven.

233. For TAR, see Christopher Barker and Anthony Schuman, *The Architects' Resistance* (New York: Common Room, 2014).

234. The Architects' Resistance, "Architecture and Racism" (pamphlet), 1969, quoted in Anthony W. Schuman, "Community Engagement," in Ockman, *Architecture School,* 255.

235. Blau, "Architecture or Revolution."

236. Goldstein, "Planning's End?" 407.

237. Vincent Scully, "Transcript of Remarks Delivered 25 November, 1968," *Novum Organum* 2 (December 3, 1968); see also "Yale Planning Emphasized by Ed Barnes on November 25th," *Novum Organum* 2 (December 3, 1968); and "Reprint of Questions Posted Prior to Ed Barnes Session," *Novum Organum* 2 (December 3, 1968).

238. The proposal submitted for the Committee of Eight on December 9, 1968, was signed by the following members of the class of 1969: Robert White, David Decker, William B. Richardson, Peter Hentschel, Robert Swenson, Paul Thompson, Stuart Wrede, Whitney Olsen, Kermit Thompson, Eric Hansen, Jr., Peter Witter, Herbert Short, Manfred Ibel, James Caldwell, Jr., and James Gage, along with three others whose signatures are illegible; Kingman Brewster Jr. Presidential Records, ser. 1, RU-11, box 25, folder 2, Yale University Manuscripts and Archives, New Haven.

239. University Council, Report of the Committee of the School of Art and Architecture, April 1968, Secretary's Office, Yale University Records, RU-52, accn. 1983-A-036, box 2, Yale University Manuscripts and Archives, New Haven.

240. Committee of Eight Proposal, 9 December 1968, Kingman Brewster Jr. Presidential

Records, ser. 1, RU-11, box 25, folder 2, Yale University Manuscripts and Archives, New Haven.

241. Ibid.

242. Stuart Wrede, "Notes from the Committee of Eight," *Novum Organum* 2 (December 3, 1968).

243. "Petition to Kingman Brewster," 28 April 1969, Kingman Brewster Jr. Presidential Records, ser. 1, RU-11, box 26, folder 1, Yale University Manuscripts and Archives, New Haven; Tom Warren, "A&A Students Demand Increased Scholarships," *Yale Daily News,* April 28, 1969.

244. Howard Weaver to Kingman Brewster, 30 April 1969, Kingman Brewster Jr. Presidential Records, ser. 1, RU-11, box 26, folder 1, Yale University Manuscripts and Archives, New Haven.

245. Kingman Brewster, letter, quoted in Warren, "A&A Students."

246. Vincent Scully quoted in Tom Warren, "A&A Protesters Hold Mock Burial," *Yale Daily News,* May 9, 1969.

247. John Jacobson, interview by Jimmy Stamp, April 18, 2013.

248. Vincent Scully quoted in Warren, "A&A Protesters." Henry Stone quoted in Tom Warren, "Brewster to Face A&A Demands," *Yale Daily News,* May 12, 1969.

249. Roc Caivano quoted in Warren, "Brewster to Face A&A Demands."

250. Henry Stone quoted in Warren, "A&A Protesters."

251. Tom Carey quoted in "A&A Faculty Agrees to Suspend Academics," *Yale Daily News,* May 16, 1969.

252. Herbert Newman, interview by Jimmy Stamp, July 20, 2013.

253. Ibid.

254. Kingman Brewster quoted in in "A&A Faculty Agrees."

255. Vincent Scully, "Modern Architecture at Yale: A Memoir," in *Yale in New Haven: Architecture and Urbanism,* ed. Vincent J. Scully, Catherine Lynn, Eric Vogt, and Paul Goldberger (New Haven: Yale University Press, 2004), 329.

256. Ibid.

257. Wrede, "Revisiting 1968–1969," 128–33.

258. Reuben Holden quoted in Eric Moore, "Oldenburg Art: Beinecke Lipstick," *Yale Daily News,* May 16, 1969.

259. Directors of the Colossal Keepsake Corporation were: Gordon Thorne; Charles Brewer; Sam Callaway, treasurer; Rob Coombs; John Allen; Peter Almond; Danny Goodrich, secretary; Claes Oldenburg, vice-president; Vincent Scully; and Stuart Wrede, president; significantly, only one woman, Susan Casteras, was a corporation member.

260. Jonathan Price, "Claes Oldenburg: Or I Spent Four Very Long Years at Yale—I Can't Remember Anything About Them," *Yale Alumni Magazine,* December 1968, 26–31.

261. Wrede's taped conversation with Herbert Marcuse appeared in edited form as front matter in *Perspecta: The Yale Architectural Journal* 12 (1969): 75; see Wrede, "Revisiting 1968–69," 128–35; fragments from another Marcuse talk were published in *Novum Organum* 3 (January 6, 1969).

262. Wrede, "Revisiting 1968–69," 128–35.

263. Ibid.

264. Björn Springfeldt quoted in ibid.

265. Vincent Scully, "The Lipstick at Yale: A Memoir" (1989), in Claes Oldenburg and Coosje van Bruggen, *Large-Scale Projects* (New York: Monacelli, 1994), 205–6.

266. Susan P. Casteras, "The Lipstick: A Colossal Keepsake Product," in *The Lipstick Comes Back* (New Haven: Yale University Art Gallery, 1974), excerpted in Oldenburg and van Bruggen, *Large-Scale Projects,* 197–98.

267. Judith Ann Schiff, "The Lipstick: From Anti-War to 'Morse Resource,'" *Yale Alumni Magazine,* February 2000.

268. Vincent Scully, interview by Jimmy Stamp, August 23, 2010.

269. Claes Oldenburg quoted in John Barton, "Oldenburg Hopes His Art Will Make Imprint at Yale," *New York Times,* May 16, 1969, 37; Schiff, "The Lipstick."

270. Wrede, "Revisiting 1968–69," 128–35.

271. Resolution quoted in "A&A Faculty."

272. University Council, Report of the Committee on the School of Art and Architecture, April 1969, Kingman Brewster Jr. Presidential Records, RU-11, box 438, folder 16, Yale University Manuscripts and Archives, New Haven.

273. Mission Statement of the School of Architecture, as articulated by Charles Moore in the *Bulletin of Yale University, School of Art and Architecture, 1970.*

274. Charles Brewer, interview by Jimmy Stamp, August 10, 2012.

275. Ibid.

276. Charles Brewer to Charles Moore, June 11, 1968, courtesy Charles Brewer.

277. Charles Brewer, interview by Jimmy Stamp, August 10, 2012.

278. Richard Dozier (lecturing at the symposium "Rethinking Designs of the 60s," the New School for Social Research, New York, March 7, 1992), in *Perspecta: The Yale Architectural Journal,* ed. William Deresiewicz, Garrett Finney, Sam Kirby, Clay Miller (Cambridge, Mass.: MIT Press, 1998), 31–36.

279. See Blau, "Architecture or Revolution."

280. Herbert Newman, interview by Jimmy Stamp, July

20, 2013; "Yale Plans Development over Oak Street Road," *Yale Daily News,* December 2, 1968.

281. The Black Workshop, "Presentation of Yale Medical Center Garage to the Urban Renewal Committee of HNC," in "A Comprehensive Proposal for the Founding and Funding of a Black Environmentalist and Planning Establishment," undated publicity material for the Black Workshop (c. 1969), courtesy Charles Brewer.

282. Charles Brewer, interview by Jimmy Stamp, August 10, 2012.

283. "A Statement from Professor Tunnard," *Yale Graduate Professional* 2 (April 1969).

284. Richard Dozier, "The Black Architect at Yale," *Design Quarterly,* no. 82/83 (1971): 18.

285. Howard Weaver, memo to Charles Brewer, Bernard Chaet, Louis DeLuca, Christopher Pullman, Ralph Tucker, and Howard S. Weaver, 23 April 1969, School of Art and Architecture, Yale University, Records RU-189, box 18, Yale University Manuscripts and Archives, New Haven.

286. Goldstein, "Planning's End?" 411.

287. Howard Weaver to Charles H. Taylor, 24 April 1969, School of Art and Architecture, Yale University, Records RU-189, box 18, Yale University Manuscripts and Archives, New Haven.

288. Black Workshop, unsigned memo presumably written to Howard Weaver, 29 April 1969. Kingman Brewster Jr. Presidential Records, ser. 1, ser. 1, RU-11, box 26, folder 6, Yale University Manuscripts and Archives, New Haven.

289. Charles Taylor to the Black Workshop, 12 June 1969, in ibid.

290. Charles H. Taylor, Jr., to E. Donald van Purnell and Joseph Middlebrooks, 2 October 1969, School of Art and Architecture, Yale University, Records RU-189, box 18, Yale University Manuscripts and Archives, New Haven.

291. Charles H. Taylor, Jr., to Donald Stull, Arthur Symes, Max Bond, E. Donald van Purnell, Joseph Middlebrooks, and members of the Black Workshop, 12 December 1969; Kingman Brewster to Donald Stull, 10 March 1970; Charles Moore to the Black Workshop, 3 March 1970; and Charles Moore to Donald Stull, 13 March 1970, all in Kingman Brewster Jr. Presidential Records, ser. 1, RU-11, box 27, folder 4, Yale University Manuscripts and Archives, New Haven.

292. Charles Moore to Arthur Symes, 13 March 1970, in ibid.

293. Henry Broude, Charles Moore, and Joseph Lieberman to Kingman Brewster, 27 May 1970, Kingman Brewster Jr. Presidential Records, ser. 1, ser. 1, RU-11, box 26, folder 6, Yale University Manuscripts and Archives, New Haven.

294. Charles Moore to Kingman Brewster, 26 June 1970, School of Architecture Records, RU-1048, accn. 2007-A-194, box 2, Yale University Manuscripts and Archives, New Haven.

295. Richard Dozier, "The Black Architect at Yale," *Design Quarterly,* no. 82/83 (1971): 17.

296. Arthur T. Row, Annual Report of the Department of City Planning, 29 June 1965, Yale University, Records of the Dean of the School of Architecture, RU-843, accn. 2007-A-193, box 13, Yale University Manuscripts and Archives, New Haven.

297. Harry J. Wexler, "The Yale Saga: From Admissions Bust to Final Solution," *Bulletin of the Association of Collegiate Schools of Planning* 9 (autumn 1971): 3–7.

298. Vincent J. Scully, "Visual Art as a Way of Knowing," in *The Fine Arts and the University,* ed. Murray G. Ross (New York: St. Martin's, 1965), 49–74.

299. Goldstein, "Planning's End?" 406.

300. Mitchell, "Imagining Digital Culture."

301. David Jacques and Jan Woudstra, *Landscape Modernism Renounced: The Career of Christopher Tunnard (1910–1979)* (London: Routledge, 2009), 75.

302. Harry Wexler, memo to Kingman Brewster and Yale Corporation, 28 July 1968, Kingman Brewster Jr. Presidential Records, ser. 1, ser. 1, RU-11, box 27, folder 7, Yale University Manuscripts and Archives, New Haven.

303. See Richard Hatch, *The Scope of Social Architecture* (New York: Wiley, 1984); and Mortimer Zuckerman, *Secrets of the Master Builders: Creating the Impossible in Stone and Steel* (Washington, D.C.: U.S. News and World Report, 2003). See also "Into the City, Seeking, Go Students from Yale," *Progressive Architecture* (July 1968): 49.

304. Rules and By-Laws of the Yale City Planning Department, 14 April 1969, Yale University, Records of the Dean of the School of Architecture, RU-843, accn. 2007-A-193, box 14, Yale University Manuscripts and Archives, New Haven.

305. Charles H. Taylor, Jr., to Howard S. Weaver, 29 April 1969, Kingman Brewster Jr. Presidential Records, ser. 1, RU-11, box 27, folder 7, Yale University Manuscripts and Archives, New Haven.

306. Charles H. Taylor, Jr., to Howard S. Weaver, 23 May 1969, in ibid.

307. Unauthorized letter of admission sent to twelve candidates for admission to the School of Art and Architecture, 22 May

1969, School of Art and Architecture, Yale University, Records RU-189, box 18, Yale University Manuscripts and Archives, New Haven.

308. Margaret Gundst to Jerome Herring, 22 May 1969, in *Perspecta: The Yale Architectural Journal*, 29 (1998): x.

309. Barton Phelps, interview by Jimmy Stamp, April 17, 2013.

310. Howard Weaver, "To the Faculty and Students in the Department of City Planning," 26 May 1969, Kingman Brewster Jr. Presidential Records, ser. 1, ser. 1, RU-11, box 27, folder 7, Yale University Manuscripts and Archives, New Haven.

311. Ibid.

312. Howard S. Weaver, telegram to twelve recipients of unauthorized letters of admission, n.d., in ibid.

313. Kingman Brewster to signatories, 27 May 1969, in ibid.

314. Kingman Brewster to wrongly admitted students, 27 May 1969, School of Art and Architecture, Yale University, Records RU-189, box 18, Yale University Manuscripts and Archives, New Haven.

315. Yale University News Bureau, press release no. 386, May 28, 1969.

316. Howard S. Weaver to Jerome Herring, 29 May 1969, in *Perspecta: The Yale Architectural Journal* 29 (1998): xi.

317. Christopher Tunnard to Howard S. Weaver, 6 July 1969, School of Architecture Records, RU-1048, accn. 2007-A-194, box 2, Yale University Manuscripts and Archives, New Haven.

318. Tom McDonough, "A Postscript to Timothy M. Rohan's 'Rendering the Surface,' *Grey Room*, no. 5 (autumn 2001): 102–11n11.

319. "Brewster Axes City Plan. Dept.; Fires Three Faculty," *Yale Graduate Professional* (August 27, 1969): 3.

320. Fred I. Steele, assistant professor, Department of Administrative Science, 2 June 1969; Harvey M. Wagner, professor, Department of Administrative Science, 2 June 1969; David Thorburn, assistant professor, Department of English, 4 June 1969; and E. S. Canellakis, professor, School of Medicine, 2 June 1969, all in Kingman Brewster Jr. Presidential Records, ser. 1, RU-11, box 27 folder 1, Yale University Manuscripts and Archives, New Haven.

321. William E. Reifsnyder to Kingman Brewster, 10 June 1969, in ibid.

322. Kingman Brewster, memo to Dean Howard S. Weaver, 6 February 1969, in ibid.; significantly, the archived copy of this document notes in pencil that changes were made in May, although the exact day of the month is not clearly legible.

323. Kingman Brewster quoted in Geoffrey M. Kabaservice, *The Guardians: Kingman Brewster, His Circle, and the Rise of the Liberal Establishment* (New York: Henry Holt), 388–89.

324. Nicholas von Hoffman, "Urban Blues," *Washington Post*, June 27, 1969, B1, B14.

325. Charles Moore quoted in Littlejohn, *Architect*, 152.

326. Charles Brewer, interview by Jimmy Stamp, August 10, 2012.

327. University Council, Report of the Committee of the School of Art and Architecture, April 1966, Secretary's Office, Yale University, Records, RU-52, accn. 1984-A-020, box 1, Yale University Manuscripts and Archives, New Haven.

328. University Council, Report, April 1969.

329. Dean Howard S. Weaver, memo to faculty and students in City Planning, 3 July 1969; and Dean Howard S. Weaver to Christopher Tunnard, 3

July 1969, both in Kingman Brewster Jr. Presidential Records, ser. 1, RU-11, box 27, folder 1, Yale University Manuscripts and Archives, New Haven.

330. Charles Taylor to Abraham Goldstein (Law), Joel L. Fleishman (associate provost for Urban Studies), Dean Francois Mergen (Forestry), Albert J. Solnit (Child Study Center), Donald Stull (advisor to the Black Workshop), Christopher Tunnard (City Planning), Henry W. Broude (director of Academic Planning), Charles Moore (chairman of Architecture), and John R. Meyer (Economics).

331. John R. Meyer to Kingman Brewster, accompanied by Report of the Ad Hoc Committee on the Future of Urban Studies at Yale, 26 February 1970, Kingman Brewster Jr. Presidential Records, ser. 1, RU-11, box 27, folder 5, Yale University Manuscripts and Archives, New Haven.

332. Charles Moore, *Sensus* 1 (November 1970).

333. Ibid.

334. Christopher Tunnard to Dean Charles W. Moore, 2 January 1969 [sic—actually 1970], Kingman Brewster Jr. Presidential Records, ser. 1, RU-11, box 27, folder 2, Yale University Manuscripts and Archives, New Haven.

335. Charles Moore to Provost Taylor, 12 January 1970, in ibid.

336. Charles Moore to Harry Wexler, 21 January 1970, in ibid.

337. Charles Moore quoted in Scott Herold, "Wexler Not Reappointed," *Yale Daily News*, January 28, 1970.

338. Harry Wexler to Charles Moore, 30 January 1970, Kingman Brewster Jr. Presidential Records, ser. 1, RU-11, box 27, folder 2, Yale

University Manuscripts and Archives, New Haven.

339. J. F., memo to Kingman Brewster, n.d.; and Charles Moore to Kingman Brewster, 4 April 1970, both in Kingman Brewster Jr. Presidential Records, ser. 1, RU-11, box 26, folder 3, Yale University Manuscripts and Archives, New Haven.

340. Kingman Brewster, memo to Charles W. Moore, Professor Jorge Hardoy, and Mr. Joseph Lieberman, 19 October 1970, Kingman Brewster Jr. Presidential Records, ser. 1, RU-11, box 25, folder 3, Yale University Manuscripts and Archives, New Haven.

341. Kingman Brewster, memo to faculty and students in Architecture and City Planning, 22 December 1970, Kingman Brewster Jr. Presidential Records, ser. I, RU-11, box 27, folder 3, Yale University Manuscripts and Archives, New Haven.

342. Joseph Lieberman, interview by Geoffrey Kabaservice, July 7, 1992, "Oral History Interview with Senator Joseph Lieberman," Griswold-Brewster Oral History Project, Yale University, RU-217, box 7 Yale University Manuscripts and Archives, New Haven.

343. Kingman Brewster, memo to faculty and students in Architecture and City Planning, 22 December 1970, Kingman Brewster Jr. Presidential Records, ser. I, RU-11, box 27, folder 3, Yale University Manuscripts and Archives, New Haven.

344. Goldstein, "Planning's End?"

345. Rubin holds a master of city planning and a Ph.D., both from the University of California, Berkeley, and is the author of an award-winning history of planning and development in Boston: Elihu Rubin, *Insuring the City: The Prudential Center and the Postwar Urban Landscape* (New Haven: Yale University Press, 2012).

346. Charles Moore, unpublished interview by C. Ray Smith, May 11, 1980, C. Ray Smith Manuscript and Research Files on the Yale Art and Architecture Building by Paul Rudolph, MS-1948, box 1, Yale University Manuscripts and Archives, New Haven.

347. Herbert Newman, interview by Jimmy Stamp, July 20, 2013.

348. Charles Moore, unpublished interview by C. Ray Smith, May 11, 1980.

349. Charles Moore quoted in Andrew P. Garvin, "Moore Starts Hammering," *Yale Daily News,* September 23, 1965, 1, 6.

350. Ibid.

351. Moore, "You Have to Pay," 58.

352. Charles Moore quoted in Garvin, "Moore Starts Hammering."

353. Ibid.

354. Charles Moore, unpublished interview by C. Ray Smith, May 11, 1980.

355. Ibid.

356. Ibid.; air conditioning was not provided until the building's comprehensive renovation and restoration in 2008.

357. Danes, "Report from the Dean," 26–27.

358. Charles W. Moore, "Notice to All Students in Architecture," 5 December 1966, King-lui Wu Archives, MS-1842, Temp. box. 2B, Yale University Manuscripts and Archives, New Haven.

359. Manfred Ibel, "Whitney Griswold: A Great Building," *Novum Organum* 4 (January 23, 1969).

360. Anonymous instructor quoted in Ellen Perry Berkeley, "Yale: A Building as Teacher," *Architectural Forum* (July/August 1967): 48.

361. Moore quoted in ibid.

362. Ibid., 48.

363. Ibid., 50.

364. Hayes, *Yale Building Project*, 24.

365. Doug Michels, unpublished interview by C. Ray Smith, 1978, C. Ray Smith Manuscript and Research Files; for more information on Ant Farm, see Felicity Scott, *Ant Farm: Living Archive 7* (Barcelona: Actar, 2007).

366. "The Revolution in Interior Design: The Bold New Poly-Expanded Mega-Decoration," *Progressive Architecture* (October 1968): 148–206.

367. Doug Michels quoted in C. Ray Smith, "Supergraphics," *Progressive Architecture* (November 1967): 132–38.

368. Doug Michels quoted in ibid.

369. Roger Jellinek, "Lively Interiors," *New York Times,* November 16, 1969, BR77.

370. Bill Grover quoted in "Tributes to Doug Michels," *Constructs* (fall 2003): 27.

371. Ken Johnson, "Doug Michels, Radical Artist and Architect, Dies at 59," *New York Times,* June 21, 2003, 32.

372. Ada Louise Huxtable, "Kicked a Building Lately?" *New York Times,* January 12, 1969, 25, 28; reprinted in Ada Louise Huxtable, *On Architecture: Collected Reflections on a Century of Change* (New York: Walker, 2010).

373. Yale University News Bureau, press release no. 173, December 4, 1968.

374. Yale University News Bureau, press release, April 10, 1968; the Griggs Collection, consisting of two hundred sixteen-millimeter prints of mostly silent movies, was the first of its kind at Yale. Though there are no surviving records of the titles in the collection, it is known to have included many early, feature-length silent comedies, including the work of Charlie Chaplin and Buster Keaton. For Project Argus, see "Revolution in Interior Design," 148–206; Patrick Clancy, "Pulsa: Light as Truth," *Yale Alumni Magazine,* May 1968, 39–43; Yale University News Bureau,

Notes to Pages 329–337

press release, April 10, 1968; and Howard S. Weaver, "Film at Yale: The Opportunity Is Waiting," *Eye: Magazine of the Yale Arts Association,* no. 2 (1968): 24–27; see also Jack Tworkov and Yale Research Associates, "The Yale Light Show," *Eye: Magazine of the Yale Arts Association,* no. 2 (1968): 36–39. Contemporary with Argus, a group of students consisting of two architects (William Grover and Jerry Wagner) and a graphic designer (Martha Wagner, who was to take the LLV studio the following semester) formed a company, the Elm City Electric Light Sculpture Company, in 1968 to produce objects conceived as both lighting fixtures and sculptures, using neon tubes. The best-known of these were the Pop heraldic "banners" for Charles Moore's Faculty Club at UC Santa Barbara (1966–68).

375. Paul Fuge quoted in Thomas Hine and Jon Coots, "Light, Sound, People Make 'Argus' Happen," *Yale Daily News,* April 26, 1968.

376. Blau, "Architecture or Revolution"; Blau is quoting from a video interview with Charles W. Moore conducted by Laurel Vlock (April 4, 1982) for *Dialogue with Laurel Vlock,* the Laurel Vlock Collection, DVD LVC Dialogue with Laurel Vlock no. 9, University of New Haven Library, New Haven.

377. Huxtable, "Kicked a Building Lately?" 25, 28; reprinted in Ada Louise Huxtable, *Will They Ever Finish Bruckner Boulevard?* (Berkeley: University of California Press: 1989), 177–81.

378. Herbert Newman, interview by Jimmy Stamp, July 20, 2013.

379. Charles Moore, unpublished interview by C. Ray Smith, May 11, 1980.

380. Timothy M. Rohan, "Canon and Anti-Canon: On the Fall and Rise of the A&A," *Harvard Design Magazine* 14 (June 2001): 24, 32.

381. David Jacobs, "The Rudolph Style: Unpredictable," *New York Times Magazine,* March 26, 1967, 46–47, 49, 52.

382. Timothy Bates, "Artists Rap A&A Building," *Yale Daily News,* May 4, 1967; the faculty signatories included well-known New York–based artists Lester Johnson (1919–2010), acting chairman of the Department of Art; Al Held (1928–2005); Red Grooms (b. 1937); and George Sugarman (1912–1999).

383. Deane Keller, "The Worst Place," *Yale Daily News,* May 9, 1967.

384. Chief James M. McNulty to Edward M. Fitzgerald, 17 June 1969, C. Ray Smith Manuscript and Research Files.

385. Ibid.

386. Thomas Lyden, Jr., quoted in Keim and Moore, *Architectural Life,* 113.

387. Robert Miller to Jimmy Stamp, 9 September 2010.

388. Thomas Fisher, "Nietzsche in New Haven: How One Philosophizes with a Hammer," *Perspecta: The Yale Architectural Journal* 29 (October 1998): 56.

389. Joseph Lelyveld, "After Fire, Yale Smolders," *New York Times,* June 27, 1969, 39.

390. Thomas Lyden, unpublished interview by C. Ray Smith, 1978, C. Ray Smith Manuscript and Research Files.

391. Paul Rudolph, unpublished interview by C. Ray Smith, 1978, C. Ray Smith Manuscript and Research Files.

392. Keim and Moore, *Architectural Life.*

393. Thomas Lyden, formal report on the fire in the A&A Building, 14 June 1969, Kingman Brewster Jr. Presidential Records, ser. 1, RU-11, box 27, folder 1, Yale University Manuscripts and Archives, New Haven.

394. "Arson Suspected in Fire at Yale Art and Architecture Building," *Architectural Record* (July 1969): 36.

395. Thomas Lyden, unpublished interview by C. Ray Smith, 1978.

396. Lelyveld, "After Fire, Yale Smolders," 39, 74; see also "Arson Suspected," 36.

397. "No Arson Is Found at Yale in Inquiry on Art School Fire," *New York Times,* July 29, 1969, 39.

398. Lelyveld, "After Fire, Yale Smolders," 39, 74.

399. Kabaservice, *Guardians,* 389.

400. Unidentified student quoted by Claire Simon, "Flames of Controversy," *New Haven Advocate,* June 11, 1998 17, cited in Kabaservice, *Guardians,* 389.

401. Thomas Lyden, Jr., unpublished interview with C. Ray Smith, 1978.

402. Turner Brooks, interview by Jimmy Stamp, July 21, 2010.

403. Peter Blake, "Yale on Ice," *New York,* August 11, 1969, 54.

404. Steering Committee to Kingman Brewster, 1 July 1969, Kingman Brewster Jr. Presidential Records, ser. 1, RU-11, box 26, folder 2, Yale University Manuscripts and Archives, New Haven.

405. Howard S. Weaver, "Developments over the Summer," memorandum to faculty and students, 15 September 1969, Kingman Brewster Jr. Presidential Records, ser. 1, RU-11, box 26, folder 2, Yale University Manuscripts and Archives, New Haven.

406. Scott Herrold, "A+A School: Boxed In?" *Yale Daily News,* February 3, 1970.

407. Barton Phelps, interview by Jimmy Stamp, April 17, 2013.

408. Moore, Report on Design and

Planning, 1969–1970.

409. Howard Weaver to faculty and students of the School of Art and Architecture, 19 June 1969, Kingman Brewster Jr. Presidential Records, ser. 1, RU-11, box 26, folder 2, Yale University Manuscripts and Archives, New Haven.

410. Charles J. Hines, "Probe Finds No Evidence of Arson in Fire at Yale," *New Haven Register*, July 28, 1969, 1–2.

411. Earl P. Carlin to alumni, 23 June 1969. Kingman Brewster Jr. Presidential Records, ser. 1, RU-11, box 26, folder 2, Yale University Manuscripts and Archives, New Haven.

412. "Yale A and A: Restructured and Still Going Strong," *Architectural Record* (March 1970): 37.

413. George Landon, Jr., to Albert H. Riese, Jr., 25 February 1970, Yale University, Records of the Dean RU-843, accn. 2007-A-193, Yale University Manuscripts and Archives, New Haven.

414. Charles Moore, "Space," memo to faculty and students, 12 March 1970, Yale University, Records of the Dean RU-843, accn. 2007-A-193, box 12, Yale University Manuscripts and Archives, New Haven.

415. Ibid.

416. University Council, Report of the Committee on the School of Art and Architecture, April 1967, Secretary's Office, Yale University, Records, RU-52, accn. 1984-A-020, box 1, Yale University Manuscripts and Archives, New Haven.

417. Jim Swiss, "A&A School: Problems of Space, Student Power, Grading, and Relevancy," *Yale Daily News*, January 15, 1969.

418. University Council, Report of the Committee, April 1969.

419. Kingman Brewster, "Interim Administrative Arrangements for Work in the Arts, Architecture, and City Planning," 15 September 1969, Kingman Brewster Jr. Presidential Records, ser. 1, RU-11, box 26, folder 2, Yale University Manuscripts and Archives, New Haven.

420. Kingman Brewster quoted in "Yale Will Divide Disputed School," *New York Times*, September 21, 1969, 56.

421. Ibid.

422. Yale University News Bureau, press release no. 49, September 16, 1969.

423. Charles Moore quoted in Littlejohn, *Architect*, 153.

424. Charles Moore quoted in ibid.

425. Ibid.

426. Ray Gindroz, telephone interview with Jimmy Stamp, July 10, 2012.

427. Charles Brewer, "A Plan for Governance, Department of Architecture, Yale University Proposal II," October 13, 1969, courtesy Charles Brewer.

428. After leaving Yale, Brewer served as chairman of architecture at Ohio State; Adams went on to practice architecture, designing some notable buildings in Columbus, Indiana, including the Lillian Schmitt Elementary School (with Harry Weese) and the renovation of the Columbus Visitors' Center; Goeters went on to serve as senior vice president of the California Housing Finance Association (1975–81), director of planning and development at the Boston Housing Authority (1984–89), and later worked as an architect specializing in home-building.

429. Moore, Report on the Faculties, 1969–1970.

430. Howard Weaver to Kingman Brewster, 31 March 1970, Kingman Brewster Jr. Presidential Records, ser. 1, RU-11, box 26, folder 3, Yale University Manuscripts and Archives, New Haven.

431. Bass and Rae, *Murder in the Model City*.

432. Mitchell, "Imagining Digital Culture."

433. Turner Brooks, interview by Jimmy Stamp, July 21, 2010.

434. Ibid.

435. Moore, Report on the Faculties, 1969–1970.

436. Charles Moore, confidential letter to Provost Charles H. Taylor, Jr., 16 December 1969, Kingman Brewster Jr. Presidential Records, ser. 1, RU-11, box 247, folder 7, Yale University Manuscripts and Archives, New Haven.

437. Ibid.

438. Walter B. Ford II, chairman, University Council Report of the Committee on the School of Art and Architecture, April 1970, Kingman Brewster Jr. Presidential Records, RU-11, box 438, folder 16, Yale University Manuscripts and Archives, New Haven.

439. Henry W. Broude to Charles H. Taylor, Jr., 9 November 1970, Kingman Brewster Jr. Presidential Records, ser. 1, RU-11, box 26, folder 3, Yale University Manuscripts and Archives, New Haven.

440. Kingman Brewster to Charles Moore, 20 November 1970, in ibid.

441. Charles Moore to Kingman Brewster, 20 April 1970, in ibid.

442. Charles Moore, "Ten Year Long Range Master Plan Guide," 1969–70, Records of the Dean of the Yale School of Architecture, RU-843, accn. 2007-A-193, box 13, folder 403, Yale University Manuscripts and Archives, New Haven.

443. Ibid.

444. Ibid.

445. *Bulletin of Yale University, Design and Planning, 1970*.

446. Moore, "Ten Year Master Plan."

447. Zeynep Pamuk, "Architecture School Receives Ph.D. Applications," *Yale Daily News*, January 29, 2009.

448. Charles Moore quoted in

Littlejohn, *Architect*, 159.

449. "Mellon Center Report," *Yale Graduate Professional* (April 4, 1970): 3.

450. Charles Moore to Kingman Brewster, 14 December 1966, Kingman Brewster Jr. Presidential Records, ser. 1, RU-11, box 147, folder 4, Yale University Manuscripts and Archives, New Haven.

451. Gibson Danes to Kingman Brewster, 20 December 1966, in ibid. In 1966, Ellen Perry Berkeley incorrectly suggested that the idea came independently from Moore and Edward Larrabee Barnes in her article "Mathematics at Yale," *Architectural Forum* (July/August, 1970): 62–66.

452. Gibson Danes to Kingman Brewster, 22 December 1966, Kingman Brewster Jr. Presidential Records, ser. 1, RU-11, box 147, folder 4, Yale University Manuscripts and Archives, New Haven.

453. See Lloyd Goodrich to Kingman Brewster, 23 December 1966, in which he recommends Marcel Breuer, in ibid.

454. Charles Moore to Kingman Brewster, 10 January 1967, Kingman Brewster Jr. Presidential Records, ser. 1, RU-11, box 147, folder 5, Yale University Manuscripts and Archives, New Haven.

455. Signatories to the petition include Doug Michels, Jeremy Scott Wood, H. Turner Brooks, F. Andrus Burr, Alexander Garvin, Susan Green (M.Arch 1969), Stuart Wrede, Peter C. Papademetriou, William H. Grover, Craig Hodgetts, Eugene Kupper, Peter Rose, Manfred Ibel, and Keith Godard (M.F.A. 1967), a graphic design student.

456. Vincent J. Scully to Jules Prown, 14 November 1968, Kingman Brewster Jr. Presidential Records, ser. 1, RU-11, box 147, folder 6, Yale University Manuscripts and Archives, New Haven.

457. Jules Prown, memo to Herbert Newman, 5 December 1968, in ibid.; Jules Prown to Kingman Brewster, 22 January 1969, Kingman Brewster Jr. Presidential Records, RU-11, ser. 1, box 147, folder 7, Yale University Manuscripts and Archives, New Haven.

458. Kingman Brewster to Jules Prown, 5 February 1969, Kingman Brewster Jr. Presidential Records, ser. 1, RU-11, box 147, folder 7, Yale University Manuscripts and Archives, New Haven.

459. Jules Prown to Provost Charles Taylor, 10 March 1969, in ibid.

460. "Concerned Citizens, Faculty, and Students" to Paul Mellon, 3 April 1969, Kingman Brewster Jr. Presidential Records, ser. 1, RU-11, box 148, folder 8, Yale University Manuscripts and Archives, New Haven.

461. Paul Mellon, "Letter to Concerned Citizens, Faculty, and Students," 30 April 1969, Kingman Brewster Jr. Presidential Records, ser. 1, RU-11, box 147, folder 7, Yale University Manuscripts and Archives, New Haven.

462. Jules Prown to Kingman Brewster, 6 May 1969, in ibid.

463. Vincent Scully to Kingman Brewster, 7 May 1969, in ibid.

464. Daniel V. Scully to Kingman Brewster, 9 June 1969, in ibid.

465. Charles Taylor to Jules Prown, 13 July 1969, in ibid.

466. Jules Prown, *The Architecture of the Yale Center for British Art* (New Haven: Yale Center for British Art, distributed by Yale University Press, 2009); see also Peter Inskip and Stephen Gee, *Louis I. Kahn and the Yale Center for British Art: A Conservation Plan* (New Haven: Yale University Press, 2011).

467. Charles Moore and Nicholas Pyle, "Preface," in *The Yale Mathematics Building Competition: Architecture for a Time of Questioning*, ed. Charles Moore and Nicholas Pyle (New Haven: Yale University Press, 1974).

468. Charles Moore, "The Scene," in Moore and Pyle, *Yale Mathematics Building Competition*, 1.

469. Moore and Pyle, "Preface," 86; Yale University News Bureau, press release no. 343, May 22, 1970.

470. Paul Goldberger, "About the Architect," *A New Math Building at Yale*, pamphlet (1972), ser. 2, RU-11, box 293, folders 9–10, Yale University Manuscripts and Archives, New Haven.

471. "Mathematics at Yale," *Architectural Forum* (July/August, 1970): 62–67; "Mathematics at Yale: Readers Respond," *Architectural Forum* (October 1970); 64–66.

472. Moore and Pyle, *Yale Mathematics Building Competition*.

473. "Mathematics at Yale," 64–66.

474. John Geesman, "Math Building Critic Given Bureaucratic Brush-Off," *Yale Daily News*, September 28, 1971.

475. Colin Rowe, "Robert Venturi and the Yale Mathematics Building," *Oppositions* (fall 1976), republished in *Colin Rowe, As I Was Saying: Recollections and Miscellaneous Essays*, vol. II, ed. Alexander Caragonne (Cambridge, Mass.: MIT Press, 1996), 79–101.

476. Serge Chermayeff quoted in "Mathematics at Yale," 65.

477. Joshua Lowenfish quoted in ibid.

478. Charles Moore's response quoted in ibid.

479. Joshua Lowenfish to Senator Hubert Humphrey, 16 July 1971, Kingman Brewster Jr. Presidential Records, ser. 2, RU-11, box 293, folder 9, Yale University Manuscripts and Archives, New Haven.

480. John Geesman, "University Accused of Fraud in Architectural Competition for Proposed Math Building," *Yale Daily News,* September 27, 1971; John Geesman, "Math Building Critic Given Bureaucratic Brush-Off," *Yale Daily News,* September 28, 1971, 1; John Geesman, "Scully Blasts Math Building Critics as 'Despicable Scum,'" *Yale Daily News,* September 29, 1971, 13.

481. Vincent Scully to Stuart Rosow, 3 November 1971, Kingman Brewster Jr. Presidential Records, ser. 2, RU-11, box 293, folder 9, Yale University Manuscripts and Archives, New Haven.

482. Joshua Lowenfish to Henry Chauncey, Jr., secretary, Yale University, 5 November 1971; Joshua Lowenfish to Jonathan F. Fanton, special assistant to the president, Yale University, 13 December 1971; and Joshua Lowenfish to Kingman Brewster, 10 March 1972, all in ibid.

483. John E. Ecklund to Joshua Lowenfish, 29 June 1972, in ibid.

484. Robert Venturi quoted in John W. Cook and Heinrich Klotz, *Conversations with Architects* (New York: Praeger, 1973), 255–56.

485. Yale University News Bureau, press release, August 10, 1970, Kingman Brewster Jr. Presidential Records, ser. 3, RU-11, box 293, folder 8 Yale University Manuscripts and Archives, New Haven.

486. Frank S. Streeter, memo to John Hay Whitney, 3 June 1970, Kingman Brewster Jr. Presidential Records, ser. 3, RU-11, box 293, folder 7 Yale University Manuscripts and Archives, New Haven.

487. For Queen's College, see Peter Arnell and Ted Bickford, eds., *James Stirling: Buildings and Projects* (New York: Rizzoli, 1984), 124–33; and Alan Berman, "Understanding the Florey Buildings, Oxford," in *Jim Stirling and the Red Trilogy: Three Radical Buildings,* ed. Alan Berman (London: Frances Lincoln, 2010), 54–67; for St. Andrew's, see Léon Krier and James Stirling, *James Stirling: Buildings and Projects, 1950–1974* (New York: Oxford University Press, 1975), 96–107; and Arnell and Bickford, *Buildings and Projects,* 107–17.

488. Mark Singer, "At the University," *Yale Alumni Magazine,* November, 1972, 44–46; Coke and Peoples to Kingman Brewster, 20 November 1972; and Brewster's reply, 29 November 1972, both in Kingman Brewster Jr. Presidential Records, ser. 3, RU-11, box 293, folder 8 Yale University Manuscripts and Archives, New Haven.

489. Jonathan F. Fanton, whitepaper, 17 April 1973; and Jonathan F. Fanton to Kingman Brewster, 18 April 1973, both in Kingman Brewster Jr. Presidential Records, RU-11, box 369, folder 8, Yale University Manuscripts and Archives, New Haven.

490. Ibid.

491. Mary E. O'Leary, "Yale Scratches Plans for 2 New Colleges," *New Haven Journal Courier,* February 13, 1975, 1, 11; Yale University News Bureau, press release no. 98, February 12, 1975.

492. "Cross Campus Plans Arouse Berkeley Ire," *Yale Daily News,* April 16, 1968.

493. Bob Mascia, "Button vs. Bulldozers Students Save X-Campus," *Yale Daily News,* June 1, 1968.

494. Bradley Nitkin quoted in "Calhoun Outcry, Library Protest Mounts," *Yale Daily News,* April 23, 1968; see also Hugh Spitzer, "A Modest Proposal for the Cross Campus," *Yale Daily News,* April 23, 1968; John Coots, "Barnes to Discuss Plans," *Yale Daily News,* November 25, 1968; Walter Langsam, "Cross Campus Again: A New Program: Old Design," *Yale Daily News,* December 10, 1968; and Manfred Ibel, "Why Do We Have to Hide People and People's Activities?" *Yale Daily News,* December 10, 1968.

495. Hunter Morrison and Hugh Spitzer, "News Analysis: Maze of Committees Keeps Dissent Quiet," *Yale Daily News,* June 2, 1968.

496. Tom Anderson, "Blum Reveals Library Plan; Students Indicate Approval," *Yale Daily News,* March 13, 1969.

497. Jeff Muskus, "Buildings Reveal Plans for CCL," *Yale Daily News,* March 25, 2005; June Torbat, "CCL Renamed for Top Donor," *Yale Daily News,* October 8, 2007.

498. Herbert Short and Manfred Ibel, letter and proposal to Kingman Brewster, 5 January 1969, Kingman Brewster Jr. Presidential Records, ser. 1, RU-11, box 26, folder 1, Yale University Manuscripts and Archives, New Haven; see also Manfred Ibel, "Whitney Griswold, A Great Builder?" *Novum Organum* 4 (1969); Manfred Ibel and Herb Short, "Away with Pointless Planning," *Yale Daily News,* November 25, 1968; and Herb Short, "A Campus Is for Students So We Must Help Plan It," *Yale Daily News,* December 10, 1968.

499. Goldstein, "Planning's End?" 408–9.

500. E. W. Y. Dunn to Charles H. Taylor, Jr., 31 January 1969, School of Art and Architecture, Yale University, Records RU-189, box 18, Yale University Manuscripts and Archives, New Haven.

501. Yale University News Bureau, press release, February 3,

1969, Kingman Brewster Jr. Presidential Records, ser. 1, RU-11, box 26, folder 1, Yale University Manuscripts and Archives, New Haven.

502. Ibid.

503. J. Goldberg, "Brewster Rejects Planners," *Yale Daily News,* April 7, 1969.

504. Moore quoted in Littlejohn, *Architect,* 159.

505. Ibid.

506. Charles Moore quoted in ibid., 160.

507. Ibid., 151.

508. Ibid.

509. Ibid., 160.

Back to Basics

Epigraph. "Perspectives," *Bulletin of Yale University, School of Architecture, 1972* ser. 68 (May 15, 1972), 16.

1. Kingman Brewster, Charles H. Taylor, Jr., John E. Ecklund, and John F. Embersits, memo to faculty and staff, "Yale's Financial Situation and Restriction of Employment," 9 September 1970, School of Architecture, Yale University, Records of the Dean RU-843, accn. 2007-A-193, box 12, Yale University Manuscripts and Archives, New Haven.

2. Kingman Brewster, Charles H. Taylor, Jr., John E. Ecklund, and John F. Embersits, memo to officers, deans, and those responsible for budgetary units, 22 June 1971, in ibid.

3. Report of the Committee on the Schools of Art and Architecture, 1 May 1971, Kingman Brewster Jr. Presidential Records, RU-11, ser. III, box 438, Yale University Manuscripts and Archives, New Haven.

4. Jonathan Barnett quoted in

ibid.

5. Ibid.

6. Yale Faculty Evaluations, Collection D: Yale University, 1959–1984, undated, box C7, the Charles W. Moore Archives: Faculty Papers, Alexander Architectural Archive, University of Texas Libraries, the University of Texas at Austin.

7. Barton Phelps, interview by Jimmy Stamp, April 17, 2013.

8. Herman D. J. Spiegel, "Personal Commentary," 1970–71 Annual Report, School of Architecture, Yale University, Records of the Dean RU-843, box 13, Yale University Manuscripts and Archives, New Haven.

9. Ibid.

10. "Safdie Named to Architectural Chair at Yale," *Interiors* 130 (March 1971): 24.

11. Spiegel, "Personal Commentary," 1970–71.

12. Roger Yee, "New Studios Offered in Architecture," *Sensus* (April 1971), Robert B. Haas Family Arts Library Special Collections, Yale University, New Haven.

13. See Moshe Safdie and Judith Wolin, eds., *For Everyone a Garden* (Cambridge, Mass.: MIT Press, 1974), 296–97; and Irena Zantovska and Irene Murray, eds., *Moshe Safdie: Buildings and Projects, 1967–1992* (Montreal: McGill-Queen's University Press, 1996), 81–82, 264; the Paris competition project team consisted of Heather Willson Cass, her class of 1972 classmates Roberta Lawrence, Martin Hoffmeister, Deborah Lee, Clinton Sheerr, and James Strickland, as well as Robert Yudell (M.Arch 1973) and Henry Wollman (M.Arch 1973).

14. Heather Willson Cass, interview by Jimmy Stamp, December 17, 2012.

15. Spiegel, "Personal Commentary," 1970–71.

16. Herman D. J. Spiegel, "Factual Report," Annual Report

1970–71, Yale University, Records of the Dean RU-843, accn. 2002-A-082, box 1, Yale University Manuscripts and Archives, New Haven.

17. Susan M. Strauss, "History VII: 1968–1981," in *The Making of an Architect,* ed. Richard Oliver (New York: Rizzoli, 1981), 243–63.

18. King-lui Wu to Kingman Brewster, 8 February 1971, Kingman Brewster Jr. Presidential Records, RU-11, ser. I, box 28, folder 2, Yale University Manuscripts and Archives, New Haven.

19. Ibid.; for Martin, see Peter Carolin and Trevor Dannatt, eds., *Architecture, Education and Research: The Work of Leslie Martin: Papers and Selected Articles* (London: Academy Editions, 1996).

20. Charles Moore to Kingman Brewster, 23 February 1971, Kingman Brewster Jr. Presidential Records, RU-11, ser. I, box 28, folder 2, Yale University Manuscripts and Archives, New Haven.

21. Joseph Passonneau to Kingman Brewster, 25 March 1971, Kingman Brewster Jr. Presidential Records, RU-11, ser. I, box 27, folder 3, Yale University Manuscripts and Archives, New Haven.

22. For Harris, see Robert Harris, "Research as an Aspect of Architectural Education," *Journal of Architectural Education* (winter–spring 1971); "Bootstrap Essence-Seeking," *Journal of Architectural Education* (November 1975).

23. Charles Moore to Kingman Brewster, 23 February 1971, Kingman Brewster Jr. Presidential Records, RU-11, ser. I, box 28, folder 2, Yale University Manuscripts and Archives, New Haven.

24. Ibid.

25. Vincent Scully to Kingman Brewster, 22 February 1971, in ibid.

26. Mrs. Robert Venturi to

27. Mrs. Robert Venturi to Kingman Brewster, 2 February 1971, in ibid.

28. Vincent Scully to Kingman Brewster, 5 April 1971, in ibid.

29. Allan Greenberg, "Introduction: Fragment of an Autobiography," in *The Architecture of Democracy: American Architecture and the Legacy of the Revolution* (New York: Rizzoli International, 2006), 21.

30. Allan Greenberg, "Lutyens's Architecture Restudied," *Perspecta* 12 (1969): 129–52.

31. Barton Phelps, interview by Jimmy Stamp, April 17, 2013.

32. Greenberg, "Introduction: Fragment," 20.

33. Marc Appleton, "New Studios Offered in Architecture," *Sensus* (April 1971), Robert B. Haas Family Arts Library Special Collections, Yale University, New Haven.

34. Ibid.

35. For Appleton's work, see *The New Classicists: Appleton and Associates* (Victoria, Aust.: Images, 2008); Appleton has also written several books, including Marc Appleton, *George Washington Smith: An Architect's Scrapbook* (Los Angeles: Tailwater, 2001); and Marc Appleton and Melba Levick, *California Mediterranean* (New York: Rizzoli, 2007).

36. Greenberg, "Introduction: Fragment," 20–21.

37. Barton Phelps, interview by Jimmy Stamp, April 17, 2013.

38. Allan Greenberg, "A Proposal for Restructuring the Yale School of Architecture," April 1971, courtesy Allan Greenberg.

39. Ibid.

40. Herman Spiegel, memo to the faculty and visiting critics, 25 February 1971, Kingman Brewster Jr. Presidential Records, RU-11, ser. I, box 28, folder 2, Yale University Manuscripts and Archives, New Haven.

41. Herman D. J. Spiegel to Kingman Brewster, 9 March 1971, in ibid.

42. Ibid.

43. Howard Weaver to Kingman Brewster, 9 March 1971, Kingman Brewster Jr. Presidential Records, RU-11, box 26, folder 4, Yale University Manuscripts and Archives, New Haven.

44. The March 5 petition also included Murray Milne and Alan Taniguchi (1922–1998), then serving as dean at the University of Texas, Austin, who received two votes each. Also included were Kenneth Frampton (b. 1930), an English-trained architect-historian teaching at Princeton; Associate Professor of City Planning Walter Harris; and Christopher Alexander, who each received no votes. Students signing that petition included Jay Bright (M.Arch 1971); Carlton M. Davis (B.A. 1968, M.Arch 1971); Gabriela Goldschmidt (M.Arch 1971); Evan Lanman (B.A. 1964, M.Arch 1971); Marc Appleton (M.Arch 1972); Roberta Carlson (M.Arch 1972); Heather Willson Cass (M.Arch 1972); John H. T. Dow, Jr. (M.Arch 1972); William N. Gardner (M.Arch 1972); David Gibson (B.A. 1967, M.Arch 1972); Marvin Michalsen (B.A. 1968, M.Arch 1972); Barton Phelps (M.Arch 1972); Jefferson B. Riley (M.Arch 1972); Clinton Sheerr (B.A. 1969, M.Arch 1972); Richard C. Shepard, Jr. (M.Arch 1972); Henry B. Teague (M.Arch 1972); Roger Yee (B.A. 1969, M.Arch 1972); Judith E. Bing (M.Arch 1973); J. P. Chadwick Floyd (B.A. 1966, M.Arch 1973); Steve Holt (M.Arch 1973); Robert Page (M.Arch 1973); Larry Thomas (M.Arch 1973); Henry Wollman (M.Arch 1973); Robert J. Yudell (B.A. 1969, M.Arch 1973); William P. Durkee (M.Arch 1974); Barbara L. Geddis (ArtA 1974); and others whose names are illegible. Kingman Brewster Jr. Presidential Records, RU-11, ser. I, box 28, folder 2, Yale University Manuscripts and Archives, New Haven; Goldschmidt's petition was signed by Ron Filson (B.Arch 1970); Carlton M. Davis (B.A. 1968, M.Arch 1971); K. Hayakaway (M.E.D. 1971); Ellen Leopold (M.Arch 1971); Thomas M. Kubota (B.A. 1961, M.Arch 1971); Paul Sparis (M.E.D. 1971); James Walters (B.A. 1966, M.Arch 1971); Hiroshi Watanabe (M.Arch 1971); Frederick Bland (B.A. 1968, M.Arch 1972); Stephen Blatt (B.A. 1968, M.Arch 1972); Jefferson B. Riley (M.Arch 1972); Richard Shepard, Jr. (M.Arch 1972); Roger Yee (M.Arch 1972); and others. For more on Shadrach Woods, see Shadrach Woods, *Candilis-Josic-Woods: Building for People* (New York: F. A. Praeger, 1968); Shadrach Woods, *Urbanism Is Everybody's Business* (Stuttgart: K. Krämer, 1968); Shadrach Woods Architectural Records and Papers, 1923–2008, the Department of Drawings and Archives, Avery Architectural and Fine Arts Library, Columbia University, New York, N.Y.

45. Ada Louise Huxtable, "Creations of Top 3 Architects Shown," *New York Times*, September 30, 1970, 38.

46. Barton Phelps, interview by Jimmy Stamp, April 17, 2013.

47. Students of the School of Architecture, letter and proposal to Kingman Brewster, 11 March 1971, Kingman Brewster Jr. Presidential Records, RU-11, ser. I, box 28, folder 2, Yale University Manuscripts

and Archives, New Haven. Students signing the March 11 letter included Jay Bright (M.Arch 1971); Carlton M. Davis (B.A. 1968, M.Arch 1971); Gabriela Goldschmidt (M.Arch 1971); Evan Lanman (B.A. 1964, M.Arch 1971); Marc Appleton (M.Arch 1972); Heather Willson Cass (M.Arch 1972); Roberta Carlson (M.Arch 1972); John H. T. Dow, Jr. (M.Arch 1972); W. N. Gardner (M.Arch 1972); David Gibson (B.A. 1967, M.Arch 1972); Marvin Michalsen (B.A. 1968, M.Arch 1972); Barton Phelps (M.Arch 1972); Jefferson B. Riley (M.Arch 1972); Clinton Sheerr (B.A. 1969, M.Arch 1972); Richard C. Shepard, Jr. (M.Arch 1972); Harry B. Teague (M.Arch 1972); Roger Yee (M.Arch 1972); Judith E. Bing (M.Arch 1973); J. P. Chadwick Floyd (B.A. 1966, M.Arch 1973); Steve Holt (M.Arch 1973); Robert Page (M.Arch 1973); Larry Thomas (M.Arch 1973); Henry Wollman (M.Arch 1973); Robert J. Yudell (B.A. 1969, M.Arch 1973); William P. Durkee IV (M.Arch 1974); Barbara L. Geddis (M.Arch 1974), and others. Kingman Brewster Jr. Presidential Records, RU-11, ser. I, box 28, folder 2, Yale University Manuscripts and Archives, New Haven.

48. Gertraud A. Wood to Kingman Brewster, 4 May 1971, in ibid.

49. Thomas R. Vreeland, Jr., to Kingman Brewster, 13 April 1971, in ibid.

50. Jaquelin Robertson, interview by Jimmy Stamp, July 21, 2011; for Llewelyn-Davies, see Noel Annan, *Richard Llewelyn-Davies and the Architect's Dilemma* (Princeton, N.J.: Institute for Advanced Study, 1987).

51. Jaquelin Robertson, interview by Jimmy Stamp, July 21, 2011.

52. Ibid. There is no documentation of this appointment. Robertson

has said that Brewster "erased" the appointment from the records. As of this writing, Cooper-Robertson is transferring its archives to Yale, but there are no letters or memos included in materials collected thus far.

53. Ibid.

54. Charles H. Taylor, memo to faculty and students of the School of Architecture, 3 September 1971, Kingman Brewster Jr. Presidential Records, RU-11, ser. I, box 28, folder 2, Yale University Manuscripts and Archives, New Haven; Yale University News Bureau, press release, September 12, 1971, in ibid.

55. George A. Dudley, Chairman's Report on the Schools of Art and Architecture, University Council, 1–2 November 1972, Kingman Brewster Jr. Presidential Records, RU-11, ser. III, box 438, folder 16, Yale University Manuscripts and Archives, New Haven.

56. "Biography of Herman D. J. Spiegel," Faculty Information Service of the Yale University News Bureau, n.d, Yale University, Records of the Dean RU-843, accn. 2002-A-082, box 1, Yale University Manuscripts and Archives, New Haven.

57. Herman D. J. Spiegel quoted in Yale University News Bureau, press release, September 12, 1971, Kingman Brewster Jr. Presidential Records, RU-11, ser. I, box 28, folder 2, Yale University Manuscripts and Archives, New Haven.

58. Herman D. J. Spiegel to Charles H. Taylor, 10 August 1971, Kingman Brewster Jr. Presidential Records, RU-11, ser. I, box 26, folder 4, Yale University Manuscripts and Archives, New Haven.

59. Dudley, Chairman's Report, 2.

60. Alexander Purves, interview by Jimmy Stamp, January 18, 2013.

61. James Kruhly, interview by Jimmy Stamp, November 10, 2011.

62. Henry Wollman, "Editorial Statement," Yale School of Architecture Calendar, November–December 1971, quoted in Ada Louise Huxtable, "The Building You Love to Hate," *New York Times*, December 12, 1971, D29.

63. Huxtable, "Building You Love to Hate."

64. Ibid.

65. Ibid.

66. Paul Goldberger, "Yale Architecture Building— Decade of Crisis," *New York Times*, April 30, 1974, 48.

67. Stephen R. Hagan and James Kruhly, "Preservation," Yale School of Architecture Calendar, March–May 1973, School of Architecture Memorabilia, RU-925, accn. 2008-A-170, box 1, Yale University Manuscripts and Archives, New Haven.

68. Herman D. J. Spiegel, "Statement of Progress," Yale School of Architecture Calendar, September–December 1974, in ibid.

69. James Kruhly, interview by Jimmy Stamp, November 10, 2011.

70. "The B.E.S.T., at Yale," pamphlet, n.d. [c. 1971], Kingman Brewster Jr. Presidential Records, RU-11, ser. II, box 247, folder 5, Yale University Manuscripts and Archives, New Haven.

71. "B.E.S.T., at Yale"; BEST students included first-year students Courtney Brown, Lonnie Odom, Maurice Parish, Josef Stagg, Hugh Thompson, and Al Tucker, and second-year students James Burris, Phil Dozier, Henry Wade Geter, and Percy Williams, as well as degree candidates Arthur Duncan, Sandra Moore, Jenkins Washington, and Ted Burrell.

72. Herman Spiegel to Richard Dozier, 22 June 1972, Records

of the Dean, RU-843, accn. 2007-A-193, box 14, Yale University Manuscripts and Archives, New Haven.

73. Herman D. J. Spiegel to Kingman Brewster, "A Brief Personal Commentary," 8 July 1974, in ibid.

74. *Bulletin of Yale University, School of Art and Architecture, 1976–1977* ser. 72, no. 4 (May 15, 1976), 45–46.

75. Ibid.

76. Ray Gindroz, interview by Jimmy Stamp, July 10, 2012; see Urban Design Associates [Ray Gindroz et al.], *The Urban Design Handbook: Techniques and Working Methods* (New York: W. W. Norton, 2002); and Urban Design Associates [Ray Gindroz et al.], *The Architectural Pattern Book* (New York: W. W. Norton, 2004).

77. James Kruhly, interview by Jimmy Stamp, November 11, 2011.

78. Ibid.

79. Elizabeth Plater-Zyberk, "The Recuperation of the Traditional Town" (William C. DeVane Lecture, Yale School of Architecture, New Haven, November 26, 2001), Guide to the Yale School of Architecture Lectures and Presentations, RU-880, accn. 2002-A-151, box 16, Yale University Manuscripts and Archives, New Haven; Harold Bloom, *The Anxiety of Influence: A Theory of Poetry* (New York: Oxford University Press, 1973).

80. Vincent Scully, interview by Jimmy Stamp, August 23, 2010.

81. Herbert Newman, interview by Jimmy Stamp, July 20, 2013.

82. Patrick Pinnell, interview by Jimmy Stamp, August 15, 2012.

83. Ibid.

84. David Schwarz, interview by Jimmy Stamp, July 26, 2012.

85. Ibid.

86. Ibid,

87. Ibid.

88. William McDonough, interview by Jimmy Stamp, July 5, 2012.

89. Ibid.

90. Ibid.

91. Ibid.

92. Ibid.

93. Ibid.

94. David Schwarz, interview by Jimmy Stamp, July 26, 2012.

95. Ibid.

96. Ibid.

97. Ibid.

98. James Stirling quoted in Stuart Silk, ed., Yale School of Architecture Calendar, March–May 1975, School of Architecture Memorabilia, RU-925, accn. 2008-A-170, box 1, Yale University Manuscripts and Archives, New Haven; Stirling addresses similar issues in his essay, "Influence of Corb on Me Now and When a Student," in *James Stirling: Early Unpublished Writings on Architecture,* ed. Mark Crinson (London: Routledge, 2009), 74–78.

99. Charles Jencks, "The Rise of Post Modern Architecture," *Architectural Association Quarterly* 7, no. 4 (October–December 1975): 3–14.

100. Emmanuel Petit, *An Architect's Legacy: James Stirling's Students at Yale, 1959–1983* (New Haven: Yale School of Architecture, 2010).

101. Ibid.

102. Ibid.

103. Ibid.

104. Stanley Tigerman, interview by Jimmy Stamp, August 25, 2011.

105. Marion Weiss, interview by Jimmy Stamp, September 28, 2012.

106. Cesar Pelli quoted in Mark Girouard, *Big Jim: The Life and Work of James Stirling* (London: Pimlico, 2000), 131.

107. Robert Kahn quoted in ibid. `

108. Alexander Gorlin quoted in ibid., 131–32.

109. Ulrike Wilke quoted in ibid.,

132.

110. Ibid.

111. Audrey Matlock quoted in ibid.

112. Alexander Gorlin quoted in ibid.

113. Ulrike Wilke quoted in ibid., 133.

114. Audrey Matlock quoted in ibid.

115. In his will, William Henry Bishop, who was an art critic, editor, diplomat, and, in his later years, a painter, bequeathed the residue of his estate to Yale for the establishment of the William Henry Bishop Fund for promoting the study of architecture in the university. "Preliminary Guide to the William Henry Bishop Papers," http://hdl.handle.net/10079/fa/mssa.ms.0083 (accessed February 25, 2015), MS-83 Yale University Manuscripts and Archives, New Haven.

116. During Spiegel's tenure, Bishop Visiting Professors included Sir Leslie Martin (spring 1974); Cesar Pelli (fall 1974); Richard Meier (spring 1975); Donald Stull (fall 1975); Noel Michael McKinnell (spring 1976); and Bruce Goff (fall 1976).

117. Cecil A. Alexander, University Council Report of the Committee on Architecture, 1976, Secretary's Office, Yale University Records, RU-52, accn. 1991-A-082, box 6, Manuscripts and Archives, Yale University, New Haven.

118. George A. Dudley, University Council's Report on the Schools of Art and Architecture, University Council, November 1972, Kingman Brewster Jr. Presidential Records, RU-11, ser. III, box 438, folder 16, Yale University Manuscripts and Archives, New Haven.

119. Allan Greenberg, interview by Jimmy Stamp, November 15, 2011.

120. Herman Spiegel, "Personal Commentary," Annual Report: School of Architecture for the Academic Year 1972–1973 (1973).

121. Allan Greenberg, interview by Jimmy Stamp, November 15, 2011.

122. University Council, Report of the Committee on the School of Architecture, November 20, 1973, Secretary's Office, Yale University Records, RU-52, accn. 1991-A-082, box 6, Manuscripts and Archives, Yale University, New Haven.

123. Allan Greenberg, interview by Jimmy Stamp, November 15, 2011. Raymond Powell (1922–1987) was a professor of economics at Yale from 1952 to 1980.

124. Ibid.

125. Ibid.

126. Spiegel, "Personal Commentary," 1972–1973.

127. William de Cossy, unpublished interview by C. Ray Smith (1978), C. Ray Smith Manuscript and Research Files on the Yale Art and Architecture Building by Paul Rudolph, MS-1948, Yale University Manuscripts and Archives, New Haven.

128. Ibid.

129. Andrés Duany, William C. DeVane seminar, Yale School of Architecture, New Haven, November 27, 2001, Guide to the Yale School of Architecture Lectures and Presentations, RU-880, accn. 2002-A-151, box 16, Yale University Manuscripts and Archives, New Haven.

130. Ibid.

131. David Schwarz, interview by Jimmy Stamp, July 26, 2012.

132. David M. Schwarz, *David Schwarz Architectural Services 1976–2001* (Washington, D.C.: Grayson, 2002); Robert L. Miller, ed., *David M. Schwarz Architect 2002–2007* (Washington, D.C.: Grayson, 2008).

133. David Schwarz, interview by Jimmy Stamp, July 26, 2012.

134. William McDonough, interview by Jimmy Stamp, July 5, 2012.

135. Murphey Pound to the dean [Spiegel], 8 August 1972, Yale University, Records of the Dean RU-843, accn. 2007-A-193, Yale University Manuscripts and Archives, New Haven.

136. Herman D. J. Spiegel to Murphey Pound, 25 October 1972, in ibid.

137. John F. Embersits to Herman D. J. Spiegel, 8 November 1972, in ibid.

138. Roger T. Jones to C. Ray Smith, 29 June 1981, C. Ray Smith Manuscript and Research Files on the Yale Art and Architecture Building; in a postscript, Jones avers that he's "not entirely sure which parts" of his letter are true. For the asbestos issue, see "Yale Art Volumes Will Be Removed to Safer Building," *New York Times*, September 10, 1974, 19; "Asbestos Called Risk," *Hartford Courant*, November 19, 1974, 26; and "Yale Removing Ceiling," *Hartford Courant*, January 4, 1975, 21.

139. Roger T. Jones to C. Ray Smith, 29 June 1981; see also Victor Osborne, Report on Asbestos Removal, 29 October 1975, Yale University, Records of the Dean RU-843, accn. 2007-A-193, Yale University Manuscripts and Archives, New Haven.

140. Administration Responses to Recommendations in the November 1973 Council Committee Reports, 24 April 1974, Kingman Brewster Jr. Presidential Records, RU-11, ser. III, box 438, folder 16, Yale University Manuscripts and Archives, New Haven.

141. Roger T. Jones to C. Ray Smith, 29 June 1981. In a postscript, Jones avers that he's "not entirely sure which parts of his letter are true."

C. Ray Smith Manuscript and Research Files on the Yale Art and Architecture Building.

142. Doug Michels, unpublished interview by C. Ray Smith, 1978, C. Ray Smith Manuscript and Research Files on the Yale Art and Architecture Building; for more on Ant Farm, see Felicity Scott, *Living Archive 7: Ant Farm, Allegorical Time Warp: The Media Fallout of July 21, 1969* (Barcelona: Actar, 2008).

143. Ray Gindroz, interview by Jimmy Stamp, July 10, 2012.

144. Individual reports were submitted by some committee members: Gerald Allen, "The Undergraduate Major in Architecture"; Jonathan Barnett, "Professional Curriculum"; Samuel Brody, "The Core Curriculum"; Heather Cass, "The Faculty of the School of Architecture"; and Cecil Alexander, "Finance." Other members of the Council Committee were Carla A. Hills, Gerald D. Hines, Donald Stull, and Stanley Tigerman. The report was revised on February 28, 1977; there was an "Administrative Response" transcribed from a tape of the meeting on May 6, 1977.

145. Herman D. J. Spiegel, "Personal Commentary," letter to Kingman Brewster, 30 September 1975, Yale University, Records of the Dean RU-843, accn. 2007-A-193, box 12, Yale University Manuscripts and Archives, New Haven.

146. *Blueprint for Leadership: Yale School of Architecture* (New Haven: Campaign for Yale, 1976).

147. Spiegel, "Personal Commentary," letter to Kingman Brewster, 23 September 1976, Yale University, Records of the Dean RU-843, accn. 2007-A-193, box 13, Yale University

7
A Brand-New School

Manuscripts and Archives, New Haven.

Epigraph. Objectives of the Yale School of Architecture, as set forth in *Bulletin of Yale University, School of Architecture, 1977–1988* ser. 73, no. 4 (May 16, 1977), 18. This description of the school's mission, first established by Cesar Pelli, is still used, with some minor changes, as of this writing.

1. Cesar Pelli, interview by Jimmy Stamp, October 5, 2011.
2. Herman Spiegel, paraphrased by Cesar Pelli, in ibid.
3. Ibid.
4. "Pelli Named Dean of School at Yale," *New York Times,* June 18, 1976, 11.
5. See University Council, Report of the Committee of Architecture, 3 December 1976, RU-11, ser. II, box 438, folder 18, Yale University Manuscripts and Archives, New Haven.
6. Cesar Pelli, interview by Jimmy Stamp, October 5, 2011.
7. Cesar Pelli, interview by Michael J. Crosbie, "Introduction," in *Cesar Pelli: Selected and Current Works* (Mulgrave, Aust.: Images, 1993), 7.
8. Eeva-Liisa Pelkonen and Donald Albrecht, eds., *Eero Saarinen: Shaping the Future* (New Haven: Yale University Press, 2006), 20–22, 357–58.
9. Cesar Pelli quoted in John Dreyfuss, "Cesar Pelli; Architect Soon to Depart for Yale University Post; Professional Skill, Imagination Will Be Missed Here," *Los Angeles Times,* December 19, 1976, 19.
10. The so-called "White and Gray" debates began with the publication of *Five Architects* (New York: Wittenborn, 1972), based on a 1967 exhibition at MoMA that included the work of Peter Eisenman, Michael Graves, Charles Gwathmey, John Hejduk, and Richard Meier—known collectively as the New York Five. The exhibition, and its accompanying publication, prompted a response from five other architects: Romaldo Giurgola, Allan Greenberg, Charles Moore, Jaquelin T. Robertson, and Robert A. M. Stern. In the May 1973 issue of *Architectural Forum,* these five architects (three of whom were former Yale students and one of whom was a former Yale dean), known collectively as "Grays," published criticisms of the New York Five, who would become known as the "Whites." The Grays believed that the modernism espoused by the Whites divorced architecture from its own history, from its context, from practical use, and from human experience; see "Five on Five," *Architectural Forum* (May 1973): 46–57; "White and Gray," *A+U: Architecture and Urbanism* 4 (April 1975): 25–80; and *Progressive Architecture* (October 1976): 70–77. For the Silvers, see *Progressive Architecture* (July 1974): 26, 29, 32.
11. For the "Four Days in May" event, also known as "White and Gray Meet Silver," held at UCLA in spring 1974, see *Progressive Architecture* (October 1976): 70–77; for the Silvers, see *Progressive Architecture* (July 1974): 26, 29, 32. The title of the conference was perhaps inspired by the Cold War thriller *Seven Days in May,* published in 1962 and turned into a film in 1964, about a hypothetical 1974 nuclear disarmament treaty and an attempted military coup in the United States.
12. Charles Jencks, "The Los Angeles Silvers," *A+U* (October 1976): 13–14.
13. Todd Gannon and Ewan Branda, eds., *A Confederacy of Heretics: The Architecture Gallery, Venice, 1979* (Los Angeles: SCI-Arc, 2013), 19.
14. Dreyfuss, "Architect Soon to Depart," 19, 22.
15. John Pastier, "Utility and Fantasy in Los Angeles' 'Blue Whale,'" *AIA Journal,* no. 67 (May 1978): 38–45.
16. Dreyfuss, "Architect Soon to Depart," 19.
17. Thomas Hines quoted in ibid., 22.
18. Cesar Pelli quoted in Claire Aldrich, "Pelli's Fame Rests on Firm Foundation," *Yale Daily News,* January 26, 1979.
19. Cesar Pelli quoted in ibid.
20. Pelli likely received this commission through the good offices of J. Irwin Miller, who had commissioned Pelli to design the Commons Center and Mall (1973), a monumental, glazed public atrium in Columbus, Indiana. See Philip F. Nelson to J. Irwin Miller, 27 February 1975, Pelli Clarke Pelli Records, 1952–2010, MS-1939, ser. III, box 67, Yale University Manuscripts and Archives, New Haven. For Pelli's proposed Music Center, see Pelli Clarke Pelli Records 1952–2010, MS-1939, ser. III box 67, Yale University Manuscripts and Archives, New Haven.
21. In 1991, Pelli would design a Music Library for Yale near the same location proposed for the Music Center. This project would also remain unrealized when space was found within Sterling Memorial Library. See Valerie Cruice, "The View from: Yale Music Library; Overflowing

Treasures Range from Bach to Benny Goodman," *New York Times,* April 14, 1991, A2; Pelli Clarke Pelli Records 1952–2010, MS-1939, ser. II box 666, Yale University Manuscripts and Archives, New Haven.

22. Cesar Pelli quoted in Dreyfuss, "Architect Soon to Depart," 22.

23. Paul Goldberger, "Museum of Modern Art Picks Architect for Tower," *New York Times,* January 27, 1977, 29.

24. Philip Johnson quoted in Dreyfuss, "Architect Soon to Depart," 19.

25. Charles Moore quoted in ibid.

26. Aldrich, "Pelli's Fame."

27. Heather Willson Cass, interview by Jimmy Stamp, December 17, 2012.

28. James Kruhly, interview by Jimmy Stamp, November 10, 2011.

29. Marc Goldstein, "A&A Students Fear Vulnerable Building, Dean Discusses Safety," *Yale Daily News,* March 26, 1981, 1, 6. For information on endowment issues at the time of Pelli's appointment, see John Tabor, "University Stock Drops; Operating Deficit Eases," *Yale Daily News,* January 13, 1975.

30. Cesar Pelli, "Personal Commentary," 1983–1984 Annual Report, Yale School of Architecture, January 24, 1983, Records of the Dean, RU-843, accn. 2007-A-193, box 13, Yale University Manuscripts and Archives, New Haven.

31. Cesar Pelli, interview by Jimmy Stamp, October 5, 2011.

32. Fred Clarke quoted in Aldrich, "Pelli's Fame."

33. Cesar Pelli paraphrased in Ray Gindroz, interview by Jimmy Stamp, July 10, 2011.

34. Aldrich, "Pelli's Fame."

35. Ibid.

36. John Kaliski quoted in ibid.

37. Cesar Pelli, 1979–1980 Annual Report, Yale School of Architecture, Records of the Dean, RU-843, accn. 2007-A-193, box 13, Yale University Manuscripts and Archives, New Haven.

38. Gavin Macrae-Gibson, interview by Jimmy Stamp, July 12, 2012.

39. Cesar Pelli, interview by Jimmy Stamp, October 5, 2011.

40. For an assessment of *Perspecta* under Pelli, see K. Michael Hays, "Searching for Authenticity" in *[Re]Reading Perspecta,* ed. Robert A. M. Stern, Peggy Deamer, and Alan Plattus (Cambridge, Mass.: MIT Press, 2004), 780–86.

41. Cesar Pelli, interview by Jimmy Stamp, October 5, 2011.

42. Vincent Scully, untitled essay, Yale School of Architecture Calendar, April–June 1979, Yale School of Architecture Memorabilia, RU-925, accn. 2008-A-170, box 1, Yale University Manuscripts and Archives, New Haven.

43. For example, Kemp Mooney (M.Arch 1963), Projected Martha Brewer Residence, Yale School of Architecture Calendar, May–August 1980, in ibid.; Morris brothers (Tim Morris, M.Arch 1978), Passive Solar Energized House, Yale School of Architecture Calendar, May–August 1980, in ibid.

44. George Ranalli, interview by Jimmy Stamp, April 9, 2013.

45. George Ranalli, e-mail message to Jimmy Stamp, February 5, 2014.

46. George Ranalli, interview by Jimmy Stamp, April 9, 2013.

47. Paul Rudolph quoted by George Ranalli in ibid.

48. Julie Peters, "Architects' Post-Postmodernism Dazzles," *Yale Daily News,* January 18, 1980.

49. For the Jahn exhibition, see *Helmut Jahn: A Yale School of Architecture Exhibition,* exh. cat. (New Haven: Yale School of Architecture,

1982); for the Pesce show, see *Gaetano Pesce: A Yale School of Architecture Exhibition,* exh. cat. (New Haven: Yale School of Architecture, 1983), Haas Arts Library, Yale University, New Haven.

50. *Raimund Abraham: Collisions,* exh. cat. (New Haven: Yale School of Architecture, 1981), Haas Arts Library, Yale University, New Haven.

51. *An Ideology for Making Architecture,* exh. cat. (New Haven: Yale School of Architecture, 1981), Haas Arts Library, Yale University, New Haven.

52. Robert Jensen (M.F.A. 1977), David Spiker (M.Arch 1978), and Kirk Train (M.Arch 1978), "Introduction," *Perspecta: The Yale Architectural Journal* 16 (1980): 6–7.

53. Cesar Pelli, ed., *Yale Seminar in Architecture Coordinated by Cesar Pelli,* vol. 2 (New Haven: Yale School of Architecture, 1981), 94.

54. Cesar Pelli, "Excerpts from a Conversation," *Perspecta: The Yale Architectural Journal* 19 (1982): 127–37.

55. Reminiscences of Elizabeth Gamard, August 6, 2012, e-mail message to Jimmy Stamp, August 26, 2012.

56. Cesar Pelli, ed., *Yale Seminar in Architecture Coordinated by Cesar Pelli,* vol. 1 (New Haven: Yale School of Architecture, 1981); Cesar Pelli, ed., *Yale Seminar in Architecture Coordinated by Cesar Pelli,* vol. 2 (New Haven: Yale School of Architecture, 1981).

57. Patrick Pinnell, interview by Jimmy Stamp, August 15, 2012.

58. Gavin Macrae-Gibson, interview by Jimmy Stamp, July 12, 2012; see also Gavin Macrae-Gibson, *The Secret Life of Buildings: An American Mythology for Modern Architecture* (Cambridge, Mass.: MIT Press, 1985).

59. Cesar Pelli to President A. Bartlett Giamatti, 24

January 1983, Yale School of Architecture, Records of the Dean, RU-843, accn. 2007-A-193, box 12, Yale University Manuscripts and Archives, New Haven.

60. Gavin Macrae-Gibson, interview by Jimmy Stamp, July 12, 2012.

61. Ibid.

62. Robert Kahn quoted in Aldrich, "Pelli's Fame."

63. Marion Weiss, interview by Jimmy Stamp, September 28, 2012.

64. Cesar Pelli, interview by Andrea Leers, "Professor Shinohara at The Yale [sic]," *Japan Architect*, no. 339 (July 1985): 46–47.

65. Ibid.

66. Gavin Macrae-Gibson, interview by Jimmy Stamp, July 12, 2012.

67. See Robert A. M. Stern and John Massengale, *The Anglo-American Suburb* (New York: St. Martin's, 1982); and Robert A. M. Stern, *Pride of Place: Building the American Dream* (Boston: Houghton Mifflin, 1986), 158. Gavin Macrae-Gibson's project for Stern's 1978 South Bronx Studio is illustrated in Robert Jensen, *Devastation/Resurrection: The South Bronx* (Bronx: Bronx Museum of the Arts, 1979).

68. See John Perkins and Kevin M. Smith, eds., *Retrospecta 1982–1983* (New Haven: Yale School of Architecture, 1983), 4.

69. Studio descriptions excerpted from Steven Marc Shapiro, ed., *Retrospecta 1979–1980* (New Haven: Yale School of Architecture, 1980).

70. Mary McLeod, "The End of Innocence: From Political Activism to Postmodernism," in *Architecture School: Three Centuries of Educating Architects in North America,* ed. Joan Ockman (Washington, D.C.: Association of Collegiate Schools of Architecture, London; Cambridge, Mass.:

MIT Press, 2012), 188.

71. Gavin Macrae-Gibson, interview by Jimmy Stamp, July 12, 2012.

72. Stanley Tigerman, *Designing Bridges to Burn: Architectural Memoirs by Stanley Tigerman* (Singapore: Oro, 2011), 19.

73. Stanley Tigerman, interview by Jimmy Stamp, August 25, 2011.

74. Cesar Pelli, interview by Andrea Leers, 46–47.

75. Kazuo Shinohara, "Contemporary Student Spirit: Japan/America," interview in *The Japan Architect,* no. 339 (July 1985): 44–45.

76. Ibid.

77. Gavin Macrae-Gibson, interview by Jimmy Stamp, July 12, 2012.

78. Cesar Pelli, interview by Jimmy Stamp, October 5, 2011.

79. Reminiscences of Elizabeth Gamard, August 6, 2012.

80. See Andrea Leers, Jane Weinzapfel, Joe Pryse, and Josiah Stevenson, *Made to Measure: The Architecture of Leers Weinzapfel Associates* (New York: Princeton Architectural Press, 2011).

81. Marion Weiss, interview by Jimmy Stamp, September 28, 2012.

82. Paul Goldberger, "Abandoning Orthodox Modernism," *New York Times,* July 11, 198, 13; see also Robert A. M. Stern, David Fishman, and Jacob Tilove, *New York 2000: Architecture and Urbanism between the Bicentennial and the Millennium* (New York: Monacelli, 2006), 985–86.

83. George Ranalli, interview by Jimmy Stamp, April 9, 2013.

84. Ibid.

85. Scott Merrill, recollections, e-mail message to Jimmy Stamp, December 22, 2012.

86. George Ranalli, excerpt from Gerald Allen et al., *Young Architects: Works,* exh. cat. (New Haven: Yale School of

Architecture, 1980), quoted in Steven Marc Shapiro, ed., *Retrospecta 1979–1980* (New Haven: Yale School of Architecture, 1980).

87. Gerald Allen, Donlyn Lyndon, and Charles Moore, *The Place of Houses* (Oakland: University of California Press, 1974).

88. George Ranalli, interview by Jimmy Stamp, April 9, 2013.

89. Ibid.

90. Ibid.

91. Ibid.

92. Philip Grausman, interview with Mark Rylander, "The Importance of Perspective Drawing in the Design Process: Philip Grausman's Drawing Class at Yale," *Crit* XV (summer 1985): 35.

93. Alexander Purves, interview by Jimmy Stamp, January 18, 2013.

94. Cesar Pelli, 1976–1977 Annual Report, n.d., Yale School of Architecture, Records of the Dean, RU-843, accn. 2007-A-193, box 13, Yale University Manuscripts and Archives, New Haven.

95. Ibid.

96. Ibid.

97. Ibid.

98. Maya Lin, "Making the Memorial," *New York Review of Books,* November 2, 2000, 33–35.

99. B. Drummond Ayres, Jr., "A Yale Senior, a Vietnam Memorial, and a Few Ironies," *New York Times,* June 29, 1981, B5.

100. Lin, "Making the Memorial."

101. Cesar Pelli to A. Bartlett Giamatti, 29 August 1980, Yale School of Architecture, Records of the Dean, RU-843, accn. 2007-A-193, box 9, Yale University Manuscripts and Archives, New Haven.

102. Gavin Macrae-Gibson, interview by Jimmy Stamp, July 12, 2012.

103. Cesar Pelli to A. Bartlett Giamatti, 29 August 1980, Yale School of Architecture, Records of the Dean, RU-843,

accn. 2007-A-193, box 9, Yale University Manuscripts and Archives, New Haven.

104. Cesar Pelli, interview by Jimmy Stamp, October 5, 2011.

105. Ellen McGarrahan, "Architecture Dean Quits," *Yale Daily News,* November 17, 1983.

106. Cesar Pelli to President A. Bartlett Giamatti, 24 January 1983, Yale School of Architecture, Records of the Dean, RU-843, accn. 2007-A-193, box 12, Yale University Manuscripts and Archives, New Haven; see also, A. Bartlett Giamatti to Cesar Pelli, 11 May 1983, in ibid.

107. McGarrahan, "Architecture Dean Quits."

108. Martin Gehner, 1984–1985 Annual Report, Yale School of Architecture, Records of the Dean, RU-843, accn. 2007-A-193, box 13, Yale University Manuscripts and Archives, New Haven.

Rappel à l'Ordre

Epigraph. Thomas Beeby quoted in Gilbert Strickler, ed., *Retrospecta 1985–1986* (New Haven: Yale School of Architecture, 1986), 1.

1. Vincent Scully to President A. Bartlett Giamatti, 1 January 1984, Records of A. Bartlett Giamatti, President of Yale University, RU-276, accn. 1991-A-053, box 1, Yale University Manuscripts and Archives, New Haven.

2. Ibid.

3. Ibid.

4. Peter Millard, memo to Herman Spiegel, 15 March 1984, King-lui Wu Archives, MS-1842, temporary box 2B, Yale University Manuscripts and Archives, New Haven.

5. Search Committee (Herman Spiegel, Kent Bloomer, Walter DeS. Harris, Jr., Herbert S. Newman, and King-lui Wu) to President A. Bartlett Giamatti, 19 September 1984, Records of A. Bartlett Giamatti, President of Yale University, RU-276, accn. 1996-A-035, box 1, Yale University Manuscripts and Archives, New Haven. For Beeby's reluctance to be considered, see Thomas H. Beeby to Herman D. J. Spiegel, 23 May 1984, and Herman D. J. Spiegel to Thomas H. Beeby, 23 July 1984, both in ibid.

6. Students to President Giamatti, 21 October 1984, in ibid.

7. Kent Bloomer to Herman Spiegel, Search Committee chairman, 15 November 1984, in ibid.; see also President Giamatti's handwritten notes made after a meeting with students, 19 November 1984, in ibid.

8. Kent Bloomer to Herman Spiegel, Search Committee chairman, 15 November 1984, in ibid.

9. Vincent Scully to A. Bartlett Giamatti, 12 November 1984, in ibid.

10. King-lui-Wu to A. Bartlett Giamatti, 15 November 1984, King-Lui Wu Archives, MS-1842, temporary box 2B, Yale University Manuscripts and Archives, New Haven.

11. Peter Millard, memo to Herman Spiegel, n.d., A. Bartlett Giamatti, President of Yale University, Records, RU-276, accn. 1991-A-053, box 1, Yale University Manuscripts and Archives, New Haven.

12. John Hejduk to A. Bartlett Giamatti, 17 January 1984; and Gavin Macrae-Gibson to A. Bartlett Giamatti, 27 October 1984, both in ibid.; and Robert A. M. Stern to A. Bartlett Giamatti, 8 November 1984, Records of A. Bartlett Giamatti, President of Yale University, RU-276, accn. 1996-A-035, Box 1, Yale University Manuscripts and Archives, New Haven.

13. Emmanuel Petit, *Ceci n'est pas une reverie: The Architecture of Stanley Tigerman*, exh. cat. (New Haven: Yale University School of Architecture, 2011).

14. Peter Millard, memo to Herman Spiegel, n.d., A. Bartlett Giamatti, President of Yale University, Records, RU-276, accn. 1991-A-053, box 1, Yale University Manuscripts and Archives, New Haven.

15. Ibid.

16. Ibid.

17. Ibid.

18. Ibid.

19. Ibid.

20. Student representatives (Frank Koumantaris, Amy Reichert, and Andrea Swartz representing the first-year students [class of 1987]; Susan Baggs, Bruce Lindsey, and John Tittmann representing the second-year students [class of 1986]; Siamak Hariri and Charles Loomis, representing the third-year students [class of 1985]; and Tim Culvahouse representing the M.E.D students) to President A. Bartlett Giamatti, 26 November 1984, Records of A. Bartlett Giamatti, President of Yale University, RU-276, accn. 1996-A-035, box 1, Yale University Manuscripts and Archives, New Haven.

21. Ibid.

22. Ibid.

23. Tigerman, *Designing Bridges to Burn*, 233–34.

24. A. Bartlett Giamatti to the Community of the School of Architecture, 28 January 1985, Records of A. Bartlett Giamatti, President of Yale University, RU-276, accn. 1996-A-035, box 1, Yale University Manuscripts and Archives, New Haven; see also Yale University News Bureau, press release no. 78, January 28, 1985, in ibid.

25. President Giamatti quoted in

Yale University News Bureau, press release no. 78, January 28, 1985, in ibid.

26. Thomas Beeby, speaking at the 2013 Richard H. Driehaus Prize Colloquium, Chicago, March 23, 2013.

27. Ibid.

28. Ross Miller, "Interview; Thomas Beeby," *Progressive Architecture* (March 1990): 113.

29. Beeby, lecture; for Mies's pedagogy at IIT, see Kevin Harrington, "Order, Space, Proportion: Mies's Curriculum at IIT," in *Mies van der Rohe: Architect as Educator*, ed. Rolf Achilles, Kevin Harrington, and Charlotte Myhrum, exh. cat. (Chicago: Illinois Institute of Technology, 1986), 49–68. See also Franz Schulze and Edward Windhorst, *Mies van der Rohe: A Critical Biography*, new and rev. ed. (Chicago: University of Chicago Press, 2012), 189–247.

30. Stanley Tigerman, interview by Betty Blum, 1998, "Oral History of Stanley Tigerman," the Chicago Architects Oral History Project, Ernest R. Graham Study Center for Architectural Drawings, Department of Architecture, the Art Institute of Chicago, 198.

31. Charles Gwathmey to A. Bartlett Giamatti, 1 March 1985, A. Bartlett Giamatti, President of Yale University, Records, RU-276, accn. 1996-A-035, box 1, Yale University Manuscripts and Archives, New Haven. The characterization of Gwathmey's epistolary style is from Vincent J. Scully to A. Bartlett Giamatti, 12 November 1984, in ibid.

32. Stanley Tigerman, interview by Betty Blum, 1998, 197.

33. Herbert Newman, interview by Jimmy Stamp, July 20, 2013.

34. Ibid.

35. Thomas Beeby, interview by

Hans Baldauf and Gilbert Schafer, *Rap Sheets: Special Project Interviews: Thomas H. Beeby*, vol. 2, ed. Hans Baldauf and Gilbert Schafer (New Haven: Yale School of Architecture, 1988), 39.

36. Thomas Beeby, interview by Betty Blum, 1998, "Oral History of Thomas Beeby," the Chicago Architects Oral History Project, Ernest R. Graham Study Center for Architectural Drawings, Department of Architecture, the Art Institute of Chicago, 103.

37. Thomas Beeby, interview by Hans Baldauf and Gilbert Schafer, 39.

38. Alan Plattus, interview by Jimmy Stamp, October 26, 2012.

39. Thomas Beeby, interview by Betty Blum, 1998, 103.

40. In 1994, his appointment became full time as associate professor of architectural design and theory. He served as associate dean from 1989 until 1998.

41. Alan Plattus, interview by Jimmy Stamp, October 26, 2012.

42. Thomas Beeby, interview by Hans Baldauf and Gilbert Schafer, 4–5.

43. Ibid., 3.

44. Mark Linder and Oscar Mertz, eds., *Rap Sheets* 0, no. 0 (November 5, 1986): 2.

45. Issues of *Rap Sheets* in the Yale School of Architecture collection include: Mark Linder and Oscar Mertz, eds., *Rap Sheets* 0, no. 0 (November 5, 1986); Mark Linder, ed., *Rap Sheets* 1, no. 1 (November 11, 1986); Oscar Mertz, ed., *Rap Sheets* 1, no. 2 (December 10, 1986); Hans Baldauf, Cary Bernstein (M.Arch 1988), Mary Buttrick (M.Arch 1987), Carey Feierabend (M.Arch 1986), Eliot Baker Goodwin (M.Arch 1987), and Li Wen (M.Arch 1988), eds., *Rap Sheets* 1, no. 3 (January 1, 1987);

Molly Hankwitz (M.Arch 1987), ed., *Rap Sheets* 1, no. 4 (February 19, 1987); Mark Linder (M.Arch 1986, M.E.D. 1988), ed., *Rap Sheets* 1, no. 5 (March 30, 1985); Charles Orton (M.Arch 1987) and Tony Ronning (M.Arch 1987), eds., *Rap Sheets* 1, no. 6 (April 17, 1987); Doug Garofalo (M.Arch 1987), ed., *Rap Sheets* 1, no. 7 (May 25, 1987); Li Wen, ed., *Rap Sheets* 2, no. 1 (October 19, 1987); Tom Marble (M.Arch 1988), ed., *Rap Sheets* 2, no. 2 (February 10, 1988); *Rap Sheets* 2, no. 3 (April 18, 1988); Lance Hosey (M.Arch 1990), ed., *Rap Sheets* 3, no. 1 (October 13, 1988); *Rap Sheets* 4, no. 4 (February 19, 1990); and *Rap Sheets* 5, no. 1 (n.d., c. 1991). See also *Rap Sheets* 1, no. 1 (April 1, 1988), an anonymous parody of *Rap Sheets* that published images of graffiti taken from the A&A bathrooms; and a two-part special issue consisting solely of an extended interview with Tom Beeby: Hans Baldauf and Gilbert Schafer, eds., *Rap Sheets: Special Project Interviews: Thomas H. Beeby*, 1 and 2 (1988).

46. Hans Baldauf and Gilbert Schafer, "Introduction," in Baldauf and Schafer, *Rap Sheets: Special Project Interviews*, vol. 1, 1.

47. Thomas Beeby, interview by Hans Baldauf and Gilbert Schafer, in Baldauf and Schafer, *Rap Sheets: Special Project Interviews*, vol. 2, 4.

48. Ibid., 21.

49. Ibid., 7.

50. Ibid., 9.

51. Tom Beeby, Strategic Plan: The School of Architecture, 1992, 19, Richard C. Levin, President of Yale University, Records, RU-832, accn. 2000-A-020, box 1, Yale University Manuscripts and Archives, New Haven.

52. See Deborah Berke, Amy Hempel, and Tracy Myers,

eds., *Deborah Berke* (New Haven: Yale University Press, 2008); and David Mohney and Keller Easterling, eds., *Seaside* (New York: Princeton Architectural Press, 1991), 118–31.

53. Deborah Berke and Steven Harris, eds., *Architecture of the Everyday* (New York: Princeton Architectural Press, 1997); for Harris, see Steven Harris, *True Life: Steven Harris Architects* (New York: Princeton Architectural Press, 2010).

54. See Turner Brooks, *Turner Brooks: Work* (New York: Princeton Architectural Press, 1995).

55. Deborah Berke, interview by Jimmy Stamp, November 28, 2012.

56. Steve Case, ed., *Retrospecta 1991–1992* (New Haven: Yale School of Architecture, 1992), 27.

57. Debra Coleman, Elizabeth Danze, and Carol Henderson, eds., *Architecture and Feminism* (New York: Princeton Architectural Press, 1996).

58. Deborah Berke, interview by Jimmy Stamp, November 28, 2012.

59. Alexander Purves, interview by Jimmy Stamp, January 18, 2013.

60. Ibid.

61. Thomas Beeby, interview by Hans Baldauf and Gilbert Schafer, 5.

62. Thomas Beeby, "Introductory Statement," in Strickler, *Retrospecta 1985–1986*, 1.

63. Martin D. Gehner, memo to Frank H. Turner, provost, 6 June 1990, Records of Benno C. Schmidt, Jr., President of Yale University, RU-281, accn. 1998-A-007, box 1, Yale University Manuscripts and Archives, New Haven.

64. George Ranalli, interview by Jimmy Stamp, April 9, 2013.

65. Ibid.

66. Gavin Macrae-Gibson, interview by Jimmy Stamp, July 12, 2012.

67. Thomas Beeby, interview by Hans Baldauf and Gilbert Schafer, vol. 2, 39.

68. Gavin Macrae-Gibson, interview by Jimmy Stamp, July 12, 2012.

69. Thomas Beeby, interview by Hans Baldauf and Gilbert Schafer, vol. 2, 16; for Beeby's Sulzer Library, see Robert A. M. Stern, *Modern Classicism* (New York: Rizzoli, 1988), 188–91; for his Harold Washington Library, see Mark Alden Branch, "Washington's Monument," *Progressive Architecture* (February 1992): 60–69.

70. Erika Belsey and Julia Williams, eds., *Retrospecta 1988–1989* (New Haven: Yale School of Architecture, 1989), 10.

71. Ross Miller, "Interview: Thomas Beeby," *Progressive Architecture* (March 1990): 113–14.

72. Dan Cooper, ed., *New Classic American Houses: The Architecture of Albert, Righter, and Tittmann* (New York: Vendome, 2009).

73. Duncan Stroik, *The Church Building as a Sacred Place: Beauty, Transcendence, and the Eternal* (Chicago: Hillenbrand, 2012).

74. Gilbert Schafer, *The Great American House: Tradition for the Way We Live Now* (New York: Rizzoli, 2011), 12.

75. Gilbert Schafer III, interview by Jimmy Stamp, February 26, 2013.

76. Stephen Brockman and Alison Hornes, eds., *Retrospecta 1987–1988* (New Haven: Yale School of Architecture, 1988), 10.

77. Schafer, *Great American House*, 12.

78. Gilbert Schafer III, interview by Jimmy Stamp, February 26, 2013.

79. Beeby, "Introductory Statement," 1.

80. Gilbert Schafer III, interview by Jimmy Stamp, February 26,

2013.

81. Belsey and Williams, *Retrospecta 1988–1989*, 6.

82. Julia Williams, ed., *Retrospecta 1989–1990* (New Haven: Yale School of Architecture, 1990), 8.

83. Tadao Ando, "Learning from the Modern Movement," in *Tadao Ando: The Yale Studio and Current Works*, ed. Tadao Ando, George T. Kunihiro, and Peter Eisenman (New York: Rizzoli, 1989), 13–14.

84. Tadao Ando quoted in Kenneth Frampton, "Tadao Ando and the Cult of Shintai," in Ando, Kunihiro, and Eisenman, *Tadao Ando*, 12.

85. Eric Chang and Paul Wang, eds., *Retrospecta 1994–1995* (New Haven: Yale University School of Architecture, 1995); J. Knoops, F. Rascoe, P. Whang, and J. Woell, eds., *Pamphlet Architecture 18: A+A . . .* (unpublished).

86. Gavin Macrae-Gibson, "Introduction," in *Design Faculty Show 1987* (New Haven: Yale School of Architecture, 1987), 2.

87. De Alba went on to edit a book on Rudolph's late work; Roberto de Alba, ed., *Paul Rudolph: The Late Work* (New York: Princeton Architectural Press, 2003).

88. Gilbert Schafer III, interview by Jimmy Stamp, February 26, 2013.

89. Vincent Scully, "Unity Temple and the A&A," *Perspecta: The Yale Architectural Journal* 22, ed. John Perks, Paul Rosenblatt, and Jennifer Sage (1986): 108–9.

90. Timothy Rohan, "Canon and Anti-Canon: On the Fall and Rise of the A&A," *Harvard Design Magazine* 14 (June 2001): 27.

91. Gilbert Schafer III, interview by Jimmy Stamp, February 26, 2013.

92. Paul Goldberger, "Yale Students Lend a Hand to an Abused Building," *New York*

Times, November 20, 1988, H39.

93. Ibid.

94. Gilbert Schafer III, interview by Jimmy Stamp, February 26, 2013.

95. Thomas Beeby, "Preface," *Paul Rudolph: Drawings of the Art and Architecture Building at Yale, 1959–1963* (New Haven: Yale School of Architecture, 1988), 3.

96. Paul Rudolph quoted in Michael J. Crosbie, "Paul Rudolph's on Yale's A&A," *Architecture* (November 1988): 100–105.

97. Ibid.

98. Ibid.

99. Robert de Alba quoted in Mark Alden Branch, "The Building That Won't Go Away," *Yale Alumni Magazine,* February 1998, 36–41.

100. Thomas Beeby, Annual Report for 1989–1990, Benno C. Schmidt, Jr., President of Yale University, Records, RU-281, accn. 1998-A-007, box 18, Yale University Manuscripts and Archives, New Haven; see also Robert A. M. Stern, "Perspective on Perspecta," *Perspecta: The First Twenty-Five* (New Haven: Yale School of Architecture, 1989), 3–4; and Robert A. M. Stern Architects Records, MS-1859, accn. 2006-M-102, box 35, Yale University Manuscripts and Archives, New Haven.

101. Thomas Beeby, Annual Report for 1986–1987, Benno C. Schmidt, Jr., President of Yale University, Records, RU-281, accn. 1996-A-072, box 15, Yale University Manuscripts and Archives, New Haven.

102. "Developing the American City: Society and Architecture in the Regional City," *Rap Sheets* 1, no. 3, ed. Hans Baldauf, Cary Bernstein, Mary Buttrick, Carey Feierabend, Baker Goodwin, and Li Wen (January 30, 1987): 2.

103. Ibid.

104. *The Search for Shelter: A Symposium and Design Workshop on Housing the Homeless, Yale School of Architecture* (New Haven: Yale School of Architecture, 1988), proceedings of a symposium on January 30–31, 1988, cosponsored by Yale School of Architecture Environmental Design Program and the Connecticut Society of Architects.

105. Mark Alden Branch, "Yale Conference on People of Color," *Progressive Architecture* (January 1992): 22–23.

106. J. C. Calderón, "Black Architects: There Are Signs of Hope," *New York Times,* October 27, 1991, A4.

107. Branch, "Yale Conference," 22–23.

108. See Richard W. Hayes, *The Yale Building Project: The First 40 Years* (New Haven: Yale School of Architecture with Yale University Press, 2007), 154.

109. Ibid., 155–57.

110. Paul Brouard quoted in ibid., 32.

111. For Church Street South, see "Low-Moderate Baroque," *Progressive Architecture* 53 (May 1972): 74–83.

112. Thomas H. Beeby to Benno C. Schmidt, Jr., 23 May 1991, Benno C. Schmidt, Jr., President of Yale University, Records, RU-281, accn. 1998-A-123, box 1, Yale University Manuscripts and Archives, New Haven; Benno C. Schmidt, Jr., to Thomas H. Beeby, 16 September 1991, in ibid.

113. Tom Beeby quoted in "Architecture Dean Resigns, Citing Practice and Family," *Yale Daily News,* October 4, 1991.

114. Thomas Beeby quoted in *Retrospecta 1985–1986,* 1.

115. Beeby, Strategic Plan.

116. Ibid.

117. Ibid.

118. Ibid.

119. Ibid.; Robert A. M. Stern, Dean's Letter, 20 September 2005, School of Architecture, Yale University, Records of the Dean RU-843, Yale University Manuscripts and Archives, New Haven.

120. Beeby, Strategic Plan, 12; for the Architecture-Forestry joint degree program, see Micah Ziegler, *Yale Daily News,* January 20, 2006.

121. Robert A. M. Stern, Dean's Letter, 19 September 2008, School of Architecture, Yale University, Records of the Dean RU-843, Yale University Manuscripts and Archives, New Haven.

122. Beeby, Strategic Plan, 14–15.

123. Robert A. M. Stern, Dean's Letter, 16 September 2003, School of Architecture, Yale University, Records of the Dean RU-843, Yale University Manuscripts and Archives, New Haven.

124. Thomas Beeby, interview by Hans Baldauf and Gilbert Schafer, *Rap Sheets: Special Project Interviews: Thomas H. Beeby,* vol. 2, ed. Hans Baldauf and Gilbert Schafer (1988), 15.

9

Toward Urbanism

Epigraph. Fred Koeter, "Dean's Letter," in *Retrospecta 1994–1995,* ed. Eric Chang and Paul Wang (New Haven: Yale University School of Architecture, 1995).

1. Alan Plattus, interview by Jimmy Stamp, October 26, 2012.

2. Alexander Purves, interview by Jimmy Stamp, January 18, 2013.

3. Ari Zweiman, "Architecture Dean Resigns, Citing Practice and Family," *Yale Daily News,* October 4, 1991; Benno C. Schmidt, Jr., to the Members of the Architecture School

Community, 30 September 1991, Records of Benno C. Schmidt, Jr., President of Yale University, RU-281, accn. 1998-A-123, box 1, Yale University Manuscripts and Archives, New Haven.

4. Search Committee to President Benno C. Schmidt, Jr., February 1992, Records of Benno C. Schmidt, Jr., President of Yale University, RU-281, accn. 1998, box 1, Yale University Manuscripts and Archives, New Haven; Robert Venturi to President Benno C. Schmidt, Jr., 9 March 1992, Records of Benno C. Schmidt, Jr., President of Yale University, RU-281, accn. 1998-A-123, box 1, Yale University Manuscripts and Archives, New Haven.

5. Philip Johnson to Benno Schmidt, 6 February 1992, Records of Benno C. Schmidt, Jr., President of Yale University, RU-281, accn. 1998-A-123, box 1, folder 10, Yale University Manuscripts and Archives, New Haven; Craig Whitaker to Benno Schmidt, 12 February 1992, in ibid.

6. Alexander Purves, interview by Jimmy Stamp, January 18, 2013.

7. Steven Holl to President Benno Schmidt, Jr., 21 April 1992, Records of Benno C. Schmidt, Jr., President of Yale University, RU-281, accn. 1998-A-123, box 1, folder 10, Yale University Manuscripts and Archives, New Haven; Benno Schmidt, Jr., to Steven Holl, 29 May 1992, in ibid.

8. Frank O. Gehry to Alexander Purves, 13 January 1992, in ibid.; for other letters of recommendation in support of Ranalli, see Records of Benno C. Schmidt, Jr.

9. Gavin Macrae-Gibson, interview by Jimmy Stamp, July 12, 2012.

10. Audrey Matlock to President Benno C. Schmidt, 18 March 1992, Records of Benno C. Schmidt, Jr., President of Yale University, RU-281, accn. 1998-A-123, box 1, Yale University Manuscripts and Archives, New Haven.

11. Joshua P. Galper, "Architecture Dean Candidate Visits Yale," Yale Daily News, March 27, 1992, 1, 5.

12. Alexander Purves, interview by Jimmy Stamp, January 18, 2013.

13. "Prominent Boston Architect and Urban Designer Is Named Dean of Yale School of Architecture," Yale University News Bureau, press release no. 329, May 7, 1992; Benno C. Schmidt, Jr., to the Members of the Architecture School Community, 30 September 1991, Records of Benno C. Schmidt, Jr., President of Yale University, RU-281, accn. 1998-A-123, box 1, Yale University Manuscripts and Archives, New Haven.

14. Alexander Purves quoted in Mark Alden Branch, "Designing the Future," Yale Alumni Magazine, December 1992, 30–35.

15. Fred Koetter and Colin Rowe, Collage City (Cambridge, Mass.: MIT Press, 1978).

16. See Alan J. Plattus, Colin Rowe, and Fred Koetter, eds., Koetter/Kim and Associates: Place/Time (New York: Rizzoli, 1997).

17. Alan Plattus, interview by Jimmy Stamp, October 26, 2012.

18. Branch, "Designing the Future," 30–35.

19. Deborah Sontag, "Yale President Quitting to Lead National Private School Venture," New York Times, May 36, 1992; Anthony DePalma, "Departure Leaves Yale in Uncomfortable Spot," New York Times, May 26, 1992; Anthony DePalma, "Schmidt's Exit Creates Worry and Hope at Yale," New York Times, May 27, 1992.

20. Ari Zweiman, "Yale Scales Back on Renovation Plans," Yale Daily News, January 22, 1992, 1, 7.

21. William H. Honan, "Yale Inaugurates Dean and Economist as Its 22nd President," New York Times, October 3, 1993, 36.

22. Jon Nordheimer, "Son of Privilege, Son of Pain: Random Death at Yale's Gates," New York Times, June 28, 1992, A23.

23. Louise Harpman and Evan M. Supcoff, eds., Perspecta: The Yale Architectural Journal 30 (1999).

24. "Yale Conference on Housing," press release, December 22, 1992, Richard C. Levin, President of Yale University, Records, RU-832, accn. 2000-A-020, box 1, Yale University Manuscripts and Archives, New Haven; Fred Koetter, Annual Report to the President 1996–1997, 1997, School of Architecture, Yale University, Records of the Dean RU-843, accn. 2007-A-224, box 13, Yale University Manuscripts and Archives, New Haven.

25. Andre Johnson quoted in Oberdorfer, "Disney Planner."

26. Fred Koeter, "Dean's Letter," in Retrospecta 1994–1995, ed. Eric Chang and Paul Wang (New Haven: Yale University School of Architecture, 1995).

27. "Roundtable Discussion with Tom Beebe [sic], Fred Koetter, Charlie Stott, and Mike Haverland," Suspecta: Advanced Studies: The Post-Professional Program at the School of Architecture (New Haven: self-published, 1994), 51–58.

28. Thomas Beeby quoted in "Roundtable Discussion," 51.

29. The Post-Professional Class of 1994, "Introduction," Suspecta.

30. Steve Izenour, "Learning from the Wildwoods," in Retrospecta 1996–1997, ed. Elspeth Cowell, Thalassa Curtis, and Bertha Olmos (1997): 55.

31. Sam Mockbee in *Retrospecta 1996–1997,* 50.

32. Stanley Tigerman, *Designing Bridges to Burn: Architectural Memoirs by Stanley Tigerman* (Singapore: Oro, 2011), 167.

33. Stanley Tigerman, interview by Betty Blum, 2003, "Oral History of Stanley Tigerman," the Chicago Architects Oral History Project, Ernest R. Graham Study Center for Architectural Drawings, Department of Architecture, the Art Institute of Chicago, 208.

34. John DeStefano quoted in "New Haven Collaborative: Graduate Students Unite to Serve the Community," *Yale Weekly Bulletin and Calendar,* December 13, 1993–January 17, 1994, 3.

35. Stanley Tigerman, *Designing Bridges to Burn,* 241.

36. Fred Koetter, Annual Report to the President, 8 July 1994, School of Architecture, Yale University, Records of the Dean RU-843, accn. 2007-A-224, box 13, Yale University Manuscripts and Archives, New Haven.

37. William Finnegan, "A Reporter at Large: Out There Part I," *New Yorker,* September 10, 1990, 51–52, 56, 58–59, 62–63, 66–70, 75–86; "A Reporter at Large: Out There Part II," *New Yorker,* September 17, 1990, 60–64, 66, 68–84, 87–90.

38. Alan Plattus, paraphrasing Nader, interview by Jimmy Stamp, October 26, 1996.

39. Ibid.

40. Ibid.

41. Ibid.

42. William Weathersby, "Timothy Dwight Elementary School, New Haven, Connecticut," *Architectural Record* (October 2005): 20–23.

43. "New Haven and Conditions of the Periphery," course description in *Retrospecta 1994–1995,* 74.

44. Fred Koetter, interview by

45. Alec Purves, interview by Jimmy Stamp, January 18, 2013.

46. Nora Davis, "Architecture Program Lacks Funding," *Yale Daily News,* November 29, 1993.

47. Michael Surry Schlabs, interview by Jimmy Stamp, August 21, 2013.

48. Ibid.

49. Fred Koetter to Judith Rodin, 25 February 1993, Richard C. Levin, President of Yale University, Records, RU-832, accn. 2000-A-020, box 1, Yale University Manuscripts and Archives, New Haven.

50. Kent Bloomer, Report on Undergraduate Major, February 1993, quoted in Fred Koetter to Judith Rodin, 25 February 1993, Richard C. Levin, President of Yale University, Records, RU-832, accn. 2000-A-020, box 1, Yale University Manuscripts and Archives, New Haven.

51. Fred Koetter to Judith Rodin, 25 February 1993, in ibid.

52. Alan Plattus, interview by Jimmy Stamp, October 26, 2012; Michael Surry Schlabs, interview by Jimmy Stamp, August 21, 2013.

53. Deborah Berke to Fred Koetter, 3 February 1993, Richard C. Levin, President of Yale University, Records, RU-832, accn. 2000-A-020, box 1, Yale University Manuscripts and Archives, New Haven.

54. Ibid.; see also Mitchell Fournier to Alan Plattus, 22 April 1991, in ibid.

55. Larry Wayne Richards, *Suspecta,* 19. See also Fred Koetter to Judith Rodin, 25 February 1993, Richard C. Levin, President of Yale University, Records, RU-832, accn. 2000-A-020, box 1, Yale University Manuscripts and Archives, New Haven.

56. See Timothy Rohan, "Canon and Anti-Canon: On the Fall

and Rise of the A&A," *Harvard Design Magazine* 14 (June 2001): 26.

57. Fred Koetter to Judith Rodin, 25 February 1993, Richard C. Levin, President of Yale University, Records, RU-832, accn. 2000-A-020, box 1, Yale University Manuscripts and Archives, New Haven.

58. Ibid.

59. Ibid.

60. Ibid.

61. Ted P. Pappis, chair of the NAAB Visiting Team, to President Benno Schmidt, 9 July 1993, in ibid.

62. For the building repair crisis, see "S.O.S. Captain Schmidt Must Heed His Crew," *Yale Daily News,* October 9, 1991; and "Complicated Choices 'People vs. Buildings' Too Simplistic," *Yale Daily News,* November 20, 1991; for the Art Library, see "Yale Expansion May Evict Gentree," *Yale Daily News,* April 30, 1992.

63. Colin Savage, "Stale Air in A&A May Cause Illness," *Yale Daily News,* April 6, 1993, 1.

64. Mort Engstrom to Rick Levin, 22 July 1993, Richard C. Levin, President of Yale University, Records, RU-832, accn. 2000-A-020, box 1, Yale University Manuscripts and Archives, New Haven.

65. Fred Koetter, "Letter from the Dean," *Retrospecta 1993–1994* (New Haven: Yale School of Architecture, 1994), 2; Archibald Currie III to Fred Bland, 4 February 1993, Richard C. Levin, President of Yale University, Records, RU-832, accn. 2000-A-020, box 1, Yale University Manuscripts and Archives, New Haven.

66. See Frederick Bland Collection of Sketches of the Yale Art and Architecture Building by Paul Rudolph, MS-1933, Manuscripts and Archives, Yale University Library.

67. Lisa Hasday, "A&A Building Gets a Makeover," *Yale Daily*

News, October 14, 1994.

68. Yale Arts Area Planning Study, 18 December 1995, Richard C. Levin, President of Yale University, Records, RU-832, accn. 2001-A-094, box 28, Yale University Manuscripts and Archives, New Haven.

69. Stan Allen, "The Future Is Now," in *Architecture School: Three Centuries of Educating Architects in North America,* ed. Joan Ockman (Washington, D.C.: Association of Collegiate Schools of Architecture; Cambridge, Mass.: MIT Press, 2012), 212.

70. Graduate students of the School of Architecture to President Levin, 12 October 1994, Richard C. Levin, President of Yale University, Records, RU-832, accn. 2001-A-094, box 1, Yale University Manuscripts and Archives, New Haven.

71. "The Digital Media Center for the Arts at Yale: A Vision and a Plan for Action," August 1997, Richard C. Levin, President of Yale University, Records, RU-832, accn. 2008-A-038, box 25, Yale University Manuscripts and Archives, New Haven.

72. NAAB Visiting Team Report, Yale School of Architecture, February 1998, 18, Richard C. Levin, President of Yale University, Records, RU-832, accn. 2000-A-020, box 1, Yale University Manuscripts and Archives, New Haven.

73. Steven Harris quoted in Marc Wortman, "The Hero Takes a Fall," *Metropolis* (October 1998): 137.

74. Fred Koetter quoted in ibid., 135.

75. Fred Koetter, interview by Jimmy Stamp, December 17, 2012.

76. Deborah Berke, interview by Jimmy Stamp, November 28, 2012.

77. Alan Plattus, interview by Jimmy Stamp, October 26, 2012.

78. Ibid.

79. Richard C. Levin, memo to faculty, students, staff, alumni, and friends of the School of Architecture, 6 May 1997, Richard C. Levin, President of Yale University, Records, RU-832, accn. 2006-A-194, box 1, Yale University Manuscripts and Archives, New Haven.

80. Nina Glickson, memo to Richard C. Levin, "re: Alan Plattus/School of Architecture," 7 May 1997, Richard C. Levin, President of Yale University, Records, RU-832, accn. 2006-A-174, box 1, Yale University Manuscripts and Archives, New Haven.

81. Alexander Garvin to President Richard Levin, 23 May 1997, Richard C. Levin, President of Yale University, Records, RU-832, accn. 2006-A-174, box 1, Yale University Manuscripts and Archives, New Haven.

82. Dolores Hayden to President Richard C. Levin, 31 May 1997, in ibid.

83. Ibid.

84. Ibid.

85. Stanley Tigerman to Richard C. Levin, August 1997, in ibid.

86. Charles Gwathmey to President Richard C. Levin, 19 May 1997, in ibid.

87. Richard C. Levin, "To the Architecture School Community," 18 August 1997, in ibid.

88. Eliza Mangold et al., "To the Dean Search Committee," 3 November 1997, in ibid.

89. Nina M. Glickson to file, cc Richard Levin, "Notes: Lunch with Architecture Students," 17 November 1997, 5 December 1997, Richard C. Levin, President of Yale University, Records, RU-832, accn. 2006-A-194, box 1, Yale University Manuscripts and Archives, New Haven.

90. Ibid.

91. Stanley Tigerman to President Richard C. Levin, 26 March 1998, in ibid.; for the Korean Presbyterian Church of New York, see Robert A. M. Stern, David Fishman, and Jacob Tilove, *New York 2000: Architecture and Urbanism between the Bicentennial and the Millennium* (New York: Monacelli, 2006), 1291; for Garofalo, see Douglas Garofalo, *A+D ser.; Douglas Garofalo* (Chicago: Art Institute of Chicago, 2006); and Blair Kamin, "Doug Garofalo, 1958–2011; UIC Professor Architecture Was on Cutting Edge of Digital Design," *Chicago Tribune,* August 7, 2011.

92. Diana Kleiner, memo to President Richard C. Levin and Alison Richard, 18 April 1998, Richard C. Levin, President of Yale University, Records, RU-832, accn. 2006-A-194, box 1, Yale University Manuscripts and Archives, New Haven.

93. David M. Childs to President Richard C. Levin, 1 May 1998, in ibid.; see also Marilyn Taylor to President Richard C. Levin, 22 April 1998, in ibid.

94. Cesar Pelli to Rick Levin, 29 April 1998, in ibid.

95. Theodore B. Whitten to President Richard C. Levin and members of the Search Committee, 27 April 1998, in ibid.

96. Raphael Sperry to Dean Search Committee, 29 April 1998, in ibid.; for Sperry, see Karrie Jacobs, "Prison Break," *Architect* (November 2012).

97. Tom Beeby to President Richard C. Levin, 5 June 1998, Richard C. Levin, President of Yale University, Records, RU-832, accn. 2006-A-194, box 1, Yale University Manuscripts and Archives, New Haven.

98. Alexander Cooper to President Richard C. Levin, 23 June 1998, in ibid.

99. Wortman, "Hero Takes a Fall," 137.

100. Students quoted in ibid., 108.

101. Ibid.

102. George Ranalli quoted in ibid.

103. Ibid.
104. Meaghan Lloyd quoted in ibid., 137.
105. Vincent Scully quoted in ibid.
106. Ibid.
107. Robert A. M. Stern quoted in ibid.
108. Bernard Tschumi quoted in ibid., 139.
109. George Ranalli quoted in ibid., 137.

10

Personal Reflections on a New Century by Robert A. M. Stern

Epigraph. Robert A. M. Stern quoted in "Alumnus Robert A. M. Stern Appointed as New School of Architecture," *Yale Bulletin and Calendar,* September 14–21, 1998, 1.

1. Julie Iovine, "Robert Stern to Be Yale's Architecture Dean," *New York Times,* September 3, 1998, B7.
2. Robin Pogrebin, "Building Respect at Yale," *New York Times,* December 16, 2007, A1.
3. Jennifer Tobias (M.Arch 2000) quoted in Glenn Hurowitz, "Stern to Head Up School of Arch," *Yale Daily News,* September 4, 1998, 4.
4. Mark Alden Branch, "Blast from the Past," *Yale Alumni Magazine,* March 1999, 24–31.
5. Kok Kian Goh (M.Arch 1999) quoted in Hurowitz, "Stern to Head," 4.
6. Reed Kroloff, "The New Old Blue," *Architecture* 87 (October 1998): 11.
7. Reed Kroloff quoted in Pogrebin, "Building Respect at Yale," A1.
8. Robert A. M. Stern quoted in Elisabeth Bumiller, "From Architectural Showman to Yale Dean," *New York Times,* September 23, 1998, B2.
9. Vincent Scully quoted in "Yale Appoints Robert A. M. Stern to Next Dean of Architecture," Yale University News Bureau, press release, September 3, 1998.
10. Bernard Tschumi quoted in Iovine, "Yale's Architecture Dean," B7.
11. Robert A. M. Stern, *Forty under Forty: An Exhibition of Young Talent in Architecture,* exh. cat. (New York: Architectural League of New York, 1966).
12. Richard Meier quoted in Arthur Lubow, "The Traditionalist," *New York Times Magazine,* October 17, 2010, SM68.
13. For the Lang Residence, see Charles W. Moore, "Lang House, Stern and Hagmann, Architects: Where Are We Now, Vincent Scully?" *Progressive Architecture* 56, no. 4 (April 1975): cover, 78–83.
14. Charles Jencks, "The Rise of Post-Modern Architecture," *AA Quarterly* 7, no. 4 (December 1975): 3–14.
15. Roger Kimball, "Making a Spectacle of Architecture on PBS," *New Criterion* (May 1986): 25–34; see Stern's accompanying book: Robert A. M. Stern with Thomas Mellins and Raymond Gastil, *Pride of Place: Building the American Dream* (Boston: Houghton Mifflin; New York: American Heritage, 1986).
16. National Architectural Accrediting Board, Yale University School of Architecture Visiting Team Report, 7–11 February 1998, Richard C. Levin, President of Yale University, Records, RU-832, accn. 2008-A-032, box 1, Yale University Manuscripts and Archives, New Haven.
17. Alexandra Lange, "Stern und Drang," *New York,* December 7, 1998, 57.
18. Philip Johnson quoted in *Constructs* (spring 1999): 1.
19. Peter Eisenman quoted in ibid., 3.
20. Daniel Libeskind, "Twilight Dawn," studio description, in *Retrospecta 1999–2000,* ed. Alexander M. Hathaway and Stella A. Papadopoulos (New Haven: Yale School of Architecture, 2000), 76.
21. Daniel Libeskind quoted in *Constructs* (fall 1999): 3.
22. See *The Work of Daniel Libeskind: Two Museums and a Garden,* exh. cat. (New Haven: Yale School of Architecture, 1999).
23. Conversation quoted in *Retrospecta 1999–2000,* 93.
24. Eric Clough quoted in Julie V. Iovine, "A Dean's Remodeling Job: Himself," *New York Times,* July 1, 1999, F1.
25. For the Hadid studio, see Douglas Grieco, Wendy Ing, and Nina Rappaport, eds., *CAC Hadid Studio Yale* (New York: Monacelli, 2001).
26. Demetri Porphyrios, "Inventive Re-Building," in *Retrospecta 1999–2000,* 80.
27. John McMorrough, "Eisenman/Krier: Two Ideologies in Review," *Constructs* (spring 2003): 10–11; see also Cynthia Davidson, ed., *Eisenman/Krier: Two Ideologies* (New York: Monacelli, 2005).
28. McMorrough, "Eisenman/Krier," 10–11.
29. Henry K. Murphy, "Paper on 'American House' Read before Professor H. N. McCracken's Class in 'Descriptive Writing' at Yale," May 20, 1912, quoted in Jeffrey W. Cody, *Building in China: Henry K. Murphy's 'Adaptive Architecture' 1914–1935* (Seattle: University of Washington Press, 2001), 17, 51n3.
30. "Americans Chosen to Advise Nanking," *New York Times,* October 15, 1928, 25, cited in Jeffrey W. Cody, *Exporting American Architecture 1870–2000* (London: Routledge,

2003), 117.

31. Alan Plattus, interview by Jimmy Stamp, October 26, 2012.

32. President Richard Levin to Robert A. M. Stern, 1 February 1999, Richard C. Levin, President of Yale University, Records, RU-832, accn. 2008-A-032, box 1, Yale University Manuscripts and Archives, New Haven.

33. Thomas Morbitzer and Irene Shum with Nina Rappaport, "The China Studio," *Constructs* 2, no. 2 (spring 2000): 16.

34. Peggy Deamer and Nina Rappaport, eds., *The Millennium House* (New York: Monacelli, 2004).

35. Robert A. M. Stern, "Dean's Letter," *Retrospecta 1999–2000*, 4.

36. Report of the Computing Assessment Committee, 28 November 1998, Richard C. Levin, President of Yale University, Records, RU-832, accn. 2008-A-032, box 1, Yale University Manuscripts and Archives, New Haven.

37. Robert A. M. Stern to Diana Kleiner, 3 December 1998, in ibid.

38. Symposium proceedings can be found in the archives boxes, School of Architecture Lectures and Presentations, RU-880, boxes 28–35, Manuscripts and Archives, Yale University Library; see also Natasha Thondavadi, "At School of Architecture, Role of Drawing in Doubt," *Yale Daily News*, April 6, 2012; Joann Gonchar, "The Afterlife of Drawing," *Architectural Record* (April 2012): 29; and Bryce A. Weigand, "Is Drawing Dead? A Symposium at Yale Poses, and Answers, the Question," *Texas Architect* (May 2012): 80.

39. Vincent Scully, "Introduction," *Cesar Pelli: Building Designs 1965–2000*, exh. cat. (New Haven: Yale School of Architecture, 2000).

40. Deborrah Glenn-Long, Financial Aid Report–Supplemental Information School of Architecture, 10 December 1998, Richard C. Levin, President of Yale University, RU-832, accn. 2008-A-032, box 1, folder 23, Yale University Manuscripts and Archives, New Haven.

41. Deborah Berke, interview by Jimmy Stamp, November 28, 2012.

42. Iovine, "A Dean's Remodeling Job," F1.

43. President Levin, Response to the Council Committee on the School of Architecture, 4 October 2001, Richard C. Levin, President of Yale University, Records, RU-832, accn. 2008-A-154, box 10, Yale University Manuscripts and Archives, New Haven.

44. "Changes Aplenty at City College," *New York Times*, December 29, 1999, B9.

45. Michael Surry Schlabs, interview by Jimmy Stamp, August 20, 2013.

46. For more on BIM, see Peggy Deamer and Phil Bernstein, eds., *BIM in Academia* (New Haven: Yale University School of Architecture, 2011).

47. Robert A. M. Stern, memorandum to John Jacobson, Peter de Bretteville, Steven Harris, Turner Brooks, and Michael Bierut, 28 September 1998, School of Architecture Records of the Dean, RU-843, accn. 2005-A-080, box 2, Yale University Manuscripts and Archives, New Haven.

48. Michael Bierut's posters for the Yale School of Architecture were collected in the book *Michael Bierut, Forty Posters for the Yale School of Architecture* (Hamden, Conn.: Winterhouse, 2007).

49. See Robert A. M. Stern, Dean's Letter, 25 September 2005, Robert A. M. Stern, Dean of the School of Architecture Records, RU-843, Yale University Manuscripts and Archives, New Haven.

50. See Mark Lindner, "Perspecta at 50: What Goes around Comes Around," *Constructs* (fall 2000): 6–9.

51. Robert A. M. Stern, Peggy Deamer, and Alan Plattus, eds., *[Re]Reading Perspecta: The First Fifty Years of the Yale Architectural Journal* (Cambridge, Mass.: MIT Press, 2004).

52. For DeVane lectures, see School of Architecture, Yale University, Lectures and Presentations, RU-880, accn. 2002-A-151, boxes 7–18, Yale University Manuscripts and Archives, New Haven; Alan Plattus, "Ideals without Ideologies," *Constructs* (spring 2002): 8–9; "DeVane Guest Lectures and Fall Lectures 2001," in ibid., 9; and Aurelia Paradiso, Edward Baxter, and Michael Baumberger, eds., *Retrospecta 2001–2002* (New Haven: Yale School of Architecture, 2002), 8.

53. *New Blue: Recent Work of Graduates of Yale School of Architecture, 1978–1998*, exh. cat. (New Haven: Yale School of Architecture, 2001).

54. Richard Hayes, "White, Gray and Blue," *Constructs* (spring 2002): 18–19; Sean Tobin, "New Blue," in ibid., 19; Reed Kroloff, "Defining a Pedagogy," in ibid.

55. Eve Blau, "Architecture or Revolution: Charles Moore and Architecture at Yale," *Constructs* (fall 2001): 6–8; Peter Reed, "Getting Real: Moore, Yale, and the 1960s," *Constructs* (spring 2002): 13–15; Margaret Crawford, "The Art of the Impossible," in ibid., 17; *Retrospecta 2001–2002*, 80–84.

56. The proceedings were not published, but the exhibition catalogue and related materials are available in the university archives: School of Architecture, Yale University, exhibit materials

from *Architecture or Revolution: Charles Moore and Architecture at Yale in the 1960s,* RU-906, Yale University Manuscripts and Archives, New Haven.

57. See Karla Britton, "Yale Art and Architecture Archives," *Constructs* (spring 2005): 13.

58. Materials from the Beinecke Library and Manuscripts and Archives can be explored using the university's online finding aid at http://findingaids.library.yale.edu.

59. Alexander Purves, interview by Jimmy Stamp, January 18, 2013.

60. Ibid.

61. Bernard Tschumi quoted in *Constructs* (fall 1999): 16.

62. Michael Surry Schlabs, interview by Jimmy Stamp, August 20, 2013.

63. For a brief account of the search for the loft, see Alexandra Lange, "Stern und Drang," *New York,* December 7, 1998, 57.

64. Peggy Deamer, interview by Jimmy Stamp, October 16, 2013.

65. Vincent J. Scully, Catherine Lynn, Eric Vogt, and Paul Goldberger, *Yale in New Haven: Architecture and Urbanism* (New Haven: Yale University, 2004).

66. "Visions in Brick and Stone: Planning and Building for the Next Century at Yale," Yale University News Bureau, press release, April 6, 1999.

67. Raymond Gastil, "Yale Constructs Symposium," *Constructs* 2, no. 1 (fall 1999): 12–13.

68. Gustav Niebuhr, "Yale to Renovate Most of Divinity School," *New York Times,* December 11, 1996, B16; Paul Goldberger, "Saving a Beloved Chapel by Cutting out Its Soul," *New York Times,* December 22, 1996, 49.

69. Vincent Scully quoted in James M. Philips, "Yale Reconstructs Architectural Conclave Ends as Scully Denounces Kliment-Halsband

Plan to Demolish Eastern Section of Divinity School Quadrangle," *Bulletin to the Members of the Foundation for the Preservation of Sterling Divinity Quadrangle,* April 12, 1999, Richard C. Levin, President of Yale University, Records, RU-832, accn. 2008-A-032, box 1, folder 24, Yale University Manuscripts and Archives, New Haven.

70. Vincent Scully quoted in Walter Kits, "Art Expert Threatens to Cut Yale Ties," *New Haven Register,* April 14, 1999, A-3.

71. Richard Levin, remarks prepared for the *Constructs* symposium, 11 April 1999, Richard C. Levin, President of Yale University, Records, RU-832, accn. 2008-A-032, box 1, folder 24, Yale University Manuscripts and Archives, New Haven.

72. Letitia Stein, "Scully Says He Could Leave If Yale Destroys Divinity Quad," *Yale Daily News,* April 13, 1999, 1; Kits, "Art Expert Threatens," 1.

73. Ibid.

74. James M. Philips to Robert A. M. Stern, 21 April 1999, Richard C. Levin, President of Yale University, Records, RU-832, accn. 2008-A-032, box 1, folder 24, Yale University Manuscripts and Archives, New Haven.

75. Vincent Scully quoted in Leticia Stein, "Yale Revises Divinity School Renovation Plan," *Yale Daily News,* September 15, 1999, 1, 6.

76. Peggy Deamer and Carol Burns quoted in Elizabeth Barry, "Yale Women in Architecture," *Constructs* (fall 2006): 18.

77. Lisa Gray quoted in Yanan Wang, "Women in Architecture Reunion Examines Gender Diversity," *Yale Daily News,* November 30, 2012.

78. John Jacobson quoted in Diana Kleiner, e-mail message to Rick Levin and

Alison Richard, 10 June 1999, Richard C. Levin, President of Yale University, Records, RU-832, accn. 2008-A-032, box 1, Yale University Manuscripts and Archives, New Haven.

79. These include the Louis I. Kahn Visiting Assistant Professorship in Architectural Design, intended to enable junior-level teacher-practitioners to offer advanced studio and seminars; the Charles Gwathmey Professorship in Practice, established by Ralph and Ricky Lauren in memory of the recently deceased architect who was their friend; the Lord Norman R. Foster Visiting Professorship, also established in 2009, to fund a professorship for international visiting faculty, with Alejandro Zaera-Polo, London-based architect, theorist, and cofounder of Foreign Office Architects (FOA), serving as the inaugural appointee; the Hines Professorship in Sustainable Architecture, established in 2008 to promote research into improving the relationship between the built and natural environments; the Edward P. Bass Distinguished Visiting Architecture Fellowship, established in 2004 to bring distinguished public or private sector clients to the school who would become active participants in an advanced design studio or seminar; the Vincent Scully Visiting Professor of Architectural History, established in 2004 with occupants serving a maximum of five years—its inaugural occupant was Kurt Forster; the Lois Alm Lenahan Memorial Dean's Resource Fund, established in 2007 to support the study of landscape architecture; and the Daniel Rose (B.A. 1951) Visiting Assistant

Notes to Pages 550–560

Professorship, established in 2007 by Joseph B. Rose (B.A. 1981) and Gideon G. Rose (B.A. 1985) to honor their father by funding a position in urban and environmental studies. Additionally, a significant gift fund in support of the study of contemporary architecture was established in 2007 by Elise Jaffe and Jeffrey Brown, friends of the school, and a fund in support of symposia was established in 2010 by the children of J. Irwin Miller (1909–2004; B.A. 1931, L.H.D.H. 1979)—William I. Miller (B.A. 1978), Catherine G. Miller, Elizabeth G. Miller, and Margaret I. Miller (M.A. 1968). And finally, I am grateful and humbled to note that in 2015 a chair in Classical and Traditional Architecture was inaugurated in my honor with a lead gift from Robert Rosenkranz (B.A. 1962), Alexandra Munroe, and significant support from the partners of Robert A. M. Stern Architects.

80. Monica Robinson, interview by Jimmy Stamp, April 10, 2013.

81. David Schwarz, interview by Jimmy Stamp, July 26, 2012.

82. James Axley, "Joint Forestry and Architecture Program," *Constructs* (spring 2006): 18.

83. "Hines Research Fund Announced," *Constructs* (spring 2009): 9.

84. Peter Eisenman quoted in Zeynep Pamuk, "Architecture School Receives Ph.D. Applications," *Yale Daily News,* January 29, 2009.

85. Kurt Forster quoted in Yanan Wang, "Architecture Ph.D. Program's Presence Grows," *Yale Daily News,* October 29, 2012.

86. Victoria Newhouse, "Architecture and Sound," *Constructs* (spring 2013): 6.

87. For the Morse and Stiles renovations, see Suzanne Stephens, "Morse and Ezra Stiles Colleges: New Haven, Kieran Timberlake's Renovation and Expansion Retails the Medieval-Modern Spirit of the Eero Saarinen-Designed Complex at Yale," *Architectural Record* (November 2011): 97–101.

88. Sid R. Bass to President Levin, 23 May 2000, Richard C. Levin, President of Yale University, Records, RU-832, accn. 2008-A-032, box 1, Yale University Manuscripts and Archives, New Haven.

89. Sid R. Bass quoted in Robert A. M. Stern, Dean's Letter, 26 October 2000, Robert A. M. Stern, Dean of the School of Architecture Records, RU-843, Yale University Manuscripts and Archives, New Haven.

90. Deborah Berke, interview by Jimmy Stamp, November 28, 2012.

91. Michael Surry Schlabs, interview by Jimmy Stamp, August 20, 2013.

92. David Childs quoted in "Out with Dead Pigeons: A&A to Rise Again," *Yale Daily News,* February 12, 2001, 1, 5.

93. "Yale Names Architects for A&A Renovation, Art History Building," Yale University News Bureau, press release, February 2, 2001.

94. Diana Kleiner to Richard Levin, 1 March 2001, Richard C. Levin, President of Yale University, Records, RU-832, accn. 2008-A-032, box 14, folder 843, Yale University Manuscripts and Archives, New Haven.

95. Robert A. M. Stern quoted in ibid.

96. John Jacobson, interview by Jimmy Stamp, May 18, 2013.

97. Richard Meier, Kenneth Frampton, and Joseph Rykwert, eds., *Richard Meier Architect,* vol. IV (New York: Rizzoli, 2004).

98. See Charles Gwathmey to Archibald Currie III, 1 November 1993, School of Architecture Records of the Dean, RU-843, accn. 2007-A-224, box 5, Yale University Manuscripts and Archives, New Haven.

99. Gracie Kim, "Sculpture Building Opens for Architecture School," *Yale Daily News,* September 19, 2007.

100. Charles Gwathmey quoted in "Restoration of Iconic Rudolph Building Is Key Step in Creation of Arts Complex," *Yale Bulletin and Calendar,* November 16, 2007, 1, 12.

101. *Model City: Buildings and Projects by Paul Rudolph for New Haven and Yale, November 3, 2008–February 6, 2009,* exh. cat. (New Haven: Yale School of Architecture, 2008); see also Timothy Rohan, *The Architecture of Paul Rudolph* (New Haven: Yale University Press, 2014).

102. Richard C. Levin quoted in "Restored, Renovated and Renamed Paul Rudolph Hall Is Rededicated," *Yale Daily News,* November 18, 2008.

103. Herbert Muschamp, "Paul Rudolph Is Dead at 78; Modernist Architect of the 60s," *New York Times,* August 9, 1997, 50.

104. John Jacobson, interview by Jimmy Stamp, April 18, 2013.

105. Ibid.

106. Charles Gwathmey quoted in "Restoration of Iconic Rudolph Building," 1, 12.

107. Vincent Scully quoted in "Back to Former Glory, A&A Named for Rudolph," *Yale Daily News,* November 7, 2008.

108. Paul Goldberger quoted in ibid.

109. "Letter from the Editors," *Retrospecta 2008–2009,* ed. Anne Mason Kemper, Andrew Smith-Rasmussen, Kyle Stover, and Emmett Zeifman (New Haven: Yale School of Architecture 2009), 5.

110. Blair Kamin, "Modernist Castle Made Livable, but Its New Neighbor Falls Flat," *Chicago Tribune,* November 9, 2008.

Index

Page numbers in *italics* indicate illustrations.

Putney School, **276**

Q

Quintana, Harry J., **299–300, 314**

R

Rae, Douglas, **350, 501,** *502,* **503–4**
Rambusch Company, **66**
RAMSA. *See* Robert A. M. Stern Architects
Ranalli, George, *416,* **430–31,** *436,* **444–46, 469, 471, 494–95, 523, 545**
Rapp, Walter L., **47**
Rappaport, Nina, **531**
Rap Sheets (journal), **465, 485**
Rapson, Ralph, **159, 160**
Rauch, John, **295**
Rawn, William, Rose Center, Yale University, **563**
Ray, Mary-Ann, **504**
Raymond, Antonin, **66, 87**
Reed, Henry Hope, Jr., **150–51, 153, 176**
Reeder, Andy, **500;** examples of work from Tigerman's studio, *502*
Reid, John Lyon, **159**
Reifsnyder, William E., **325**
Reinecke, William, **229;** Sibley House, **229,** *230*
Retrospecta (annual), *428,* **430, 455, 465, 492, 498, 541, 542, 548, 549**
Richards, Larry Wayne, **258, 509**
Richards Medical Research Laboratories, University of Pennsylvania, Philadelphia (Kahn), **191**
Rickart, Charles E., **360**
Ricker, Nathan, **9**
Righter, James Volney, **279, 337, 447, 475;** Art and Architecture

Building elevator design, *338;* Pavillon Soixante-Dix Ski Resort, *278,* **279**
Riley, Noah, Proposal for an Extension to the Whitney Museum in New York, *532*
Ritchie, Andrew C., **202**
Robbins, Mark, **519–21**
Robert A. M. Stern Architects (RAMSA), **529–30**
Robertson, Jaquelin T., ix, **103–4, 119, 179, 193, 208, 291, 292, 378–80, 384–85, 387–89, 401–2, 427, 435,** *436, 438,* **439, 456, 457, 465, 475, 518;** Dormitory for Old Campus, **179,** *180*
Robinson, Monica, **559–60**
Roche, Kevin, **235, 358, 361, 385, 425, 441, 551**
Roche-Dinkeloo: Coliseum, **398, 413;** Knights of Columbus Building, **398**
Rockefeller, John D., **46**
Rockefeller Apartments, New York City (Harrison), **62**
Rockefeller Center, New York City (Associated Architects), **62**
Rockefeller Center, New York City (Harrison & Abramovitz), **87**
Rockefeller Center, New York City (Hood), **49, 62**
Rodgers, Robert Perry, **62**
Rodia, Simon, **294**
Rodin, Judith, **507–9**
Rodriguez, Susan, **557**
Rogers, Ernesto Nathan, **158, 160, 161, 189**
Rogers, James Gamble, **37, 41, 57, 149, 154, 219;** Harkness Memorial Quadrangle, Yale University, **35, 37;** Harkness Tower, Yale University, **154;**

University Theatre renovation, **281**
Rogers, Richard, **188–89, 191, 199, 206, 209, 211, 377;** A New City, **209,** *210;* Pierson-Sage Science Complex, *190,* **191**
Rogers, Su Brumwell, **189, 209**
Rohan, Timothy, **201, 215, 217–19, 339–40, 481, 510, 568**
Rohm and Haas (company), **91**
Rome, **46, 504, 505, 543**
Rome, Harold, **53;** A Greek Doric Hexastyle-Peripteral Temple, *54*
Romney, Hervin A. R., **430**
Roofless Church, New Harmony, Indiana (Johnson), **115**
Roosevelt Memorial, New York City (Kahn), **119**
Rose, Peter, **276–77, 279;** Pavillon Soixante-Dix Ski Resort, *278,* **279**
Rose Center, Yale University (Rawn), **563**
Rosenblatt, Phyllis, **219**
Rosenkranz Hall, Yale University, New Haven (Koetter Kim & Associates), **563**
Rosenstein, Mark, **431**
Rosow, Stuart, **363**
Rossi, Aldo, **439**
Rotch Traveling Scholarship, **37**
Roth, Alfred, **67**
Roth, Ed "Big Daddy," **294**
Roth, Harold, **431, 444, 473**
Roth & Moore Architects, **431**
Rotheroe, Kevin, **557**
Rotival, Maurice, **67, 69, 70, 150;** City of New Haven Redevelopment Plan, *70,* **71**
Rouse, Irving, **109**
Row, Arthur, **319**
Rowan, Jan, **222**

Rowe, Colin, **362, 429, 432, 463, 464, 476, 494, 495, 500, 508**
Rowen, Daniel, **505**
Ruben, Marshall, **488**
Rubin, Elihu, **330**
Ruble, John, **279**
Rucker, Thelma, **394**
Rudofsky, Bernard, **194, 303**
Rudolph, Paul, **96, 97, 160–61, 164–241,** *166, 182, 186, 214, 224, 232,* **246–49, 267, 271, 279, 285, 287, 319, 330–31, 343, 357, 385, 392, 402–3, 413, 430–31, 461, 479, 481,** *482,* **484, 529, 564, 568;** Art and Architecture Building, Yale University, **xiii, 38, 167, 187,** *214,* **215,** *216,* **217–19,** *220,* **221–23,** *224,* **225, 254, 284, 311, 330–48,** *334, 342,* **391, 402, 412–18,** *416,* **431, 451, 477–85, 490, 509–13,** *512,* **517, 527, 530–31, 533, 543, 562, 564–71,** *570;* Blue Cross/Blue Shield office building, **165, 189, 248;** Crawford Manor apartments, **295;** Government Service Center, **225;** Greeley Memorial Laboratory, School of Forestry, Yale University, **215;** Married Student Housing, Yale University, **177,** *180,* **215, 265;** Mary Cooper Jewett Arts Center, Wellesley College, **165, 248, 413;** Tastee-Freez Ice Cream Stand, *166, 167;* Temple St. Parking Garage, *204,* **205**
Ruedig, Adam, Millennium House, *538*
Ruml, Beardsley, **69**
Ruscha, Ed, **294**

Illustration Credits

The photographers and the sources of visual material other than the owners indicated in the captions are as follows. Every effort has been made to supply complete and correct credits; if there are errors or omissions, please contact Yale University Press so that corrections can be made in any subsequent edition.

Unless otherwise indicated, all images are courtesy Yale School of Architecture.

Adam Anuszkiewicz: **8.16**
Marc Appleton: **6.3**
Architectural Design: **5.11**
Thomas Beeby: **4.37**
Roy Berkeley: **5.35 (right), 5.36, 5.37**
Steven Brooke: **6.5**
Carpenter's Company: **7.5**
Charles Moore Foundation: **5.1, 5.2**
Leslie Cheek: **2.31**
Robert Cole: **3.23 (top)**
Columbia University Archives: **5.35 (left)**
Design and the Public Good, ed. Richard Plunz (Cambridge: MIT Press, 1983): **5.5**
École nationale supérieure des beaux-arts: **2.5, 2.6**
Elliot Erwitt/Magnum Photos: **4.12, 4.15, 4.16, 4.19, 4.20, 4.35**
Norman Foster: **4.38**
Gary Fujiwara: **4.51**
Gregory M. S. Gall: **3.23 (bottom)**
Leonard Haber: **2.30**
Craig Hodgetts: **5.20**
© Sue Ann Kahn. Photo by Paul Takeuchi: **3.5**
Raymond Kaskey: **5.4**
Robert Knight: **5.44**
Koetter Kim: **9.12**
James Kruhly: **7.4**
Library of Congress Prints and Photographs Division, Washington, D.C., Bain Collection: **2.4**
Library of Congress Prints and Photographs Division,

Washington, D.C., Paul Rudolph Archive: **4.2**
Library of Congress Prints and Photographs Division, Washington, D.C., Vietnam Veterans Memorial Fund Records, ca. 1979–84: **7.25**
William McDonough: **6.6**
Norman McGrath: **4.36**
Estelle Thompson Margolis: **2.42, 2.43, 3.30**
Hansel Mieth and Otto Hagel: **2.38**
Robert Mittelstadt: **4.48, 4.49**
Moshe Safdie Architects: **6.2** (Jerry Spearman and Martin Hoffmeister)
New Haven Register: **3.37**
Arnold Newman/Getty Images: **3.29**
Oscar Nitzchke: **2.36**
Mark Ostow: **10.24**
OTTO: **10.31, 10.35**
Pencil Points: **2.19**
Progressive Architecture: **5.6, 5.9, 5.16, 5.38**
Marvin Rand: **3.35**
Richard Meier & Partners Architects: **10.29, 10.30**
Robert A. M. Stern Architects: **4.46** (Robert Perron), **5.7, 5.17**
Sonia Albert Schimberg: **2.41**
Ben Schnall: **3.16**
David Sellers: **4.52**
Shunk-Kender/Getty Trust: **5.32**
Jimmy Stamp: **8.3**
Courtesy Robert A. M. Stern: **3.11, 10.2, 10.34**
Stanley Tigerman: **4.14**
University of Pennsylvania Archives and Records Center: **5.21–5.26**
Van Alen Institute (formerly B.A.I.D.): **2.18, 2.22–2.25, 2.28, 2.32–2.35**
Venturi and Rauch, Architects: **5.47**
Vogue: **5.15**
Jeremy Scott Wood: **4.54, 4.55**
Yale Daily News: **3.50, 5.30** (Stephen Koch), **5.31** (Stephen Koch)
Yale University Art Gallery: **2.26, 2.37**
Yale University Library, Manuscripts and Archives: **1.1–1.8, 2.1–2.3, 2.7–2.17, 2.20, 2.21, 2.27, 2.29, 2.32, 2.35, 2.39, 2.40. 3.1–3.4, 3.6–3.10, 3.12–3.15, 3.17–3.22, 3.24–3.28, 3.31–3.34, 3.36, 3.38–3.49;**

4.1, 4.3–4.11, 4.13 (Stanley Tigerman), **4.17** (Stanley Tigerman), **4.18** (Stanley Tigerman), **4.21–4.34, 4.39–4.47, 4.49, 4.50. 4.53, 5.8, 5.10, 5.12–5.14, 5.18, 5.19, 5.27, 5.28** (James Righter), **5.29** (James Righter), **5.33, 5.34, 5.39, 5.40, 5.41** (James Righter), **5.42** (James Righter), **5.44** (Robert Knight), **5.45, 5.46** (George Pohl), **5.50, 5.51, 6.1, 6.4, 7.1–7.3, 8.23, 9.1, 9.9–9.11, 10.17**
Yale University, Visual Resources Collection: **5.3, 7.2**
Yale Urban Design Workshop: **9.6, 9.7**